AF608032

Prince Twins Seven-Seven

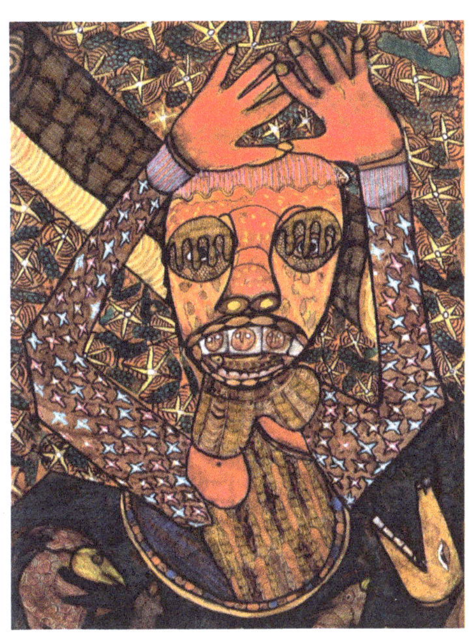

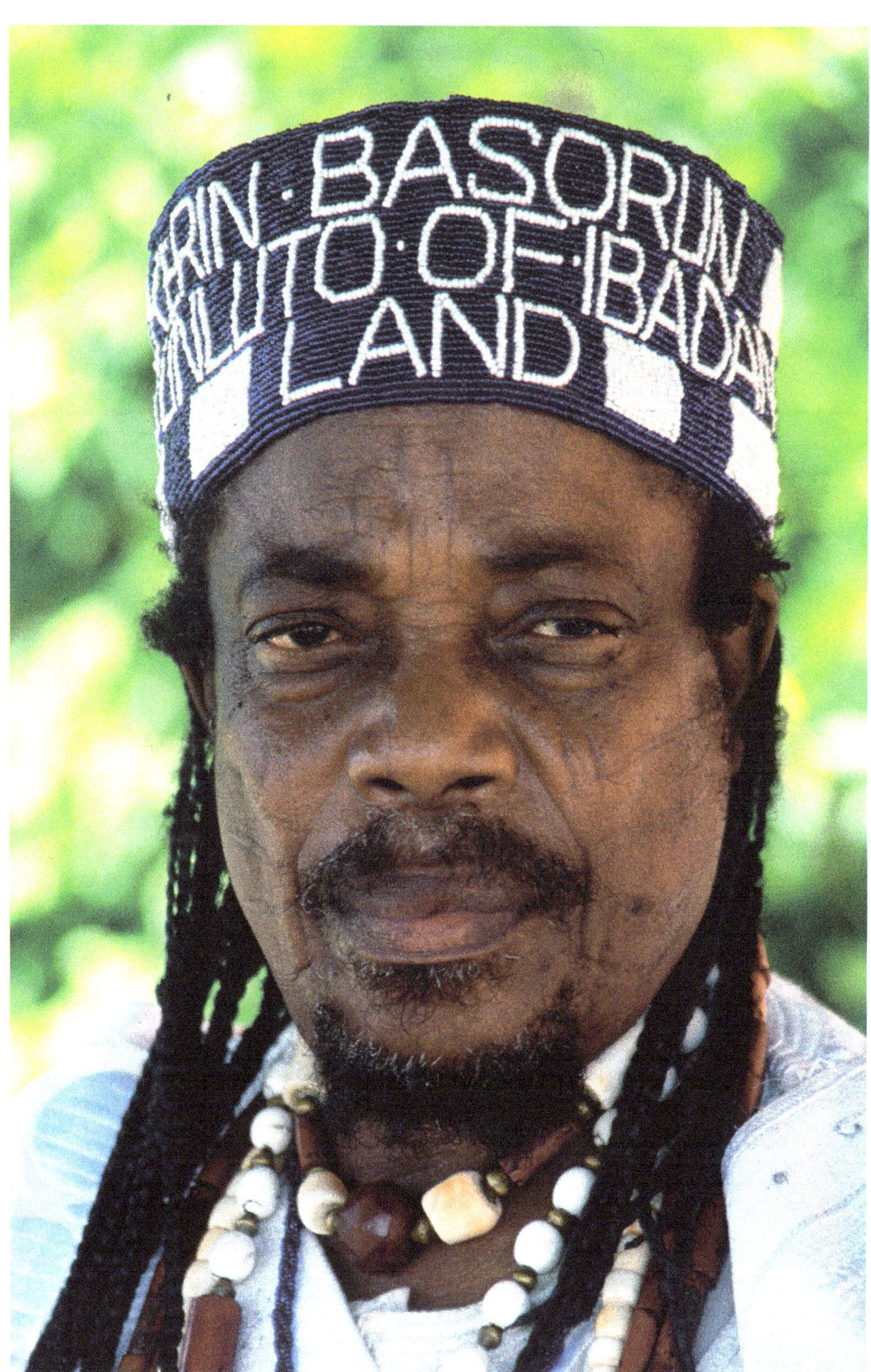

BASORUN
OF
LAND

Prince Twins Seven-Seven

His Art,
His Life in Nigeria,
His Exile in America

Henry Glassie

Photography, Drawings, and Design by the Author

Bloomington and Indianapolis

Indiana University Press • 2010

Material Culture

This book is a publication of

Indiana University Press
601 North Morton Street
Bloomington, Indiana 47404-3797 USA

www.iupress.indiana.edu

Telephone orders 800-842-6796
Fax orders 812-855-7931
Orders by e-mail iuporder@indiana.edu

∞ The paper used in this publication meets the minimum requirements of the American National Standard for Information Sciences—Permanence of Paper for Printed Library Materials, ANSI Z39.48-1992.

Manufactured in the United States of America

Cataloging information is available from the Library of Congress.

ISBN 978-0-253-35439-6

1 2 3 4 5 15 14 13 12 11 10

Contents

Part Two: Prince's Art

Works by Prince Twins Seven-Seven

Henry and Twins dedicate their book to

George Jevremović,

yoldaş, kardeş, dost

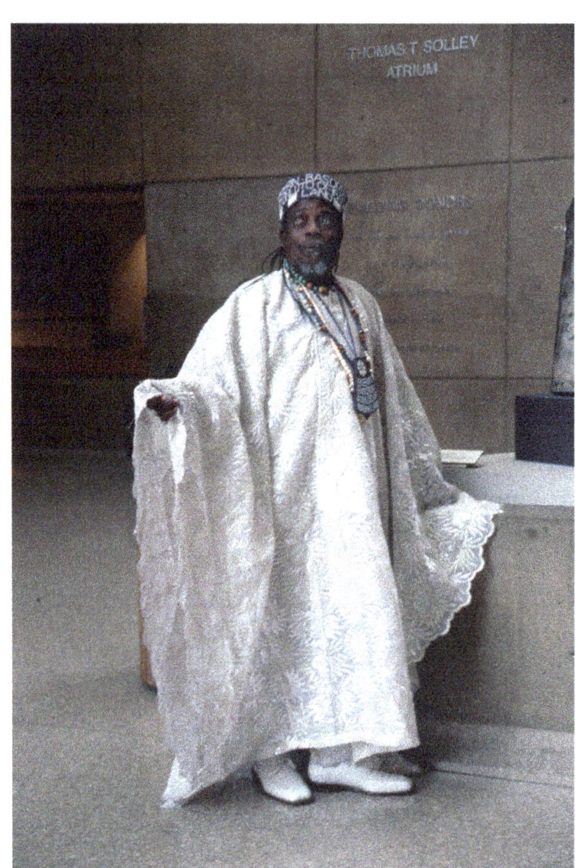

Prince Twins Seven-Seven.
Indiana University Art Museum

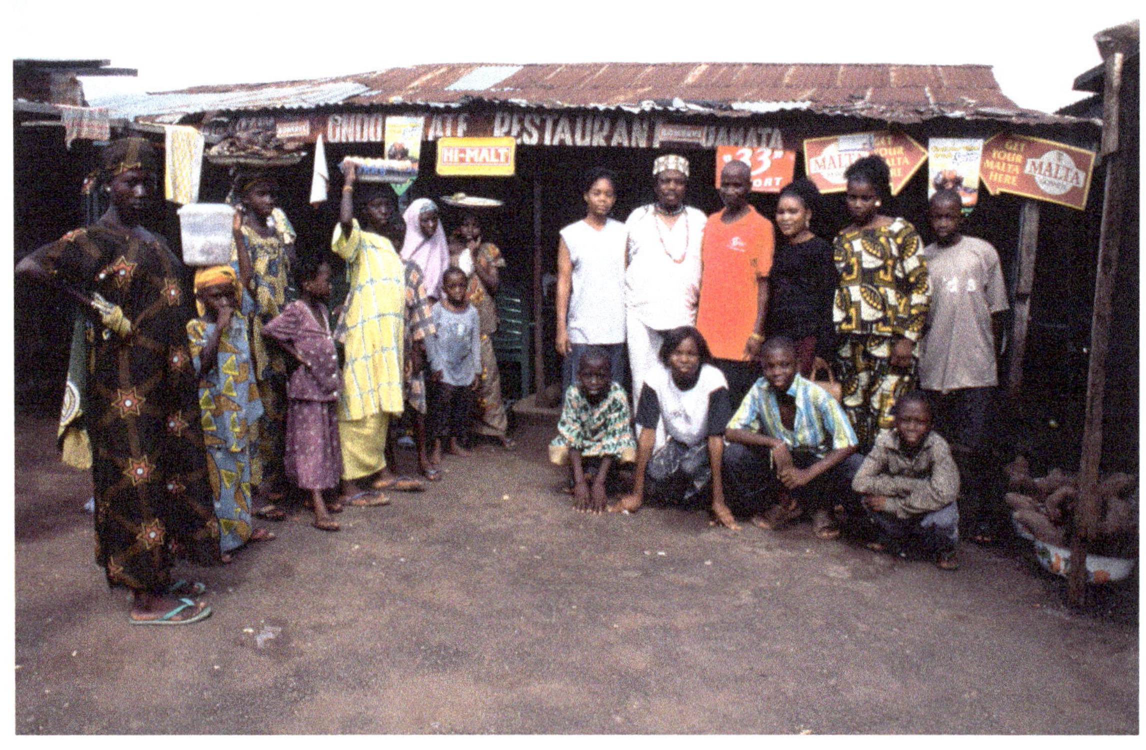

Prince and his people. Lokoja

Twins Seven-Seven

His father named him Bamidele. His grandmother named him Olaniyi. When he left home and took to the road, he named himself Twins Seven-Seven. Seven times he came into the world, each time as one in a set of twins. Six times he returned to the spirits who sent him, but after his seventh birth his mother managed, with the water of the goddess Osun, to keep him on the earth.

A boy from the bush, Twins Seven-Seven came to town as the dancer in a traveling medicine show. Crashing the gate at a literary event, he astounded the crowd with his spectacular moves, and Ulli Beier, a man dedicated to the advancement of African art, invited him to stay. At the time, Beier was organizing a series of workshops for young artists. In the third of them, as Ulli Beier put it in a letter to me, Twins Seven-Seven "found himself."

The town was Osogbo, in the Yorubaland of southwestern Nigeria, the year was 1964. Twins was twenty. He wandered into the workshop conducted by Georgina Beier. The others were painting, but Twins called for pen and ink. His first picture, *The Devil's Dog,* the first he had ever drawn, already displayed the style—imaginative, decorative, and ripped from within—that would carry him to sudden renown.

The artists discovered in the workshops made up the Osogbo school. In Nigerian published opinion, it was "the most important art movement in contemporary Nigeria," and Twins Seven-Seven was "undoubtedly the most talented" of the Osogbo artists. Within a year his works had been exhibited in Nigeria, Czechoslovakia, and the United States. International exhibitions followed at the rate of better than two a year. While he mastered new media and his fame as an artist spread, Twins was also the lead singer in a band, an actor in films. He threw himself into the turmoil of Nigerian politics, learning by accident that he was the descendant of a king, and deserved to be addressed as Prince.

Like all of his friends, I call him Twins, but he prefers the formal title, so from now on in this book Prince it will be.

Prince courageously tests himself in diverse spheres, excited to have several unfinished projects going at once. But art is the base and frame of his fame, his pleasure and consolation.

When we got to Osogbo, in 2006, Victor Akpan, an official of tourism development, told me, "Twins Seven-Seven is the number one artist of Nigeria. He is an icon."

An icon:

We are sitting in a roadside restaurant outside of Lokoja, eating pounded yam and *egusi*, a savory soup of greens and ground melon seeds. A tall, slim girl, maybe twelve, walks slowly from the back and sits at the edge of a bench across from Prince, staring at him, thinking hard. Then she breaks into a sunburst of a smile, claps, stamps her feet, and names the character he played in a film she had seen. She waits, fidgeting with excitement, until we are done—the *egusi* is excellent—then she assembles her friends for a photograph with the great man. Laughing, Prince hands CDs of his music through the crowd, and we are gone.

The back country roads are lined with wrecks, crushed cars and battered trucks, dragged to the verge and rusting into a long, silent warning to careless drivers. Our road is rutted and gullied, interrupted by temporary barricades thrown up by the police. Not wanting to waste time in pointless interrogation, Prince directs Sunday, his driver, to slow down so he can hand a few naira to the armed men who stand back and smile, pleasantly waving us on. Near Kabba, we downshift through another checkpoint, money passes from hand to hand, but a young man, burdened with a rifle, runs along beside us, panting and calling out, "Kabiyesi, Kabiyesi." It is the proper greeting for a high chief, meaning, Prince says, "Nobody has the power to challenge your authority." We pull off the road, so the policemen can gather and have their picture taken with Prince Twins Seven-Seven, attired all in white and carrying the horsetail whisk of chiefly authority.

At the edge of Sekona, we sit with old friends in the shade. There is a bowl of bony, tangy bush meat on the table and many black bottles of stout (Nigeria has surpassed Ireland as a consumer of Guinness). A young man walks by, touches the ground with both hands, thrusting one leg back in honorific semi-prostration, and saying, "Seven-Seven is the number." Then he stands, steadies himself, and turns to join his pals in the red-eyed haze of an afternoon of palm wine.

In the parking lot of the sleek government buildings outside of Osogbo, young men cluster at the car, asking for a blessing. They kneel around him, and Prince improvises a prayer, advising them to shun fashionable, foreign materialism and hold to the noble culture of their ancestors.

We enter a dimly lit nightclub in Ibadan. Beyond the tables of the drinkers, across the floor swaying with dancers, a tight band plays in the spotlight. We skirt the rim of darkness, and without a change of tempo or melody, the singer's song segues into praise of Twins Seven-Seven, artist, musician, and hero to his people.

An icon at home, Prince rose to the top of public life when, in 1996, he was awarded chieftaincy titles in Ibadan and Ogidi, the places of his parents. As an artist abroad, his fame crested at the end of the nineteen-eighties with exhibitions in France, Finland, and Japan. All that success came coupled with troubles, troubles in politics, troubles with the police, with women, with jealous friends, with wild armed robbers—troubles that heaped into such a burden that he fled Nigeria in 2000, crossed the black ocean, and settled in Philadelphia where he had been garlanded with honors in the past.

He arrived with an immigrant's hope. He met with an immigrant's defeat. Beaten down by repetitive failures, he drifted toward despair, feeling, he said, as though he were tied up in a sack and sinking in the sea. At this lowest of low points, with all hope gone, his funds exhausted, George Jevremović appeared in his life, much as Ulli Beier had forty years before. The proprietor of a vast emporium called Material Culture, overflowing with select artifacts from throughout the world—furniture from China, textiles from Ghana, ceramics from Romania, carvings from India, splendid carpets from Turkey—George bought what Prince had to sell and offered him a job.

So, Prince came to Material Culture. Strangely enough, he had been there before; he had been hired as the security guard of the parking lot that served the store, then fired for sleeping on the job. Now George paid him, and he worked, doing menial things at first, then applying his tremendous talent to small tasks: decorating old Turkish pots, painting pictures on brown paper bags that George gave to good customers. Prince was relieved, but hardly happy, and George, who cares deeply about artists and art, gave me a call.

We have been best friends, George and I, bound together like brothers, for a quarter of a century. When George told me that he had hired a mercurial character named Twins Seven-Seven, I was shocked. How could this man be down and out in Philly? I had admired his work since the early nineteen-seventies when colleagues and friends who were experts in African art—Roy Sieber, Robert Farris Thompson, and Robert Plant Armstrong—told me about a young artist who was reshaping the Yoruba tradition into modern masterpieces. With Bob Armstrong I was especially close. An anthropologist and phenomenologist, Bob wrote a brilliant trilogy on the nature of art, guided by close study of Yoruba creations. The first volume, *The Affecting Presence*, had claimed my admiration before we met. The third volume, *The Powers of Presence*, he dedicated to me. *Wellspring*, the book in the middle, about which I published a laudatory essay, opens with a painting by Twins Seven-Seven and offers a superb analysis of his work. Bob's home in Dallas was filled with a lifetime's collection of Yoruba art, the most exquisite masks, the most refined figures, and, passing through the front door, the first thing you saw was a huge painting by Twins Seven-Seven. Bob left us too suddenly, too soon, but he bequeathed to me a deep appreciation of Prince's art.

In verbose excitement, I told George what I knew. George gave Prince a space on the second floor of Material Culture, among the pots and rugs, freeing him to paint what he wanted, and Prince entered a period of intense productivity. His is not the kind of work that gets done nine to five. He retreats through the fissures in time, closing his eyes to make contact with his spirit. He chats constantly on the cell phone, maintaining connection with Nigeria. He appears, disappears, reappears. His coworkers groused, complaining that he was being given special treatment, so, eventually, George struck a deal with Prince about profits and cleared out a small, well-lit room by the carpenters' shop, allowing him to come and go at will. Prince now had a studio, supplied by George without cost. And that is how it remains, but when George hired him first, knowing nearly nothing about him, but trusting his instincts, it marked the beginning of a fresh and hopeful phase in Prince's turbulent life.

That was late in the fall of 2004. A new deal had been made and Prince was on a roll. At Paris, on May 25, 2005, nominated by Olusegun Obasanjo, the president of Nigeria, Prince was named the UNESCO Artist for Peace, "in recognition of his artistic contribution to the promotion of dialogue, tolerance and understanding among peoples, particularly in Africa and its diaspora." Those were the words on the certificate signed by Koichiro Matsuura, Director-General of UNESCO. Matsuura had written to Prince, saying, "Your ability to shape new artistic paradigms and your capacity to move beyond conventional forms of proportion and perspective have been hallmarks of your genuine artistic approach." After half a decade of misery, Prince had a victory at last.

His international stature as an original and important artist had been reaffirmed. Soon the UNESCO Artist for Peace sold a major work to the Philadelphia Museum of Art, and in the autumn of 2005 George Jevremović mounted a joint exhibition in his new gallery at Material Culture for Prince Twins Seven-Seven and Mister Imagination. A star within the class of creation called outsider art, Mister Imagination assembles industrial detritus into figurative sculpture, often tangential self-portraits depicting a handsome, bearded black king, picked from his dreams and ornamented with bottlecaps. Mister Imagination had his throne and statues on one side of the gallery. Prince had sixty-four paintings, most of them brand new, on the other. Wanting to meet both of these men, I flew to Philadelphia. Both artists had good shows, selling much, and the night ended with Prince's band playing and all of us dancing, Mister I in a cowboy hat made out of bottlecaps, Prince's women in lush Yoruba dress, moving in subtle, startling excellence.

Over the next nine months, Prince once came to Indiana, giving a gallery talk at Indiana University where I teach, and I got to Philadelphia several times. Who had the idea first no one remembers, but as we talked, George, Prince, and I, it became my responsibility to write this book.

We all had our motives. As the producer of the world's finest new carpets and the owner of Material Culture, George Jevremović had no screaming need for money, but he wanted to help, a book would announce that Prince was alive and well in Philadelphia, and he had no objection to selling the paintings he had bought to keep Prince afloat. George had supported the publication of scholarly books before, believing it is an obligation of his firm to increase general understanding of the abounding art of the world.

Prince, for his part, had given hundreds of quick interviews, leading to hundreds of notices in print, all much alike, and he already had a book. As he describes it, he visited Ulli Beier in Australia, where he now lives, and read to him from his diaries. Beier edited his reminiscences into an excellent book, *A Dreaming Life*. But much time had passed, things had changed. Prince had seen thick books of mine lying around; he attended a lecture I gave about Ireland on Saint Patrick's Day in 2006. He was anxious to tell the whole story, to describe his life as he views it now. He wanted to create a permanent record for the future, and he felt that a new book would bring him new admirers, new buyers: an artist has to live.

As for me, I was in the midst of a project on Japanese figurative ceramics, not looking for work, but I had learned from my writings and the writings of friends—the fine books on Southern pottery, for example, by Ralph Rinzler, John Burrison, Terry Zug, Mark Hewitt, and Nancy Sweezy—that scholarly books can benefit their subjects, encouraging them to keep at it and bringing them, through serious attention, financial gain. Understanding something of Prince's predicament, I suspended my project (my Japanese friends are doing well, fortunate to live in a nation where tradition and art are valued), and I took up this task, hoping it would help Prince during his struggle in my difficult country, knowing it would help me.

Money was not at issue: if this book earns royalties, they will go to Prince. My profit lies in the writing. By writing I would get to learn about him, to learn more about Africa and

African art, and I could demonstrate how I think vital arts should be studied. I had written about great masters of traditional art from the United States and Ireland, Turkey and Bangladesh. Prince offered me a challenge and a chance.

The challenge was to learn enough to write with confidence. The chance was to show how living artists ought to be approached for understanding. My work is founded on the conviction that famed painters in big Western cities, unknown potters in small Eastern towns, old farming men who sing in the pubs on the border, young women who weave in the far mountain villages—all artists should be brought into the record by means of the same method. My method, refined through more than four decades of practice, requires time. It requires observing the process of creation and participating in the unfolding of events, sharing intimately in the lives of the artists. It requires many long and unfettered interviews about art and life. It requires exacting formal analysis of the objects—the works, the texts—through which artists express at once themselves and their cultures. As the poet Seamus Heaney said of poetry, all art is simultaneously a "revelation of the self to the self" and a "restoration of the culture to itself." And things like poems and paintings are all we have. People cannot be studied directly; there is no hole in the head through which we can enter and poke about. Known only through their communications, people are rigorously, courteously, compassionately understood by study of the sensate things they offer through bodily motion into the world: their postures and gestures, the clothes they wear, the words they speak, the artifacts they shape out of mundane substances, clay, wood, wool, apples, ink. Such things are all we have to know about other people.

My purpose then was to learn about Prince. My purpose now is to get enough of what I learned into prose so you can meet him. Prince is not an example of some force or process or condition. He is a man. Real, complex with contradiction, ultimately unknowable, he is, for me, a man, as George Gudger was a man for James Agee. I am not an Africanist with a need to reconcile the conflicting authorities and make of Prince a representative African man—though he is a man of Africa who offers glimpses through a slim aperture of Nigerian history and Yoruba culture. Nor am I an art historian with a need to fit his works into some scheme, reducing them to examples of African art or Yoruba art or traditional art or heritage art or self-taught art or outsider art or folk art or fine art or modern art—though they are, in part, all of those things, calling us to consider our categories of inclusion and exclusion while encountering creativity, unblinkered by academical convention. I do not intend a historian's biography, testing his statements against ostensibly objective evidence for their veracity. A folklorist, an ethnographer, I am after a subjective revelation. The truth I seek is the truth as Prince sees it.

Inspired long ago by autobiographies of Native Americans elicited by anthropologists, books like *Sun Chief* and *Two Leggings*, I believe it is a sufficient achievement to meet another individual, a fellow traveler on the long road. Study will expand to groups, movements, communities, societies, whole nations, but all understanding begins with real people, with individuals and their acts of creative will.

This, then, is how one man—extraordinary like everyone—talks about things, conducts his life, practices his religion, and makes his marvelous art.

The author of the future who composes a full biography, like Ellmann's on Joyce, will find useful Ulli Beier's book and mine. That author will be glad that we talked with the man at length and published our divergent versions of his life, incorporating facts to be found in no other document.

I write out of three sources: the garrulous notes I took while I watched Prince work and traveled with him through Nigeria; the tape recordings I made of his story during ten long sessions in July of 2006, four in October of 2007, two more the next April, one in June, and a last two in November of 2008; and the hundreds of prints and paintings I have seen, some in books, others in Prince's homes and the homes of his collectors, most of them at Material Culture in Philadelphia, where George Jevremović has assembled a massive collection of his works that spans the whole of Prince's career. The key texts are of his contriving: his pictures and his story of his life. Represented in photographs and transcripts, they provide us a shared basis for interpretation, the means for a patient approach.

In writing, I will probe Prince's art for his creative principles, then I will present his life as he told it, as much as possible in his own words. I asked few questions, and let him talk on. What he said I transcribed exactly from tape, spelling names and Yoruba words as he told me they should be spelled. Then I edited tenderly. When he composes an artful narrative, his myth of the origin of Osun, for example, what you read is what he said, precisely, word for word. But in the rambling informational passages, I have, without altering words or splicing statements together, omitted disorienting digressions, tightening the text to sharpen his point, while guiding his speech to the page. He deserves to be heard, read, understood.

This book's first part carries the story of Prince's life, which I analyzed and arranged, directed by his priorities, to make his order and emphasis clear. It is his truth, I repeat, that I am after. Next I consider his works to capture the patterns and connections of his personal style. Last comes a gallery of his creations, arranged to display his worldview and accompanied by his explanations. In them, Prince will get the last word.

All of it is designed to get the two things together—his words and his works, his life and his art, so you can gain some feel for the man, a signal artist of our time.

Part One: Prince's Life

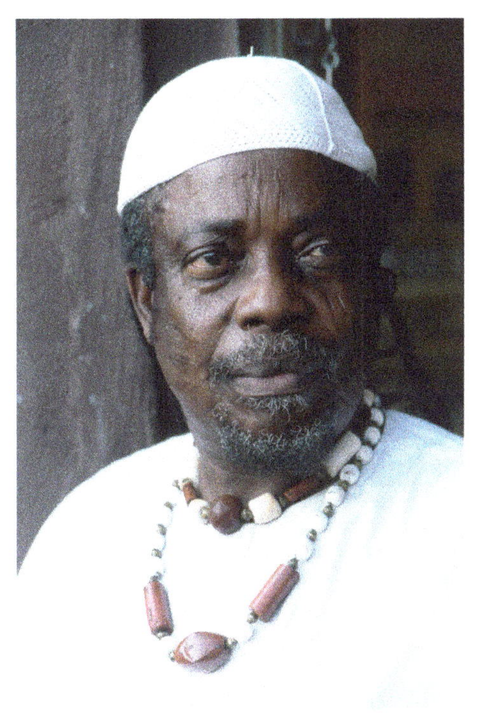

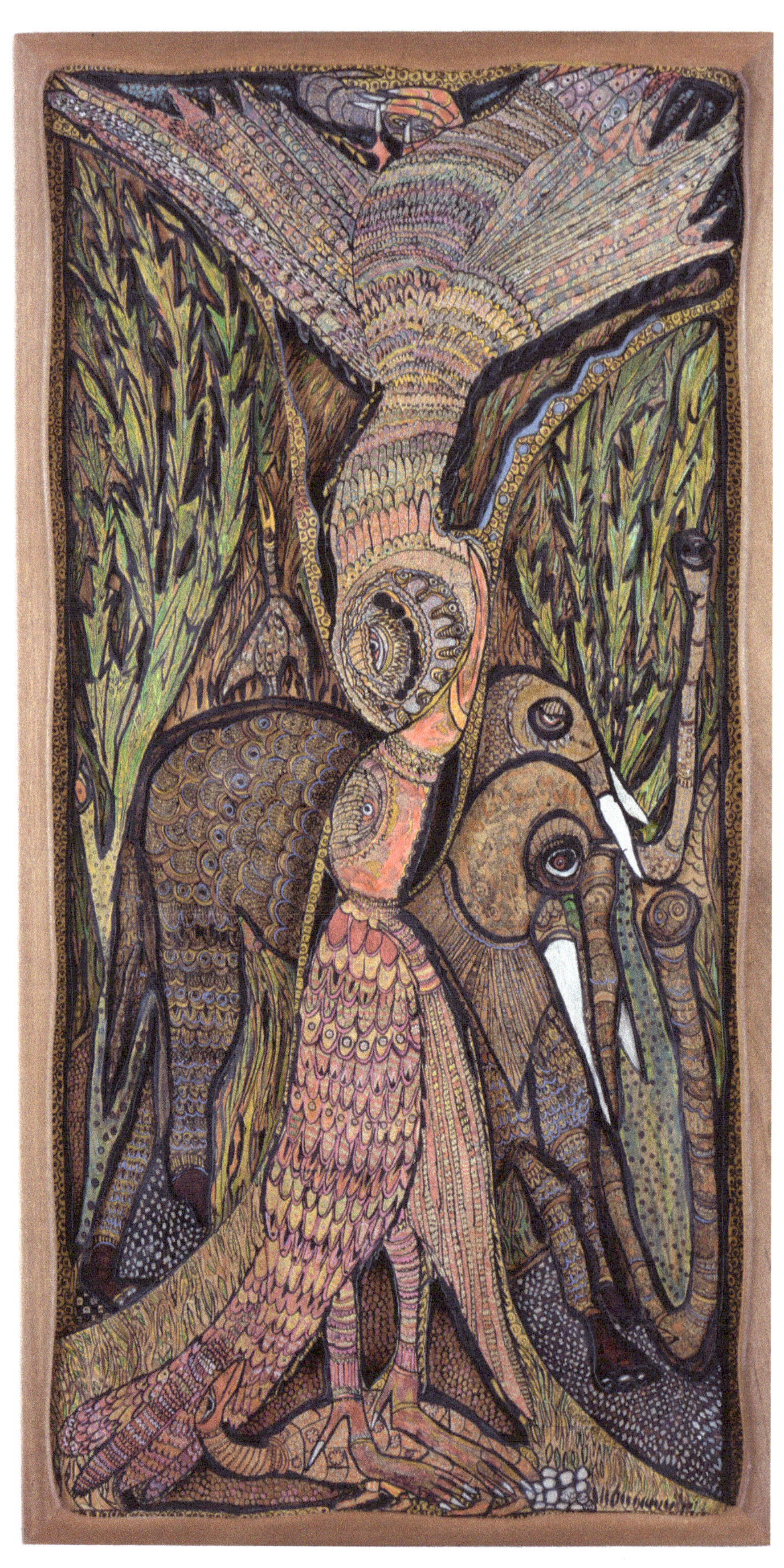

Kissing Birds. Ink, pastel, watercolor, acrylic, and oil on wood; 3 layers. 4'4" x 8'4" (framed). Philadelphia, 2006

·1·

Kissing Birds

Before Prince begins the story of his life, I will describe the creation of a painting he calls *Kissing Birds*. I start there because the man is a painter, revealed as much by his works as his words, and I have chosen this from all the pictures I watched in progress for good reasons. It is the painting he made while we talked, and he will refer to it as our interviews roll forward. A more important reason for my choice is that *Kissing Birds* is characteristic and complex, exemplifying his procedures at their fullest, and it is most important, at this stage in the story, because the principles he used in his painting are the principles he will use in composing his autobiography. The principles of his thought and action, they bring us near Prince Twins Seven-Seven.

To begin at the beginning: in the summer of 2006, George Jevremović, seeking to beautify his store, asked the men of the carpenters' shop to cut ogee-arched panels out of plywood to place above the doorways, and seeking to get a little cash to Prince Twins Seven-Seven, he asked him to decorate them. Prince painted them pink, applied beads and bits of glittery glass, then brushed around them in black. His decorative program followed and reinforced the bilateral symmetry of the forms, in the manner best suited to architectural ornament, but he did not measure. Prince glued and painted spontaneously, and the asymmetries of his action contradicted the symmetry of his concept. Look at his work and you will see what Edmund Wilson saw when he looked along the classical colonnade on the lawn of Mr. Jefferson's university at Charlottesville, or what James Agee saw in the austere wooden buildings of rural Alabama. The stable symmetry of the mind is wrenched by the swift motions of the hand, and in the tension between idea and act, plan and performance, inert material objects vibrate with life.

Agee spoke of symmetries sprained and sprung. Sprung symmetry is the artisan's way to bring life into things, things into life. When two women sit between the hewn beams of a loom on a mountainside in Turkey, they follow no drawn plan, no cartoon. Their design, assembled in experience, comes out of their heads—*kafadan*, they say—through their fingers into knots of wool, tied and cut quickly, color by color. The women differ in skill; one is teaching, one is learning. They differ in their inviolable selves, but improvising and compromising, they bind their separation into the unity of a carpet. Their shared concept is symmetrical, and perfectly so, but its appearance in the world is syncopated by the differences in the women whose habits of hand and impromptu decisions abide in the pile. When a carpenter at the edge of a town in Pakistan shapes on the lathe four legs for a stubby chair, he gauges his turning by eye, measuring little, working fast. Wood spins, contracts, and swells. Each piece is patterned like the other, but the yield of the practiced, active hand, no two are exactly the same.

Carpet and chair, apparently composed of identical parts, but vitalized by difference, are, in this, like the things of nature. Like a pine tree, like the human face that seems the same on both sides, though it is not, the artisan's creation, its symmetry sprung, belongs to life. By contrast, the artifact of impeccable symmetry erases the human, becoming, like the geometries of Islam, symbolic of the transcendent perfection of the divine, or, in the tool machined to intolerant exactitude, an object to employ, without pause or guilt, in some self-serving endeavor.

But the artifact of sprung symmetry, in asserting and subverting the power of repetition, escapes reduction to symbol or tool. It stands as a human presence, allied to the energies of the world. In the middle of the nineteenth century, John Ruskin praised the imperfections of Gothic architecture as signs of the worker's humanity. Ruskin got it right. When the expectation of repetition is upset, when repetition's mirrored closing into symmetry fails, a gap opens between concept and appearance. During contemplation, the mind grips the embracing order, while the senses wander pleasantly among the subtleties of free variation, and slowly the ghost of another appears, a human being whose plan is found in symmetrical design, whose momentary performance registers in variable detail. Order and disorder coexist in quiet unresolution. So it is in the English parish church, for example, the Turkish carpet or the Japanese teabowl. That bowl contains the geometry of its concept in its form, then the gritty clay, the tracks of the potter's fingers, and the glaze that broke and flowed in the kiln, tell the tale of its making. In teetering balance, the creation establishes a pattern, teaches it, then alters it to exhibit at once the creator's planning mind and performing body.

Symmetry makes the beginning, the ground and frame, revealing a deep commitment to balance and wholeness. Then the artist's departure might be nonchalant, playful, compelled by contingency, or—following the line of argument in Wole Soyinka's essay on ritual—it might be heroic. Refusing to be confined, even by plans of their own, artists become free, abandoning things to the world that propose a relation between the mind and the body, theory and practice, timeless concepts and historical actions. Their works feel human. As Robert Plant Armstrong argued, they are not objects, but subjectivities that fill in for the absence of their makers by capturing a fragment of the universally human while aligning themselves, of necessity, with the cultural particularities of people called Japanese, say, or Serbian or Yoruba.

Sprung symmetry is a key trait in the art of Prince Twins Seven-Seven. And it is a trait in the goods—the Turkish carpets, Pakistani furniture, and Japanese pottery—that George Jevremović selects for sale at Material Culture in Philadelphia. At some point there is a deep meeting of taste between these men of strong will, enabling George to offer, and Prince to accept, a place to work at Material Culture. As surely as George makes decisions about Prince's work in the frame of general appreciation, Prince frankly comments on the things arrayed in George's shop, strongly favoring the conspicuously handmade.

George and Prince connect in respect and exchange. They need each other. The merchant needs goods of quality, worthy of his customers. The artist needs liberal and sympathetic patrons. At once advancing his financial interests and striving sincerely to help Prince, George bargains hard and buys his paintings, and he commissions Prince to ornament his store. In 2007, George paid Prince to decorate a gigantic fiberglass dinosaur; now it stands high in George's vast showroom. In 2006, the carpenters cut them, Prince decorated them, and when the arched tympanums were set in place they fit the store's prevailing style.

Then Prince walked into the carpenters' shop and there he saw, leaning against the wall, the four-by-eight sheet of plywood from which the arched tympanums had been cut, one from each side. In it he saw, instantaneously, an image of two birds kissing. He took the board, shaped roughly like an hourglass, into his studio and placed it on the table in the sun. At the time, he was working on a large painting on paper, but inspiration had struck. He rolled the old picture up (he would finish it six months later), and after fourteen long days of labor in the month of July, he had completed *Kissing Birds*.

At the beginning of his career, Prince made no sketch. His pictures grew, detail by detail across the sheet. Now he begins with a sketch, drawing quickly in long sweeps of the pen, in hasty gestures that will be confirmed and blackened as the picture progresses, preserving the spontaneity of his first motions. His sketch for *Kissing Birds* traced the geometry of two triangles, poised point to point, that might have represented any paired forces, equal, oppo-

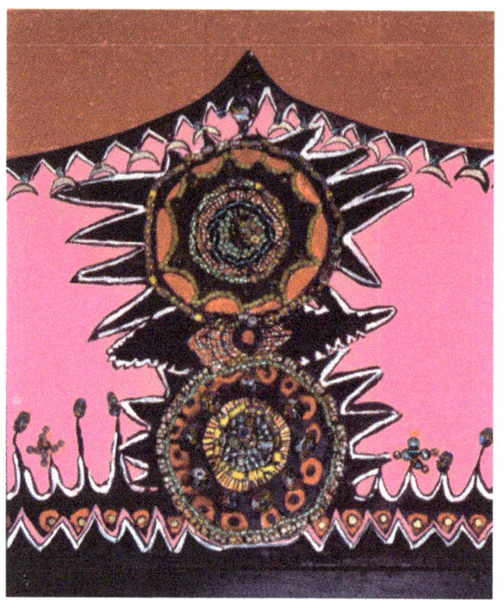

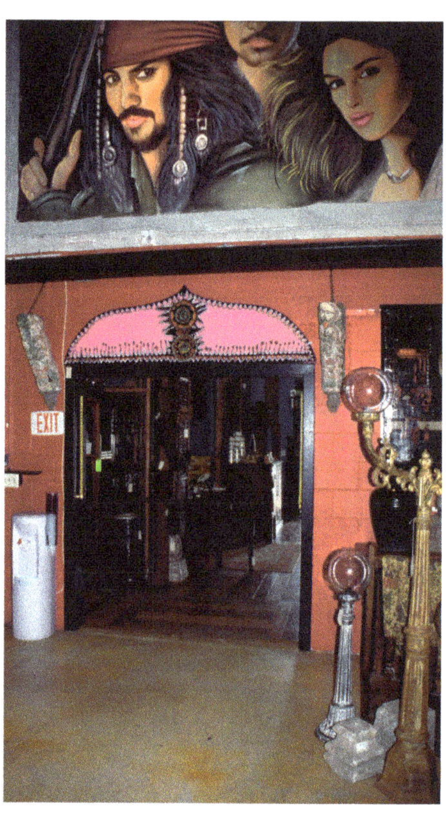

Pink tympanum by Prince.
Material Culture

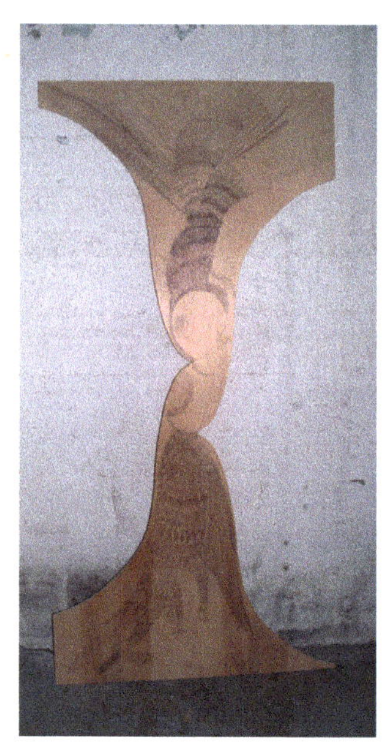

The board with the sketch

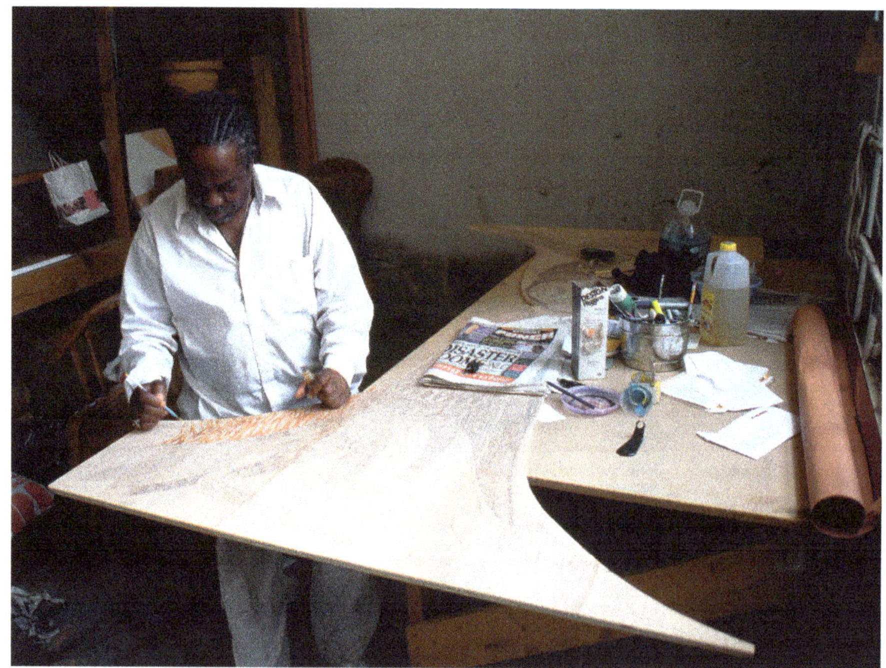

Painting begins

site, and balanced. But as he drew, Prince distorted the geometry, sprung the symmetry by refiguring the triangles into birds, one stretching up from the ground, the other descending from the sky, the two meeting in a kiss.

The forms of the birds lead us into Prince's process of creation. Once, at a party in Philadelphia, a pleasant woman asked him a question artists often get. He was sitting with Ade Oyelami, a friend from home who was visiting from Atlanta. Prince was wearing a satiny white robe and drinking red wine. The woman asked which artists had influenced him; did he admire Picasso? "I'm bigger than Picasso," Prince said with a smile, and then he explained. Picasso developed modern art in Europe by borrowing ideas from Africa, but Prince is an African man and his ideas for a modern art come directly and effortlessly from his own tradition. "The only person who inspire me most," Prince concluded, "is God." He smiled again, commenting in an aside to Ade and me that by God he meant Olodumare, the great Yoruba creator.

On the matter of influence, Prince was clear. No other artist sets a model for him, though he is open, wide open, to the influences that rise up from his tradition, the tradition of the Yoruba people, and to the influences that flow through him as he moves attentively among the wonders of God's creation. Amid these crosscurrents of inspiration, the only artist upon whose work he builds is the one called Twins Seven-Seven.

Prince soaks up ideas as though there were no skin between him and his sources, then he works and reworks them. Sometimes he starts with a small, quick picture, trapping an idea that he elaborates into a masterpiece. Sometimes in an instant of high excitement, he paints that masterpiece first, then explores it by creating small pictures out of its parts. His own work makes his base: through practice he has shaped for himself a little artistic tradition of one. Before he began *Kissing Birds*, he made a small watercolor on paper, *Fish-eating Lover Birds*, showing a slim female bird, light in color, beneath a darker, hefty male bird who was catching fish from a river. Their postures and positions are different in *Kissing Birds*, but these are the same birds: a slender female reaching up from the earth, a burly male dropping out of the sky. The opposition implied by the triangles, point to point, one above, one below, has become specific. Presenting the separation and unity of forces in bird form, the picture could represent—to borrow from Soyinka again, this time from a poem—the wedding of sky and earth. For Prince it represents the joining of female and male powers into an image of power itself, the power that divides among creatures like people or birds who are merely male or female, the power that unites in love and nature and God: the one and enduring power of the universe.

The jigsawed board with the sketch lies on the table among tubes of paint and bottles of ink, pastels, colored pencils, and felt-tipped markers. As for media, Prince says, "I will use anything that comes to my hands." Three tasks lie before him: blackening the outlines, filling them with ornamental detail, and filling the ornament with color. He will begin all of these tasks, shifting from one to the other, before finishing any of them. Painting the outlines in black, he darkens and sharpens his sketch and defines areas on the board that need to be cut away. These he marks with a quick X, or he writes "cut out" on them. As the outlines thicken and blacken, the forms become more detailed. The earth's bird is standing on a tortoise, and when Prince turns to the bird in the sky, he draws a snake in its grasp. Watching, I ask, and Prince says that from the beginning he planned to have the female stand on a tortoise, but he had not planned on the snake. It just showed up when the hand with the pen was moving.

The black outline, like the sketch beneath it, is gestural: quick, loose, and bold. It sets up a contrast with the ornamental infill, a contrast that baffles his many imitators and stands as a defining trait of his style. It might seem that a loose sketch would be followed by a loose, painterly attack, impressionistic or expressionistic, wild and free. Instead, Prince bears down on the ornament like a craftsman, using two techniques to render the feathers. In one of them, seen plainly on the wings of the male bird, he draws long, swift vertical lines, then inserts between them chains of repetitive geometric motifs. In the other, seen on the wing of the female, he draws a horizontal sequence of lappets, like the scales of fish, like rounded shingles on a roof, then fills them, row by row, with geometric forms that alternate rhythmically in descent. By these means, while feathering the birds, Prince divides space, then divides it again and again. The pen more than the brush is his tool, shapes and lines concern him first, and he keeps drawing until the empty spots, all trimly confined, are the size of the smallest peas and beans. Then he touches with the brush, filling the tiny voids with color to create contrast, balance, and an overall tone.

The bodies of the birds exhibit strong, simple outlines, black upon black, that fence the wide fields of delicate patterning Prince likens to textile designs. The artist's act, Prince feels, is an act of connecting. Just as he joins male and female power in his image, he combines in his action two sides of his personality. He is an artist as bold and free as his outlines. He is a craftsman as patient and caring as his ornament. His art brings the opposed forces within him into vibrant association.

Prince is a practiced master. He had forty-two years of making pictures behind him when he started on *Kissing Birds*. His process is set. Before he finished drawing the lower bird,

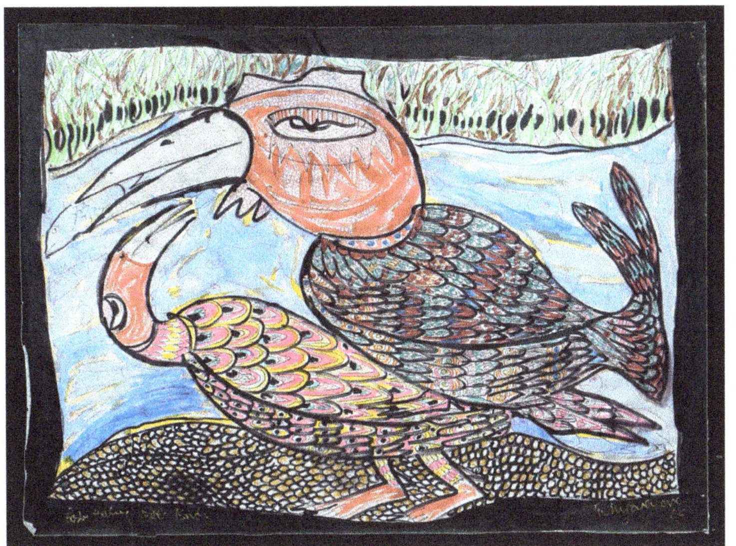

Fish-eating Lover Birds.
Ink and watercolor on paper. 24"x18".
Philadelphia, 2006

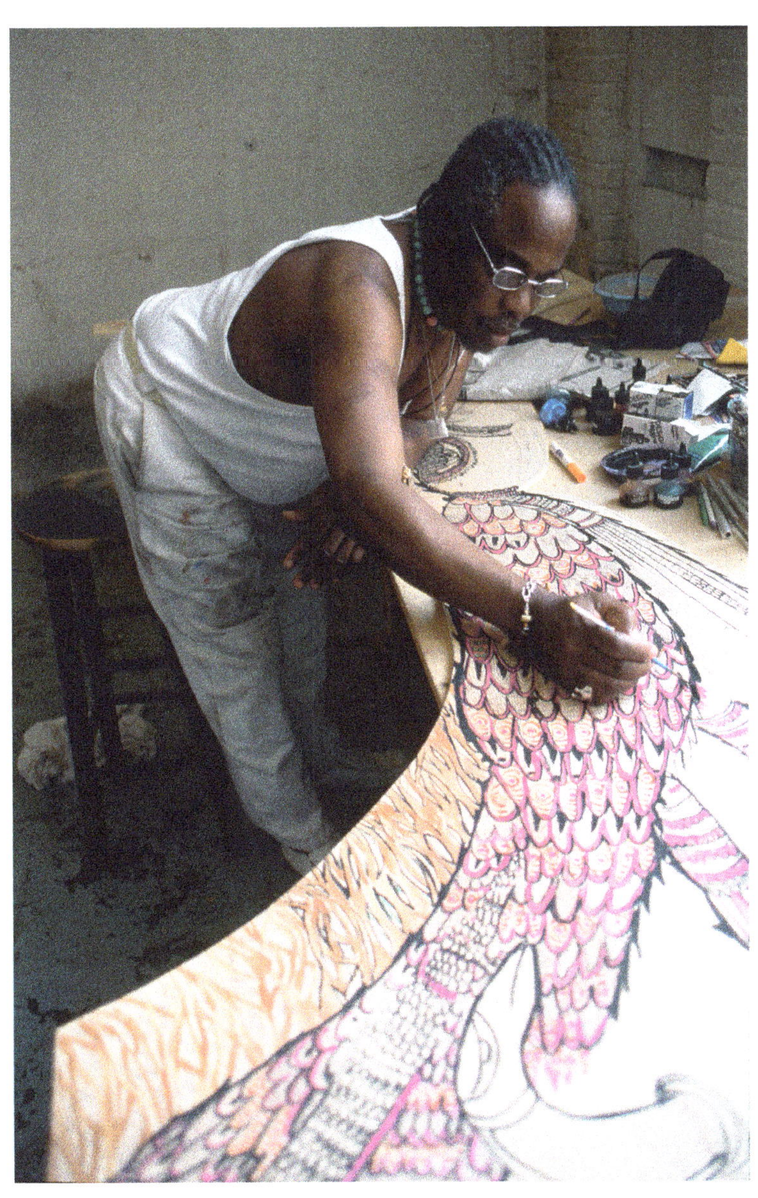

Kissing Birds.
Painting the female's wing

he began drawing the upper bird. Before he had finished painting the lower bird, he began painting the upper bird. He moved back and forth, alternating from side to side, now drawing, now painting, and before he had finished the birds, their faces still undone, he borrowed a power drill from the carpenters and punched holes through the board. Then he took up an electric jigsaw and let it run while he rammed it through the holes and ripped sections of the board away in swift, imprecise sweeps like those of his original sketch. He painted the board's raw edges in black, and the birds were finished enough.

While he was working, I asked why he turned to a second job before he had completed the first. Prince replied that it would be best to finish each phase of a project, refining it to perfection before turning to the next, and then to assemble finished parts into a finished whole. But, he said, that is not how he does it, and he had reasons for doing it his way.

First, if you work as quickly as he does, submitting to the momentum of the moment, you are bound to make mistakes. You will spill paint, as he did on the face of the male bird. You will saw off a piece that ought to have remained. Mistakes, he said, are easier to rectify if the work remains imperfect, ragged to the end, since repairs blend smoothly into rough passages. Prince did not say, but I noticed that when he made a mistake or reached a dead end, he did not pause to ponder. He turned to some incomplete portion of the picture, drawing more little motifs or dabbing them with paint, doing something easy before returning to what he was doing before. It is useful to have some unfinished business to attend to while you figure out how to fix what has gone wrong.

His second reason is continuity. In a big project like *Kissing Birds*, what you create in a late stage will force you to return to earlier work, modifying it to better fit the drift of the whole. This return ensures continuity from part to part, and it would be a waste of time, Prince said, to bring an early phase to perfection when later work will require its revision. I understood his point from my craft. If you fret about polishing every clause in an early chapter of a book, it will prove to be time lost because something written in a later chapter will drive changes back through the manuscript. It is wiser to bring each chapter near completion, tolerating roughness in them all, until the final draft when the book as a whole makes sense. That is how Prince does it: by pushing on to the next phase before the last one is done, he can move backward as well as forward while creating continuity from point to point, balance in the whole.

Continuity and consistency, balance and wholeness are goals in Prince's craft. Incompleteness helps him forward. When drawing the ornament, he shapes one motif here, another there, then links them across empty space, establishing the pattern. Next, he draws motifs inside the motifs, checks for consistency, then goes back to add more details—radial lines spring from the circles in one row, spirals surround the circles in another—until the complexity of one passage matches the complexity of the others. When he adds the color, he experiments in one patch, then another, closing the gaps color by color. He started on the birds with pastels, colored pencils, and watercolors. The colors were pale; he called them fragile. Then he mixed red and black into yellow ink to get a brown that he applied with a brush to one side, then the other, moving back and forth. If he painted steadily from one side to the other, Prince told me, he might run out of the color he had mixed. He could mix up another batch but it might not match. So he alternates from side to side, leaving the middle empty, to ensure balance, a symmetry of hue in the picture as a whole. The brown he uses in this work is a prime color for Prince; it throws over the picture a veil of consistency that blends with the wood beneath, that fuses with the ambering varnish he applies at the end, that modulates between the black of the outlines and the brighter colors they contain, the red, the orange, the green. "I'm trying to find what color the bird is," Prince said, then he added purple to the female, yellow to the male, creating contrast between them, before bringing them together with dots of black.

As unfinished passages disappear, the picture spreads with patterns consistent in scale, with colors that differ in hue more than value. It comes into balance, takes on a tone of wholeness. The visual effect is calming, reassuring. In many of Prince's paintings that effect, the result of his craft, contrasts dramatically with the content. Prince's relentless imagination directs him to draw images from the other world: spirits and ghosts with stretched necks, spiky feet, multiple eyes, and displaced heads. In his spontaneous drawings, these figures are strange, passing strange, even frightening. They remain so in his quick pictures, but when he sets out to paint a masterpiece, they are subdued by symmetries, trapped in a calming environment of repetitive patterns and balanced colors. Fear drains away, and the work meets Prince's desire to picture images from his tradition, while gentling into accord with his predominantly cheerful, unfailingly positive view of the world.

Gathering much, a picture by Prince can be disturbing and amusing, wild, frightening, fanciful, disciplined, and restful all at once.

The birds of the picture in progress are not disturbing like the ghosts of other pictures, but they are strange. They certainly do not resemble birds you have seen. Departing in form and ornament from the birds of the air, they prompt symbolic interpretation. A year after his picture was done, I asked Prince why birds feature so frequently in his work, and he answered while the tape recorder ran:

"In Yoruba belief, human beings are like birds, flying birds. Because we believe that we have birds in our spiritual thinking. In the sense that, even from your dreams, you can find yourself very very far away from where you sleep. Because we believe the spirit in us can fly like a bird.

"At the same time, you know, the birds represent the witchcraft. In your thinking, in Western thinking, the bats represent witches. But in our culture, in Yoruba traditional thinking, the birds, any flying birds, represent the influence of witchcraft.

"They are good and bad at the same time."

These birds are more than birds. They symbolize human beings, depict the soul in flight, and evoke witchcraft, a multivalent force in the world. The other animals, Prince said, also carry meanings. The tortoise is the Yoruba trickster, the small, wily hero who beats the big beasts in the old stories Prince learned from his mother, but in this case, he said, the tortoise stands for the lowly, weak people in society. The snake brings to Prince from Christianity feelings of deception and evil, since Satan came as a serpent to the garden. But in the Yoruba tradition, he said, the snake associates with Ogun, the god of iron, the god of the warriors. It means power, not evil, and yet for Prince personally the snake slithers with the odor of death, for his father died after the bite of a snake. So, the bird who grips a snake in his talons is a mighty bird, stronger than death, and the bird who stands on the tortoise is one who tramples the weak. The powers of the birds increase, but their force and passion and frenzy diminish in the comforting balance of his rendition.

Now the picture of the birds is finished enough. Drawn, painted, and jigsawed, it is ready to become the top sheet in a laminated work of the kind Prince calls a sculpture's painting. He invented the technique in 1969, and though he paints on paper, canvas, and cloth, the sculpture's painting of wood, large or small, remains his signal creation.

This one is large, and his studio is too cramped for the next step in the operation. Beyond the studio's door, out in a wide storeroom, we place two new four-by-eight sheets of plywood side by side on sawhorses, making an eight-foot square. We set the kissing birds across them, athwart the seam. Prince had found another scrap in the shop. Its shape suggested a seated beast, and he sketched an animal on it. He said it could become a dog or it might be a leopard. Either one would fit the theme of power, for the dog is Ogun's beast and the leopard is an emblem of chiefly authority. He places the scrap to the right of the birds. Deciding immediately that it wrecked the picture's balance, he leans the scrap back against the wall, where it will remain until, months later, he will build it into a large sculpture's painting, *Imaginative Dream of George's Dog*. We place one clear sheet of plywood on the horses and align the birds precisely atop it.

Prince draws lines around the birds, then he stands and looks and thinks for about five minutes while patterns on the lower board shape an image in his head. Such natural patterns, he told me, are gifts from the world to his imagination, just as his dreams are. Two lines in the grain of the wood outline in his mind an elephant's head and the descent of its trunk. With amazing speed, he draws the elephant's face, gives it an eye, sketches its trunk and front legs, outlines its rear, puts a bird on its back, and another elephant behind it. The second elephant was not part of his plan; it just came, he said. The birds and elephants arrive in pairs, like twins in double power. Prince ends his sketch in long strokes, raising a leafy forest above the elephants.

Elephants appear in Prince's work nearly as often as birds do. They limit human power in his paintings, killing the hunters who try to kill them for the ivory of their tusks, and earlier in the summer of 2006 he painted a small picture of an elephant with birds beside it, reversed but quite like the one he sketched first on the board. The elephant fits the painting as well as a leopard would, because, Prince said, the elephant is the king of the jungle, a symbol of regal power in human affairs.

We lift the top sheet, the one with the birds, and carry it back to the studio where Prince paints in the details of the tortoise, thinking. Abruptly he stands and returns to the lower sheet, the one with the elephants, still resting across the sawhorses. He has decided to cut the first elephant out and add a third sheet of plywood below. He draws around the elephant with a ballpoint pen, marking the areas that must be cut away. The drill wails, the jigsaw whines: holes open between the leaves of the trees, and the front elephant, all but its eye, is gone. We gather the scraps so Prince can make repairs once the second and third sheets of his picture get glued together.

Building additively upon itself, as Prince's process generally does, this laminated technique would seem to be a way to accomplish something like perspective, the lower sheets indicating depth in space as they recede, layer by layer, in the manner of a Chinese or Japanese landscape. But that is not exactly what Prince produces. In this case, the birds of the top

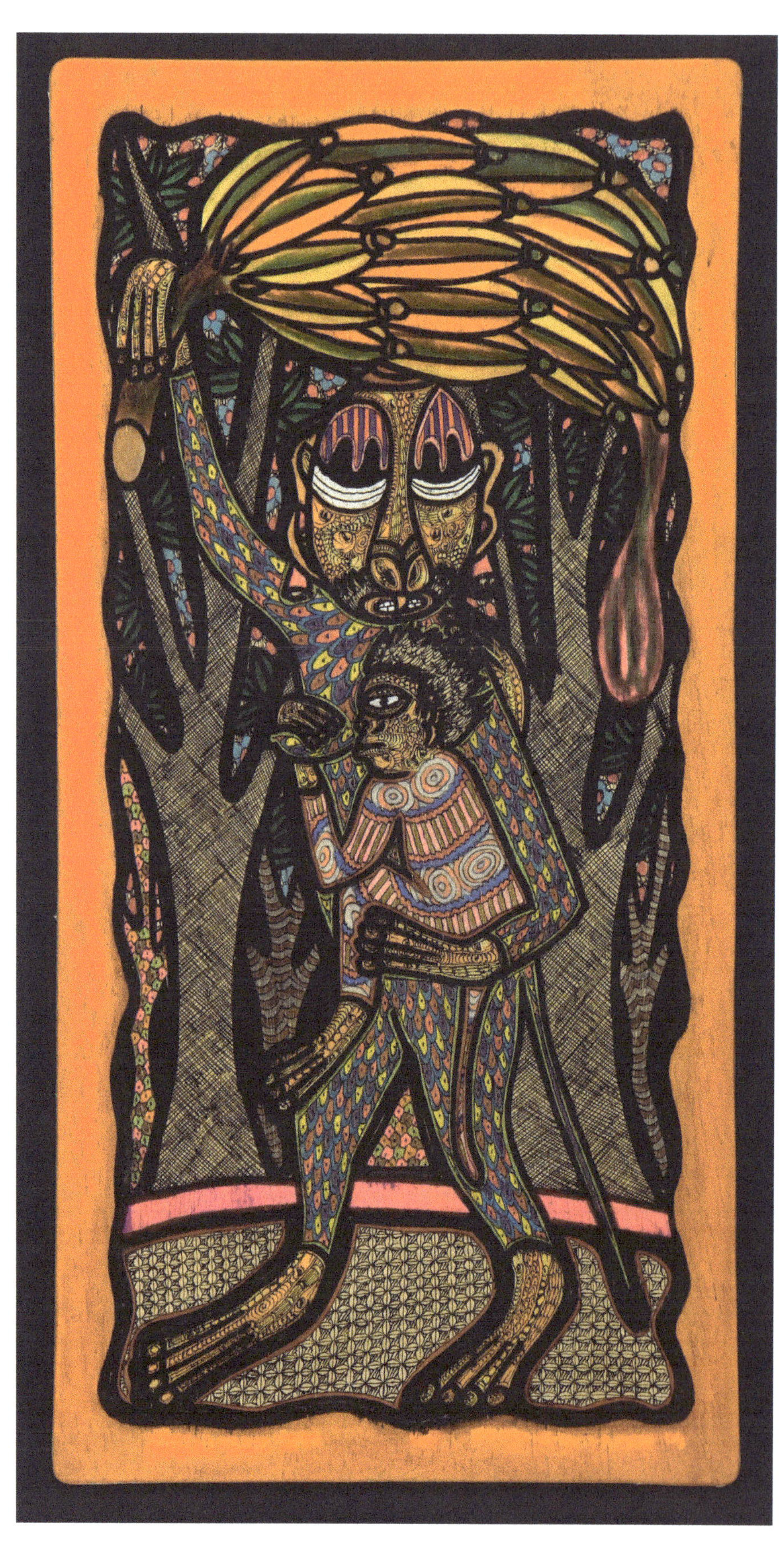

Baby-caring Mother Monkey (Edun).
Ink and oil on wood; 2 layers. 12"x24". Osogbo, 1998

sheet will kiss in front of the elephants, but the first elephant will be painted on the bottom sheet, apparently closer but actually further away, while the elephant behind it will be painted on the middle sheet, deeper in space but nearer the viewer. Spatial distortion of the sort is normal in sculpture's paintings by Prince Twins Seven-Seven. Here is another example, a small painting, one of several with orange borders in a vertical format that Prince made at the end of the nineteen-nineties. Composed of two layers, like most sculpture's paintings, it compares with the bottom two sheets of *Kissing Birds*. Both pictures read as figures in front of a forest, but instead of an elephant this one shows a densely patterned mother monkey, a baby in her arms, a bunch of bananas on her head. The front board carries the monkey and two of the trees from the forest behind her. The back board carries the rest of the forest and the geometrically configured ground beneath her feet.

Pieces of the background step forward, bits of the foreground retreat, and the work at once represents visual depth and invites an awareness of spatial interconnections, much as the increasingly small motifs in Prince's repetitive patterning, receding in relation to one another but all lying on the same plane, provoke a sensation of an interlocked, infinite expanse of the kind that the masters of Islamic art reveal in their intricate geometric assemblies. In Prince's work, foreground and background interact to effect compression at the pictorial surface where a subjective, visual experience merges with an objective, intellectual understanding. Things happen all at once and close to us, as they do in Persian and Indian miniatures. Depth and flatness coexist, and the mingling of the viewed and the imagined, the seen and thought, take us through his art toward the man himself.

It is time to assemble the whole, to check for errors. The second sheet lies on the third, and we bring the birds back. Prince scans and discovers that he had accidentally cut off the back of the second elephant and with it the bird. Freehand, he cuts a new back and a new bird. He told me that the forest rising behind the elephants would be full of birds, but this is the only one that will make it through to the end. When he cut the first elephant out, the scrap took the sketch with it, so he draws the elephant again.

We lift away the top sheet, and Prince glues the middle and bottom sheets together, adding the limbs of the trees that had broken off, the elephant's back, and the bird. He piles on heavy blocks of wood to secure the bond, abandons the lower section of his picture for two days, and returns to the birds on the table in his studio. Plenty remains to be done. There are always feathers to pick out with paint, and he must devise a design for the birds' faces to disguise the dribbles of paint he spilled across the male bird's cheek.

When he returns to the lower sheets, now glued together, his task is to blacken the edges, raw from the rip of the saw. First he paints with an acrylic black that gives him a deep gray, then he follows with india ink that is truly black. The blackness of the outlines—aggressively dividing form from form, demarcating zones in wholeness—is of special importance to Prince. When in 2006 he found an old sculpture's painting, made in 1989 for sale in Finland, he immediately freshened the black with new ink. Now he continues the chore of blackening the edges of the boards, switching for interest to outlining the big elephant. As he does he finds mistakes. So, he saws out a piece for the missing tusk—he calls it the ivory—and glues it on. Then he cuts slender scraps to glue between the elephant's trunk and front leg, its tail and back leg. Though the elephant is drawn on the bottom sheet, these additions will lie on the plane of the middle sheet. All come physically forward, as the tusk visually should, but the other bits belong to the background; conceptually they recede.

Complications accumulate. Bold outlines and delicate patterns, weird figures and harmonious colors, spatial depth and pictorial compression, visible objects and visionary imaginings—things come together, and Prince keeps going. "Back home," he said while he blackened the edges, "there is nothing like working for certain hours. You work until you are tired or some event comes up." He keeps at it, whistling and singing snatches of Yoruba songs, switching from task to task, repairing things that went wrong. "Mistakes," he said, "always come up when you are in a hurry. Sometimes you have to move. If there is a hole in your roof, and the rain is coming, you don't wait till the rain comes before you start moving the things the rain will mess up."

Prince keeps moving. He has cut up the scraps and glued them on, and now he gets back to the black. The edges darken. The forest and elephants take shape.

When the birds return, they will form a vertical mass that gathers from each side then sweeps from the top and bottom to a narrow point at the middle. At that point, the backs of the elephants will transcribe a rolling line that divides the design of the background into horizontal bands. Vertical motion—the upthrust of the trees, the elephants' trunks on the right, the bird on the left—will connect his composition, echoing the curves of the birds as they rise or fall, but Prince approaches the background as separate tasks in horizontal zones. The forest above makes one task, the elephants below make another. It will not be news that, during four days of work, Prince will move back and forth, up and down, beginning both tasks before completing either, urging far-flung parts gradually toward union.

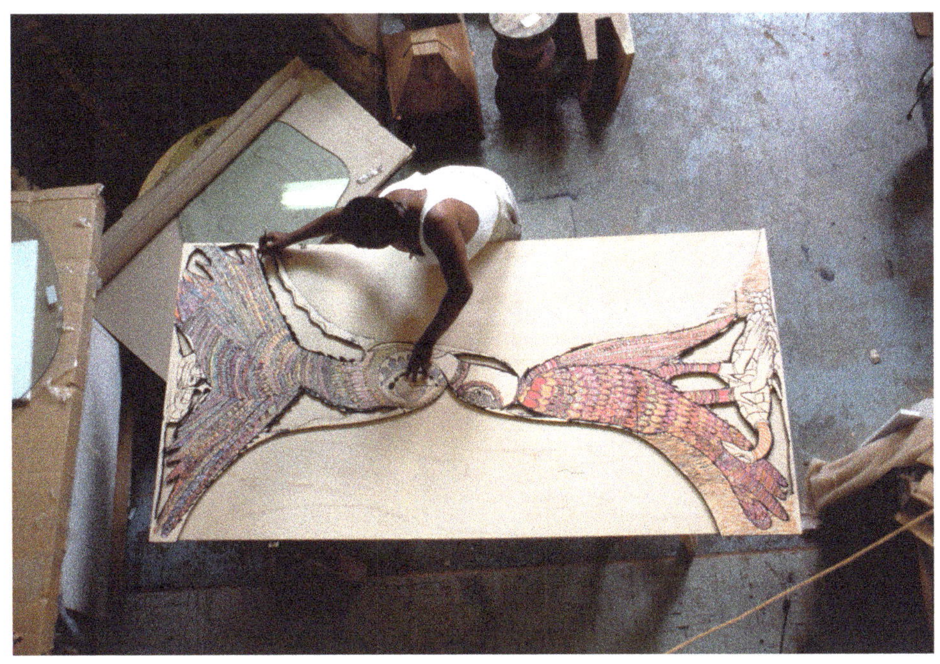

Placing the birds
on the second sheet

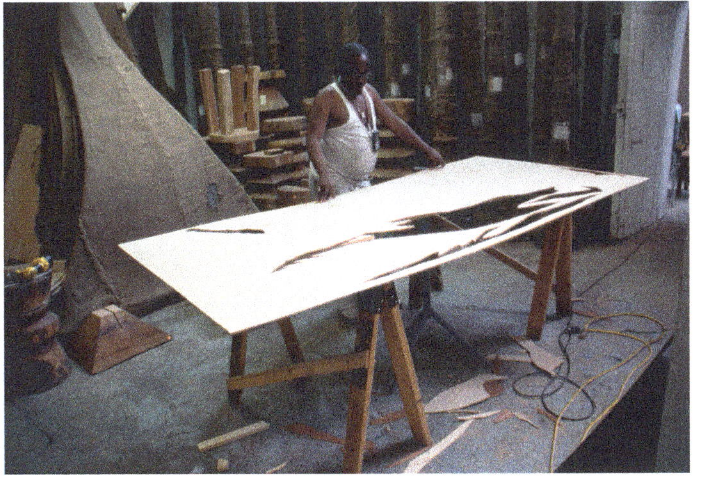

Planning the cuts of the second sheet

Sawing pieces to apply
to the bottom sheet

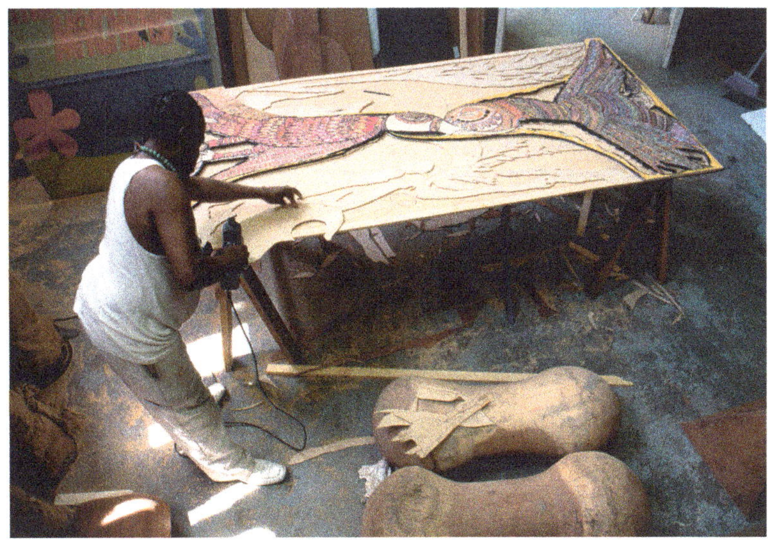

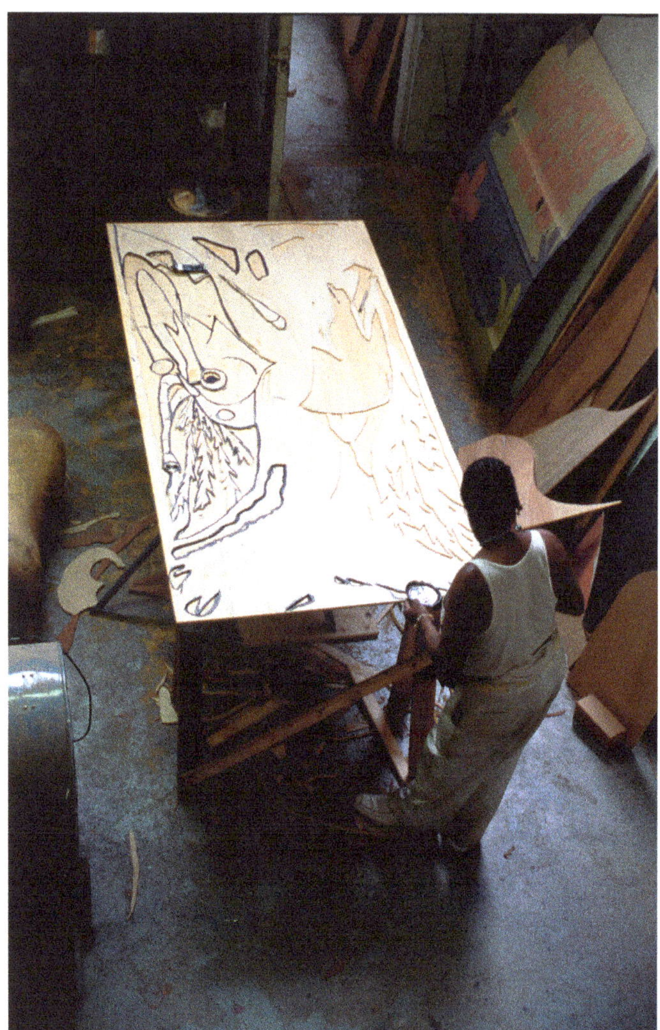

Blackening the edges

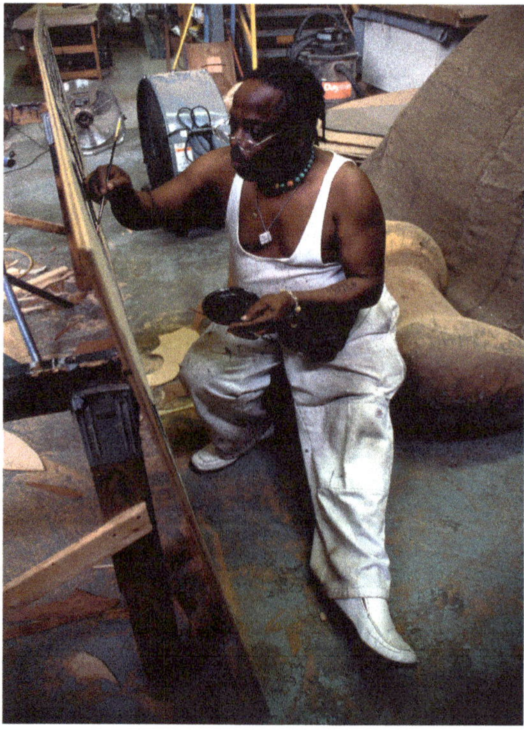

Drawn with a ballpoint pen or a green pencil, outlined in black paint and ink, the forest breaks vertically into four sections. On each side, the sections are larger, the leaves are larger, the colors are brighter. Prince mixes an acrylic green to paint the leaves, adds yellow to the green and paints again, the fluttering color suggesting depth. Then he quiets the green with dashes of red and brown, moving from side to side, back and forth, to frame and balance the picture with identical hues. "See," Prince says, "the forest is coming slowly." He fills the smaller, interior sections with smaller leaves and darker colors, providing a channel through which the male bird will descend.

"I might paint the background some color, but it will not look perfect without putting some drawings there," Prince tells me, and then into the slots between the leaves, he begins drawing tiny flowers onto the bottom board with a ballpoint pen. Circles surrounded by semicircular petals, they match in form and scale the tiny circles that represent gravel on the ground under the elephants, which Prince started drawing, to give himself a break, before the black outlines were finished. These minuscule circles, each touched with pastel or paint, create subtle balance between the picture's top and bottom and imply a solid background of colored dots. Almost completely obscured by the trees and beasts, but glimpsed through the gaps, this background establishes a far plane, so deep in space that its forms nearly elude recognition or perception.

The forest lies over the ultimate ground of tiny circles, flowers above, gravel below. Its parts display no infill of pattern: the leaves are drawn in black, spread with color. Here Prince's method is as much the painter's as the draftsman's, but when he began with the elephants, where he concentrated his effort, he ornamented them with the same techniques he used on the birds, and the repeat of the patterns will pull his picture together.

Prince started his work on the front elephant's rump. The forest had yet to receive its color when he drew one rounded scale to the right of the first row, a second to the right of the third row, a third to the left of the third row, a fourth to the left of the fourth row, a fifth to the left of the second row, and then he linked them into a sweep of seven rows that rolled over the elephant's rear. Now he begins to detail the scales, placing circles in the first row, swags in the second, angled waves in the third, black dots in the fourth, small scales in the fifth, circles in the sixth, small scales in the seventh. He will return to draw swooping lines between the rows, finer detail inside the scales, and smaller scales coursing down the elephant's legs. A flat pattern of scales, of lappets in rows like roofing tiles, will cover both elephants and match the pattern of the female bird's wing. The other pattern, the one begun with vertical lines and seen on the male bird's wings, Prince will apply to the elephant's ear. These are, for Prince, versions of one technique, derived from the design of batiks. Both are slow; both involve intricate geometric drawings, filled between the lines with spots of color. Another in this set has a grid like a checkerboard as its base. Prince contrasts all of these with a quicker technique he calls tattoo, in which drawings in black are made upon a swath of paint. That is the technique he will use on the big elephant's head.

When he moves from the elephant's back to its front, Prince finds that he has to cut little scraps to surround the elephant's trunk, slathering the gaps with a filler of sawdust and glue. "By the time it dries, and I apply the color," he says, "you don't see the joints." Finding, too, that a stretch of the sketch was misplaced, Prince sands it off and paints heavy black lines around the elephant's head and eye. He begins the decoration with random arcs and curls of brown ink. Then he spatters black with a brush, outlining the spatters in ballpoint pen, affirming his acceptance of accidental effects. Next he splashes dots of brown across the elephant's face and down its trunk, smearing the dots with his fingers. He dips a pen in india ink and begins to outline the irregular shapes of the smears. Some remain amorphous, but one turns into a rat, another into the head of a dog. The work is quick, but it absorbs the mind while the penpoint plays, discovering tiny figures at a level of detail few viewers will ever notice. Prince says as he draws:

"If I spent six months, I will bring a lot of things out there. This is a time-consuming process if I want to do that.

"That's why I have to be careful. Because if I start, I can't stop. I want to make it so people will keep looking. The more you look, the more you see. I have to be careful or I never finish. I bring out more, but I hate these things coming to me. I don't want it, or I never finish.

"I intentionally kill all the small figures that start coming. Because it would take months to finish the elephant. I try to avoid it, but still it comes out.

"You can't stop. It call you."

Little figures pop out despite him. His work draws him in and holds him. "It's coming fast; my mind is moving fast," Prince says as one brown spot turns into a fish, another into the head of a cow, and small spirals emerge between the smears.

These splashes of black and brown, these wee creatures, black on brown, combine into a passage of tattooing that Prince will trap between patches of geometric patterning when he

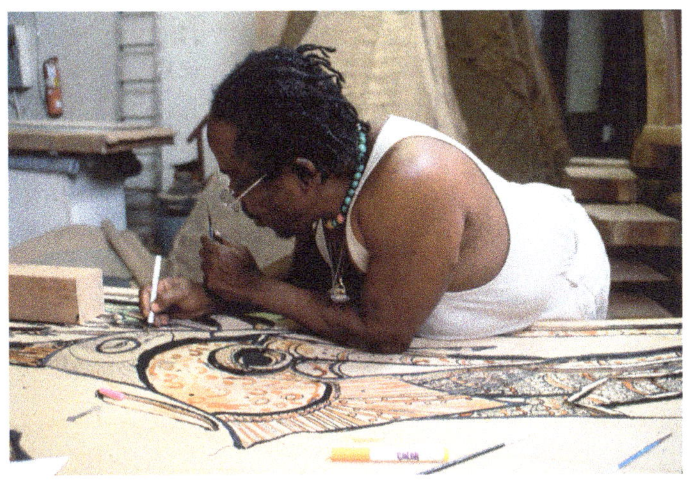

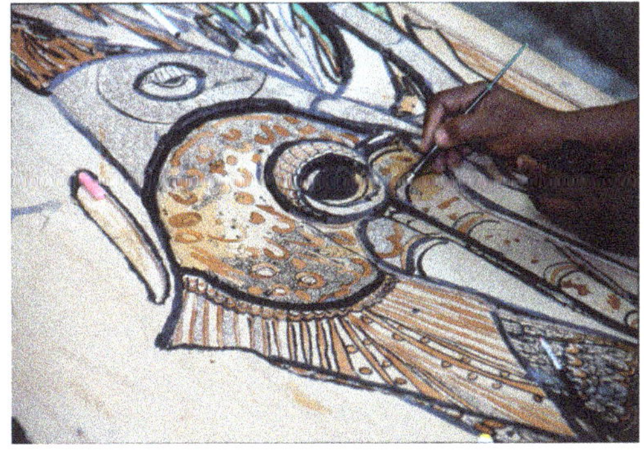

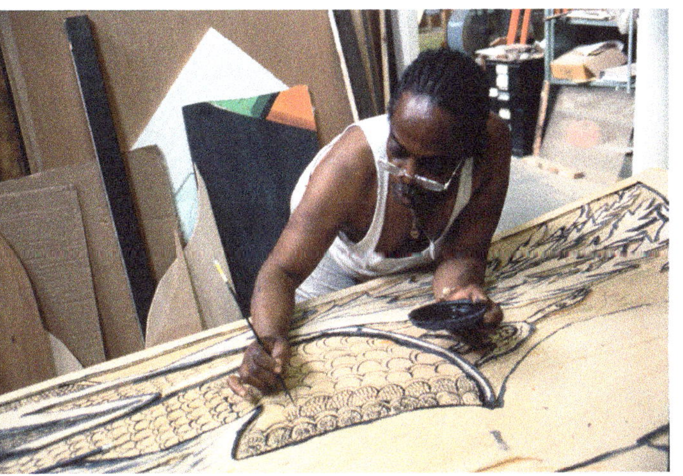

Painting the elephants

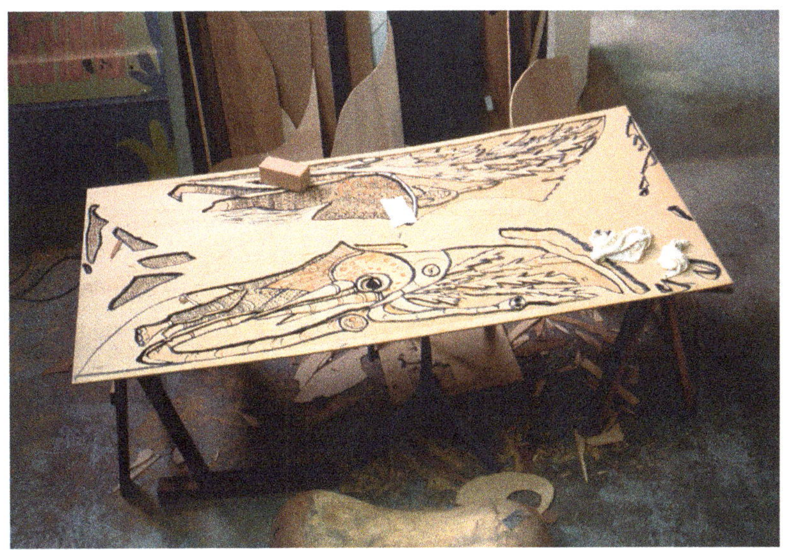

covers the back elephant's face with a checkerboard and finishes the front elephant's trunk with lines that separate rows of motifs: spirals, scales, waves, circles, and one upside-down dog.

The end is in sight and Prince is in "a finishing mood." They are two pleasures, working and finishing. He whistles while he works and separate tasks go forward simultaneously, but he is silent in finishing and he rushes with determined haste, too much haste at times. In reaching to paint the leaves of the trees, he spills yellow across the elephant's rear. Earlier it would not have mattered, but now the elephant's patterns have filled with color. Prince wanted to have the elephants "brownish" to make a dull backdrop for the brighter birds, but when he wipes the yellow off with his hand, enough remains to force him to add yellow and orange to the elephant's patterns to hide the error. It was not in his plan, but "It looks good," he said. That accident was a gift to the picture.

Prince smiles and keeps going, drawing gravel, painting grass, ornamenting a tree with a checkerboard pattern, but this is mostly a time for black and brown. Outlines thicken and darken, spots of brown dance into cohesion. Then he squeezes white oil paint onto his finger and smears it on the elephants' tusks and eyes. Watching, I laugh with understanding: black and brown with counterpoints of thick white on a spread of fine pattern; the thing now really looks like the work of Prince Twins Seven-Seven. No other hand could have done it.

On the last day, July 29, 2006, we assemble the parts on the big bench in the carpenters' shop at Material Culture. Prince glues the top sheet on. At home, he drives nails through the layers with a hammer, clinching them on the back. Now he borrows a nail gun and shoots nails in great numbers through all three sheets; their heads are lost in the maze of patterns. The birds have joined the elephants. Ian Jones, a carpenter in the shop, has made a mahogany frame for the picture. It fits, and the picture seems done, but "You never finish a painting," Prince says, echoing Yeats who said he did not finish poems, he abandoned them.

The black is never black enough. Back home, Prince grinds charcoal and mixes it with water and kerosene to get his black, but it fades, so india ink is a blessing, as are felt-tipped permanent markers. He takes up a black sharpie, stretches over the frame, and runs black once again around the birds, the trees, the elephants. Then he sprays the picture with varnish, believing it will protect the fragile colors in his blend of media, knowing it will pull the black lines to the surface and provide a unifying sheen and golden tone to the whole. Prince looks

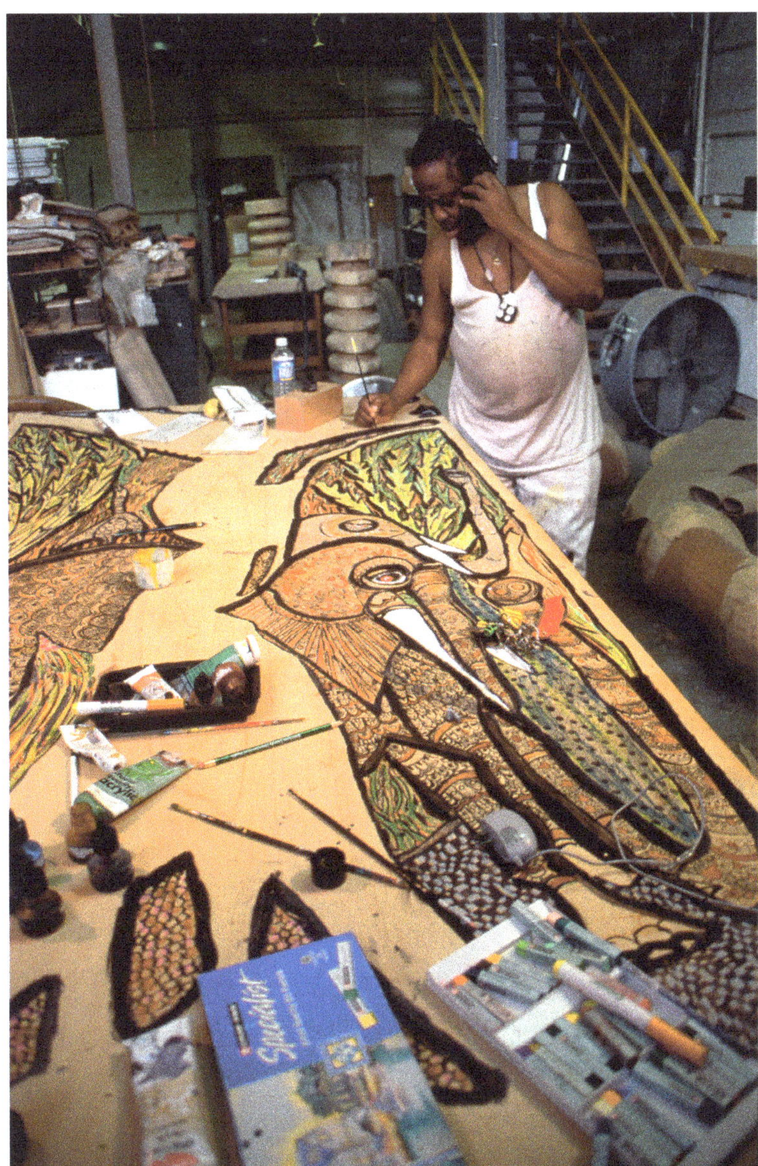

Prince in a finishing mood

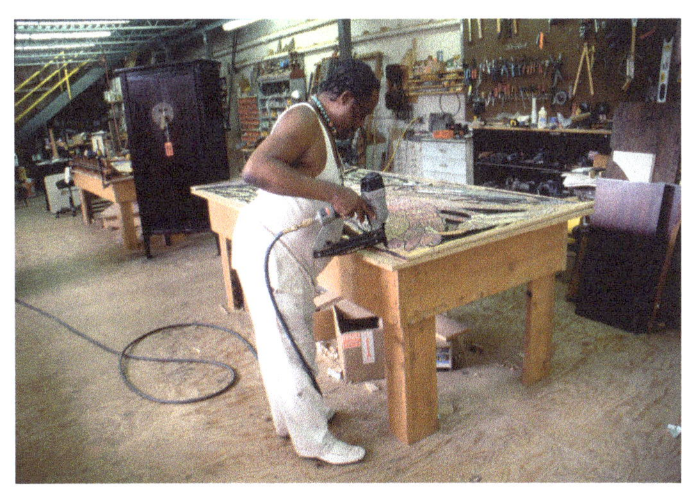

Nailing the sheets together. *Kissing Birds* is done

it over, adds touches of black, another coat of varnish, and he walks away from his picture. It is ready for sale; the price is seventeen thousand, five hundred dollars.

Now, having answered Paul Klee's request to describe the artist at work, as one must in studies of material culture, I look back to look forward. In Prince's creative procedure, as displayed in *Kissing Birds*, lie three principles that he will use in telling the tale of his life.

Acceptance is first. It brings connection between the artist and the world. Prince accepts ideas that come from beyond him and builds his acts upon them. Ideas arrive in found objects. He accepted a jigsawed piece of scrap plywood as the base for his work. He shaped the elephant's profile from the grain in another piece of wood. Not in *Kissing Birds*, but in many of his other paintings he incorporates bits from the world—beads and shells and sequins, strips of cloth, printed pictures, and locks of hair—in the images he creates. In this, as in much of his work, Prince follows old African precedent and aligns with tendencies in the late West, where pastiche, collage, and assemblage figure in the art of both insiders and outsiders.

Sometimes Prince forces things to reveal their ideas. He will pour water on a board and leave it in the sun to raise the grain in which he finds the forms he draws. Other times, gestures of his own—intended accidents—bring him ideas. He spattered ink on the elephant's face, then smudged it to discover the little animals lurking in the brown smears. During 2005, he proceeded like that in many paintings, spilling paint on the canvas, turning and tilting it so the color would run, and then rationalizing the spills into representational images.

Mistakes also come from beyond; they are not intended. Some Prince scrapes away or hides with repairs, but, he told me, mistakes are gifts from the spirits. Turkish artists say proverbially that a mistake is a new design. Prince agrees, and usually his mistakes, like his free gestures and the patterns in woodgrain, provide new points of departure in the restless onrush of action. He accepts them and they remain, along with the designs he draws, in the finished product.

When Prince told his life's tale, he moved rapidly as he did in painting his picture. Word followed word as motif followed motif. Unlike some others whose stories I have recorded, he never stopped in uncertainty and called on the aid of published texts. He gave me documents, some rare and ephemeral, which I used in my writing, but he spoke on without them, comfortable in English, secure in his knowledge. What he gathered from beyond and used to press his story forward were dates and names, especially the names of places. These facts, lodged in his memory but not his invention, Prince used, as he used my comments and questions—as he used the scrap sheet from the carpenters' shop—as places to begin. He accepted them as points of departure in composing his narrative.

Acceptance is first. Balance comes next. With pattern and paint Prince ratified his commitment to balance, but its base lay in the sketch he made at the beginning. Two triangles meet point to point at the midline of his design, dividing it into halves. Both triangles subdivide, revealing a broad base with a reptile—a tortoise in one, a snake in the other—before narrowing through birds to the point of their conjunction, a kiss. During the first four days of our interviews, Prince sketched his life, and its form matched the plan for his painting exactly. He broke his life into halves that balanced on a midpoint, the moment in 1964 when he drew his first picture. The first half narrows from the broad base of culture, through his arrival in Osogbo, to that moment of creation. The second half widens from that point, through his exhibitions, to the broad sweep of his accomplishments and problems. Both halves subdivide by events—the death of his father, his coming to America—to establish four segments in his chronology: 1944 to 1952, 1952 to 1964; 1964 to 2000, 2000 to the present.

The scheme is symmetrical. But when Prince refined the outlines of his story, adjusting them to follow the contours of events, and when he returned during six more days of talk to fill his sketch with life's surprising details, he sprung the symmetry, just as he did when he transformed the triangles into birds and spread them with flat patterning. Symmetries lie in his mind, but he responds to chance. Making no measurements, he acts swiftly and draws freely at the large scale of his plan and the small scale of his ornament. The big triangles sway, the little motifs trip along, no two exactly alike. The whole work begins to flutter and flow, to match nature in vitality.

Sprung symmetry, I repeat, is a key trait in the art of Prince Twins Seven-Seven. It is visible in his picture, audible in his oral autobiography, both of them symmetrical in concept, spontaneous in execution. Sprung symmetry is the link between the principle of balance and the principle that governs Prince's mode of composition. Astute students of art, both Robert Plant Armstrong and Henry Drewal, have recognized that a particular compositional dynamic—the one Prince employs—is a defining characteristic of the creative force of the Yoruba people.

Drewal calls it seriate composition. Armstrong calls it syndesis and contrasts it with synthesis. In synthesis, oppositions resolve in closure: life is confined by form. In syndesis, distinct entities accrete: life is released to proceed, to go on and on, as though to the beat of a drum. Both dynamics abide and combine in the thought and action of all human beings (which positions sprung symmetry centrally in creation, for it opens synthesis to syndesis), but one or the other rises to typify the creative output of different cultures and eras. In the West, the shift from the Middle Ages to the Renaissance was marked by a shift from syndesis to synthesis (as I have labored in books to explain through the example of architecture), and then modernist action in the twentieth century was guided by attempts to retrieve syndetic energy: Picasso turned for inspiration to Africa, Pollock dribbled paint to a soundtrack of jazz, and Beckett, the greatest of modern playwrights, put it directly when he said that he wished to eliminate form in favor of movement.

Among the Yoruba, as Armstrong and Drewal argue comprehensively and convincingly, syndesis prevails. Prince is a Yoruba man. His work fits his culture, displaying signs of syndetic, serial thinking in the black outlines that separate forms, in the motifs that stream in sequence, in the boards piled one on another, but his process is most obvious when you watch him at work.

Prince's process of open, unpredictable, serial composition operates at the level of form. He drew the birds without knowing the male would grip a snake. He completed the design of the birds without knowing an elephant would stand behind them. He drew the first elephant without knowing a second would stand behind it. The form evolved in the midst of motion, and meaning followed along. A year after his painting was done, I asked Prince to explicate his text, and he said:

"It's called Kissing Birds.

"I don't need to tell you about this, because you know how it started, how I picked the woods—woods they were going to throw away.

"This is just something to do with social thinking. This is social thinking. Everybody believes that the elephant is the king of the jungle, the father of all the animals.

"And the birds are kissing in order to multiply.

"It's about human beings.

"And this one is standing on a tortoise.

"You know the tortoise; it is a very weak, weak small animal. You know how big powerful people here"—in America—"do with the poor people. It's very political in a way.

"The lower bird is standing on a tortoise. The upper bird has a snake, a symbol of the end of the world.

"And the powerful one is kissing the smaller one, while the father of the jungle was looking on, unconcerned.

"The upper bird is more powerful. It is he. The lower bird is she.

"And then the elephant who is supposed to say, Don't do that—he doesn't pay attention. They were just on their own."

Prince laughs and concludes:

"Kings don't pay attention while people make love and step on the poor ones. They don't care."

While the powerful make love with the weak and the weak trample the weaker, while human beings exploit their powers—witchcraft is one—to mistreat one another, the most powerful do not care; they fail to use their inherited or usurped authority, as they should, to bring society into peaceful balance. Prince's "political," critical interpretation of the disturbing content of his balanced, decorative painting cannot have been the meaning he intended at the beginning. For then he did not know the snake would appear, or the elephants. It is a meaning made in retrospect as he looked back on a work that grew incrementally through an additive procedure—syndetically Armstrong would say.

Prince formed his story like that. He regularly apologized for sudden shifts of topic, for bringing forth a new subject before he had finished his previous thought. Ideas thrust themselves upon him while he spoke, just as they did when he painted, and it was not until he had traveled far along a narrative line that he came upon the larger meaning that bundled past words into the coherence of significance, that made his speech act interpretable.

Prince's spontaneous, improvisational process of serial composition worked at the level of form and interpretation, and even more conspicuously at the level of ornament. He filled the outlines with patterns, going over them and over them again, inserting finer and finer details, discovering yet more figures in the smears of brown ink. He will do that in his narrative, returning to topics introduced earlier and elaborating them with increasing complexities.

Prince used two main techniques to decorate his birds and elephants, one geometric and borrowed from textile design, the other figurative and called tattoo. When he fills the outlines of his story, he will also use two main techniques. In one, he begins a chronological sequence of events, continuing until he discovers a theme. Then he forgets time and illustrates the theme with an open-ended series of distinct, apposite examples. In the other, he tells a tale, then explores its implications through an open-ended sequence of explanatory comments. In both, his life's story unfolds toward an end that remains unreached.

In his picture and his narrative, at the levels of both form and ornament, Prince exemplifies and employs the Yoruba tradition of serial composition. The result, profound with integrity, displays a wholeness of totality more than unity; it is less a fusion of parts than a concatenation of contradictions, a simultaneity of actions.

It is time for Prince's narrative, a tale built of acceptance, balance, and syndetic energy.

· 2 ·

Born at the Edge

On the table before us, a sheet of plywood fills with pattern and color. Bottles of ink, tubes of paint, pens, brushes, and scraps of paper scatter in the summer's light. I fold a newspaper on the board to receive the recorder, flick the switch on the microphone, and tell Prince to take his time, to tell his story as he wishes. He is sitting on a high stool, pen in hand, I am sitting on a low chair beside him, and he begins:

"I was born in a town called Ijara. Now Ijara is in Ijumu, Kogi State, which is, at that time, part of northern Nigeria. During the military era, it was known as Kwara State, but now it is called Kogi State, which is about two, three hours south drive of Abuja, the local capital of Nigeria.

"My father was a prince from Ibadan, from the royal family of Osuntoki. The man Osuntoki is a warrior who traveled, fighting along his way to Ibadan from Offa. And I learned that he is a direct descendant from Olugbense, which is the most renowned warrior in the Offa hierarchy.

"I was born on May third, nineteen forty-four; on Thursday according to my mom.

"My mother suffered from the disease of abiku. I was an abiku child.

"Abiku is a child that when they born them, they died in infancy. An abiku child can even die when he is about thirty, forty years old. Depends how much the parents can hold on to him.

"In my case, my mother, who was supposed to be from Ogidi; it is a small town. In those days it is being invaded by the Nupe warriors, the people from the North.

"And during the time of my birth I believe they didn't have enough doctors and nurses, but they have the traditional medical herbs that they used to cure kids. It was believed that during the period of my birth, my mother was supposed to be carrying twins, and she have to dance.

"Because you have three type of twins. One of them they call the alarinjo. Alarinjo are twins that they have to dance in the streets. Beg for money. Even though the parents are rich.

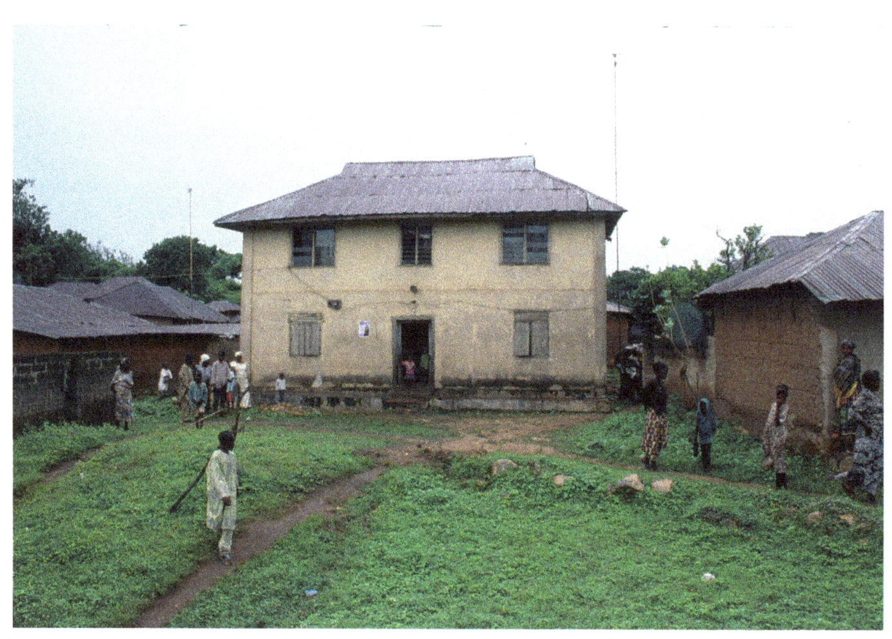

The house in which Prince was born

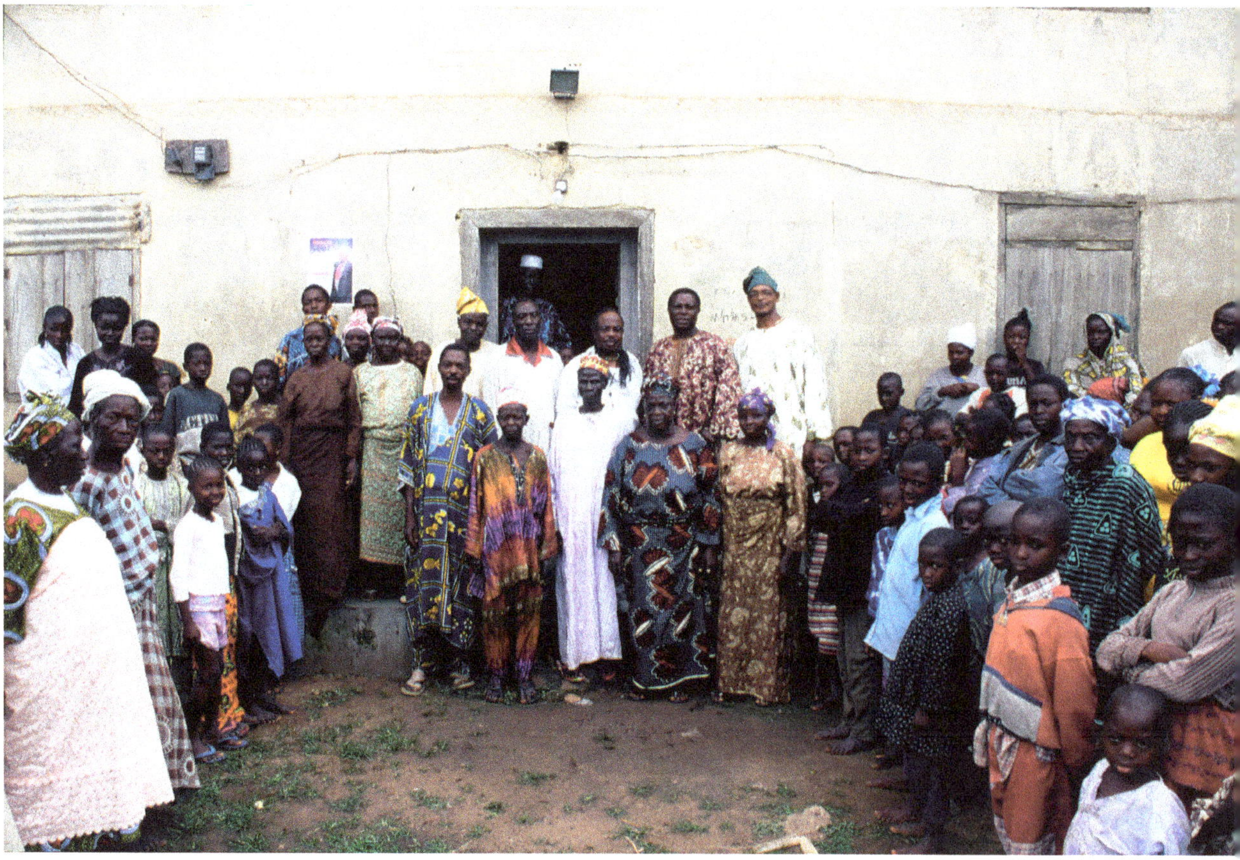

Prince and his people at his birthplace. Ijara

"But because my grandmother was—my father's mother was a trader, a very successful circuit trader—she would not like to see my mom go about in the streets, dancing, asking for alms.

"When I was in the womb, my mother told me, she had visited thirteen, fourteen different high chiefs, like obas—kings—in that area. Because she was told that the visitor, which means the baby in her womb, is going to be a great, great person.

"Eventually, they lost all their children, except me.

"So, the first set of twins died, according to my mom, when they were like about three months old. The second set left after a year. The third set—about two years. The fourth set: three years. The fifth set died in the womb; they didn't see the daylight. The sixth one—one survived; the other one died. Then when it was my turn, I was lucky to see my sister, who was a girl—that's why I wear my hair braided—living up to the age of three. But she died.

"And then my mother insisted that this one—that's me—will go nowhere. That's why they call me Bamidele—Ba-mi-dele, which means Follow me-reach-home. Because my father is not from that town. And my grandmother is not from that town. And my mother, too, was not from that town. So, they were like a visitor, living in another domain. So I was named Bamidele, which is a ritual name for an abiku child.

"In respect of when someone is an abiku, let me put it this way:

"In every family, when an old man dies, like the head of a family, and a baby was born, that boy would be named Babatunde, means Daddy has come back or Father has come back. And if it is a woman that died in the family, and a girl was born, the girl would be named Yetunde or Iyabo—Mama has come back again.

"See, there are so many beliefs that surround the recognition mythology in Yoruba thinking."

Prince pauses for the first time. He speaks quickly, without effort, his words tumbling and flowing like a swift mountain stream. Now he stops. He has completed the overture to his life, announcing his theme at the end: the recognition mythology of the Yoruba people. His theme incorporated a series of topics. To each of them he will return, shifting from one to the other, developing and detailing them in later conversations. Space came first.

The date will come later; he began with a location. He was born in Ijara. The house, though much modified, still stands, the home of a retired military man. The front door gives into a corridor, flanked by files of rooms, a plan, analogous to the English Georgian, that is common in the towns and countryside of southern Nigeria. To the right of the door, at the foot of the stair, his grandmother's tomb extends through the wall. His father's tomb has been razed, but he was probably buried in a back room to the left. Prince's ancestral spirits, he says, protect the house of his birth.

In breaking the story of his life into four segments, of which this is the first, Prince began each of them with a place, a location on the earth. Time followed space, then chronology broke down as he found the theme that organized events meaningfully. Location, the beginning, is a given, not a flash of the imagination, but a fact from the world, found in the environment as the plywood sheet for *Kissing Birds* was found in the carpenters' shop.

Set in space, the arc of time carried Prince from the margin to the middle. Born at the northeastern edge of Yorubaland in Ijara, he was raised in nearby Ogidi, his mother's town, where he built his first house. Then life took him westward, first to Osogbo, where he built a grand house, where his mother lies buried, then to Ibadan in the heart of Yorubaland, his father's birthplace, where he built a pleasant country home. From the northeast to the southwest, he crossed a landscape that erupts with rocks then levels away from the Niger in swaths of bush. He came home to Yorubaland, a nation within a nation, a place famed for its art, a place of ancient cities and long royal dynasties, of agricultural villages strung along dirt roads, a place of motion, culturally linked by the travels of warriors and traders, artisans, diviners, and laborers in search of gainful employment.

Prince's pattern of motion parallels his ancestor's: Osuntoki fought along a southwesterly track from Offa to Ibadan. More generally it parallels the trail of his people. The Yoruba, he believes, came from Arabia, moving westward across the Sudan, then southward into the territory embraced by the bend of the Niger, eventually, during the nineteenth century, making Ibadan, in his words, "the capital of the whole southwestern part of the country." Ibadan is the end of the trip, and its beginning. Of the towns to the northeast, he said, "I was born there. I only grew up there. But I'm from Ibadan." Since that is his identity and destiny, some writings, based on hasty, journalistic interviews, name Ibadan as the place of his birth. Now he waits in exile in Philadelphia, fourth in line to the throne, hoping to return and crown his life by becoming the king of Ibadan.

The Yoruba traveled west from Arabia, Prince says, along with the Hausa. He calls them, the Hausa and Fulani, the people of the North, while the people of the South are the Yoruba to the west, the Igbo to the east. The people of the North are Muslims; the Southerners are nominally Christians and Muslims, though the old religion retains power among them. As he put it one night to a group of off-duty policemen who had come to have a beer with him

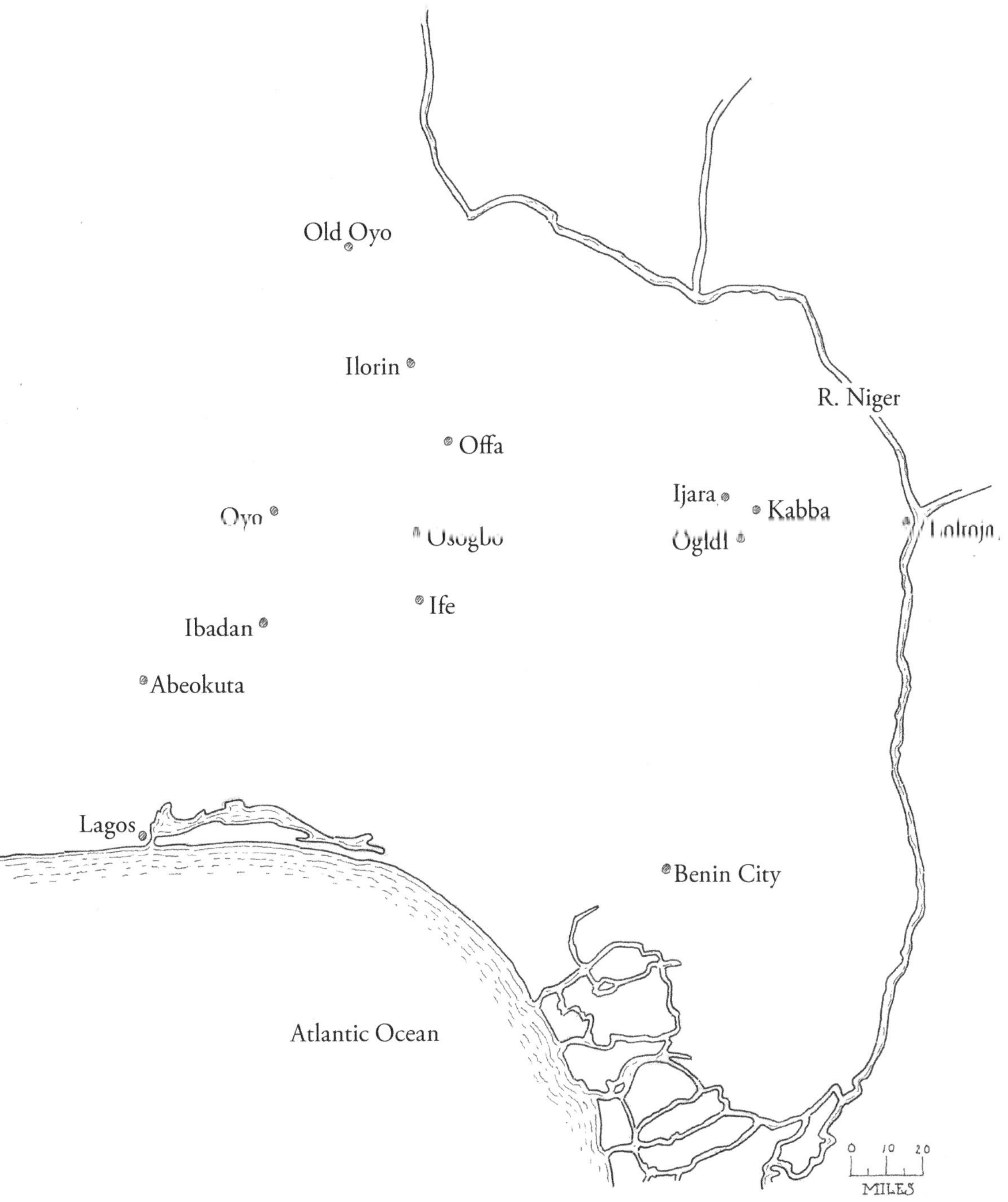

The Yorubaland of southwestern Nigeria

in the town of Kabba, "You people sing Hallelujah to Jesus in church in the morning, then you pray to Obatala at night." They all laughed, shifting a bit nervously.

The quip is conventional with him, though usually he says people pray to Jesus in the morning, Sango at night. His observation tallies with academic opinion. Islam entered Yorubaland in the seventeenth century, Christianity in 1843, but as Wande Abimbola, a great Yoruba scholar of the Yoruba tradition, said in a published interview, complete conversion from the old religion to one of the new ones "hardly exists among the Yoruba."

In religion, as in art, Prince is firmly centered and freely inclusive in the manner Edward Gibbon attributed to polytheistic belief in *The History of the Decline and Fall of the Roman Empire.* The new religions mix casually in his speech. He says *Inshallah,* if God wills, when looking ahead as a Muslim would, and he thanks God like a Christian when looking back on a blessing. He admires the honesty of the Muslim and believes Nigerian Christians to be more sincere in their devotion than American Christians. Then he faults them all for abandoning the old faith:

"The Muslims hate me. The Christians hate me. The older generations don't like me because, to them, I am reviving the dead culture.

"I'm trying to bring back the religion they don't like. That belongs to them, but they don't care about it. Because some of them who are Muslim, who are in Muslim religion because they want to make money, because, being Alhaji, they go to government to get contracts. And the Christians, because they are Christians, they can get money in the bank. So this is the reason why most of them are religious. There are some serious religious people, but ninety percent of them are liars. Because in the night they still go to all the native doctors—to get something done for their life."

For Prince, the spatial unity of Nigeria breaks by region, North and South. The population divides by religion: Islam, Christianity, and the old native faith. He is a Nigerian—a "pure Nigerian, to the core"—overarching all division. His father, Aitoyeje, was a Yoruba, a Southerner from Ibadan, and a Muslim. His mother, Mary, was a Nupe, a Northerner from Ogidi, and a Christian. He was born in the North, educated in Muslim and Christian schools, then he moved to the southwest and dedicated himself to reviving, through ritual and art, the "traditional" religion of his people. He is a Nigerian, as Whitman was an American, embracing multitudes, but he was from the beginning a man of the Yoruba.

He calls his people, the Yoruba, a tribe. That term has lost favor in polite academic discourse, but its replacement, ethnic group, seems little improvement, inadequate for a population of something like thirty million. Nation would be better. The Yoruba are an *ethnos*, a people like the English or Turks, though their territory in southwestern Nigeria and adjacent Benin is not coterminous with a nation-state like England or Turkey. Born at the edge, Prince was given "tribal marks" that identified him as a Yoruba from the center, permanently establishing his cultural (tribal, ethnic, national) and spatial (regional) frames of belonging. On some of the carved wooden *ibeji* figures of the Ibadan region, these marks are reduced to three horizontal cuts on each cheek. Prince explains:

"The mark is an inborn thing. Any Yoruba person will give this mark to their child, particularly in a family that is royal. You see this, you see these"—Prince touches his cheek—"these are family tattoo.

"You see, if by tomorrow I become king, now they know me. Let's say nobody know me, and I came to the country. Let's say I've been living in America all my life; I have this tattoo, and they invited me over to come and take my father's position. If there is another person who happened to grow up in our family, who is not a son of our family, who is not related to us bloodwise, because he has money now and he wants to challenge me, to take my father's position, the first thing you ask him is to remove his dress, and you ask him where is the family tattoo. And when he don't have it, so, even if he spend millions, they would just take his money for a lie.

"So, the mark was given to me. And another thing is that, in Yorubaland, when a woman is not from their clan, they sometimes mark the child so that woman cannot run away with the child. That is number one. And number two: during the time of war in those days, if I'm a soldier, and you are a soldier, if you have the same mark like me, and you are on the other side, and I am on the other side fighting, when we met face to face, you would not hurt me because you know that we are bloodly related. And if it is a woman who has the same mark like me, I would not date her because I would know we are bloodline related.

"Then the Yoruba sing this song:

Taba sonu
Karirawahe.

"We mark our children so that if he is lost, we can find him back.

"That's why we mark ourselves. That is the song.

"If we are lost, we can find ourselves. That's why we have tribal marks."

The marks Prince received positioned him in his family and separated him from the other children of his boyhood. He could not learn from his father about his heritage, but he could find himself when lost. Prince travels the world, but his mind abides in Nigeria; he moves within a Yoruba body. Marked, named Bamidele, he could follow his father home to the Yoruba core, the place of the Oyo people, the territory of the Oyo Empire that once spread north of Ibadan:

"I didn't grow to know my father. My father died when I was seven. I didn't know my father.

"But the marks on my face distinguish me out of other children. That I'm not—wherever I am in Yorubaland—I'm not from that place.

"The people there don't have mark. The Yoruba people, the typical Yoruba people, have mark. Even though in these areas they speak Yoruba, but they are not typical Oyo people."

Prince's marks are one of the kinds of skillful incision once practiced by the Yoruba. He calls them "identification marks." Others, including circumcision, were medical in purpose; still others were aesthetic. These last, the cicatrices of beautification, called *kolo*, were received voluntarily, amid pain, and read as signs of bravery as well as beauty.

In many African societies marks of identification were part of a ritual of initiation, marking the passage to adult status. Among the Yoruba, beautification marks were courageously chosen, usually by young women moving into maturity. There seems to be some correlation between marks and age, so I ask Prince when he received the marks that distanced him from the place of his childhood, and he replies:

"It is done by the same time as circumcision, when they do that. When the baby is seven days old, with a special medicine, and it is by tiny needles they do it.

"But today they don't do it much because of a lot of interracial marriages. But they do it with this tiny kind of object that when the baby is growing, it grows with it; it is showing. And when you get older, it starts to get away. You need to look—even, like, even President Obasanjo have the mark, but you need to look very, very closely to be able to see, because the age that you become they disappear; they become too disappearing.

"But today most people don't do it, but they still do the one, either on the stomach or the arm, because it is important. But because of religion, Christianity and Islamic religion, and because we are trying to be too modern, imitating your way of life, a lot of our traditions are dying out, or people are forgetting.

"But this, they cannot stop it; they will do this until tomorrow."

He pauses and concludes, "I know who my father is, and my father's home, and who I am."

He does. At the end of his first week of life, Prince was marked, inscribed on the flesh with an identity that pulled him out of the marginal place of his birth and located him in the Yoruba heartland, within a noble family line.

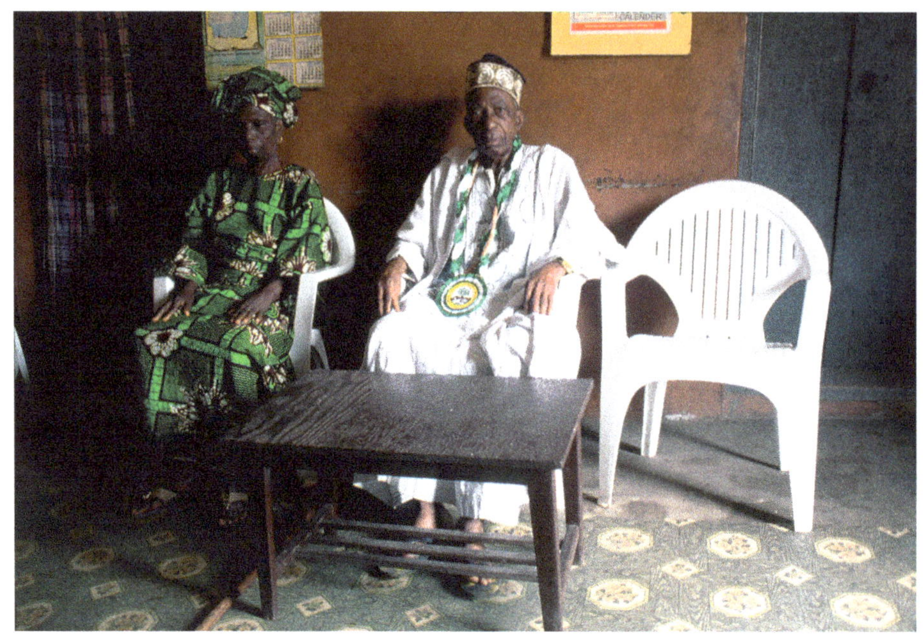

Moniniola and Chief Busari Odunoye Osuntoki
in the audience hall of the palace

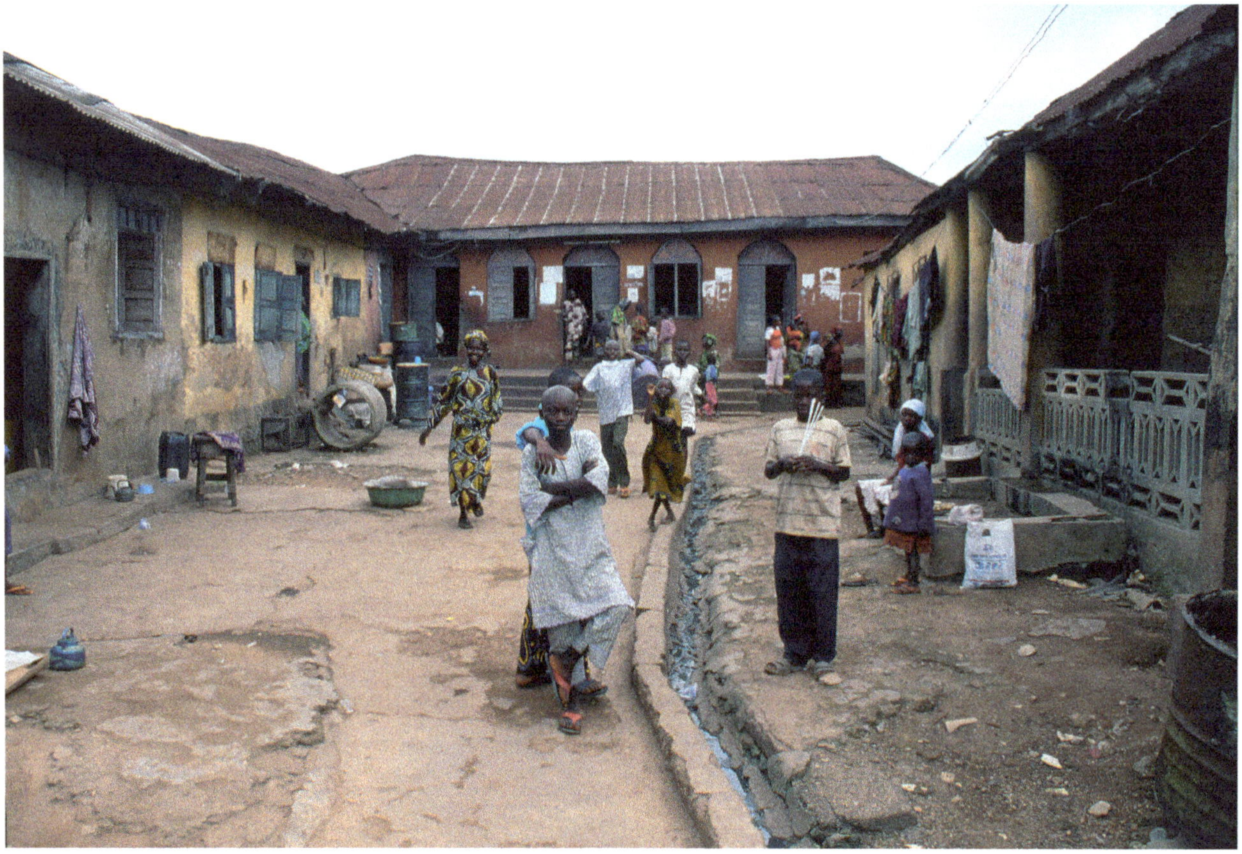

The palace, Olosun compound. Ibadan

·3·

The Line of Osuntoki

When Prince began the story of his life, space was his first topic, lineage his second. The place of his lineage is Ibadan, in the Agbeni Market, a long traffic jam thronged with buyers and sellers. In the middle of the market, across from the spiring Methodist church, a narrow bent passage breaks through the stalls of vendors into the courtyard before the earthen walls of the palace. Another courtyard opens along the right, turning the corner to connect with a courtyard on the left where Prince's father was born. Wooden steps rise to the palace. The door to the left leads into the shrine of the goddess Osun. The doors ahead take us into the wide waiting room, beyond which, in the audience hall, Chief Busari Odunoye Osuntoki, the Mogaji, the head of the family, sits with his sister, Moniniola, leader of the compound's women. Framed family photographs hang on the walls, including one of Chief Busari with Prince Twins Seven-Seven. The opening formula of the Holy Koran, the Muslim prayer of beginnings, In the Name of God, the Merciful, the Compassionate, is chalked in Arabic script above the door.

Chief Busari offers me a seat beside him and tells me he is ninety years of age, next in line to the throne of Ibadan. He calls for the ruins of an old book, turns the pages, and says that his grandfather, Osuntoki, was crowned king of Ibadan in 1895 and ruled until 1897. As Prince has done, he tells me that Osuntoki was a warrior from Offa who brought peace to Ibadanland. The Chief leads us into a parlor in the back, curtained and dark, lined with chairs. A television stands in one corner, Osuntoki's tomb lies in another. "Osuntoki sleeps here," he tells me. "His spirit helps me rule."

The compound fits the pattern of Yoruba palaces, an expandable system of buildings grouped around courtyards. Through zones of narrowing access, it presents a domestic version of the organization of Yoruba sacred space, outlined by Robert Farris Thompson and J. Omosade Awolalu: a long public courtyard, followed by a familial territory of courtyards and rooms that enclose the inner sanctum—the *igbejo*—where Osuntoki sleeps in power.

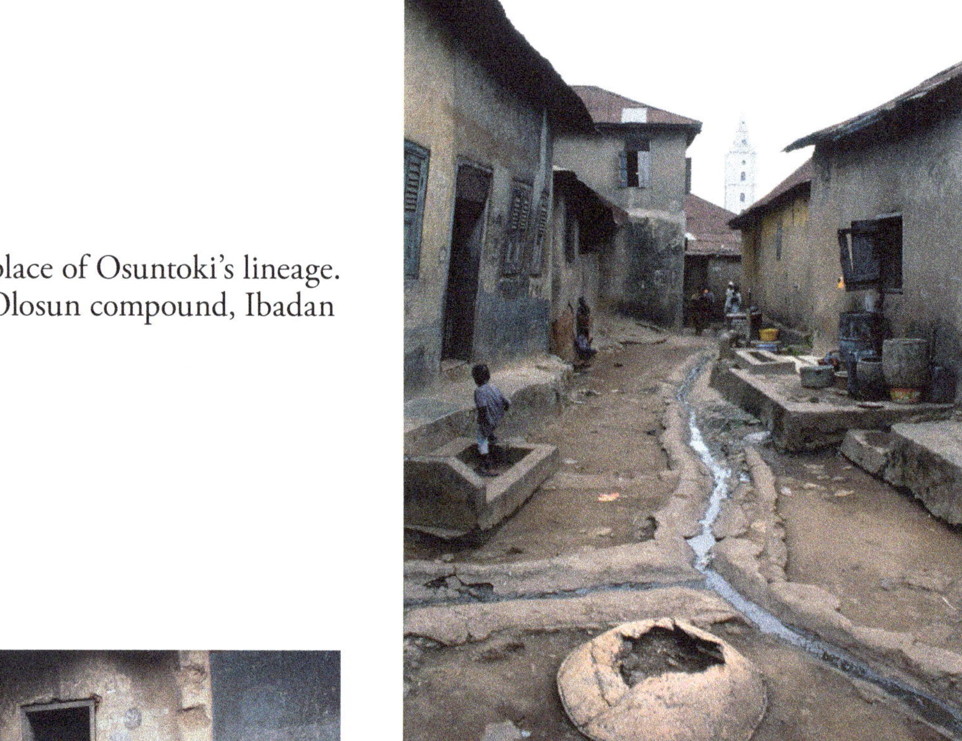
The place of Osuntoki's lineage.
Olosun compound, Ibadan

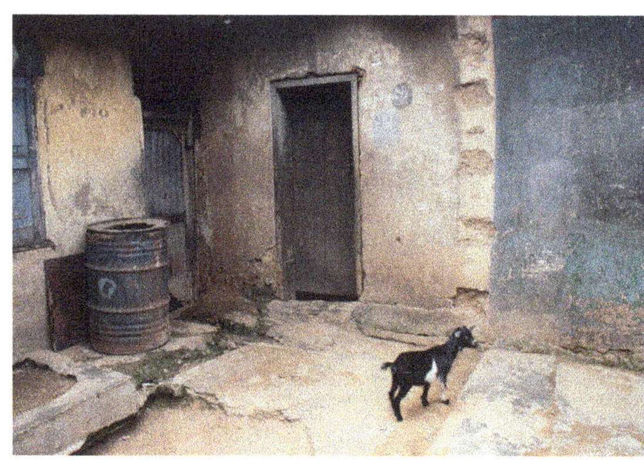
The birthplace of Prince's father, Aitoyeje

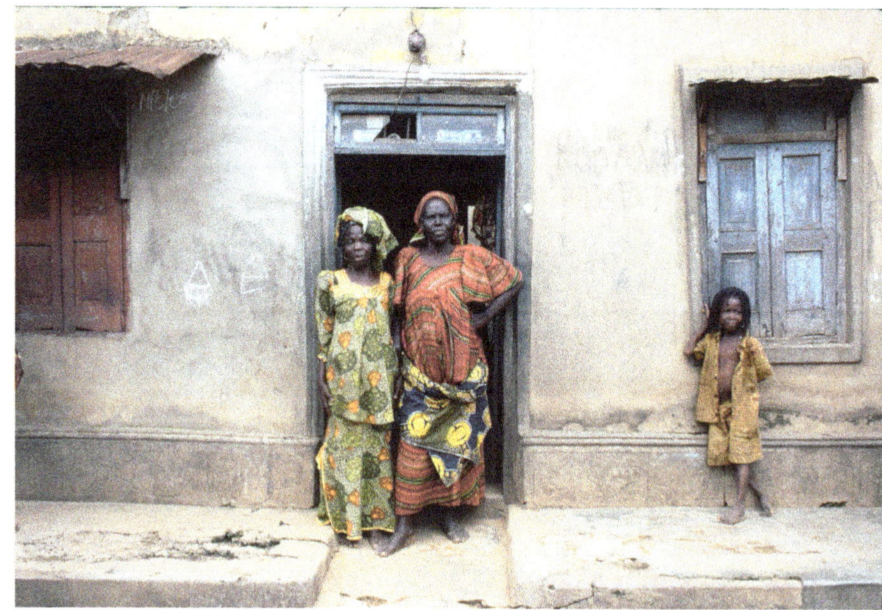
Falasade Osuntoki and
Sidikat Osuntoki

This is the place of the lineage that Prince sketched in our first taped interview. He expanded during our eighth:

"My great-great-grandfather, Olugbense, is a king in Offa. And he have so many children, like me, and among those children my great-grandfather, Osuntoki, is one of his children.

"He became a fighter. Then he moved to Ibadan. He is like somebody who is a troublemaker here. In those days the troublemaker may become like people in the bush who goes against the established order, what you call a rebel.

"Okay, maybe he started as a rebel, Osuntoki, a rebel for a purpose, and then when he came to Ibadan he had a lot of followers, fighting against the Northerners who wanted to take our land.

"Okay. Then he became popular, and became powerful. At the end of it he became king in Ibadan.

"But he came all the way from Offa. He fought, not as walking: he fought through, and, in fighting, he has a lot of people following him, as battlers and fighters, maybe to attack powerless people, attack villages and make them become his own domain. Then he rode over them. Because in those days, before the British came, that's what people do. Africans, they fight each other, they grab each other's land.

"The most powerful become the leader.

"Anyway, my lineage is Osuntoki. Osuntoki have eight children. Out of eight children, my own grandfather is the first, which is Oyekale. And my own father is Aitoyeje.

"But people believe I am the spirit of the *old* ancestor guy who came from Offa and fought in Ibadan. Because everything I've been doing since I became a recognized person shows I have some quality of leadership, spiritual leadership, in my attitude towards my people.

"I am the reincarnation of the old father, of Osuntoki."

Since Prince is the reincarnation of Osuntoki, we need to know more about the old king's character. I ask, and Prince tells me first that his reign was distinguished because, during it, paper money was introduced by the British, replacing the old currency in cowrie shells. He goes on:

"And then at the same time they stopped the slave trade, so he became a very respectable king. He only reigned for two years, but that two years was the most peaceful period in the history of Ibadan.

"Before that time he was a very powerful warrior who grabbed land, fighting. And my ancestor was the one who led the conqueror warriors of Yorubaland against the Northern soldiers, and the war at that time is called Jalumi War. Jalumi means: when they were running, some people were running, they fell into the river and they could not run across, and they butchered them in the water.

"But when he became king, he tried to make the radicals, the young radicals in Ibadan city, to stop fighting. And it was written in a book that his time was the most peaceful period in the history of Ibadan."

Rebel, warrior, man of peace, Osuntoki has returned in Prince Twins Seven-Seven. Prince's view of reincarnation is narrower than the Hindu. The soul migrates from body to body in sequential lives, but it passes strictly from person to person within a family line to form the basis of an individual's character:

"Because of the ancestors, when I first came to the world, I was a fighter. I was a serious warrior. But today I am a peaceful person, never fighting. But I think some of the fighting I have done in the past has been haunting me."

The thought amuses him. It is not an easy blend. He is a rebel in the cause of the old religion, a fighter and a lover of peace. Though evil people do not return through reincarnation, good people are complex, and, as in the Hindu theory, rebirth carries karma. It may balance in the generational succession. Prince, ever the optimist, misquotes Shakespeare:

"One of the English proverbs says, The good men do lives after them. I think all these things, when you come into life—maybe you came before and you are not successful, so this time around you have to be very successful. Or maybe last time around you were very successful, but this time you have to share.

"So that's the way I think about it."

Balance is possible, balance is the goal, but unbalance is the normal state of affairs. Peace is the desire, conflict the reality. Wrongs in a past life bring unsettling difficulties in this one. His own troubles, he believes, might be explained by the deaths of innocent people, killed in the wars of his ancestors. Life's troubles have a cause, and one cause is an unknowable evil committed in a past life. There is nothing to do but to do the best one can, striving for balance, for atonement, paying off the karmic debt through sacrifice and extravagant generosity, then enduring the disappointment. Life is hard, its troubles, though caused, inexplicable at last:

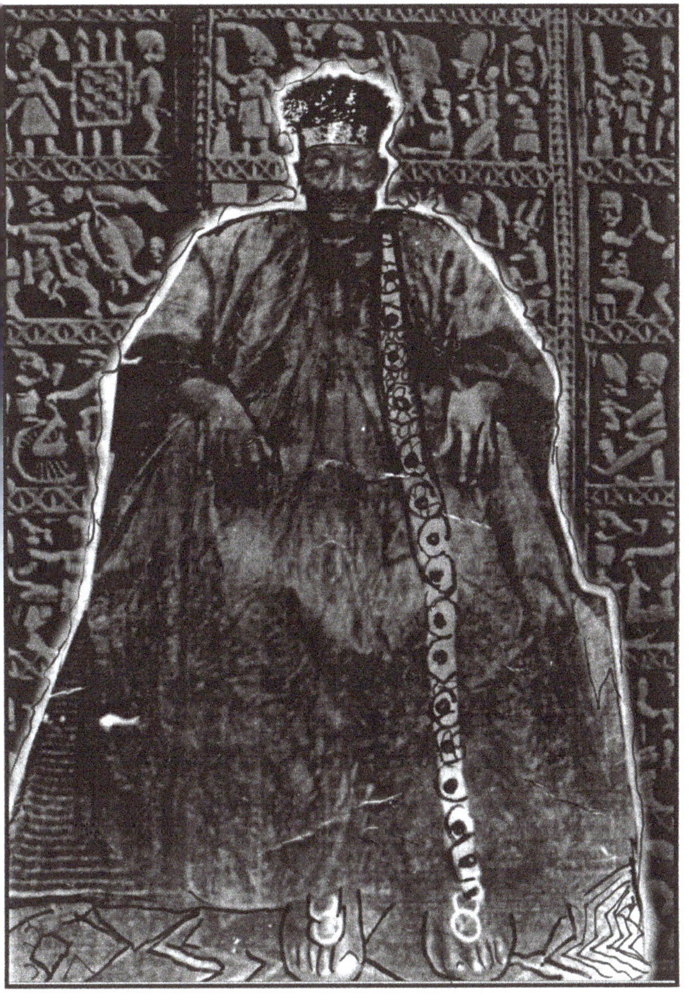

Osuntoki.
To create this image, Prince cut his great-grandfather from a faded old photograph, gave him a crown, sharpended the details, and placed him in front of an old Yoruba door

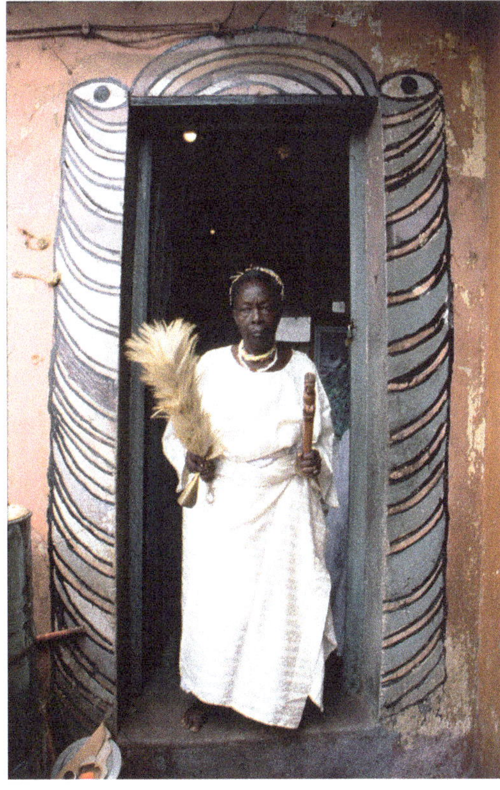

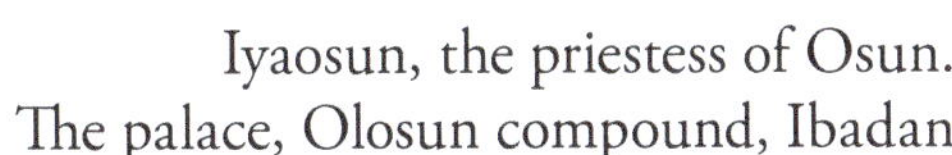

Iyaosun, the priestess of Osun.
The palace, Olosun compound, Ibadan

"It is not easy to all of us who look at it. This man is very successful. But behind the successfulness, he must be fighting something. Either illness, body pain, trouble in the brain—something is going wrong somewhere. Nobody can have it smooth all the time.

"It is like—take the case of President Bush. He started he was a young man. Within a short time he was a governor. Within a short time he became president. Now, in his mind he has something. He has money. He has everything. But there is something wrong there.

"Or take the case of Muhammad Ali, when he was boxing. He was very famous. He was big. He was respected, but still, at the end of the day, he cannot box no more. And he didn't deserve to be that way. And he has money to cure himself, but it is an incurable disease. You see? So, that's the way I see life."

We have traveled with Prince from the specifics of reincarnation to a general view of life. All of us strain for some balance in an unbalanced world, beset by inexplicable travail. In Prince's large painting *Barefoot President in a Fragile Boat with the World Tears Apart*, finished at the beginning of 2007 and usually called *Bush,* President Bush stands barefoot, like a poor man, in a small, rocking boat. The world on his shoulders, a collage of maps, cracks into pieces, while in a boat beyond him men in African dress protest against war, and beyond them a mass of faces spreads, the eyes watching, the minds judging. Some of the watchers, Prince says, favor war, some are opposed. They judge; Bush wobbles. The picture, like the traditional dilemma tales of Africa, offers no conclusion. Members of the audience build their own opinions, deciding while the man of power, an incompetent Atlas, confounded by his own troubles, rocks and sways, seeking balance, faltering in unstable distress.

In distress, the Muslim remembers and calls out to God, the Christian yearns for divine signs of assurance. At the intersection of force and counterforce, amid conditions that spin beyond full control or knowing, Prince seeks assistance through sacrifice and obeisance to the gods of his ancestors. With the soul of a king, he venerates Sango. The deified fourth king of Oyo, Sango is the god of thunder, the lord of lightning, the heavenly force of swift retribution, the scourge of evil. Prince made a lifesize, lifelike concrete statue of Sango, his axe raised in judgment, that stands guard over the entry to his house in Osogbo. With the soul of a warrior, the mind and hand of an artist, Prince calls upon Ogun, the god of iron, of creation and destruction, the deity of those who employ iron in their trade, warriors, carvers, and smiths.

Behind the palace of Osuntoki's family in Ibadan, a passage leads to a lane. Four turns, and we enter an iron-roofed smithy. The crowd packed inside, men more than women, leaves

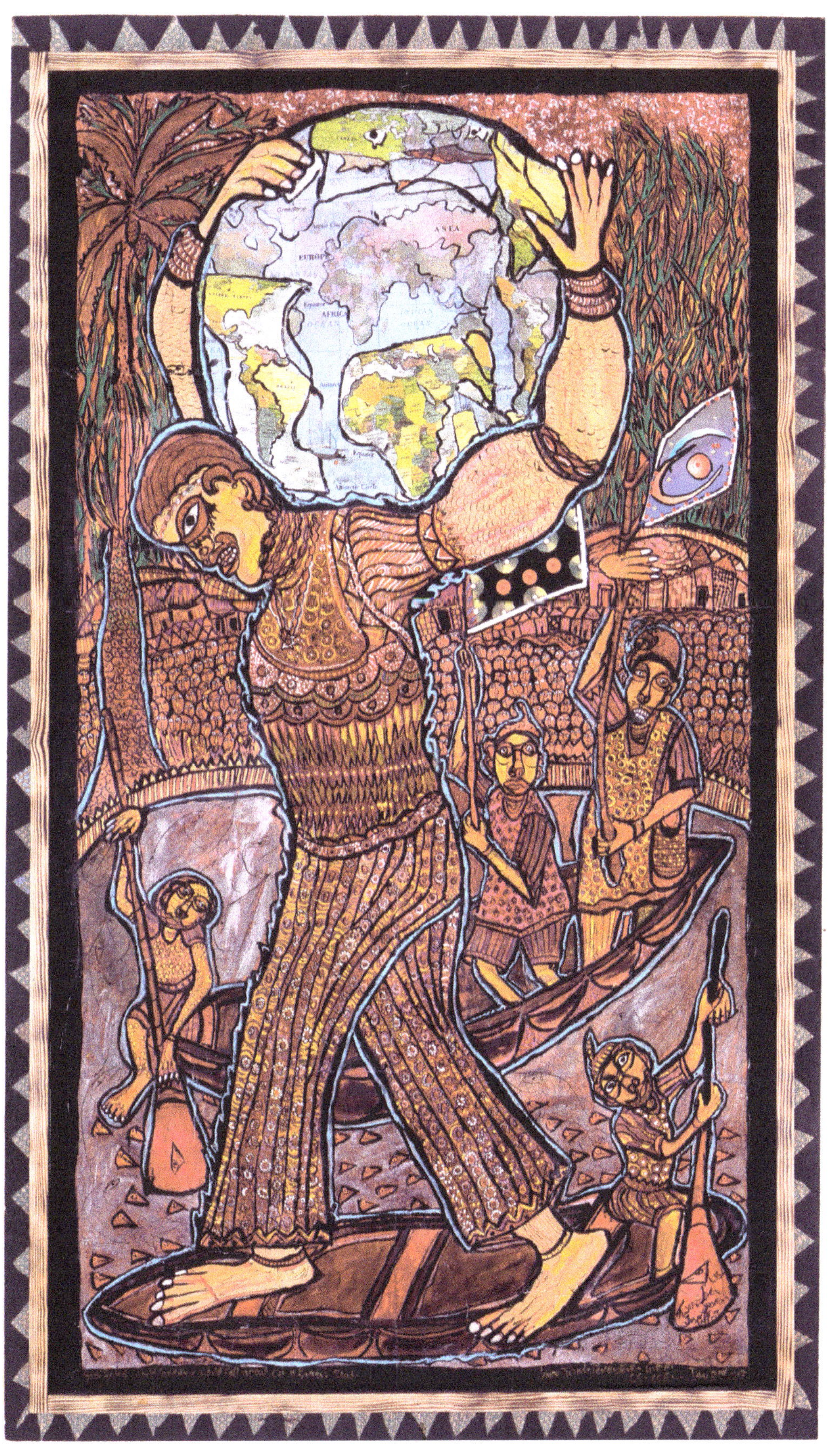

Barefoot President in a Fragile Boat with the World Tears Apart.
Ink, pastel, acrylic, and oil on paper, glued to a board. 44"x73". Philadelphia 2006-2007

a small space around the anvil. On it two Muslim blacksmiths tap out a rhythm. Like drummers, they create variable tones that match the sound and swing of speech, hammering a riff over and over, calling Ogun. Prince hands money to the young priest, so do I, and the men and women standing thick to the walls begin wadding up bills and tossing them toward the anvil, while the priest sings praise to Ogun, warrior and healer, and his little son dances.

The priest hands a black cock, its legs bound with twine, to his son, and dresses the anvil, an altar now, with white flour, red palm oil, and black-eyed peas. He takes the cock back, unties its legs, gathering its feet and fluttery wings in one hand, and passes it to Prince who points it toward the anvil and gives it back. The priest has become his agent in sacrifice. Putting the big toe of his left foot on the cock's head, the priest twists the neck and pulls the body free. The head, its astonished round eye still staring, lies in the dust, while the priest adds blood from the body to the dripping mix on the anvil, food for the god. Next he touches a kola nut to Prince's forehead, to the back of his neck, breaks the nut in four pieces and casts them at the base of the anvil, noting the pattern of their fall. He breaks another kola, casts again and reads again, receiving a message from the god in the relation of backs and bellies upturned on the ground. Then he and Prince turn their backs to the anvil, shaking their butts in dismissive disdain for Prince's enemies. They have enlisted Ogun in Prince's struggle to get his troubles behind him so he can step forward on his quest for success.

The priest drops a dot of red cock's blood on the big toe of Prince's left foot, then on his own. A pot of black-eyed peas passes through the crowd. We all take a pinch and eat in communion, feasting together, dining with the deity. The service is over, the congregation disperses.

In the street, on the way back, Prince tells me that Ogun's beast is the dog. It would be better to sacrifice a dog than a rooster, but, laughing, he says that Americans love dogs and if they read in this book that he killed a dog, they would hate him. More quietly, he tells me that killing dogs upsets him, so he chooses priests who are willing to substitute chickens for dogs. The sacrifice suffices, the god has supped the red blood of a black cock, and Prince is at peace.

Sango and Ogun befit the aggressive, ambitious side of Prince's nature, but he is, prevailingly, a man of peace. "I can do acting," he said. "I can act angry, but I am not violent. I can't even kill a chicken. If someone beats a child, I cry. I am too emotional." He concludes, "I am an Osun." People in Brazil, where the gods of the Yoruba live in art and ritual, comparably identify by personality with an *orixá,* the beautiful who love beauty saying, I am an Oxum. By nature, Prince is a devotee of the goddess Osun.

"Osun," he says, "is for peace, fertility, and assistance for a lot of positive things between the human being. She is unlike Ogun, the god of iron. God of iron is different from Sango. Sango is different from Obatala. Obatala is the creator. He is the person who creates the heads. As when a human being is coming into the world, you go to Obatala's garden to pick the head. Some people pick the right one. Some people pick the bad."

He laughs, and I comment that he seems to have picked the right one.

"Well," he says, "I think I do. But I still have a lot of forces out there that make my road not be very smooth, the way it is supposed to be."

Prince chose his destiny, his head. The head of an artist, it seems to me, combining wild creative energy with a diligent respect for beauty and peace, as though Ogun and Osun met in his makeup. That head leads him to trouble as well as success. Compatibly, as a consequence of reincarnation, he joins the karmic debt of a killer with a dedication to Osun. He follows Osun, like his great-grandfather Osuntoki, whose name, Osun-toki, means Osun is worth following. He said:

"Osuntoki is an Osun worshiper. Osuntoki means Osun is worth following, worth bow down for, worth worshiping. Osuntoki means Osun is a god worth worshiping, worth greeting, worshiping."

Osuntoki was a protector of the goddess:

"You see, my great-grandfather was called Olosun, the owner of Osun. He has five or six shrines in my family home, and this guy is a worshiper. And he so much adores to Osun that whenever he was going to the war, he asked for a sacrifice to Osun. And our home is named after Osun, Olosun compound that has been in Ibadan."

In Ibadan, Chief Busari told me that, though he is a Muslim, it is a responsibility of the master of the palace to maintain the shrine to Osun where an elderly priestess officiates. She wears white, the devotees she gathers for prayer, men and women, all wear white, and Prince, as an Osun, always wears white, white underclothes and robe, white trousers, white socks, white shoes. Once he was awarded a chieftainship that required him to wear a red beaded crown, and everything went wrong until he designed a white one to replace it. Red is the color of danger and death; he said, "I have to avoid the red forces troubling me. I wear white to swim through life with Osun."

His father was born in Olosun compound, and as Prince followed him home to Ibadan, Osun directed his steps. The main stop on his journey was Osogbo. The capital of Osun State, Osogbo lies by the River Osun where the major shrine to the goddess stands and the

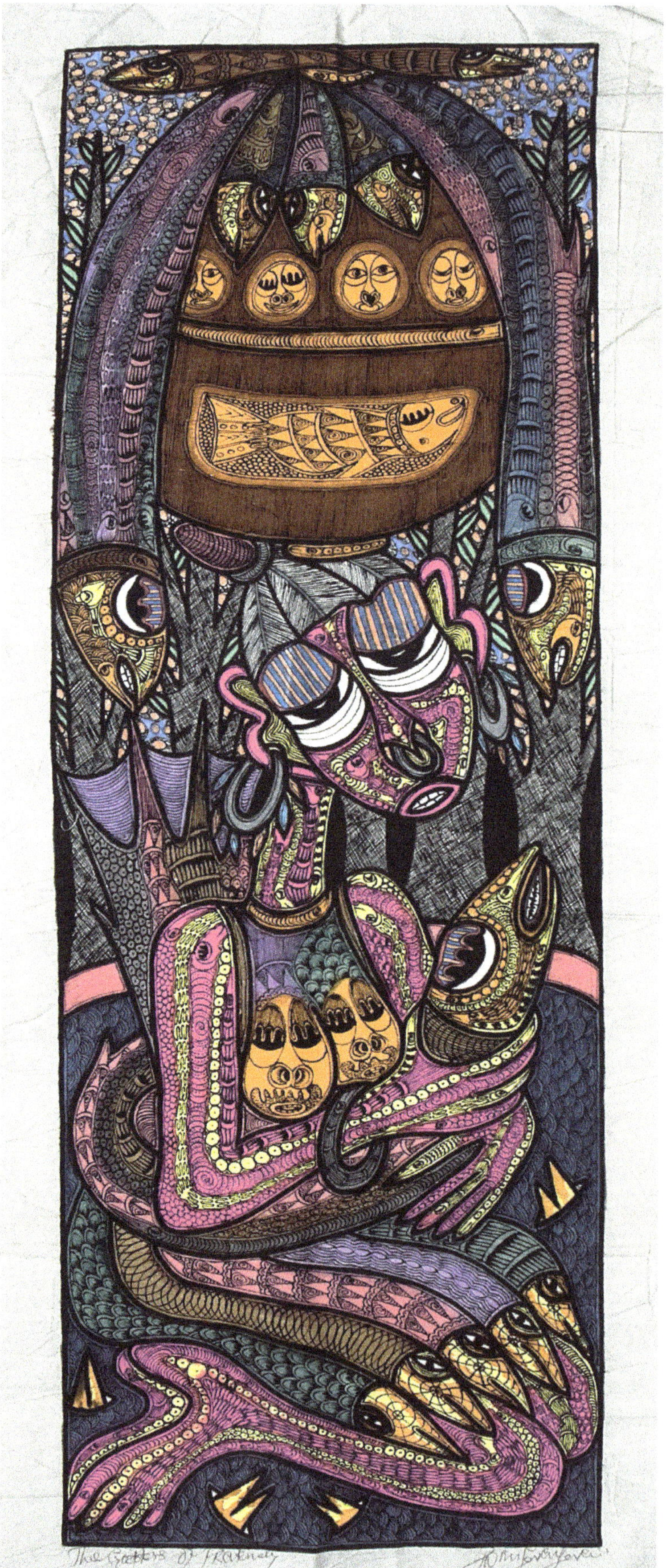

The Goddess of Fertility.
Ink, dye, and oil on cloth.
12"x33". Ibadan, 2007.
This is Osun,
a calabash on her head,
the fish of fertility in her arms.
See chapter 20, nos. 8–10

Osun Festival gathers thousands every August. In Osogbo, Bumi, Prince's daughter, the fourth child of his second wife, told us that when she was about four years old she rode on her father's shoulders down to the riverside, and Osun, Mami Wata, revealed herself. Her hair was beautiful; she was the size of a normal woman, slender, and she rose from the river, revealing herself down to the belly, so Bumi could not see the part of her that is shaped like a fish. That was about 1978. Since then, Bumi said, some white people tried to capture Osun, so she no longer appears. Bumi became a Christian in 1991. She is married, a mother, and the ordained pastor of a church. "Jesus Christ is our savior," she said. "But all that other stuff is real; I was raised with it. Osun is real." Barren women, she tells us, go to the Festival, drink water from the river, and return the next year with new babies.

In his paintings, Prince has depicted all of the great Yoruba deities, Sango frequently, and he has made many renditions of Obatala's garden, abloom with a vast display of heads to select. But Osun is the most usual of his sacred images, and he pictures her so often that, not wishing to seem repetitive, he rarely puts her name in the title. An early etching is labeled *The Goddess of Fertility*; one masterpiece he calls *Rainbow Wealth Goddess*, others he titled *Mami Wata* and *Mermaid of Peace*. Osun appears in his prints and paintings as a mermaid, her body formed by a swarm of fish that can disperse, leaving no shape in the water. The water is the goddess herself. Not every mermaid he draws is Osun, but she has inspired them all. She is the sweet water running to the sea, carrying the power to heal, to bring life. Her water flows with fertility. "I have used my Osun potion to have so many children," Prince said, and when his youngest wife, Aliratu, lost her daughter and was struggling to conceive, Prince brought her Osun water to drink.

To explain it all, Prince tells the myth of Osun's origin:

"Osun is one of the wives of Sango. Sango is the god of thunder.

"And you know Sango; before the arrival of the British, he is a very well renowned, *powerful* king in Yorubaland.

"He owns, geographically, towards Timbuktu and Ghana. It used to be part of Oyo Empire.

"And Sango himself, when he didn't hang himself and become an invisible person, he's a very *powerful,* powerful magician. People believe when he talks, fire comes out of his mouth. When he is angry, his voice also turns into flame and fire.

"Anyway, he has so many wives. He has Oya, who is the whirlwind. He has Osun. Then he have Yemoja.

"And when Sango is angry, the only person who can appeal to him is Osun.

"And he love Osun so much. Because Osun prepared the *best* food for him.

"But nobody knows—even Sango himself, how powerful he is—he doesn't know that Osun has been cutting a part of her ear, into the soup, for him.

"Because, according to people who have eaten—even when you touch your body, like this"—he licks his wrist—"when you sweat, you find some taste of salt on your skin. So, it means human flesh is very delicious. So, every time when the woman cuts part of her ear into the soup, it tastes better than the other wives' food.

"So, Sango never eat the other wives' food. Only Osun's food.

"And then one day, Sango asked Osun, My wife, how do you cook this beautiful food for me? What do you put in the soup that makes it so delicious?

"She said, My husband, don't worry about it. It is not your business to know.

"*Then*. Osun loved Oya, the whirlwind. She loved her so much that they used to exchange secret discussions together.

"So one day, Oya asked Osun, Mama—because she is the most senior wife. The junior wife will not call the senior wife's name. So they either say Mama, or call her by the name of her children.

"So, say, Mama, it is too much the way God makes it possible for you that you take care of our husband. I wish that I could be lucky to do the same kind of cooking that you are doing.

"Then. So, Osun said, If I tell you, you will not say it to everybody.

"She promised, she swore by the name of God, that she will never tell anybody.

"So, Osun removed her headtie and showed her ear. Because Osun have large, long ears."

Prince gestures the sweep of long ears, down to his shoulders, ears as long as a dog's, saying:

"And the woman—"

A shocked look comes to his face, his eyes wide, his hand covering his open mouth.

"Keep your mouth shut. Please don't tell anybody. So she park her hair back.

"*Then*. Oya, now, out of jealousy, she cooked and take it to Sango. Sango have a taste; it doesn't taste like Osun's food. And so he throw the plates away.

"She said, Why do you throw my plates away? If I be like Madame Osun who used to cut her ear into the soup for you—that's why her food is better than the rest of us.

"Out of jealousy. And she promised she would never say it.

"So, in the evening Sango invited Osun to the room for romance—trick her to make her think he wanted to have sex with her. The moment she came into the room, he tried to untie her headtie. The woman resisted and pulled back.

"He said, Why are you hiding from me? I want to see your ear. Since the time I marry you, you never show me your ear.

"Then the woman realized that her secret has been revealed, and she opened it, and Sango see that part of her ear is hacked off.

"Osun got angry and fell down.

"And turned into a river.

"But before that time, Osun has been a woman curer. She cured for women. She cured for children. Anybody who has problem with pregnancy, they bring her to Osun, and Osun give her water.

"You see, like, because she was a powerful woman, when she put the water in a bowl and touched it, with her will for curing, it happened.

"So, she turned into water, and turned herself into a river.

"And then Oya, too. She got disgraced, like the story of Judas and Jesus Christ, and turn herself into a whirlwind.

"So that is how Osun became water.

"And then all the women that she had helped in life started to sing about her:

> Ekoreyeye yeo
> E-ko-re-ye-ye, Osun.

"When you go to the Festival, you will hear all the women singing that song:

> Olomoni yami
> O-lo-mon-i yami.

"Our mother, she left us. She is the mother of her children.

"Then they started crying and singing about her. Since ever that day, Osun became a deity.

"In many communities in Yorubaland, people have Osun shrine in their home. But when the British came and they bring the Bible, and Arabic people bring the Koran, they made us lose most of our very important religion.

"But some people still stick to it. And God used me to immortalize the name of Osun."

At the beginning of his narrative, Sango and Osun are people on the earth, living in a polygamous household like Prince's. Sango is the king of Oyo. Perhaps six hundred years ago, perhaps a thousand, shamed by an act of his own, Sango went alone to the bush and committed suicide by hanging. Then the priests deified him as the god of thunder, lightning, and justice. His cult spread with the expansion of the Oyo Empire that reached its peak in the eighteenth century and held power into the nineteenth. As the Oyo Empire declined toward its collapse in the eighteen-thirties, Yorubaland shattered into the wars among the city-states relentlessly documented in Reverend Samuel Johnson's *The History of the Yorubas*. The losers were sold into slavery, sent in captivity to Cuba and Brazil, where the worship of Sango continues.

The earthly Osun is a healer whose water ensures fertility. Betrayed, enraged, she melted into a river. Then her female followers deified her as the goddess of healing, fertility, and peace. Her worship, too, was carried across the Atlantic to Cuba and Brazil.

Prince calls them both powerful. Both took themselves out of life. As deities, both connect with water. Sango unleashes the storms that crack with thunder, strike with lightning, and drench the earth. Osun is the water that comes from the sky, gathers in lakes, and flows to the ocean. Father above, mother below, they join in the damp cycle of life.

Through his telling, Prince identified with both of them, with the powerful king and magician who has many wives, with the powerful healer betrayed by a jealous friend. In making Osun the wife who cut her ear into the soup, Prince's version differs significantly from the usual story. William Bascom, a noted anthropological student of Yoruba culture, gathered and compared sixteen examples of this Yoruba myth from Nigeria, Cuba, and Brazil. In the usual story, which Bascom analyzes, which Wande Abimbola says is known throughout Yorubaland, it is Oba, not Osun (or Oya), who cuts off her ear. She is tricked into doing so by a co-wife, often Osun, to separate her from Sango who, disgusted by the ear in his stew and by his disfigured wife, shuns her and turns his affection to another, often Osun. The tale in its diversity describes the tensions among co-wives, but in Prince's version Osun's rage, not Sango's, is the focus. He does not stress trickery, but jealousy, the betrayal of friendship and the breaking of a vow made in the name of God. He tells of a woman who willingly sacrifices her own flesh for love. Back in the world, Prince Twins Seven-Seven, a man of a royal line with many wives, a magical artist, endures among the jealous, sacrificing his wealth and energy to gain the love of others.

He ends his telling with a return to the critical issue of decline and revival. During the chat that followed, Prince told me that when he cooperated in the restoration of the Osun shrine at Osogbo, "people hated me for it. The Muslims thought I'm bringing back the dead religion. The Christians felt I'm bringing back a dead religion." Remembering their enmity, Prince put his opinion into a collaged painting entitled *The Beginning of the End*, in which a looming human figure forces the Bible and Koran into the eyes of the beholder. The new religions brought the beginning of the end, but despite aggressive proselytizing, the end has not come. The old religion thrives, and Prince has accepted the task thrust upon him by his belief, his mission from God, by his historical awareness in a postcolonial context, his social concern in a scene riven by division, and by the inner force of reincarnation. He honors Osun through art and ritual acts.

Ogun wants the slaughter of a dog. Osun wants no blood. A goddess of peace, she dines on vegetarian fare. At Prince's request, women prepare *ekuru* (black-eyed peas, pounded without oil and steamed in leaves) or *akara* (black-eyed peas beaten into a batter, balled up, and deep fried). He carries a heap on a tray to the edge of the lake at Sekona, distributing a third to his followers—the *akara*, smaller and tangier than the *acarajé* of the Brazilian streets, is really delicious—and he stands, pinching the food into bits and pitching them into the water. The food is his sacrifice to Osun, his request for assistance and affection.

It is a familial duty to serve Osun, and it is a personal statement of gratitude. Osun saved him when he was born an abiku child.

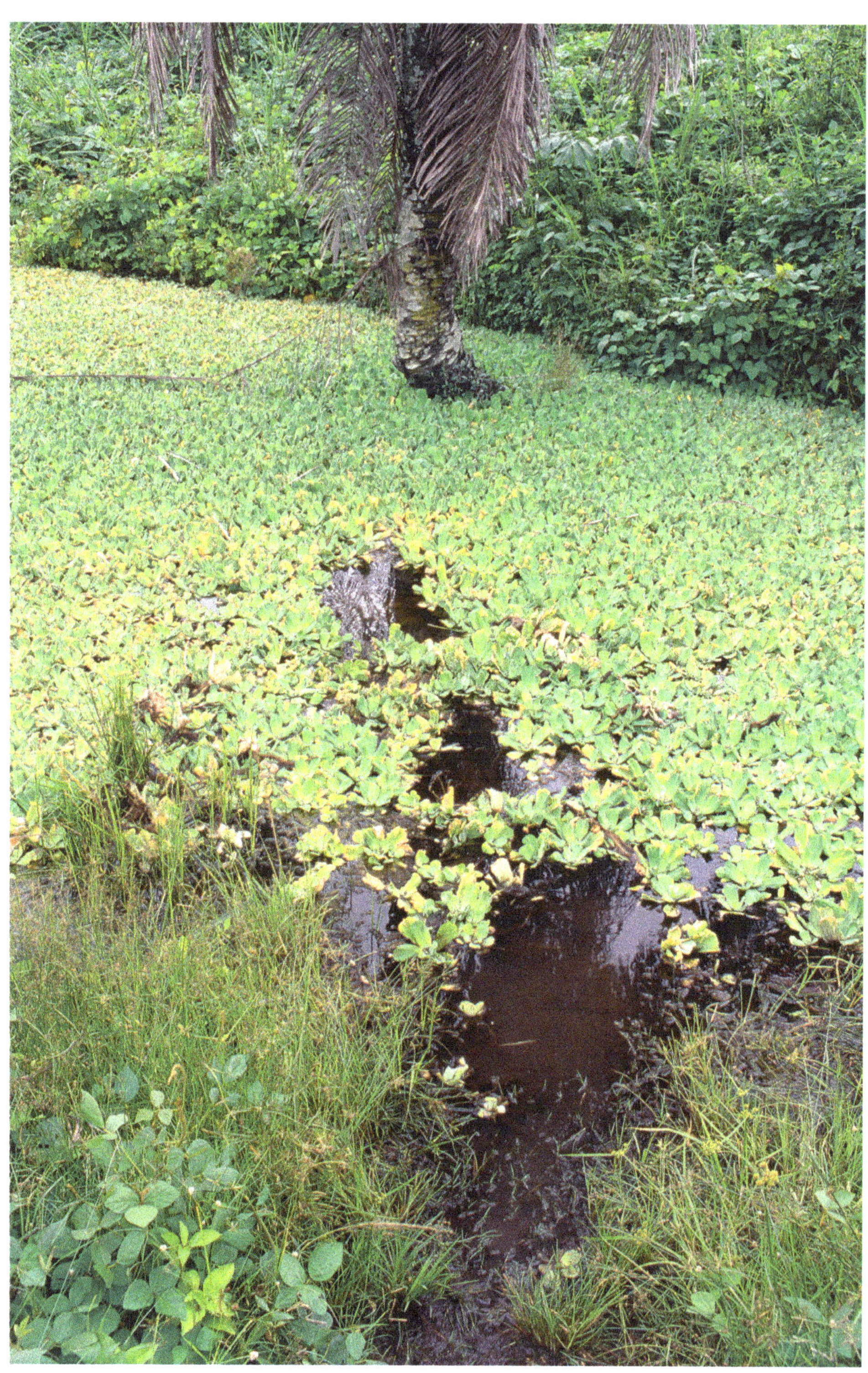

Omielja, Ijara

· 4 ·

An Abiku Child

Prince set himself in space, then in a familial line, and then, he said, he came into the world, on a certain day in 1944, as an abiku, a child born to die.

The abiku is sent from the other world. Two worlds exist simultaneously, this and the other, the seen and the unseen. We live in this one, the world of sun and dust, rain and mud. In the other world—the parallel universe called Orun and likened to Heaven—live the gods, the ancestors, and a host of spirits, many bent on bringing misery to humankind. Communication between the worlds is constant. Individuals gauge their relation to supernatural power by the good and bad that befall them, and they seek clarification by consulting diviners—Prince calls them soothsayers, more often readers, still more often babas—who use a wide variety of techniques to receive messages, messages they interpret to provide their clients with information that will aid them in conducting their lives. Diviners, Prince said, could foretell a baby's future:

"I remember: even before a baby was born, there would be a soothsayer who would tell you what the baby is going to do, in life. They know he is going to be a doctor. They know he is going to be a businessman. But today they don't do it anymore.

"The minute the baby is born, they would take a look at his palm, to read it, to say this boy is going to be a traveler, he is going to be successful, he is going to live long, he is going to die young—all these things.

"So, the parents prepare themselves. And they tell you what kind of a man you are going to marry, if it is a girl, what town she has to go to. But today—because of civilization, because of we are trying to copy your culture—we are losing most of the things that belong to us.

"These are the people who could tell you, these soothsayers; they can tell you if you have an abiku child. And if the child is not going to live, no amount of medicine, herbs, you give to him—they let you know in advance, so you don't bother yourself. And if that baby dies, the husband and wife are prepared to have another baby because they know, already, he is going away. So, they don't have to be thinking about how to save this kind of baby.

"And whenever they are going to have another one, they would prepare to find out what they should do to stop the other one from going back again."

The diviner diagnoses the problem—this is an abiku, sent from the other world, destined to return—and prescribes a procedure for its solution. Divination is followed by sacrifice, a human communication to the gods, just as the patterns of cast cowries or cracked kola nuts or traces in the sand encode a communication from the gods. Sacrifice requires loss, a willed decrease of personal resources. Prince gives money, money he could use in the mundane swill of things, to the women who prepare the food. Sacrifice is a social act. He gives some of the food to the people around him, benefiting them through sustenance and bringing power back to himself through their esteem. Sacrifice is a sacred act. Most of the food is thrown into the lake to be consumed by Osun who will help him move toward his desire. It is not exactly a reciprocal exchange that yields a balanced account, but it entails a loss for a gain.

Blood is the clearest sign of sacrifice. The chicken that might feature at a private feast is sacrificed, beheaded to provide food for the god. Ogun wants blood, and he wants palm wine, palm oil, and black-eyed peas. Food, essential to life, is one thing that is sacrificed, abandoned to possibility. Money is another. The diviner is paid, the farmer who owns the goat is paid, the man who butchers the goat, the women who cook it, the priest who conducts the ritual—all are paid. Further, the ritual demands a sacrifice of time and energy that could be spent in directly profitable pursuits. Like Native Americans who diminish their wealth in potlatches and throws, gaining the favor of their neighbors and the spiritual powers of the universe, the people who sacrifice in Yorubaland deplete their own bounty of food, cash, and energy to enhance their prestige, solve their problems, and bring them boons.

The mothers of abiku children sacrifice themselves, as Osun did. Abiku children are classified by the kind of sacrifice required of their mothers. There are, Prince says, three kinds:

"You have the alarinjo, those whom they have to survive by dancing, or begging for alms. Then you have the ones that their parents have to be doing petty trading—petty trading, either in fabric, either in wood carving—anything have to do with trade. Then you have the others who are just babies that got sick all the time, and the parents would run from one native doctor's home to another native doctor's home. Because they want to exhaust the resources of the parents."

They, the ones who want to exhaust the family, are the spirits who demand sacrifice. For one kind of abiku child, the *alarinjo*, the mother sacrifices herself by dancing in public to amuse the crowd and by asking for alms, lowering her status to that of a beggar. For another, she becomes a trader, buying and selling to benefit her suppliers, her customers, and the people of her household. The third sacrifices time and money by running in hopeless frenzy from doctor to doctor. All humble themselves, diminishing in this world to influence the powers of the other, losing to gain life for a child the spirits wish to retrieve. Without a pause, Prince continues:

"And you have to do rituals to make them survive.

"And in the rituals of the Yoruba people, we don't throw away kids. Some family have kids that is not presentable in public. Like, some people have kids with big heads, like a lion. They keep them in the house; they won't kill them. Because they believe it is a gift of God. So, the Yoruba people have a special likeness for children.

"Some people have their kids born blind. Abiku child can come like a blind person. They can come like these deformed kids; all kind of those children are abiku. They come from this unseen world. They are not from the normal-normal world where other people are born, where you have good hair, good nose, good everything. So, the belief of the Yoruba person is that abiku—sometimes you can see them as very negative, semi-positive, and positive. Depends on how lucky the family is.

"And some people are lucky that they know that they have abiku in their family."

"The parents have to work to keep the baby in the world," I say, and he answers:

"They have to. And sometimes it is the kind of baby that will not survive no matter how much money you spend, no matter how much of ritual you go through. It will still go bad.

"That baby is taken back to the spirit world.

"And that is why, when I was an alarinjo, when the trouble was too much for my mom, she has to go to a river, go to a lake; it's called Omielja: the lake that protects spiritual holding fish.

"So my ma has to go there and drink the water. During the time of this last pregnancy.

"And it helped a lot. Fortified."

The lake is in Ijara, a short walk from the house where Prince was born and his grandmother lies buried. In the past, the lake was regularly drained, revealing a big rock. Turtles, snakes, and fish, the devotees of Osun, were lifted out of the mud and put in boxes and pots to be returned when the lake filled with clear water. One time Prince said that his mother knew that her husband's line was charged with the protection of Osun, another time he said she did not know, but what matters is that the lake holds the water of Osun. Omielja, Prince said, "means the water that have a holy fish. And Osun is the holy fish." By drinking the water, along with the medicine provided by a native doctor, she was able to keep her boy in the world:

"Before I was born, my mother has have six sets of twins. The seventh set is when they realized that I am the same child who has been coming and going since all these years.

"Then my mother, who could not stand losing another child, went to the native doctor. You people call them soothsayers, or you call them palm readers. But we call them babalawo.

"We call them babalawo because they have special objects that they can use to read and tell the destiny of new-born baby, of a baby in the womb, of a grownup person. And they tell the kings when to do sacrifice. This is their job.

"So, my mom now went to this babalawo who told my mom that what she is looking for is in her husband's pocket. Which means: instead of her looking far away, what she can use to cure this abiku problem is within her vicinity.

"And this lake is not far from where I was born. So, because they told my mom I'm an Osun—a lot of people, they started telling her to make peace with the goddess of the water or river. That water I would take as a little person.

"So, the man told my mother to go and do sacrifice at that lake, and the priest at the lake gave her water in a small pot. And the pot was supposed not to get dry. Anytime it would get dry, she would have to come back and get water to put in it.

"I suppose there was some kind of potion in it.

"So, whenever my mother want to feed me, she would use that water to feed me.

"Anyway, to cut a long story short, my mother now ended up going there and getting the water.

"And anytime I'm, like, sick: go there, give some sacrifice, take the water. Till I grow up.

"Up to today, a lot of women still go to that water."

Omielja's water, the power of Osun, the gift of Osun, was the key to his survival because his mother could not enact the sacrifices required for an *alarinjo*. In Yoruba society, women normally manage the commerce in the markets. Prince's grandmother, his father's mother, Morenike Apeshigidibarin, was a wealthy trader. She took her daughter-in-law into partnership. They hired other women as their employees. And his grandmother and mother agreed that it would be unseemly for a member of such a prosperous family to go dancing and begging in the streets (which is the point of the sacrificial demand). Prince explains:

"My grandmother was very successful textile trader. She brought clothes from the South and sell to the people in the place where I was born. And imagine a woman, who has about ten, twelve girls carrying clothes from house to house to sell to people, starting dancing.

"But she cannot avoid dancing in the house with me when I am crying. She burp me and sit down in the compound. But it's a big letdown for her to go to the streets, begging. Because nobody will even give her money because they know they were doing well. You know, she was like the righthand person to my grandmother in terms of the business they were doing.

"In the Yoruba culture, your wife will be even closer to your mom than you. Let's say you are just a farmer, and you have this, your wife, and your mom goes to the market, the place where they sell, and your wife will be with her. The only time she is with you is when you sleep or you want to rear your children. Otherwise, she's a wife to your mom. That's the way we are. Before the British bring their civilization attitude to our life and things start going apart.

"That's the way it is."

He sums it up, saying, "Alarinjo is a child you have to carry and walk about and dance. My mother refused, refused to do it. And that's why I end up dancing for years."

Her refusal shaped his future. He paid off her debt to the powers by dancing in the streets, and, as a dancer, he came to Osogbo where his career as a painter began.

Prince's art, his dancing and singing and painting, owes some of its force to his birth as an abiku child. Like all human beings, he was shaped in the spirit world. Olodumare, who is, like Allah, without form or gender, the ultimate power, gave him the breath of life. Obatala, the creator of living form, offered him flesh and a choice of heads. Then the spirits sent him to this world, only to take him back, bringing grief to his parents. But they interrupted the cycle by means of ritual:

"I am not supposed to be here. But my parents forced me to be here. They snatched me away from these people, and the system of life is somewhere in between.

"They snatched me away to make me survive, so that I don't go back to them. But they still haunt me to this day.

"Like, you see the way I walk. I had a terrible car accident in nineteen eighty-two. And on several occasions I have been involved in different car accidents, but I never die. I will go one day, but—

"Some people are trying to take me away from here. And some say, No. They don't allow it. Maybe because of the rituals of the past. And because my time hasn't reached yet."

There are two worlds. Human life is sprung between them, conditioned at once by natural and supernatural forces. The tensions of connection are particularly strong for an abiku child. The people who sent him want him back. The people who have him want him to stay, and their rituals engender contention among those who sent him. The abiku is caught in a war of the worlds, and pulled toward the unseen, he is haunted by spirits. They cause him harm, warn him, and send him messages. Prince hears voices that direct his actions at crucial junctures in life. Songs and ideas for paintings come to him, seemingly from nowhere. He dreams and his dreams come true. I ask him if abiku children have a connection to the spirit world that gives them special powers.

"Yes, they have. You lose some if you are not concentrating; you can lose some. But if you pay attention to it, it can still come back. Like, I'm gifted in one thing: if I dream about something now, before three months it will come to pass. So that's the opportunity tomorrow. And it is a dream, a big thing, as large as the sky.

"So, things like that still happen, but, like, in terms of songs, in terms of thinking about something for tomorrow and it happens. Okay, let's say I am doing this painting, and I put my energy on it, and I learn the whole thing: this painting is going to be sold to somebody from London.

"You're going to London," he says to the painting in progress on the table before us.

"That's an example.

"Like, it happens when I'm broke. I need to help some people. Because a lot of people come to me for help because they assume I have a lot of money. And I cannot say no to those people.

"So, you cannot believe in that, but, at that time, I'm dreaming of a person that tells me to go to Lagos. Go to street So-so-so-so. And I will find somebody who will help me.

"It happens to me like that.

"So, the abiku child are gifted."

When I ask Prince about the source of his creativity, he stresses two entwined things. First, his connection to the traditions of his people and place, a matter of a rebellious, revitalizing will. Second, his connection to the dead, the ancestors, the spirits. The second is a gift to the abiku. It decays with age, with distance from the spirit world and entanglement in quotidian concerns, but it can be preserved through determination; it is a matter of will—concentration—as well as fate:

"When I started painting, I tried to bring out everything that is in my mind, and focus on the mythological thinking of my people. When I started, maybe you'd think I'm crazy, because I remember when I was a very young man, I used to hear voices. I would sing songs, but I don't know where they come from. And even when they asked me to do it again, I will not be able to do it.

"But some of these things are going away when I started having properties. When I had a lot of money and started building houses here and palace there. Or cars. Earthly things. I started to lose some of it. But I still have it, but not as strong as when I was, like, about twenty, or between eighteen to twenty.

"The most aspect of it is my special connection to our part of the world. My belief. My communication with unseen hands. Like, I still do that today. I still do a lot of prayer. I still believe that one can reach the influence of the dead people. I talk a lot to people I don't see.

"I talk a lot to people I don't see.

"Because I have the feeling that we don't see them in flesh. But they can see you. They can hear you."

Prince offered the conclusion in a later conversation:

"God has been very helpful to me. And I go to the shrines in the past to pray. Meditate. By two or three A.M. in the night, I talk to the spirits. Because I believe I don't see them, but I believe that if you believe in them, they can save you in a situation. And that's the way I have been all my life."

Our Prince was born with powers he calls special and golden and spiritual, powers he understands through the aspect of his culture he calls mythological. Before birth, in Obatala's garden, he chose his Ori, the head and destiny of an artist. The reincarnation of Osuntoki, a warrior who followed Osun, Prince was born a fighter and a child of peace, identifiable as an Osun. Arriving again as an abiku, he knew both life and death, and born to die, he was preserved in life by Osun, the goddess he had worshiped in a former life. It is essential to his understanding of himself that he is an abiku, saved by Osun. To the abiku blessed by Osun, the two worlds are revealed: by nature he connects to the supernatural. That is the base of his *ase*, the life force he displays in incessant, compulsive creative action, but there is yet more in the charmed composition that was set at his birth. He was born a twin in double power, male and female, worldly and supernatural, positive and negative. Prince continues:

"When my mother was pregnant, they thought that she was going to have two girls. Because there is no scanning machine, so the babalawo, the priest, will use his oral procedures to read, and at that time he told my mom she was going to have twins, and the twins are coming to be women, and if anything happens that this child does not come as a woman, he is going to come as a man with a lot of woman in his life."

She had twins. The elder was a girl, the younger was Prince, a man with a lot of woman in his life. His many wives provide the conspicuous example, and once he told me, after talking to one of them on the cell phone, a tool perpetually in use, that he needs to talk with women, to argue with women, to find the energy to create his paintings. More profoundly, he told me that when his sister died, her soul united with his. She is one of the spirits with whom he speaks, from whom he benefits. Thinking again of the blend of Ogun and Osun, I ask if his absorption of his sister's spirit gives him at once the power of a man and the power of a woman. His response is quick:

"It give me both. It give me both. Before I started to discover whom I am as an artist, up to this morning, I still talk to my sister. I feel that she is around me all the time. And when I went to the reader, he used to tell me that somebody died a long time ago because of me, and she's always with me. And there are so many instances that I am close to death and somebody take the beating for me. It never happened.

"So, she's always around me—very very protective of me. Very, very. Very, very."

The feminine in him, reinforced by his devotion to Osun, guides him to beauty and doubles his creative resources. I was standing on the balcony of his house in Ogidi when the drummers came through the gate. The crowd gathered, pulsing to the beat, thickening to shape a vast turning swirl, a spiraling nebula of humanity with Prince, in white, at the center. When he began to dance, a sudden excitement spread outward, rippling into a collective wave of delight. He is not the dancer he was before a car wreck left him with an iron hip and a limp, but his tight, intense moves thrilled the musicians and dancers knotted around him. What struck me as I watched was that he danced like no other, that he freely fused in his body the conventional postures and motions of both male and female dancers. The man is a touch outrageous, happy at the edge.

Driven by male and female forces, Prince puts figures in his pictures who are doubly sexed. People and beasts exhibit the breasts of a woman, the genitals of a man—both are sources of white, life-giving fluids, signs of power and creative energy.

Prince commemorates his dead sister, honors Sango, and positions himself for social interaction by having his hair braided in cornrows as few men but many women do in Yorubaland. His hair, woven with cowries and elaborated by braided extensions for great events, sets him apart. His hair set him apart at birth.

In the past, he said, the details of birth were recorded in the names given to children. Babies born wrapped in the umbilical cord or shrouded in a caul, born feet first or face down, were given special names. So was the child born with hair matted into the dreadlocks of a Rastafarian:

"When a baby is born with braids, from the baby time, lots of people will name that baby Dada. Dada. I'm not talking about the braids people do today by putting soap in their hair, but naturally. And if you have that long hair like that of Bob Marley, in my country in that time before Bob Marley was known, they would say you are crazy. Because it is not usual to see people with that kind of dreadlock, uncombed and so long, because people you see with that kind of dreadlock are crazy, mad people—people who are mad for over eighteen years or twenty years, whom are incurable. So, these are the people you see that are that kind of rasta.

"Even mine was shining and it was well-braided, but, oh my God, people would call me all kind of names. There was a lady I was supposed to marry. Beautiful. She has a beautiful voice. I love to marry her, but the parents said, The man couldn't afford to get one naira to buy a comb.

"They need to say something to discourage the girl from following me: A crazy man who doesn't have money to buy a comb."

As he grew, rebel, dancer, and artist, he lived with the accusations of insanity, with the snarls of disapproval that surround a buoyant youth with long, unruly hair, a Yoruba hippie. He was born that way, a dada child, "rasta right from the womb." At birth his hair was matted with meaning because, he says, dada children become "very very powerful, and very rich, and they turn out to be successful in everything they touch."

Prince's powers expand. Dada children, like him and one of his sons, he says, are "very powerful, spiritually."

The circumstances of birth, remembered in names, are borne forward in life. On her tomb at Prince's home in Osogbo, Madam Mary Aitoyeje is called Iya Ibeji, Mother of Twins. Her son, an abiku, came to the world seven times, each time as one in a set of twins. The name he gave himself records that fact. Our topic is twins, and the man called Twins by his friends says, as the books do, that Yorubaland has the world's highest instance of twin births:

"In the time before our time, in the east before the missionary came to Nigeria, anybody who have twins at that time, they would kill the children. Because they thought they were bad luck. It's only the Yoruba people who see twins as God-given, good-luck kids.

"And today, all over the world, the Yoruba are the biggest twins-bearing people. Because the Yoruba believe that twins are special, gifted kids. And sometimes some people want to have twins, so that if they only want to have four children, two twins, they will stop having babies. But in those days people don't care; the more children you have the better, because they can go to the farm to help their family. Unlike today when children become too lazy and watch movies, and everybody just stay in the house, playing with computer and all that. But in those days, the more children you have—and that is why most men want to have boys, because they can help them on the farm with their farm products."

Twins are prized, special, gifted. Prince captures their qualities in his work. In a small sculpture's painting, *Mother of Twins*, the twins help their mother sell fruit, displaying the mundane virtue Prince raised when he spoke of boys helping their fathers on the farm. Usually, though, the stress is spiritual. In a large painting, ink on canvas, fantastic birds swirl around a basket holding swaddled twins. Prince calls it *The Coming to the World and the Golden Birds* or *Coming to the World of the Twins and the Spiritual Birds*. It shows, he said, "the coming to the world of the special twins, and these special golden birds are singing, welcoming the babies to the world." The birds represent witchcraft, Prince said. They are good and bad. So are we all; Prince speaks for twins:

"You know when we come to the world, we come with the two. The baby is good luck, then the thing you cut from the mother, the bag, that's the bag that contain the evils that come to the world with us.

"So, when we are coming to the world, we come with both the left and the right, the negative and the positive."

The left is the spiritual side, the right is the earthly side. Both are mixed. The physical doubleness of the twins recalls the doubleness of existence: spiritual and material, good and bad. In the picture, forces of doubleness—birds who are witches who are good and bad—welcome more doubleness to the earth.

Prince points to the top of the picture, saying, "And this is the sunset here, at the top. Because nobody come to the world without the influence of the sun. And when you are about to go away, the sun sets. When the sun sets, naturally, the sun sets for the human being—means: at the end of the journey, when you die."

The twins are welcomed into the double world of life and death. This is a picture of birth, of human beings born to die. The journey through the natural world from basket to sunset, from womb to tomb, will be hard, but twins have helpers. The monkeys in Prince's

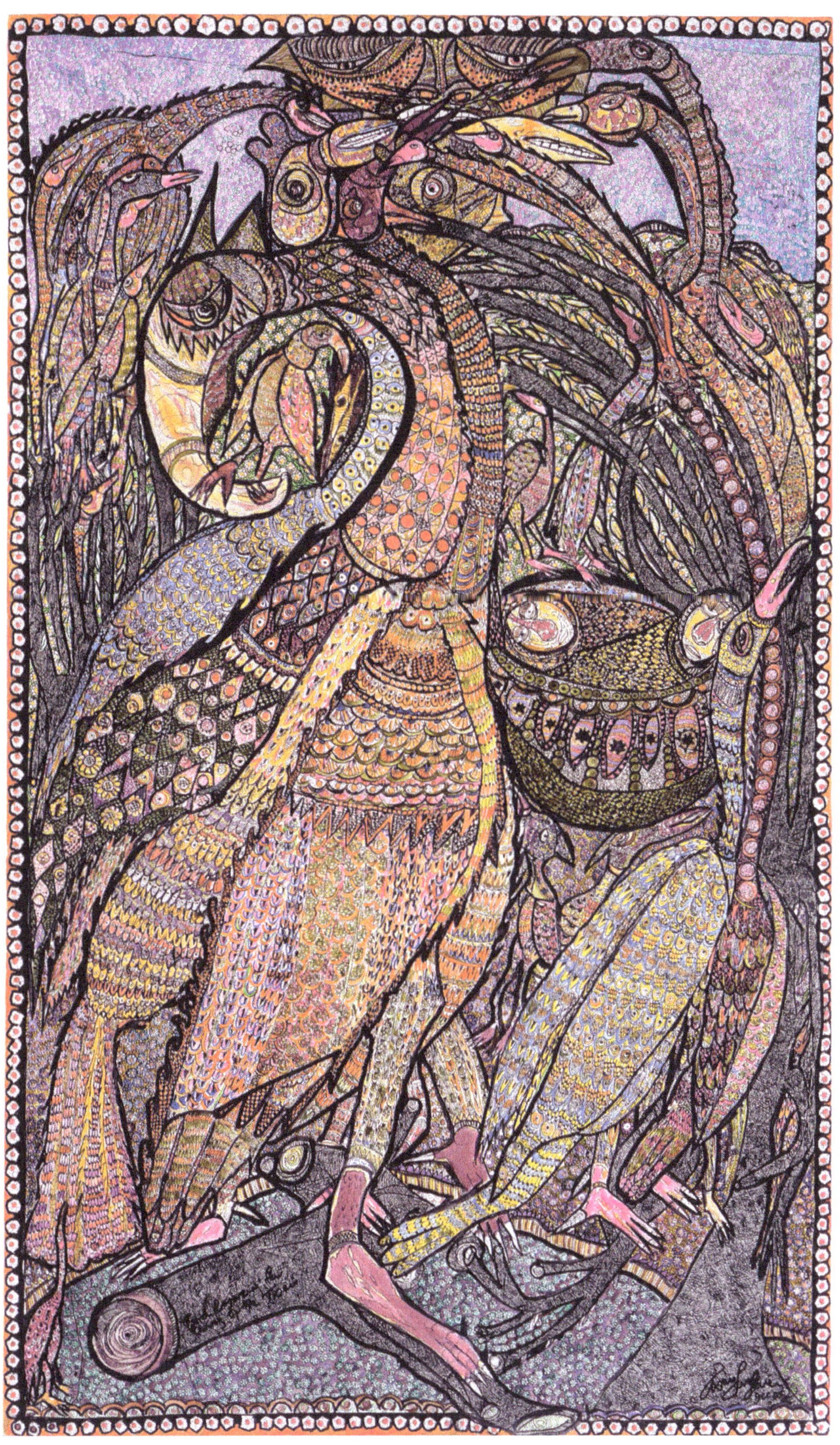

The Coming to the World and the Golden Birds.
Inks on canvas. 3'x5'. Philadelphia, 2006

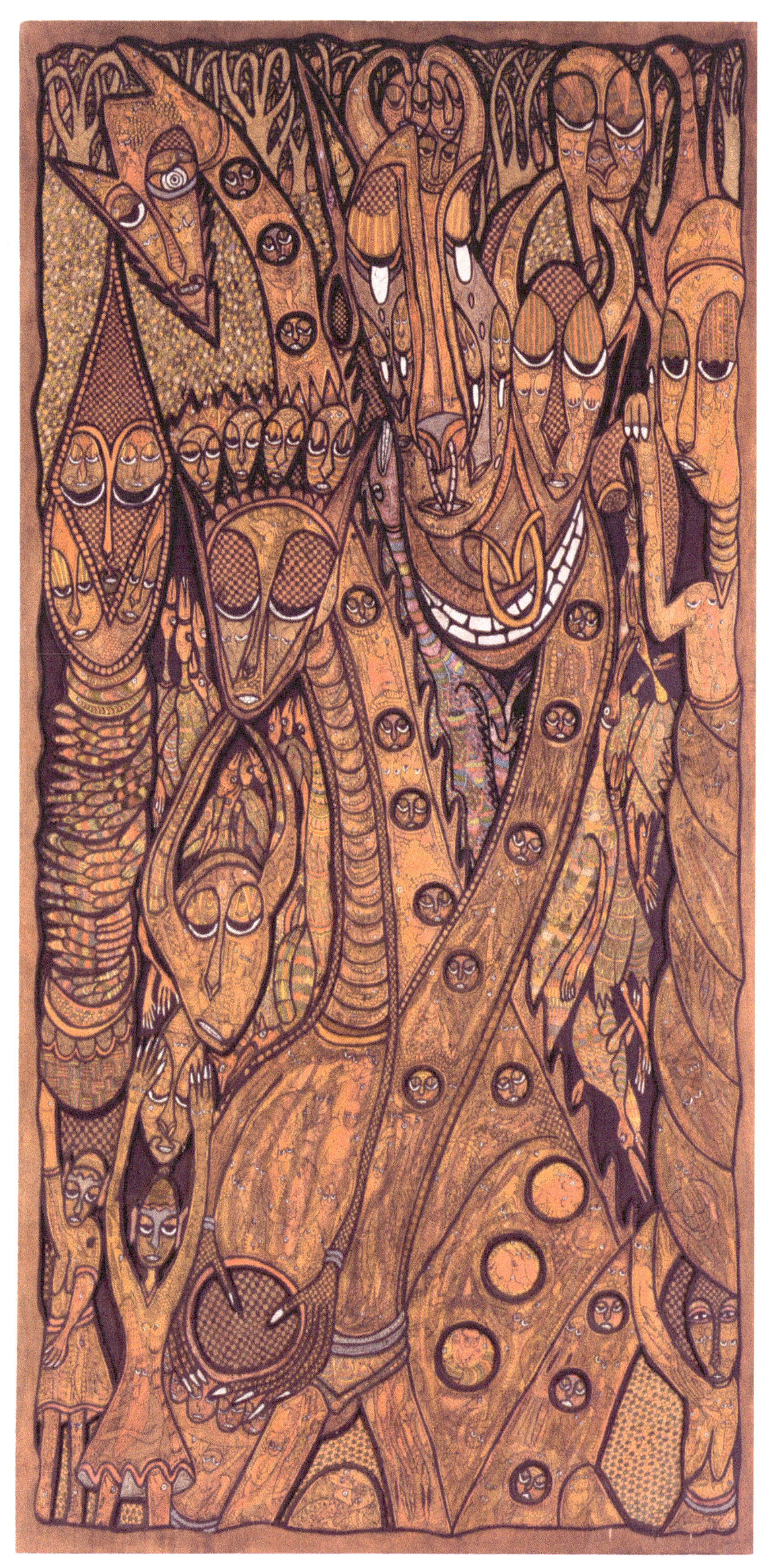

Ghosts in Political Conference
Ink, watercolor, and oil on wood; 2 layers. 4'x8'. Osogbo, 1978–1979

paintings represent one of two kinds of small simian, not the silvery gray one, but the one who has "a white small face and a beautiful white beard." This is Edun, "the protector of twins." Prince said:

"You know the yellow monkey, the one that can leap so far, with white face and white stomach; that is the one we call Edun.

"It represent twins, and they do protect twins, because people believe it was them that actually came as human being into the stomach of the pregnant woman. That's why we never touch it. We don't eat. No twins would eat Edun; no twins would eat monkey.

"They would not protect somebody who eat it. They would curse. Some people would eat, but twins never would."

In this world, the monkeys called *ijimere*, named Edun, run from people, leaping in the treetops. Sometimes they gather and chatter. Prince has seen them at the Osun shrine, assembled placidly and gazing into the river. Some people understand their speech. Prince does not, but he feeds them bananas, knowing that, in the other world, Edun pleads on behalf of twins, providing them spiritual protection.

Prince in solitude is not alone. A twin, he has helpers in both worlds. Osun, Edun, and the dead, his twin sister, his martial ancestors, come to his aid, and his pictures fill with gods and ghosts, with birds and snakes and monkeys.

As Robert Farris Thompson and John Pemberton III tell it, a cult of twins developed during the Oyo Empire in association with the worship of Sango. Once thought monstrous, twins, under Sango's protection, came to be revered for their power. When a twin died, the mother commissioned a small carving that, in Pemberton's words, embodied the living dead: it was bathed, clothed, and fed. Abounding in Yorubaland, wooden *ibeji* figures represent the dead who abide in the other world, not through portraits, but as conventionalized human beings, in proportion like a baby, with a large head and short legs, differentiated by the sexual characteristics of an adult. Wooden carvings image spirits as people, but Prince Twins Seven-Seven, empowered as a twin and an abiku, knows that the spirits differ radically from the people of the world. God, Prince says, has given him a gift that permits him to transfer the appearance of the spirits from his mind, through his hands, to the pictorial surface. The spirits in his pictures are mobile, not stable like the *ibeji* figures; their necks stretch and sway, and they are marked by the doubleness of twins.

The eyes get you first. Spirits have enormous double eyes. The lids are lowered, leaving arcs of black and white, or they are slit, half veiling the dark eyes behind. Open and closed at once, the eyes look in and look out, seeing simultaneously into both worlds. In many of Prince's paintings, the contrast is sharp. Human faces fill the background, their simple eyes staring in stunned wonder, while the spiritual being in the foreground sees everything through split lenses. Doubleness spreads to the body, to heads with two faces, to creatures who are both female and male, then doubleness extends to multiplicity in the spirits who have faces in their eyes, eyes in their necks, their breasts and bellies, all awake, all aware. More is more: this multiplicity of form, like the four arms of Shiva and Kali, the ten arms of Durga, bespeaks a power beyond the human, a power brought to the earth in the doubled phenomenon of twin birth.

A twin by birth, Prince is a twin by name. *Ibeji*, he says, is the general word for twins, but twins are named by the order of their birth:

"You know, when you have twins, the last one is supposed to be the elder. The last to come is the one who sends the first one, Taiwo, to the world, to investigate the world and report back. And when the baby say, Mwaaa, mwaaa, then the elder one will come because he told him the world is good."

Logically, Prince says, the first to come would be considered the elder, since he is longer in the world, but the second born is—"spiritually speaking"—the senior twin and she is named Kehinde. (The pronouns are right for Prince's birth; the names are the same for both genders.) The younger is Taiyewo, which means, he says, "Go to the world and see what it is like." Taiyewo can be shortened to Taiye, the word tattooed on Prince's forearm, or contracted into Taiwo, the usual name for a junior twin. In the past, the first, second, and third children born after twins were also given special names. "But," he says, "because of modernization, most women who have children today—because they don't have time or because there's nobody to tell them, because everybody is trying to imitate American way of life, so most of these names are not being used anymore. Most people use Christian names, like Samuel, Joseph, different things like that."

One class of Yoruba name, determined by the convulsions of nature, records the circumstances of birth. Taiwo, the younger, firstborn twin, is one of his names. The others were chosen. His father gave him the abiku name Bamidele. His grandmother named him Olaniyi. He was also given the Muslim name Husseini, which he rarely mentions. Prince tells of his naming in one long sweep:

"Bamidele is the original name given to me because they want me to survive and go back to Ibadan with my father. Then Olaniyi is from my family; we have what you call family appellation. Oyewale shows that the honor and prestige has come back to the family.

"You see, when a baby is born in Nigeria, Yorubas name their children from their ancestors to the present generation, and each family can give a child a name. The mother will give the name. The father will give the name. The auntie, the whoever is in the family at that time—and even if it is an uncle or a father who is far away, he will call and say, I name the baby So-so-so.

"But the other name that I am supposed to have, that they don't call me all the time then, is Oyekale. That is my grandfather's name. And my own father's name is Aitoyeje, which means He came back to the truth.

"This Oyekale was the father of all the eight children, but my father was the most senior among them.

"So, Oyekale was the son of Osuntoki.

"If I am lucky to become king in future, I would like to be called Taiwo Bamidele Olaniyi Oyewale Oyekale Aitoyeje Osuntoki. Then I should be Osuntoki Two, Osuntoki Two, the second Osuntoki.

"I'm using the name because I want people to know who I am. I want them to remember my descent from my great-grandfather.

"But there is no way I can run away from Twins Seven-Seven. Because everybody knows me that way, and they will put Twins Seven-Seven somewhere. But they may not call me to my face, but when they mention my name on the TV or anything.

"Some people pick up their own name. They don't use family name, and that situation is because you have nothing to relate back to. But if you have something to relate back to in terms of history, you have to let everybody know *all* these names. Then they know who you are.

"It could have just been Taiwo Olaniyi; like, in some places, in checkbook, I just have Twins Olaniyi. You have Twins because I believe my dead sister, the two of us are in me. So that's why I take the name Twins.

"In my language Twins Seven-Seven is Ibeji Meje-Meje. Ibeji means twins; Meje means seven. Some people will call, Meje-Meje Baba, Baba Meje-Meje. But when I started having all these chieftaincy titles, and people know I'm from a royal family, most people call me Baba.

"The people we grew up together, or they are my age group, they call me Meje-Meje, when we are in a very enclosed area. But if we are outside, they will not call me that. They will say Prince, or they will say Chief.

"I started calling myself Twins Seven-Seven right from the time I started traveling. You see, when I got the gramophone and danced, that's the name I used. You see, I have Ibeji Meje-Meje, Twins Seven-Seven, in Yoruba and English."

His names carry facts from his birth as a junior twin and an abiku child. They bring him a lineage running back to his great-grandfather, a king, and embracing his hopes for the future, aroused by the discovery, made in maturity, that he belonged to a royal family and deserved to be called Prince. They incorporate the identity he adopted as a young dancer and painter. The names go with him and drop him into the flow of time.

·5·

Pattern in Time

By starting his story with a place, not a date, Prince departed from the biographical pattern governed by the academic historian's dedication to chronology and allied himself with alternative histories in which space dominates time. Academic histories flurry with dates that break time's line into sealed periods; the past recedes, period by period, decreasing in relevance, fading into the haze of unknowable origins. Spatial history, in contrast, fills with the names of places. The past is not vanished or prologue; it is palpably present in landmarks, and time on the narrated landscape is as repetitious as it is developmental, as cyclical as it is linear, as continuous as changing, as blended as split.

In his fine writings, N. Scott Momaday, poet, novelist, and man of the Kiowa, describes and exemplifies the orientation to space generally held by Native American historians. During a decade of study in Ballymenone, a rural community on the Irish border, I learned that the local historians comparably gave precedence to the spatial dimension. The wisest of Ballymenone's historians, Hugh Nolan, taught me that spatial emphasis renders history relevant, that spatial restriction helped him in his task, which he defined at the end of his life as keeping the truth and telling the whole tale. By setting his tales firmly in place and breaking them out of chronological alignment, Mr. Nolan built his history typologically by theme to clarify for his neighbors the dread dilemmas of their existence. In advancing toward material comfort, they were retreating from social order. In struggling for armed victory, they were risking eternal defeat by breaking God's commandment to love. Like Ballymenone's historians, Prince acknowledges chronology, but he lets time drift while expanding on themes that trade sequence for significance.

The emplaced view of history, shared by Scott Momaday, Hugh Nolan, and Prince Twins Seven-Seven, is caught in William Faulkner's declaration that "The past is never dead. It's not even past." Faulkner's great novels combine into the tale of a place, Yoknapatawpha, illustrating how events of the past—the displacement of the native people, the settlement of the land, slav-

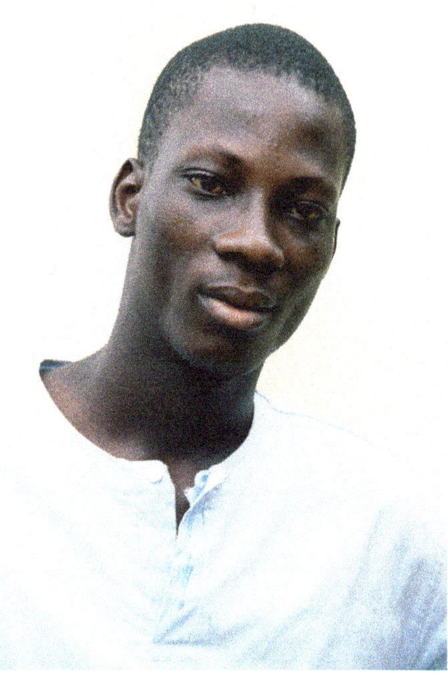

Sunday Ayantoye

ery and the Civil War, the arrival of noisy machines and the obsession with cash—continue to drive events in the present. The Faulknerian view (Sartre wrote that it is like speeding forward in a car while looking into the rearview mirror) is not alien to Nigeria.

It was one of those nights spent hurtling along a narrow road while the black bush sped backward on both sides. No feature marked progress: the old Peugeot was going as fast as it could, but it felt as though we were getting nowhere, as though we were furiously holding steady in space. The topic was reincarnation. Prince told us that he was troubled today by the innocent people killed by his ancestors in the past. Sunday Ayantoye, Prince's driver, a trained engineer and a Christian from Abuja, said that his mind could not accept what Prince's mind did. He did not believe in reincarnation, but he understood why others might. Sunday began with a proverb: Wicked people bring good people into their wickedness. Then he gave an example. If a man is a thief, he will harm his children by giving the family a bad name. After his death, aggrieved people will still approach his children, angrily seeking redress for past thefts. Old acts have consequences in the present, but for Sunday this historical continuity was not a matter of mystical connection, but of communication through time in social life.

The past is alive for Sunday as it was for Faulkner. But for Prince it is literally true: the people of the past—the deified dead, the ancestors, the spirits—live and act, though unseen, in the present. Academic history features linear development and keys upon human agency; it befits a secular cast of mind. Spatial history swallows time into the present; it welcomes both natural and supernatural causation and befits a spiritual worldview.

The past is present. Prince is the descendant and the reincarnation of Osuntoki. The old king lives again in him and burdens him with karmic debt. The spirits who sent him from the other world want him to return, and they intrude in his life with disastrous results—car wrecks and lingering injuries. He talks with his dead sister who protects him, who comes between him and death. He talks with his ancestors who, though invisible, inspire and inform him:

"The dead give me powers.

"They give me ideas. They give me ideas. And sometimes they warn me too. If there is somebody I should deal with, they tell me.

"They tell me."

He hears the dead, and he sees them. The dead, he says, are all around us, though we do not know it. He wonders, as one might in a crowded airport, how there can be so many unknown people in the world, and, to make his point, he tells a story he learned from his mother (which in the manner of spatial history is exact about place, vague about time; where the events happened, Kaduna and Ogidi, is clear, when they happened is not):

"I look in some areas in Nigeria where we have civil war. The whole place was perished. But today there is a very very explosive market place. A lot of people. I don't know where these people came from. You know what I mean?

"Because we believe that people can die here and appear in another country. We have that belief. Through reincarnation.

"They can die in one place and still surface in another place.

"But when they see somebody who knows them, you cannot see them, but they see you.

"Unless you don't know this man has died, he will appear—like, we have a story where a woman married a man, in a town called Kaduna.

"And they have six kids together. And every time this woman bothered the man, saying, Why are you not taking me to your family?

"So, when the pressure was too much, he decided to come south.

"As they arrived in my mom's home town, the man said, told her, I want to call one of my friends here to let him know I am back. That's why I will go there.

"So, the woman with the six kids, when going inside, she said, I am here.

"Who are you?

"I am married to Mister Kolade.

"They say, Which Kolade?

"She said, We are together in Kaduna.

"Then, the man could not believe it. He said, Which Kolade?

"And the woman mentioned the name of the Kolade, the son of the woman who knew that her son had died for over five years ago.

"And then they said to the woman, That is impossible. They allow her to come inside. They said, Put down your luggage. And the woman said, Are you serious?

"You see, my son Kolade is the very man, Karin Kolade.

"The woman fainted.

"And later on, she was all right. But the man doesn't come again.

"The man who they are traveling together, who they had been living together for six years in another town, he never came back into the house with her. Only to tell her, Go; I am going somewhere.

"That is just an example of how my beliefs—like, even when my father died, somebody saw him miles and miles away, and he told that person he was on his way to buy some leather. But he died a natural death. He died naturally, no accident, no nothing."

A violent death is not necessary (as it frequently is in American ghost lore) to free the spirit and force its return. People die, but they can come back in the flesh, visible to those who do not know them, capable of procreation with earthly partners. The dead inhabit this world as well as the other. Ghosts and spirits make rich subjects for paintings. Prince does not stop there. He goes on to say that the spirit can depart from the living body and, like the wraith of European tradition, it can roam the world:

"You don't have to be dead.

"Even me, even me. If I am not there, people will see me. I was in America last year, and some people were fighting in Nigeria. One man said, It was Twins; I saw him. The person told him, It was one of his children. No, it was him. So, it happens like that."

The spirit is real, separable from flesh, separable from time. The past, through the dead, acts in the present.

The future, too, can be brought into the present. That is the work of the diviners.

Diviners can foretell a child's destiny at birth. Prince calls them soothsayers, but they are more than fortune-tellers who can predict the future. All of time is their province. Diviners, Prince says, are "four-eyed people." With two eyes they see the world, with two eyes they see into the world of the spirits. They see by reading signs; he calls them readers. They are wise and powerful; he calls them babas, fathers.

Prince goes to them with a problem. They look backward in time to discover its cause. They look into his current state to analyze his complaint. They look forward in time to learn how his life will unfold, and then they recommend and perform acts that will influence the course of events. Diviners gather all of time into the present to shape the future, to ensure that predicted blessings will come to pass, that predicted evils will be averted. Like the ancestors, diviners help Prince on his struggle forward.

Since the problems people bring to them are often physical ills, since diviners are, in process and effect, like healers of disease, since they are usually herbalists as well as seers, Prince groups them loosely with "native doctors" and says he consults many of them, just as a man with an ailment will consult many physicians, weighing conflicting diagnostic advice in his quest for health. He consults many because "some of them are—some are fake, some are good. Some are good.

"Because the world is just too materialistic. When you go to soothsayers that have cars, who is having rugs in his house—he's too modern. Maybe if you need to spend only one hundred dollars for his services, he ask you for three hundred because he need money for his cars."

In harmony with his critical view of historical change, in which a coherent past contrasts with a fragmented, duplicitous present and the blame for change is placed on colonialism—British soldiers and missionaries in the past, American mass media today—Prince says that once diviners were honest men in the bush. They read accurately, supplied "medicine" made of roots and herbs, "potion" to drink, soap for ritual washing, and they prescribed the sacrifices necessary to a fruitful future. In return, they received modest sums and agricultural produce. Now, materialistic like the rest of us, they demand large quantities of cash and extravagant gifts, often automobiles. Still, hounded by problems, desperate for answers, Prince visits them frequently.

He consults many diviners because they vary in reliability, and because they differ in kind. "I am," he often says, "a man of many doors." His doors open into a wide array of spiritual realms. To a Christian in Nigeria he said, "You have Jesus Christ in your life, but I have everything." To me he said, "I play everything against everything, so no one can catch me." He dodges the frauds and locates the skilled people who will give him the right advice.

Diviners are also women, but the ones Prince visits are male. They cluster into two main groups.

One kind of diviner he calls babalawo, the father of secrets. The babalawo makes a cast and reads the pattern. The specific pattern connects to one or more specific verses in his

Suleiman Badmus

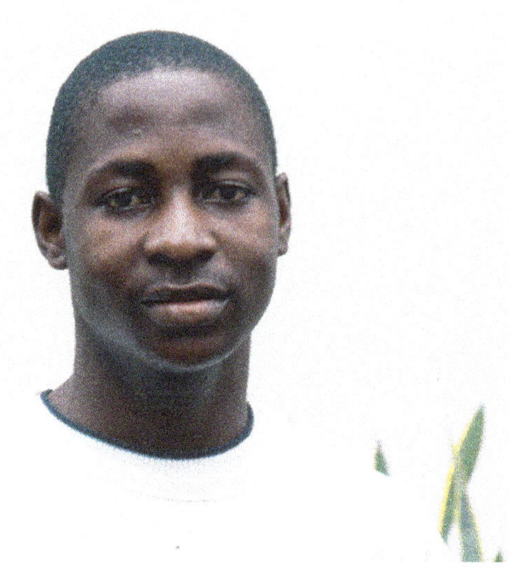

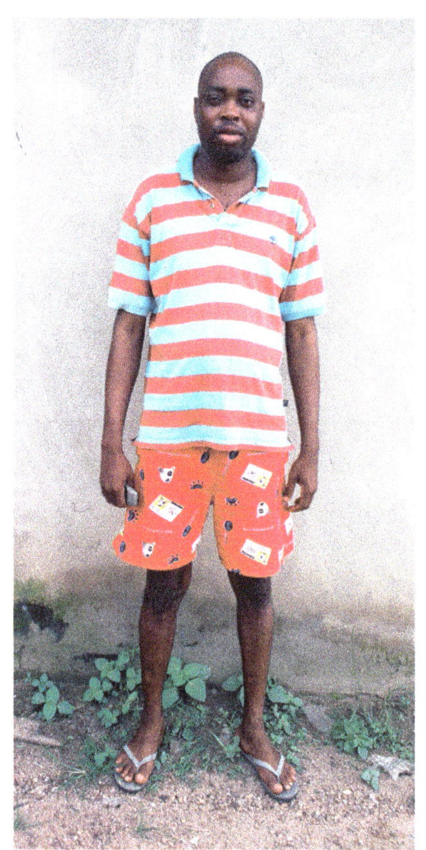

Diviners

Suleiman Abbakir

Alhaji Oladeji

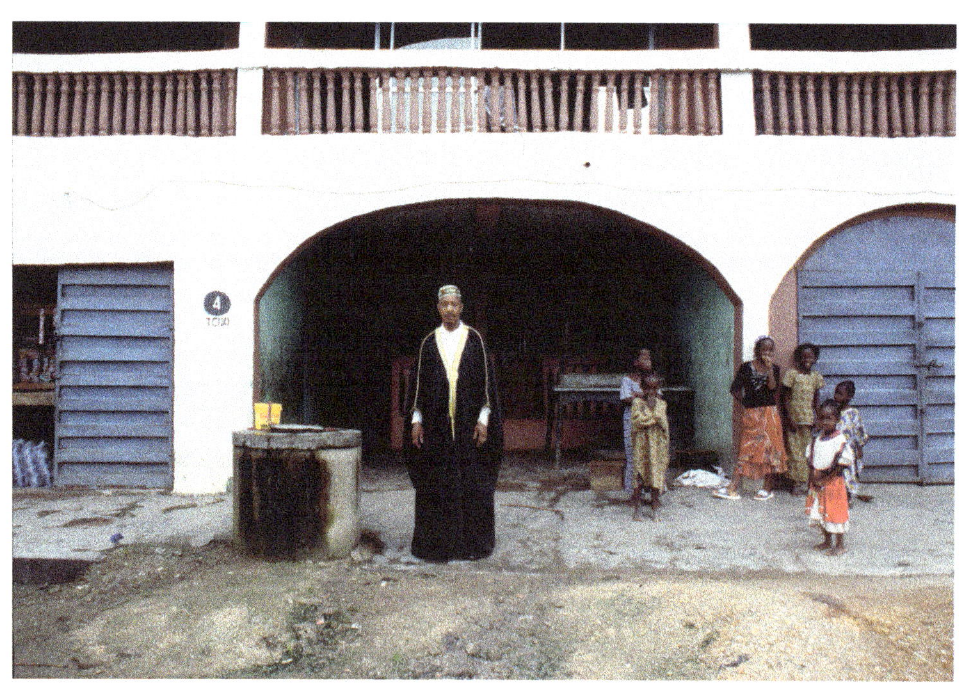

mind. The verses are communications from Ifa, the god of wisdom. This is the classical divinatory procedure of the Yoruba people, and, in acting as a conduit between the worlds, reporting directly from Ifa, the babalawo should be trustworthy. The system is perfectly valid and efficacious, Prince says, but the babalawo, anxious for cash, might perform perfunctorily and tell the client what he wants to hear, or Ifa, offended by the babalawo's worldly motives, might send a false message. So other readers must be consulted.

Prince calls diviners of the second kind seers, oracles, and most often spiritual readers. Classically, the babalawo divines with palm nuts or a chain. Spiritual readers use different techniques. They read with knotted string, paper and pens, bowls of water, trays of sand. They read leaves and palms and holy texts. They pray. The babalawo receives messages from Ifa. Spiritual readers have other sources of power. Some of them are herbal healers, some are priests at the shrines of deities other than Ifa.

One of Prince's readers is a Christian, Elder Adewolo, the minister of a rural church to which Prince has donated musical instruments. The members of his congregation wear white and they go barefoot because Moses climbed barefoot up the mountain to meet the Lord and Jesus went through the world without shoes. Prince regularly calls him on his cell phone for advice. Elder Adewolo prays with him, Prince responding with repeated Amens, and he makes predictions. Before he met me, Prince said, the Elder told him that a tall man would enter his life and support him in his work.

But most of Prince's spiritual readers are Muslims. Alhaji Oladeji reads for him from a bowl of water placed beneath his desk in the room in his large house that is set aside for consultation. Suleiman Abbakir reads for him from marks he makes in sand, which, Prince says, is an "Arabic" method brought by the Fulani to Yorubaland. Suleiman Badmus, called Sule, travels with Prince. Sule's father was a great reader, and when he was a little boy, Prince says, Sule had the wise, deep eyes of an old man. A quiet, steady presence and still a virgin, Sule possesses pure power. He evaluates the readings and medicines provided by other diviners, advising Prince when to accept, when to reject. He performs the orthodox Muslim namaz, praying for peace in Prince's household, and he prepares the "concoction" that Prince consumes in quantity. Using the juice of a berry for ink, Sule inscribes Koranic texts in the Arabic script on a narrow writing board—the classical form of Muslim Africa, tipped by a diamond. Then he tilts the board, pouring water down it, and the sacred words dissolve into a pinkish fluid that fills the used plastic bottles Prince carries on his journeys, drinking from them to increase his power and protect himself from evil.

They are, for Prince, all readers, all babas, but some of them, the priests who channel Ifa, he also calls babalawo. Others he calls witches, witchdoctors, magicians, and juju men. They deal with evil. "Every Yoruba man believes in witches," Prince said. "There are positive witches and negative witches."

Negative witches work to destroy, replacing beneficent sacrifices with magical acts designed to bring harm. The technique Prince usually mentions involves speaking a charm to an open padlock, then closing it to trap the spirit of the targeted individual. The witch hangs the lock on a tree in the bush so that it can be retrieved and opened to release the spirit, or he throws it into a river, permanently stifling the spirit while the stricken person, overcome with illnesses of body and mind, shrivels toward death. Positive witches read to discover the witchcraft at the source of a client's problems, then they engage in a war of the witches, using craft of their own—sixteen dead rats spread at a crossroad, for example—to counteract the witchery of their client's enemies. Prince sums it up:

"Black people don't build airplanes. We don't have all this technology, but we have much we can do.

"We don't have electricity. But we have the darkness."

The literature on African divination, and Yoruba divination in particular, is vast and excellent. Philip Peek edited a particularly useful volume titled *African Divination Systems.* Generally it is written that diviners begin without information; they must divine to learn about their clients and their problems. That is not true for Prince. In the past, he said, families retained particular diviners and normally he consults readers who know him and something about his problems. But traveling with him I was able to experience the early phase of the process. The diviners began by telling me things about myself that no one could have told them. Two of them told me that I have four children, and one of them said that one of the two middle children was enduring, just then, a time of trouble about which I did not know. That turned out to be true. Their information was intended to be a convincing demonstration of their powers. Then several of them went on to say that I had an enemy who was causing trouble in my life, blocking the success I deserve. One said it was a man, another said it was a professional colleague, another said I would not learn my enemy's identity until the day of my death. With this information, they invited further (and expensive) readings that would lead to (expensive) sacrifices.

Only once did we visit a diviner Prince had not met before. He gave Prince much information and advice about himself. It was accurate enough, but Prince is a famous man, easy to know about, and the diviner knew one of Prince's former wives and one of his friends (who stood to gain materially from the advice he supplied), so his knowledge was not, to me at least, particularly convincing. It mattered little to Prince, one way or the other. Readers have powers and what he wants from them is information about things he does not know, about hidden causes and useful solutions.

Sunday tinkers the car into action, and we pile in, Prince and his junior wife, Princess Aliratu, my wife, Pravina, and I. We leave Kabba, traveling the dirt roads to the farm where Alhaji Suleiman Otitoloju lives with his three wives and many children. On his business card, Alhaji Suleiman calls himself an "alternative medicine practitional herbalist." Prince calls him a babalawo. Behind his house, in a long range to the left of the courtyard, he has, as most diviners do, a small, tight room for consultation. With a broad smile and an elaborate handshake he welcomes us in.

We sit, two couples, on a plank bench shoved to the wall by the door. Shelves rise up the wall to the left, bearing bottles, jars, and tin cans, gourds and earthenware pots. The floor beneath spreads toward us, jumbled with more containers filled with the raw materials of medical practice. The pelt of some bush beast and a large calendar hang on the wall before us, and across from us on the right, Alhaji Suleiman sits on a low stool in the soft light of a curtained window.

Wrapped in a cloth, he has four chains. Classical diviners at the heart of Yorubaland use a single chain, but we are at the northeastern edge where four chains are normal. Linked into each chain are four half pods of a dried fruit, not the *agbigba* that gives its name to northeastern divination, but the inedible *esoepa*. Women in the area use cowries in divination, and cowries hang from the ends of Alhaji Suleiman's chains. He spreads the cloth before him and casts upon it, lifting one chain in each hand and tossing them forward together, so that the bottoms land where the tops had been and the pods spin freely. After the cast, some of the pods lie with their rounded backs exposed, others with the flat belly turned upward. In his detailed account of Ifa divination, William Bascom asks us to think of them as the heads and tails of coins. Alhaji Suleiman repeats the cast with the other two chains. Now sixteen pods, four chains of four, two casts of eight, transcribe a pattern of backs and bellies. He reads the pattern from right to left, from the first chain thrown with the right hand to the second thrown with the left. The pattern brings to mind a verse he has memorized. The verse, a message from Ifa, he repeats and interprets to provide the information his client needs.

For me, the procedure was at its simplest. He asked my name and no more. Then he cast the four chains, read the pattern of sixteen, and told me I have a jealous rival who is blocking my route to success. He asked me to touch the earth and swear that I would keep every promise. I did, and then he told me that, by sacrificing a ram, I would clear my way forward. Things, in my case, turned out to be negotiable. I told him that a blood sacrifice might enrage the Hindu gods, possibly precipitating, since my wife is a Hindu, a war in the heavens between the gods of India and Yorubaland. He was happy to accept as my sacrifice money enough to mount a vegetarian feast for the poor people in his neighborhood.

Alhaji Suleiman has read for Prince before. He knows him and his concerns. Prince knows who he is, knows his problems; he wants solutions. So, nervous and deferential, Prince begins a long narration. While he speaks, clasping his hands in passion and gesturing broadly, Alhaji Suleiman watches him closely. He had done the same with me. His body is still, his attention complete. His gaze is steady and deep, unblinking and probing, his smile is warm and comforting. I felt that it was useful for Prince to tell his story at length and in detail, useful for Alhaji Suleiman to play the role of the ideal psychiatrist. While he listened in rapt patience, Prince spelled out three problems. First, he said, there is trouble in his household. Dissension among his wives, brought on, he believes, by witchcraft, has separated him from Shola, the stately, beautiful wife who accompanied him to America. Second, Aliratu, his youngest wife who sits beside him at the end of the bench, lost her seven-year-old daughter in the spring. She cannot stop grieving. With no child, she has no position in the household, where mothers are named for their children. She wants a baby but has been unable to bring a pregnancy to term, and, depressed, she has threatened to leave for Lagos. Third, Prince is miserable in America, where he gets no respect, where he has been reduced to menial tasks, even washing his own car. He hopes that President Obasanjo, for whom he campaigned, will arrange for him a position in Nigeria that is sufficiently remunerative and worthy of his talents.

These are the problems that demand Ifa's wisdom and a babalawo's art. As soon as Alhaji Suleiman began to cast for the answers, Chief Umoru, splendidly dressed, filled the door and squeezed onto the bench beside me. He, too, is a babalawo, a prosperous landlord, and he has come for a reading. Diviners serve others; they cannot read for themselves. Prince had repeated a proverb to me: The elephant never eats the grass under his stomach. Then he glossed it: "The babalawo can solve other people's problems, but not their own." Alhaji Suleiman is a Muslim. Chief Umoru follows the old native faith. But their discipline as diviners is the same, and they are close friends.

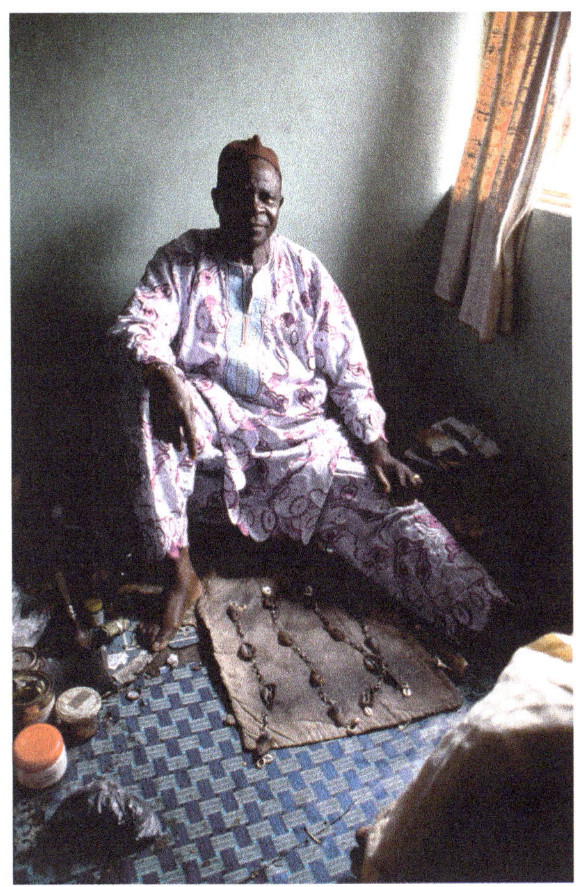

Alhaji Suleiman Otitoloju
with the four chains for divination

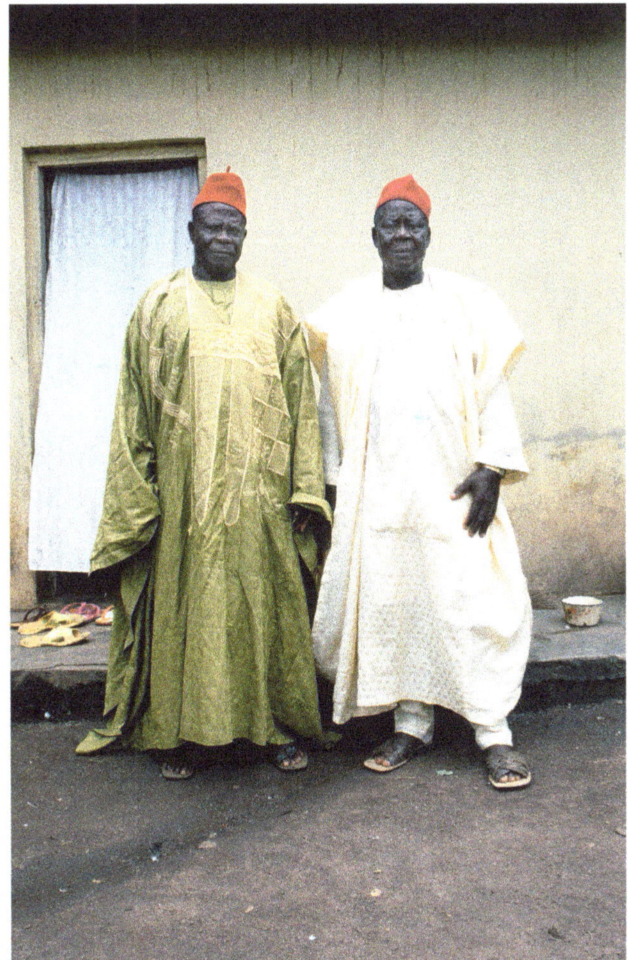

Alhaji Suleiman and Chief Umoru.
Kabba

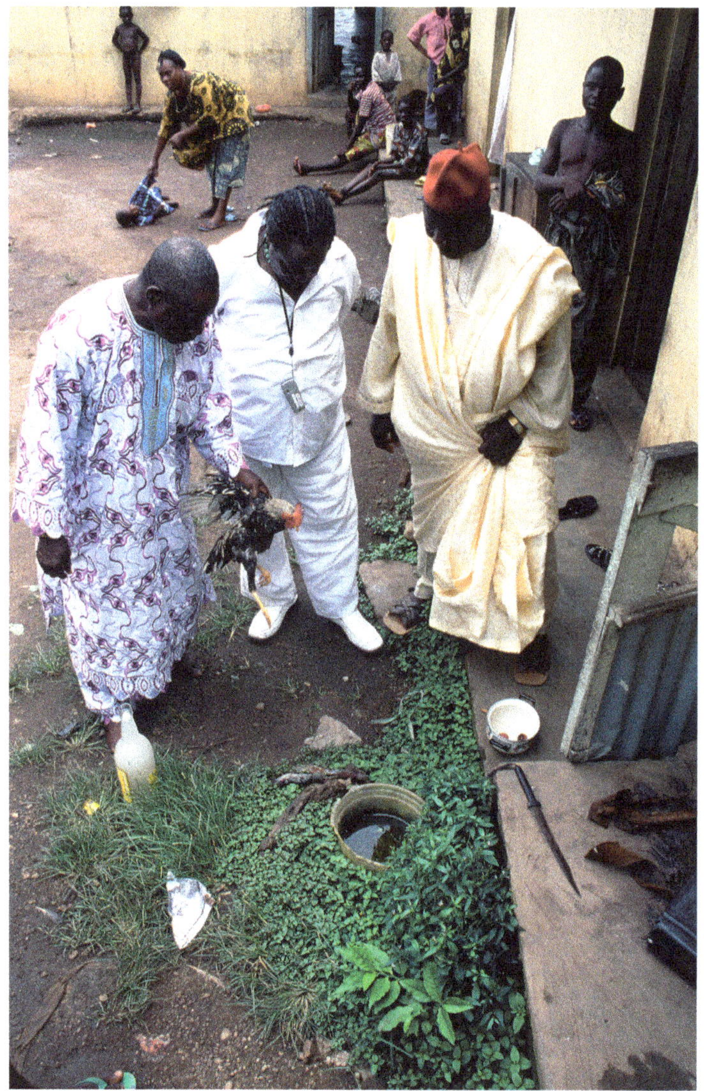

Alhaji Suleiman, Prince, and Chief Umoru, sacrificing to Ogun

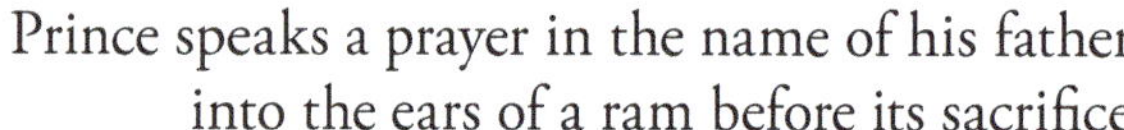

Prince speaks a prayer in the name of his father into the ears of a ram before its sacrifice

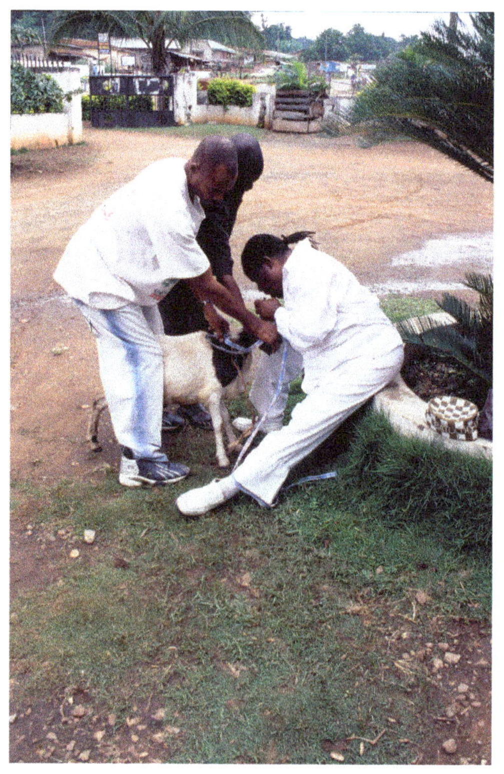

When Alhaji Suleiman casts the chains for Chief Umoru, sometimes they read the pattern silently together, smiling in mutual comprehension. Sometimes Alhaji Suleiman, after reading the pattern, chants a verse, and sometimes they chant the verse in unison. Once Prince knew the verse too and chanted along. There was no need for interpretation; the patterns and verses sufficed. They received the message in independent, professional accord. Chief Umoru has learned what he wanted. They shake hands, kissing their own fingertips at the end, laughing heartily together, reminding me of Sufis in Turkey, joyous in a oneness of spiritual understanding.

When Alhaji Suleiman turned back to Prince's case, Chief Umoru joined in, seconding his colleague's interpretations. The chains are cast. They read the pattern together. If the answer is unclear, the fourth chain, the one on the far left, is tossed again. Without reciting the verse indexed by the pattern, Alhaji Suleiman goes straight to the conclusion. The evil that separated Shola from Prince can be obliterated by the warrior Ogun. The sacrifice of a dog would be best, but a cock will do. Someone has marked Aliratu. Sacrificing a she-goat will erase the mark and return her to fertility and wifely balance. Some jealous person has worked magic, causing President Obasanjo to forget Prince. A ram must be sacrificed. As in the reading for me, a ram's death can cancel jealous opposition.

The divination is over. The event is not. There is a long chanted prayer, Prince pounding the beat with his left fist on his right foot. There is a song sung by the diviners. When the bush burns, it says, there is no place for the tiger and elephant to hide. The only safety is found in running water, an idea that would make sense to a follower of Osun. The song ends by stressing the need for sacrifice. The work of sacrifice remains.

Princess Aliratu, fashionably dressed in American clothes, is forced to kneel, trembling, and hold the rope tied to the black she-goat's neck. Alhaji Suleiman and Chief Umoru recite a long prayer to which she rhythmically responds, *"Ase,"* power, as a Christian would repeat a compliant Amen. Chief Umoru then gives her a lecture on the duties of a wife, saying she is fortunate to be married to a famous man and she should learn to be respectfully obedient. He tells her of his own life, how one of his wives left him and he cursed her. When she wanted to return, he refused. Later, Aliratu will tell us it was a terrifying experience; she had no intention to leave, but she feared the tiger in Prince's eyes, and all she wanted was for him to stay with her. Alhaji Suleiman gives her black soap and coils of raffia to scrub the mark from her body. The she-goat will be sacrificed to protect her child of the future.

We went outside then, taking a hobbled cock. During a long prayer, Alhaji Suleiman points the cock toward the altar, a stub of earth against which iron blades lean. He beheads the cock with a knife and tosses the body aside to flop in the dust while its blood runs down the iron. Chief Umoru adds a white paste to the blood. The boy who was sent for palm wine returns with a recycled bottle full of cloudy liquid. A bowl is sent to circulate among the young men who stand back in the shade, and we all take a sip, then pour the remainder of the palm wine into the blood. We eat bits of bitter kola, then four pieces of kola are cast and cast again at the base of the altar to confirm the reading of the chains. Ogun has been fed, asked to battle evil, to aid Prince in his quest for a future of familial peace.

Finally, the imam of the mosque in Kabba will butcher the ram after Prince has spoken into each of its ears a prayer in the name of his father, Aitoyeje. The sacrifice will carry the prayer to the other world. The ram's meat will make a feast to which all will be welcome.

We stand in the dry heat. Alhaji Suleiman asks for a token. I find in my camera bag a silver medallion, a souvenir from a Hindu temple. I give it to him, he gives me his business card, and we all shake hands. Sunday, who has been sitting in the car for a long time (such things do not interest him), gets it going.

What can be done has been done. The future, it is to be hoped, will be better.

· 6 ·

A Throwaway Boy from the Bush

Prince began his story with culture, thematically linking the aspects of his life explained by the "recognition mythology" of the Yoruba people. Marked, he is a man from the heart of Yorubaland. The reincarnation of Osuntoki, he is a rebel, a fighter, a devotee of Osun. A twin, an abiku, a dada, he is spiritually gifted; he lives between the worlds, struggling in this one, receiving messages from the other—directly from the dead, indirectly through the diviners. Past and future collapse into an enchanted present when Prince, his head roiling with notions, sits down to paint.

In every person, the learned and innate meld inextricably. Every word or gesture, every painting, expresses an integrated self, uniting the learned and innate, nurture and nature, the dimensions of the individual customarily labeled culture and personality.

The work of art is one, it is both, but scholars analyze it into difference. Anthropologists stress culture and social motivations. Art historians stress personality and individual talent. Categorical distinctions—fine and folk art, say, or elite and popular, insider and outsider, Western and Eastern, cosmopolitan and primitive—arise more from academic presuppositions than from phenomenal realities. Art is art. In full presence, all works of art combine culture and personality. Art might as well be defined as a complete revelation of the human, a concentrated, devoted work of fusion in which culture and personality are both insistently manifest.

The life, too, is one, but modern biographers, persuaded by the disciplinary conventions of history and psychology, begin with the personality that develops in time, looking briefly backward to genetic inheritance, then forward from the moment of birth to track the career chronologically to death. Prince, by contrast, began with culture. It was an unusual, but not unique, move. The first full biography of Robert Burns, prepared four years after his death, featured at the beginning—before the narrative of his life—an essay on the Scottish peasantry. That reversal of norms is basic to a rhetoric of cultural authenticity. Burns, Currie argued in

1800, spoke with an authentic Scottish voice. Prince argues for himself. Abiku, dada, Osun—marked—he is an authentic, grounded and committed, man of the Yoruba. Like Burns, he is an emplaced creator, bringing tradition forth and twisting it personally into new works of art.

Stressing belonging in a way that fits with a spatial rather than a temporal take on history, Prince began with culture. I have followed him, tracing his theme to the end. The summer sun falls through a tall window and flows over the table, the pens and brushes, unopened envelopes, a box of pastels, a plastic container of red, savory lunch. He pauses, smiling, tapping a beat with his pen. Then, beginning again, he turns to personality, to the life of a child he calls, not a prince from a royal line, but "a throwaway boy from the bush."

Getting back into his story, and putting us on a familiar autobiographical track, he starts with schooling. Like any child at the beginning of a career that runs beyond the home, he was sent to school, an ordeal he endured fitfully while his creative personality developed and with it family opposition:

"As a Yoruba person, the fact that I was an abiku does not stop my parents from encouraging me to go to school.

"First of all, I was supposed to go to Islamic school, to study Koran. But I hate anybody touching my head.

"The Islamic teacher, he used to use the worry beads, what you call the worry beads—you know, the thing that you count, like. He put them together in order to hit me on the head. So, I hate that. Because of that"—Prince claps his hands sharply—"I ran away from Islamic Koranic school.

"Thank God, my mother have a cousin who is now like an archdeacon, Reverend Martin Ogbonnewo. Then when my father died in nineteen fifty-two, he took me to a town called Iyamoye."

Though his father was a Muslim, his mother was a Christian, and the school where her cousin taught was a Christian school. Prince continues:

"From there I came back to Ogidi.

"It's a long story. All I remember is that during my youth age, I hear voices.

"When I arrived home from school, I would go to the mountains and make music, singing to whoever. I don't know who I'm singing to.

"But whenever I go to the class, when the exam time comes, I would pass, I would come first. And the teacher does not care for me. So, people believed that there were some spiritual other people from that place with me.

"Even this art work I started doing at a later stage, my prayers used to carry me, because when they give me Bibles in school—in those days there were Bibles with illustrations, of Jesus on the horse going to Galilee—I would cut it, and take scissors and I would cut Jesus's head, put it in another place, and I would make, like, a paper collage."

Prince laughs, saying, "And then my parents would beat me because they felt the Devil is giving me the idea to do what I am doing.

"They never look at the creative aspect of my life. The only person who noticed was this teacher that I was living with"—Ogbonnewo in Iyamoye—"who was able to see that I am going to be a great musician. Because I make music in the house with anything. From beating the chair, to the table, to the tree.

"He was very very helpful in my life.

"But then I never know I am going to be an artist. I never know I'm going to go to the point of doing what I am doing today.

"But I remember in my young age, I used to—like, I would make houses with sands. Houses I never see before that stack up, buildings like I got to see when I started traveling to oversea. I was doing that when I was very young without seeing anything like that, no pictures, nothing.

"I would take sand, move them off. I put windows. Sometimes I put matches box. You know, we have this tiny matches box. You have the big one and the smaller one. The smaller one I would put in between the sands, and when the sand would dry, I would remove them, and I would put castor fruit. You know, there is a tree we call castor. This castor thing, it has white seeds, and it is very oily. When you put three, four together, they bloom when you get light on it. The oil make it bloom. Shoots. But it is sort of like candlelight. And I put it in, in the evening.

"Then I make lamps from pawpaw tree, pawpaw fruit. I would cut it, remove the fruit inside, and put this castor thing inside, and put light. We used that, as kids, for an oil lamp in my mother's village, to make little lamps.

"So, a lot of things like that I started doing at that time. But my parents, particularly my mom, whom I grew up with, doesn't see anything creative in it. She thought something's wrong somewhere.

"At that time I was just following what my mind asked me to do. I happened to believe that somebody was telling me to do these things, and I was doing it.

"But my mom was another person entirely. Because she grew up to be a lady who go to school not a long time, maybe for a short time. She can read Bible, and she ended up being

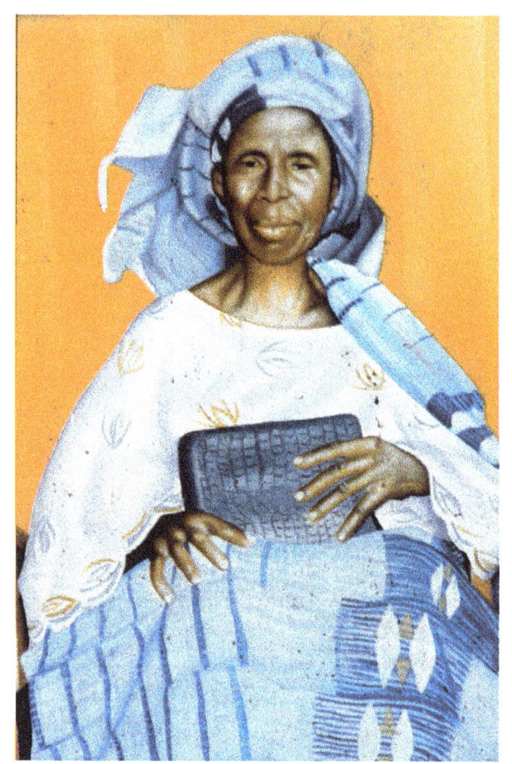

Madam Mary Aitoyeje. This is a detail from a painting of Prince's mother, made from a photograph by Fattai, an artist in Osogbo. It hangs in her tomb at Prince's house in Osogbo

married to my father. And she worked with her mother-in-law, who was a trader, to learn about business, trading.

"So, my mom would like to see me as a very successful businessman. Or a lawyer. Or a teacher. These are the kinds of careers my mother was looking to. She does not like to see me wasting my time carving or making music.

"Even when I started painting, she keeps telling me, All your colleagues are learning to be lawyers, teachers. Because that was the hope at that time: to be a teacher, lawyer, administrative officer, government worker working for the government, a civil servant.

"So, these are the areas that my mother was looking to—that I'm going to be one of these people. Because those are the paying job at that time. And when I started painting, she didn't like it—until nineteen sixty-seven when I was invited to London. Then she started rolling on the floor, singing, thanking God.

"Because at that time, anybody who travel out of Nigeria, returning to your own country, you are a hero."

For the second time in our first taped interview, Prince pauses and turns to me, smiling. When young men he does not know stop him in the streets of Nigeria, asking for a blessing, receiving a few naira, they hail him with stock phrases of praise. "Seven-Seven is the number," they say. "Twins Seven-Seven: from zero to hero." Zero to hero is the narrative now in motion. He began with his formal education, first in a Muslim school, then in a Christian school, only to stress its irrelevance, his creative preoccupation, and his mother's objection to the direction his head was carrying him.

Prince has quickly found the theme in which chronology dissolves: in his boyhood, his creative energy owed nothing to human authorities, neither parents nor teachers. His schooling was culturally irrelevant:

"In this system of our education, because we were brought up by the British, there's nothing like technical education, whereby, like today, you have people who became very successful in technology, or in scientific pursuits."

The British, he says, "only came to divide and rule." He faults them for fomenting contention among Nigeria's regional, ethnic, and religious groups, as they did in Ireland at one end of the empire and India at the other, dividing to rule. On our travels in Nigeria, I once made the mistake of admiring the architecture of a bridge, built in the British period and still carrying the traffic of modern times. Prince said, "The British came with book. They came with gun and sword, and destroyed our civilization." The education they provided did not prepare the people for the technological future, and it flooded their minds with foreign trivia. The irrelevance of his schooling bored him and inspired him to work for cultural revival:

"That's one of the things that pushed me into what I'm doing, this work. Because in those days, when you are taught about King George of England, I don't pay attention. I don't pay attention."

"British pressure," I say, "pushed you back into Yoruba culture." Never satisfied with a single cause, Prince responds:

"Not only their pressure. The pressure of my people too, embracing religions that they don't even understand.

"You see, my people are embracing Islamic religion. They are embracing Christianity religion.

"Like, I went to a Roman Catholic church. They were talking in Latin. The father was praising God and doing some prayers in Latin. And I don't understand what he said. So I asked the father, Speak what I can understand. Because I love to pray. I love to meditate. But how can I meditate with a language that I don't understand it?

"So, this is what pushed me again back to my background.

"And when I started making music, I based my music on the traditional aspects of what I know. In the beginning, before five years, I still have a lot of performers. I still have a lot of people pay attention to what I'm doing. I still have people, critics, writing good things about what I am doing.

"Because most of my words, most of my compositions, are based on the mythological thinking of the Yoruba people.

"What really pushed me more into music was because most Nigerians, the intellectuals, the well-to-do, they don't understand my painting. They would like to see me painting butterfly, like the things in the literature books: fish, tsetse fly, butterfly, the things they see in the literature books in school.

"So those kind of drawings is what they know. So, by the time I started doing what I am doing, and I put the face of a human being on animal, and I give a title to it, call it Devil's Dog, or this and that, today, they start writing against me.

"Then I started singing songs, talking about what I am trying to do. Talking about Sango. Singing about Osun. Singing, I tried to use some of our very valuable proverbs: Yoruba, typical Yoruba proverbs. I put these in my songs. Because at the time I started to play my music, we had highlife. The highlife music was influenced by music from Jamaica.

"So, I tried to do my kind of music with the background of my people."

In later days, songs in the dialect of his birthplace, songs filled with Yoruba references and rolling to Nigerian, not Jamaican, rhythms, became popular, played on the radio, favored by the students in the universities. In his earliest memories, Prince is singing, beating on tables and trees, cutting up Bibles, building castles of sand. His formal education was culturally irrelevant, and it was irrelevant to the construction of his creative personality. He did what his mind told him to do. He listened to voices from the spirit world. And he was born into the household of a craftsman. Prince introduced his father as a prince from a royal line, but he did not know that when he was a child. His father was a leatherworker. He tanned hides and decorated them with naturally dyed designs. Prince begins to tell about Aitoyeje by distinguishing among his fathers, the father of his reincarnation, the father of his mundane birth:

"My father was a warrior, but my own father-father-father, my real father, was a leather designer.

"My father was a leather designer.

"But I would not see his influence in my work. Because at that time I never thought I was going to do anything like that. I don't pay attention to him. But I remember he would buy a lot of skins, put them in special chemical vats to remove the hair. When they are dry,

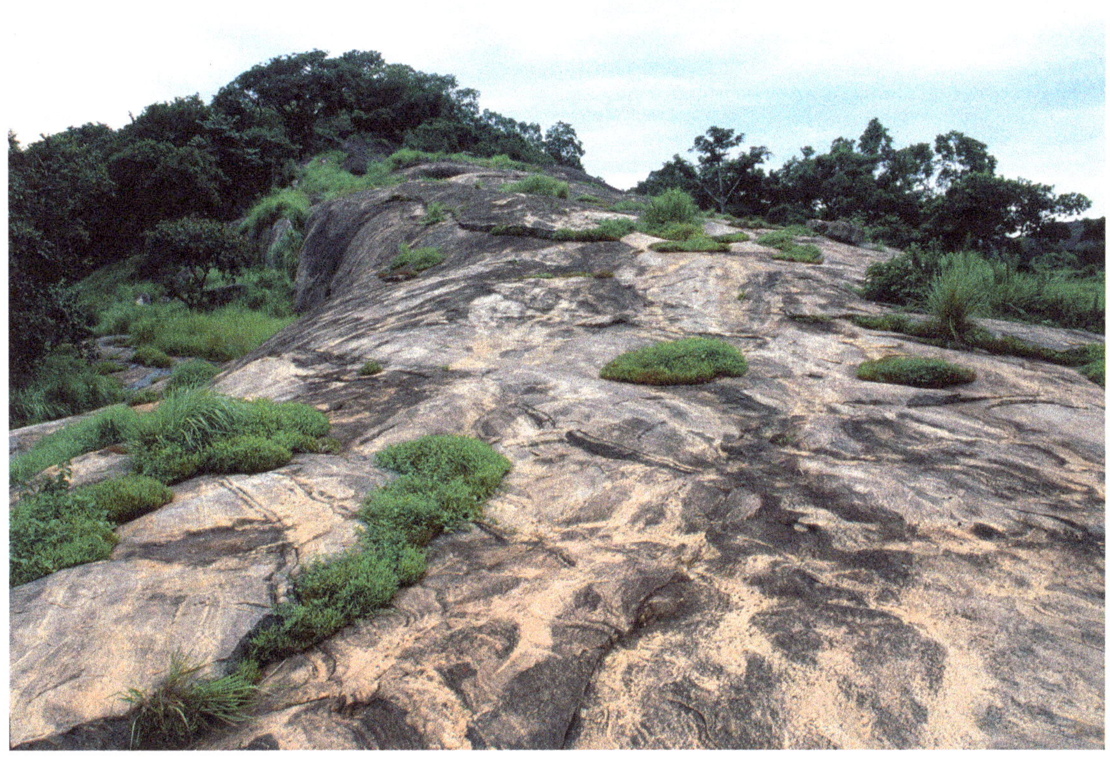

The rock, Ogidi, where Prince learned from the ants

he used the millet—you know the millet—he put millet, he soaked in the pot to give him different colors, like brown, red, and all that.

"Then he designed it. And he would sell it to the Northerners, and they would make bags out of it. You have seen the bags before. My father just used the skin, designed it, and sell it to the Northerners, the Muslims in the North. And at that time, a couple of years or a couple of months later, when they would come back, and you would see the bags they had made, with a kind of flap over, and the design on the leather. But I don't see them no more today."

Prince's uncle, his mother's brother, was also a craftsman. He embroidered caps and shoes, using fine thread wrapped with glittering metal, a skill that flourishes from Turkey to India. Though I see an artisan's care in his work, and though Prince accepts the possibility of a genetic predisposition to creative activity, inherited from both sides of his family, he feels no influence from the early experience in his father's shop, just as he feels no positive influence from his schooling. His art is his own. His education as an artist began in nature, on the rocks of Ogidi:

"I used to hide on the rock. When I ran away from school, I would go to the rock, and I watch all the animals on the mountain, the animals, the small-small animals.

"Sometimes I watch the ants. The ants, how they would build houses. The white ants and the black ones. Sometimes I follow ants and see them go to invade other ants.

"And then the termites, the termites, the ones that eat wood. You know, they have soldier ones that have big-big heads. Then you have soldier ants. They go in millions where they walk, black and very big. And they would go to attack the termites. They go there, and sometimes you see the black ants cut the termites in two.

"Things like that interested me.

"I used to watch the ants build houses, and I used that in building the houses I have in Nigeria. And I do it bit by bit, bit by bit.

"And I learned from them, too, as an artist. The way they carry leaves, big leaves, and take it to their house, and make nests. When I see them going, going, going, I take my cutlass, and if this is where they enter, I go and dig about one foot away, and come to the hall. They have sitting room, and, oh my God, they have their own sitting room; they have storage. They have new babies, new eggs. When they keep it there, no animal can touch it. They are so brilliant. Very intelligent.

"That's the way I work. Like the ants."

I have often been with Prince when, in galleries or the homes of collectors, he meets new people and introduces them to his art. He regularly plucks out for narration a few of the episodes he embedded in the flow of our interviews. This is one of them. He tells how he prepared his own food and went up to the mountain to watch the snakes, the bush beasts, the ants. He always tells of the ants at war with the termites, of the ants as builders of homes, amused that the creatures of nature are as violent and domestic as human beings. An architect in Philadelphia, standing before several of Prince's paintings, praised two things: the strength of his personal style (the variety in the pictures that patently came from the same hand), and the rich vocabulary of ornament in his repetitive patterns. Prince told him of his time on the rock, watching the ants, and he attributed his style to them, calling his process of creation "my ant work."

Ant work has three facets: persistence, finish, and a compositional dynamic. The ants keep at it, and so does he. Long practice has given him complete confidence. If he begins, he will, through perseverance, finish. Forty years ago he began building his house in Osogbo "bit by bit, bit by bit." It is not finished, but that does not worry him. Beginning is enough; it will be finished. I am used to students who are daunted by the size of the writing task before them, unable to figure out a way to begin. Prince begins effortlessly. Scale does not block

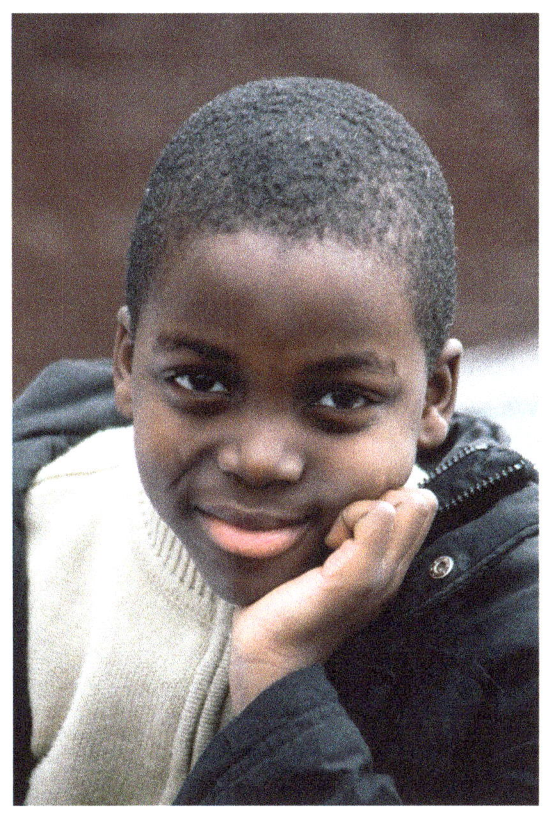

Timi.
Prince's youngest son

him; starting with a slim ballpoint pen on a vast sheet of plywood, he knows he will eventually finish. His work fills with pattern, and past the point at which it could be declared done, he keeps going like an ant, adding the finer and finer layers of decorative detail that the Philadelphia architect admired. He touches every spot, leaving no voids, and the works of his own that Prince considers most important are completely finished, filled, as a Muslim artisan's masterpieces are filled, with a webbing of geometric patterning. Without obscuring the overall order, his patterning increases in intricacy, receding, through the minuscule, toward infinity. Toward infinity, he marches like an ant, adding and adding and adding in the serial compositional dynamic that Robert Plant Armstrong and Henry Drewal consider a key to Yoruba aesthetics. Ant work is Prince's way to say syndesis.

The ants work in their millions. Prince works in solitude. He went alone to the mountain, observed alone, learned alone, and he stands before a painting, watching it happen, singing to himself, lost in his work, beyond time, engaged, content in solitude. He is like that now, was like that as a boy in the bush. I imagine him happy in oblivious concentration, delicately contriving a mansion of sand. At the same time, he is now, as he was then, excited by social exchange, a leader, a person on whom others depend. He had just received another of the innumerable phone calls from Nigeria: a man in distress, pleading for his assistance. Prince clicks the phone into silence and says:

"That's one thing I was talking to God about my life: is being like that from when I was very young. In fact, at the age of six, according to my mom, I used to have a lot of other children following me places. And then we'd make music with cigarette tin—you know, they call it Guinea Gold, Guinea Gold cigarette, and there's some cigarette called Bicycle in those days. So, they come in tins. So, I'd make music with that, and the children would follow me everywhere. That's how it has been my life, ever.

"That's how it has been, my life.

"Even with this age, I still have my age-group of those days still hanging around me. Friends or nonfriends—but I could not run away from it. I ran away from it; but they still keep coming. They run after me."

His life pulls him into himself and throws him out into the throng. After a wild party in Osogbo, Prince, weary, told me that when the loud crowd fills his house, dancing and drinking, he yearns to rest in his quiet country home outside of Ibadan. But, smiling, he said that when he is alone for a few days, he misses the crowd, the racket and action, the endless demands, the bracing adulation. When he paints, though, it is always good, he said. His mind is occupied, his hand in motion. He forgets, never worries.

Months later, at a low point in his life, he called me from Philadelphia, saying he felt dreadfully, miserably alone. Shola had gone to New York, taking the boys, and he was pained by the absence of the youngest one, Timi, "a wonderful spirit." He longs to be in Nigeria, where people know him, people need him, where he is energized by the turmoil, the wheeling and dealing, the quick give-and-take in the midst of the mob. "Thank God," he says, "I have my painting. It's the only thing that keeps me going."

This, the first segment of his story, is done. From the standpoint of personality, Prince is solitary and sociable, given to the patient craft of an artisan and the imaginative freedom of an artist. From the standpoint of culture, he is a Yoruba man, the reincarnation of a king, devoted to Osun, drawn to spiritual explanations, committed to the revitalization of the religion of his people. From any perspective, he is rare, gifted, unstoppably creative. As a little boy in an obscure, marginal place, on a rock, in the bush, he possessed the powers of the future. He was ready for the road.

· 7 ·

The Road to Osogbo

Prince's story began in Ijara, the place of his birth. When he started again, narrating the second segment of his autobiography in our second taped interview, he began again with Ijara, the place of his father's death. Aitoyeje died after a snake bite, and his death set his son in motion. Prince traveled for education, traveled as a trader, then, driven by the spirits, he abandoned schooling and commerce and took to the road as a fantastic dancer:

"After my father died in nineteen fifty-two, we moved from this town called Ijara, back to Ogidi.

"I have to put it summary by summary, and I will tell you everything.

"I lost my father in the year nineteen fifty-two. Then I have to go—I started living with this, my uncle, whom I told you was a teacher. His name is now Archdeacon M. O. Ogbonnewo. He wanted to become a bishop, but he was, like, one step before bishop when he retired. He now lives in Ilorin, the capital of Kwara State.

"So, by nineteen fifty-two, when my father died, I moved with him to a town called Iyamoye. I was attending a school called Saint Paul's School, African School, near Iyamoye, for one year. Then I moved back to Ogidi.

"My father's mother was a business woman, who imports clothes from the South to sell to all the people in that area; they were all farmers.

"So, in nineteen fifty-four, I was attending Saint George School in Ogidi, to nineteen fifty-six. I was living with a reverend father as a missionary boy, in the church.

"And the guy was not treating us well. I was one of those who protested, and he taught me it was too rude of me to be rude to the pastor of the church. So this gentleman sacked me, sent me out of school. Like: Go away and come back in two weeks' time.

"Instead of going back to that school, coincidentally, I went to take exam. And because of my tribal marks, I would not be admitted to most of the renowned institutions in the

North. Because at that time the Northern government promoted what you call Northern ideology—against the western, southern people.

"So, I went to a town called Epinmi. There I was enrolled in school for two years. Coincidentally, I don't know how I managed: I find myself in Teacher Training College, taking a course in history and geography. And I taught; after that I taught a while in a town called Ifira, Saint Andrew's School, Ifira. I taught there for a year. I teach English.

"During all this time, I was helping my mom. Because that time I used to help my mother to sell the wares—things like earrings, different items for women. My mother sell them. And she bought me a bicycle. And I would put a big box like this"—Prince gestures a wide headload—"full of items to sell and travel village to village, every market day.

"And one day I heard this music.

"The guy was I. K. Dairo. He was the first to make music with accordion. He was the first to introduce accordion to juju music in Nigeria. And this music came out, and it became a *big hit*. And they played, like, two thousand times on the radio.

"And I hear this music; I don't problem what other wares I am selling. And I have a gramophone; you know, this thing you wind. I brought this music; from then, I started traveling from village to village.

"That's what I am talking about: spiritual pushing. The spirits pushed me now to start doing this, forgetting the things I am selling for my mother. My bicycle was very expensive; not everybody had that kind of bicycle in that area at that time. I dropped the bicycle. I dropped the wares. I picked my gramophone.

"And I picked boards, and I wrote, Come watch Seven-Seven's way of dancing.

"And I placed that on the trees in the village.

"And, believe you me, everywhere I performed—full house."

Prince claps his hands for his first public triumph. Dancing, the boy from the bush was on the road to success. I ask him to put his dancing into words and he makes a game effort:

"I am a dancer from youth. You see, as a creative person, as an abiku child, I danced—even the breakdancing; it has become big here, but I have been doing it before they paid attention to it.

"So, the breakdancing has become big here in sixty, seventy; that's what I was doing.

"Somersaults. And put my head down on the road; remove the stones from my skin. I would dance on broken bottles. Or the cement. Or, like, I would sit down, lie down, and they would put pounding box—it is a big wood, and they hollow it, and they put yams in it to pound—they put it over my chest to pound.

"I was just doing it. Sometimes I come and sit on top of a tree. Or dance on a moving vehicle. Oh, my God.

"At the time, some forces are trying to direct my attention away from going to school, from giving importance to education.

"Because the way I was going at that time, so many people think I am crazy. They think something is wrong with me, because even when there is no music, I would be hearing the music; I would be dancing.

"But at that time I do not know anything about control. Because I felt I'm happy. And I do what I am doing. And I don't know what I will do. It might be that sometimes I put powder here"—he touches his face—"like when you watch people now watching the sports.

"I put red here, blue here, green here, and I walk in the streets, and dance. And people give me money. And then I went and give the money to people who doesn't have.

"And I had a gramophone. It has a black box, and you wound it. After you wind it, you put the record, and this thing that turns its head like a snake, and it had a little needle, and you put the needle on it, and it played the music.

"Sometimes I would have young guys who would carry it on their head, in the streets. They would play it, and I'm dancing.

"But whenever I would come to my family home, I would not dance."

Compelled to dance, to let music propel his body, Prince forgot about schooling and trade, he paid off his mother's debt to the spirits, and he learned. Happily out of control, he learned to release his talent, letting it fly to the edge and beyond. He learned that flamboyant acts—flamboyant is his word for himself—bring him attention. Some thought him daft, but the crowd gathered, the young men began to follow him. He learned to love the limelight, to feed upon the reactions of others. Dancing gained him recognition and cash, but when he says he gave the money to people in need, a merry outlaw, I believe him, for I have, too often, watched him work hard to accumulate money, money he needed, only to give it away, winning with his generosity, his sacrifice, what he wins with his art: the attention and admiration of others. As a dancer, it seems, he would do anything to please the crowd—climbing trees, painting his face, letting them pound yams in a mortar on his chest. Amid all this extravagance, there was, even in the early days of his dancing, a craving for response, a giddy will to the risky, an undeniable talent.

Prince said
of this painting:
"Somebody is lying down
backward, and they put
pounding box on his chest.
I do that before, when I
was very young. I do a lot
of that to attract crowds."

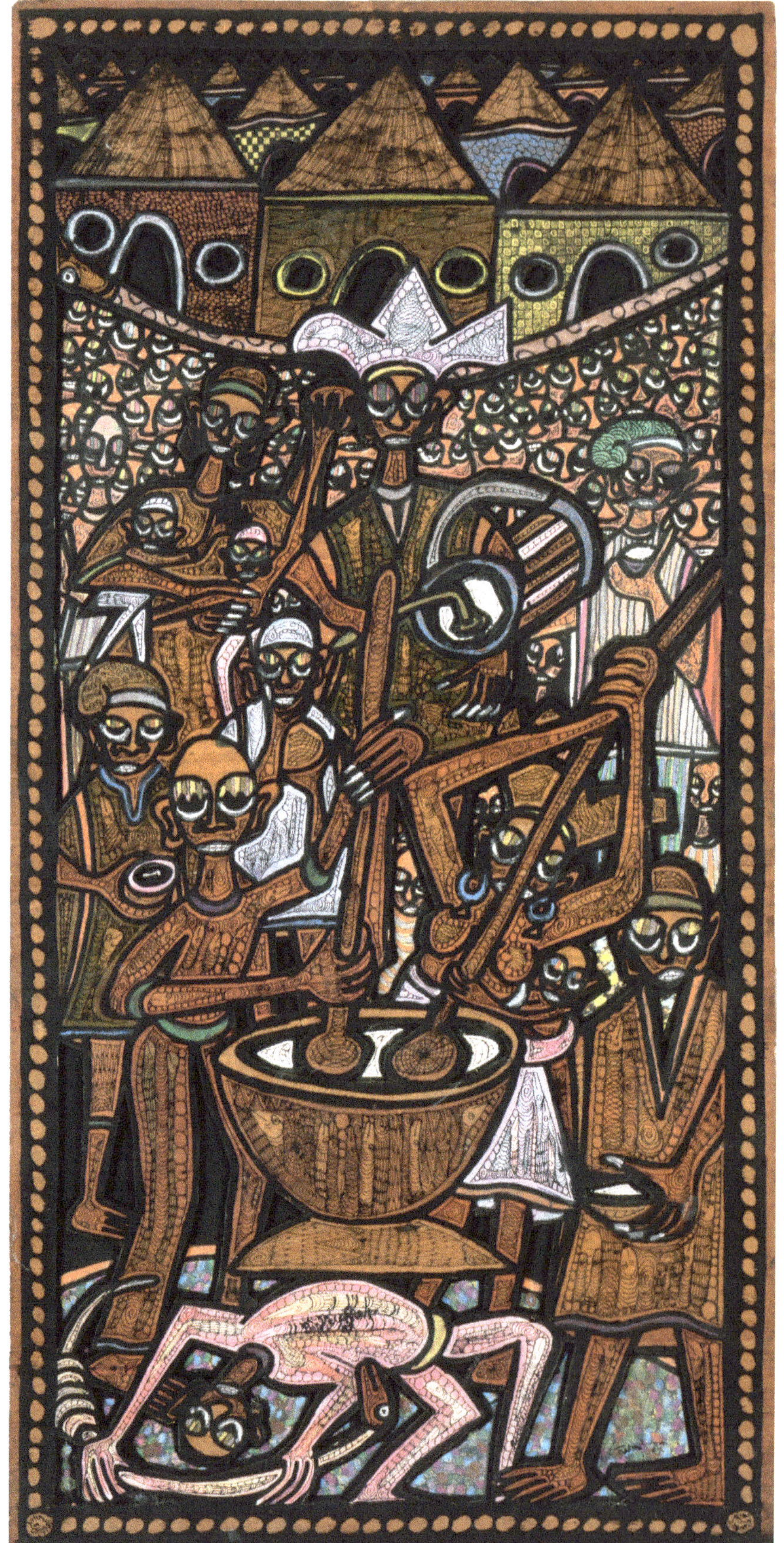

Villagers in Festivity Mood with Dancers.
Ink, acrylic, and oil on wood; 2 layers. 24"x48". Osogbo, 1969

Prince has a follower in one of his sons, Busoye, who has gained fame as a dancer. The son of Prince's first wife, Bintu, he is, he says, number seventeen among the children. Prince showed me the slight cleft behind his right ear that proves Busoye to be an abiku who came first to the world as a girl. He is spiritually gifted. When he was two in 1982, Prince wanted to take him for a trip in the car, but he ran away and hid, so he was not in the car when it hit another, almost killing his father. The spirits who caused the wreck had warned him to flee.

One of his father's problems, Busoye told me in Osogbo, is that when he gets money, he distributes it among people he does not know, leaving the household short of funds. Another problem is that, having so many children, he can give none of them the attention they want and need, but Busoye is not resentful. His father is a great man, he says, his model for life. Busoye, a handsome young man, has grown a beard like his father's, and he has taken his artistic name for his own: Olaniyi Busoye Seven-Seven. A dancer himself, he told me that he had always heard that his father was a great dancer before the wreck that Busoye hid to avoid. He thought it was an exaggeration until he saw an old film of his father dancing. "He was really really great," Busoye said. "He lives in the wrong time; he is like somebody from the past world in the modern world. But he was futuristic. He was doing everything dancers today think they invent."

As scouts can watch a boy play one sport and gauge his general athletic ability, his speed, dexterity, and strength, a series of observant men saw in Prince's dancing a deep and general creative capacity. Ultimately it would be Ulli Beier in Osogbo, but the first was a man who arranged Prince's first "solo concert" as a dancer, an entire success. Then in the town of Mopa, "an educationalist guy, who was writing a play on the life and death of Jesus Christ" as part of a missionary effort, hired Prince as the manager of his theatrical troupe, tasking him to teach the other actors about music and dance:

"I became very successful, but in the end, this guy turned us into farmers. He went to buy a *large* land. Weeks when we don't perform, he made us go to his farm and work. Turning us into a kind of slavery. I just revolt and get angry.

"Then one day I saw these people, selling medicine in the streets. They have a van. There were no elements, like you have elements here. These are people who made their medicine themselves. Maybe they are lying. Because later I got to know they are lying. You see, they had sugar boiled; you know, melted. And they put some sweet in it. And they put iodine or whatever, some pepper or peppermint, and they ground it and mixed it. It smell good, spicy. And they would tell you that this medicine would cure stomach problem. It can cure woman's menstruation problem. It can make you potent. And people are buying it.

"Because they believed it.

"So anyway, I walked up to these guys, and I said, If you find a dancer, will you take him?

"They say, Yes.

"I started dancing for them. When I'm dancing, I would dance in the streets. Children would run after me. Everybody would run after me. I would bring them to these guys. And I would demonstrate how you use the medicine: three times by spoon. And they would be buying this medicine.

"And that is how I got to Osogbo."

They called it Superman Tonic. The medicine men would stop their van before a town, fill two or three dozen bottles with river water, add the ingredients, largely caramelized sugar, and glue on the labels. In town, Prince would dance to attract the crowd and sell packets of detergent and bottles of tonic, claiming it would calm backaches, stomachaches, and menstrual cramps. It made men potent and women fertile. The road winding from town to town led to Osogbo, where the medicine men built fine houses for themselves and Twins Seven-Seven shared a room with their driver, Sunday Makanju, who, the charismatic dancer's follower, named himself Nine-Nine.

Osogbo is the end point of this segment, a bridge from Ijara to Osogbo, from 1952 to 1964, from boyhood to the beginning of Prince's career as a painter. In narrating this phase of his life, he began with a sequence of dates. They vanished with his schooling, but he maintained temporal order, leaning forward. The story is paced, its destination is clear:

"When I came to Osogbo, I was dancing with the people who were selling medicine, who were going everywhere with a van, with a jeep. It is a kind of a military jeep, British jeep, imported British jeep, that was sold at auction.

"So, these people, I was dancing, and I would go places with them.

"Until one day I happened to drive one of the cars, and I collided with an electric pole. And the electric pole broke. Because, naturally, I wanted to be a driver; one of the greatest things I wanted to do in my life is to be a driver.

"Apart from my dancing, the only thing I wanted to be, I wanted to be a driver. Then I went to a reader who told me that I never drive no car for nobody in life. I never know what it means.

"He told me, If you want to be a driver, you will drive, but never under nobody.

"I don't know then that I'm going to have miles of cars.

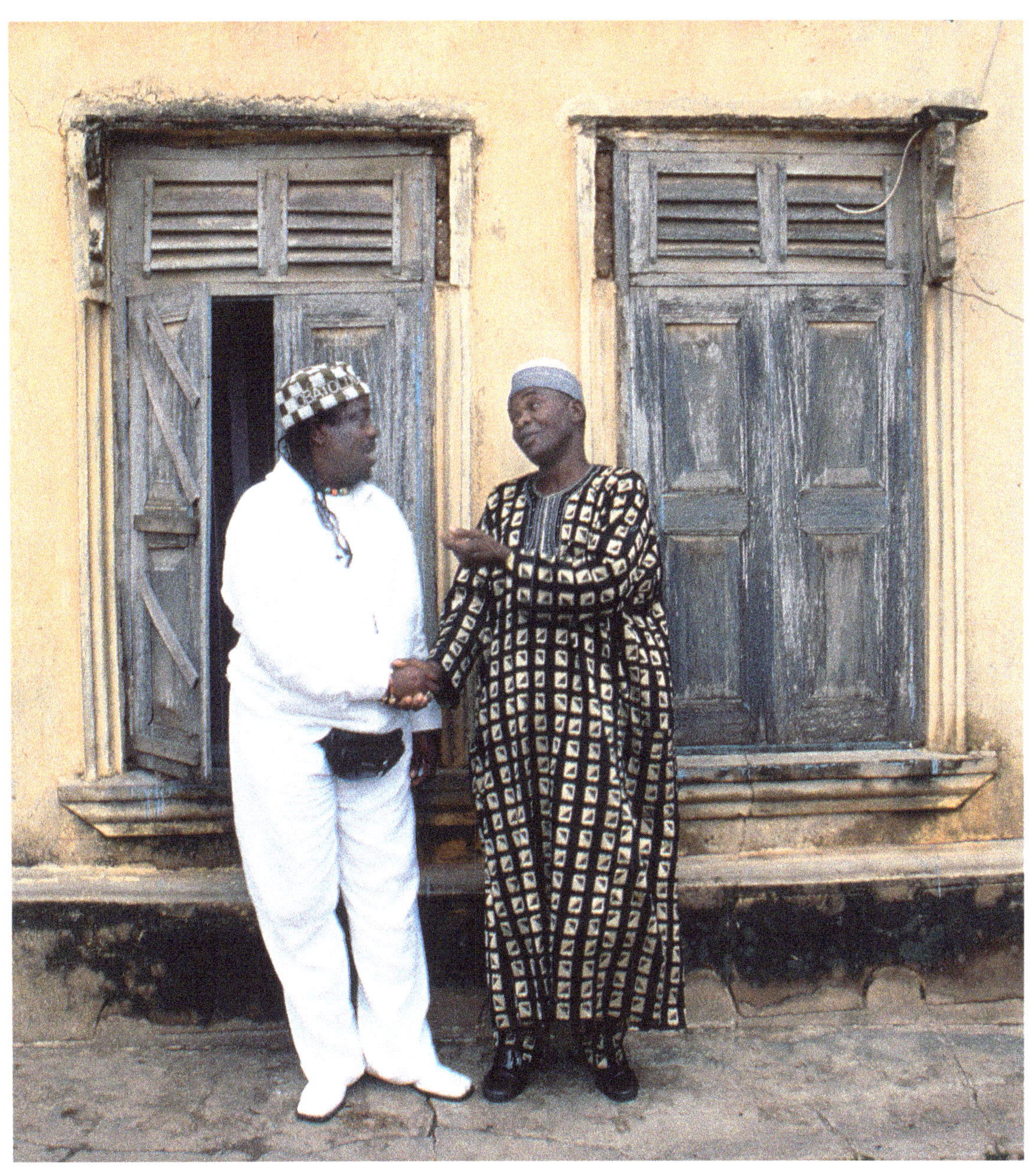

Seven-Seven and Nine-Nine,
reunited in front of the room they shared
in the early nineteen-sixties in Osogbo

"So now, when I got to Osogbo, and I was dancing, and I collided with the electric pole, public electric pole, and the police say I am liable for the cost. When the jeep meet it, it broke into two, but the wire doesn't let the pole fall down."

The medicine man, Prince's employer, was, he said, rich. He eliminated his wild driver's liability by getting the proper amount into the proper hands of the officials who valued the utility pole at ten thousand pounds:

"So, this guy now wanted me to work, so I started dancing without them paying me, for the cost of this electric pole.

"And one day I was crying. As I was walking away from the compound of these people I was dancing for, I saw this white guy in a Citroen—you know, it is a French car; we call it Chicken Cage. The car broke down, and I had went there to help, to push.

"That was Ulli Beier.

"I don't want anything; I just help him.

"We didn't talk. And then he left.

"Then two weeks later, I was walking by the ministry. I heard music in the hall. And I gatecrash.

"It was a party, an entertainment, a sendoff party for one Mister J. P. Clark and Peggy Harper, a South African teacher-dancer at the University of Ibadan. They were invited for our Independence, and they were leaving now to go away from Nigeria.

"And Mbari Mbayo was a writer-artist's club that Ulli Beier founded. That's where the party was taking place.

"And I walked in there to start dancing, and everybody was surprised. What kind of dancing is this?"

We have independent corroboration of their surprise in Ulli Beier's account, which I quote, with his permission, from his book of 1968, *Contemporary Art in Africa*:

"Seven-Seven appeared one night at a dance held at the Mbari Mbayo Club. His appearance fascinated us at once: a blouse of rather bright Nigerian cloth which had 'Seven-Seven' embroidered across the back, narrow trousers with pink buttons sewn along the seams, zigzag edges cut into sleeves and trousers, pointed Cuban-heel shoes and an embroidered, tasseled cap. Even in a colourful town like Oshogbo he caused a minor sensation. But his dancing was even more exciting than his appearance: his imaginative variations on accepted highlife dancing proved so spectacular that the large crowd cleared the floor for him—a rare happening in a community where nearly everyone is a born dancer. I felt attracted by the young man's personality and was somehow reluctant to let him drift away again. I called him over and asked him what had brought him to Oshogbo. He told me that he had been hired at £3 a month as a dancer to advertise the medicines of a travelling quack doctor. Without having any plan in mind I offered him a higher salary if he would agree to stay. He asked for a day to think it over and then sent a letter the next day announcing that he would be happy to become my 'backroom boy.'"

We return to Prince's voice and version. He continues:

"So, after the party, Ulli invited me over and he said would I like to join Duro Ladipo's theater as an artist in residence at that place.

"And I said, okay, he should give me three days to think about it. When I came back, I was hired.

"But I used to have a follower, and that guy called himself Nine-Nine, because I put Seven-Seven, because of my story of being born seven times before I survived. I put Seven-Seven on my pants. On every dress I wear, I put Seven-Seven on it, and I have buttons sewn to my dresses. I have flamboyant kind of dresses, like a politician.

"Anyway, so when Ulli Beier invited me over, this guy was not employed. And I said to Ulli, if he is not employed, I will not work for them.

"After some persuasion, I decided to work for them."

The year is 1964. Prince has just turned twenty. He has landed in Osogbo, found a paying job. In a few weeks his career as a painter will begin, bringing him international renown and a train of personal problems.

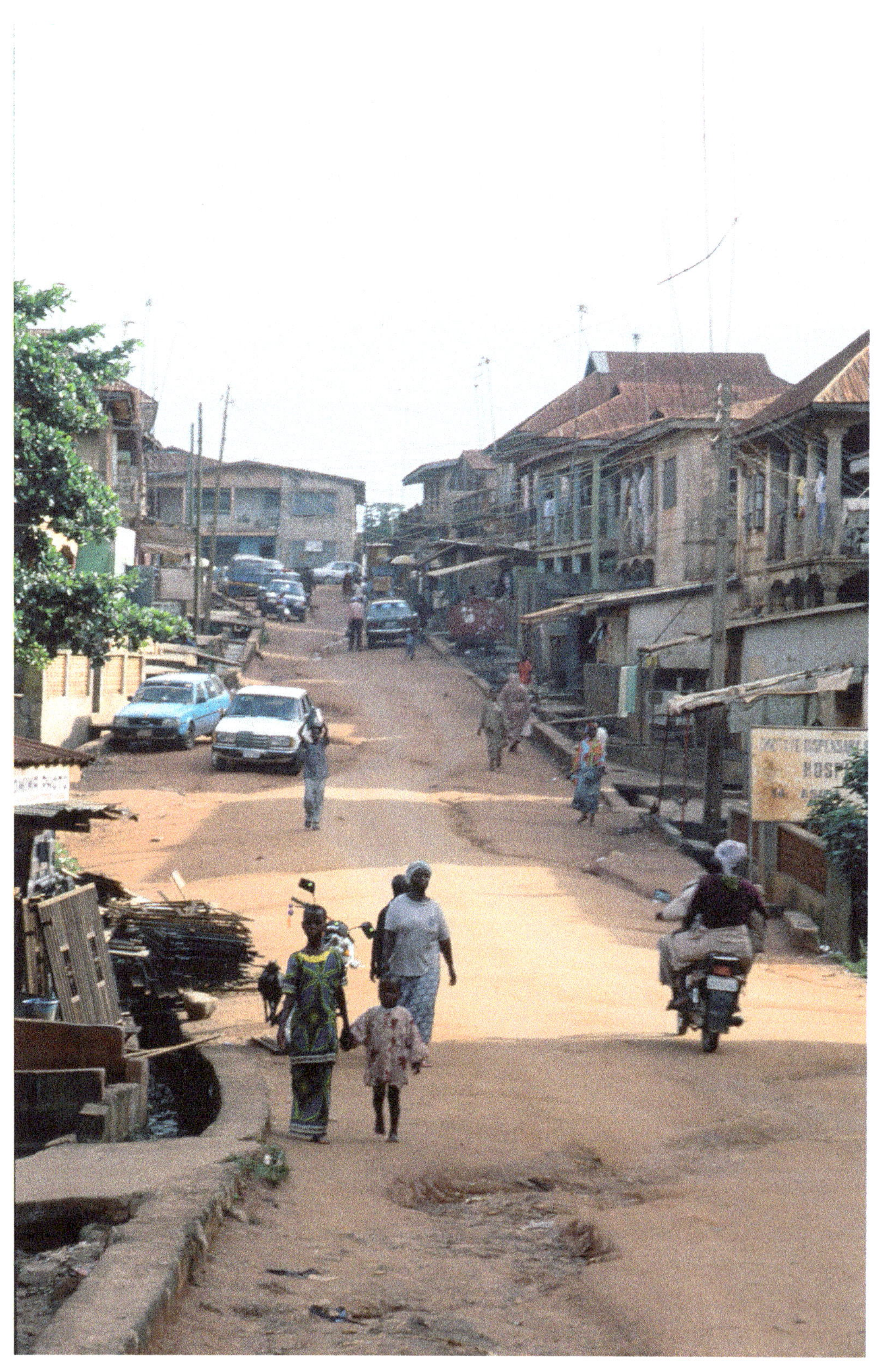

Osogbo

· 8 ·

Prince's First Picture

Osogbo was the place, the nurturing ground of Prince's success. He describes it, a city of unsettled diversity and commercial activity:

"When I came to Osogbo, it is like a city where there is war, and all the people run away from the warfront, or when there is no more war, people settle. They become encamped. So, Osogbo was not like Ibadan; Osogbo was like a war camp. After the war finishes, everybody settles there. It became a big commercial city because of the railway, because the railway pass through there to the North. Osogbo became very popular. And then the adire, the tie-and-dye cloth; it is a town where the women there were dyeing the clothes in those days. And then people come then to buy and take them to the North, to sell them to the Northerners. That what makes Osogbo become famous.

"Okay, let me put it this way. There is a war going on in Iraq. Okay. There may be a town where some people run, like refugee, and they ran any way from the war-torn area, and they settle, and it become like a peaceable little city. That's how Osogbo is.

"So, fifty percent of the people from Osogbo are from my tribe. They are Yoruba people. Today now we have Igbo, we have Hausa, we have all kinds, because it is a capital, the capital of Osun State."

Central to the intellectual life of this city in flux—and to Prince's creative development—was the Mbari Mbayo Club, where Prince crashed the gate and astonished them with his dancing. Prince said the club was founded by Ulli Beier. A German by birth, but a citizen of the wide world, Ulli Beier came to Nigeria in 1950 when he was twenty-eight, and he stayed for sixteen years. He taught at University College Ibadan, then in 1957 he founded the journal *Black Orpheus*, which under his editorship became a critical force in Nigerian literature. The next year he settled in Osogbo, continuing to deepen his knowledge of Yoruba culture while applying his organizational skills to the advancement of African art. Modestly (for he was instrumental in the effort), Ulli Beier credits Duro Ladipo and says that their club

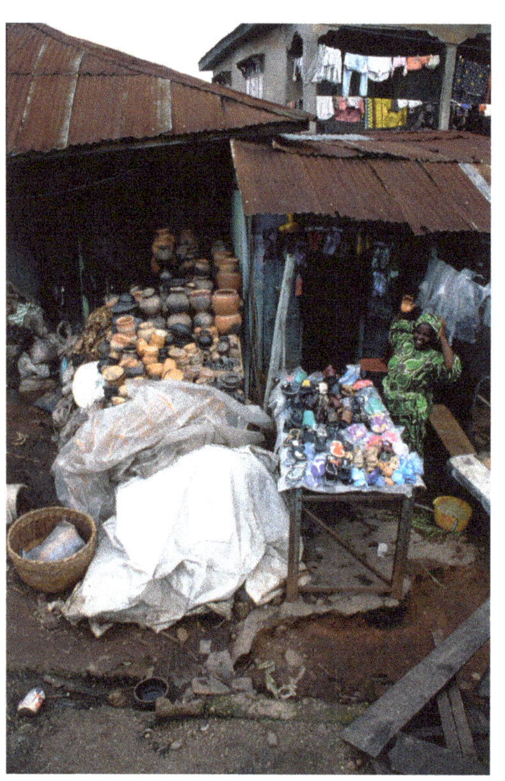

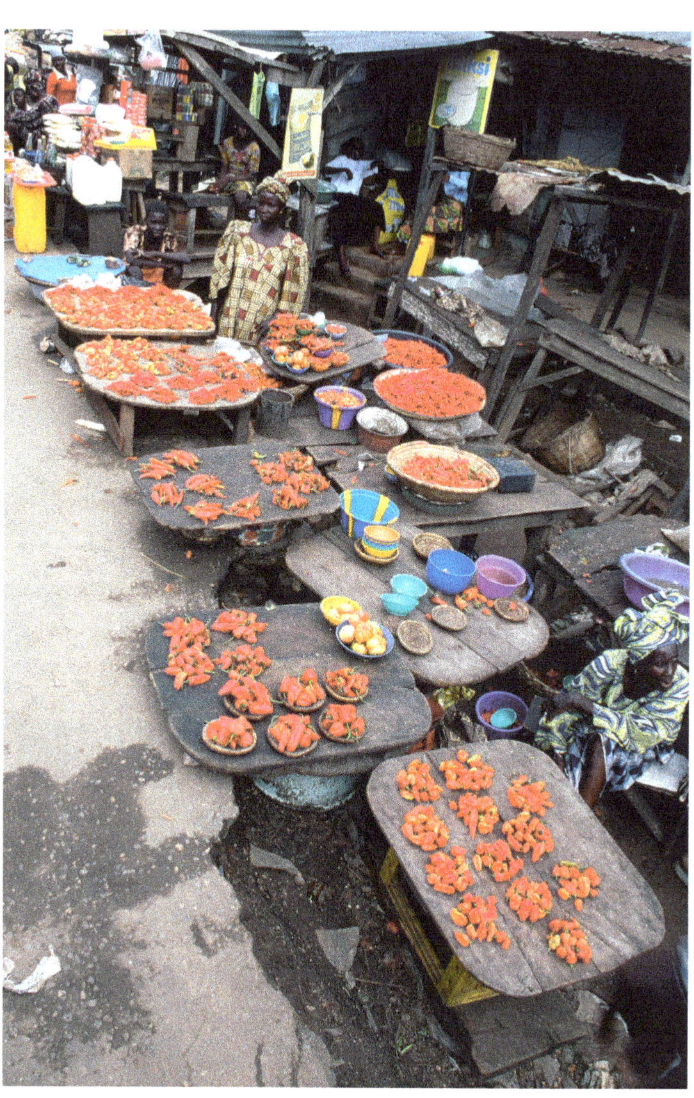

The market, Osogbo

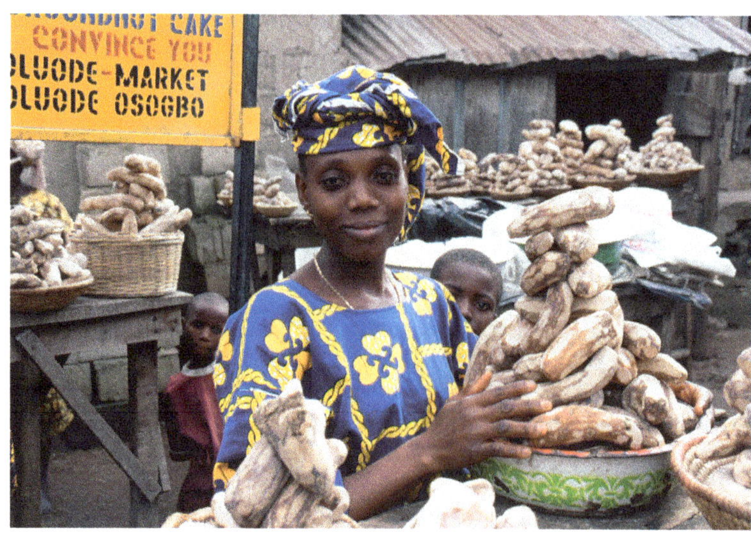

Adijaz at the yam mill

in Osogbo was inspired by the Mbari Club, founded in 1961 by the dramatist Wole Soyinka, the poet J. P. Clark, the novelist Chinua Achebe, and other young writers in Ibadan. In his memoir *Ibadan*, Wole Soyinka calls the Mbari Mbayo Club an "offshoot," the "hinterland outpost" of Ibadan's Mbari creative arts movement. Soyinka associates Osogbo's club with his fellow playwright Duro Ladipo, and recalls his unease when heading to Osogbo to see a new play, to drink palm wine, to eat pounded yam and bush meat, to hear "Twins Seven-Seven and company, playing till the late hours."

As he tells it in another memoir, Wole Soyinka returned from England in 1960 to conduct field research on traditional drama. He knew the plays of Greece and Ireland, of Sophocles and Synge; his intention was to learn from West African tradition and create a modern drama fit to its place and time. To say he succeeded would be a grotesque understatement. Soyinka is one of the great writers of our time, the first African to receive the Nobel Prize for Literature.

While Wole Soyinka was working toward mastery, Duro Ladipo, a composer of original musical works, turned to the writing of plays that explored and exposed his heritage. Both of them would construct dramas out of an event that took place in Oyo in 1946. Ladipo's *Oba Waja* is stark and abrupt. Soyinka's *Death and the King's Horseman* is expansive, tense with foreboding and psychological nuance. Both are modern, musical, beautiful in their language. Both are revelations of Yoruba cosmology, mythic in power.

Thc king of Oyo is dead. His horseman is obliged to end his life and serve his king in the other world. The British district officer intervenes, preventing the suicide. The horseman is disgraced, vilified, relieved. His son, a modern man—in Soyinka's version, he is a man like the author, educated in England—appears and, horrified by his father's failure, kills himself. His father is beyond redemption; the son acts to effect continuity, to maintain the cosmic order. Then, too late, the old horseman kills himself. Meaning well, ignorantly meddling in the lives of others, the district officer recognizes the evil he has done.

The play incarnates principles that Wole Soyinka outlines in his critical essays. It brings the elder tradition into modern form, symbolically exemplifying Soyinka's proposition that cultural survival, which shapes the basis of political resistance, often requires a shift in medium. It is not the old man following an ancient custom, but the worldly young man who becomes the vehicle of cultural continuity, just as it is not the old tale told at a fire in the bush, but the modern play, open to international influence, that bears today the power of myth. It would be like that, too, with Prince Twins Seven-Seven. Recasting the Yoruba tradition he shared with Soyinka and Ladipo, he put old ideas into new forms, using—"unfortunately," he told me—the alien medium of painting to express the "mythological thinking" of the Yoruba people.

My point is not narrow influence, but broad context. Nigeria won its independence in 1960. According to Wole Soyinka, the exuberant celebrations of the period, featuring traditional arts, "forgave anthropologists their obsession and challenged a new generation with an embarrassment of riches." The new generation quickly formed the Mbari and Mbari Mbayo clubs and took up the errand of creating a new art for a new nation. Their work, Soyinka wrote, involved selective revival, "artistic retrieval," and it was grounded on knowledge of the traditional religion that preceded Islam and Christianity. Soyinka would do that on the stage. Prince would do it in his paintings.

Wole Soyinka's feisty, elegant writings permit us to return in time and shape a context around Prince's beginning. Soyinka was born in 1934, raised in a prosperous Christian home, and educated in the best schools in Nigeria, then England, graduating from the University of Leeds in 1957. He performed as a singer of folksongs in Paris, met Pete Seeger, and admired the "blues saint," Mr. Huddie Ledbetter of Louisiana. Back home in Nigeria, he studied the tradition and collected old works of African art; he became a leader in a wide artistic movement, a professor in the university. Prince, in comparison, was younger, far less privileged, a lone actor. But both were Yoruba men, men of a time and a place.

Soyinka called his colleagues bohemians. His novel of 1965, *The Interpreters*, allows me to imagine them. They are, like Stephen's companions in *Ulysses*, young and educated, witty in repartee. They drink all night; they discuss the old religion. One is a journalist, another a teacher, and one is a painter who chooses the Yoruba deities for his subjects. Young men like them founded the Mbari Club, where writers met, art was exhibited, and plays were performed. Osogbo's Mbari Mbayo was comparably broad in its reach. There, Ulli Beier organized a series of workshops for artists. The third of them, conducted by the artist Georgina Beier, opened in August 1964, a few weeks after Prince danced himself into employment.

Now the story is his again. Prince remembers:

"They had an art workshop at Mbari. Everybody was painting. They give us brushes, colors, all kind of things to work with. But I—for whatever I am, from what I told you, like, from listening to myself—I requested for pen and ink.

"You know, during my school days, in our desk there was a hole made in the desk, and there was a small plastic cup you put there for ink, and you had this kind of pen. So I requested that. And it was given to me.

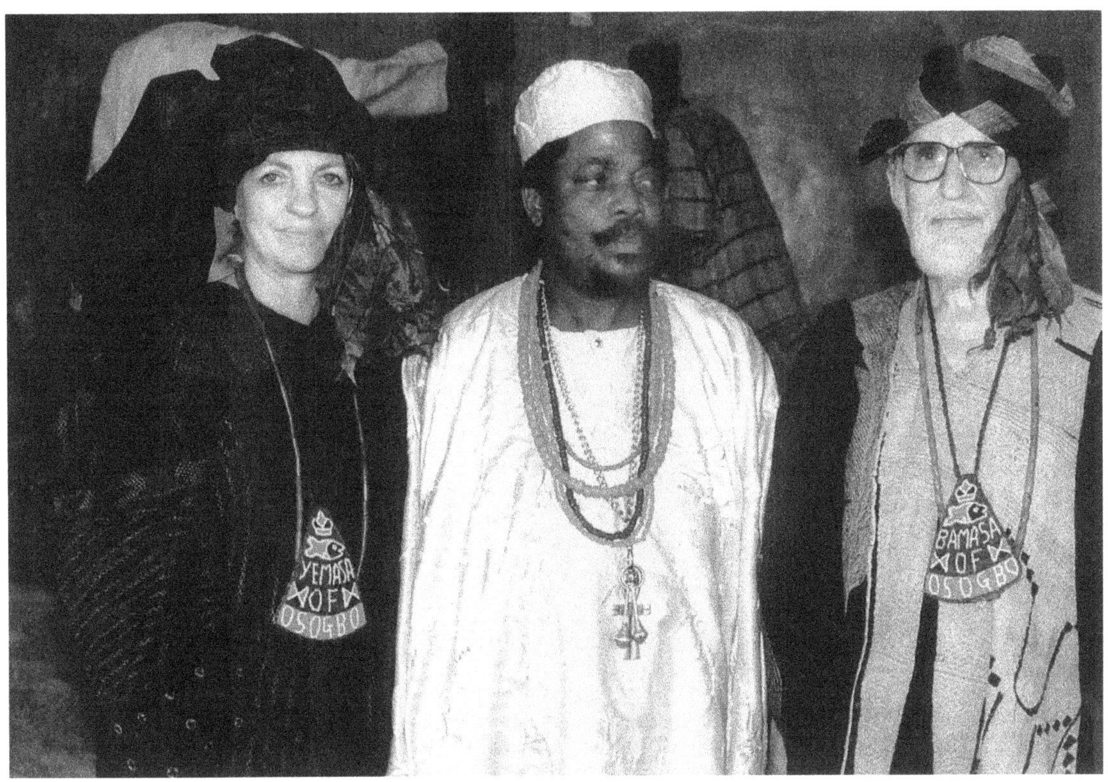

Georgina Beier, Prince, and Ulli Beier, about 1994.
Prince's photograph collection

"And I swear to Almighty God, what I am doing today started like playing. I was doodling, and I have a *large* brown paper. Like, you know, today I do the sketch. Then I don't do no sketch.

"There is no sketch. I just started from one corner, keep working, working, listening to myself, and continue, continue, and by the time I finish I have this *big* brown paper filled.

"And Ulli Beier asked me, What is that?

"I said, Devil's Dog.

"You know why I used the word Devil's Dog? Because I felt it might be the Devil that is making me do what I do, without doing what everybody was doing. Because I have been lazy. I thought I was lazy.

"Ulli cannot believe his eyes."

In Ulli Beier's account, Prince, having nothing else to do, joined the workshop. The others were painting, but Prince began to draw black lines with a twig. A twig is the primitive tool of a boy from the bush. A pen befits the schoolboy in Prince's mind whose parents thought the Devil was guiding him—that he was the Devil's pet—when he broke from the educational routine to follow his creative instinct, as he did on the first day of the workshop in Osogbo. Supplied with pen and ink, he worked like an ant, gradually filling a large sheet of paper. The result, *The Devil's Dog*, a symbolic self-portrait, his very first picture, already bore, in Ulli Beier's words, "the typical Seven-Seven stamp." Prince continues:

"So, from there Ulli went to bring me books in Yoruba literature. Books like My Life in the Bush of Ghosts, Palm-Wine Drinker, books like what we read in school. And I found very interesting stories, mythological stories about ghosts, about things like that. Then, the things I have known from my childhood, the stories I heard from my mom, I put these together."

The books Ulli Beier gave Prince were novels by the Yoruba writer Amos Tutuola, a member, along with Soyinka, Achebe, and Clark, of the Mbari Club in Ibadan. In *The Palm-Wine Drinkard*, published in 1952, the drinkard goes in search of his dead tapster. The book slides from episode to episode, accumulating—in the order he came to them, Tutuola said—traditional tales, tales of marvels and frustrating tasks, tales familiar to folklorists, familiar to Prince. It is a wonderful, funny book. Tutuola's first, it marked the beginning of modern West African literature, Chinua Achebe said, and the end of the dominance of derogatory stories about Africa told by European writers. Tutuola's second novel, *My Life in the Bush of Ghosts*, published in 1954, fumes with fear and disgust, unreeling in masochistic horror—surpassing Beckett at his most grim—as the narrator escapes enslavement during a war, only to be put in a bag by a ghost, transformed by juju into a horse, baptized in hot water, covered with flies, with spit, trapped in a pitcher, coated with rotten blood, caught in a spider's web, put in a coffin, buried, beheaded, captured by slave traders, sold, flogged, and then, after a lapse of twenty-four years, saved by his brother, returned to his mother. Both novels describe travel between the worlds, interactions between the living and dead. Both, like Prince's paintings from the beginning, exhibit the dynamic of serial composition, of syndesis, of ant work.

Ulli Beier gave Prince those books and asked him to illustrate them. Many of his early paintings respond to Tutuola, and Tutuola's words have continued to inspire the occasional painting right to the present. That connection has prompted some critics to reduce Prince to an illustrator, as though Tutuola were his prime influence. But Ulli Beier briefly, and Robert Plant Armstrong at length, have argued cogently that their similarities are owed to independent expressions of a shared Yoruba heritage.

The nature of illustration is at issue. In his comprehensive study of Albrecht Dürer's life and work, Erwin Panofsky describes pictures in which the great artist illustrated specific, usually sacred texts, then he argues that in many instances Dürer did not work like an illustrator. Rather, he "proceeded like a musician extemporizing on a given theme," extending from a fragment of text—a sentence or lone word—and sometimes slipping beyond any textual referent, guided not by lines of found words but by the inward drift of imagination. Like Dürer in his middle passage, Prince is concerned with technique and ornament as well as content, and his relation to his literary sources is even freer. A word of Tutuola's might ignite his imagination, but usually what he takes from the page is a mood, a feeling that he shapes into images of his own, generally less fearful than Tutuola's. *My Life in the Bush of Ghosts* is Prince's favorite of Tutuola's writings, and when I asked about illustration a year later, he used it as his example and said:

"I'm not doing an illustration, but I use that book to give me guideline toward my feeling of my own thinking.

"If I'm to do an illustration, then I'm adding more to what Tutuola says. Because there are so many things he writes, but he doesn't say it. But my picture is saying it.

"I'm getting a feeling of what he is saying to direct me what I see in my mind.

"His work, his writing is like a torch light. Like, I'm in a *big* black cave, and there's a light to enable me to see what is inside. And I'm saying what I see in what he has wrote.

"The picture is my *own* making—from *his* own writing. It is like somebody has a vision: it is going to rain. And another person says, Yeah, when it rains, *big* thunderbolts or stones are dropping."

They stand together in one place. Tutuola scans the sky and says it will rain. Prince looks too and sees that it will rain thunderbolts and stones, signs of the god Sango. Then he puts what his mind's eye saw into a picture. He does not illustrate Tutuola. His work, he says, "is not a copy of anything. It's an inspiration that come from thinking about that book." He renders an inspired thought of his own, as though he and Tutuola shared one memory, one vision. Tutuola refers to that vision in prose. Prince realizes it in a detailed depiction. They share a Yoruba tradition, which Tutuola stretches into stories, which Prince, a musician, extemporizes into visibility.

Prince surely learned from Tutuola's novels that others might be interested in the mysterious matters that interested him, but few of the works in his long career refer to Tutuola. Their closest, most lasting convergence lies in the titles Prince gives his pictures, which sound—as he acknowledges—like the titles Tutuola used to break up his narratives. Here are a few titles from early works, mostly from the nineteen-sixties—some inspired by Tutuola—that were exhibited at the Smithsonian in Washington in 2000: *The Anti-Bird Ghost in War with the Red Crews*; *The Baptist Church of Bush of Ghosts*; *The Lively Ghost in Spider's Bush*; *The Long Eared Ghost*; *Procession to the Shrine of Oshun*. And here are a few titles of recent works, painted in 2005 and exhibited that year at Material Culture in Philadelphia: *The Anti-Bird Beast of No Planet*; *The Spiritual Bird of Wealth and the Golden Eggs*; *Leafless Herb Roots on the Red Planet*; *The Tree of Life in Obatala's Garden*; *Ogun, God of Iron, and His Bird of Wisdom*. But, as Prince said, Tutuola's tales blended with those of his mother, becoming tales of his own—a matrix of narrative for the play of the visual imagination.

The creative acts of Amos Tutuola and Twins Seven-Seven unfolded along parallel tracks. Both took up European media—Tutuola the novel, Prince the painting—without deep knowledge of European practice and precedents. Wole Soyinka, by contrast, knew the Greek dramatists of antiquity and studied with a Shakespearean scholar in England. His plays incorporate the music and dance of African ritual, but they are built on the dramatic unities of the Western tradition, tightly plotted from conflict to resolution. Tutuola's picaresque novels and Prince's ant-work paintings, though, embody an additive Yoruba principle of order. They mix humor and horror, revealing a Yoruba vision of human existence. The "system of life," Prince said, lies "between," mingling the shocking mysteries of the unseen world with the humdrum doings of the visible world. Tutuola's writings and Prince's pictures both calmly depict betweenness, not bringing conflict into resolution but imagining conflicting forces into perpetual coexistence to match the spiritual and material duality of experience.

Now, having mentioned Amos Tutuola's novels, Prince goes on, turning upon his predilection for the linear to the topic of media. His account begins in accord with Ulli Beier's:

"And then, Ulli see the way I do my painting. He suggested I would be very good at etching. So, he went to Europe. But before he come back from Europe, I have done a lot of black-and-white drawings. I've done about forty pieces.

"So, he took it to Prague, in Czechoslovakia, for my first exhibition outside Nigeria. And the second one was at Wesleyan University, here in Connecticut. That was nineteen sixty-five.

"So then, Ulli Beier now create a studio for me, and I started doing etching. You know, the type of etching you remove the plastic sheet, and you use candlelight to have the flames give you a darker shade on the mirror-like part of the metal. Then you do the drawing by little kind of tool, needle-like, with needle. And then afterward you put it in the acid. Then the acid does the biting of all the place you put the lines.

"That's how I started. Then I was working on etching. But this technique was developed by myself."

Prince taps the jigsawed piece of plywood on the table before us. It will be mounted on another, then another to make what he calls a sculpture's painting. He developed the technique to distance himself from aggravating imitators:

"After about four years, my exhibitions and publications here and there, a lot of people started to copy my style. And I'm not happy about that.

"Then I moved from there to create batiks. And my band has become big, and I have to end up having seven women, young girls who dance for me. And any time I have performance, I have the problem of the police. Because whenever I went to perform, the girls run away from school to come to my house. The police would come outside"—Prince raps on the painting as they would knock on his door. "So after I have these girls as my wife, that problem is solved.

"So then, I started the sculpture painting in nineteen sixty-nine. I call them sculpture's painting.

"I don't have a jigsaw then; I don't have an electric jigsaw. I would use a hammer with chisel, like. When I wanted to cut someplace, I would make a hole with the chisel before I use a handsaw.

"Until when I came to Haystack in nineteen seventy-two. I was invited to Haystack as an artist in residence, teaching etching. And when I went back, the money they paid me, I got some tools. I was able to buy a jigsaw, and that's how—then it became easier, and then I can produce so many sculpture's paintings.

"So, by the time I went to go to Haystack, a lot of my other artist friends have become very jealous of me.

"Before I was invited to Haystack, I was invited to London in nineteen sixty-seven, through the influence of Ulli Beier who have a big show at the Commonwealth Art Institute. That was the time the book came out, Contemporary Art in Africa.

"Since then, it is one thing after another. I started seeing various places in different parts of the world—for exhibitions, for artists in residence, you know. Toward the end of nineteen seventy-two, Barbara Ann Teer"—founder of the National Black Theater in Harlem—"invited me to the U.S. To New York. To work with her. She tried to have what you call Cultural Gap, bringing artists from Nigeria, artists from America. We worked together here, and then, later on, they would go to Nigeria.

Barbara Ann Teer and Prince Twins Seven-Seven,
Margaret and Ajani, in Ornette Coleman's home, New York, 1985.
Prince's photograph collection

"And during that time, a big art festival for all of Africa came up, and Barbara was able to bring some of her performing artists to this program in Nigeria. And they were living in my place for about three months.

"Then, in between, I was trying to be involved in politics. I was like a power broker. I organized events for all my friends. Until nineteen seventy-six, when I contested myself. And I won as a member of the Local Government Council in Osogbo.

"And I was privileged to be able to get a lot of development done, like the development of roads. A lot of people doesn't have job to pay their tax, and they arrested them. You know, they don't have what you call income tax. It's a kind of paper. You pay as you earn. So, I used my own salary, which is about two, three hundred dollar now. I helped people.

"And then I have a lot of problems too. In every year, I would have one problem, either with police, or either with some friends.

"But I just keep going."

Prince's narrative has found its theme: the distress that accompanies success and brings on the struggle to endure. He just keeps going. His style was set in his first effort. His progress was marked by shifts of technique: pen-and-ink drawings, etchings, paintings, batiks, sculpture's paintings. His success was confirmed by exhibitions, invitations, opportunities to travel. Success as an artist, and as the lead singer in a band, won him fame. Fame brought him careers as a politician and as an actor in films. It brought him chieftaincy titles. And it brought him problems with women, with the police, with jealous friends, problems in the vexed sphere of Nigerian politics.

In telling the story of his beginning as an artist, Prince composed an overture, as he did in telling of his birth, raising topics that fit his theme and deserved elaboration. For the interviews that followed, he arrived ready to explore some aspect of the theme he discovered by narrating directly, chronologically, the tale of his beginning. The theme will govern the whole third segment of his life's story, and by emphasizing the distress that attends success he will do more than describe the complications of his life. He will build a rationale, looking forward to explain why he left Nigeria, why he abides in exile in Philadelphia. Prince just keeps going, a man of the ants, enduring troubles now as he did in the beginning.

If we trace a single line, the one most important to the study of his art, it seems that an innate ability coupled with a dedication to Yoruba culture, shared with other artists of his era, swept him with amazing speed to fame. But it was not easy. You will recall that, while Ulli Beier wrote in *Contemporary Art in Africa* that he had no plans for him, Prince said he was hired to join Duro Ladipo's theater company. He did; he immediately became an actor in Ladipo's troupe. In the Introduction to *A Dreaming Life*, Ulli Beier says blandly that Prince and Ladipo "were two personalities who were incompatible." Their incompatibility makes a story, set in the year of his first picture, which Prince repeats with passion:

"When I started working for Ulli, I become so popular that the man who owns the theater group could not stand looking at my face. He started getting jealous.

"So, in nineteen sixty-four, he was invited to go and play at Berlin Festival.

"He dropped me.

"He would not take me.

"The spot where I have my house today is a big yard. I went there to hang myself.

"Because one of my dream in life is to go to Europe, any European country. And this was my opportunity. And this guy would not take me.

"So, I went to hang myself.

"And I hear a voice.

"It says, Do you think this is the end of your world?

"That's where I have my house today. But it is a small house I bought, and I keep developing it and developing it, and it is a *big* compound. I have a theater there. I hope to have a nightclub, other things to do with nightlife.

"The voice says, This is not the end of the world for you if you don't travel where you want to go.

"I listen to that voice ever since. The same voice I hear when Duro Ladipo didn't take me to Germany in nineteen sixty-four.

"That shows you the irony of what human beings go through to survive. I go through—if I would tell you everything, millions and millions of instances—things that are just supposed to finish me, and I just cross it like you cross a stream.

"So, when I heard that voice, I have a rope around my neck, and I remove it, and I come down.

"And there was a gentleman that walked over to me; he was powerful, he was a witch-doctor, and people are scared of him, and he said, Twins, I know you have problems. I will help you."

Prince keeps going. He has help from the spirits, help from the readers. But it was hard from the start.

·9·

Big Shows and Changing Markets

Autobiographical writings are often engaging in their childhood sections, since their authors have gained distance enough to see themselves as individuals and as members of families and societies, distance enough to compose compelling narratives about youngsters growing within historical conditions. In later sections, though, when authors enumerate their adult accomplishments, narrative energy gives way to lists, context fades, interest narrows, diminishes.

It is not like that with Wole Soyinka. He preserves distance, in one of his memoirs speaking of himself in the third person, and he tells good tales from the first to the last. In his latest memoir, *You Must Set Forth at Dawn*, the story of his attempt to repatriate a Nigerian work of art is a small literary masterpiece. Soyinka is, in his autobiographies, a valiant political activist. If the critic is surprised that his fictional writings are not always similarly political, I would say, guided by Fernand Braudel's theory of historical time, that all of his writing is political. Even when Soyinka's dramas do not connect at the busy, surficial level of parties and policies, they operate at the slow, deep level of the long duration, arguing for cultural survival, against imperialism. Soyinka's autobiographical writings throw a context around his creative effort. In them he does not boast of his artistic achievements, nor does he talk much about writing, about the inner task and the lonely, long hours at the desk that fill such a large portion of his life.

For some reason that must have to do with culture, with time and place, Prince Twins Seven-Seven, his younger contemporary and fellow Yoruba, does much the same. He speaks of his accomplishments with innocent pride, but folds them into stories that have goals beyond the recitation of victories. His stories spread context around his art, but he rarely talks about art. He does it.

When Prince told about his start as an artist, he carried the story forward for less than a decade, mentioning along the way a few early exhibitions. But the sequence of his exhibitions provides the backbone for this, the unwieldy third segment of his oral autobiography. His shows shape the buried armature of success in his theme of endurance.

The program printed when Prince assumed his chieftaincies in Ibadan, in 1996, lists his accomplishments. The list is repetitive, hard to interpret, but from it I gather that his works had been shown in sixty-six exhibitions between 1964 and 1996. From him I know of eighteen others that were omitted from the list or that took place between 1996 and 2000. The majority, forty, were mounted in the United States; next comes Germany with twelve, Nigeria with eight, England with six. The rest are scattered: Spain, Italy, France, Finland, Holland, Czechoslovakia, Ghana, Canada, Mexico, Argentina, Japan, Australia. Some are group shows, some solo. Some are major, some minor. Though most happened in America, many of the American exhibitions were small displays at universities, and I had heard him speak most enthusiastically about exhibitions in England, Finland, France, and Japan. I wanted his take, wanted to know which shows he remembered, which ones mattered to him. So I disrupted his normal pattern and asked for a list, reminding him that he had yet to speak of the exhibitions since the seventies. It was not our best moment together, but the friendships that grow during ethnographic exchange bring mutual obligations. Friends help friends. He was willing to help, to take up the burden I placed on him, trusting me that a list of exhibitions was a necessary part of our work.

Prince began, Yoruba-style, with a proverb, set up a general preamble, then marched forth, using dates and locations to prod his memory. He stopped often, tapping a tattoo with his pen on the table, now softly, now sharply, now in agitated irritation, while he remembered and I kept quiet. Then, recovering from silence or digression, he would suddenly name another show, getting back on the track that ran generally onward, right to the present. He says:

"There is one Yoruba proverb that says, Priests never be honored in their own village.

"If you are doing anything in your country, and the other countries, renowned reputable countries in the world, does not show interest in what you are doing, then you are a failure.

"The most value is in something you started on your own. It's not something you bring back from the other part of the world. See, like a singer: if you sing and you cut a disc, and the disc does not come very very successful outside—unless America plays or BBC plays your music, then, to them, they still look at you like a failure.

"And today every artist does want to come out, to have their show. Even if you don't have the full writings in foreign paper, the fact that you are able to go out and have the show is very very encouraging.

"And then, by the end of the nineteen-seventies, letters were falling upon each other—from dealers, countries, from museums and galleries, inviting me over. And when I know I could not do a solo show, I call one or two other artists to join me for a group show.

"So. And then, in the nineteen-sixties through the seventies, the Goethe Institute in Nigeria did a good job in our work, giving us a lot of exposure in Germany, Europe, and all that.

"One of my first major exhibition was at Commonwealth Institute, in nineteen sixty-seven, in London.

"There's another one in Prague, at a gallery that I do not know how to pronounce the name, in nineteen sixty-four.

"In nineteen sixty-nine: a big show in London. Nineteen seventy-four: a big show here in America, at Corcoran Art Gallery.

"So: so many very very important exhibitions.

"And the other one that really become very very big was in nineteen eighty-nine at Georges Pompidou Center, in Paris. That was the time they have the show called Magician of the World. Magician of the World. And after that we have Africa Now exhibition that tour around the whole world through the collection of Mister Pigozzi, an Italian-American collector. I think he live in Switzerland.

"So then, in nineteen ninety-one, I have a very big one in Las Palmas. In Spain. *Lots* of them.

"A lot of very very important shows.

"But the show I love the most was the one at the Commonwealth Institute in nineteen sixty-seven, whereby there was a policeman on a horse, guiding people for not touching the paintings. And when I was coming nearer, the horse raised up his foreleg to push me away. That's what really discouraged me, and I went back home.

"That was the day I said, If I am doing something so important that the horse rider will not allow me—because the guy doesn't know I'm the artist. That's how I went back to Nigeria.

"So, lots of very very important shows."

Prince taps on the table.

"And the other show that was very very good to me was organized by myself in Finland.

"Taidemuseo Hameenlinna. It was very very successful. Not successful in terms of how many paintings I sold, but the paper coverage, the television coverage."

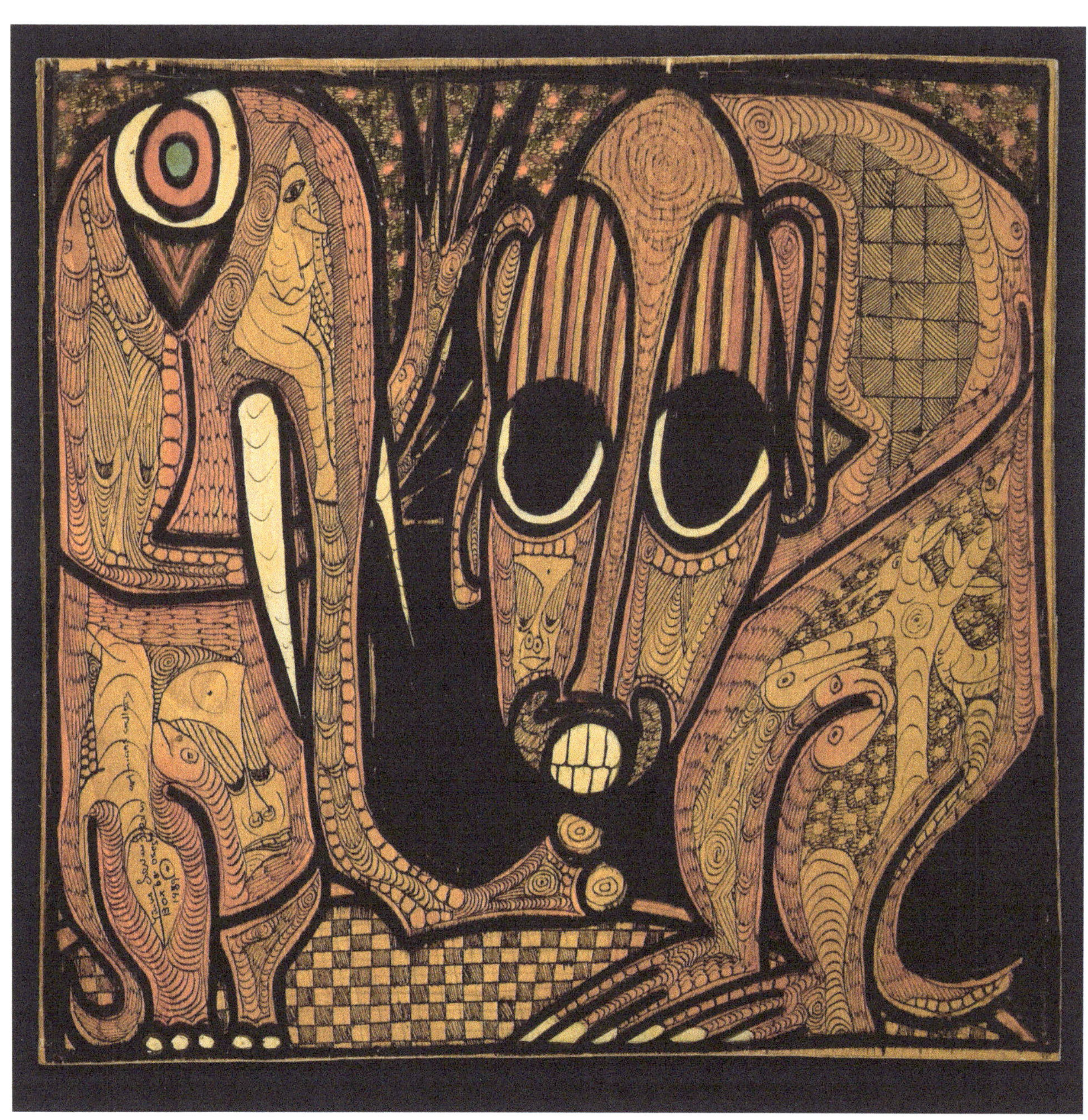

Elephant and Mr. Baboon in a Far Away Discussion Imagination. Ink, watercolor, and oil on wood: 2 layers. 22½"x21½". Osogbo 1989. Prince made this painting for his exhibition in Finland in 1991; see chapter 20, no. 13, and p. 475

Another time he said the show in 1991 was a financial triumph. He was then in his "brown period," exhibiting sculpture's paintings of wood, varnished to a golden-brown hue, and the Finns loved them:

"It was a very very successful show. I came back with about twenty thousand dollars. One of my greatest shows ever.

"Because that country, you know, they deal in wood. They love wood. So my wood paintings they love. The museum bought a lot; private art collectors bought a lot."

Without a tap of punctuation, Prince continues:

"And then, also, between nineteen seventy-two to seventy-four, I did a lot of successful shows in Holland. There's a gentleman there—he's late now—Mister Fopma. He buy cocoa. He import cocoa from Nigeria, and he really want to do something for the country.

"So, he got to know me through the introduction of the Netherland ambassador then. So, he invited me over to Holland on several occasions, and through him that's how my work got to Tropical Museum in Holland.

"Then, in nineteen seventy-four, my group was invited to take part in a very big festival in Germany, and I have a very successful show. And then, in nineteen eighty, there's what you call Book Fair, in Frankfurt. My paintings were exhibited in that show. The critics were coming there for me, and it was very big, big-big breakthrough; they covered it in Switzerland and in Sweden, and in Nigeria as well.

"A lot of times I have shows in both Italian embassy, or Goethe Institute, or French Cultural Center in Nigeria."

He taps on the table, takety-tak, takety-tak, tak, tak.

"And there's another exhibition in nineteen sixty-nine, in Ghana. At the German Cultural Institute. It was very big, and very successful. It was a group—an Osogbo group of artists show. In the beginning, they forced me to go, to have a show together. But, you know, when they have shows, most of the time, they buy my paintings; they don't buy any of the other guys'. So they get angry, and then don't do a show with me anymore.

"But, it's interesting. It's interesting.

"But sometimes when I sell my paintings, I'm very sad. Because it is like you are selling your children. But because there is no other way for me to survive in this life of art, I have to end up selling my paintings."

Takety-tak, takety-tak, he taps, takety, thinking.

"Then there's this guy, this guy that the American government was looking at for some time. I think they say he didn't pay tax. And he ran to Spain. He was rich, and he was a great admirer of my work. There was a time he sent me to Spain to live for about six months. He give me a studio, put money in my account, and I produced beautiful lithographs.

"And then I did a painting for him that I call Mister Cash. It's a man carrying a basket, and the basket is full of coins. And I put coins, all the coins I have from my various travels in my pocket. I put some Spanish money, American money. And I have to cut part of my hair, to make hair braid for him. I think—yeah, he bought the painting for fifty thousand dollars. In nineteen eighty-four."

Mister Cash is one of two pictures he frequently mentions, the other being his first one, *The Devil's Dog*; both are veiled self-portraits. In 2000, our "multi-talented Nigerian artiste from Ibadan" was interviewed for the magazine *Nigerian Videos*. The NV interviewer asked him how his journey has been, and he answered, "The road has been very rough, but we thank God who has kept us moving." When asked which paintings "shot you into the limelight," he replied, "I have a lot of works that are of international standard, but I can remember vividly that in 1967 *Devil Dog* one of my early works brought me fame. Another painting, *Cash Man* made of beads, cowries and currency. The piece was sold in 1984 to an oil magnate, Jack Achwell who resides in Spain at the whopping price of $50,000."

Prince smiles with the memory. "So, Mister Cash was you, making money," I say, and he laughs:

"I think it is me in a way. He really look like me, with beads; he's like my portrait. Very beautiful painting."

He laughs once more, taps, turns serious:

"I think God create these worries in my life to enable me to create. Because sometimes when I have worries—now I don't do fearful pictures any more. In the beginning, I do a lot of very *weird* looking paintings, and then some critics in Nigeria, Nigerian writers, were making me look like I'm painting people from different world.

"I paint people from the unseen world because otherwise I would do realistic painting. And I knew before me there is so many realistic painters. What can I paint that would look different? That's why I decided to do what I am doing, and what I love to do best.

"Some are frightening. Some have to do with the fact that I'm dealing with the story about ghosts, about invisible objects, and things like that. Sometimes from my dreams.

"Here"—in America—"where I'm in environment where I see so many cars, so many colorful things, it is unlike back home where you have to close your eyes to come up with imagination."

Prince taps on the table, long and loud, annoyed, urging himself back to the topic:

"So, talk about big shows. The show in Las Palmas was very big. Then in Japan, everything was going like that"—he snaps his fingers—"at Seibu Ikebukuro Museum in Tokyo."

During another taped interview, he told the story of the Japanese exhibition in 1989:

"We went to Japan under the auspices of the Nigerian government when they have a show, a Nigerian antique show.

"You know, they were showing with these antiques that Nigeria had years ago.

"I think the exhibition came here, then it went to Japan. And the gentleman who was in charge, he came to Nigeria to visit Obasanjo, who is the president now. He has an organization called African Forum Leadership. And the members are ex-presidents from various countries, professors who used to be there to do some thinking for the world. He has a home on his farm. Then he has an international hotel. There's a big farm. I think he was influenced by Carter, by President Carter, the former president.

"Anyway, these people came to him. They already had in mind that I am the one they are going to invite to come and perform. They asked President Obasanjo, can he recommend to them any artist that is involved in art and music.

"He said, Twins Seven-Seven.

"So, the Japanese, they can't believe it. The person they have already picked to go to Tokyo is the person Obasanjo recommended.

"Anyway, that's how we got invited to Japan."

Prince taps lightly, briefly, adds an old show in Rome to the list, and arrives at the present, ending his task, finishing the work. He is now in Philadelphia:

"And by the time I was here for six years: no shows. A lot of people who doesn't know where I am before I got the award"—the UNESCO award in 2005—"would be thinking maybe I'm dead.

"Six years. But it is good because, like, when I come back now it will enable my work to have better value.

"The other thing is that, you know, people, because of all these troubles in the world, people who have money are very skeptical, very afraid to touch their money. Because they don't know what is going to happen. They get afraid, maybe they don't buy art.

"But, all said and done, I thank God, and I thank people that make it possible for me, because, like, it's not very common for some artist—that is why, in this country, when some people get *down*, and there is nobody to bring them *up*, they resorting to violence, or drug, but I thank God I was able to stand still."

In 2000, Prince thanked God for keeping him moving. In 2006, he thanked God for helping him stand still. Standing pat is victory enough in the circumstances. No big shows for six years, but he is at work again. There will be new shows, a quickening in the market, new sales. But people with money are reluctant to release it at a time like this, a time when President Obasanjo's second term is ending and the Nigerian government will have to thrash through a turbulent transition, a time when President Bush's second term has not ended and the American government, dispensing with democratic values, has rigged the economy to benefit the very rich at home while spreading the horrors of war abroad. Prince has hope, fear, and an immigrant's complaint. When I recorded the life history of Hagop Barın, an Armenian who left Turkey and immigrated to the United States, suffering through a spell of depression, then deciding to make Philadelphia his home, he told me that he was stunned by the absence of community spirit in America. No one helps. America, Hagop said, is a place where nobody belongs, where you succeed or fail on your own. Or, Prince adds, you turn to criminality, to violence and drugs. But he has managed to stand still, to resist surrender, to hold to the art that carries him on.

From 1964 to 2000, Prince's exhibitions continued, coming one after the other at a pace of better than two a year. The smooth flow of shows, though, conceals disaster and change.

On July 3, 1982, Prince was coming home from a political meeting. At Abaigbira on the narrow Gbonga-Ikere Road, a truck swung into his lane to pass a car. He swerved to avoid a head-on collision, plummeting into the bush and ramming into another car that had left the road to skirt the crash. Local men pulled him from the wreck. The radio announced his death. For thirteen days he lay in the hospital without opening his eyes. He was given an artificial hip and confined to bed for eighteen months. His wives, one by one, abandoned him. Prince's dancing days were done, and it would take a mighty effort to recover the momentum of his artistic career. That is one reason why he recalls so fondly *Mister Cash*, the painting of 1984, and the exhibitions in Paris in 1989 and Finland in 1991—all of them announced his return as a creative, money-making artist.

Still, the eighties were hard. In a brief but perceptive history of the Osogbo school, written in 1989 and published in *Seven Stories about Modern Art in Africa*, the artist Tayo Adenaike calls Twins Seven-Seven "undoubtedly the most talented" of the Osogbo artists, then goes on to say, "Sadly Twins is no longer the prolific artist today that he used to be." But you cannot count the man out. The critic's mistake is extrapolating the future from the present and seeking a developmental trend that will unite the whole career. In one of his few formal statements on art, Picasso took a stand against simple evolutionary schemes, saying that art and the careers of individual artists follow "certain ups and downs that might occur at any time." Prince's pattern illustrates the great artist's generalization: his course pulses in waves, marked by recursion, by lingering and leaps, by moments of high and low productivity.

Prince is a man of many talents and interests, many troubles. His artistic output rises and falls. In the nineteen-sixties, musical performances took him away from painting. In the nineteen-seventies, it was politics, and he believes that involvement in politics brought on his wreck. The spirits nearly killed him to warn him that the political path was not for him. During his recuperation, there was little time for art, but, despite Adenaike's assessment, he knew periods of great productivity in the late nineteen-eighties, the late nineteen-nineties, and again, after a miserable dry spell in Philadelphia, during the middle of the first decade of the twenty-first century.

Quantities fluctuate over the course of his career, qualities shift. Prince is drawn at once to craft and imagination, to the disciplined skill of the hand and the wild wanderings of the mind. Both signal his originality, his personal authenticity, but they engender differential response.

Writing in 1968, Ulli Beier praised Prince primarily for his imagination, sensing a general decline when Prince concentrated on richly crafting an old vision in the manner of a folk artist rather than straining for novelty as modern artists do. It could follow that Prince's great period of creativity ended with the sixties. In that, he would hardly be alone. He had, in the sixties, developed his range of techniques, from pen-and-ink drawings to sculpture's paintings, but he has continued fitfully from that time to this, alternating between the qualities that combine, in different proportions, in every work he makes.

Visionary imagination jumps him forward, then he consolidates vision with skilled concentration; then he leaps again, chasing the phantoms in his head. Things go on. Sometimes imagination leads and the unexpected erupts. Sometimes craft leads and repetition follows. Duchamp replicated his old works without destroying his reputation as an innovator. Manet painted more than one version of Maximilian's execution without tumbling from the lofty position he most assuredly deserves in the history of art. Duchamp and Manet—not to mention Michelangelo and Rembrandt (all those self-portraits)—were craftsmen too. It is no failure when a young man, recently a dancer in a traveling medicine show, draws a second Devil's Dog, or a third or a fourth, or when an aging man, scrambling to pay his bills, renders another image of Osun as a swarm of fish. Money is a necessity, and it is useful to take a second shot at a good idea, making it better. There is no art without craft. Craftwork keeps the hand moving while the mind patiently awaits a strike by the muse. And this too: the well-wrought artifact, like the imaginative flash, has its admirers.

Prince feels that, generally, foreigners like the strange works that bubble out of his imagination, while Nigerians are more apt to appreciate excellent craft. It is logical, if ironic, then, that foreign critics, who disparage him for playing to a foreign audience, seem to have lost interest in his work at exactly the time when, shortly after his wreck, Nigerians began to collect and commission his paintings. To appeal to this new market, Prince (a man who rejoices in foreign approval, but who is, at last, a man of his culture and place) brought his skills to perfection and let drift the fearful imagery—he calls it weird, Ulli Beier calls it bizarre—that welled up in him when he was young, that attracted foreigners, but no longer dominated the churnings of his mind.

As they spin on, his exhibitions string together, running past the time of his disaster in 1982 and the time of his achievement of a Nigerian market in about 1985. His first serious Nigerian collector was a Yoruba man, a prosperous lawyer, Chief Oyekunle Alex-Duduyemi, who advised his business associates in Holland to purchase paintings by Prince. We met up with him and his Hungarian architect at Haja Fausat Ogunkule's open-air restaurant, our favorite stop on the road to Osogbo, not far from the site of Prince's wreck. In 1991, another Nigerian patron became "the first Northerner, the first die-hard Muslim" to collect Prince's art. His name was Alhaji Dangote; he was a wealthy businessman who commissioned Prince to paint three portraits of him on horseback, playing polo.

"I have many Nigerian collectors," Prince said. "Too many of them. But they didn't start collecting my work until around nineteen eighty-five upward. Those who were collecting—there was, like, some businessmen, some politicians. For example, a brother-in-law of mine, he is a lawyer, he is a politician; he is late now. He commissioned me to do a lot of political events in his house, and I believe those paintings are still in his house now. And I did a lot of beautiful things for him.

"The reason why local people were not able to buy paintings is because they are very poor. That is why when I do my music, those who cannot buy my paintings end up buy my music, buy my plastic's plates.

"Even then, that's why I created the batik. Then I make dresses. That's why I bring in my wives now. To help them to do something for themself. So, they started creating fabric wares we got from batik: we have bedsheets, children wares, sarong.

"Then, through God, and through whatever we are doing, help us to internationalize the tie-and-dye, the local tie-and-dye, and the one done with wax, bee wax and candle wax.

"Most people, they don't know what I'm doing to make money. Some of them are just wondering: where does he get his money, he's in drugs, and all that. So, I started doing things that is in their reach, financially. And they were very happy about it.

"And today, seventy-five percent of my people wear—and in the beginning, many religious people, like Muslim, would not touch this fabric. Because to them it's like paganism. But today they wear it."

He laughs quietly, pauses, musing:

"Ah, Nigeria.

"My people, they will criticize many, too many things you do. But when you are very successful, then you have a lot of friends. They want to hang around you."

Early on, Prince won fame abroad with his painting, fame at home with his music. Then by designing fabrics for the masses and making paintings for the rich, he changed local opinion, gathering his people around him. He addressed that change in his own way, when, five interviews later, having thought it over and gotten it together, he announced his topic as the commercialization of his art—not a sin in his mind; a man has to live—and told the whole story. An admirably orderly narrative, it came easily, streaming with none of the halts and lurches that disrupted his list of exhibitions. In the telling, he was inspired to ponder his style, twice expanding into unusual and valuable general comment on the nature of his artistic work.

He began by returning to 1964, quickly repeating how he made his first picture at the Mbari Mbayo Club, how Duro Ladipo refused to take him to Germany and he went to hang himself in the place where his house stands in Osogbo, how Ulli Beier gave him books of Yoruba literature, how his drawings were exhibited in Prague. The story is rolling:

"Then I started receiving a lot of guests. To you, you may call them tourists, but to me: guests. Because their coming to Osogbo has to do with the fact that they want to see my paintings. They want to be involved with the Osun. I took them to the shrine. I become like a guide to everybody that came to Osogbo.

"And I started having friends, people coming from various parts of the country, the world, to see what I am doing—ambassadors to Nigeria, cultural attaché—everybody was falling over each other just to meet me. And I was becoming very flamboyant. And rosy. And beautiful.

"Before that time, when we do any paintings we just give it to Ulli. Because none of us"—the artists of the Osogbo school—"even was painting to sell. Nobody thought that what we were doing was worth anything, that there was pay in it. Just the idea of just that I'm dealing with something.

"And then Ulli would show us pictures of exhibitions, writings in various papers in Europe.

"Then there was a time in nineteen sixty-five, a gentleman, an Israelite who works with a company that treat water; they create drinking water in Nigeria. We seemed to be more advanced than the rest of the countries in Africa at that time, so we have all these Israelites in building construction, engineering construction—all kind of things.

"So, this particular person came to my house, and he saw this painting I was working on, a big one, like this"—Prince gestures at *Kissing Birds* in progress on the table. "I think he bought it for sixty pounds. Sixty pounds. At that time—God, sixty pounds.

"But I didn't know he was a good friend of Ulli Beier's. So, when Ulli came, he showed this painting to Ulli. Ulli got frustrated and annoyancy. But he told me, Maybe you want to live by your painting. Because at that time he was paying me, like, small money, like pocket money. He was paying all the artists then.

"So, he says, It seems that you are mature enough to live by your painting.

"So. He said, Anytime you do anything good, let me see it. If I like it, I buy it for Mbari. If I didn't like it, you can sell it to someone else.

"Anyway, I kept working. More Israelites are coming to buy my painting. But they are not flamboyant buyers like Americans. The Americans will pay your price. Any price, they'll pay. But the Israelites—if you want to sell a painting for one hundred dollars, they try to get it for ten dollars.

"Because they have become Nigerians themselves. They so mixed with our culture that—you know in Nigeria, if somebody want to sell for one hundred dollars, he start from six hundred dollars. Because eventually he knows you will cut his price down. Because it is part of the system.

"Anyway, then the Americans, the British—everybody started coming, and I started having events of exhibitions.

"Then our first exhibition after the one Ulli Beier arranged was at the Goethe Institute, which is a German cultural institute, where they encourage writers, musicians. It's a kind of diplomat institutional place. And the Osogbo artists were their major artists that they really put pressure to promote. I think it is because Ulli is from Germany. And it is a pride to them that somebody from their country discover this group of young artists. And they want to give some kind of encouragement to them.

"So, we have an exhibition there. From there: the British Council, which is similar like the Goethe Institute; they invite us for exhibitions. United States Information Center also. So, it become a kind of competition between all the diplomats.

"So, by and by, we started becoming *big* and having exhibitions in various parts of the world. That is how it started.

"But Nigerians don't start to buy my paintings until nineteen eighty.

"That's how we started. And then we end up even having people coming to you to dictate what they want. You know, like, I want you to paint me the god Ogun. Osun. Or paint me a man on a horse. You know, that kind of commission started rolling in.

"And when I see that life was becoming rosy, and I got a lot of jobs coming in, then my wives are going into batiks. My house now become like a big commercial center. Because when you come there, there are so many things to buy. If you don't buy my paintings, you either buy my music, or get me performing. So, that's how the commercialization of my artwork started.

"And I started receiving commissions from, like, the Italian embassy, the Argentina embassy, Brazilian embassy. In fact, I was so close to one of the ambassadors, I even had my first baby in his house. He was the Brazilian ambassador to Nigeria. But he was a white guy; he likes me. Anytime I'm in Lagos, I always stay in his embassy, stay in the guesthouse there.

"So, that's how the commercialization of my work started.

"But before that time I never know that I could make a dime from whatever I am doing.

"Anyway, that's how it started.

"And from all these commissions, my thinking started getting broader and broader. But I try as much as possible to remain myself—that I don't get carried away, because I am getting commissions, to forget my style. Because I know the style is what makes what my work is.

"I tried to develop—when I started I was working only on a flat surface, on plywood. And when I started having a lot of commissions rolling in, I go to this, in nineteen sixty-nine, that I call sculpture's paintings."

Prince points to the jigsawed top sheet of *Kissing Birds*. Local artists do attempt to repeat its cut and laminated technique, but never, in my experience, with much success.

"The British call it third-dimensional; the Americans call it sculpture paintings.

"The idea came to me because I'm jealous of people trying to imitate my work. I don't like it. You see, when I become so successful, many art students would go to my exhibitions, and take their pencil and copy. Then I have a lot of people tried to copy my work, and that doesn't make me very happy—in the beginning. But now I'm happy because I know that the more people copy me, the more they push me to think deeper, to come up with new ideas. And then it shows that I have been accepted by my people. Because if I'm not accepted, nobody want to touch my work."

While working, Prince says, he strives to preserve his personal style, but, at the same time, he wants reaction, acceptance, approval. For him, the main benefit of his foreign exhibitions is the approval and prosperity they provide him in Nigeria, among his own people. He goes on smoothly:

"So then, surprisingly, the first exhibition I did with sculpture paintings was like putting fire on dry wood. *Pshu!* Everything sold out in ten minutes.

"So, from there I just continue, continue, continue. And several of these big works are in museums all around the world.

"But one of the paintings I cannot forget in my life is the one I sold to this guy in Spain. Mister Cash. I love that painting. It is just like myself, holding a bag full of money. And I cut part of my hair to make the beard for the painting. And my hairdo, I split my hair and glue it on it. Incredible."

It is fitting that Mister Cash makes another appearance, for this is a story about commercialization, about art transformed into money. His painting is an icon of hope; it shows a man like him, fully recuperated and rich. The money in his hands is a sign of approval. Payment for the artist who works in solitude is like applause for the musician who performs in public. It signals the completion of a successful communication. And money enables artists, like the other people trapped in the world, to do what they want. Prince continues, raising the issues of race and widening markets:

"And then by the time I came to America with Barbara Ann Teer in nineteen seventy-two, I have a lot of people through her connections that collected my work. Like a lot of black Americans collected my work.

"In the beginning I thought I was doing these paintings for the white people alone. But from nineteen eighty, I started having a lot of Africans collecting my work.

"Some Nigerians purchase my work because some of their very successful white partners in business have my paintings. They just want to show that they understand it, even if they don't understand it.

"And there's some that bought it because they felt, in future, my work is going to be very very valuable, and they were investing. And there is some who just bought because they like me. Or because they want to be part of the system.

"But with the Europeans, some people are into very very scary looking paintings. Some people just bought because it is painted by me. And some people just buy anything, provided it looks like my work—not from me, but from my imitators. Because they are dying to buy my paintings, and maybe they don't see me, or because they cannot afford my price.

"Whoever buy my painting in Nigeria, they buy it because it is my painting. They don't like the scary ones; they like decorative. Some like things with animals. Some like things that look like they are abstract. Some like things that have to do with landscape. Some just purchase because they want to have my painting. Because it is done by me.

"Some people will say, Oh, I would like you to paint me this—like some people have a special interest in certain things. Like, I remember a very rich guy who gave me a picture of him playing polo. You know polo; it is a game of very rich people. The British brought that sport to Nigeria. So, he give me three pictures of him playing polo. And I painted him in three different ways, the way I feel about it.

"So, there is a very beautiful abstract painting that I did, that does not have any eyes—just design. He picked that."

I ask if Prince thinks his patron, Alhaji Dangote, chose that painting, a display of craft, because he was a Muslim.

"No, because he loved the painting I did for him as well. He just liked it because he has a beautiful, well-furnished home, and he was looking for something that was very decorative.

"And you don't expect him to have a snake with something, or Ogun with something, in his house."

Prince pauses briefly for a thought. He is relaxed, comfortable with me after two weeks of talk, and he pivots on the painting to offer a rare description of his process, pulling together observations of the sort that usually arrive in scraps of random commentary while he works:

"I didn't do it for him. The painting just came by itself.

"That's part of what I told you the spirits can do for me. It just came by itself. The work came by itself. I didn't plan it. It just—by accident.

"You know, sometimes I want to do something, and it doesn't come the way I want to have it, and I go back to it, and work on it, like playing, and by the time I finish it, it become a nice object, a beautiful object.

"It is like this"—he gestures again at *Kissing Birds*. "I came here, I saw it there, and I followed what my mind was asking me to do. But in another situation, I just experiment, and from experimenting, whatever I'm doing, it comes out different from everything that everybody knows I used to do.

"Such work is possible. You will find people argue over it. He did it. He didn't do it. He did it.

"I have a lot of different styles.

"Sometimes I'm lazy. And sometimes when I'm lazy, from my laziness, something terrible, wonderful can come out.

"And sometimes I'm in a hurry. I want to finish quick, and by the time I finish it, something wonderful come out.

"Those are the same way.

"And there's a time—sometimes I stay long on a painting, and by the time I finish it, it is so complicated that whoever is collecting it will find it difficult to know what it is, or even me to give title, except if I have already put a title before I paint it, the work. It has changed so much, and there's a lot in there, and I put too much in there. It is hard to just caption it and give it just one single title.

"When I make a mistake, I don't accept it. I just turn it into something else.

"It's a style now. A new mistake is a style now. A new mistake is a style now.

"That's why I don't like to carve. Because when you carve, you see something in the wood, and by the time you are carving, you will see something else somewhere, and something has come out, and you have another face. And then you have two things to fight against, either to repair the mistake or to continue with the original thing of what you are doing. And then it is too complicated."

Wood carving, the prime medium of Yoruba traditional art, presents Prince with problems. A wood carving is hard to repair in the midst of a process that unfolds without plans, that yields objects through a sequence of spontaneous acts. His paintings, even more radically than the old statues of wood, emerge from the Yoruba tradition of serial composition.

Another time Prince told me he does not like wood carving because it demands hammering, pounding, driving the chisel into the flesh of the tree. Like people, like birds and beasts, trees, too, have spirits, and if he pounds all day, the sound of the pounding haunts his dreams, as though the spirit of the tree were, in revenge, pounding his body. Now he goes on, saying that lost-wax casting is another traditional technique he has used:

"I do brass-casting as well. When you melted the brass, the spark that went into the eyes discourage me from doing it. Unless that you have very good goggles.

"I used to do a lot of brass-casting as well. I did it for ceremony purposes.

"When I do the wax, I make clay to cover it, and I leave a small pass-out. And when you dry it, you dry it for a couple of weeks. Then you put it on the fire, and blow it. And when the wax melted out, you just pour the melted bronze into it.

"Sometimes it comes out fantastic. And sometimes there's a kind of mistake in the mold, and it came out with another shape, which is great too.

"The mistake is a gift from the spirit for you to create something new.

"I think the work of art belongs to another world entirely. Because sometimes, as an artist, you create things that, by the time you finish, you ask yourself, Now, how did I do this?

"Most of my paintings, some of them, I don't even remember how I do them. Seriously.

"People think I'm sleeping.

"When you see me sleeping, to some I'm sleeping, not looking at the paintings in my mind. I can create something good for you. But if you want me to do any idiot thing, I will. But I worry for my reputation.

"Like, this wood, when we were coming, immediately I saw it. I saw the two birds.

"In some cases, let's say, I do not see anything. I pour water on the wood, and I put it in the sun. By the time the patterns come out, I need to sit down, meditate, and I have my eyes half-closed to be able to come out with some shapes.

"And then I ask the spirits to give me good names, a good title for the painting. Like most people who bought my paintings, some people are fascinated by my titles. I have heard somebody told me that I have poem-like titles for my paintings.

"So.

"Art is an interaction between me and the other part of the world. You have to join it together."

The words cease. He has ended with a grand conclusion. Art records an exchange between the creator and the world. Artists transform old substances and ideas, assembling them into new unities. Art is a joining together. A sensate display of human completeness, art rises from an act of connection: what was divided is joined to reveal the human. For Prince, to be human is to live between the worlds. His work joins the gift of the spirits with the gift of a maker on the ground, combining the strange imaginings that seem to float from nowhere with the dedicated labor of the crafting hand. By joining the spiritual and material worlds, by listening to the dead and working like an ant, Prince developed a style all his own. Works in that style join personality and culture, materializing his simultaneous desires to follow his own head and to express the tradition of his people. His works embody the fullness of his presence as an individual, and they serve to position him socially, bringing connections to other people who buy and exhibit his pictures. With money and appreciation they confirm the effectiveness of a communicative effort, an open and devoted act of the will, in which the worlds commingle, the visionary imagination fuses with mundane materials, the natural and nurtured sides of the individual come into productive alignment, and the social separation of the self and the other—the boy from the bush and the rich patron, the native man and the foreigner—is overcome. All that joining is Prince's success.

Success frames the third segment of Prince's life history, the era from 1964 to 2000. He was, all agree, the star of the Osogbo school in the sixties. The exhibitions that followed, numbering something like eighty-four, carried his name and paintings around the world. His time of success was also a time of disaster, and beyond the realm of art there were other triumphs, other troubles.

· 10 ·

Political Involvements

Triumphs and troubles: that is how it is. Prince says: "It's like the Yoruba proverb that say, Tibi tire lada aiye. Means: The world is created with both negative and positive."

Take the story of Prince's discovery of his lineage, a story that will drag us into Nigerian politics. Prince's values are egalitarian, but he believes in upholding what he calls "the established order," the tradition of respect for authority—for the gods, the ancestors, the kings and chiefs, the elected officials—and he felt that by joining the conservative, capitalistic National Party of Nigeria, he could work within the system to advance art and benefit the common people, the people on the farms and city streets with whom he identified. (His father, the leatherworker, had died without explaining to him how he belonged to a royal line.) In 1983, Alhaji Shehu Shagari, leader of the NPN, was re-elected as president, and Prince, not fully recovered from his car wreck, stood for election as an NPN member of the House of Representatives. He won. But the party's local reporter of election results, bribed, Prince thinks, by his enemies in Osogbo, removed his name, and sent forward the name of another:

"When it comes to election in Nigeria, forget it. There's no election in Nigeria; it's selection.

"So, this guy removed my name, and put his own favorite person there, who does not even contest at all. So we contest—we started protesting. We started sending petition. I started taking my youths to the party leader secretariat in Ibadan, three hours drive, making trouble, throw stones on the window to stop them from making meetings.

"Then, one day, they asked me to go and see one of the prominent Islamic leader. But he is very young, dynamic, rich, well-connected young man. But he is more of a Muslim person. But at that time because Shagari, who was the head of state, was a Muslim, so they were seeing the National Party of Nigeria as a Muslim party. It's more pro-Muslim.

"But in the *South*, many people don't want to be with him, because they felt he is anti-Christianity. But to *me*, I believe in national unity of the country. I believe this party can cause a lot of beautiful things to happen for the unity of the country.

"Because Obasanjo, the present president now, was in military and he hand over the government to this gentleman at that time.

"Anyway, to cut a long story short, they sent me to go and see this gentleman. I went to his house. His name is Alhaji Arishekola; he is a very very powerful Islamic leader. And he is a close political friend, Islamic friend, of our political leader in Ibadan, in the person of Chief Adediba, Alhaji Adediba, very very powerful. He is a man who can sit in his house, with his political maneuvering, and remove the governor from his position. By going through the House of Assembly, he got the governor impeached. Just like that"—Prince snaps his fingers. "That show you how powerful that man is.

"Anyway, I went to see this man to complain to him that I've been elected to go to the House of Rep in my constituency in Osogbo. And my name was removed, and somebody else name was put in my position.

"So, they calmed me, appeased me that I should not worry. The party is thinking of giving me a better position. And they would give me something more stronger. Even though I don't go to the House of Rep, they would give me a good job, or something.

"Then, after he left me, he went into the room, because they always give you money to give to your supporters. So, he came back with about, say, about one thousand naira; at that time that thousand naira is about ten thousand in our money at this time. He says, This is for your gas, for petrol.

"So, when I was leaving, I saw a copy of my petition that I wrote to them. I saw it on the floor. And I pick it."

Prince plucks a piece of paper from the table, and holds it before his eyes as though he were reading it, down to the bottom:

"Underneath they have names of all the kings that have reigned in Ibadan.

"Then my own grandfather name was third on it. Circled.

"*Then* I realize that they discover about me, whom I am.

"Because the people of Osogbo were discriminating against me, because I am not from Osogbo. I'm from Ibadan.

"And they were saying, If I need a position, I should go and run for election in Ibadan.

"And I live all my life in Osogbo. Everybody know me as artist Twins Seven-Seven of Osogbo. And Osogbo is part of Ibadan. They haven't even created the new state out of Ibadan yet.

"You know what I mean?

"You are American and some people are discriminating against you because maybe your father come from Czechoslovakia, or your great-grandfather come from Turkey, and they say you can't do anything here.

"Which is wrong. So, I stand my feet, and I start fighting this injustice.

"So, this is the day I discover the importancy of my ancestor in Ibadan life. In Yoruba Nigeria as well."

He has reached the conclusion, the paper still in his hands. I remain interested, asking no question but repeating what he had said. The men were leaders in the ruling National Party of Nigeria. After a pause, Prince runs over it again:

"The ones that were in the house of the man I met, they were top-top, notable politicians, and they were like king-maker at the same time. They were trying to find out: who is me? Why am I so strong in Osogbo? And then they said, His grandfather is So-so-so, and I think they were discussing me, and that paper, the photocopy is circled.

"And somebody drop his copy. But that person doesn't know I'm coming there. It's like you're going out, and you see a piece of paper, and you pick it, and, surprisingly, it's part of my petition. We call it petition in Nigeria; you call it write-up here.

"You see, I wrote to explain how I won the election, how they remove my name, and I'm not going to take the injustice, and I'm going to fight it to the last national level of the party, to the president.

"So then, this guy now was supposed to be like a peace-maker to see what they can do to reconcile with me. And the paper I used to write to them, the last page of it is where they wrote the names of the different kings, the obas of Ibadan. The top is my great-grandfather.

"That was the day I got to realize the importancy of my father in Ibadan, in Yorubaland."

Prince has finished again, coming to the same conclusion, then telling me that he checked the facts in a history book he found in the university bookstore. It is true: he is a direct descendant of Osuntoki, and the leaders of his party knew it. Perhaps they had been informed by his enemies who felt he should run for election in Ibadan, not Osogbo, or perhaps they had discovered it for themselves when his boys rioted and Prince, interrogated by the police, refused to make a statement, offering instead a small, intricate, incomprehensible drawing. He was a man to be reckoned with, and someone had traced his genealogy in an effort to understand his power. Now, accidentally it seems, he knew who he was, and he stood at a dramatic point in his life: his wreck in the past, his wives scattered, suddenly a prince in line to the throne.

The event holds critical significance in his life, and his story illustrates the mingling in all life of the positive and negative. Denied election, he learned of his lineage. Belonging to a royal line could benefit him as much as election to the House of Representatives. The regional leaders of the NPN, learning of his power, had promised to reward him in some way. In this case, the positive and negative come into balance. But if we survey the temporal swing of his political involvement, the scale tips to the negative: distress outweighs success.

In 1976, the winner of a local election in Osogbo, Prince gained power among the youth and the poor, enmity among the political elite. Their enmity increased when he joined the National Party of Nigeria after its victory in 1979, believing "the only way you can be successful in Nigeria at that time is to work with the Northern people." The people around him—Southerners, Christians, affiliates of Chief Awolowo's old UPN—felt it was traitorous of him to cooperate with Muslims from the North, but it paid off. He was named the Youth Leader of the NPN, and when he met President Shagari in 1980:

"He shook my hand, and he said, Twins, what can I do for you?

"And I say, Your Excellency, I would be glad if I got a plot of land in Abuja, to develop a gallery in the future."

He got the land, scrambling through financial tangles, from 1982 to 1991, to build a house in Abuja, which he later rented to the government of Osun State, making a little money.

In 1982, returning to Osogbo from a political meeting in Ibadan, he was nearly killed. Usually he says the spirits caused the wreck to warn him away from politics, but sometimes he explains the disaster as the result of witchcraft worked against him by his enemies from Osogbo. Not heeding the warning, he ran for office in 1983. His victory was thwarted by those enemies from Osogbo, but he had come to the attention of the leaders of the NPN—king-makers he called them—and he could look forward to something, a lofty position perhaps, maybe another gift of valuable land. But three months after the election, a military coup ended the rule of the NPN. Prince's hopes evaporated.

That coup was followed by another in 1985, which brought General Ibrahim Badamasi Babangida to power. In time, Babangida announced a return to civilian rule and scheduled

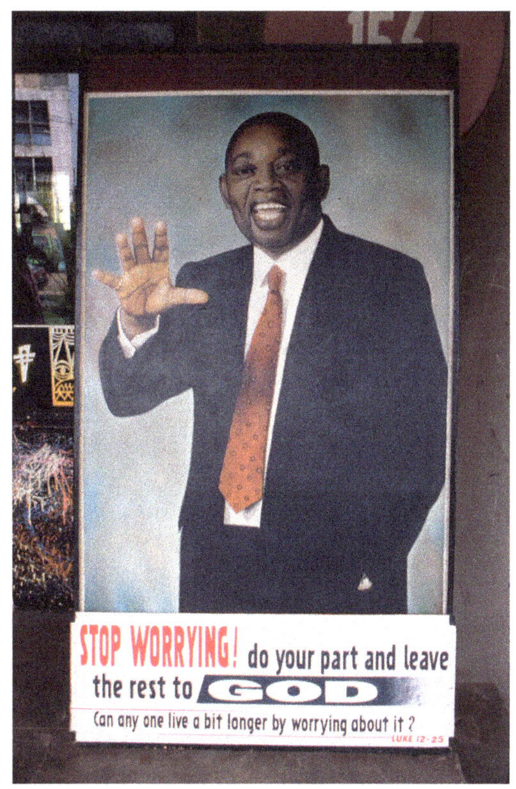

Chief M. K. O. Abiola. Photorealist painting on display at the Topfat Gallery, Ibadan

a presidential election for 1993, assuming that his man, Bashir Tofa, would win. Tofa's token opponent was Chief M. K. O. Abiola, a founder of the NPN, who left his party and politics after he was not nominated for the presidency in 1983. He was a Yoruba, a Muslim, a wealthy businessman, and a bountiful philanthropist. Prince remembers him as fearless and honest. "People lined up to vote for him," Prince said, and Chief Abiola's victory was clear and complete. While some old-timers claimed it as a victory for the Yoruba people, it was, Wole Soyinka said, a national victory. Signaling a repudiation of oligarchic military rule and a rejection of the British division of Nigeria by region and religion, the election of Chief Abiola marked, in Soyinka's words, "the birth of a nation."

Abiola won: Nigeria won. In fury the dictator Babangida annulled the election. The violent reaction forced him to set up an interim government that was taken over, three months later, by Babangida's sidekick, General Sani Abacha. A year after his election, Chief M. K. O. Abiola declared himself president, and Abacha threw him in jail. In the midst of Abacha's tyrannical reign, Wole Soyinka wrote *The Open Sore of a Continent*, in which he labors to find words fierce enough to denounce Abacha, but sees hope in the fact that Abacha is so monstrous that he will be "the last despot who will impose himself on the Nigerian nation." When he wrote, Chief Moshood Kashimawo Olawale Abiola was still alive, and Soyinka ended his book by arguing that Nigeria's "civilian president-elect" should be released from prison "to head a government of national unity and restore the nation to a democratic path."

Chief Abiola was never freed. He died in prison, killed, Prince believes, by American secret agents:

"I think the American government leaders want him dead. Because he was—he's not a radical Muslim, but he dabbled into what doesn't concern him. Like, when he came here to America, he met members of the Black Caucus, and he was talking about reparation for the blacks.

"Otherwise, he would have been the president. Before he died, he was in jail; the military put him in jail. And they want him to renounce his mandate, but he refused.

"And he was having tea with one of your ambassadors. And he have a drink of tea, and a couple of hours later, he has a heart attack.

"And everyone believes he was killed by poison."

The more we learn about American clandestine activities, the less far-fetched it sounds. Abiola died suddenly in his cell in 1998. If he had lived, he might have been president, because Abacha had dropped dead a month before, and properly democratic elections were held in 1999. Had he won, it might have been good for Prince, since he had been a firm follower of Abiola's, serving as "a member delegate" for his election in 1993. In the event, the winner was Olusegun Obasanjo, who brought a bright record to the election. When he was a general in the army he supported the NPN, though he was a Yoruba man, marked as Prince was, and he managed the transition from military to civilian rule, preparing for the election of 1979, won by Shehu Shagari. Obasanjo had been imprisoned by Abacha in 1995, surely winning him credit on the street, and now a civilian with genuinely democratic values in politics, he was a popular choice, and as history attests, a good choice. During his two terms in office he did not betray Wole Soyinka's hopes for an end to despots.

Prince had known President Obasanjo since his military days, for his band often played at army galas. He campaigned enthusiastically for Obasanjo's election in 1999, and his band was invited to perform at the inauguration, three days of euphoric celebration.

Prince had known other presidents of Nigeria: "We have met personally. But I have not been privileged to benefit financially from all these connections." Though disappointed, Prince kept working: "I'm not doing what I'm doing because I want money from the government. I just follow my intuition. I follow that spirit that talks to me to do this, do this, do this."

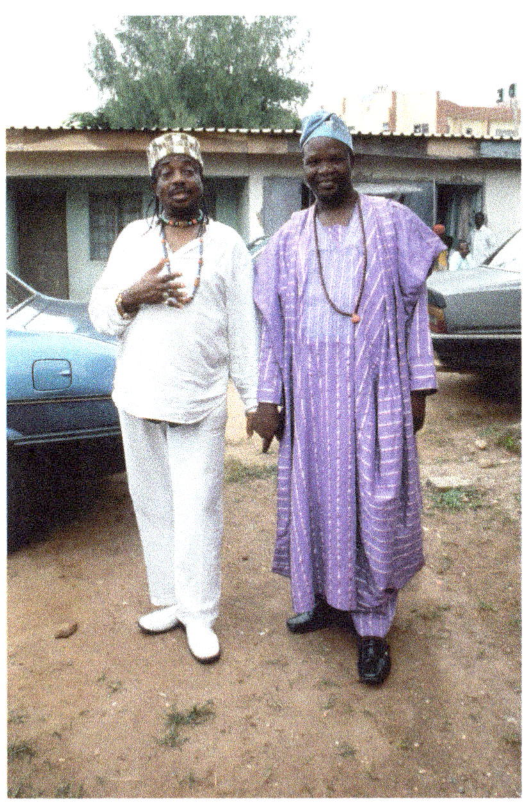

Prince and Chief Bio Taiwo. Abuja

But this time it was different. The connection was old, he had worked for Obasanjo's election, and he allowed himself to dream. An ambassadorship would be nice; it would let him live outside the country, with a staff to do all the work, so he could concentrate on his painting. Nothing happened. Envious enemies of his must have prevented his portfolio from reaching the president's desk. Somehow Obasanjo had forgotten him. No letter came, nothing.

Prince's expectations were great, his disappointment was extreme. In the realm of politics, the scale, always tipped to the negative, came down hard on the wrong side. And the accumulation of disappointment, ending in 1999 with nothing to show for his steady support of the established order, had become one reason for his decision to leave Nigeria and head for Philadelphia:

"God does not want me to be politically involved," he said. "God wants me to be in America."

Now the shape of events in the political realm becomes the shape of things in the whole third segment of Prince's life. Good on one side, bad on the other, but the weight of the bad has fallen, fallen so heavily that, by the end of the nineteen-nineties, there was nothing to do but escape.

When we stopped in Abuja, in 2006, to visit an old friend, High Chief Bio Taiwo, he asked why Prince had left Nigeria. Prince replied that he had worked hard for President

Obasanjo, but he had gotten no position, and, he said, he could no longer abide the strife among his wives at home. Later, outside of Kabba, when he told the story of his woes to the babalawo Alhaji Suleiman Otitoloju, he described the misery he was enduring in America because President Obasanjo had neglected him, and he told of the troubles he was having with his wives. The political story is over; trouble with women comes next.

Our interviews have found their pattern. I have been conducting interviews for as long as Prince has been making paintings. My style is not the journalist's. I do not come with a set of specific questions, seeking short answers to pepper my prose with quotes. My style is ethnographic. General questions and productive orientations lie in my mind, derived from a lifetime of reading and matured through the experience of fieldwork in the United States, in Ireland, England, and Sweden, in Turkey, India, Bangladesh, and Japan. Wanting to understand in depth, to see the world as others see it, I request long stories and spontaneous verbal essays, waiting through the silences, letting people lead me, going where they will. I speak to keep them moving or to turn them back to what they have said, making comments that will get them to repeat things in greater detail, asking questions to clarify topics they have raised, then I relax attentively while they go forward, knowing that they know best. The work takes, as the great folklorist Lady Gregory said, patience and reverence.

Prince has learned that I will listen. We have time, sitting together in his high, narrow workshop. He need not rush and hustle, trying to get it all said at once. He comes now, having thought it over, with a particular story to tell. His stories have a shape, a shape like a drop of water falling, or a comet crossing the night sky. A well-rounded narrative comes first, then a trail of commentary follows, sometimes coalescing into small tales, sometimes lengthening into a stream of facts and scattered thoughts. The wrought, leading narrative, generally a story of origins, a myth of the self, is marked by the traits that Dell Hymes, folklorist and anthropologist, linguist and poet, has taught us to expect (though Prince's patterns are not so trim as those of the Native American narrators Hymes studied or the Irish narrators I recorded): there are repeated words of beginning and linkage—So, Then, And, But, Anyway, Because—and pauses that pulse the flow, creating distinct lines, the strings of speech I represent as short paragraphs.

In telling about the commercialization of his art, Prince worked like that. The leading narrative recounted the sale of a picture to an Israeli and Ulli Beier's decision to let Prince separate himself from the other artists of the Osogbo school. Then the history of his commerce followed, ending unpredictably (for his narrative style is a kind of ant work) in an account of his practice. When he came to politics, he told the tale of discovering his lineage, the one positive event that did not overbalance all the rest, and he ended with disappointment and a resolve to leave Nigeria. Now when he chooses to tell about his troubles with women, or about his achievement of chieftaincy titles, his pattern will be the same. A narrative will come first, the end will be a reason to leave, the whole will be an expressive, meditative soliloquy on the causes for exile. Next comes the story of the women.

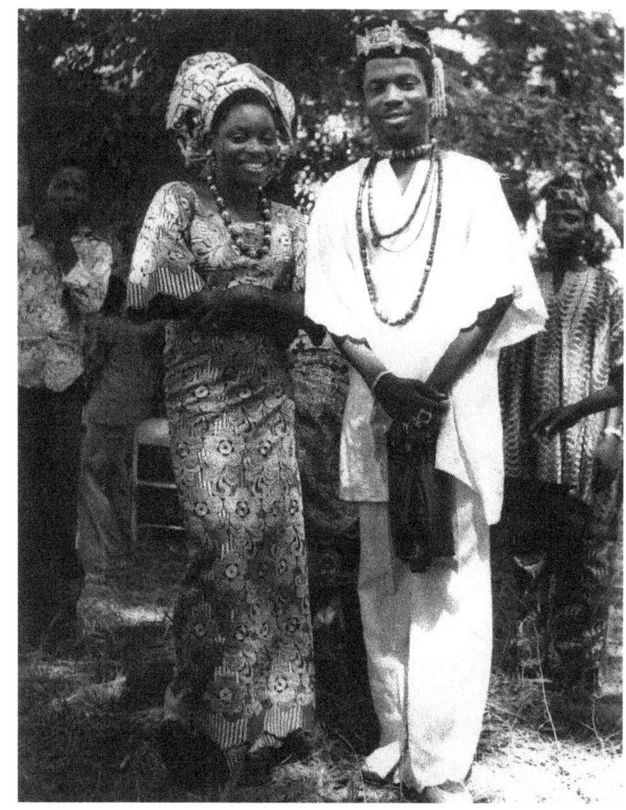

Prince and Bisi, 1978.
Prince's photograph collection

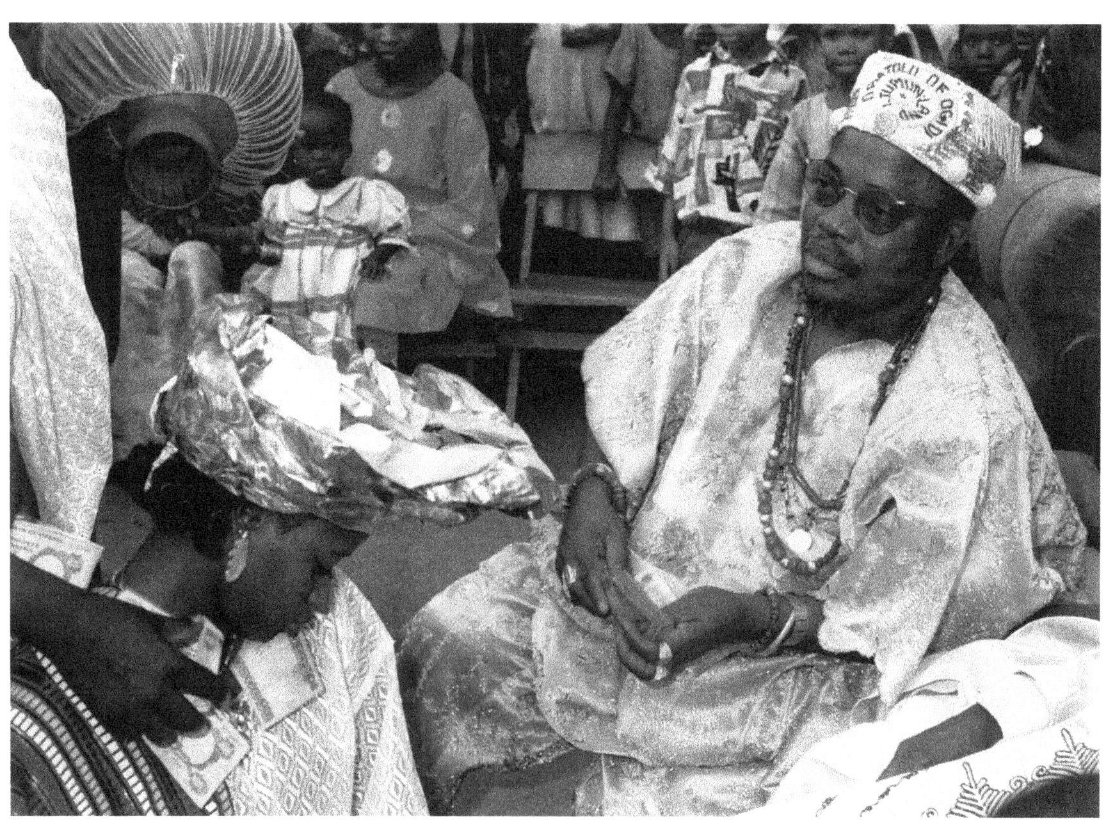

Prince marries Aliratu, 1998.
Prince's photograph collection

• 11 •

Troubles at Home

"The story today will be the event that turned me into a polygamist.

"All my life, I've wanted to be a man with one woman, a woman that would love me so much, that I would love so much, and I never thought of having more than two to four kids.

"But, from the story that my mom used to tell me about how she go through pain, all the trouble she go through before she could have me as an abiku child, encouraged me to find out what it is to be a father.

"So, when I started playing music in the sixties, I started becoming very, very popular, and I have engagement running over each other—like, they invite me to play one town for one event; we would not finish before we have other thing happening. And then we would play every evening at the nightclub. It's called Mayfair Hotel.

"So, every time we went to perform, my musicians, the gentleman who is more closer to me, and we have been friends from childhood time, his name is Samuel Omonaiye—Omonaiye, which means The child owns the world; that's what the name means. So, we be friends for so many years. Before we ever met in Osogbo, we are friends in my mother's place. He plays my bass guitar.

"And I've already got—I've got a wife, and I've got a couple of girlfriends; maybe I don't sleep with them, but they follow me everywhere. And this guy doesn't have any woman.

"So, one evening when we were playing at the Mayfair—it's my habit when I'm singing, when I close my eyes, anytime I open my eyes, if there's anybody in the crowd, a girl most especially, who look into my eyes at that particular time, she's going to be catched by some kind of charm."

Prince laughs, remembering:

"So, then I make a sign to one of my boys, and say, I would like to get that girl for Samuel.

"So, my friend went—one of my boy called Olu; Olu means Honor—went to the girl, and after my performance, around four A.M. in the morning, I'm riding a Yamaha motorcycle. And the rest of my guys doesn't ride anything. But when we have a long trip, we hire a truck to take our equipment.

"Anyway, when we arrive home, already I've got my wife, my first wife, Bintu, very nice woman. Very very beautiful woman. But I marry her at the age of, probably, nineteen. She's too young to understand the life of the bandleader.

"I don't know that then. It was not until I grow that I realize the mistake that it means at that time. And then God has destined that such would happen.

"Anyway, when I got home, my wife was in the house. She was sleeping, but whenever I went to perform, she would not sleep until I arrive.

"So, when we come now, I came to my room to sleep. *But* my wife realize there's another girl was behind me. But she never knew the girl was not on my bed. She never knew the girl was for Samuel, and the girl for Samuel was a young girl too. She never knew.

"But, definitely out of jealousy, out of ignorance of finding out before you react, she came with a lamp. You know, the lamp with kerosene, with glasses. When she came into the room, she does not see properly. The fact that she just saw me lying down, and the pillowcase behind me. She just started hitting me, with the lamp. And I have this cut here."

Prince points to the scar on his shoulder.

"So then, the kerosene from the lamp spilled onto the pillowcase, and the bed caught fire.

"So, from there, my mother beat her. Which I'm sorry, because my mother didn't supposed to beat her. But, as a woman, and I am her lone child, she didn't supposed to come between me and my wife. But, as a woman, she did.

"And then, after we finish the quarrel, my mother sit me down and say:

"Look, I don't do circumcision for you because of one woman.

"And that: she got another five wives for my father, which means herself, another four wives, married to my father.

"And that: when I was born, she has been told that I'm going to be a man with so many women.

"That: why one woman would kill me just because somebody came to the house, and she doesn't even *see*.

"Anyway, unfortunately, my wife did that act, and my mother, I'm sorry, my mother encouraged me into polygamy.

"So, because of that incident, I have to marry—I pick another wife. My mother went to her village to bring me a girl through her brother, whom I told you does needlework. That is how I started having a bunch of women around me as wives. Otherwise Bintu should have been my only wife in life. And I respect her today, even though we got separated in nineteen eighty-two, after my car accident. She never marry other man up to today. And she got four kids for me—five kids; one died in the first day of life.

"If I need anything, she still come to the house. The children are very helpful to me.

"That's how I started my life as a polygamist."

Polygamy is part of his life, and like everything else in his life, in all life, in the world, it is at once positive and negative. The chief positive consequence of polygamy is children. Many wives make many kids. Casual questions get casual, inflated answers, but Prince, of course, knows the number. As of the fall of 2007, he had thirty-seven children and twenty grandchildren. Prince says his wives give him children or get children for him, and children in abundance are a visible sign of his power as a man. He is a man, a particular kind of man: an artist. He says:

"I don't know why all artists have that problem with the women. And we cannot survive without women. It is women who admire our work. Like, all my life, when I have exhibition, you will find that it is wives that always insisted that, I want this, and the husband would buy it. And then, sometimes the husband would say, No. And then, you have to go and pick the more expensive one, you know."

Women give him the response he craves. Prince takes women seriously, feeling it is wrong to sing love songs in public, for they trivialize deep human emotions. When he depicts women in his paintings, they are goddesses and mothers, never provocative. He does not like to see women dressed immodestly, with their flesh exposed, and he prefers the beautiful, wrapped dress of Nigerian women to the scanty, sexy dress of American women. Prince admires women, women admire him, and that makes for trouble:

"And I don't know how I have this magic that attracts this audience.

"And the women, they annoy me, because it ends up I have too many of them. Even those I don't want, they would just slip around, and they won't go away.

"Some girls would run away from their home. And then the police would come and arrest me—that I am the one that abducted these children.

"And that's why I stopped performing in schools. Because, before, I loved going to schools to perform, but any time I perform in schools, I end up having problems. Some girls would run away and follow my group. Some of my boys make eyes; you know, do goo-goo eyes to them. Or tell them I need them. I don't need them, but sometimes the girl is at the end of her wits because she wants to see you. But I have some guy in my group who uses his sweet, sugar-coated mouth to bring them."

That problem he solved by giving no more concerts in schools, and, as he said, by marrying the girls who ran away to follow him: "I would marry any girl who is a good singer, a good dancer, because of my profession." (Lest you get the wrong impression because a man in his sixties is speaking: the girls in question are seventeen or eighteen, the bandleader is twenty-two or twenty-three.) Prince legalized his relationships and consolidated his earnings by gathering into his household the girls who danced, dressed in traditional Yoruba fashion, in front of his band. The young girls were one problem solved by polygamy, married women were another:

"Being a polygamist helped me. It saved my life, because it stopped me from looking at other people's wives. In Nigeria, whatever destroy you, as a famous person or a powerful person, is when you started dating married women. When you date somebody else wife, they can kill you or they can put some kind of medicine, juju, voodoo on that woman."

Prince looks at me, horror in his eyes. He had told me of jealous husbands who put medicine on the bodies of their wives, and when their lovers touched them, they fell ill, swelling up, shriveling in pain, impotent. He concludes:

"It saved my life, but at the same time it caused me a lot of trouble.

"But sometimes the trouble enable me to know the world."

Polygamy is good, and it is bad. The trouble from which he learned was the trouble brewed among the wives assembled in his home. He lists them:

"I have Bintu, then I have Muni, then I have Nike. And then I have Yemisi, then I have Bisi, and I have Risi. Then I have Tinuke. That's how I have my first set of wives, but all of them dancers.

"And when we started performing and life was becoming very beautiful for us, I thought I need to do something to keep them busy. Because Fela Kuti in Lagos—you know about Fela, the musician; he has a bunch of dancer wives, but his women would go and do anything; they can go and sleep with other men and still come back home. But my wife don't do that. Not until when I started to have a lot of feminist art lovers visiting me, and then they break my first home."

Prince laughs heartily in this stew of art and politics. Fela Anikulapo Kuti, dead of AIDS in 1997, was five years older than Prince and a cousin of Wole Soyinka's. A Yoruba man

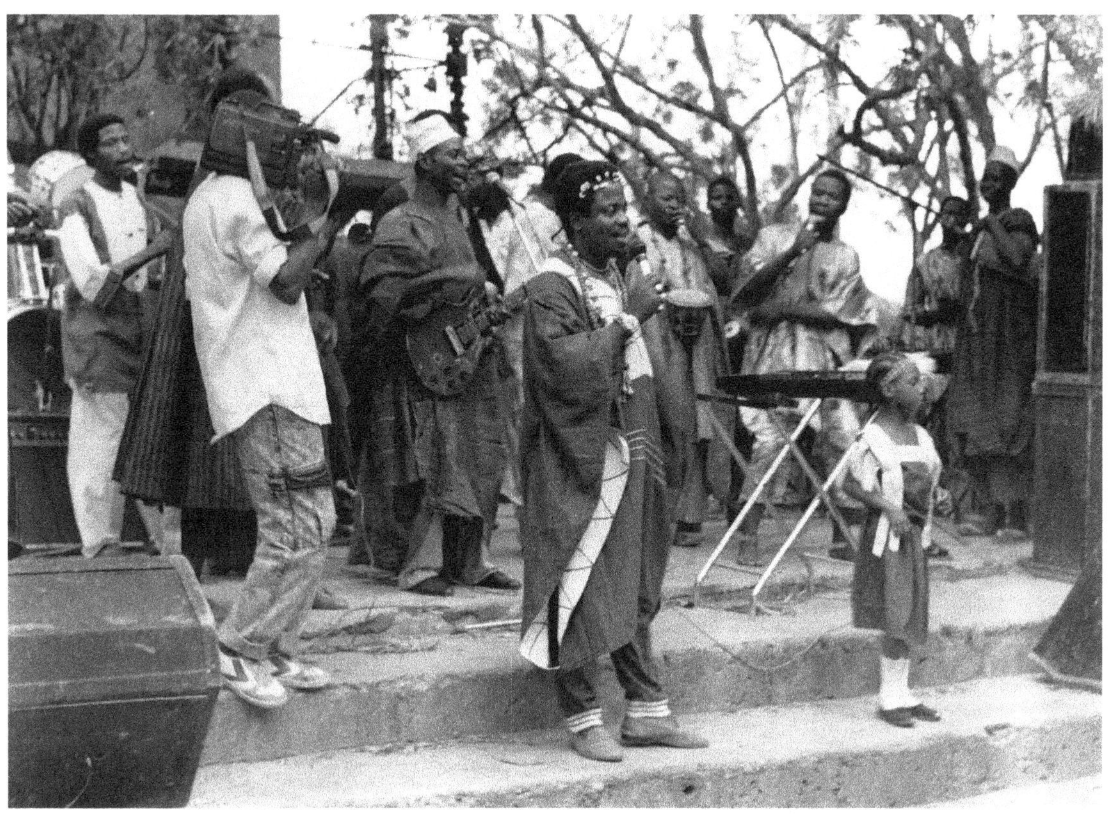

Prince and Kemi perform with his band. Osogbo, 1990.
Prince's photograph collection

from a solid Christian family who studied music in England, Fela played the sax, fusing highlife with jazz, and he was, along with King Sunny Ade, a leader in the scene when Prince formed his band. Fela was a model by contrast. Fela bent his music toward the West, Prince bent his to the Yoruba tradition. Politically, Fela was a radical, while Prince remained a supporter of the established order, as he said on another day:

"When my band was playing, we would go to ceremonial performances, like if somebody dies. You know, back home, everything is ceremony. When somebody died, a band would perform. When you have a new baby born, a band will perform. When you have somebody in the family graduating, then they would throw a party.

"We would be engaged to come and perform. There is nothing we don't dance to. Everybody is merry, merry, merry. Even when you cry, you wipe your face and go dancing.

"So, my band was opportuned to get performances. And I am making music. I'm making records. Sometimes I sing about the political situation in the country. I try to be very very careful. I'm not as critical as Fela. Because Fela, who he is, he was trained to be stubborn from baby. He sing about the military. They beat him. They kill his mom. I don't want to take that kind of beating. I have my culture, and I present the government in a very very positive way. It worked fine for me."

Fela Kuti was a rebel, and he suffered for it. In a paroxysm of maleness, Fela married twenty-seven wives. Prince Twins Seven-Seven stopped at the requisite seven. And as for those foreign feminists who found their way to the compound at the end of the lane on the outskirts of Osogbo: they could do no more than add heat to the unhappiness simmering in the household. Prince's laughter fades slowly:

"They pretend to be art lovers, because they *read* about how I have these wives, and they involved in art and batik-making. So, I tried to encourage them in making batiks. When they were fighting, what caused the fight is that, when we have visitors, those who could not afford my painting, they would buy small things from them."

His wives were fighting over money, jealous of the ones who sold best. Whatever Muni made—"sometimes she would just slap color on fabric"—sold quickly, but Nike was the wife with talent. She embroidered pillowcases with flowers and names, she produced handsome wall hangings, and she is the one who would rise to fame as an artist. In the house, the wrangling continued:

"So, I have to give them what you call division of labor, and it worked out very successfully. And all of a sudden, you will find somebody was lucky that they would ask her to do three dozen of skirts that they taking to Kenya, or they taking to Cameroon. So, life was—until I have an accident, and they thought I would die.

"When I have the accident, I did eighteen months, on the bed. So, the women have freedom of—just go anyplace they want. And I don't know why none of them even thought I would survive. But, though, anybody who see me at that time would never think I would survive it.

"So, whatever it is, all of them left.

"Nike and Bisi came here to America, because they know I am very popular here. And they tell people I am paralyzed, they need money, and they said some children are starving. And they were able to go back with good money, and Nike have a *big* art center. But when she came back, she started befriending a Welsh contractor, a retired Nigerian soldier person who is from British, but he is Welsh. So, she went to marry this guy, and I think the guy must have used some of the money he gained from the contract to build a good center for Nike. But now she's got a very big place, too, in Abuja. She's very very successful.

"She's very very successful."

Nike Davies-Okundaye manages elegant galleries in Abuja, Lagos, and Osogbo, selling her work, the work of other contemporary artists, and old pieces of African art, masks, carvings, textiles. She has said hard things in print about Prince. Everyone has a story to tell. Prince owns up to the errors of his passionate youth—being out of control made him an artist and a terror—but he is not now a man who speaks ill of others. Nike was the artistic star; he remembers his first wives as "Nike and them" and remains proud of her as a creator of wall hangings in batik (which owe more than a little to his distinctive style). He goes on:

"After I have my accident, then, when the first set of wives left me, a lady who stay by me then, I end up marry her, and her name is Bose. And through her, I have another set of five wives, in which the one who came to America"—Shola—"is number three.

"I don't make it seven this time. Five. But I was careful that I don't bring them into art."

He had learned from his troubles. Art fetches money, and it builds self-interest, pride and envy, precipitating the conflicts in the household that caused him to say at the beginning that he was sorry he became a polygamist. He set up his new wives as traders, selling things he bought on his travels abroad:

"Between nineteen eighty-five and nineteen ninety-nine, used items from Europe became very popular in Nigeria. Used cars. Used refrigerator. Used radios. Used anything used, electronic. So, whenever I come to buy cars, I would buy a van, and I would load it with different kind of electrical appliances, sending to Nigeria, and when they get to Nigeria, I would give it to my wives to sell.

"So. But in the end, by the time I become very, *very* successful, I became *very*, very successful, then another trouble come into the family. Things start falling apart."

This is, in some form, something he often says, referring to Chinua Achebe's novel, its title taken from Yeats's "The Second Coming," the great emblematic poem of the twentieth century. "Things fall apart; the centre cannot hold." The slouching beast is, in the context of an Africa still under assault, the force that destroys the established order: the Christianity and colonial aggression that divide the people and lead to Okonkwo's suicide in Achebe's novel, the alien thinking that breeds dissension in a traditional polygamist household. Among Prince's new wives, it was neither art nor commerce, but an inner clash of values, angry arguments over domestic duties, jealousies that drove them to physical violence and subtle witchery, that dragged him—an optimist who passes through troubles as one would cross a stream, who was, just then, at the crest of success—down into the murk of despond:

"The only time I am depressed totally is when there is a big problem in my house. My wives started fighting each other. If I go out, I don't have peace when I come back home.

"And I made a mistake.

"See, I married this girl, a very flamboyant girl from the governor's office. She's a typist.

"And because I felt that with her knowledge as a typist, I'll use her to write a lot of letters, and use her to do a lot of things in terms of communication. Because then we didn't have fax—we have fax but we don't have internet in those days.

"So, when I marry her—she is even younger than the rest of my wives—she came to my house with all these administrative habits of being pro-feminist. She's too pro-feminist. You have all these things that she read in the magazine about feminist activities in America. She brought that to my house.

"So, my other wives now, they start fighting each. Shola, she nearly killed her. So, I decided to give peace a chance.

"With what has happened to me, I cannot take it no more. I decided to get away.

"Then I tell Shola to come: Bring your American-born baby, bring two other children, making three of them. So I know she cannot throw away the kids and go somewhere else.

"So, that's how we got here."

Trouble in the household, like political disappointment, drove him away. He took Shola, hoping she would be the one wife he had always wanted, who would love him as he loved her, and he settled into exile in America.

· 12 ·

Chieftaincy Titles

Late in the twentieth century, when political disappointments and battles in the house were gathering into a burden too heavy to bear, Prince experienced an exhilarating triumph. It will follow; now he announces the day's story as an explanation of how he began receiving chieftaincy titles, and proceeds:

"As a throwaway boy whom people doesn't think he has any future, who at that time doesn't have any meaning to his people, and the fact that I'm living in another land"—Osogbo—"that is not my home town—how did I become a chief?

"And to become a chief in that sort of environment, where you are not an inherited person to a throne, a personality to the family, and, like, you are a tourist in a place—and people start giving me recognition.

"By the year nineteen seventy-four, as my habit, I used to go to the local pubs to eat. Because back home I don't eat much of the food that my wives prepare. Not for any other thing but because of what I call my own safety. Because I have too many wives. I have four, five wives, or seven wives, at that time, and you never know who is jealous. So, when they cook me food, I give the food to my children.

"But I end up going to the street to buy the food. I sit by the roadside, get them to make me bean cake, and things like that. I would go to the local restaurant to eat.

"So, I was in this restaurant. And I order food with my entourage.

"*Then*. Another group of four people were sitting on the other table. And when they finished eating, they don't have enough money to pay what they have et.

"And the owner of the shop want to embarrass them.

"And because it is my regular place where I used to eat, and I used to say, Serve everybody. And when I say, Serve everybody, whatever they eat, I will pay. Anything.

"So, I said to the lady, Don't bother them. I'll take care of the bill.

"I never know that this gentleman is going to become a king, six months after that date.

"He was a medicine seller. You know, at that time we don't have premises. So, some people would buy medicine, some of them, and they would go with their bicycles to sell to people, from house to house. This is what this guy does. But he's from a royal family.

"And at that time, he himself never know that he was going to become a king.

"So, I picked up his bill. But among of his entourage was one young man who has been in my theater group before—about two, three years backward. And he is now a follower to this gentleman. He is now a king himself in another small village, very close to Osogbo.

"Anyway, six months after, the gentleman, whom I told you that has been in my theater group, he came to me, and he said that this king want to see me.

"So, I went with him. When we go there, he said, You never remember me. Couple of months ago, I et in a restaurant; I couldn't pay. And you take care of me. I want to honor you with a chieftaincy title.

"So then, he gave me the—he wanted to give me the Babalawo Awise of Ilobu, which means the head of the native doctors. I look like somebody who has power, magical something. But I don't practice it. So I said, I prefer to be called Amuludun, which means somebody in charge of social development of the community.

"So, he gave me the Amuludun of Ilobu.

"That was nineteen seventy-four. And it become a very big, big-big news in Nigeria that a musician, an artist, is honored with this chieftaincy title.

"So, that was my first chieftaincy title."

Prince's tale tells of himself. He is wildly generous. "That's what gives me joy. It give me happiness." Others, he says, delight in traveling or womanizing, but God placed him on the earth to be kind, and he likes giving money away. It is, in itself, a pleasure, and he believes that cash scattered freely in society will benefit him. People will remember him, pray for him, and in this instance a small, casual gift earned him a big, formal honor. He is, to say the least, a complex individual. The title he was offered befit the solitary, mysterious, spiritual side of his personality; the title he accepted met his public, gregarious side, serving his need to be socially useful. His benefactor was a man like himself, a worker from a royal family who was unaware of his destiny. At the time, Prince did not know he was the descendant of a king, just as the new king, when he was—as Prince had been—a seller of medicine, did not know that in half a year's time he would ascend to the throne. If Prince had known then that he was a prince, he might not have consented. "Because," he said, "in our concept of thinking, it is not usual for a son of a king to be taking chieftaincy titles, because, as the son of a king, you are bigger than those high chiefs."

The ambitious man accumulates titles, building a position of power in society. After his first chieftaincy, Prince said, "my prestige, my honor become higher among the other artists. And everybody don't call me my name again. They call me either Baba or Chief, because when you become a chief, you are like a father."

Twenty-two years pass. His fame increases, recognition arrives in the form of "diploma awards from various institutions all around the world." He accepts them "because it's only paper." Those honors demanded nothing from him, but the subsequent offers of chieftaincy titles—many in number and including one from Osogbo in 1988—he refused:

"Because the more chieftaincy title you get, the more responsibility involve, the more people you have to cater for. If they make you a chief in four different local areas, you have to be responsible to a lot of people there. Because my own responsibility is with my family, my musicians, my followers. To take all these chieftaincy title, I tried to dodge. And whenever they want to make me a chief, I either found a way, or God found a way, for me to travel out of Nigeria."

By traveling he was able to run free, escaping the responsibilities that would tie him down and drain his energy, until 1996, when he took titles "in the royal line of my ancestors" in Ibadan:

"Early nineteen ninety-five, a couple of gentlemen came to my house and told me they discover that I am the son of the most powerful king in Ibadan, and the Oba of Ibadan want to honor my ancestors by giving back part of what belongs to my ancestors, and that was at the time when it was exactly ninety-nine years when my great-grandfather was king in Ibadan.

"So, by January nineteen ninety-six, I was given two titles. One as Ekerin-Basorun of Ibadanland; Ekerin-Basorun is, like, the fourth into the rank of general, the general of the warrior of Ibadanland. Then Atunluto—which is not common for them to give two titles at a time—Atunluto is a man in charge of social and cultural development in Ibadanland.

"So, it was a *great* day in my life.

"Then I have—for about thirty-two miles line of cars, of people screaming, shouting, singing, drumming to where I went to build my country home.

"Because I could not afford to build another palace in Olosun compound. Because there I have an uncle who is older than me"—Chief Busari—"who is the head of the family. He is called the Mogaji. Mogaji is like the head of a certain family, particularly a royal family. As Mogaji, you move, step by step, up to king. It is very political.

"So anyway, I have to move away from my family home to where my great-grandfather used to prepare himself for war. The village is still there. And then most people who went to war with my father, like the soldiers who used to fight with him at that time, he gave them spots where to live. We have about sixteen villages under the leadership of this village.

"And I went there to acquire my great-grandfather land. I found my own father land, and some land as well that shared the property that belongs to me. And I developed miles of land. So, I went there to build a beautiful house.

"And the day of my chieftaincy title, I have *all* the diplomats in all the embassy in Nigeria in attendance.

"And then we have what you call *all night* party with about four bands playing."

Prince glows with the memory of January 27, 1996. It is one thing to get honorary degrees from foreign universities, quite another to be honored at home. The crowd, the shouting and drumming, the gorgeous ceremony: this is his triumph. The boy named Bamidele has followed his father home to Ibadan, purchased Osuntoki's land, and built there a comfortable house. He has been formally recognized as a prince from a royal line; he has secured a position of authority in his lineage with twin titles. The celebration has drawn a throbbing throng, affirming acceptance by his people. There are diplomats, too, acknowledging the international stature he has achieved as an artist. Within the year, triumph upon triumph, the people of Ogidi will honor him with another chieftaincy.

Ogidi breaks into three sections. "You know how Africans divide themselves," Prince says. "They speak the same language. They eat the same food. But they still believe that you are this, you are that, you are that, that." Ileteju lies at one end, Ilaere at the other. Ogidi's middle piece is Okoro, his mother's quarter, and there Prince was made the Obatolu, "second in command to the king of the village" in December of 1996:

"Obatolu means The king who has come to make the town dwellable.

"So, I was given that title."

Honored in Ibadan and Ogidi, Prince was confirmed as a leader in the places of both his father and his mother. His divided points of origin united in a wide territory of belonging. Prince was home: he could, at fifty-two, relax amid approval, settling into success. A pleasant old age waited to wrap him in contentment. But soon he would flee, flying by the nets of connection.

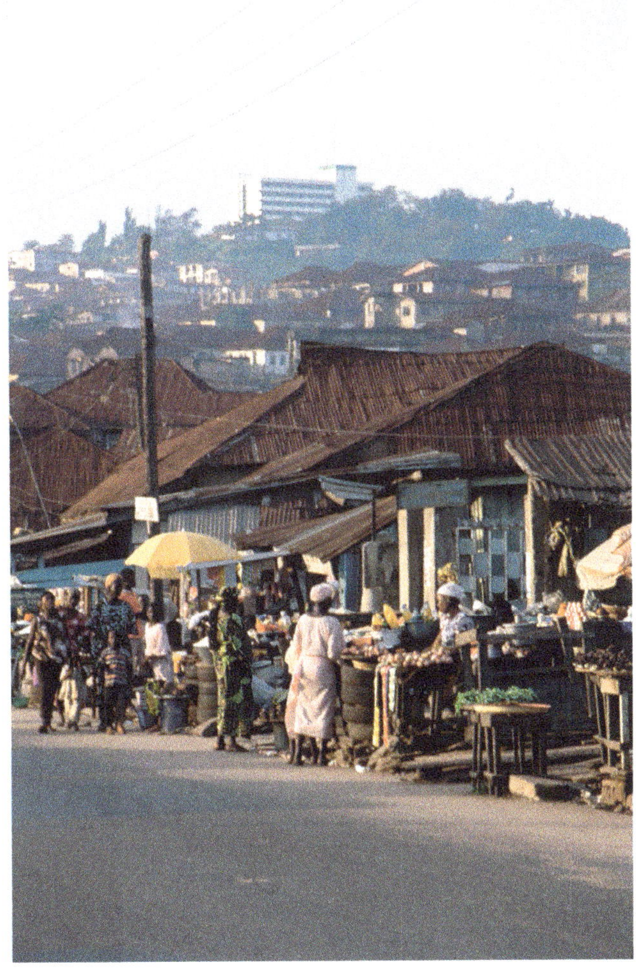

Ibadan

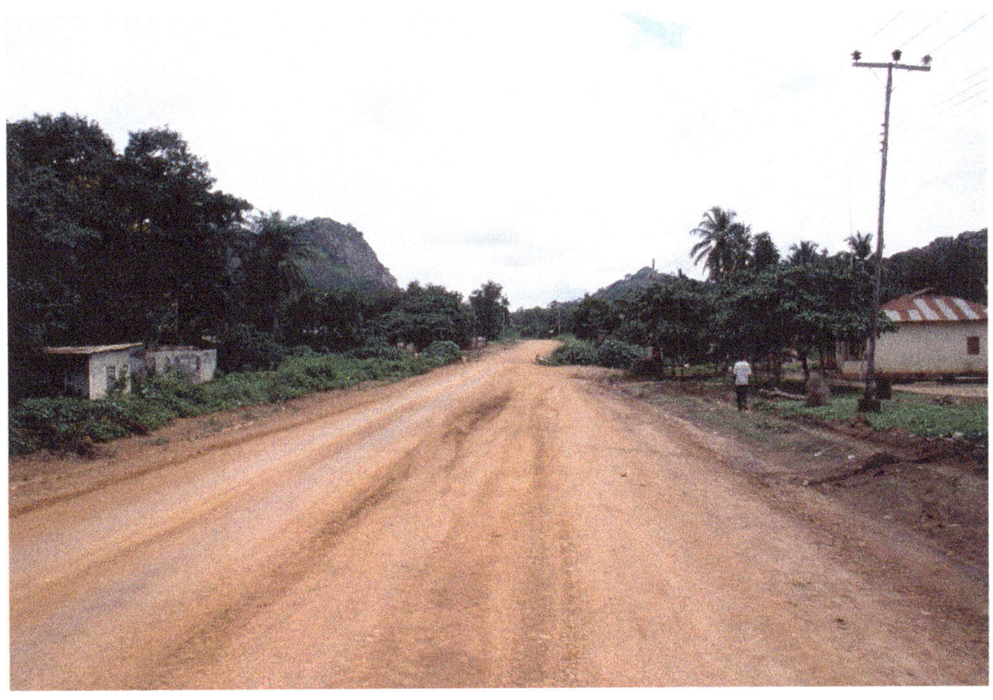

Ogidi

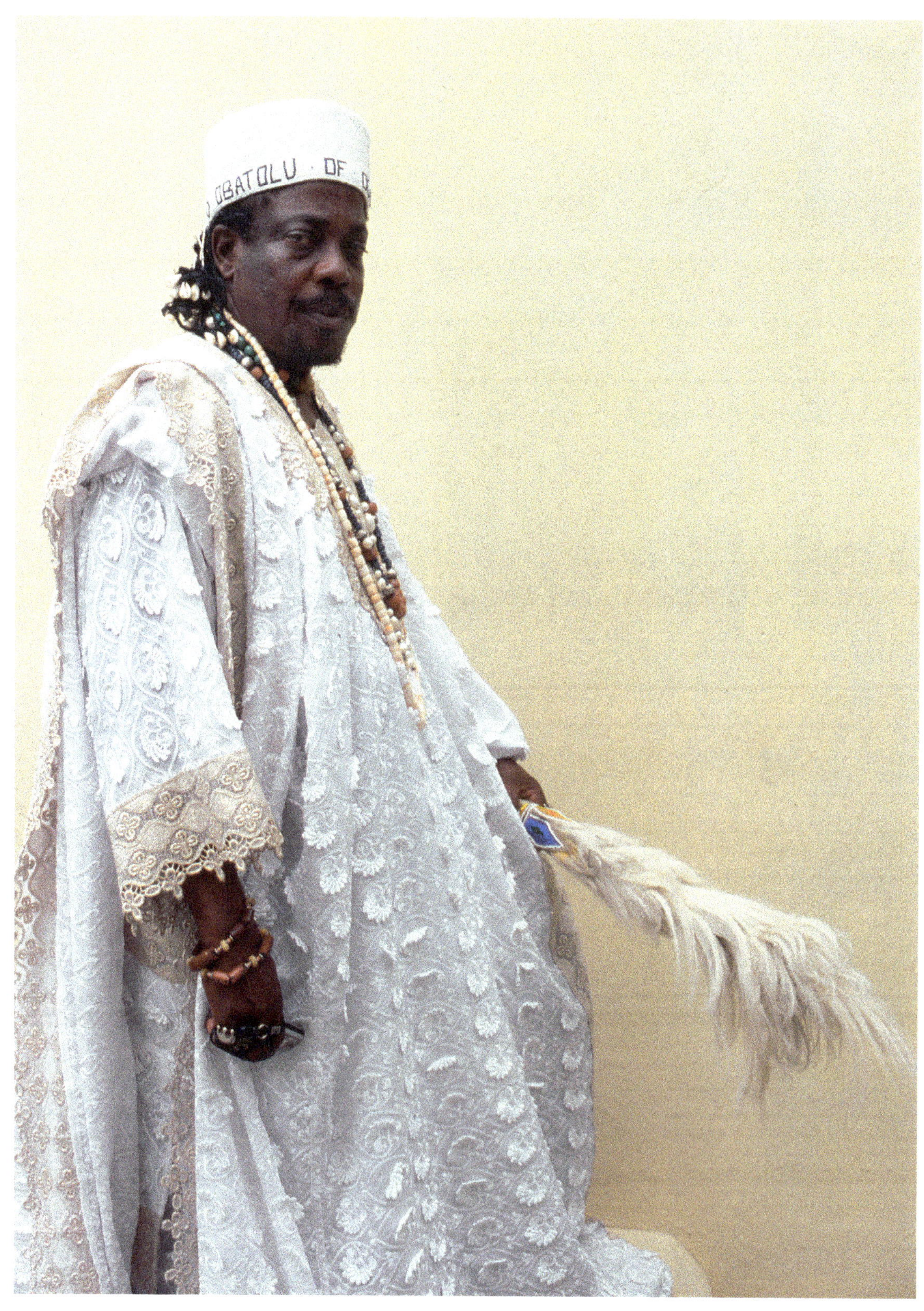

Prince Twins Seven-Seven, the Obatolu of Ogidi

Many titles and many children are, in Prince's system of values, the main signs of worldly power. They bring pride, distinction, prestige. They bring noisome, burdensome obligations.

As the Amuludun of Ilobu, he was put in charge of the community's social development, and both of his new chieftaincies carried social responsibilities. As the Atunluto of Ibadan, he commands social and cultural development. As the Obatolu of Ogidi, he must make the town dwellable. Prince has houses in Ibadan and Ogidi, but Osogbo is his primary place of residence. When he shows up in the places of his chieftaincies, he is edgy, ill at ease. People stand out of the crowd to laud his fame and to upbraid him frankly for not doing more to help them. He earnestly tries when he visits to promote improvements. His ideas are good, but he does not stay to guide them to implementation, and he knows he does not do all his honors demand. He should bear down on the local problems—the market in Ogidi needs to be rebuilt—but, while such work would suit his sense of civic duty, it would require ceaseless, tedious, tiresome, delicate, political negotiations, stealing time from his spiritual and artistic obsessions. He needs time alone, time to meditate, time to paint. The young artist still kicking inside him screams for release, for freedom from social obligations. He was happiest when dancing solo on the road.

Prince's social success, so fulfilling in the moment, baffles his desires and brings on the problems he locates, actually and symbolically, in the crown he was given as the Obatolu of Ogidi:

"So, I have to have a crown from there. Unfortunately for me the most renowned crown is *red* cap. They are red cap people, chiefs. I cannot wear red cap because of my spiritual beliefs.

"For two years that I started wearing the red cap, things are going backward for me. Before I realize I am touching what is no good for my spirit, a lot of things have gone down.

"That's what resulted in all the problem I have in ninety-six, ninety-seven, ninety-eight, to nineteen ninety-nine.

"So, I *stopped* wearing the red cap, and I used my artistic imagination to design a crown for myself with the name of the chieftaincy title on that cap.

"So. Otherwise I was supposed to be wearing a red cap with feather on it. But because of Sango and other things in me, red is a taboo for me. I cannot wear red.

"In the past, when I don't know, the priest told me that, as an Obatala-Osun, all my life I must wear white. *All* the time. Even when the white is dirty, I still wear white."

Within him, the red and white powers interlock in combat. Both serve him, making him who he is. The red powers tell him to seek general acclaim; they counsel ruthless action, pricking his ambition, urging him to be a mighty, violent, self-destructive king like Sango, the god of thunder and justice. Crowned in red, he rose in pride and power. But he is an Osun, a wearer of white who must turn away from the red. The white powers call him to peace, to calm, to quiet creativity. When he put on the red cap, he denied the white powers, forgetting his reverence for the creator Obatala, chief of the white deities, including Osun, the goddess of fertility and healing, the placid river sliding toward the sea. Crowned in red, he stood tall in power; he swayed dizzily, teetering in unbalance.

Something was wrong. In his painting *Barefoot President in a Fragile Boat with the World Tears Apart*, the big figure rocks while the people watch. The president is powerful, Prince said, but something is wrong inside of him. Perhaps like *The Devil's Dog* (a boy not doing as he is told) and *Mister Cash* (a man recovered and wealthy), it is an image of the self (an artist not doing art). The chief is big with power, but something is wrong inside.

Prince's terrific task—assigned to him by all he is, mind, body, and spirit—is to balance the red and the white, to bring the Sango in him into proper accord with the Osun in him. In myth—thunderbolt and sweet water—they are husband and wife. In Prince, their positions must be inverted; Sango must submit to Osun. These inner forces embrace fruitfully when he is alone and singing, the painting before him subduing wild thoughts with patient craft, but they slip out of control and into conflict when he goes among others, seeking power and fame, receiving praise and demands. Then things fall apart.

Crowned in Ibadan, then in Ogidi, he had reached the peak of his life, but lifted out of the crowd and bearing red upon the head Obatala gave him, he attracted the troubles that would bring him down—public troubles in the realm of politics, private troubles in the household—and, out of balance, untrue to himself, decentered, he had become vulnerable to the grinning, evil people who flocked to him:

"Life was becoming too buoyant, too flamboyant, too successful for me. And the more successful I am, the more enemy are going around me."

Successful people, Prince said, always have people around them, bored, grasping, flattering, demanding people. "My people are so greedy," he said. Now he laughs softly, saying:

"So, that's now about all the chieftaincy title. And I was lucky to reject *a lot*—some very very important ones from different towns, which I'm not related, which I don't have anything to do with them, but because they see what I have done as a Yoruba person.

"Every Yoruba man is very proud of his clan. They very proud—some people, some intellectual people, like you, professors, lecturers in the university who value what I am doing, they are very very proud of my achievement. But the local people who doesn't know the meaning of art, who doesn't believe somebody who walk in the street, who danced in the street a couple of years ago, who dress crazy-wise, wearing dreadlocks, can become somebody."

"You proved them wrong," I say. He replies with no enthusiasm:

"I proved them wrong. And I paid a *big* price for it.

"That's what resulted into what happened to me before I come here."

The titles, that is, were a cause of the causes, bringing on the troubles that drove him into exile. By wearing the red crown, he stumbled into difficulty, but wearing a beaded crown of any color—blue for Ibadan, white for Ogidi, once he had designed a new one—he found himself surrounded by enemies, by jealous people who felt that a throwaway boy from the bush, a dancer from a traveling medicine show, a crazy pagan artist who got rich in some mysterious way, had risen up too high in life and needed to be beaten back down.

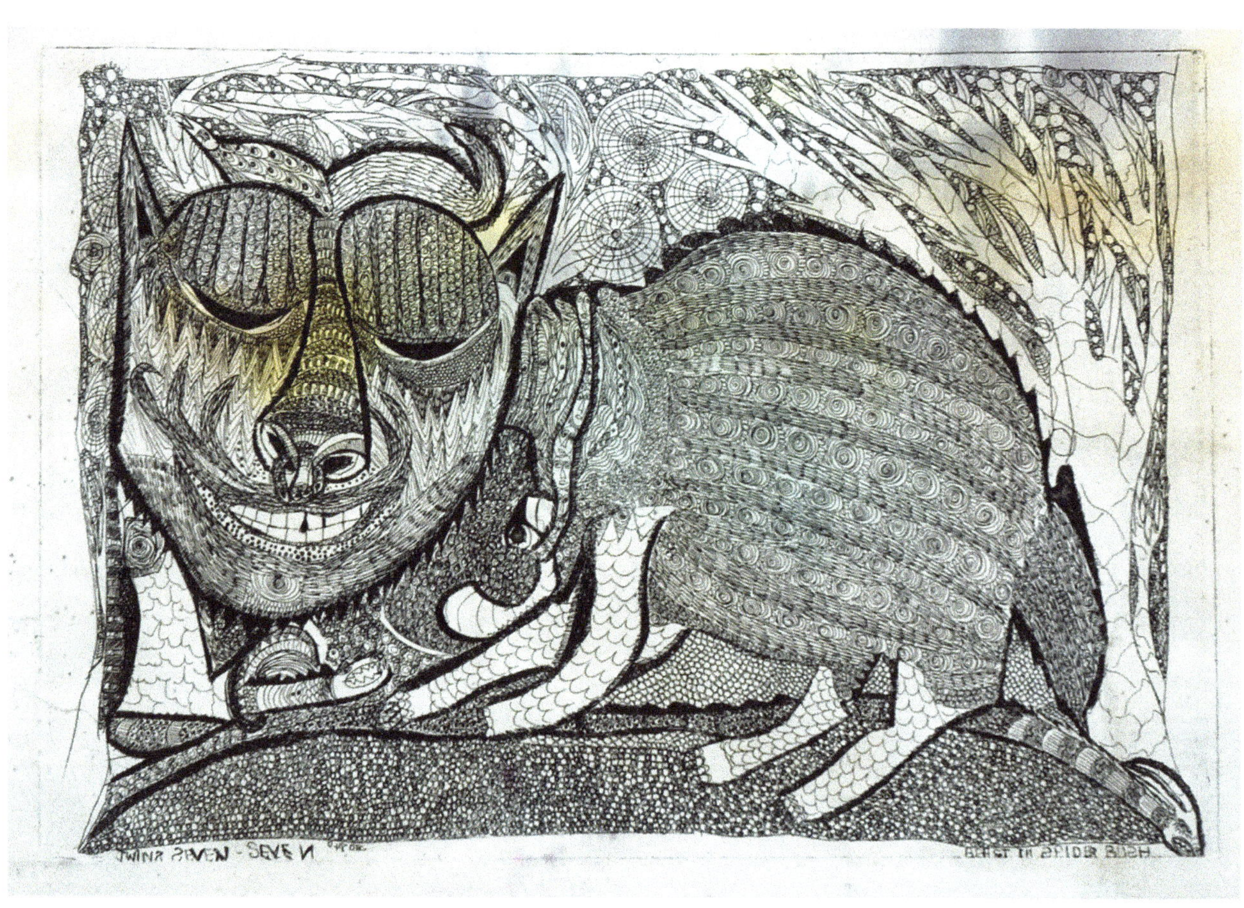

Smiling Beast in Spider Bush.
Etching. 17½"x12". Sydney, 1984.
This print was stained by color runs when Prince's luggage was left out in the rain at the airport in London in 2006. A clean impression can be found in Ulli Beier's *A Dreaming Life,* plate 15

· 13 ·

Reasons to Leave

Two pictures by Prince shape a visual preface for this chapter, the last before America. When I saw them first, I took both to be indirect self-portraits, one alone, one in company, but it is my discipline to check my thoughts with the author, turning interpretation collaborative and pushing it from speculation toward understanding.

When we were going through a pile of papers in his house in Osogbo, hunting for old photographs, we found an etching entitled *Smiling Beast in Spider Bush.* More than a year later, when we sat down to discuss his works, Prince said that there is a Spider's Bush in Amos Tutuola's *My Life in the Bush of Ghosts*, but this image was not drawn from the novel. It shows a beast, snakes slithering around him, spider webs stretched behind him. The beast hunches into himself, tight in his frame, trapped, but smiling. He reminded me of the Devil's Dog, and I thought of the etching as an autobiographical reference to his first work, an icon of revival, a metaphorical representation of the self. I asked Prince if he thought the beast resembled the Devil's Dog. He replied:

"Yeah. Sort of. It is the same relation in terms of thinking. The only thing about Devil's Dog is it have sixteen legs, and the Devil's Dog was the only one on the sheet; there was no background. There was nothing like snake coming out of the hole. There's nothing like birds."

The beast seems threatened by snakes, tangled in webs, and yet he seems content, delighted by some inner thought, serene and happy. I told that to Prince and he said the beast was safe:

"The snake is not coming to attack. Because in the Spider's Bush there is so many things in the bush. You go in, and you see one here, a *long* one here; you see, with the horn? It's a snake. And this one is going outside."

The horned snake slides along the bottom of the picture, exiting to the right. Another enters from the left. Prince turns to the web:

"He is not tangled in the web. Because when he shakes his body, the spider web will leave him alone."

Summarizing, I said that, though beset by troubles, the beast keeps smiling. Prince agreed: "Smiling, in trouble."

I asked when he made the picture. "This is one of my early works, in my time of Ulli Beier, when I do the etching," Prince said, and he guessed it was from the nineteen-sixties. Then I pointed out that it was dated 1984, two years after his wreck, and I said it looked to me like a symbolic self-portrait, a depiction of victory, showing him healthy and happy, despite the disaster of the past, the problems of the present. I asked what he thought. Positive or negative responses to an ethnographer's questions prove nothing, but when questions prompt expansion, a route to interpretation has opened, and Prince expanded: he picked up my idea and carried it forward, identifying with the smiling beast:

"Even though that happened to me, I'm safe, smiling.

"You're right in your explanation. You're right. Because it is just after my car accident. And it is just a couple of months after I started working again. Because I had the accident in eighty-two. And I was doing bed riding for eighteen months.

"Which means—just exactly." Prince speaks with the sudden excitement of a discovery: "It was just about the first thing that happened to me after the accident. I was invited to Australia, with crutches. So, I made this there, one of my first works after the accident."

"Despite all your troubles, you made it," I say, and his excitement continues:

"You're right. You're right.

"You're right.

"He's smiling."

The bush beast smiles. Troubles surround him, but the man endures, prevails, lit from within and grinning.

Smiling Beast in Spider Bush, etched in the wake of his wreck, is a portrait of the artist in solitude, drawn into himself and happy amid danger. Prince turned to his life's other side, portraying the artist in society in two distinct versions of a single image titled *The Spirits of My Reincarnation Brothers and Sisters.* He had used a similar title before, for a painting on cloth made at the end of the nineteen-sixties and picturing an assembly of spirits. The new pictures, brightly painted with batik dyes on large pieces of cloth in Philadelphia during the winter of 2006–2007, exhibit a symmetrical arrangement of figures in columns. The figures to the sides sway and twist, like those in the old painting. The central figure, absent from the earlier work, stands stolid and straight, a shaft on the midline, capped with a sad, aging face. That central figure, the axis of the whole, plays a stringed instrument. It is clearly Prince, and he says:

"That's myself there. I'm in the middle with my traditional guitar, like. It's called goje—the Hausa kind of instrument. It's sometimes made out of a calabash, and you can use this part of it"—the resonant calabash—"to drink palm wine; that's why there's palm wine in the calabash.

"But this was a calabash with strings; strings from the horsetail are used."

The figure squatting below him to support the *goje* licks palm wine from the calabash, consuming the yield of his effort while Prince plays on. "You look sad," I say.

"Yes, I'm sad. Because of what life is around me *here*"—in Philadelphia. "But in the end I'm glad I can make myself look like a mask *there*."

Beneath the mask-like face, his beard, the beard of an elder, shapes into a mask that fails to conceal his sadness. Some of the figures who flank him are smiling. All have the stretched necks and multiplex eyes—eyes capable of seeing at once into this world and the other—that, in his work, indicate supernatural beings. These are the title's spiritual reincarnations of his brothers and sisters. He says:

"All the people around me are ghosts and spirits. And they are happy. Because I'm not happy, they get happy. Because even when I'm not happy, the money I get I send it to them.

"So. After my unhappiness, they are happy."

To render the people around him as ghosts and spirits, distinguished by his "trademark" eyes, is to remove them from the visible world and provoke a symbolic interpretation. The figures turned frontally to the viewer, like a band on a stage, make up a musical ensemble, recalling his old band, the first group of people who depended on him. He stands in the middle, the leader, playing the melody. The others follow, most of them drumming, one with a horn, all of them dependent. But drawn as spirits, not men, the members of his band can stand for everyone who makes demands on him: the women of his household, the "brothers and sisters" in the towns where he is a chief. In the painting, only his eyes are not the eyes of a spirit. They are the sad eyes of a human being, but Prince has given himself a "spiritual breast" to feed those who crowd around him. They are:

"All the people who are demanding from me." Prince points at the figure who licks wine from his calabash, saying, "And this one is wearing a clock, calculating the hours of the day when they would call me to ask for money."

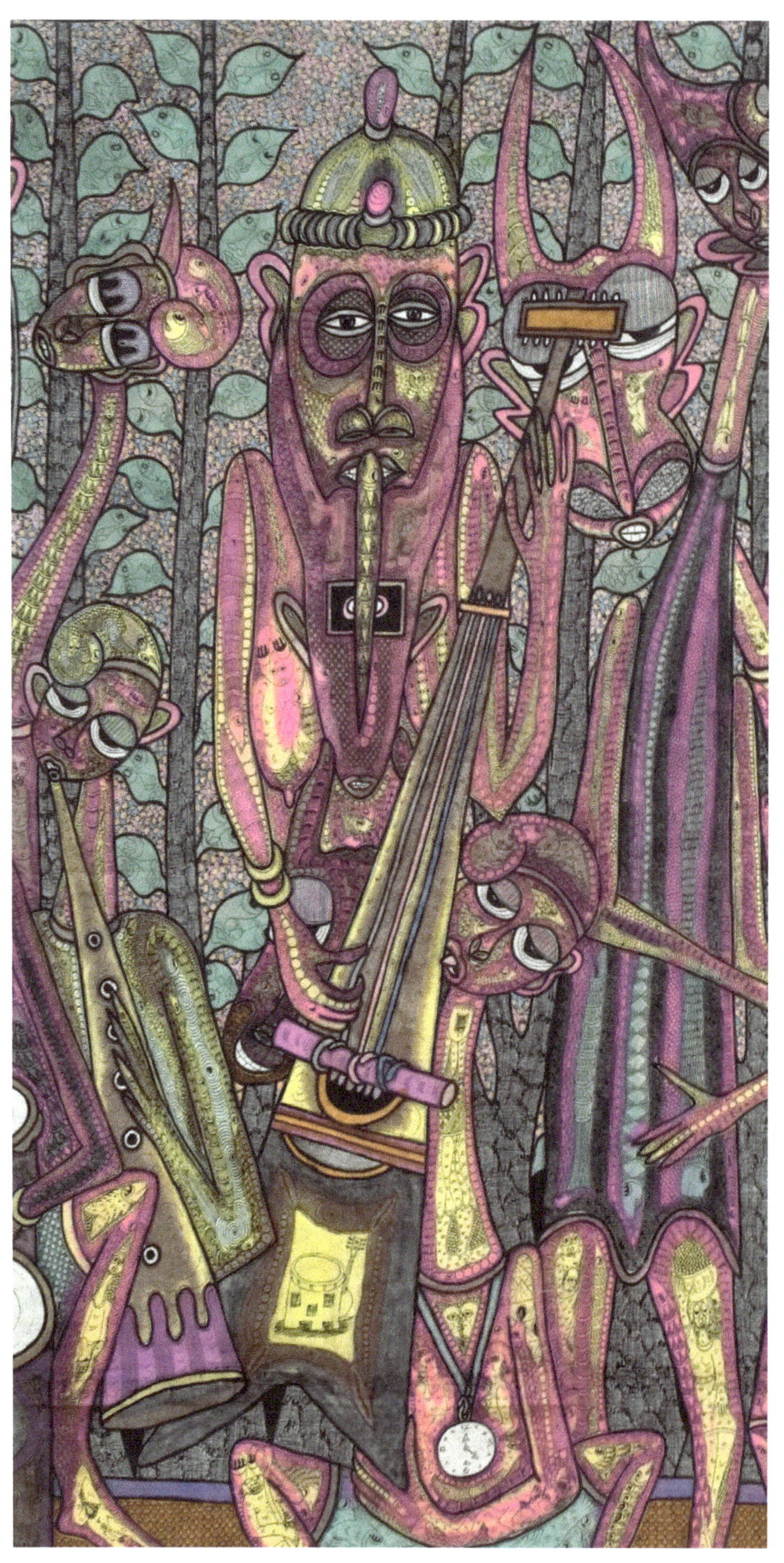

Prince's self-portrait.
My Reincarnation Brothers and Sisters, 2006–2007. Chapter 20, no. 29

There is no escape, nothing to be done. Prince is, like all of us, free and not. He works alone in his studio in Philadelphia, singing and painting the pictures he wants to paint, taking his time. He worked three weeks of long days to create each version of *The Spirits of My Reincarnation Brothers and Sisters*, earning five thousand dollars and half of any profit from future resale. His work brings him money. His money brings him the constant interruption of phone calls from Nigeria. Back home it is worse. He is greeted with requests. His wives need clothes, his children need school supplies, his house needs repairs, his friends want loans that will never be repaid.

Two pictures. One reveals the personality of a man who holds to his course and smiles through travail. The other reveals his social situation: he is crushed among others who happily make him sad. Inner directions and external pressures interlock, shaping the dialectic of his life.

As Prince tells it, his character has maintained itself consistently, continuously over time. He has always been creative, making music and sand castles then, making music and paintings now. He hears voices, meditates, and follows his own head. A wayfarer on the long lonesome road, he goes his way, smiling and touched with melancholy. Yet, from the beginning he has attracted others, seeking their approval, and the great change in his life has developed in time as he has become enmeshed in widening social networks, pleased by expanding fame, pained by expanding demands.

When he was a little boy, pounding out rhythms on used cigarette tins, he gathered followers as he did later when he danced on the road. Boys carried his gramophone and wound it so he could excite the crowd, adding new lads to his entourage. He felt obliged to them, the ones who were loyal to him, buying them meals and pleading with Ulli Beier to give Nine-Nine a job too.

When Prince formed his band, now a leader by name, he became responsible for the lives of his boys, getting them gigs and pay, bringing troubles into his house when he tried to snag a chick for his lonely bass player, his pal from childhood. All these followers, the boys in the band and the band's fans, proved a burden. They slept in his house, touched him for loans, and some of them pressured him to use the connections he had made through his art to foreign embassies in Nigeria. To get them visas he had to swear they were artists, though few of them were. Some of them traveled and rose to wealth, others drove cabs; some returned, many did not, and the work he did for his followers made it hard, in the end, for Prince to get visas for himself. He paid a price for loyalty.

The visa problem was the example Sunday Ayantoye used to explain Prince's personality one night in Ibadan. Prince, he said, is "innocent," never intentionally bad, never thinking ill of others, incapable of recognizing the badness in the people swirling around him. He is "honest," too honest. He tells everything, and holding nothing back, he gives out too much information, becoming susceptible to subtle manipulation by evil people. He is "generous," far too generous with his money and power. "Twins," Sunday said, "has an open mind, and he helps everybody, even bad people." Once he secured a visa for a man who turned out to be a dope dealer, and afterward he was not sly enough to deny that he knew the man well. Such acts, Sunday said, "spoiled his name." Innocence, honesty, generosity—all are virtues, as loyalty is, and all are sources of his distress. Prince is always anxious to help other people, but by helping them, Sunday said, he brings troubles on his head.

The men Prince classes as followers, he addresses, and refers to, as brothers. They make up a family of sorts for a man who was a lonely child, and Prince's web of responsibility, spun first among his followers, widened and tightened when he married his band's dancers. Then he was not only responsible to his wives and their children, and eventually to his grandchildren, but also to a broad sweep of in-laws. The parents and brothers of his wives, the wives and children and cousins of those brothers, all felt free to make demands on his powers, his funds and social connections. Polygamy in Yorubaland, like *compadrazgo* in modern Mexico or fosterage in medieval Ireland, links families to families, sending out tendrils of association that bind people together, yielding general social cohesion. Prince's family ramified through society, knotting him into a vast network of need.

That stretching of social connections, the consequence of polygamy, continued, stretching still more with the political positions that gave him a constituency in Osogbo, with the chieftaincies in Ogidi and Ibadan that dropped him into whole communities of people he calls brothers and sisters, who call him Baba: the women of Ogidi greet him, singing in unison and repetition, "We have a father." Yoruba political orders shape along familial lines, and as a chief Prince plays a paternal role in families that extend into unknowable complexity. Ibadan, where his title charges him with social development, is, it seems (precise numbers are hard to come by), the third-largest of Nigeria's cities, after Lagos and Kano, with a population of, maybe, eight million.

Caught at the center of embedded, expanding social circles, Prince gets and gives. A father, he should get respect, and he does: people listen when he speaks. A man of power, he must give. The people around him make demands on him, and he freely makes demands on them. Such exchanges of imposition serve to tie society together. The demands he makes are followed by gifts, generally gifts of cash that outweigh the demand, keeping people indebted to him, social relations intact. The demands he gets should be tempered by reason, framed by respect. But, he feels, they rarely are. They are, instead, built out of greed and self-interest.

When Prince was a young man, Colin Turnbull, the author of an artful ethnography on the people of the Ituri Forest, wrote a book more general in scope, *The Lonely African*, to account for the abundance in modernizing African society of amoral self-interest. Turnbull describes several lives, offering texts that hew too smoothly to the line of his argument to be trustworthy, but his argument makes anthropological sense. No longer dedicated adherents of the old native faith, not fully integrated into the new religion of the missionaries, people fall into a spiritual void and come to embrace a self-interested materialism. By Turnbull's lights, it is in Africa as it was in Europe after the Reformation, when religion fragmented and capitalism sprouted through the cracks and spread, snarling society in greed.

Turnbull's characterization aligns with Prince's. The demands made by the people around him—the ghosts and spirits of his musical painting—are not part of society's reciprocal functioning. They are greedy and selfish. Prince, though, explains it differently. Greed and self-interest are normal, eternal human traits, usually held in check, but released by his presence. In his mind, Prince is an opportunity for others, a resource to exploit. His mere presence generates demands. Demands are a burden. But his presence also generates jealousy. Jealousy is another normal human trait, which Prince frankly ascribes to himself, but jealousy, when allied with witchcraft, is more than burdensome. It is destructive. Jealousies in his household and jealousies among his political rivals are the forces he attempts to counter through the advice of his readers and the sacrifices they prescribe. It is jealousy, the seam of evil snaking through social relations, that Prince, entangled in his sticky web, must struggle against.

His many children, Prince believes, are the major cause of the jealousy that boils in other people. But there are others. Artists are jealous of his success, his exhibitions and cash. Many are jealous of his honors and fame, his chieftaincies and the writings published about him. When he spoke of his political activities, his wives and titles, jealousies figured in his failures, and he ended with his reasons to leave, but when he faced jealousy directly, his words rolled stories of his envious enemies toward his most emphatic conclusion.

Jealousy is perpetual, the consequence of social success—a perduring source of hostility in others, distress in him—but, characteristically, Prince chose to reveal its impact through self-expressive personal narratives of specific events. The first took place in the early nineteen-seventies when he was invited to teach in America and jealous artists, colleagues of his, tried to ruin him:

"Some group of Osogbo artists petitioned the police that I am too flamboyant. I must be doing drugs, not the cocaine, but what was popular then was grass, marijuana.

"They said anytime I travel, I must be hiding marijuana in my paintings."

Prince laughs, shaking his head.

"So I was arrested at the airport. They don't let me fly.

"They took me back to Osogbo the second day.

"Okay. I'm a smoker, but I don't sell.

"So, when they would get to my house, they would find it everywhere.

"But before that time there was a magistrate who lived next to me, a woman. She loved me. She loved my wife. She was so happy because she grew up in London, and she loved the way I encouraged my wife to do batik. And the tourists come to buy from her. To her, no Nigerian man would do that.

"So, the woman loved me for that.

"She always come and sit by my wife when they do the batiks.

"So, the police cannot search your house without a search warrant, signed by the magistrate.

"They went to see her in court.

"Then the magistrate send her driver to my house. To warn my wife that they should clean everywhere in the house, so they would not find anything.

"During the civil war, there were people by accident or plan made it look like they have mental trouble, and they let them go. And maybe they would foment trouble in some places. But they don't touch them because they believe they have papers that show they are ex-soldiers, fighting the war, and they are wounded. And the police cannot arrest them.

"So, thirty of them drew up and stand in front of my house, because when I play music, people smoke free in my compound.

"So, they love me for that, these ex-soldiers or war veterans.

"So, they came and stand by. I don't invite them. I don't know how they came. I don't know who told them.

"The police who came from Lagos were four. Fully armed.

"And they told the police, If you find anything, or if you ever try to do anything with Twins, we are going to kill you and kill ourselves.

"So, anyway, thank God, the police didn't find anything. They went away. Then I gave money to these ex-soldier people. Then I flew into Haystack.

"So, there are so many instances.

"But to let you know: people are trying to destroy me. For no reason."

Prince's prominent position in society is good and bad. It is bad because people get jealous and try to destroy him. It is good because, as a result of his powers and deeds, there are people who are loyal to him, who "love" him in the Elizabethan sense of the word, and come to his aid in times of trouble. The magistrate, his neighbor, loved him and so she signed the search warrant, but only after warning his wife to clear the house of illegal substances. The vets who loved him for his hospitality rallied to protect his house, and Prince rewarded them with money.

The second event, which he narrated as a pair with the first, was structured comparably. The time is fifteen years later, a few years after his wreck. Some vandals had stoned a cocoa factory. One of his estranged wives conspired with the king of the town, who was jealous of Prince's fame, to place the blame on him, since it was rumored that the leader of the vandals was a man with a limp, and Prince was then a man with a limp. He was arrested and forced to walk in a police line-up for identification. Had he been convicted, he would have been executed. But the trickery of his enemies was dashed by help from his friends. His enemies did not know that the man they bribed to name him as the culprit, an ex-soldier who worked as a security guard, was, in fact, an uncle of his from Ibadan. Another friend was the policeman who advised him to remove the distinguishing ornaments of his flamboyant persona, so he would be harder to recognize:

"So, the police came to arrest me. That was the first time that I was so close to death. I was put on, what you call, identification parade.

"So, on the day of my being taken to the police for identification parade, the police officer, who was supposed to interview me, told me, Remove all these rings and those things you put on your head.

"He said, Remove it. I didn't know he was doing me a favor. I dress artistic. I have earrings, bangles, everything.

"I removed them, and when I removed them, I looked different.

"I had my hair braided. He said remove my hair. I remove my hair. It is cut.

"It was three years after I have the accident. I was limping.

"They said that the guy who led the vandalizers was a limping man. How would a limping man lead some group of crooks to attack a house, and the police cannot find them? If they cannot catch those who run, what about the guy who cannot run, who have one leg?"

Prince stops. It is quiet, a rare moment in the onrush of our interviews. He turns to me, a tear in his eye, and addresses me directly, formally, reaching out to touch me, holding my eyes in his:

"Doctor Henry.

"Do you know that day I know there's God.

"That day, I know there's a God.

"When it was my turn to walk, I have an iron hip. An *iron* hip.

"I was walking *straight.*

"Maybe it's because I don't want to die. Or maybe God don't want me to die.

"The person who led the vandalizers had to be shot.

"You know, when they kill somebody outside for everybody to look. A firing squad. They tie you on the pole, and they shoot you.

"So, I am walking straight. All the police were looking. Some do this. Some do that. The man said, No, not him. Not him.

"The man is an uncle of me.

"Because I was not limping at that time. It's my turn. I don't know how I have the energy to stand up.

"Anyway, that passed.

"They left me off the hook.

"I was released. And the second day I flew to Amsterdam to perform."

Successful people draw others to them; some are friends and admirers. Perhaps the officer who got Prince to remove his rings and cut his hair was a man who appreciated his music. But it seems too much of a coincidence that the man who was paid to pick him out of the parade was his uncle, and since the limp in his gait is extreme, it was nothing short of a miracle that he was able to walk straight for a few critical minutes. Prince thanked God that the police found nothing incriminating in his house in Osogbo, and he took it as a sign of God's existence and God's favor that he could walk with a steady stride. Some people are ranged against him, but others support him, and the powers—the spirits, his sister, the deified dead, and God (Olodumare, Allah)—have determined that his day has not yet come.

Those were not the only times that his enemies intrigued to have him imprisoned, but he was always set free. Prince is not alone on his journey. God directs his destiny, sending friends to help, and, early on, he helped himself by winning the affection of the authorities. Since he honored the established order, his band was often engaged to play for the military and the police. Once, having been released after another arrest:

"I invite the police to see my paintings. From there, the police have a lot of respect for me.

"And then in my early stage, around sixty, seventy, my band used to go and play at military camps.

"They have what you call wassail night. Wassail is like a military weekend something. So my band—that's how I got to know General Obasanjo when he was a junior officer. Nobody know at that time he was going to become head of state.

"So, I used to play, and the police used to hire me to entertain the community.

"So, I was in good book of the police. That is why when some people try to destroy me—I believe there is over a thousand letters written against me to the police, and they don't act on it.

"So, we are moving on, moving on."

Moving on in his life, Prince limped through a world pitching in disequilibrium, eternally unsettled by the seethe of positive and negative forces. Moving on in his story, memories of his arrests provoke a rambling rumination on his troubles. Gliding through some, lingering on others, the tale of his troubles will build to an attack by armed robbers in 1999. It was the last straw; he left. Now he recalls that the people of Osogbo were mystified by his riches:

"Most people don't know what I do to make money; the ordinary people in the street, in the town where I lived. So, there's a lot of jealousy."

Envious, they spread nasty rumors about him, so he started dealing in used cars to provide them an acceptable explanation. But:

"I'm not a good businessman. I'm too generous to be a good businessman. Because many people end up buying from me without paying me.

"And when they come crying, I say, Go."

To say that managing money is not one of his skills would be to put it mildly, God knows. To say that generosity is the cause would not be wholly wrong. He gets money, then he gives it away, willing himself to forget the debts, so he can hold steady on a positive course, juggling the red and white into order, walking straight despite jealousy, sorcery, and disorienting fame.

The harshest thing I ever heard him say about an acquaintance came after a man, a foreigner, arrived by surprise at his home in Osogbo. Prince welcomed him in, gave him food and drink. Once he had gone, Prince told me that years before he had given the man several paintings to sell on consignment. Prince never saw the pictures again, never saw a penny of profit, and he called the man a crook. Crook: he said the word sharply, with vehemence, then he smiled and waved the memory out of his head.

A smile, whether happy or ruefully resigned, is Prince's little victory, celebrated in *Smiling Beast in Spider Bush*. Emotions wash swiftly through him: now laughing, now sad or serious, he continues his litany of complaint, remembering money troubles, then troubles in politics:

"So I started as an artist, but eventually I became a very very powerful politician, because of inroads to a lot of these big people.

"Because of my magic abilities, I was able to become like a king-maker.

"At the same time, I have some people that doesn't like my face. That is life.

"Then, before I left Nigeria, I was doing a lot of very interesting things that has been very helpful to my people.

"I used my influence with the embassies to bring people to different parts of the world. I would go to the embassy, if I have a show, and I would take people along with me. But unfortunately, in long run: no good. They were supposed to go back, but they didn't go back.

"But I'm glad that some of them doesn't go back. Today they are doctors, very successful business people.

"But not all of them remember to compensate me for it.

"But I'm glad that I was able to do something with my reputation.

"Then it came to a point where some other people want to be doing the same thing I am doing. Then they start writing; they go to the embassy and tell the embassy they should not give me visa because the people I have helped are not artists. Whereas, they want to do things like I do themselves.

"So, when I cannot take the heat no more—and on three occasions I was attacked by armed robbers in Nigeria.

"But the armed robbers are not real armed robbers. I think it is like they are preplanned armed robbers.

"There was even an occasion when I have to face two of them. I don't know where the energy come. I hold them to myself and *bang* them and push them back.

"Then. I'm a military person in thinking. Anytime I travel in Nigeria, I always carry arms. Because I have learned to carry arms.

"So, anytime I leave this country, I have a pistol in my clothing, and a pump-action.

"So, my driver—I don't really remember I have all these things on me. I don't *remember.* That show you how terrified you can be if you are overcome by armed robbers.

"So, my driver was saying"—he speaks in a hurried whisper—"Baba. Hey Babo. Hey Babo, have your guns, have your guns.

"So, when he gave the gun to me, there is no bullet in it, because you need to pump the action to put a bullet in it.

"These four of the armed robbers: *Lare, lare lare*—they are speaking the language; they are from the southern part—Lare, lare: Let's go, in Bini language, not Yoruba: Let's go, let's go. The man have a double-barrel, double-barrel.

"And they started running.

"And I stood up, and I cocked the gun and I said:

"My father used to eat human flesh.

"Why don't you wait till I shoot three shots?

"But, after that, my God, my body was shaking. Because they put stone on the road. Our car hit the stone, and the tire got bursted. And when we were putting on the extra tire, I didn't notice that the extra tire in the boot of my big Mercedes is the tire for my one-ninety, so it doesn't work.

"But while we are there, all of a sudden we hear: *Pow.* Pow. Everybody lie down. If you get up, you are dead meat.

"So then. A lot of things like that.

"That is what happened last that made me decide to leave.

"I left the house, thinking I am going away for six months.

"I left Nigeria in November. I arrive here November four in the year of the election."

His sentences have slowed. He pauses in thought, sadness in his eyes. When he said the armed robbery was preplanned, I understood him to mean that his enemies sent the robbers, just as they had reported him to the officials in the embassies, and I say, "The reason you left is because all these people were jealous." Without lifting from his mood, he says to himself, "Jealousy," and then slowly takes up the story again:

"False accusations eventually were clear, because at the end everybody can see.

"Then, in between, I become number four to the king of Ibadan. In nineteen ninety-six, my mother's village, they make me high chief there.

"In between, I am having problems, even though I am having success. It is just A and B.

"Something happens, I becoming bitter; something happens, I becoming sweeter.

"But the last part of it when the armed robbers—first they came to my house. Second time, they throw stones on my car. The third time, I fight them. The first time was nineteen eighty-nine, when I came back from Japan."

The first time, he says, was a "coincidence." The robbers were looking for a banker who had made "money deals with people, and he doesn't pay them their share." But, it turns out, they had been watching him too, taking note of the gold jewelry he wears. Suddenly robbers appear in the courtyard of his house in Osogbo. Prince is standing high above them on the balcony:

"I challenged them. Because my house is three stories. And I said, Who goes there? Who are you?

"They said, We are armed robbers. Don't you know we are armed robbers?

"I had never heard that in my life before.

"And the torch light they put into my eyes. I only talk into the light, because I don't see the person who do the torch light.

"I said, What are you looking for?

"They said, We want money.

"I said, I don't have any money.

"They said, What about all the gold? Because we see you at the airport yesterday.

"And I just came back from Japan.

"Then I started using incantations, spiritual words with English. And I said, What are you going to do with the banana ropes?

"All of a sudden, I'm aware it is an incantation, spiritual words. There's a word you can use that will appease a negative force.

"So then they said to show them the rich people in the neighborhood.

"I said, All the families in this neighborhood, we are all thieves.

"I don't know why I'm saying that. I swear, I don't know how it started coming out of my mouth.

"I said, Everybody in this, my neighborhood, we are all thieves. We steal gold. We steal human beings.

"Then they said, Give us money then.

"Then one of the guy that followed the armed robbers, he said, Let's go. That man, he is a good man. He always gives money to everybody.

"Leave him. Let's go."

The tale's pattern is clear, and clearly self-descriptive. Prince is threatened by others. Now he is threatened by armed robbers, as he had been threatened when jealous artists told the police he had dope in his house and when his enemies contrived to accuse him of leading the vandals. The robbers, like his friends and followers, want his money. But he is an abiku, a man with spiritual powers. Mysterious words spill from his lips, stopping the robbers. Energy comes from some source, enabling him to walk on parade and push the robbers back. The powers help him and he helps himself. He is a generous man who tosses money through the crowd, apparently wasting it, but bringing friends to his side. Out of nowhere, one among the robbers declares Prince to be a good man who gives money to everybody. Without being asked, the vets assemble and stand guard at his house. A policeman he does not know warns him to remove his jewelry. He is generous, and he is brave. He lifts the shotgun and scatters the robbers by saying his father was a cannibal, "which means, I am the son of a warrior who can kill his enemy and eat their flesh." Now he stands firmly in the light and the robbers go. Prince continues:

"Anyway, because of that the police in Osogbo give me a valid license to have a gun. So, that's how I got my first double-barrel. Because I risked my life to save a lot of people. Because even if I told them that there was not anybody in my neighborhood who was rich, they would have robbed, but I said we were like them too.

"So, the police in Nigeria are not like here; anytime they come, they would be asking a lot of unnecessary questions. Indeed, sometimes they arrest people who are innocent and doesn't know anything.

"So, the police were leaving, trying to turn the table against me. But the neighbors say, No, no, no. If we didn't have this gentleman, we would have been in trouble.

"So, from there, the police gave me license, so I was able to buy my first double-barrel.

"So, that was nineteen eighty-nine.

"But the other time I fought, it was nineteen ninety-nine.

"So, the last one sent me out of Nigeria.

"Because they shoot me. At close range.

"But the bullet just came, but it doesn't touch me. And that scared them.

"I was wearing an amulet."

The amulet hangs around his neck; it augments his spiritual power. Prince lifts it out of his undershirt, showing it to me and saying:

"I was wearing this. Once in a year I must kill a ram, and I put it in the mouth of the ram, and the blood soak into it. Very powerful.

"So, thank God I was wearing this. Thank God I got this one. The power. They fired at close range. Close range: *Pow, pow.*

"That scared the armed robber; they had never seen anything like that in their life.

"But the *one* thing that scared me. This, my daughter—they go to her too. She's Dupe. Dupe. She's, like, maybe—she's sixteen now; she was about eleven then.

"And then she was lying down on the floor, and she look up and say, In the name of Jesus. They said, If we *ever hear you say Jesus*—and they threatened to cut her. But they never cut her head.

"I hold them.

"I don't know where the energy come from. I *push them together.* I push them back."

Prince speaks fiercely:

"What do you want?

"Money, money, they said.

"I go to the front of the car. I used to sit in the front. I give them a leather bag containing about fifty thousand naira. Then he wanted my rings.

"That's when I got angry.

"Then my driver said, Baba, Baba. Baboni, Baboni. Then he gave me the gun.

"Then I pump it.

"Then one of them said, Lare, lare, lare—"

Prince pauses.

"It was really too close, too close."

He pauses again.

"That's why I said, Okay. Enough. Enough of Nigeria now.

"That's how I left.

"Because if they go back to their place—they've got to have a place where they meet to discuss the operation—you never know if somebody send them to come back.

"But, it's over."

Prince stops for a thought. His narrative took a spiraling course, a pattern I have found as well among storytellers in America, Ireland, and Turkey. He narrated the core event, spun away from it to entail others, then circled back over the same ground, telling of the event in greater detail, and reaching the same conclusion. It's over, time to go. The pause is brief. He speaks again, reaching out and sweeping together his reasons to leave:

"Sometimes, I don't know. I think there are those who are angry, or those who felt I'm too successful.

"I don't have enemies in other places; it's just the town where I grew up"—Osogbo—"where I started this thing, all these art monuments, and it has become a *big* thing.

"Some of the artists who are part of those who are jealous—because, like, you know, in Africa there are so many things people are jealous about. If you are too rich. Like, at that time I was making good money, and I have properties everywhere. I have good children. I have a lot of children.

"So, those are the things that make people jealous and envy you.

"But you do what you are doing.

"And I never hurt anybody in my life.

"But I thank God I was able to leave home. I don't even know how I left home.

"Then, before I left home, my wives were making trouble against each other. Because then everybody has known President Obasanjo is going to give me position. And I'm eyeing that. I want to be an ambassador. I'm thinking that if he would give me a post as ambassador, I could be outside and do my painting.

"And I'm close to getting it. Then some of my detractors, political detractors, they hide my portfolio. They never give it to the president.

"Maybe I'll still get it. Because he ask me what I want."

He pauses, thinking, then says:

"It was a very very interesting period.

"I was fighting three different wars. War of survival. War of achievement. And war of conquering my enemies.

"I was involved in politics. People were trying to destroy me. And I'm escaping the strategies of every plan they plan against me. And I'm doing well.

"I'm doing well."

His enemies send the police; he is arrested, then released. They send armed robbers. Incantations baffle them. His amulet stops their bullet. He stands bravely, and they run. He is doing well, but the last time was too terrifying. They shot at him, threatened to cut his daughter, and they are still at large. Their attack in 1999 was the last act, but it was the last act because of the troubles that preceded it, troubles in politics, troubles at home:

"Between nineteen ninety-eight, nineteen ninety-nine, I was seriously involved in campaigning, touring with the ruling party of Nigeria. I got a letter from the president that I am being commissioned to perform at his inauguration.

"So, I came back to perform in nineteen ninety-nine at Eagle Square. Eagle Square is a big ceremony park. It is a park in remembrance of the people who died in the civil war. So, that's why we have a big stadium and everything. So, I was performing there three days.

"After the performance, then things fall apart.

"I am talking about my decision to come to America.

"Then, things fall apart.

"The cars I'm selling, I could not get them sold anymore.

"All embassies in Nigeria, they won't give me visa because I've got a bad record of people that I've helped to come to London, or go to Germany. They never did come back.

"So then, in my house, the wives believe the young wife, the youngest wife I have—the other wives believe that since the time of this young lady that this bad luck befell the family.

"So, they believe that this young girl that I married, she the one that brought bad vibes to the family. And then the other wives believe that the wife who is here with me now is a witch. And she's the one that block my way of success.

"So, there was *big* palaver in the house.

"I have, all over, about fifty people living in the same compound with me.

"So. Every day when I go out, and came back, there is a *big* fight. A lot of fight.

"Anyway."

Prince's tone is weary, whipped.

"I'm tired of it."

He left for Philadelphia.

· 14 ·

An Immigrant's Tale

Philadelphia was his destination. When I asked Prince to account for his choice, to tell about his association with the city, he said:

"This story go back to how I started having contact with a city called Philadelphia. In nineteen seventy-two, I was invited to America by a French art collector, by name Mister Roderique. He lived then at ten West Sixty-Sixth Street, near Central Park in New York. He came to visit me in Osogbo, and he invited me for an exhibition of my work. And the exhibition took place at Merton Simpson Art Gallery on Madison Avenue in New York.

"So, when I came, then there's a dancer in this city"—Philadelphia—"called Arthur Hall. He's a dancer. And he was at my exhibition, then he invited me over here for the special opening of his theater, called—at that time he called the place Ile-Ife Museum. This at the time when a lot of black Americans were trying to retrace their historical connection to Africa.

"Ile-Ife is a town; it is like about one hour south of Osogbo. So, he named the place Ile-Ife Museum. So, this the time I was first invited to this place, as a special guest for the opening of this Arthur Hall cultural center known as Ile-Ife Museum.

"Then after that I met Lois Fernandez. Lois Fernandez was the founder of Odunde Festival. That is the black American festival that has been taking place"—in Philadelphia—"ever since, in every June of the year. And it does attract a lot of people, both Africans, Americans to Pine Street. It surely have the same thing with the Osun Festival in Osogbo, because I got Lois Fernandez initiated into the Osun-worshiping thing in Osogbo in nineteen seventy-two. She came back and started talking about Osun, and now there is beautiful place, group of people go together for worshiping. They have a center, places for kids to *learn* about Yoruba culture.

"Ever since, I've been invited over and over. And I have seen Philadelphia as my second home. Then by nineteen seventy-five, I was given the key to the city of Philadelphia. I was specially invited to perform at the Afro-American Museum then. Then by the year nineteen ninety-two, the Odunde people invited me over again for the Odunde Festival; I did ritual at the riverside, praying. And then I was given another citation about Philadelphia"—by Mayor Edward Rendell—"and that they would declare June twenty-third as my day.

"So, that's how my journey with Philadelphia started. And whenever I come to the U.S., whenever I go, I always end up taking off from Philadelphia.

"I think I am at home here, but I miss my other home, on the other side. It's very interesting, a very interesting adventure.

"Since then, since nineteen seventy-two, hardly a month go by, pass by in a year, that I am not in America.

"Not because of any other thing, but because, like, whenever I come here there's a lot of spiritual things I take back with me, spiritual in terms of freedom of expression. Freedom of my work. And back home, too, it's a *big* prestige when they heard you went for exhibition in America. That you have been accepted in America is, like, Oh, look at the things we don't care for here, but it is a big thing now in America. It is very very important.

"Very very important. *Both* spiritually, artistically, economically."

Prince tapped with his pen at each of those words—spiritually, artistically, economically—and laughed at the end. Philadelphia had been the scene of success in the past; it could be the scene of success in the future. It was the logical choice.

Philadelphia was his destination. Now Prince begins an immigrant's tale. At the end of the nineties, an honored chief, he entered a productive phase in his art, but troubles in his unquiet house drove him out, drove him to drink. It was time to leave, to get out, to go, if only he could get a visa. He tells it:

"Every day I would travel to Lagos. I would stay in the casino, looking, or go to the club. Then I started drinking. I started drinking because the drinking would make me forget all these horrible events around me.

"Anyway, one day this, my wife who lives here with me, came back and told me she went somewhere to pray. And they told her I should forget about anything medicine: no juju, voodoo, or whatever. I should not touch it.

"Instead: go to the Celestial Church. Celestial Church is the denomination of another kind of Christian movement in Nigeria. You have the Seventh Day Adventists. You have the Anglicans. You have the Roman Catholics. And then you have those that when they pray, they shake their body. They can tell you what you did thirty years ago. They hear voices, and they say things about the time that is about to come to pass."

Rooted in Nigeria, these Christians rival the diviners, knowing, like them, what has happened, what will happen. Prince continues:

"And anyway, this is the kind of church my wife said I should go: get to the door, bow three times, and I will get my visa.

"And it was one whole year that I could not travel out of Nigeria. A whole year. From May, nineteen ninety-nine, when I came back to perform for the new government, till two thousand.

"So. October of two thousand, I went to American embassy, and they gave me a two-year visa. It was the time that President Clinton came for the inauguration. And he asked some people—because we have a big show coming up at the Smithsonian, and my band is supposed to be there to perform, and I have a program at Indiana. But I couldn't come because of the visa problem.

"So anyway, the gentleman who was with Clinton saw me at the luncheon for the president. He asked him, Why is he here? He's supposed to be in Washington, D.C. I don't know what he said, but he made sure I got the paper.

"So, the same week I got my two-year American visa, I got two-year German visa; Australia: two year. Which means: I went to that church, and I bowed three times, and it miraculously worked."

Spiritual and temporal powers run together in Prince's life: prayer and the president got him a visa. He goes on:

"So, my intention is to come to Germany. Because my son is living in Dusseldorf. So, because of the tension of my waiting for a whole year—because all my life, hardly I stay in Nigeria more than three, two months; I always have visa application to one country or the other; or I go on my own.

"So anyway, when I came to Germany, I stayed with my son thirteen days in Dusseldorf. And early November I left Dusseldorf to come here. I land here on the fourth of November, two thousand, and that was the election day.

"And when I arrive here, I don't have any money, but I stay at an apartment with two Nigerian boys that I helped to come here, who paid the rent. So I stay there.

"But while I was in political, financial, spiritual problems in Nigeria, I have a property in the capital, in Abuja. It's a house I built through selling my paintings to these Germans in Nigeria.

"So, I gave this house to a gentleman to sell for money for me. So this, my wife, called me to let me know that there was some money for me, and it was about fifty thousand dollars.

"So I said, That's okay. Go and get the money and go to the black market, and change the money on the black market. But she could not get that big an amount of money on the black market. She had to go to the bank, and the bank, they pay her less than what you would get on the black market.

"Anyway, she changed about forty thousand dollars.

"Then, inside me, I said, I'm not stupid. What if this woman get to Amsterdam, and make another trip, and lie to me that I lost the money or somebody attack her? I said, Please don't come alone. Take your son, take your two children, take another child from the other wives, so the four of you come and join me.

"So, when she was coming, she bring her son, and bring the other girls, three of them. They arrived.

"And when they arrived, I talked with a friend of mine—he's back in Nigeria now—who has been living in Philadelphia for a *long* time. He's like my second brother. He look like me; he has the same tribal marks. But we are not from the same family; he is from the northeast of the country.

"So, he introduced me to this gentleman who is in the real estate business."

With that sentence, Prince's tale turns sour. Like most immigrants, he relied on people who had come before, who knew the strange ways of the new world. He stayed in the house of Nigerian friends until a Nigerian brother introduced him to another Nigerian who bought old houses, repaired and sold them. Knowing nothing about the American mortgaging system, tricky and usurious when legal, Prince trusted the realtor (who was his fellow countryman), innocently unsuspicious when he made an extravagant downpayment and agreed to clear his debt in a year:

"But the happiness that I am going to have a house in America. I was so carried away. All the papers they give to me to initial, I would just put my initial without reading it, without finding out what it means.

"But what left me that up to today I have a house in America is that the manager of the company love art. So, he took one of my canvas, a large canvas painting, which I told him the price is fifty thousand. That if I could not pay within a year, they would take that painting to offset my loan.

"That was my understanding about everything. That's what helped me that I'm still here. Otherwise by now I would be in the street or go back to Africa—lose all that money."

In time, he would lose it all. First, Prince bought a small house as an "investment property." He rented it to young Nigerian men to provide a steady income, though their payments proved erratic. A week later he bought a house for himself. I drove with him to see it, a trim brick bungalow, set back in a spacious, shady yard. We parked at the curb, and Prince told me it was perfect. It had a back porch he planned to convert into a gallery and plenty of room for his boys, Victor and Timi, to play. But the money he paid to the realtor, his countryman, was never transferred to the bank, and just before the sheriff came to evict him, he packed his belongings into a truck, banished his tenants, and moved into the house he had rented for profit.

That was where he lived at the time of our interviews, a slim rowhouse of two stories, the usual Philadelphia type. You step over the threshold into the front room. The stairs ascend on the left. The couch on the right stands across from a new television sitting on an old television. Prince tunes the one that works to CNN, daily reminded that "the world is all killing." A metal disc by the front door carries a picture of Mecca and a prayer in the Arabic script. A cross hangs over the space at the back, partitioned into a narrow kitchen and a dining room where Prince's chiefly crowns rest on shelves in curatorial array. No works of his are on display. The pictures on the wall are framed photographs, one showing Prince with President Obasanjo, others showing him in Paris when he was named the UNESCO Artist for Peace. One is a portrait of Shola, the beautiful wife who lived there with him, with two of his sons and three of his daughters. Shola danced and sang with his band in Nigeria. In Philadelphia, she was the lead singer in a church choir, who made her living by braiding hair in an African style.

Things will fall apart, but for the moment the housing problem had been solved. The money problem remained:

"So, by the time I was in process of saving myself, I went for bankruptcy. Because I was, like, about two, three years doing nothing. I don't even paint. And what caused that is: one day I and my wife, in March, two thousand and one, we went to casino. My wife won twenty-five thousand dollars."

Prince laughs, a sad, amazed laugh:

"From slot machine, five-dollar slot machine. So that—I don't want to do anything, just go to casino and win my own twenty-five thousand. And we lost it all."

Prince laughs again. It was silly to think gambling was the answer. Casinos reduce the American economy to its essence: they take the consumer's money, and then, without the distraction of a shoddy product, they keep it. And yet, money seems to flow freely in America, and the glittery casinos at the Jersey shore still call him. Later in our conversation, after running through his failed attempts at employment, Prince stopped to say:

"I still believe I can make my money back from casino. The only thing that helped me is the fact that whenever I go to Atlantic City, and I look at the lights and see a lot of people listening to music, most of the time I don't gamble anymore, but I still go. It is exciting and I met different people, and there was a day I see somebody, and then I know you have ghosts in here too.

"Because at midnight in Caesar, this guy I don't know at all. And he have two tiny eyes like owl, owl eyes. And everybody, not only me, was looking surprised. The minute I saw him, everybody around me shaked. I was so worried, and my wife, too, saw him. So, he have the black hair, and all his face is like the back of a toad. Unbelievable.

"But since, I haven't seen that person again. Very tall, very very tall. And everybody was moving away from his way."

The eyes, the bright little owl eyes, revealed him for a ghost, just as the weird eyes with slit lids mark the ghosts in Prince's paintings. America is not so strange. It has ghosts. There are no readers who can intervene in time and call the gods to the aid of people in quest of wealth, but there are lawyers who can mysteriously intervene in the legal system and bring a client wealth without labor. Prince knew of a taxi company, run by immigrants like himself, that enlisted lawyers in its cause. Its drivers cruised the streets, not looking for fares, but for luxurious automobiles. Then passing in front of some Mercedes or Cadillac, the driver would step on the brakes, brace to bounce with the crash, and wait moaning for the ambulance that would carry him to the hospital. The next step was the courtroom where a suit yielded cash. Thus the company prospered.

Prince was learning about America. Once, when crossing the polished floor of a bank, he slipped on a slick of snow, and lying there, flat on his back, he felt a thrill of joy. The bank was jammed, crammed, mounded with money; some of it would be his. While he did not pursue that excellent opportunity, another time his car was hit in traffic and he hired a lawyer. Pleading that the collision had disrupted his artistic imagination and his sexual vigor, Prince thought he had a case. The lawyer took his money, assured him on the phone that his suit was going forward, took his money again . . . nothing happened, but another case paid off:

"I was working with Parkway—you know, where you park the cars. I was like the attendant. When the car goes out, they pay money and all that.

"So, one evening, a Nigerian, an Igbo guy who happens to know about me from the sixties, who told me he was nearly becoming an artist because of my career, because of reading about me—he is a big accountant with a company—while he was talking to me, I was supposed to do my timing. That was the first time ever I was fired because I didn't do my timing."

Prince was supposed to punch the clock on his arrival, but, lost in chat about home, he forgot:

"So, when I put the time in—I got to work at seven; I worked from seven P.M. to seven A.M. in the morning. So, I do this, after I was talking to the guy for one hour, so I took my pen to write seven P.M., to put the time. Then the Afghanistan guy, who liked me very much, fired me because of that. Not because of that, but because he want people from his own country to replace me.

"Thank God before that time there was a day in the storm time, in the snow. The thing that go up"—the arm of the gate—"doesn't go up, so I go to use my hands to make it go up, and I went to go back to my kiosk. The wind blew me with a big gust. I fell down and broke my arm. And it was swelling. And this Afghanistan man took me to the hospital on Broad Street for treatment. They were about to do surgery on my hand the day I went to the bankruptcy court.

"So, I went to the compensation court to sue them. I told them I am a painter. I could not paint. So, I was able to get eight thousand, something.

"And I got that money after I started working for George."

Prince laughs. This is America. The citizens go by the clock. The immigrants try to figure it out. Prince understood why a man who liked him would fire him to hire one of his own countrymen, and his boss understood why an employee, a fellow immigrant in need of cash, would sue his company for falling in the snow. That is the system: a loop of law and insurance. It gives—in this case, eight thousand dollars—and it takes:

"I was keeping going, keeping going, keeping going. Some days: food. Some days: no food. Some days—then I have problem with police. Traffic lights. Because I think too much. When it's a red light, because of my worry in my mind, I would be seeing green light. And when I move: *boom*.

"Then, there's one day I was driving out during winter; I want to move the snow in my house. As I pushed back, some old man was coming. He hit my car"—Prince claps. "Then the second day he brought letter to the house. And my wife put the letter from him, not knowing he was going to make case with me. Then he went to look for a mechanic who told him the scar is going to cost about thirty-eight hundred to repair. A little scratch.

"Because I'm black; I'm living in the *white*, deep white American neighborhood. Because I'm black, and because this guy has been in the military before. He felt he had to suffer a lot to save the war, so he had to put it on *me*. Because that's what he told me.

"So anyway, he took me to court. And we went to court, and the court asked me to pay, but the damages is not as much as he wanted to collect from me. And at that time I don't have insurance.

"So, they told me I must be paying two hundred every month. But I only pay two times. Two times: four hundred. I couldn't pay the rest. Because I was supposed to pay one thousand, six.

"So, a letter came: my driver license was suspended because I couldn't pay him.

"While we were on that, then the bank found me to eject me from the house."

Trouble upon trouble. In this place, it is hard when you are black, and when you are also down and deep in debt, it is nearly impossible. Prince was not going to survive by gambling and lawsuits. He had received letters, telling him he could be the winner of big sums of money. He replied, sending many checks away, but, never a winner, he realized that letters addressed to T. Sevenseven and sent from Singapore were part of a scam. Prince lost much money that way, but he learned there was no easy road to wealth. He would have to enter the workforce of immigrants, willing to labor for low wages, sacrificing themselves for their families—the power at the base of the top-heavy American economy. He needed a job, and the loss of his driver's license was a hard blow, for Prince has told us that when he was young he wanted to be a driver, and all the jobs he found in Philadelphia required him to drive. The first was as a guard for the vast parking lot that, among other businesses, served Material Culture:

"So, anyway, by and by, I was working here as a security guard. And I never know George is there. And I never knew Material Culture has something to do with selling or whatever. So, what I do is sit, sit in my van, both in winter and in spring, see cars that go in and go out. They pay me six-fifty dollar an hour.

"And one day I was—like I love to meditate. That's the very thing I do every morning is to meditate. Talk to my ancestors, talk to myself, to guide me, to give me wisdom to do the right thing."

Prince was parked at the top of the slope at the northern edge of the lot:

"So, I was meditating. Because this hill become *higher* when I was meditating. It's like I'm on top of a higher mountain. And I closed my eyes, not knowing my manager is around. And they said I am sleeping.

"So, he fire me.

Prince laughs it off. Next he got a job with the social services administration, driving "foster home kids" to visit their parents. Then, needing "a source of income to sustain my bankruptcy," he got a job delivering auto parts. It, too, did not last. Prince, thinking back, tries to remain upbeat: by driving, he got to know the city. But his life had lost direction:

"That enabled me to do much area. I would travel a lot to so many places in this area. But my art doesn't come back to me. I never think about my art. I don't even remember whom I am. I don't even know people like you is somewhere that I can call for help."

It was a grim time, and Prince, jobless, uninsured, unlicensed, bankrupt, and evicted from his first house, was nearing despair. His tale, though, has reached bottom. Things, having changed, will change again:

"Then, all of a sudden, somebody call me from the Philadelphia Museum, that they are surprised that I am here. They visit me; they came to see some of the paper work that I did. Then they pick some and bought it for the Philadelphia Museum, for their shop, like a gift shop, where they sell little-little things. So, they bought—and, thank God, everything they bought was sold.

"So then, the guy there whom I remember to thank God for making him come into my life, Mister John Zarobell; he was a student of art. Now he is head of the department of European painting at the Museum. He happened to study my work; he happened to be following my career. So, he's the one that recommended my meeting George."

John Zarobell, now Assistant Curator of Painting and Sculpture at the San Francisco Museum of Modern Art, was then an Associate Curator of European Painting and Sculpture at the Philadelphia Museum of Art, but he had a strong interest in African art and he was assembling an exhibition called "African Art, African Voices," which included an old picture by Prince. As he explained in a letter to me, John first heard about Prince Twins Seven-Seven in a course on African art taught by Rowland Abiodun at Amherst College, and first saw his work at the Studio Museum in Harlem in 1990. Oliver Franklin, a member of the Community Committee for the exhibition, told him Prince was in Philadelphia, Tony Fisher of Indigo Arts gave him Prince's phone number, and Kathleen A. Foster, Senior Curator of American Art, suggested contacting George Jevremović. John writes, "I went to George to solicit a donation to make possible some programming for the African show and I knew Twins was hard up. George turned me down for the donation but he told me to have Twins call, so I gave Twins George's number and the next thing I knew, I was invited to the Material Culture Christmas Party as a guest of Twins."

A crucial link in this chain of chance, John Zarobell wrote, "If I have been some help to Twins, I am very grateful to have been." Prince is also grateful, and he continues the story:

"So, he called me and said, There's a gentleman who love art, but he doesn't have anything from Nigeria, but he has been doing a lot of business in *Ghana*. So, he give me his number. So, I'm a very fast person when it comes to business, very very fast. I don't slow down. If I need to contact somebody ten times in a day, I keep calling until I get that person.

"So, I called George. He took just two or three hours to find my house. Because the way I described the place to him, my accent and everything, he couldn't be able to find my house. But he tried, and definitely he got me. And when he got me, he said, Is that what you have? I say, Yes. He said, Bring everything, everything you have, bring them. Even some that I haven't finished, like the one I am working on—he would buy it.

"Then, the painting I selected for him was about twenty-five thousand dollars. And it's not in my nature to go down for anybody—but because of the situation I am at that time, I need money badly. I need money for my lawyer to sustain my bankruptcy. I need money for my kids, so that they will be able to eat. So, he says"—Prince's voice slows and lowers—"I will pay you seven thousand."

Prince turns sad eyes to me:

"Then I started weeping, because I am too emotional person. He said I should stop crying. That he will help me, and if these thing can sell, he will eventually come back to buy.

"So, he give me one thousand from his pocket, and he wrote for me a check of seven thousand. It was like seven million."

Prince softens his tone, drawing the words slowly into the air:

"It was like seven million to me. I couldn't believe it.

"The reason is: when I woke up that morning, I could not even buy bread for the kids. Thank God my kids were very good boys. When they go out to play, they don't steal, they don't remove pocket books.

"Then, my wife: I would carry her from house to house to braid people's hair. But what she is charging one hundred and fifty dollars for now, then if they give her thirty dollars, she would take it. Because she is the one who came to the house, but now she has got her own shop that people have to come.

"Anyway, I got the check. I was able to take care of my lawyer. I was able to pay some money to these bankruptcy thing."

Prince's tale of immigration has come to its climactic instant. George Jevremović has entered his life. "I couldn't believe it," George said, "the day I pulled up there. Broke my heart. I'm serious. It was like I stepped into a tragedy. That's how it felt that day." With the money George gave him Prince fed his children and paid his hungry lawyers. Money matters, but what is most important is that this is the moment when Prince relocated his spirit and recovered his career, becoming an artist in America:

"George lift me back from my down period in life. I look at him as someone who can resurrect me back. Because before I met him, I don't think about my painting anymore. I was just like this—"

Prince hunches and slumps, a dead look on his face.

"Like some kind of force is blocking my vision. I don't think about anything. I don't think of good work. I don't think I will go back. I was just living.

"Like if you put somebody in a sack and tie the rope. And he's in darkness. Though he's still breathing. That's the way I was.

"The only thing is: I know I'm alive, but I don't have no inspiration, no initiative. Nothing. No.

"I think it has to do with the fact that I'm not destined to die, but maybe I'm destined to stop.

"And the spirit in me said, No. You can't stop.

"That is why something moved me away from home, and bring me here.

"Probably had I been in Nigeria, maybe I would have died. Because I was at the end of the road."

The road did not end. It stretched to America, to Philadelphia, to Material Culture and a new life in art. To tell his tale, Prince drove it down, steadily down through failure after failure, to the afternoon he met George Jevremović, but when he turned back, filling his story with detail, the reversal in his fortune was not quite so sudden. Referring to George, as he normally does, as my friend, Prince says:

"I was so grateful that I met your friend. And I'm so grateful to my wife, even though, right away, she's behaving like an American woman. She was a very special person in my life.

Because, like, when I was supposed to not really know where I am coming from anymore, she said, No. Why don't you do some painting?"

In a conversation a year later, Prince explained that several months before he met George in the autumn of 2004, Shola, sensing his distress, told him to take up painting once more:

"This is one thing that my wife did for me that I will never forget her for. When I was so *down*, when I'm not painting, she called me to sit down, say, Look, whatever happens to you, you go back to your painting. Because this is what people know you, all over the world.

"I was down, doing all kind of jobs, and either I got fired or I don't like it. So, I go back to painting."

The painting he began was a large cut and laminated oil on wood, the first work created in his American house, other than small pictures on paper. It took him, as he recalls, two or three months. Entitled *The Golden Bird and the Unnoticed Crowd*, it shows "the father of the birds; he is the head of all the birds." Thinking of the genders bent and blended in his paintings, I note the eggs at the bottom of the picture and ask how a father could have laid them. Prince answers:

"Because some of the spiritual bird can lay eggs. Like, there's some kind of bird that lay eggs, like she-birds. Some he-birds both lay eggs too, because he is so powerful."

I comment that in many of his paintings, even those representing himself, figures exhibit both male and female traits as a sign of spiritual power. "Yeah," he says, pointing to the painting:

"That was the story of Alokolobo—is a human being who have man thing and woman thing. But in our culture we believe that they are like witch.

"The witch can be black witch or good witch, like Alokolobo: he and she."

For his painting, Prince chose a spiritual image from Yoruba tradition and lavished it with fastidious care. A pure instance of Prince's mature style, it was his first American masterpiece. He had, of course, made paintings and etchings during many of his visits to America, and earlier in his period of immigration he met up with an old friend, a sculptor in Washington:

"By the year two thousand and three, thank God, I went to Washington, D.C. I run into a black guy who has visited me in the sixties in Nigeria. He was surprised to see me at the gas station. Says, Twins, what are you doing here?

"So, this guy invited me to his house. He has a show for me. I do some paintings. Part of the paintings I did is part of the ones that George bought the first time when we met.

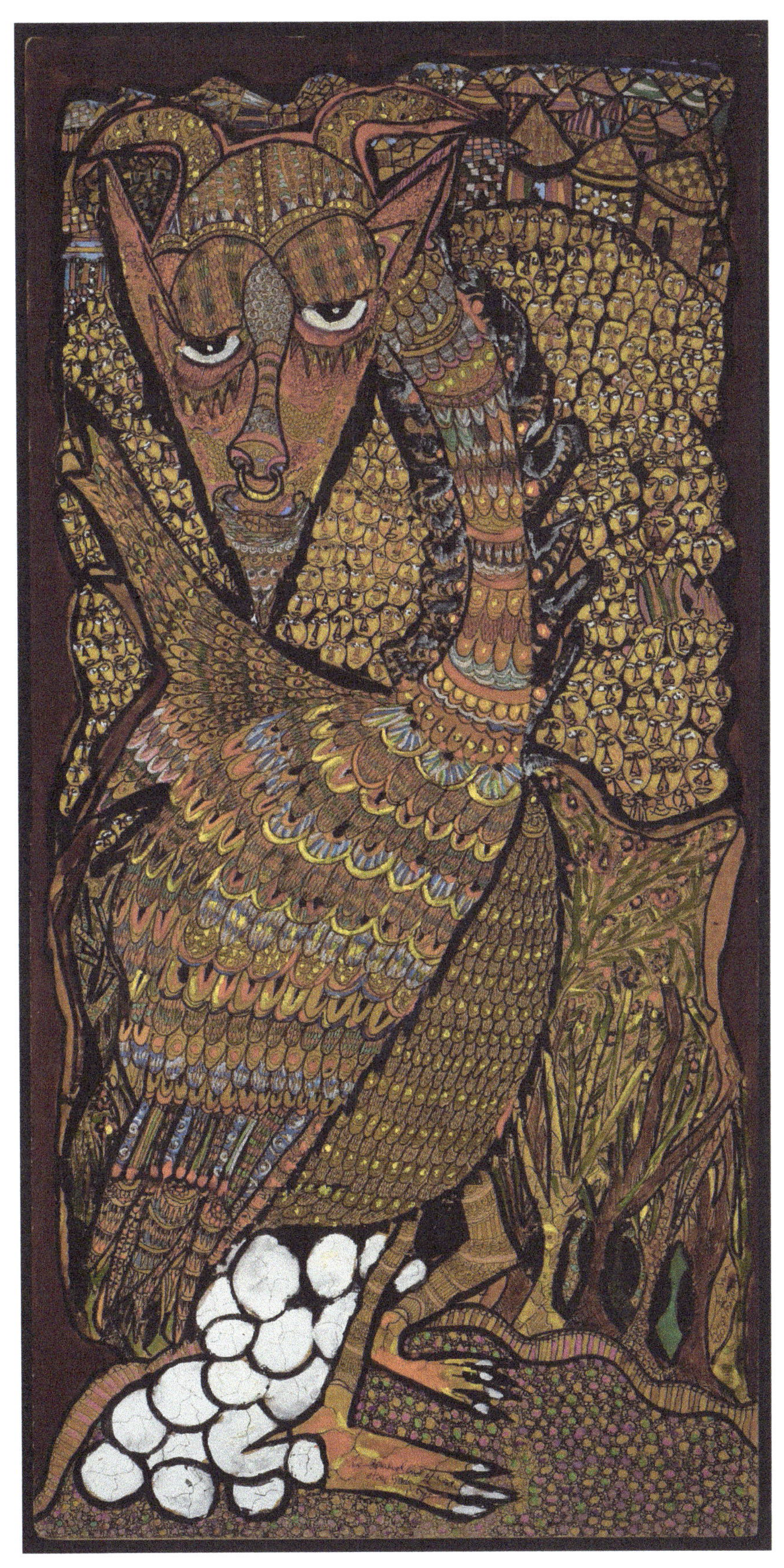

The Golden Bird and the Unnoticed Crowd.
Ink and oil on wood; 2 layers. 23"x48". Philadelphia, 2004

"So, when the guy told me he is going to have a show for me in about three months, I work hard, day and night; I was able to get fifteen paintings together."

Some were new, some old. As a wily investor will scatter his funds among the world's financial institutions, Prince, wary of the political instability in Nigeria early in the nineties, left paintings in Finland and Germany, shipped others to friends in Washington who had an art center named Mbari Mbayo after the club in Osogbo. The pictures were banked assets to use if he were forced to flee. Prince collected the Washington pictures for the show in his friend's house, and once he felt secure in Philadelphia, with a job at Material Culture, he retrieved the others. He had painted in America before he met George Jevremović, but without George his art might have faltered and failed. As he said, he might have stopped. Prince reveres powerful men, readers, chiefs, and politicians in Nigeria, George in America. Now his tale of immigration, of adaptation to America, moves forward from the moment he and George met:

"Then my lawyer told me he is going to court next week, and I must show proof of source of income. Because if I said I'm selling paintings, he said, the trustee can't believe a painting every day; like, it's not something you sell everyday. But I should go and look for a job.

"So, I came here. Thank God I told George our problem. Then my wife, she sell wares; you know, she sell traditional African old fabrics that we bought a long time ago. So, George bought everything; I think it is worth about five thousand, but he gave her two thousand. That's the money we used to rent the shop where she is using now."

Shola's shop, Princess African Hair Braiding, occupied a slot off Roosevelt Boulevard, where she and the daughters, along with other women from Africa and one from Jamaica, braided hair for black ladies in a long row of barber's chairs. Prince continues:

"But eventually she paid me back in a bad manner: she is becoming too American.

"But anyway, I thank God that I was in position to help her. A lot of things get damaged in my life: position-wise, property-wise, family-wise. But that's okay.

"Anyway, she got her own shop. Then I told George, I'm looking for a job. He said, You think you can work here? I said, Whatever you have. He said, Come back—it was Friday, and he said, Come back Monday.

"So, I came back on Monday. Then he called the gentleman here and said does he need help at the workshop"—the carpenters' shop at Material Culture. "The reason I was so happy to come here is because I know I'm going to see *woods*, to work with. But I was not expecting the man here to give me an odd job.

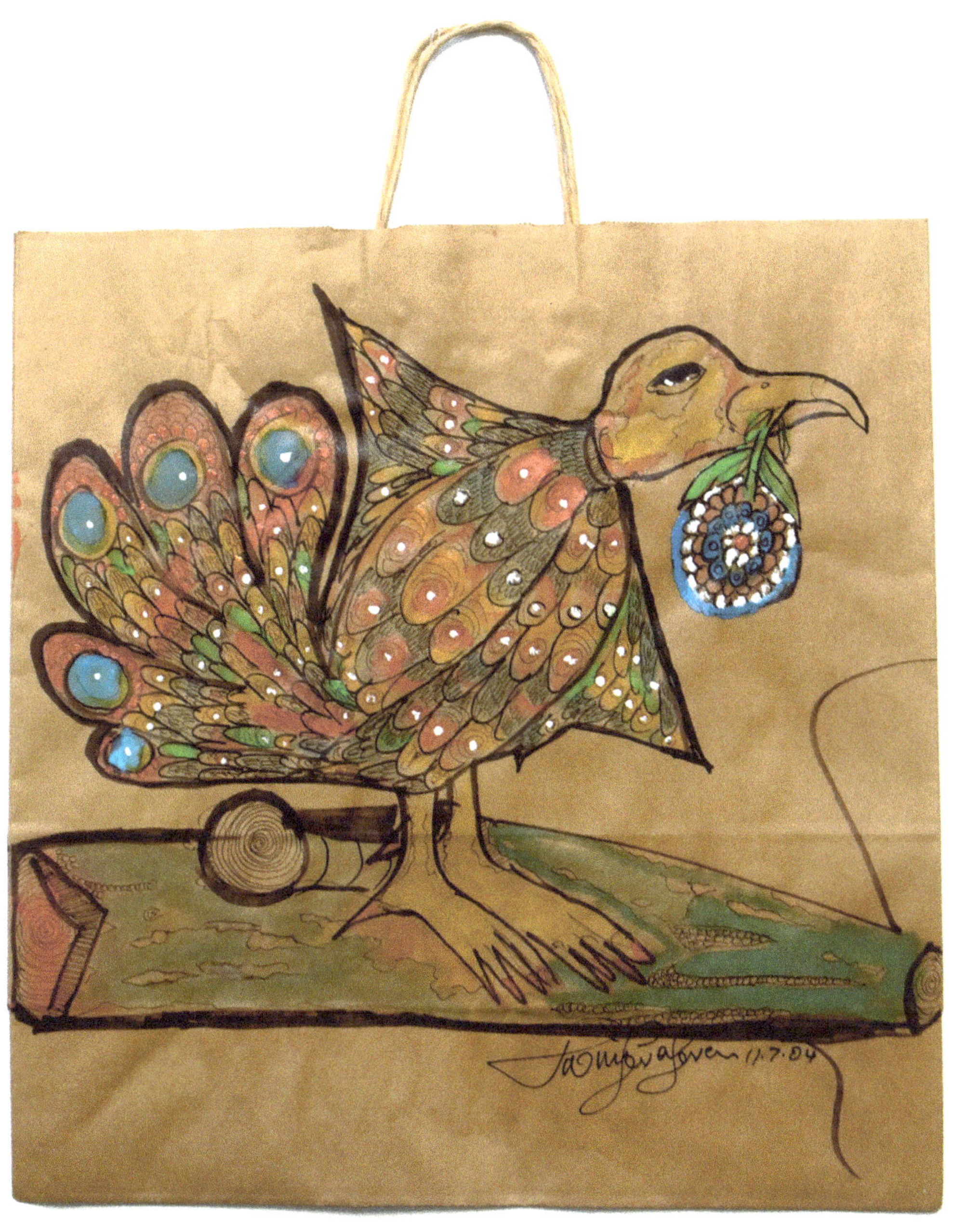

Paper bag painted by Prince.
Measuring 18"x18" and dated November 7, 2004, this bag carries a turkey, a reference to Thanksgiving in America, and it records the beginning of Prince's association with Material Culture, since the first creative job George Jevremović gave Prince was decorating paper bags that he gave to favored customers

"When George put me here, I don't know what he talked to the man. But the man give ten hours making sandpaper of the wood, using these machines to sand-smoothe it. Then another time he gave me irons with oil on it—the chairs they brought from India, in wintertime, I was cleaning them with hot water. But I am happy because at least I have got something.

"Anyway, one day, I don't know who told George whom I am, but I think it is you, he got the story behind my reputation. And he said, Look, why didn't you tell me? He said, I don't want you to do this job that you are doing. He said, I think about the idea; I'm going to get some paper bags. You put any design you like on them. I will be giving them away to my customers.

"So, that's how I started painting again. But the credit go to my wife, because without her who wake me up, I forget about my painting.

"I don't know what kind of a block; I don't know what you call it. But I was, like, in another world entirely. I was down. I was like inside an ocean, in a sack. That I was put in a sack, tied it, and drop me in the ocean. Because everything blocked. I don't have any thoughts anymore.

"Thank God, meanwhile, I started painting. And George told me, If we are lucky to sell something good, I will give you commission for all the paintings you do for the show. And I thank you for coming between us, because since I met you, he has really become interested in my work.

"It is a long, long story. Long, long story."

It is a story of immigration, the great American story of arrival, adjustment, and struggle. It is a story of art. Prince's career had entered an excited, productive new phase, which began, three years after his arrival, with a chance encounter at a filling station in Washington, issued its first masterpiece at Shola's insistence, then took off when George gave him a place to work at Material Culture in the fall of 2004. At Paris, in May of 2005, Prince received the UNESCO award, and exhilarated upon his return, he worked with steadily increasing success until the end of July in 2006, when, with *Kissing Birds* done, we left for Nigeria.

I saw the new work of Prince's American phase first at the show George mounted at Material Culture in November of 2005, then in February 2006 at Jayne During's Kuaba Gallery in Indianapolis. Both exhibitions mingled the new and the old, and during comparison, I noticed, as one must in historical evaluation, both continuity and change.

The continuity lay in content and drawing: scenes of rural life, images of animals and spirits, all pulled away from retinal realism and centered upon conceptual formulations that invite spiritual interpretation. The most conspicuous change lay in the palette. The old pictures painted in Nigeria were earthy: black and brown, brownish red and reddish yellow, with slashes of green. Many of the new American pictures were gaudier, electric with pink and blue. It was our first conversation about art; we were standing together in Indianapolis, and I asked Prince about that contrast. He said I was right: he casually pulls the colors of his surroundings into his work. (Picasso once said much the same thing.) The Nigerian tone, Prince told me, is dull and dark, the American is bright and light. He was right: when I traveled with him to Nigeria, I saw his palette in the shadows and leaves of the forests, in the rust of the tin roofs, in the earthen walls, the dirt roads, the wide dry fields, and I returned to look with new eyes at the hard artificial colors and shiny surfaces of the cars and clothes and commercial signage of America.

Prince sets no other artist as a model for his work, but, observant and visually acute, he casually absorbs influences from his environment, an environment made by artists as well as farmers, carpenters, and God. When George gave him a place to work upstairs at Material Culture, Prince was surrounded by carpets and ceramics, and when George suggested that he paint borders on his pictures to save the cost of having them framed, he borrowed freely from the artifacts around him. The spring of 2006, Prince says, was a good time for him, and the masterpiece of the period, *Scientist in Animals' Kingdom*, has the borders and overall look of a Persian carpet. I asked, and he said:

"Yeah, you can tell. You can see the influence of George carpet. It is just like one of the carpets. It is from the influence of the carpet. Because I see too many of those carpet designs too much, and they sticking to my brain."

The ceramics, too, offered borders. Material Culture sells plates painted underglaze on a composite white body by masters in Kütahya, Turkey. One of their traditional designs for borders derives from the wave-and-rock pattern of Chinese porcelain, and one of the masters, Mehmet Gürsoy, inspired by the decorative settings of Turkish calligraphy, extracted an element from the old design and repeated it in cloud-like forms that billow around the central figure. Prince picked up Mehmet's idea and applied it when running borders around small paintings on canvas.

These Middle Eastern touches drifted into Prince's work, gifts from the environment that marked his period of high creativity in 2005 and 2006. This was also the time when, seeking new sources of inspiration, he shaped many paintings out of spills. He continued to start work with a sketch, as he had in Nigeria, as he would in *Kissing Birds*, converting an idea into a communicative form during a rapt engagement with materials (as Ben Shahn would have it in *The Shape of Content*), but he also spilled paint onto canvas and then teased the accident into a picture, a process that, like his palette, distinguished his new American pictures from his old Nigerian ones. Prince was back, recalled to life, ceaselessly creative and productive. The bleak era of depression and deprivation was over, a new era had begun, and I return us to Prince's story:

"Anyway, I was here"—at Material Culture—"working and working and working, praying—I used to pray—all of a sudden I got a telephone call. I got a cell phone sound, and I pick it. It's from the office of the president of Nigeria, looking for me because they nominated me to get this award in Paris.

"And they sent me a letter in that respect. So, a letter was sent to my home in Nigeria, because they didn't know I'm here permanently.

"And I show it to George. That is one of the things I will never forget him for. And he gave me, I think, five thousand, which I pay him back when I get back. He gave me five thousand so I could go to Paris.

"I am very grateful to him. He has been very wonderful in my life.

"Anyway, I went to Paris. I become the UNESCO Artist for Peace, or Ambassador for Peace. And that opened up a *big* room for me. And when I came back that's why your government know I am here. They invited me and my family, and they gave me a ten years' green card. Ten years. And I learnt that they don't give anybody that kind of visa; they always give, probably, two years or one year."

A green card is the immigrant's prize. An award is the artist's pride. In the press release announcing the award, it says, "UNESCO Artists for Peace are internationally-renowned personalities," and it says that Prince Twins Seven-Seven is "the most famous representative of the renowned Oshogbo school of painting, which is at the heart of Yoruba civilization . . . . His varied style, using different techniques and astonishing materials, is the most copied in contemporary Nigerian art." On *Crossover*, the next CD he released, Prince billed himself as "The Singing Ambassador." With the award and the card, we have come to July 2005, and Prince goes on:

"Then by October the Philadelphia Museum give a big luncheon in respect of the award. Because they said if I live here and I got that honor, it is good for Philadelphia. So, they throw up a *big* party for me at the Museum. That really developed to the point of them buying one of my paintings."

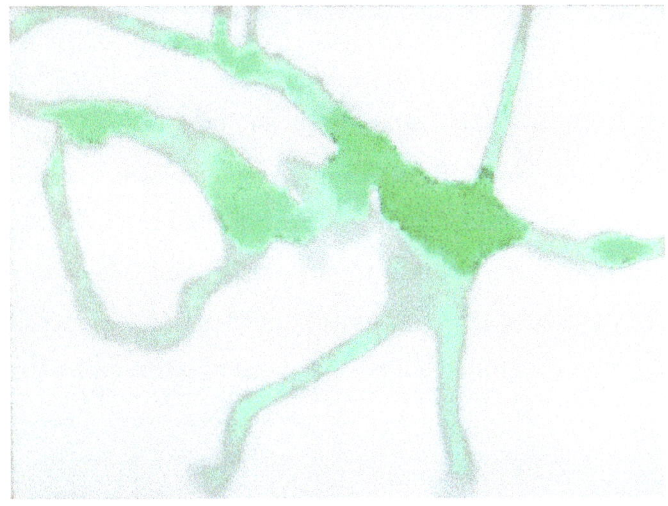

The green spill at the beginning

The Race Mates.
A painting in Prince's "American style."
See chapter 20, nos. 16, 26

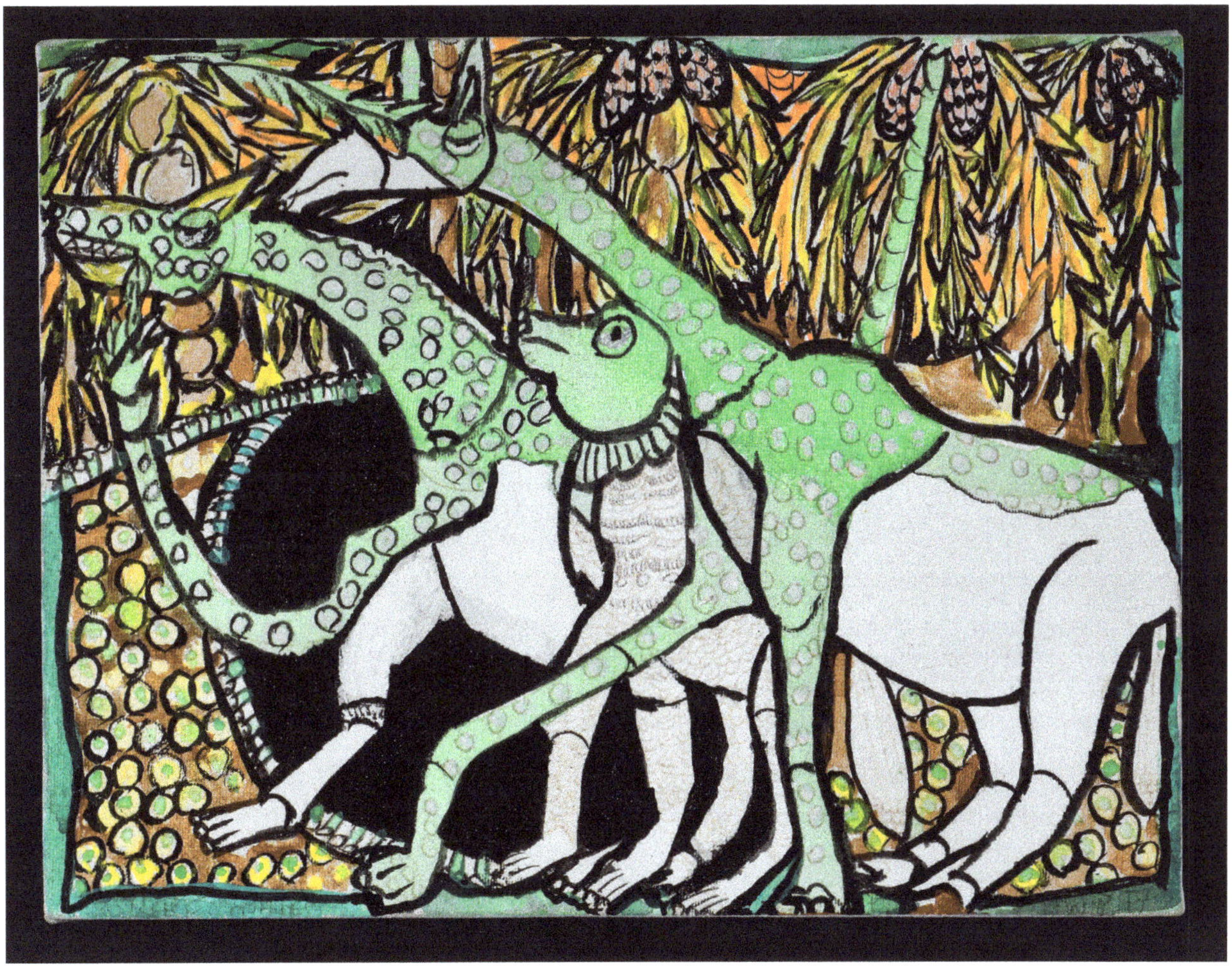

The Race Mates.
Ink and acrylic on canvas. 12" x 9". Philadelphia, 2005

That painting is the early version of *My Reincarnation Brothers and Sisters*, dated 1968–69 in the Museum's report for 2006. Led by Carlos Basualdo, the Museum's curatorial team selected the picture at Material Culture. The cost—fifteen thousand dollars on Material Culture's list of prices—was covered by a gift from Material Culture and funds contributed by John McFadden, a trustee with an interest in African art. On display at the Philadelphia Museum of Art for six months, the early picture contrasts with the later versions Prince painted in 2006 and 2007. It lacks Prince's self-portrait, and the spirits, according to the Museum's statement, represent his deceased brothers and sisters, the twins who accompanied him into life, then left, while those in the later paintings, according to Prince, represent the people around him who hound him for money. Now Prince goes on to the show where the picture bought by the Museum was exhibited and sold:

"Then in November, we have a lot of music here"—at Material Culture—"and then we have the big exhibition, which was my *first*, big, major exhibition in probably about eight or nine years. It was well attended. And, thank God, we met, and with your golden touch you were the first collector of my painting that night.

"And after that, sales continued."

There he stopped, the tale ended. It is quiet, the recorder spins, and I ask Prince how he sees his life in America. He begins slowly:

"In fairness to myself, I think I know that with the support of people like you and support of God, if I choose to live here, I will be okay. But—nowhere like home.

"Nowhere like home, and now events is happening around me that make my life more horrible. My wife has packed out of the house, and she's picking American habits in a non-acceptable way. It's very hard and painful, but I swallow it, because I know something greater is coming for me. Because many times I have things that are happening to me; something great has come out before.

"Like, after the show"—in November of 2005—"some people at George place were envying me. This guy complained to him that I'm always on my telephone, you know."

Complaints of the sort caused George to move Prince's place from the second floor of his store to the studio by the carpenters' shop in the summer of 2006, so he could come and go unnoticed, working as he wanted. It is in America as it was in Nigeria; Prince continues:

"I have a lot of jealous people around me all the time. It's a part of what I brought from the world, from my own other world.

"But I thank God because through Him and through you people I was able to discover myself back to my artistic career. Because if I do not meet George, probably I would not even remember that I used to do something with my art and with my brain.

"And I do hope God will make it possible that this, our trip, will be very successful and you will be able to collect enough material to make a very very interesting book for the people of the world to read."

Prince pauses, looking forward to our trip to Nigeria, without which I would have had information, but not the feel that makes the writing flow. Prince hopes that book, this one, will help him rebuild his career. Something greater is coming for him, he believes, and in America he has changed for the better. Earlier he told me:

"My life is different from what it was eight years ago. Eight years ago, I am very aggressive about life. Lot of smoking. Lot of drinking. Womanizing. Then, now I am a bit mellow, slow down, and my spiritual power is coming back again.

"But about ten years ago, I was just living for life."

Once again, he is living for art, living with purpose. If he stays in America, he will be, he said, okay—not excellent, not wonderful, just okay. Life here is hard. Things in his household have fallen apart, and there is no place like home. He abides in exile, in hiding, far removed from the social situations in which, by offending some person of power, he might lose his chance to follow Osuntoki and become the king of Ibadan. Prince can make it here, but he is waiting for a great victory so he can go home in triumph.

Now, having paused in thought, Prince returns to my question about life in America, expanding this time from his personal position to the state of the world. In horror, Prince watches the newsworthy violence that burns across the screen of his television. America's war in Iraq appalls him, as it should, and the whole world seems shaking in pain:

"I think this is a very beautiful society. I'm sorry that the world, that the things in the world now confuse me. I don't know where we are going. I'm confused.

"And my own country, too. Even though we don't have terrorists, we have young school-leavers who have no jobs, who are trying to imitate what they see overseas—to act in Nigeria; you know what I mean? Even though they are not terrorists, but nothing is stopping them from going and starting bombing places, like what they see on CNN, and all that.

"I think sometimes: if the world want peace, my idea is that they should not always show these calamities. They should not show all the calamities. Probably they have it, and put it in government records; don't show it to the people.

"If the filmmakers or the newscasters can try and show positive responses, events, it will reduce all this problem in the world."

Prince speaks of a popular film that detailed a robbery, providing a plan for fools to copy. He blames the newscasts of suicide bombings for encouraging dreadful acts by deluded young men seeking "cheap notoriety." He offers the world his solution:

"We should gather all the elders, from all the religions, who have the traditional wisdom, so that people can learn from them. So that they will be able—because when they die, they take most of these things away. But if we can do that, it will enable us to find out—to solve all these problems in the world.

"Because all the wisdom in the minds of these respectable religious leaders can be used in other political situations.

"Okay, like I remember the former pope was trying to do that by bringing *all* different religious leaders together so they can exchange ideas. If they do that, it can help the world.

"And then you have too many young people now becoming head of state, head of this political leadership in every country. Like Blair is too young, Bush is too young, Putin is too young. And the guy now in Iran is a young radical from the university.

"I think it is about time that they go back to the old days when they put more seasoned, older people in power. Because they know they will die, and they know they have seen too much of the world. They would not just go and press the button for war.

"So, most of these young people, they don't even care about whatever happens. They don't care."

They are like haughty, oblivious monarchs, like the elephants in *Kissing Birds*, the painting he had in progress when he spoke. They don't care, but stand aside in unconcern while people mistreat one another, and the world burns. Mellow, an elder himself, who works for the restoration of sacred tradition, Prince continues without a pause, turning back to my question, retreating from the wide world into the confines of the self:

"So, like my life here: I pray and wish I can continue to do more good job. And I hope and I dream that I will be able to leave a good legacy of my work in America.

"So, I do a lot of things here. I do a lot of odd jobs.

"The older you are, the better you produce more work. Because it will come at any time when I don't think about selling anymore. I will be thinking about what you leave behind. And I started bringing the best out of me, because I am not keeping this for myself.

"I thank God for giving me this ability, and I thank God that I was gifted. I was blessed that my life has benefited the life of other people in my country."

With that, Prince concludes. If he stays in America, aging in success, he hopes to work without the burden of commercial worries, making the best art of his life and leaving a grand legacy in America, but his final desire is to benefit the people back home, his people. Our talk is done, *Kissing Birds* is complete, and we are off to Nigeria.

Home in Nigeria

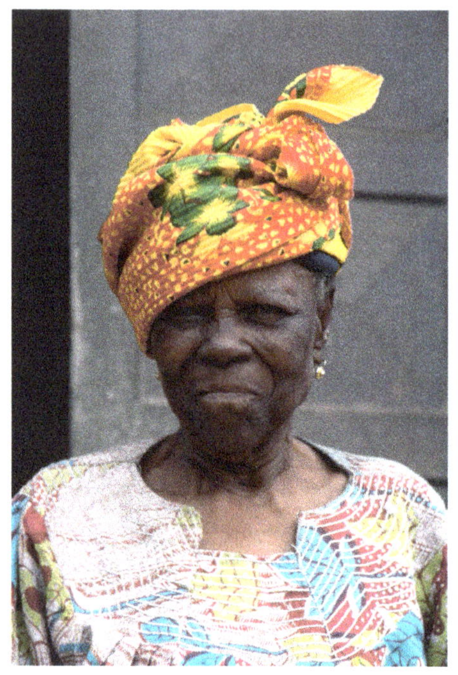

Shijuwoye Osuntoki

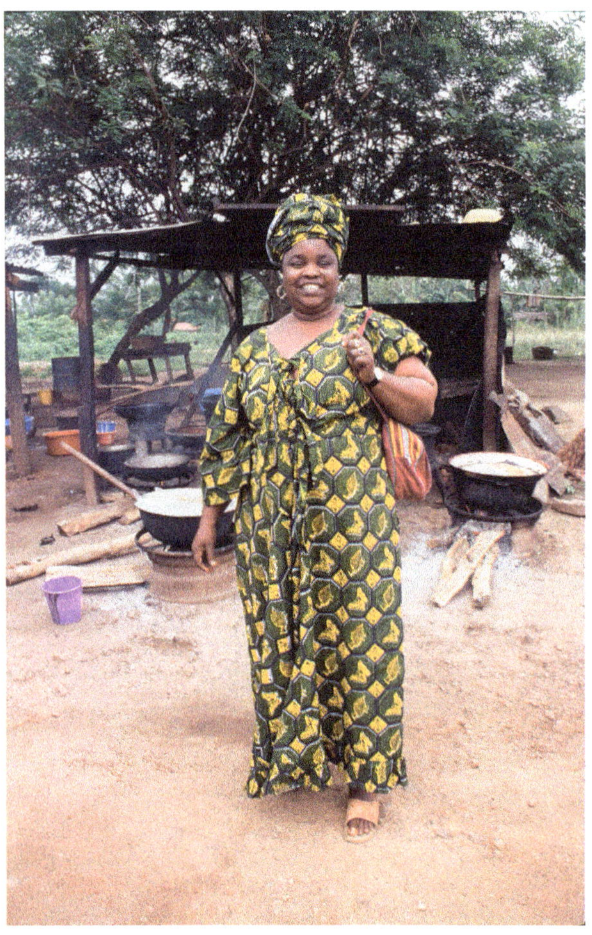

Haja Fausat Folasade Ogunkule

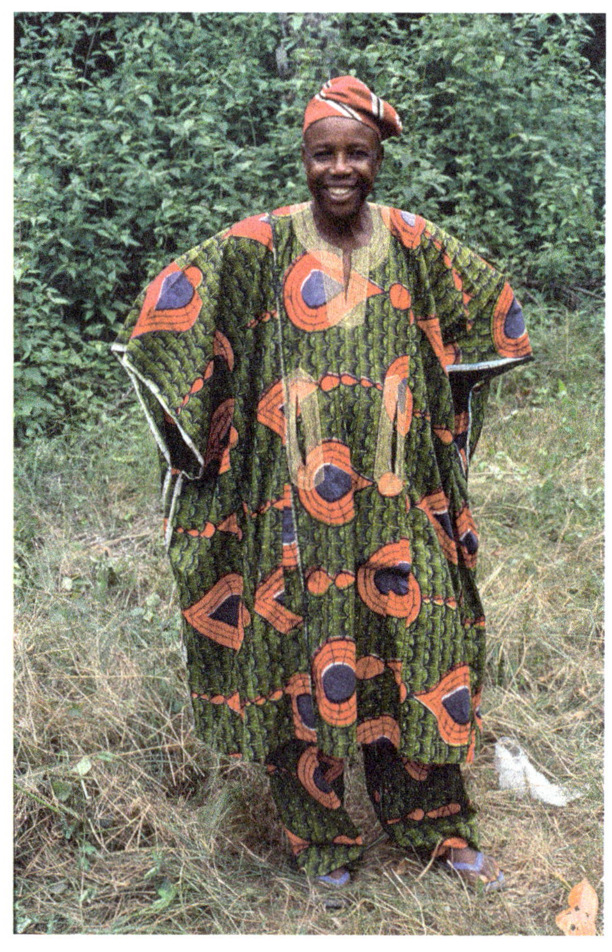

Prince Oladosu Emmanuel, J.P.

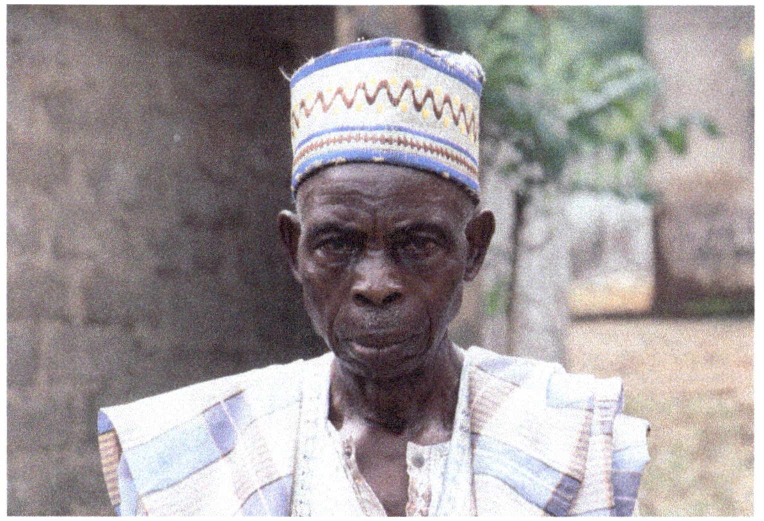

Joseph Abiodun.
Prince's uncle, his mother's brother,
who died in December 2006

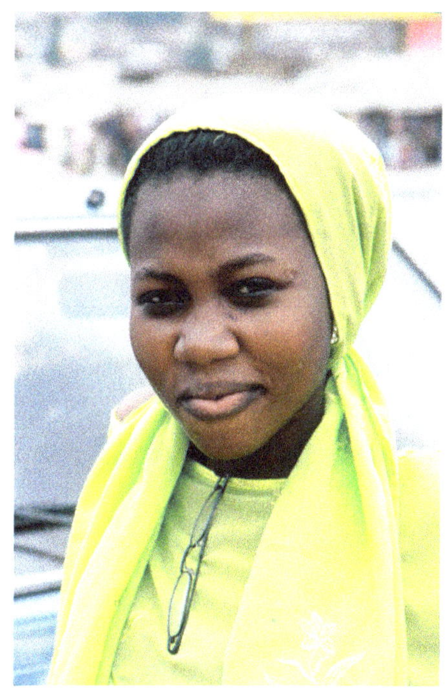

Keji.
Prince's granddaughter

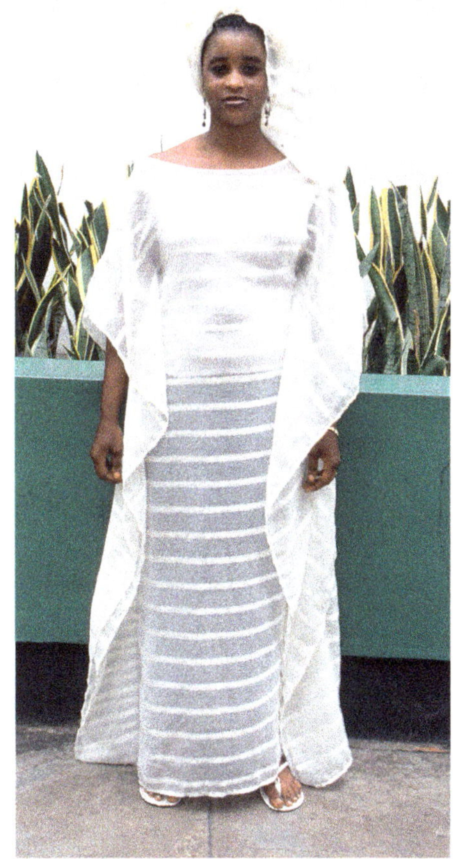

Princess Aliratu

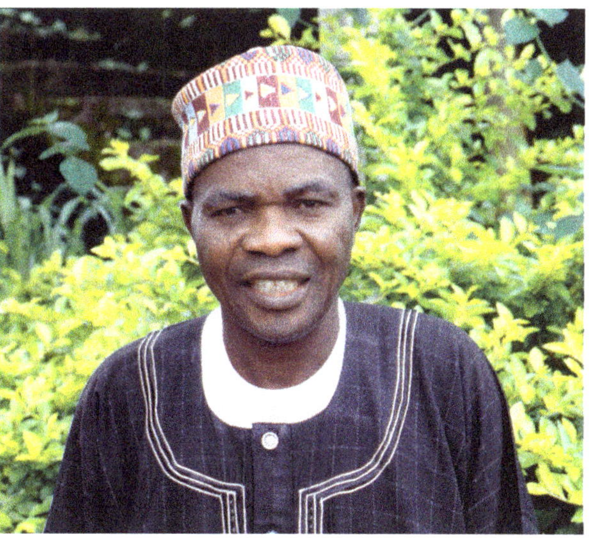

Nine-Nine

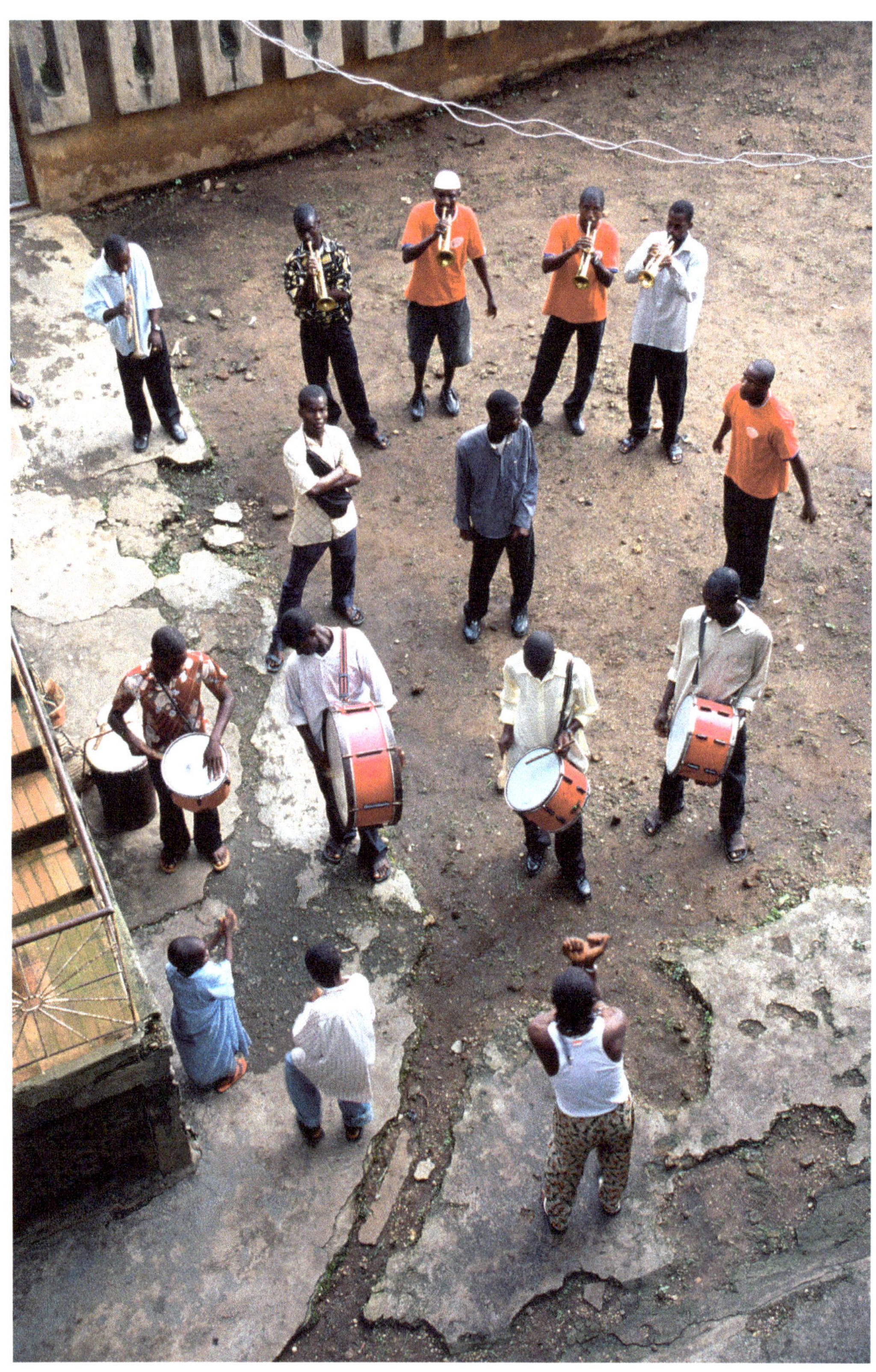

A brass band welcomes Prince home to Osogbo

· 15 ·

The Hero's Return

We planned our trip so Prince could make a glorious return on the day of the Osun Festival in Osogbo. Earlier in the summer he had attended a conference, sponsored by UNESCO, in Abuja, but this would be his first trip home, to the places of his family and followers, in six long years. His hair was freshly braided, his beard was blackened, his clothes were crisp and white. He looked robust and youthful; he was ready.

Prince's intention was to appear with sudden drama, to exhibit flamboyant vitality and then disappear, having repositioned himself in the Yoruba scheme of things, a twice double, fourfold patterning of power: material and spiritual, beneficent and malign. The human universe splits into two worlds—the material realm of the living, the spiritual realm of the dead and the gods—both driven by positive and negative forces. The worlds interpenetrate: the dead act in this one, the living influence the other by deeds, prayers, and sacrifice. Positive and negative forces are eternal; there is no option for an earthly rebirth into purity. "Some people are lucky to be able to be very very good," Prince said. "They have power to subdue the negative spiritual aspect in them. But, at the same time, they still have little devilish things hiding somewhere." The devilish things creep out when good people get envious or angry. All human beings are flawed and corrupt, the spirits tend to malevolence, and even the deities can be forgetful and devious. Only God, called Olodumare, is pure in goodness. Existence inevitably entails the negative, so it must be bravely checked, carefully balanced, or controlled with strength, as when a man of power manages the negative forces of jealousy, greed, and ambition, channeling them through competitive aggression to win wealth and prestige.

We traveled so Prince could connect with the men of power. The diviners supplied him information from the other world, prescribed sacrifices that carried his requests to the gods, and advised him how to handle the positive and negative forces during his quest to recover his strength and get on with his life. Prince trusts the diviners, the native doctors, but not the doctors of the West. A German physician offered to repeat the operation on his hip, decreasing his pain and eliminating his limp, but, he said, "I don't trust anybody who sticks knives in my ass." White doctors, he believes, use black patients in medical experiments, rendering them worse, not better, and the German doctor, a collector of his art, might have killed him on the operating table to increase the value of the works he owned. In Prince's mind, Western practitioners, narrow in their specializations, give you a second disease while curing the first, but the native doctors practice within a wide system that recognizes the interconnections of mental, physical, social, and spiritual ills, that acknowledges the simultaneity of good and evil, so the bad medicine provided by one native doctor can be countered by the good medicine provided by another, and the troubled patient can proceed in balance through a world of perpetual strife.

We met with the men of spiritual power, and with the men of temporal power. The high point was a pleasant hour in the wide office of the affable governor of Osun State, Prince Olagunsoye Oyinlola, whose father, Prince said, "was a great scholar, and he was a teacher, and he was a king too. He has done a lot of things for the cultural value of the Yoruba people."

Engaged with the chiefs and political leaders, Prince strove to relocate his position in the chain of being that links society vertically through the crosswinds of circumstance. To those above, Prince was polite, deferential, and entertaining, bringing the shock of laughter into solemn scenes. From those below, he expected the respect owed to a chief, and to them he was generous, as he hoped the men of power would be to him. He gave out food, and he gave out money in astonishing quantity.

In this context, the context of home, hierarchy, and fourfold power, Prince's extravagant throws of money, which seem irrational to his American friends, make perfect sense. The free gift of money is a sacrifice, diminishing his resources to achieve benefit. That benefit is general. He gives money away, helping others, to pull positive energy into the world. When I asked my friends in Ireland, poor Catholic farmers, why they fed everyone who entered their houses on the hills, why they gave more than they would ever get, they said it was a sacred duty. Their hospitality was not part of a reciprocal exchange, but a valorous attempt to keep goodness alive on the earth. Prince thinks like that, giving more than he receives. By upholding the positive he counteracts the negative and contributes to cosmic balance. In addition, Prince feels that gifts to the poor are a social obligation. By giving, he compensates for the wrongs done by his ancestors, and he works for human harmony by repaying society in general for the good that has befallen him, a poor boy from the bush who has become a prosperous chief. Social connections follow the gracious gift, and, as A. D. Nuttall argues in his philosophical analysis of

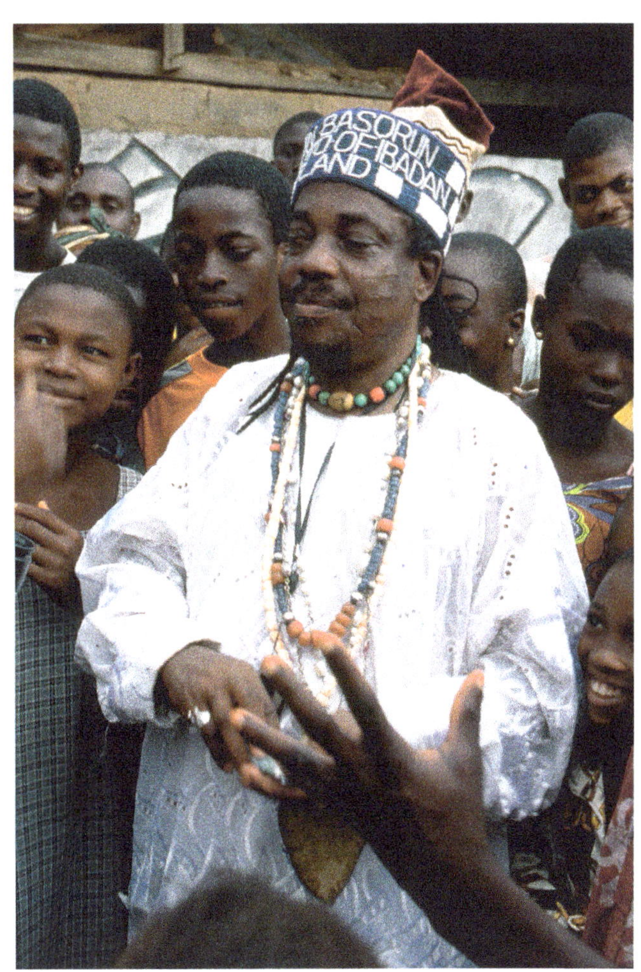

Prince gives out money in Ogidi

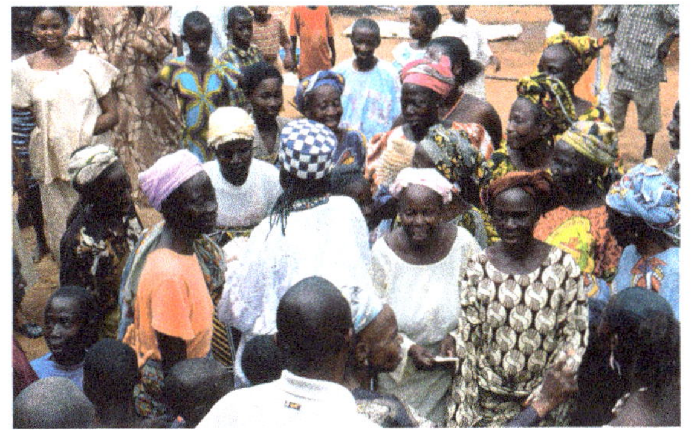

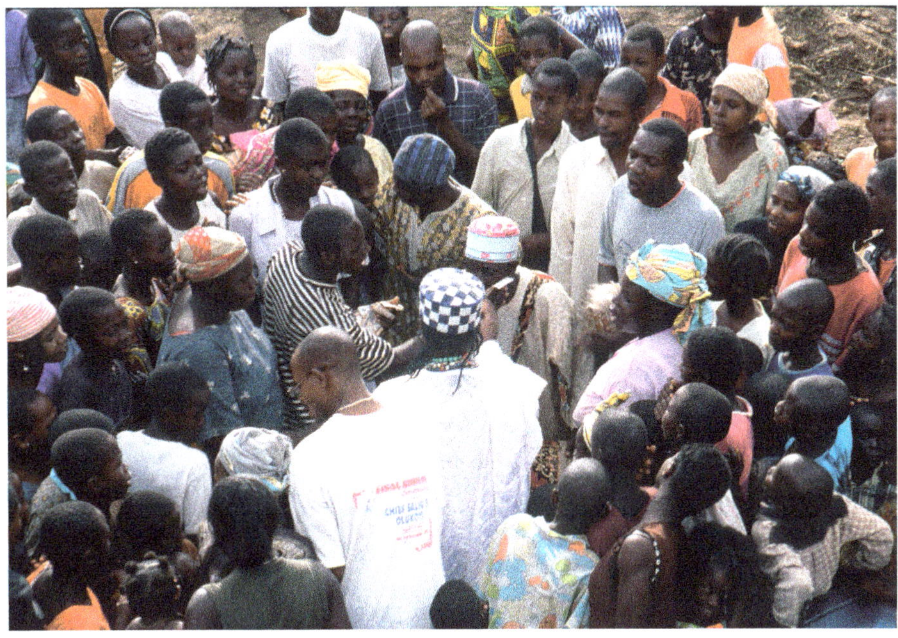

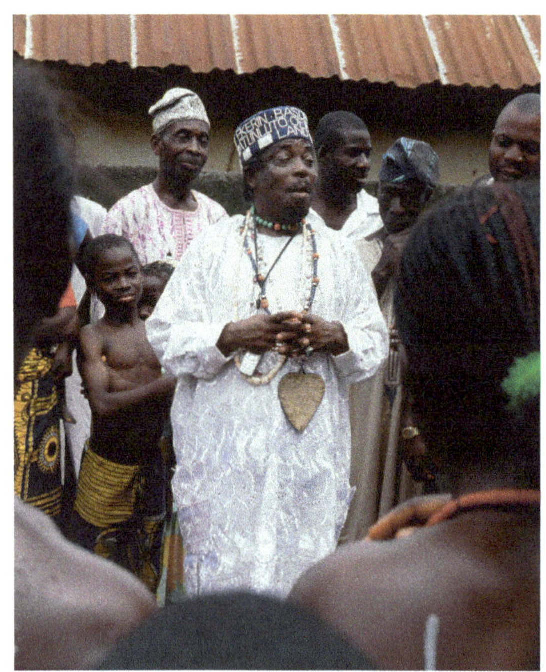

Prince gives his speech at Ogidi

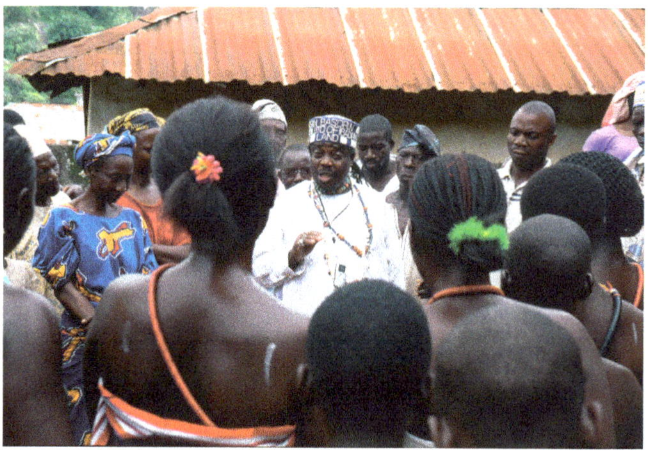

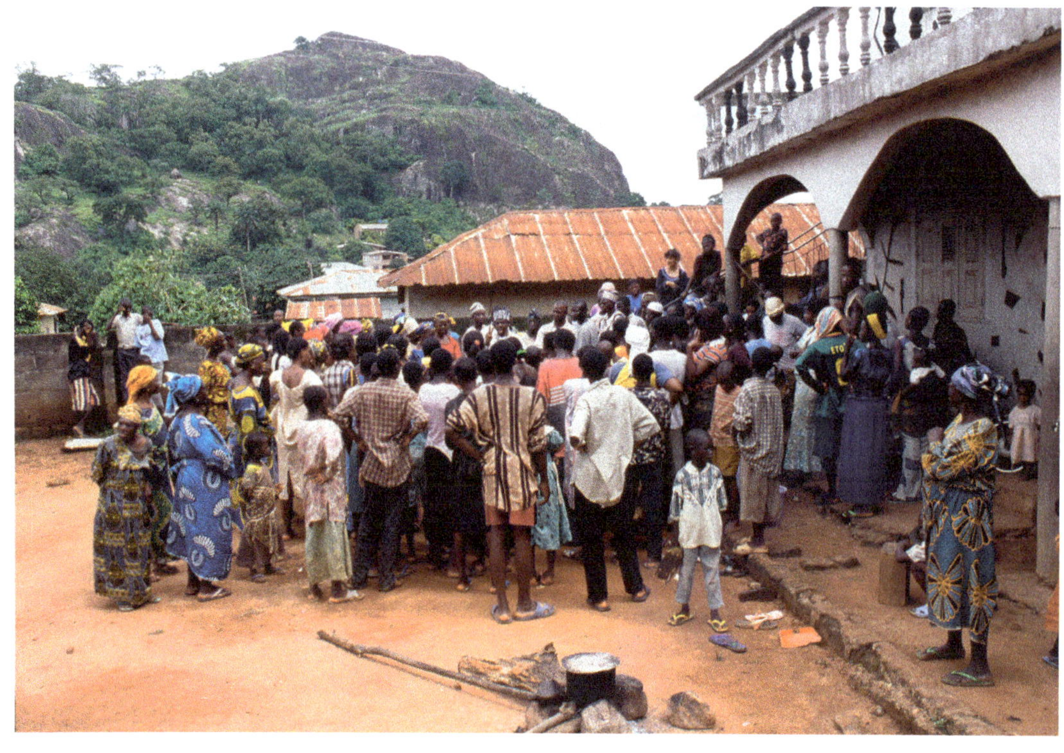

Shakespeare's *Timon of Athens*, though the giver does not expect a material return, he does expect an ethical return, a mutuality of association and aid. And further, Prince believes his gifts benefit him personally. If he does not give, sullen people will slink away and curse him, but if he does give, grateful people will admire and honor him, remembering him in their prayers. Curses and prayers register in the other world, thwarting and supporting him during his struggles in this one. Money brings prayers; prayers bring the gods to his side. Cosmic, social, and personal benefits condense in his gifts. Prince is a generous man. He likes to give, but the constant demands for money, though they reflect his high status, drive him mad.

As we traveled, his visits, gifts, and sacrifices helped Prince reestablish his presence in the Yoruba universe. Our journey followed the westering course of his life. When we got to Ogidi, where he passed his boyhood, the women greeted him with songs of praise.

Prince had on his "big clothes," the chiefly robe called *agbada*, which screens the body and expands its scope, like the ceremonial attire of the old Japanese warlords. Big clothes signal the men of station and wealth, from whom wisdom and gifts can be expected. He stood in placid splendor while the young women danced for him. Then he gave them money and called the crowd around him.

It was a scene he would repeat throughout our travels. As I watched I was reminded of spontaneous assemblies on the streets of black neighborhoods in big American cities, when a man of experience gathers the wild boys to coach them, lecturing them on respect and duty. Prince began by warning the young to stay home and hold to the old values. He admonished them to shun the cities that suck young people into the sink of immorality, causing them to disrespect the elders and disintegrate into licentiousness. Then he told the story of his life, how he had been, like them, impoverished in Ogidi, how he had fought for success. He had been everywhere, he said, to many African countries, to every corner of Europe, except Russia, to India, Brazil, and Argentina. On his travels, he had seen every kind of art, but when he came home he forgot it all. His art, the first modern art in Africa, he said, the base of his fame and fortune, was built out of the tradition he shared with them, the people gathered quietly around him. This is the modern age, Prince said, so we can return to tradition. What we need for success is already ours. We can turn away from the seductive flash of the West, turn back to our own deep heritage, and succeed through righteous struggle.

They stood without moving, listened closely, then came to receive the blessing of cash. He gives more than he gets, Prince told me at the time, because his people are poor. But money moved in both directions. Late in the day, when the drummers had come and the dancing had begun, a handsome young politician pulled his sedan to the edge of the compound and walked straight through the crowd to Prince. There he stood, smiling, peeling bills from a thick stack and showering them over Prince's head while the boys scrambled in the dust to snatch fallen notes. Then as quickly as he came, he left. Money circulates, comes and goes, balancing in the cosmic account.

His people took his money, took his food, settling into his house with beer, *akara*, and bowls of stew made from the flesh of a sacrificed ram. Prince began building this house when he was eighteen, a dancer on the road. On one of the doors, in 1965, he painted an elephant, a premonition of royalty. He has not lived here for years, so he rents it out in the belief that houses, like people, have spirits; their spirits abide in the people who move within them, keeping them alive. "Houses are like human being," Prince said. "When you go, your spirit stays there, but if you leave for a long time, the spirit goes out, the walls start cracking."

While the people of Ogidi ate his food in his house, we walked away to pay our respects to the king, His Royal Highness Oba Rabiu Ola Sule. In the parlor of his fine home, the king and his retainers listened in gracious patience as Prince burst with the tensions built up during six years of silence and failure in America. They sat. He gestured and laughed, repeating blustery old tales of the self.

As we were returning to the feast in Prince's house, Yahya Jinabu, called Yayi, backed out of an unfinished concrete building, followed by Agbo, a mound of green and brown leaves. A line of men in martial array, chanting while they marched, came up behind, and Yayi danced in front, wielding a stick to control Agbo. Four is the usual number, but this time Agbo came alone, came like a thing torn out of the bush, a dashing, erratic fragment of nature. The men, culture's agents, tried to drive Agbo along a straight line, but it dodged and fled, moving without limbs, no hands, no feet, making no sound, no screech or grunt, but only the sibilant shimmer of dry leaves in a breeze. Sometimes it flattened into a leafy disc, pulsing, then springing again into the shape of a haystack blown by the wind, skimming over the ground. Agbo's acts, like the fairytales and folk drama of the European night, were coded for differential response. The women stood away, back at the village. The boys scattered up the slope, laughing in fascinated fear. The men came close, greeting Agbo with a hug, feeling the smooth coolness of the palm fronds, perhaps struck, as I was in embrace, by the absence of a face behind the hood and the silence, no whisper, no breath.

Agbo sped through the crowd, up the stairs and into the house, vanishing into a closed room, waiting to be forgotten. Then suddenly it reappeared to glide among the people, swish-

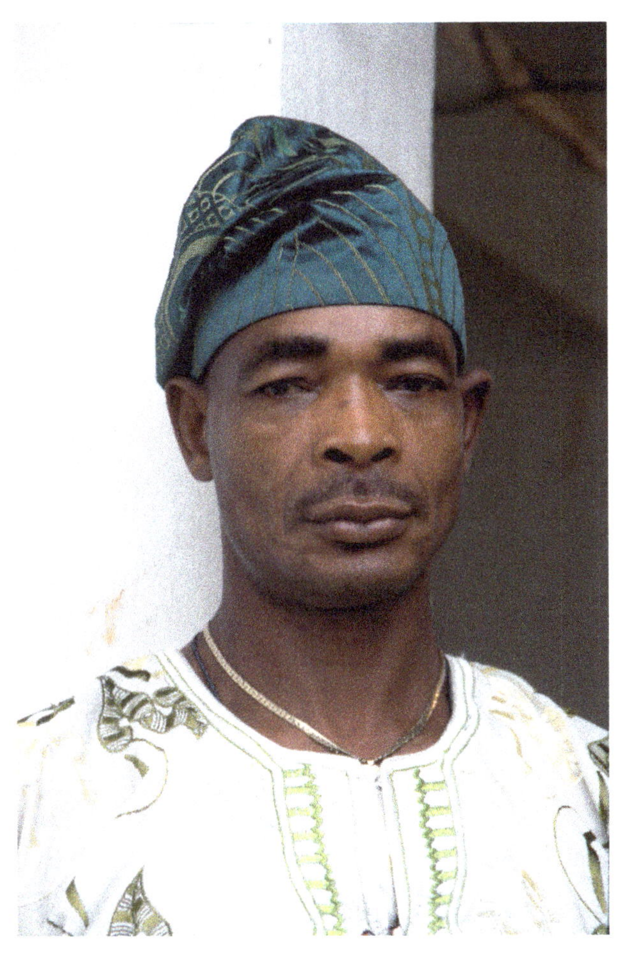
Yahya Jinabu, called Yayi

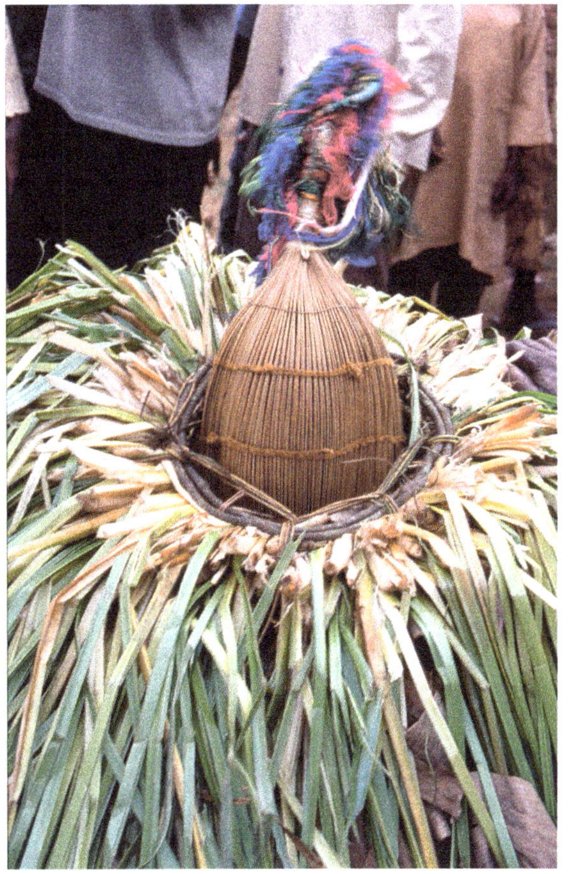
Agbo

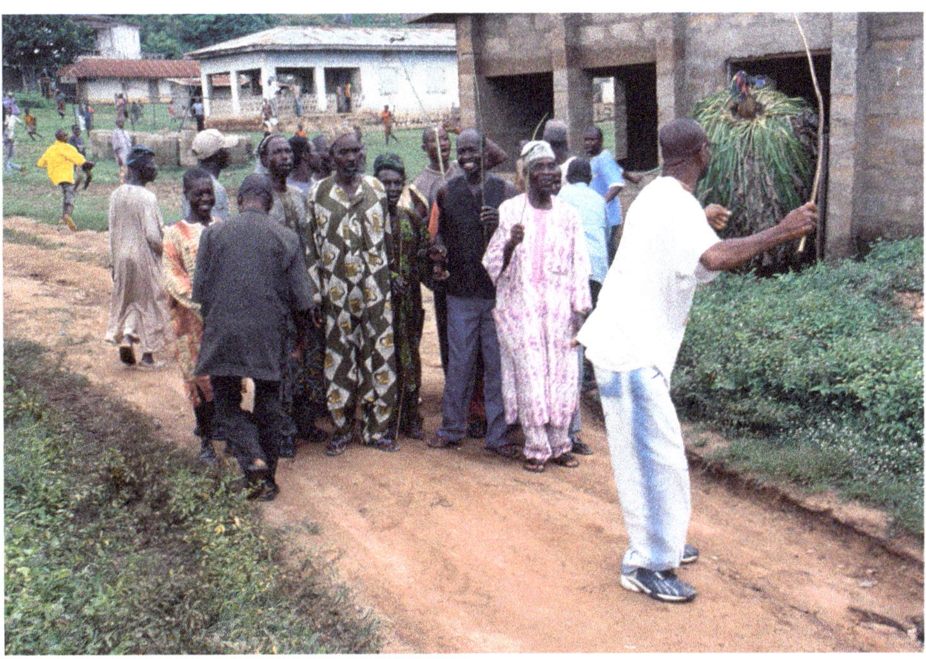
Yayi leads, Agbo emerges

ing through their pleasures of drink and dance, much as the forces of the other world sweep through this one, in a flash like Sango's lightning. Agbo maintains mystery and provokes uncertainty by antic acts, by appearing and disappearing. So does Prince, and when he was young he played Agbo, the Ogidi masquerade who uses the power granted by society to swing in disguise beyond the frame of conventional interaction.

At the time, I asked Prince what it was like to impersonate a spirit. I expected a mystical answer. He said it was hot, hard work and hot. Nearly two years later, when I asked him to tell me about Agbo, he said it was a male spirit, playfully threatening to women, frightening to children, and he explained that each of Ogidi's three sections has its own masquerade. Ilaere Agbo, Okoro Agbo, and Ileteju Agbo differ in the details of their masks. Prince used the word mask for the hood that hid his face and for the whole costume, including the heap of leaves that hung from a ring around his neck. When he was "a young radical" he belonged to Okoro's masquerade society, and what he remembered was that the costume was heavy, the work was hot, but the performer was given a "concoction" to drink—gin mixed with roots, over which an incantation had been spoken—so "you don't feel the weight, you don't know you carry anything; it feel light like a spider web." No one knows who you are, except the other members of the society and your wife, but they say nothing, so you can do what you want.

Agbos come in swarms at the time of the yam harvest, and many appear when great men die. While the tape unreeled, Prince said this, lending support to Marcel Griaule's generalization that African masquerades embody the spirits of the dead:

"The *old* belief is that when the masquerade comes out, they were representatives of the dead. They supposed to be the person that comes from the other part of the world. Like today, when modernization has come, they use them as a jamboree, but in those days they were very scary. Some of the masks—you know, most of them have meanings. There are some they have to wear when the king dies. There's some they wear when you have a new king. And there's some they wear when they want the rain to come. So, each of those masks has a purpose and a reason.

"The Agbos are different. The one that came out for me, that was a blessing. The one for the dead, you cannot even look at the face because they have a certain mask, made out of broom sticks. It have eyes and cowrie shells. And then the broom—they weave it and make it have a scary face, and it have three faces, one here, one here, and one on the other side, so that when he is looking at you, at the same time he is looking at somebody else. So, you don't know which of them has the wearer's eyes, except the way he walks. Then you can know he is looking directly.

"That one is for the dead, but the one they brought out for me is for a symbol of progress and revival of life.

"And that's why you see some very beautiful, fresh leaves on top of the dry leaves, shiny and yellow.

"Whereas the one for the dead, it wouldn't be yellow. It would be scary leaves. And sometimes when they touch your body, they scratch.

"And sometimes the one for the dead: ten times of that size. So *huge* that when you look at it as one small person, it does not seem possible.

"But the one that came out for me that day, it came out because, like, as a high chief of that community, that they thought is dead, I'm alive, and I didn't die, so that's why you see that mask that day.

"You see, there's a time they become two. When they go down, there's supposed to be a small one coming out. It is a symbol of the continuity of life.

"But it's not just anybody they will do that. That's because of my generosity, because of what I have done for the community. I've helped so many people there: children, scholars, students. Somebody couldn't pay his school fees, they came to me in Osogbo; I pay a whole year for them. Somebody who married, and they couldn't take good care of their business, I give them money. I buy them machine to sow crops so they can support their family. So, *all* these thing, that's why they *love* me in that town.

"Agbo show the love to me, and then appeasement to the spirit that somebody they love forever is back again alive."

When Agbo came on the day of the feast, running between life and death, incarnating the dead and giving birth to the young, it came, as the dancers did, to honor the town's favorite son, Prince Twins Seven-Seven, the Obatolu of Ogidi, and, like the dancers, Agbo was rewarded with money. That money keeps going around, and as it does, Prince reclaims his place.

On our trip, during trades of food and cash for respect, Prince announced his return. He was not dead, and he set out to exhibit his *ase*, his life force, by revitalizing projects that had crumbled in his absence.

In 1987, returning with profit from a musical tour of the Netherlands, Prince began to develop a piece of "bushy" land outside the village of Sekona. Where a natural spring bubbled up, he had a lake excavated in the shape of Africa; it filled with clear water that, miraculously, attracted no mosquitoes. Prince stocked the lake with carp. "At that time," he said, "I have Japanese carp. They leap and come to me like chicken when I feed them. But as an Osun person, I never eat fish." It is here that Prince sacrifices to Osun, and the healing power of the goddess has spread; mud from the lake's bottom cures skin rashes. At the edge of the lake, Prince set a stage, and when his band performed during the nineties, this country place throbbed with crowds of happy dancers.

Near the entry he opened a playground for kids, with a swing and seesaw plumbed out of pipes. Above the lake, Prince arranged a meandering, seriate sequence of spaces into a guesthouse. Okido, a musician in his band, an acrobatic dancer who played the masquerade in his hometown, decorated the facade with naturalistic reliefs, and he created a statue of Sango in concrete, like the one at Prince's home in Osogbo. Prince added to the ornament in "my style," the technique he used for the exteriors of his houses in Ogidi and Abuja. To his design, a carpenter cut strips of wood that were embedded in the wall as it rose, then removed once the concrete had set, leaving impressed slots to blacken. His style for buildings—black on white and surprising—is a skeletal version of his style for paintings.

At the point of the lake stands the wonder of the place, the "fish house" Prince designed as a lodging for guests in the shape of a carp with a toad in its mouth, a dragonfly in the mouth of the toad. Inside, three steps lead down from the bedroom in the head to the bathroom in the tail. This emblem of nature's chain of nutrition is the beginning of an architectural menagerie. Once Prince told me that he planned to add a house in the shape of an elephant. Another time he said he planned three more houses, one in the form of a crocodile, one like a lion, the last like a big bird with its wings spread wide.

The place is a marvel. A cultural attaché at the French embassy named it Resort de Paradise, the name now on the gate. Prince calls it the Resort. When he left Nigeria in 2000, the rumor was out that he was dead. Boys vandalized the buildings, and the bush rolled in. The smooth lawns disappeared beneath a gnarly tangle. The lake choked with vegetation, swamped and shrank. We stood, hip deep in weeds, and Prince said sadly, "I have poured millions into this bush." Then he poured more.

He gathered a team of local men (which included, he thought, some of the boys who vandalized the Resort) and gave them his speech, advising them to pray and work hard. They waded in with machetes, and every time we came back, the land was cleaner, the water level in the lake had risen. Prince's vision was practical. Improvements, he hoped, would interest

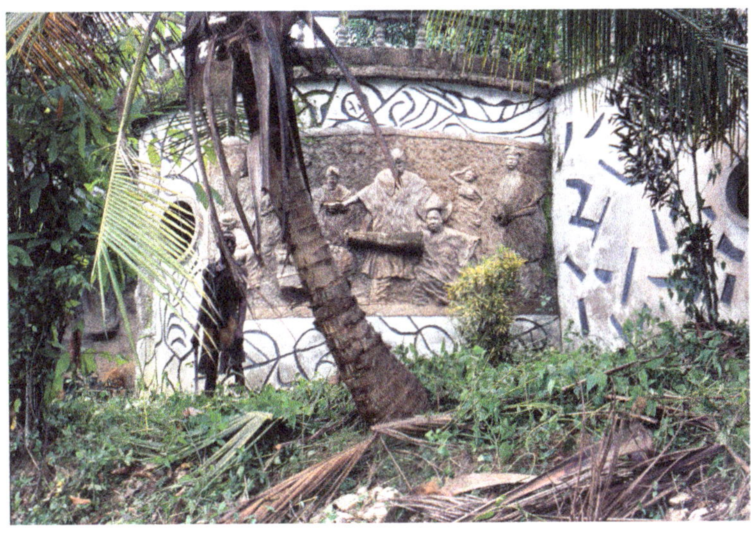

The guesthouse

The Resort

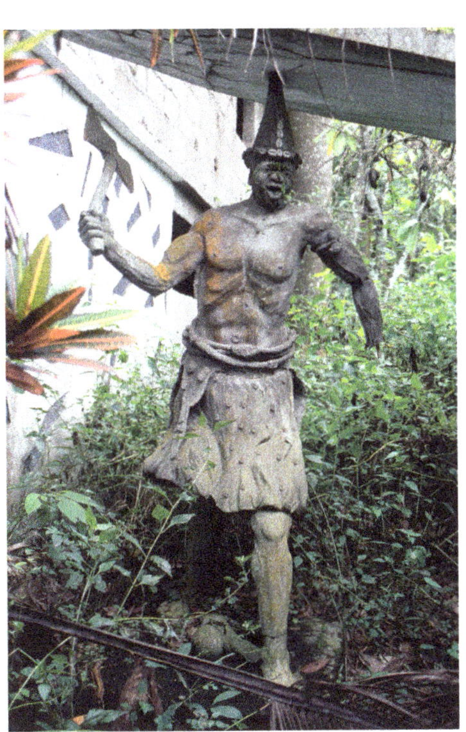

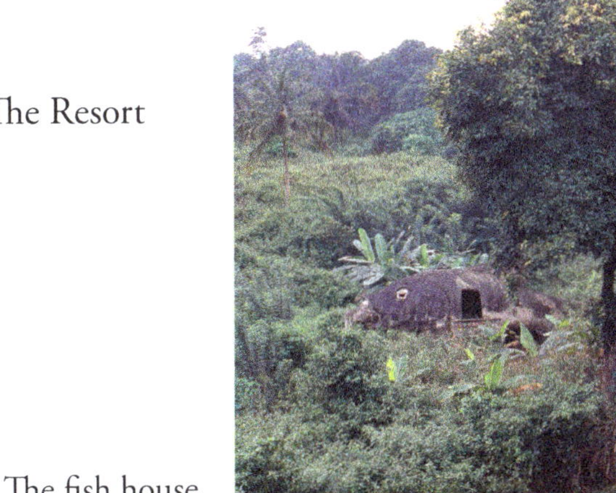

The fish house

Sango by Okido

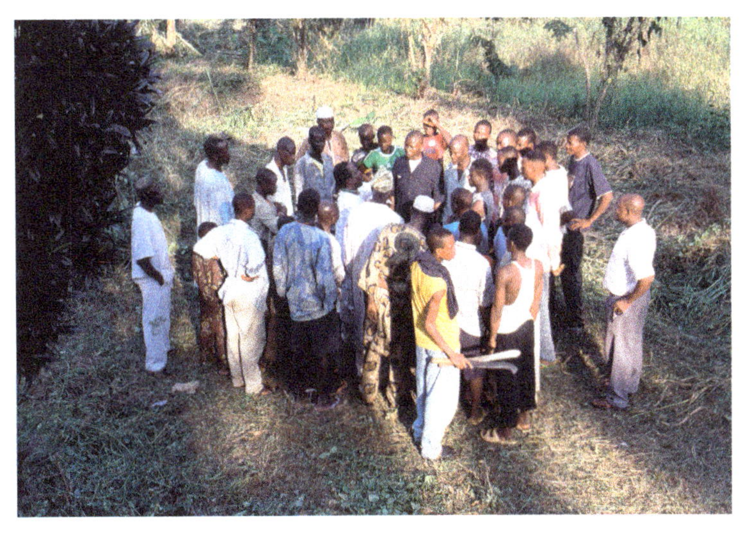

Prince gives his speech

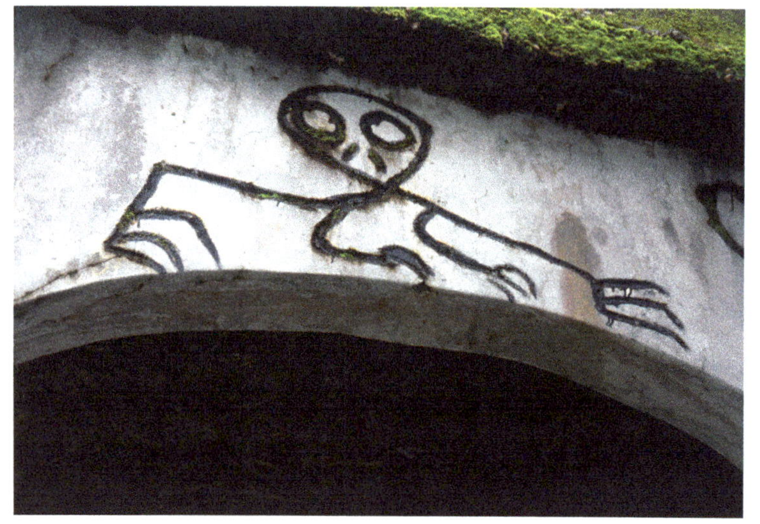

The Resort

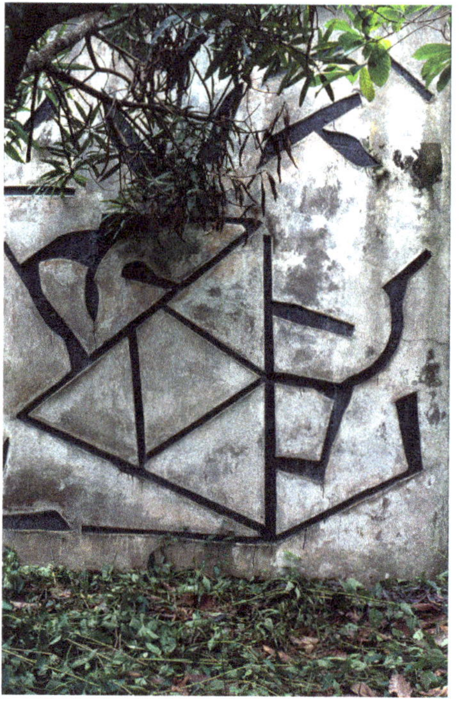

Prince's black-and-white ornament

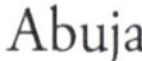

Abuja

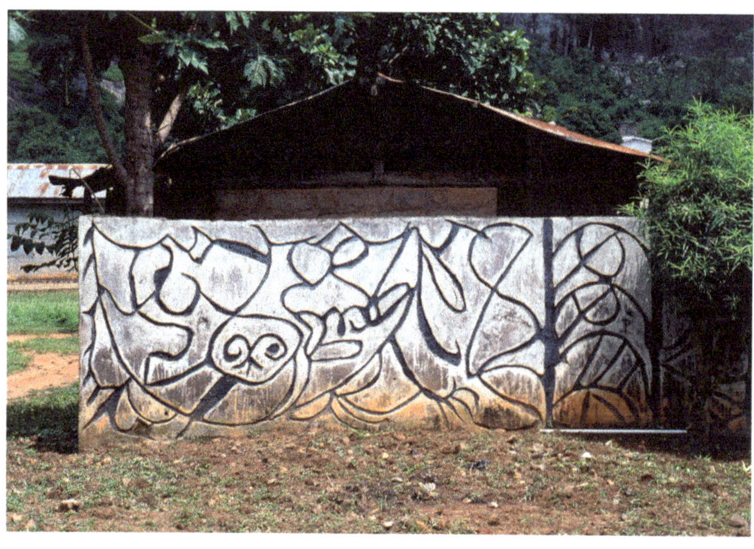

Ogidi

the governor of Osun State in the property, and during the next eighteen months, the state graded the road to the Resort and a plan for the land's use was formulated in the governor's office. In the future, perhaps, Prince will recover some of his investment, but what is more important, right now, this project, never to be complete, is once again moving forward, a sure sign of his continuing vitality.

"Somebody who is not as powerful as God thought he could kill me," Prince told me when we stood in the weeds. But he was alive, and he would show them. Why this urgent need, you might ask, why all this talk of death? People in Ogidi and Sekona might have thought he was dead, but more to the point, only two years before he was sinking in the sea, his energy sapped, his mind blank. His spirit was drifting toward death, but he had risen; he was painting again, and, honored once more, he was home in full force. The cleared fields and rising water are visible proofs of his existence. He acts, he commands others to act, and the actions yield material evidence. The far goal is of less importance. In the moment: he acts, therefore, he is.

Prince was back. On the day of the Osun Festival in Osogbo, the first Friday in August, the drummers came to his house, beating in the courtyard, then leading him into the crowd that moved quickly away from the main road. Some people were already leaving, a few families in fine automobiles lurched in the procession, making slow progress, but we went with the people, walking quickly, turning into the lane that passed through the grove, onward, down toward the pavilion. A light rain was falling, a good sign on Osun's day; it was hazy overhead, slippery underfoot.

At the temporary fence before the pavilion, police officers turned most people back, but they instantly recognized Prince and welcomed him heartily. We left our drummers and pressed through the gate. The order inside, the ranking and placement, had become familiar to me from meetings of local government councils. Straight ahead, the pavilion sheltered the king and his court, the governor and other political officials. Distinguished guests sat along the left, the men and women of Osun, and there we were given, Prince, Pravina, and I, white plastic chairs. An arc of newsmen with television cameras swung from left to right, obscuring the view of the people who filled the hillside, clustered around drummers whose cadences meshed and clashed. To the right, as though at a parade or powwow, an announcer spoke into a microphone, naming each group of performers—mostly women in identical attire, accompanied by male drummers—who squeezed through the gate on cue and danced in front of the pavilion. Then they fell in prostration, rose to receive gifts of money from the great

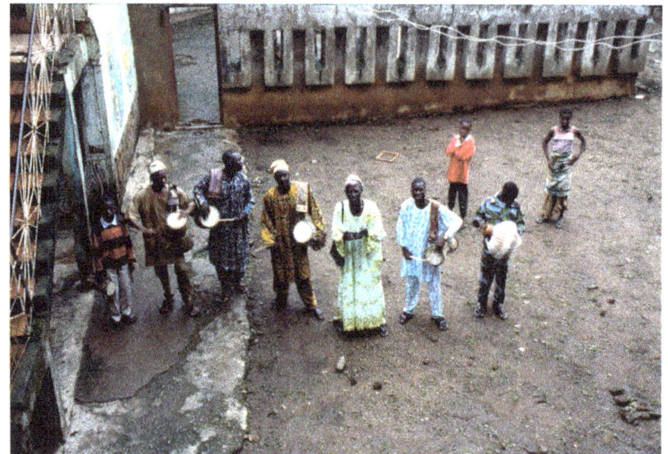

The drummers arrive at Prince's house to lead him to the Festival

Osun Festival

Prince arrives at the Festival

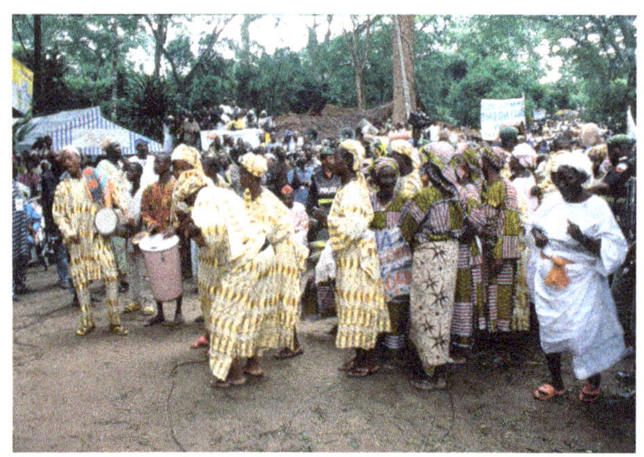

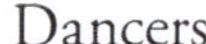

Dancers

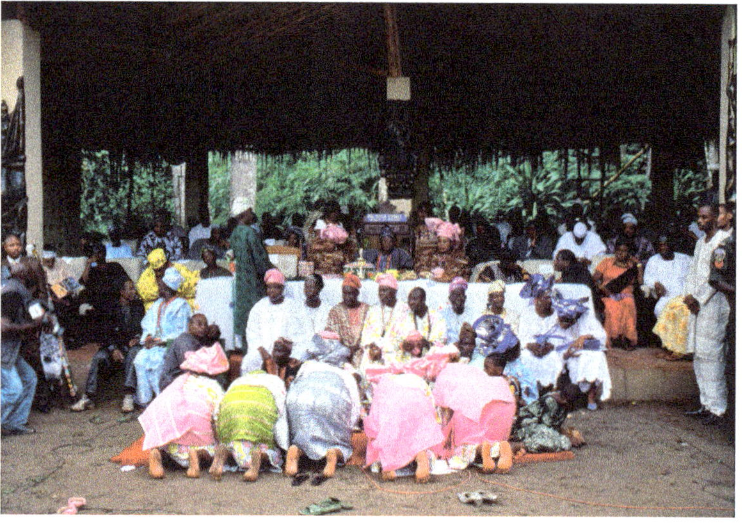

Prostration before the king at the pavilion

men before them, and exited to the right. It was a grand version of small events I had seen: people honoring Prince in performance and receiving cash in return.

While the dancers came and went, the reporters nearby turned their attention to Prince, kneeling before him, welcoming him home, recording his words. Needing footage to fill airtime, they turned to me. I could not hear what they asked or I said, but I told them that, as a result of unsubtle prejudice, when their nation figured in the newscasts of the West, the tone was invariably negative, but I liked Nigeria: the people were warm, the music excellent, the food delicious. What Prince and I said was featured, along with a statement by Governor Oyinlola, on the televised news that night and repeated frequently afterward. During the rest of the trip, young men greeted me in the street with bright smiles, calling me Prof and giving me high fives, though I had only said what was so.

The event's final act began when Governor Oyinlola stepped forward to the podium, acknowledged in sequence the people of significance, and spoke of the cultural importance of the Festival. He was followed by a man who declared Jesus Christ to be our Lord, and spoke of the economic importance of the Festival, its capacity to attract tourists to Osogbo. Tourism is a relatively clean industry that extracts wealth from people in motion and distributes it among the people in place, some of them modest in means. The Festival's catch from the West was small, statistically irrelevant, but conspicuous, as I was, by color: two bewildered girls from northern Europe, two mature women of the Africanist sort, one jittery kid who liked drumming, a dealer in traditional art, five arty videographers. As in every place where I have attended to tourism—the United States, Turkey, India, Japan—most of the tourists here were not rich foreigners (whose intrusion inspires simplistic critique) but native people who had come for more than the spectacle. They were, like Chaucer's folks on the road, both tourists and pilgrims.

After the speeches, the climax came with Egungun. For the first time in a long day, people in the audience shouted for the television boys to squat down. This is something they wanted to see. Egungun, like Agbo, is a dancer of the ancestors. Prince said:

"Egungun is representative of the dead. In those days, when there's no police, it is the Egungun that the oba used to punish whoever must have done bad things in the society. People called them Araorunkinkin—somebody that come from heaven with clean hands.

"So, they are a representative of the dead. When we were very young, we always believed there's nobody in the costume. Because, you know, they cover everything, and they're very scary. With a mask—unlike today when, modern times, you have masquerades with only cloth on their face, a net, and they talk. Then you know somebody is inside.

"But during the time I was growing up, we don't think that there is anybody inside.

"So, when I was growing up, nobody know that Egungun has a wearer. But now we say, The eyes are not on the knee, but now the eyes have left the knee to come up here." Prince points to his face and smiles. "Which means: when you are very young, as a baby, everything scared you. And when you grow up, the eyes are no more on the knee.

"If somebody dies, you have different type of Egungun that would come out. Now, many women does not know where Egungun come from; they don't allow women to go to the forest, where they usually dress up. Because they believe that women can't keep the secrets. That's the reason.

"And then we have Oro. When the Oro thing is done, no woman can come out. Like in Ibadan, there's a particular masquerade, when he come out, no women can come out; every woman would be indoors. Oro"—a whirling roarer—"make noise, and when they do that, these cult members, when they hear it, every woman would go inside and lock their door.

"Because many years ago, before the white man, any woman that would see it, they would take her away and kill her.

"Some Egunguns are for festival. And some Egunguns we cannot use for festival. There is an Egungun that comes for rain. There's an Egungun that will come out when they want to do special blessing for the community. But, like, in some big cities today, Egungun might be just for carnival, and things like that. The Egungun at the Osun is a festival one, for performance, for the fun of it.

"But the real Egungun thing, the one that was sometimes coming for special occasions, some can be caning, beating up people."

This Egungun whirled in one costume, colorful flaps flying, then transformed, like a Northwest Coast mask, opening to reveal an inner spirit in a dappled suit that danced magnificently with an elder wearing an *agbada*. The crowd was roused, and the king reappeared. He had been sitting in the front, calmly watching, but now he walked in from the back, beneath a wide parasol, still wearing his crown with the beaded veil. The king was followed by a last band of drummers, and the dignitaries dispersed, leaving Osun's place to her people.

Prince called the Osun Festival a "three-in-one" event, at once political, commercial, and sacred. The pattern is general in festivals: politicians and businessmen seize upon the people's gatherings and bend them toward their own ends; meanwhile, the people mingle and mill, enjoying the music and enacting holy rites. From above it looks like history. One motion, the one tracked by journalists and conventional historians (the procession to honor

Osun Festival

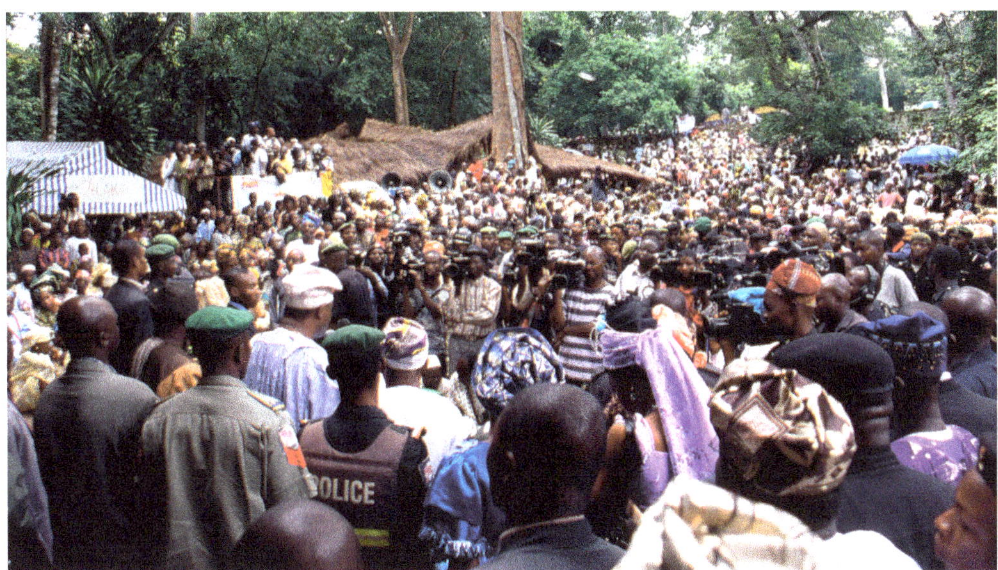

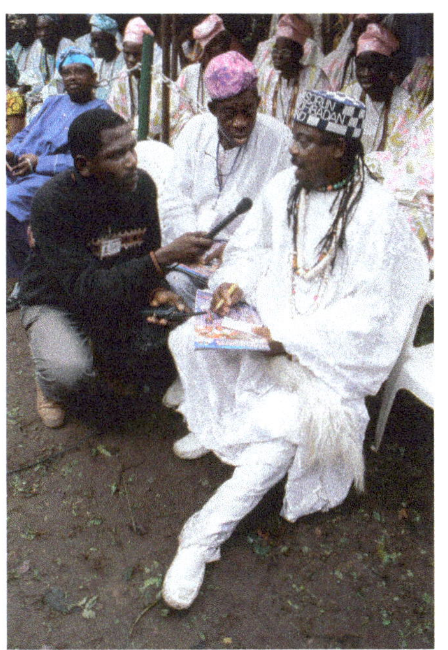

Prince and the media

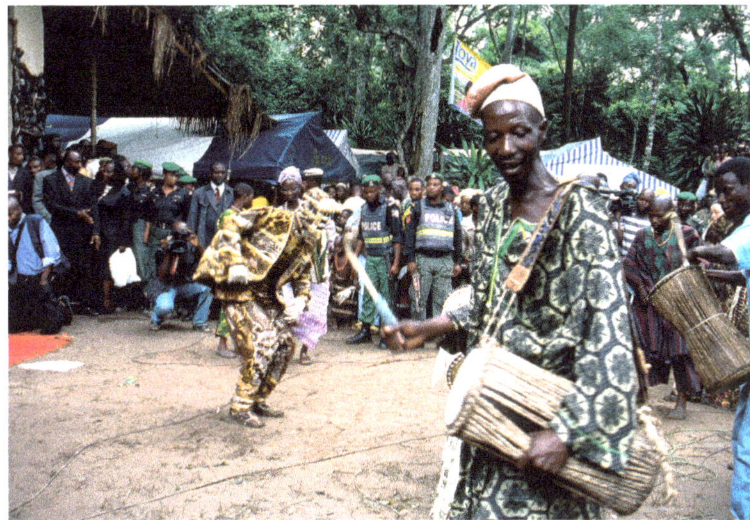

Egungun

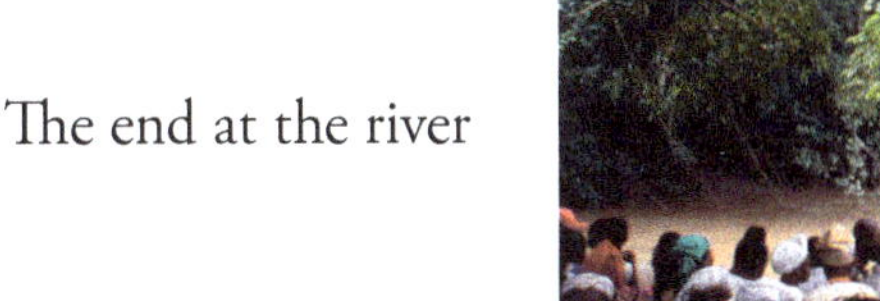

The end at the river

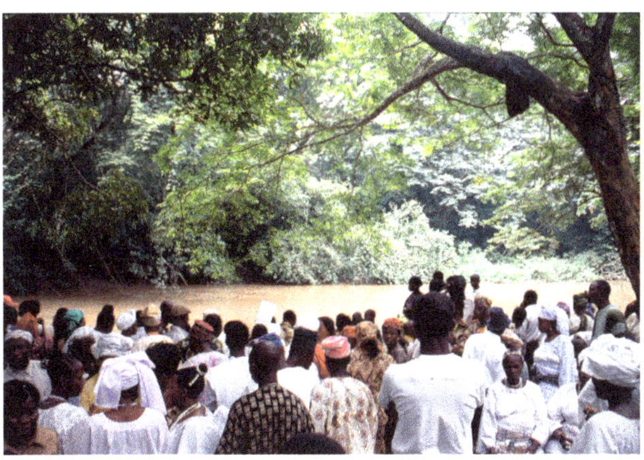

Aji-Ogbe pray for Prince in his house in Osogbo

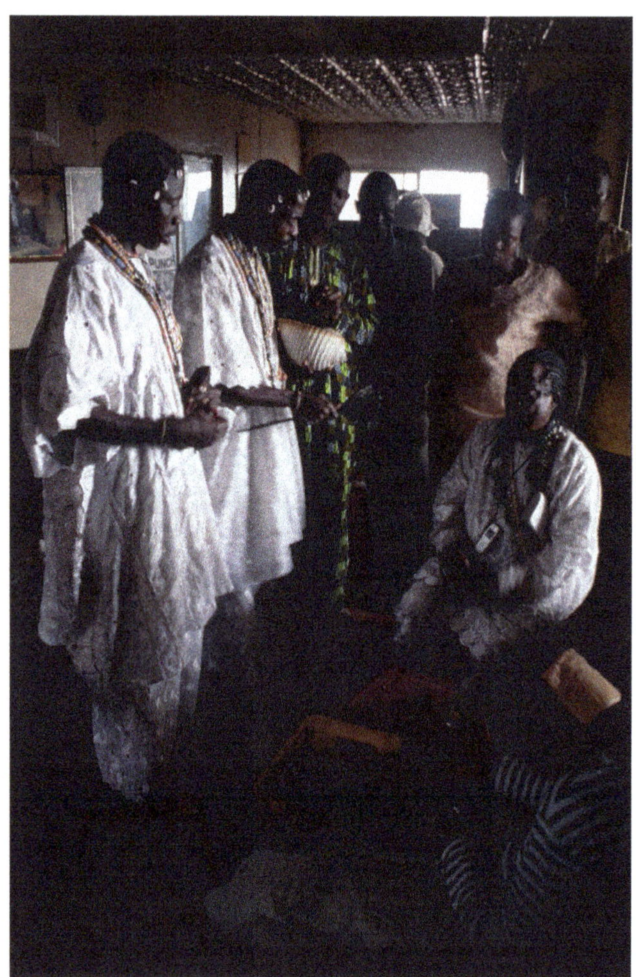

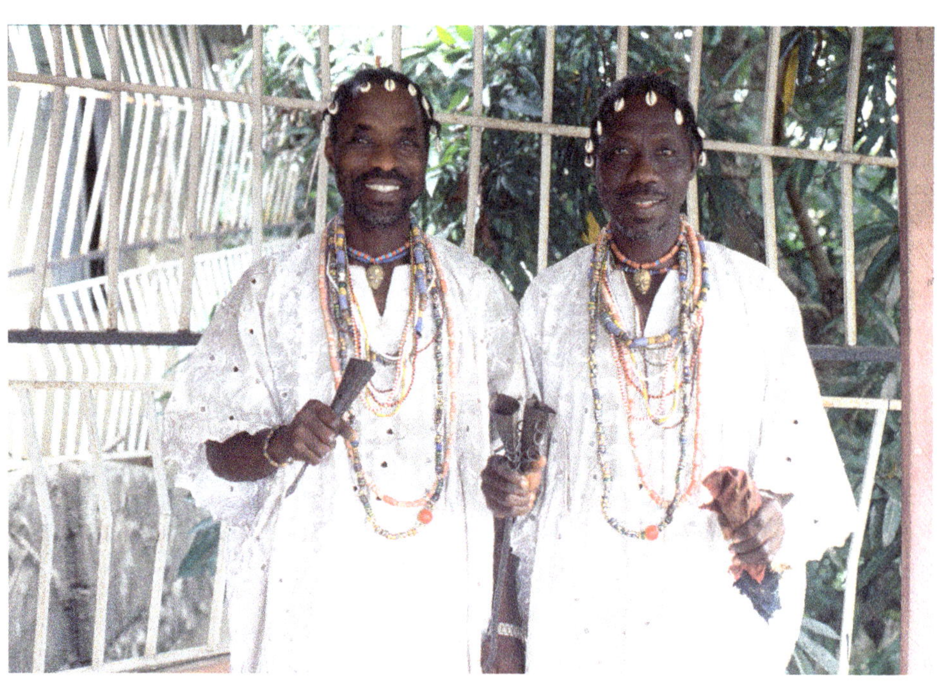

Aji-Ogbe, priests of Osun's shrine, Osogbo

temporal power), is mapped over another, usually lost to the record (the scatter and surge of the people's sociable assembly, motivated by small pleasures and sincere devotion). The historian's problem, the great historian E. P. Thompson told me, is how to get that second motion, the people's own actions, into the chronicle. Ethnography, I think, the patient procedure of folklorists and anthropologists, is the solution.

While the costumed performers knifed through the crowd, headed straight for the pavilion, most people, nearly all by percentage, were blocked by the fence that divided them from the media, the rulers, and the bureaucrats with plans to boost the economy. They turned back uphill to sit around their own musicians, then filtered down and turned right. We followed them through the narrow gate of the thatched shrine, shoes off, feeling the damp earth beneath, inching slowly forward, shoulder to shoulder, belly to back, at last meeting with the priests, twin men, dressed like Prince in white, their hair braided with cowries like his. They gave us a pinch of spicy yam to eat and a sup of Osun's water from a coconut shell, and we gave them offerings of money. It was theologically like communion, since by drinking the water we took the goddess—not metaphorically, but actually, sacramentally—into ourselves, and it was experientially like the exchange at a busy Hindu temple, where the priest gives *prasad* and receives a donation. Prayers were brief. We shouldered our way back through the crowd, squirming through the slim slit of the gate, as though reborn, and followed the loose procession that skirted the pavilion and ended at the bank of the River Osun, where Bumi saw the goddess rise from the water. The river is Osun herself. This is where barren women come to drink, returning a year later with healthy babies. Prince dipped a jar full of water for Princess Aliratu, and we retraced our route, pausing on the way out to throw behind us, over our heads, the troubles others had shed upon us during the Festival.

Back home, there was blood in the courtyard, spilled during sacrifice by the ram whose meat simmered into a tangy stew. The party in Prince's house had already begun. He seemed tired, maybe disappointed that his reception at the Festival had not met his dreams, but he was back, Osogbo knew it, and his house was full of people, eating his stew, drinking his beer, and dancing to the drums. Soon the twin priests of the shrine, Aji-Ogbe, arrived and they stood above Prince, chanting over and over in Yoruba: Mother rescue me, Mother Osun, Mother rescue me, Mother Osun . . . . Then they danced with him when a brass band appeared in the courtyard to honor Osogbo's hero.

The hero was weary, and it was not late when we left. To avoid danger and preserve mystery, Prince did not stay in his house. He and Aliratu shared a suite with Pravina and me in a modest hotel where the band down below continued in amplified aggression through the night. Prince's plan for the next day was to appear suddenly in different parts of the town, making people believe he was staying, though he intended to decamp quickly for his quiet country house outside of Ibadan.

A man's power in public is measured by the size of his entourage. I did not make much of an entourage, but I was all he had, so early the next morning he took me along to the vast auditorium where Governor Oyinlola was holding a televised question-and-answer session. The hall was full, every seat taken. High on a stage to the left, the governor sat on a couch, cooled by oscillating fans. One by one, his people stood at a microphone, down on the floor to the right. A woman said that moving the school would disrupt the economy of the women who sell food to the students. A man complained about the sporadic flow of electricity. Another asked for buses so workers could get to their jobs. Direct, pragmatic needs, not abstract matters of ideology, dominated the talk. The governor replied with warmth and wit, amusing the audience with puns in Yoruba, saying that, with the grace of God, he would solve the people's problems. As soon as we arrived, Prince was invited to the mike. Interrupting the train of complaint, he called the drummers to his side and sang, uniting the crowd in a call-and-response performance that swelled up and held. Then he spoke to thank the governor for the improvements wrought by his administration, new roads, new schools. At the end, Governor Oyinlola passed down the aisle, shaking hands with the people who lined up to greet him, and, having picked up a few followers—Adeagbo and Nine-Nine—we were off to our next stop. It was Prince's duty to visit Susanne Wenger.

Susanne Wenger met Ulli Beier in Paris in 1949. She was a painter in an up-to-date abstract manner with a strong interest in the world's traditions of art and myth. They visited museums together, and the next year they married in London and moved to Nigeria. In time, Prince told me, they separated. She married a Nigerian drummer. He married Georgina, an English artist who was the age of the young men she taught in the Mbari Mbayo workshops. "It was strange," Prince said, "to see a white guy in our community practicing polygamy, so they respect Ulli for that." When Ulli and Georgina left Nigeria in 1966, Susanne Wenger moved into their house, the house Ulli had bought in Osogbo in 1958.

The exterior of the house was ornamented by artists of the Osogbo school. Prince told me that they were shown photographs of works by Paul Klee, and Klee's linear sensibility merges easily with the Yoruba inclination to the figurative on the railings outside. Inside, across the hallway from a small shop selling local craft, is the studio where Prince made his first etchings. A narrow stair in the back rises through an Afro-fantastic assemblage of twisted limbs and old carvings to the third floor where Susanne Wenger, ninety-one years of age, waited to receive us. Like a shadow out of Dickens or Faulkner, this ancient lady sat gently amid decay, a dark, deep collection of wood and dust. Prince sat on a low stool beside her, like an affectionate son, humble in posture and uncommonly quiet. They spoke of Ulli Beier, then, as a mother would do with a son who had returned after a long journey, she asked about his trip, commiserating with his hardships, pleased when he told her I was writing this book.

Wole Soyinka remembers Susanne Wenger in two of his memoirs. In both, ambivalence resolves in respect. He was repelled by the filth in her house, attracted by her tranquility. She and Ulli Beier had "gone native," Soyinka wrote, Susanne Wenger "viscerally and spiritually": "this strange Austrian woman," heroic during the dark ages of the Holocaust, "had found a home among the Yoruba, found her goddess and become her priestess." Devoted to Osun, she led the movement to restore the shrine by the river, filling the sacred grove with her own peculiar concrete statues. Sometimes Soyinka felt reconciled to her works, other times hostile. Osun's place had become "one of the weirdest yet most meditative spots in the nation," a serene site of serious pilgrimage. In Soyinka's accounts, her sincerity trumps her strangeness, and Prince's opinion tallies with his.

When I asked Prince to tell me about Susanne Wenger, he twined their lives together. Like her, he is a follower of Osun who was saved by the water of the goddess. Like him, she is an artist who shapes her creations to a personal vision. Both of them worked to retrieve the old faith and protect the place of Osun—hated when they began, respected once the Festival had become a success. Prince put it like this:

"What I heard from Susanne Wenger, and what I heard from Ulli: when they first came to Nigeria, Ulli was working at the University of Ibadan, at the extramural department. And they happened to love to live in Osogbo, rather than stay in Ibadan at the university. And I think Susanne Wenger was sick. I think she got small pox or something. And she happens to go to the river, and one of the priestess, of Osun's priestess, take good care of her. And she got well. And that is when she started get attracted to the river.

"And maybe she is somebody who love nature. She end up staying in that forest"—Osun's grove—"by herself alone. Probably meditating, whatever she is doing at that time. Not many people know it, and not many people thought that place is going to become what it is, through her contribution.

"So, I think that is how she started. And then eventually she got into the love of the area, and started doing her sculpture work in the forest there. But many people thought something is wrong with her. And they call her an idol worshiper.

"But she attracted herself to a lot of these Osun worshipers, and she became part of it. And they give her chieftaincy title, and that's how she began doing her work at the shrine.

"But most of the sculptures she was doing has to be a reflection of her own thinking. Like the animals, the face, the nose of the sculptures you see; it is from her own personality way of thinking. Like in my drawing too.

"So, what I'm trying to say here is that when Susanne Wenger started her work, not everybody thought or believed what she was doing was good, was going to go toward what it is today.

"So, I think I call her an artistic missionary. That's what I would call her, rather than a religious missionary.

"At the beginning, not everybody admire what she is doing then. I have never met them then"—Prince had not yet come to Osogbo. "She must have got a lot of enemy among the Muslims and the Christians. Because to them, at that time, she is bringing back an abandoned religion. Because, like, you know, in those days if you don't go to church, you can hardly get your children be admitted to school. And later, in the seventies and eighties, if you are not an Alhaji, somebody who has been to Mecca before, you have no connection to government officials to get contract. That's why. And many Yorubas are not serious Muslims, my people, because in the night they still go to the native doctors, they still go to their secret cult meetings, and all that. But they can be Alhaji Yusuf, and some of the Christians can be called David, Samuel, but in the night they are behind somewhere, doing the right thing for their people.

"Later, Susanne Wenger started getting a lot of respect. And then, the aspect of it is when a lot of international people started coming to Osogbo, during the Festival. But before that time, you see a lot of people, either Muslims or Christians, love to be at the river. They don't want to throw over what belongs to them.

"Then, when I came in, apart from the fact that my great-grandfather was known as Olosun, the man who really owns Osun. So I went to the shrine, for my *own* thinking, for my own spiritual way of thinking. I bought a cow. Which nobody ever did before, and I gave it to the shrine.

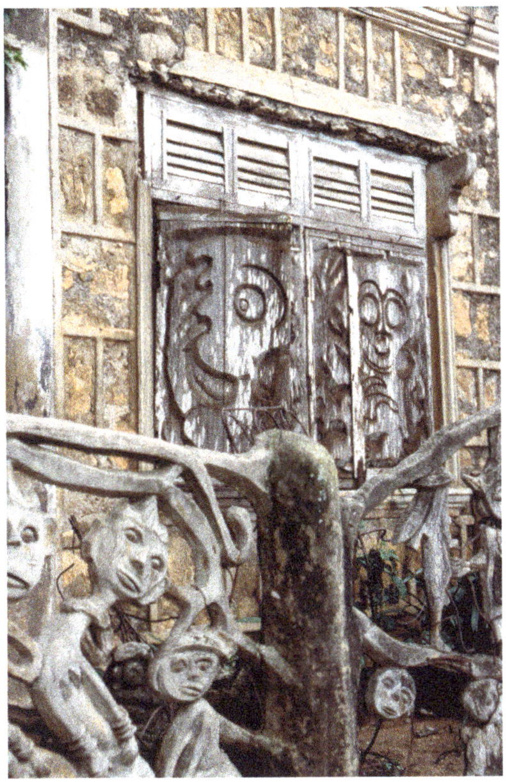

Susanne Wenger's house, Osogbo, 2006

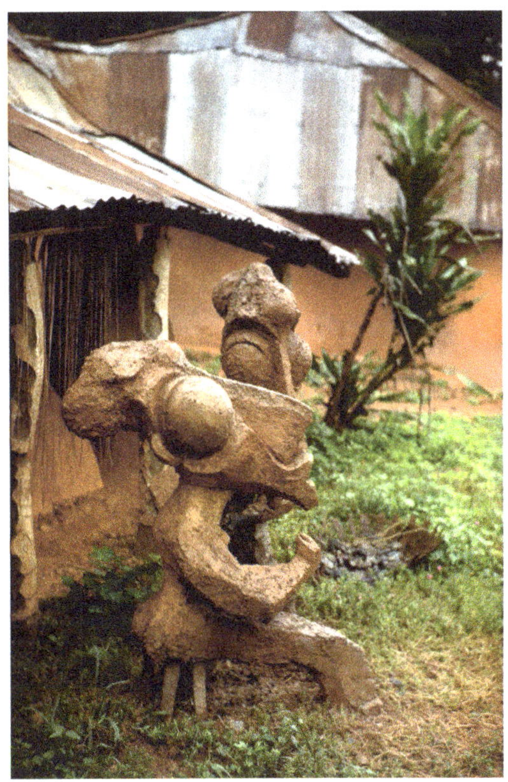

Susanne Wenger's work at the shrine, Osogbo.
Photographs taken by Philip M. Peek in 1965

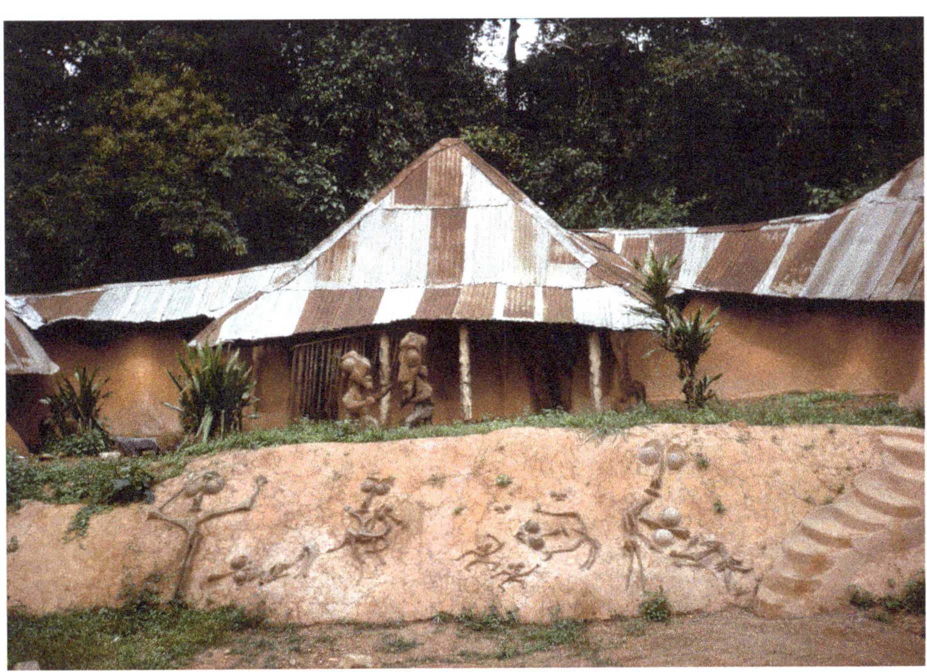

"And I pledged that if I become successful in my work, if I become successful and my work took me to every country of the world, I will always remember to worship her, as my ancestor did.

"And when I have my first baby, I didn't have money for Bintu to take medicine in the hospital. So, I used to go there and take the water. And I go there midnight to talk to the river, to the goddess. So, I used that a lot. And that is why, most of the time, I have river goddess in my paintings.

"I think I can probably tell you that I'm the *most* closest person, as a young artist, after Ulli Beier and Susanne Wenger, that got close to the Osun thing. And my name was more pronounced with the popularity of Osun in the *whole* local area. And during the Festival, I would bring the band, like Sunny Ade or other band, to perform, *eve* of Osun day. So, it become a big jamboree thing.

"So. I don't want to sing my praises, but even when I am not at the shrine, some people will see me. I can be at home painting during the Osun day, and some people will say they see me at the shrine.

"That show you how my spirit is so close to the place.

"And it come to a point where some people hate me too. In Osogbo. Because they thought all these international people came and bringing millions of dollars because of Osun. So, everybody now want to be Osun worshiper, to gain what I have gained.

"But eventually, at the end, they realized that whatever is happening is just my love of Osun, not for my material gain from it. The only time I gain from Osun is when people visited me, they invited me back to their country for an exhibition. That's the only gain. It's not that when people come to the Osun Festival, they bring me money, as their priest. No. But many people don't know that.

"Because, at that time, the fire of my acclaim, popularity, become so big, and it was like striking matches together.

"And then there was a point of time that I organize what you call shrine guide. To stop people from coming there to kill fish. Because the fishes in the river were *big*, big, big. And some land intruders want to be taking the land. And I have my journalist to do my underground writing, to support the protection of that place. The Nigerian government push to acquire the land there, to stop people from eroding in on the land. Otherwise, they should have sold all the land.

"And some people hate Susanne Wenger, because they said, Where does she come from? Because today the place is, like, Susanne Wenger property. Because without her that land should have been eroded away and sold by people.

"So, everybody is grateful to her. She is like a big, big, big respectable symbol. And, you know, the government did a fantastic birthday party for her; she was ninety. The Osun State government did that. They spent a lot of money, invite people.

"And I respect her a lot, because she seemed to have a soft spot for me. She did; she was like a mother to me. She call me Edun. Edun means the name you call the monkey that represent the twins. That's what she called me. She never call me by my name; she call me Edun.

"She is a wonderful person."

The visit was brief, soft and sad. We left Susanne Wenger with her women—a priestess of Sango with a red feather in her hair, an artist who practices her father's craft of brass-casting—her colleagues, companions, and keepers. Our next destination was the grand home of the reader Alhaji Oladeji, at the edge of the city. He led us into his room for consultation. A picture on the wall above his desk showed him in Saudi dress, a souvenir of the hajj to Mecca that earned him the title Alhaji. The title, Prince told me, marked him as a man of wealth, capable of making the trip, and it gained him permanent respectability, a convenient cover for his work as a diviner.

Prince sat nervously on a bench to the side, rubbing his hair and telling the tale of a life turned upside-down. While he spoke, Alhaji Oladeji looked directly, steadily into his eyes, smiling angelically. Prince asked him to use his Muslim name, Husseini, to clear an Islamic channel to power. Alhaji Oladeji placed a naira note on Prince's forehead, then set it in front of the bowl of water hidden in the kneehole of his desk. With stunning speed and clarity, he repeated a long incantation and gazed into the water where he could see people and things invisible to others. He told Prince that he would receive an award from the president, that his troubles were brought on by witchcraft worked by his wives, that he would become a king. The first and last were not predictions exactly, but provisional forecasts requiring actions to counter the cause of his distress. Prince had to purchase the supplies, dead rats and dead fish, in the market downtown, which Alhaji Oladeji would use to battle the witches hired by his enemies, and if he proved successful—if Prince got the award, if his life straightened out, if he became a king—then Alhaji Oladeji expected a fine gift. What he wanted was a convertible, so that, with his top down, he could be seen driving through the streets of his hometown, Osogbo.

The gift of an automobile seemed reasonable, since Prince once dealt in used cars, but the cost of the procedure was more than he could manage. This reader, Prince said, was "expensive"; he recommended three sacrifices, each costing sixteen thousand naira. Alhaji Oladeji bade us farewell with a sweet smile, but Prince left in a state of agitation that would only increase when he got back to his house.

They had seen him at the Festival, seen him on television, and they were already gathering in the expansive, cross-shaped room on the third floor of his house, waiting to greet him. Prince had set a task for himself, and it alone would have caused him unease. He was leaving, staking his hopes on success in America. Together we went through the heaps of sodden paper, illegible citations and yellowing newsprint, hunting for photographs that documented his career, for minor works of art that had escaped the damp and might be sold. He filled a shotgun case with old photos, removed old paintings from their frames and rolled them up. The people, sitting in small groups, did not watch, but waited quietly, then approached, some bending a knee, some touching the ground with both hands, others lying face-down, flat on the floor before him. Old acquaintances, distant relations: he shook their hands, heard their stories, and gave them money. The people of his household watched the money fly, and they lined up to repeat their requests. The plumbing needs repair, the children need clothes, the mosquitoes are swarming and bug spray costs money.

Night fell. Prince kept sifting through the wreckage of his life, finding photographs faded, stained, and stuck together, etchings spotted and foxed, record albums in ruined sleeves, fused clumps of paper. He is not a drinker, but he was drinking, trying to think, trying not to think, while new groups of men formed on the couches, waiting, while the women of his household waited too, all ready to pounce when he rose from his job to pace in agitated distraction through the room. They pretend to love him, he told me as we peeled away layers in the midden of his achievement, but they take, take, take, never give. His money was going. He paced and drank, the demands did not stop. At last, he snapped.

To new experiences, we come half-prepared. Reading about Yoruba culture prepared me for certain details of my experience in Nigeria, but in trying to get a grip on the whole, I fell back on Shakespeare. The comparison of Shakespeare's England with Prince's Nigeria is not trivial. There are kings, witches, and ghosts, jealousy and greed, revenge, trickery, generosity, and stoic heroism. In the background lies the wrenching change from the old religion to a new one, and the problem of political succession in a nation shifting from hereditary power to power won by money and force of will. In the foreground opens a mind, liberated and fearful, driven by private ambition, yet anxious about social connection, about loyalty and love.

Late one night, we arrived at the palace of a paramount chief, a king who held sway over fourteen lords, all rivals for his crown. The place, beyond a small town, was dark: the electricity had failed, the king was asleep. We knocked, and the porter lit a lamp and led us into the deep, black audience hall. While we waited for the king, Prince limped the length of the hall and slouched into the high throne; I could not but think of Richard the Third. Now, feeling betrayed by his family and friends, Prince raged like Lear on the heath. Damning them all for their greed and false affection, he stormed in fury and ran screaming into a small chamber to weep against the wall. Remembering from the sixties how to handle bad trips, I followed and held him while he sobbed.

Cultural difference counts for little in times of human pain. We were men of the same generation, embraced in sweat, his tears soaking into my shirt. As he settled down and grew calm, he told me that the ceaseless demands for money had caused him to crack, but his anxiety ran deeper than cash.

Prince had told me before that the root cause of his trouble was the curse of a powerful reader, a baba who lived far to the east. His farm flourished, apparently without labor, yielding bumper crops of corn and the largest yams. His neighbors were baffled by his success, but one day a boy who was still a virgin chanced to wash his face in the water used by the baba, and when he looked up he saw the fields full of dead children at work on the land. He told the neighbors. Believing the baba had killed the children to use their labor, they destroyed his house and had him imprisoned. After three years in jail, he moved to another town and prospered. I found this to be a common motif in the biographies of the babas. Their neighbors burn their homes, forcing them to flee, doomed to wander until they find a place where they can practice in peace. Once, this powerful baba came all the way to Prince's house in Osogbo. In fear, Prince hid, pretending that he was not home, but the baba knew he was, and for this discourtesy he demanded the gift of a car. Prince refused. The baba waxed furious and cursed him. Though later he made peace with the man, Prince still felt that the curse had not been lifted, that it was the cause of his political problems, the cause of the attacks by armed robbers that drove him out of Nigeria.

But now he has new information. Last night, after the Festival, Aji-Ogbe, the twin priests of Osun's shrine, told him that the source of his distress was, indeed, a curse—not a curse by the baba to the east, but a curse by the baba in the bush. (In this passage, my constant rule of ethical delicacy directs me to suppress the names as well as the details of a personal nature that might bring harm if frozen in print.) The baba in the bush is even more powerful than the baba to the east. Prince calls him a witchdoctor, a juju man, and says that he knows the future and can change it at will. If he wants a palm tree to die, it will die that night.

Prince has known the baba in the bush for years. One time a European collector sent his agents to buy paintings from Prince. Art was not their only concern, and while they were enjoying a night with prostitutes, their passports were stolen. This baba worked magic to locate the thieves and recover the passports, which held high value on the black market. Another time, Prince was arrested; the baba sent him a "talisman" that secured his immediate release. When all his wives left him in 1982, Prince wanted nothing more to do with women or children, but the baba told him he would marry again and gave him a black soap to use in ritual bathing. He had five more wives, twenty-eight more children. The last time that Prince was considering marriage, he went to the baba for advice. He told him to marry, but when he married Aliratu, the baba cursed him because he wanted Prince to marry his own daughter. And that was the curse, Aji-Ogbe said, that had ruined his life. The time was right, late in the nineties when things began to fall apart. Prince was convinced. He had at last learned the cause of his decade of failure—the arguments among his wives, the attacks by armed robbers, the steep decline of his fortunes in America.

Yesterday Aji-Ogbe told him that the baba had sent two men to talk with him. Spies, Prince called them. But they found his house too crowded and noisy for a serious conversation, so they left. It was clear to Prince that he would have to go to the bush and speak with the baba. The prospect terrified him; it filled his brain and drove him to drink, but he had no choice, and he asked me to go with him, to give him support—support is one of his key words; he is flamboyant, others fill supportive roles. By midnight, Prince had gathered his courage, and, with Sunday at the wheel, we were away to the bush, the dense domain of shadows that rolls beyond control.

A long way out of Osogbo, we turn off the main road and into the bush. The headlights cut a track through the black, turning the black walls green, for an instant, the black road red, while we slip through the thickness that looms before us and closes behind. For mile after mile, brushed on both sides, we splash through streams and spin in the mud, finding the slit in the tangle that carries us through a brief clearing, then plunges us back into the bush for miles more, until, at a second clearing, the car stops. There is no moon, no stars.

Sleep lies deep in both of the mud-walled houses. It is perfectly silent, utterly dark. Then a small light moves behind a window, and a tall man emerges from the doorway, holding a kerosene lantern. This is the baba, elderly but erect, bare-chested and handsome. He stands, smiling serenely as powerful readers do, while Prince embraces his knees in Homeric supplication, weeping and spilling out the tale of his troubles. Enough is enough, he cries. Calmly, gently, the baba of the bush tells him that the past is past; it is over: everything will be all right.

Maybe, but a delicate personal matter demands debate and resolution. Twenty people have roused themselves and gathered. They huddle back in the dark, while the baba settles onto a bench, in the dim light of the lamp, to sit in judgment. He sends a boy out through the night to call a key witness. Prince stands and delivers his version of events. Fresh from sleep, a young man appears, and, at the baba's command, offers his version. Questioned, he steps out of his sandals, stands barefoot on the earth, and tells the truth. His tale no longer contradicts Prince's. As in any court case, it has been a contest of narratives, and Prince, the victor, is suddenly his giddy old self. Now, breaking all the rules of decorum, he moves and laughs freely, talking on and on, while the audience slowly surrenders composure and laughs along. The laughter swallows the dangerous, painful information that reasonable speech had released. Prince has become a humorous healer of social ills.

God is a wonder, a boy told me in Ogidi, that He has created someone like Prince Twins Seven-Seven. Prince is a little wonder himself, a passionate disruption in sober scenes, a personified contrast to the Yoruba virtue of cool restraint. Merrily, Prince opens a black plastic sack stuffed with naira notes in small denominations. He hands some to everyone in the crowd—so they would not curse him for being forgotten, he told me later—and gives a thick wad to the baba, repaying society for allowing him to be who he is. He is a wild artist, a masquerader at play beyond the bonds of the normal, and he is a wily self-made man who complains about money lost and given away, but always—nearly always—seems to have held enough back to meet his immediate needs.

Prince moves in laughter, then, abruptly serious, he kneels before the baba's wife, the mother of the girl he did not marry, and pleads for forgiveness. She smiles, and he turns to her husband. Weeping once more, he hugs the baba's knees. Unruffled, disdainful of all this unseemly emotion, the baba looks down into his eyes, smiling the smile of an indulgent father, and tells him all is forgiven: henceforth his life will be free of trouble. At the end, the baba intones a prayer, calling upon the black powers to protect Prince.

The night has begun its slide toward dawn. In the car on the way home, Prince tells us that, though the baba had cursed him, he had now reassured him that his route to the future lay clear. It was not a reader's prediction, Prince says, dependent on sacrifices and acts of the gods. The baba holds in himself the power to make things happen. His closing prayer meant everything, Prince says. If he could believe it, what a relief it would be. His return to Nigeria would have been a monumental victory. Connected again to the powers, he has cleaned up the past; he can go forward in confidence.

It is sweet to believe, to abide in pure faith, but our Prince is a meditative man. His mind turns in an overdetermined universe of multiple, simultaneous causation. His life has been a mighty struggle. Rising from poverty, battered by defeat, he has learned to be engaging and brave—it was surely brave to face the baba in the bush—and he has learned to retreat into the citadel of the self. Happy outside, a colorful and talented entertainer, he is tight, wary, and distrustful inside. He has been told his troubles are over; now he sets out to test what he has learned.

Two days later we are in Suleiman Abbakir's room for consultation. Before him on a table he has a rectangular tray of fine, dry sand. Prince gives him a twenty-dollar bill, and using two fingers at once, moving left to right, Suleiman makes four rows of double dents in the sand, as though he were writing. Then he counts backward from the bottom, striking vertical lines through the pattern, reads, and tells Prince that there will be no death in the near future. He advises Prince to live near water that abounds in fish (which is right for an Osun), and he says that water and wood are essential to his success. That is right, Prince whispers to me, since sculpture's paintings on wood have brought him fame, and he finds pictures in the grain by spilling water on wood. Suleiman Abbakir ends the first phase of the reading by telling Prince that, though jealous enemies surround him, he protects himself by generosity, by giving his wealth away.

For the second phase of the reading, Suleiman uses seven mysterious objects, each crafted out of a guinea hen feather stuck into a tiny, tight bundle that looks like an amulet. He arranges them into a standing circle on the sand in the tray, and tips them over so that they overlap at the center of the circle, in a shape like an asterisk. Then he covers them with a hemispherical section of a calabash. Suleiman sits back and speaks a prayer. Prince places his hands on the dome of the calabash and repeats the prayer. When Suleiman lifts the calabash, six of the seven feathered bundles have sprung up to stand erect. More money is necessary. Prince gives Suleiman a hundred-dollar bill. Suleiman circles the feathered amulets, tips them over, and covers them with the calabash. Prince places his hands on the calabash again, repeats Suleiman's prayer again, and asks his first question. Is it true that the baba in the bush will trouble him no more? The calabash is lifted. All seven of the feathers are standing upright. The answer is yes. Prince is elated.

The procedure repeats. Prince asks the second question. Will I become the king of Ibadan? The calabash goes up, the feathers all stand. The third question is: will Shola return? The feathers stand. Suleiman tells Prince to ask this last question. Will I die soon? The calabash is lifted. All the feathers still lie in the sand. The answer is no, a confirmation of the message Suleiman found in the sand at the beginning. The divination has circled into symmetrical closure.

It has been a marvelous reading, and Prince is thrilled. He can look forward to a long life, a peaceful household, a royal crown, and, best of all, the baba in the bush has truly lifted the curse that wrecked his life. Suleiman gives him packets of medicine to take with black stout and soap to use in ritual washing, so his strength will continue, his wishes will come true.

No reading, no single act, of course, is enough. That evening Prince sacrificed to Osun at the lake, and that night he asked Sule Badmus, his reliable reader, to evaluate Suleiman Abbakir's prescription. The soap is efficacious, Sule said, it will help Prince overcome his enemies, but the medicine, while harmless, is worthless. It is like an advertisement or a calling card. By taking it Prince would be reminded of Suleiman, prompted to return to him for further readings.

Prince might have been reassured, but the next day we went again to the baba in the bush, finding him this time in a house he owns in a village. Sunday, Pravina, and I sat in one room. Prince went with the baba into the other. Through the closed door, we heard only a low, rhythmic murmur, punctuated by Prince's stressed voice repeating, *"Ase,"* power. He came back to us, drained and weak, shaken but ready to believe. He has done all he could with the men of spiritual power.

He had one more move to make, this one designed to bring the men of worldly power to his side. "I want to be the king of this place," Prince said when we got to Ibadan. Alhaji Oladeji and Suleiman Akkabir both read a kingship into his future. As the Ekerin-Basorun of Ibadan, he stands fourth in line to the throne, but, he said, the kingship rotates among sixteen families in Ibadan, of which his is but one, and the final decision rests with Ifa, with acts of divination interpreted by the babalawo and the men he calls king-makers. To advance his chance for selection, Prince planned to please the people and leaders of Ibadan with a day of entertainment.

The palace, Olosun compound, Ibadan, on the day of Prince's entertainment

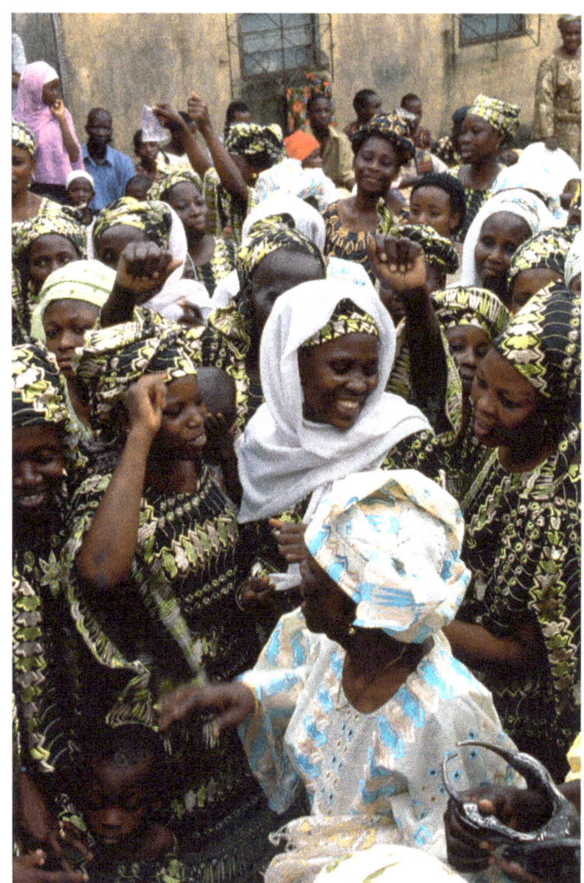

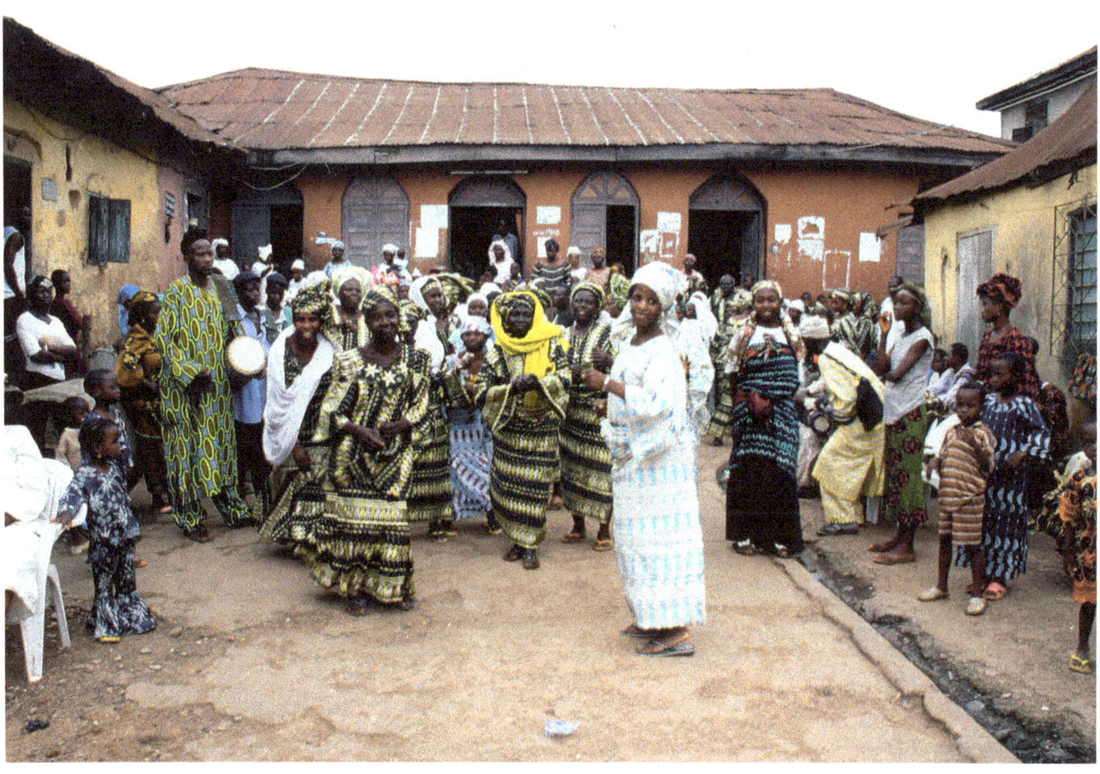

On the big day, Prince rose early in his country house outside of Ibadan. He was nervous and irritable, shouting out orders to the women who had come from Osogbo to prepare the food. He fretted and paced, fuming in a Sango mood, but the women were used to it, and with his pleasant, efficient daughter-in-law Iyakeji in the lead, they made a mound of *akara* and a vast chicken soup to serve the guests at the Olosun compound. Prince was anxious to go, but reluctant to leave, and he delayed his departure until noon, then delayed his arrival by stopping to chat happily with an old friend in the New Gbagi Market.

Blocked by the traffic in the Agbeni Market, we walked the last few hundred yards, and turned into the compound. Straight ahead, Chief Busari Odunoye Osuntoki sat in front of the palace. Up the steps behind him sat a long row of Osun's devotees, men and women in white. To the left sat the invited dignitaries, the king-makers: Chief Obiaruku, the Olorialagba of Ibadan, and Olanipenkun, the Baale of Apata. The compound's married women, dressed in matching green outfits, stood back to the right where they would serve the food and drink provided by Prince. The independent women of the family, prosperous traders, ladies with no need for men, sat in a proud line at the edge of the courtyard, defining the open ground for performance.

Prince had hardly finished greeting the great men when the drummer arrived and set the place to dancing. When the sound of the drum comes to a street, everyone, as though choreographed, begins to move subtly to the beat, and now the public courtyard of the palace vibrates and fills with bodies in slow, stately, rhythmic motion. A pulsing white swirl sweeps around Prince, and he dances with the followers of Osun.

When the drumming stops, the dancers go off to get their food, and Prince takes his seat beside Chief Busari, the Mogaji. Prince had arranged for the Ajagila acrobats to perform, and now the show begins. To the beat of the drum, boys spin cartwheels down the courtyard and turn somersaults in the air. His routine complete, each boy comes to Prince for pay. At the end, a slim lad stands while his feet are tied together and the crowd showers him with money. Then, his feet bound and the people amazed, he bounces through back flips from one end of the open space to the other. The show is over, the drumming is not; the dancing begins again. Prince had told us to be ready to move. He gives us the sign and walks swiftly out of the courtyard, away from the palace, and into the market. Sunday is waiting in the getaway car. He nudges it through the crowd that had followed Prince out of Olosun compound. A boy screams Seven-Seven, money goes out the window, and we are gone.

Just beyond the market, free at last, we stop at an open shed by the roadside and sit in the shade with cold sodas. Prince looks exhausted. "This place takes all my money," he sighs.

I was with him, and I would guess that he gave twelve thousand dollars away, had three thousand left in the bank. But whatever the count, some money remains, the Resort is back on track, and he has retraced the course of his life, reconnecting with the powers in Ogidi, Osogbo, and Ibadan. There is nothing more to be done: we sit in a long restful silence. It is a lovely day, hot and bright, and we have a whole day to get to Abuja and catch the plane to America.

· 16 ·

Farewell

Our trip, he says, was a great achievement. Prince has done what he could. The road before him looks straight and smooth. It turned out, of course, to be twisted and rough.

We got a late start, took a wrong turn or two, and drove through the night, arriving shortly before our flight. In Abuja, we were told of a terrorist scare in London, our first stop. We could take on board only our cash and passports. Prince bought a green plastic sack into which he dropped three quart bottles of Sule's "Koranic water" and a tub of slippery black soap. Grimly I stuffed my cameras, shot film, and fieldnotes into a suitcase, surrendering my work into the void. In London, all flights were cancelled, producing an ideal situation for terrorists: people without visas were let into the city, travelers were separated from their luggage, misrule and confusion prevailed. We were stuck in London with the worried blues, not much money and no changes of clothing.

Prince got out first. Beneath his white shirt he had a brown one with Koranic inscriptions of the kind worn by hunters and Muslim warriors. He was stopped by a security guard and ordered to remove the contents of his pockets: three tight, furry balls, wrapped with tape. Asked what they were, he said they were his "voodoo stuffs." Told he could not take them, he politely said they protected him and everyone else on the airplane. Unyielding, he waited for the supervisor who called him, repetitively and condescendingly, "sir," and told him that the regulations made it impossible for him to take such things on board. Prince was firm, calmly adamant. The supervisor asked him what the little bundles contained. Fragments, Prince answered, of the shirt his great-grandfather wore in battle. The man looked aghast, imagining, perhaps, an international incident since this man in a beaded cap and a white robe had told him that he was an African prince. He looked away and waved him on, voodoo stuffs and all.

We followed him three days later. We were told that our bags were still in Abuja, that they were in New York, that—don't worry, sir—they were traveling along with us. Some turned up at Prince's house in Philadelphia, one stood on our doorstep in Indiana. To my great relief—I could not have written this book without the materials they contained—they all got through, but they had been left for days on the tarmac in the rain. The books I bought had congealed into a damp mass. Many of the old prints and paintings Prince had brought to sell were ruined: colors had run, paper was stained. It was not an auspicious beginning for the new era in Prince's life.

Over the next two years, the period of this book's writing, we stayed constantly in touch. When he came to Philadelphia, I came too, asking the questions that arose as I wrote. Like Prince's paintings, like the Resort de Paradise, my writings linger in revision until they are abandoned. When he was in Nigeria, he called two or three times a month, keeping me, his Boswell, informed. I took notes when we met, kept a log of his calls, so I can report what happened. Through the report's chronology, these threads can be traced: the ups and downs of his productivity, the descent of his domestic affairs, his quest for a position in Nigeria, his struggle to make a living as an artist.

September 2006. After three weeks in Philadelphia, Prince returns to Nigeria. While we traveled through Yorubaland, Prince frequently called the office of the president, knowing that President Obasanjo's second and final term would end the following May, and hoping that, before he left office, the president would arrange a position for him, so he could draw a steady salary and paint in peace. That position would be the victory Prince is waiting for, the victory that would permit a triumphal return. When he got to Philadelphia, he found a fax that gave him an appointment. The date had passed.

Now Prince flies to Nigeria. He waits for ten days in Abuja to meet with the minister of culture who tells him that, before the end of his term, President Obasanjo—"a lover of art" Prince calls him—intends to establish a Nigerian museum of modern art. For the museum, they will buy twenty paintings by Prince at fifteen thousand dollars apiece. All that money would not be his; he would have to give some to the officials capable of bringing the project to fruition, would have to share the profit with George Jevremović who owns the pictures, but this sudden rush of cash would enable him to settle comfortably in Philadelphia, paying off the back taxes on his house and recovering the painting he left as collateral with the mortgaging company. A delegation from Nigeria will come in late October or early November to select the paintings.

December 2006. Prince is back from Nigeria. One of the men in the Nigerian delegation was able to get a visa, and he has at last arrived, assuring Prince that all of the money has been appropriated, but because the sum is so large they will buy ten paintings now, as soon as the funds have been transferred to an American bank, then ten more later. He also plans an international traveling exhibition of Nigerian modern art that will feature Prince's work. Foreign critics might have forgotten him, but Prince's fame at home endures. Meanwhile, Prince is at work in his high, narrow studio at Material Culture, creating a large painting on pink wrapping paper.

When he began this painting last summer, he called it *The Man with the Weight of the World*. Now he calls it *Barefoot President in a Fragile Boat with the World Tears Apart*. It shows, Prince said, "The way I see Mister Bush. He's walking on a very *fragile* boat, with a *large* world on his arm, with all the countries tearing apart." The world is a "collage" of cut up maps. An old African village of round, thatched houses spreads in the far distance, because, Prince says, "All the world is a village to Bush; he just throws bombs there."

The pink paper provides a unifying tone like the tan ground of his paintings on wood. Working along, Prince finds mistakes, places where the paper blistered above the board to which it was glued. He slices them with a carpet knife, squirts glue beneath, and tamps the spots, trusting that the painted patterns will hide the repairs, as they hide the nails in sculpture's paintings, and telling me with a savvy smile, "I'm destroying to rebuild." His main task is to bring the figures forward with contrasts of value and hue. With a paper punch, he makes tiny white circles and glues them onto the eyes of the people who stare while Bush wobbles. The eyes spray bright white specks across the pink-brown surface. He mixes up a purplish blue ink so that Bush's loud trousers will be red, white, and blue.

As he switches from medium to medium, from ink to pastel to acrylics, and as he switches from color to color, Prince uses this picture to exemplify his process, telling me that he starts with one idea, then finds others as he goes: "Sometimes I have an idea, but then the object itself asks for something, and I give it, and it is perfect." As for color:

"It is like a closet of clothes. You look in and something says, Wear me.

"So, I look at the painting, and it will ask for a color. I put it on, and it is perfect."

Prince will finish this painting in January. He planned to follow it with another one inspired by the televised news that causes people of peace, like Prince, such distress. Entitled *Imagination of the Returnees*, it would depict soldiers returning from Iraq, bearing camels and boxes on their heads, symbols of the terrible memories of war they will have to carry throughout their lives. He never made that painting, but by working hard on *Barefoot President* he picked up the momentum that would lift him to the peak of his American achievement, the

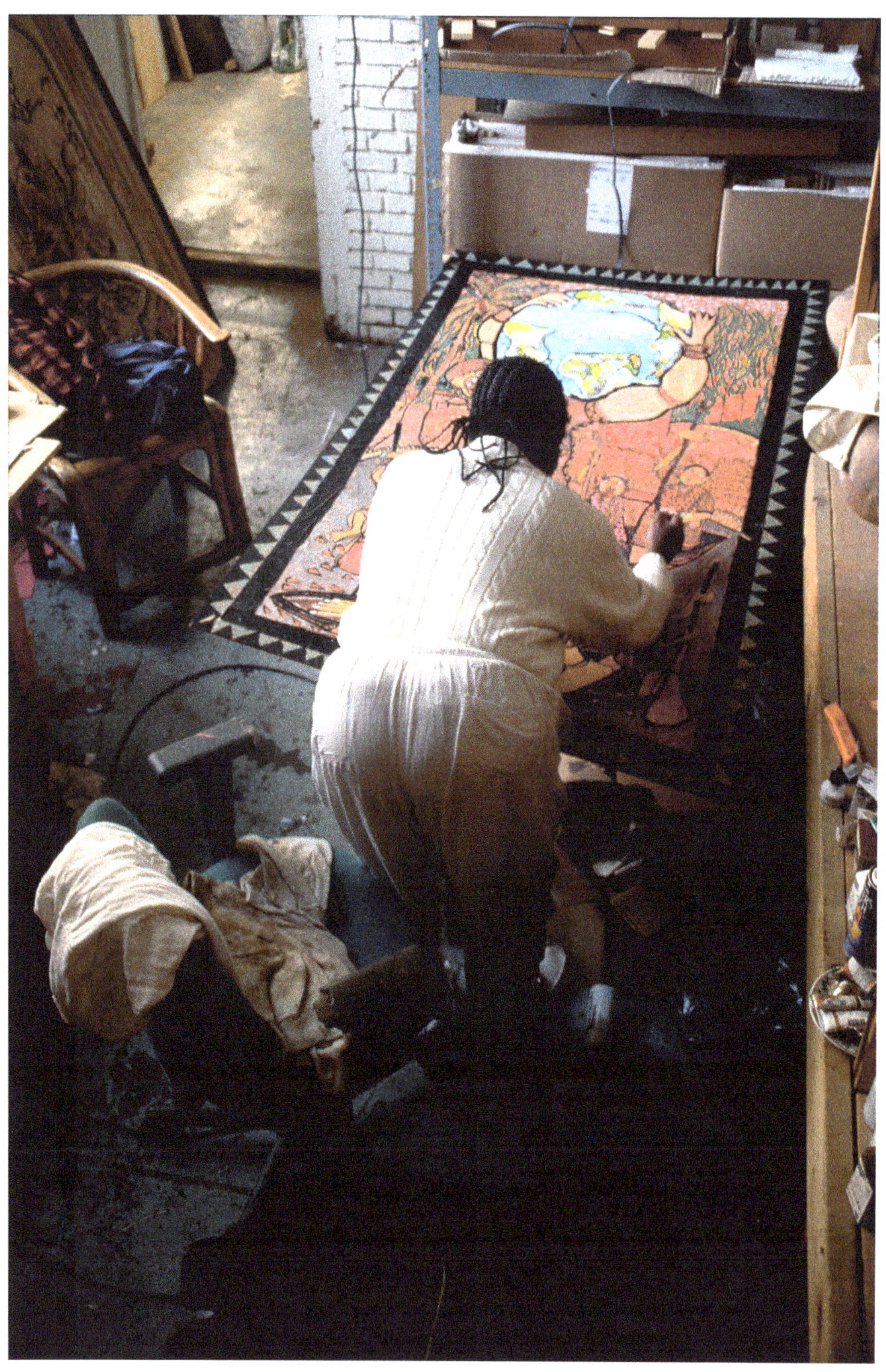

Prince painting *Barefoot President*. December 2006

two versions of *The Spirits of My Reincarnation Brothers and Sisters*, which stunned George Jevremović with their excellence. Like other American critics, George prefers Prince's early work, but in his opinion these new paintings on cloth are as exciting as anything Prince has ever done.

February 2007. Prince calls from Philadelphia. The Nigerian buyer was supposed to come in January. He never came. He promised to send the money in February. It has not come. Princess Aliratu called with sad news from Nigeria. She miscarried, losing twins, and Prince has always wanted to be the father of twins. Shola has escaped the cold, returning to Nigeria, leaving Prince to care for Victor and Timi. Fortunately Timi likes the Nigerian food his father prepares, and fortunately George has advanced Prince money to paint his portrait.

March 2007. Prince calls to say the bank is threatening to evict him from his house. Prince's word is eject. The money George paid him for the two versions of *My Reincarnation Brothers and Sisters* is gone, sucked up by bills: the water bill, the electric bill, his accumulated credit card debts, his legal fees, a tax payment to the city. It seems that the Nigerian buyer is still in the process of transferring the funds, and Prince needs nine thousand to prevent eviction. His only hope is to make a series of paintings in the "rainbow" palette he developed early in the nineties and applied to the paintings George admired and bought, but it is cold in his studio.

April 2007. Shola has gone to New York, taking the boys. Aliratu cries on the phone, pleading with Prince to bring her to America, but he is worried about what she would do if she came. "America," he says, "changes everyone." Shola has left him; he fears that his boys will run with a bad crowd in New York. The Nigerian buyer seems to have disappeared. A rich American collector wanted a major work for little money; he bought nothing. Everything costs too much in America. Credit cards are a disaster.

May 2007. Prince leaves for Nigeria. Having heard nothing from the Nigerian buyer, he is going home to find out what happened. He calls to say he has settled happily in his country house outside of Ibadan, and he is painting with much success in the style perfected in *My Reincarnation Brothers and Sisters.*

July 2007. Prince is in Nigeria. The Nigerian buyer is in Philadelphia, at Material Culture, looking again at the paintings. Prince's daughter Kemi calls to say they are being evicted from the house. Maria Murphy, the considerate, informative lawyer who is handling Prince's case *pro bono*, calls to say that the judge has decided against Prince. She understands that he was caught in a scam and cheated; he paid, and paid too much, but his payments were never recorded. Back taxes have piled up. The house is lost. But she has submitted an appeal for a stay of eviction so that the two girls in the house can pack their belongings into the Material Culture truck and scatter them into the basements of Nigerian friends. I tell her Prince is worried about the painting he left to secure his loan. Maria says that, though there is nothing in writing, she will appeal and she expects that, in the case of the painting, she will succeed. On the phone, Prince asks with a laugh, "Why does the bank love my painting so much?"

August 2007. In Nigeria, the election held in the spring is still being contested in court, the president-elect, Alhaji Umaru Yar'Adua, has not formally taken office. In general Prince respects Muslims for their forthright honesty, and Yar'Adua, he believes, is an honorable Northerner sincerely committed to the nation's welfare. Prince tells me that Yar'Adua intends to establish a ministry of art and culture. Hoping for a position within it, Prince calls his office incessantly. At last he gets an appointment and meets for four hours with one of the president-elect's deputies who tells him that there are twenty-two positions in the new government for which Prince might be suitable.

Prince tells me on the phone that he is "keeping a low profile" and "hiding his head" in his country house. He has sold some land in Ibadan, and he has sold the office of his old car dealership in Osogbo. With the money, he is buying food for his family in Osogbo and a shop for Aliratu in Ibadan. Business will give her something to occupy her mind. His daughters in Philadelphia, he says, have jobs and they have found places to stay—"to squat" is how Kemi put it to me—with their friends from church. Prince wonders about the fate of his painting.

October 2007. Prince is in Philadelphia. He came back on the twelfth of September to find his old house empty. Assuming that the sheriff thinks he will never return from Nigeria, he is staying quietly in the house, cleaning it up and painting it so he will not be charged for ruining it. Prince brought from Ibadan a set of paintings on cloth, created with the rainbow palette and tattooed ornament of *My Reincarnation Brothers and Sisters.* All excellent, they mark the end of the momentum built up with *Kissing Birds* and *Barefoot President.* His period of high productivity and creative fervor carried into Nigeria, lasting from the fall of 2005 until the summer of 2007. A low period begins. George Jevremović bought all of Prince's new pictures, and understanding his needs, George commissioned him to decorate a monstrous fiberglass tyrannosaur that he bought in Karachi, Pakistan.

"It's better to do this than do nothing," Prince tells me when he begins on the dinosaur. He gazed into its whiteness, received a vision of a zebra, and decided to do it in black and

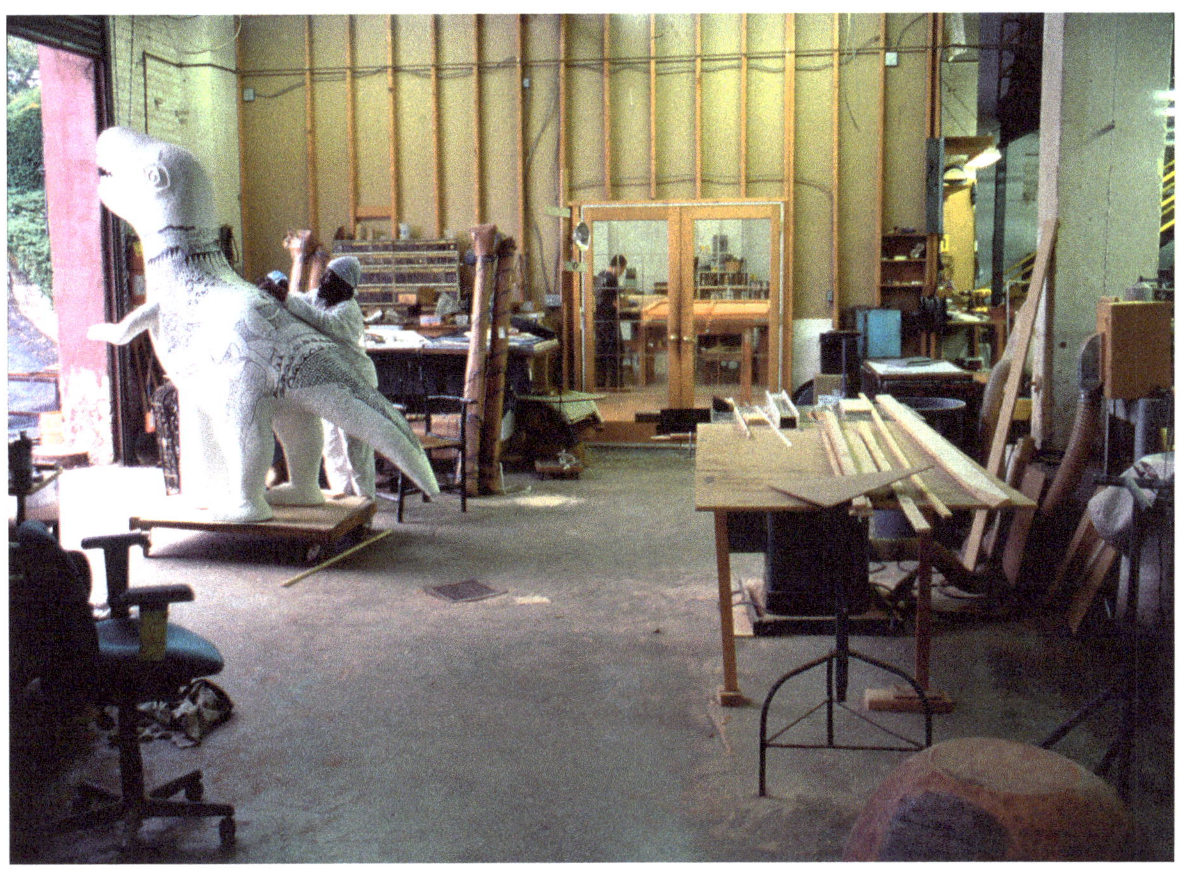

Prince painting the dinosaur. October 2007

white. A zebra-dinosaur seems a good idea, something no one has ever seen. He loves black-and-white work, he says, that is how he began, and furthermore, if he fills his black drawing with color, the job will take too long. Time is one condition. Location is another. Prince tells me that George plans to give the dinosaur to a children's museum or a children's library. It will be seen by kids, so it should not be frightening; he will give it no weird eyes, and he will calm the fearful form with whimsical pictures. And since it will stand in public, its craft must be fine.

I have found Prince's concern for appropriate contextualization to be general among artisans. Just as we stand and speak more formally on public occasions, craftsmen are particularly meticulous with works destined for public spaces. Hindu sculptors in Bangladesh knock out little molded images of the deities for domestic settings, then they model by hand and paint with precision when they craft the great images for temples. Turkish weavers make wild things for their homes, loose in drawing and hilarious in color, but they confine harmonious hues in symmetrical designs on the carpets they send to market, making them signs of their skill and their courteous regard for the unknown others who will meet them through their creations in public. All art is rhetorical, a message designed to grip and persuade a viewer, whether that viewer is the artist in action or someone far removed in space and time.

Prince says he can piss on powder and sell the result. He keeps no little notebooks filled with ideas, makes no preparatory sketches. Every sketch becomes a finished piece, every idea goes into works for sale. But they are ranked in his mind. At the bottom, there are swarms of small, quick pictures, casual in line and color. In the middle, there are small finished works, fewer in number. At the top, there are a very few masterworks, always large and charged with devotion, detailed down to the vanishing point. Size matters, as any potter will tell you. This is a big project, and in its public location the dinosaur must stand as an exhibit of care. Prince's process remains spontaneous and swift—surprising figures pop out, a python wraps around the clumsy base—but he is unusually deliberate, measuring with his hands, drawing straight lines with a ruler, and tracing around an iron washer so the circles will be regular in size, exact in shape. The circles become flowers, coating the terrible beast with sweetness, but, as I watch, spontaneity takes over and he fills a row of flowers with bright colors.

The pause is brief. He could paint over the flowers in white, he tells me, keeping to his black-and-white scheme, but it is clear that the work wants color. So much for the zebra idea. He filled his drawing with color, and it took him exactly a month to complete.

November 2007. Prince calls from Philadelphia to say the dinosaur is beautiful, but he is disappointed with the amount George paid him. Three years have passed since they met. Prince understands that George is a businessman, the manager of a vast operation, and he must hold his costs down. George understands Prince's need for money. Affection frames their relation, but when money is at stake, tensions rise. George is weary. Prince is hurt. "Why am I in America?" he wonders aloud, then answers his own question. Because George would never come to Nigeria, Prince had to come to America so George could own the largest and best collection of his work in the world. That is the first reason; the second is that we met in America, making this book possible. It is cold, his hip aches. Prince leaves for Nigeria.

January 2008. Prince calls from Nigeria to say he is praying for my health (I had been in the hospital) and for the success of George's business: "We are not powerful technologically, but we are powerful spiritually." George saved him when he was down, and he is going to "witchdoctors, church people, and Muslim people," getting them to pray for his American friends. Since he is staying in his country house, with no rental expenses, he has money enough to pay for the prayers and to keep his family going. He attended a meeting with government officials in Abeokuta, still hopes for a position. The money appropriated to buy his paintings has been spent on an archaeological project, but a line remains in the budget. Someday, *inshallah,* they will buy the paintings, but the government works very slowly, he says with a sad laugh.

March 2008. In Nigeria, the matter of the election remains unresolved, but Prince believes and hopes that soon Umaru Yar'Adua will be confirmed as the president. Prince must wait until a decision is made to learn whether or not he will get a position, but he is going to Osogbo to sign an agreement that will divide the ownership of the Resort de Paradise into thirds: one for Osun State, one for the local government, one for Prince. With money promised, Prince is at work again, cleaning up the Resort.

April 2008. Prince is back in Philadelphia, staying with friends. There is no word on a position, no word from the Nigerian buyer, no word about the painting he left against his debt. They have taken his houses; taking his painting too would be—no softer word will do—robbery. We meet a couple of times for taped talk, but he is "just wandering around," he says, "trying to figure out what to do with all the junks." When his daughters were evicted, the furniture he had bought was left on the street. It is gone, but he has things stored in the basements of friends, including some games for children that could be useful at the Resort. His friends want the stuff removed. He is finding it hard to manage because his car was parked for months on the street, and the police towed it away. He wonders what they thought of all the letters and papers piled inside. That small car, he says, served as "the office for my gallery." His casual personal archive has vanished, a loss for the history of art.

June 2008. Having no car, he was stuck in the house. "That is life." Unable to travel, Prince worked during May, creating twenty-six sketchy pictures in colored ink on paper: birds, elephants, snakes, a snake charmer, Sango, Osun, and Obatala's garden, his usual subjects. They earned him enough to repair his Plymouth van; it is not new but it is in excellent condition. He will fill it with his possessions and ship it to Nigeria. He does not say it, but it does not need saying. America has beaten him. He is not bitter, does not complain. He imagines a painting as big as the sky, but he never quite mastered what he calls "the system under the flash in America." He lost what he brought, lost what he gained. His houses are gone. His family is scattered. He is alone. The friend he is staying with grumps that he does not contribute enough to the household. He has no place. His paintings remain unsold. It is over. He is going.

Once more I fly to Philadelphia, and we meet at Material Culture where his colorful dinosaur is lofted across from the entrance to the main showroom. Prince is wearing the blue

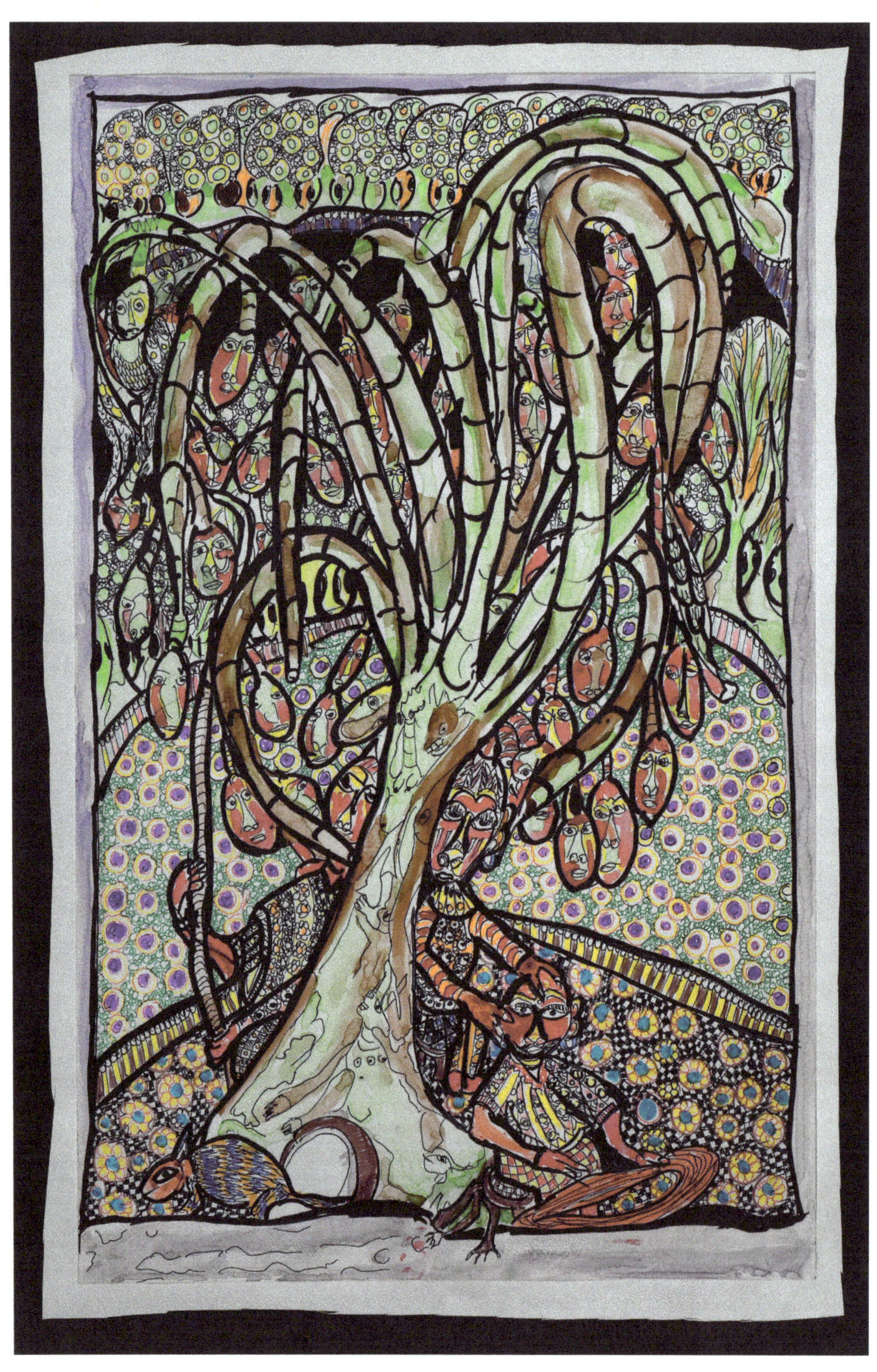

The Tree of Life, Obatala's Garden. Inks on paper. 14"x22".
An example of Prince's quick pictures, done in one night, May 2008

beaded crown of the Ekerin-Basorun of Ibadan, many strands of beads, and a sparkling white robe. He looks great, happy and energetic: the past does not depress him, the future excites him. The pictures might yet be sold, maybe a paying position awaits him. He might become the king of Ibadan. God alone knows.

We sit in George's office for a last talk on tape. I have drafted this book up to this chapter, and I have a few questions that will spatter improvements back through the text. Oddly, while I was recording Prince's life, Barbara Truesdell was recording mine for an article in *The Public Historian*. Her last question, at the end of eight sessions, forced me to look backward and generalize. I tell that to Prince and ask him to craft a conclusion.

What he said was ripe with truth. The world abounds in excellent artists who die unrecognized, many more talented than he is, many more powerful. He works like an ant, steadily on his own anthill, but luckily the head he chose in Obatala's garden allied his quiet, ant-like creativity with a bold, flamboyant personality that brought him fame, causing him to be accepted for the man he is. He could do what he wanted to do—what could be better?—and doing it, he was able to travel the world and live the life of an artist. He is grateful to God for making it happen, grateful that his mother lived to see his success, grateful that, a man of renown, he could serve as a model for others, inspiring people, and especially his own people, to release their creative energies and become what he has become, a fully realized human being. That is his triumph: he is entirely alive, undefeatable, a vital presence in a battered old world. This is what he said:

"What I believe most is that, number one, I'm very grateful to God that I was able to be used by whoever sent me to this world to rediscover a lot of creative minds in my country.

"Today, hardly any family in Nigeria you don't find an artist, you don't find a singer, you don't find an actor. That's number one.

"Number two: I'm happy that I was able to be accepted for what I am, by the world. Because there's thousands of people can do better than what I am doing. But they don't accept them.

"So, I'm very grateful to the world, because they accepted me for whatever I love to do, and I do it.

"Like sometimes I put muddy water on paper, and put my name. Somebody is there, says, Oh, I love it, let me have it. So, that's one of the things.

"And then I was able to encourage young people in my country. All over Africa, and the world over. Because I know a lot of people got started because of my work. Like, I saw some paintings somewhere; it's just like somebody sit down and copy what I have done, and it is done by an American. It's done by an American artist.

"So, I thank God that God give me that opportunity. And I thank my mother too, for letting me do what I love to do. Because in those days she would sit down and cry. She want me to be a lawyer or a teacher. And she told me, You beast, you go to school, but you sit down here, playing with pencil and all these stupid things. Where do you think this will take you to?

"That is why I bury her where I bury her in my home in Osogbo. Because when I do music, in the beginning, she hate it. But every time she remember all these things they tell her about me, when she was carrying me in the womb. So, she would sit down there"—where her tomb is today—"and watch us performing.

"And there was a day I have members of British Lawyers' Association, in the Commonwealth. I don't know what they came to do in Lagos—about three hundred of them; they came and visited me in Osogbo. And I put on a performance for them.

"And my mother was crying.

"And after they left, I asked why she was crying. She said she was so happy that this thing happened in her lifetime.

"And she never know it is going to be this way.

"So, I thank God, and I thank you people for making it possible for me.

"Well, everything is not—everything is not what you want it to be. But the fact that I was able to touch a bit, and that bit spread all over the world.

"I thank my God.

"I thank my creator."

At that, Prince claps and falls silent. The tape recorder continues to do its little job. I say nothing, and after a long pause, Prince says:

"Sometime people have energy to break stone, and nobody knows that. You know what I mean? Somebody carry big hammer to break a stone to make a *sculpture* out of it. Nobody cares.

"But the little I do, like *ants*, like ants walking on ant heaps, you know."

Prince laughs. That is the end. Three days later, on June 9, 2008, he left America, went home to Nigeria.

Part Two: Prince's Art

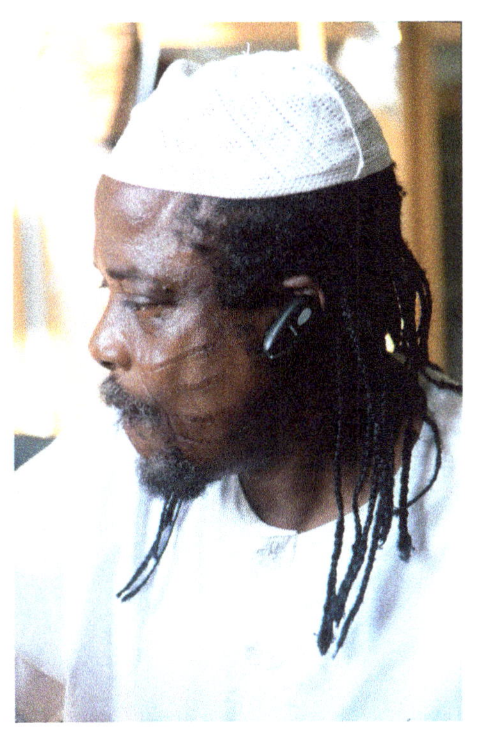

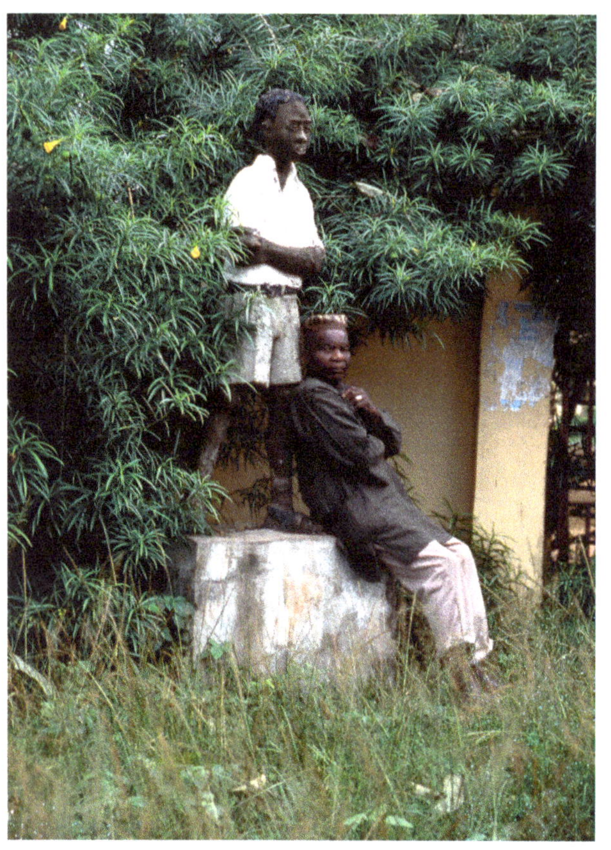

St. Charles School, Osobgo

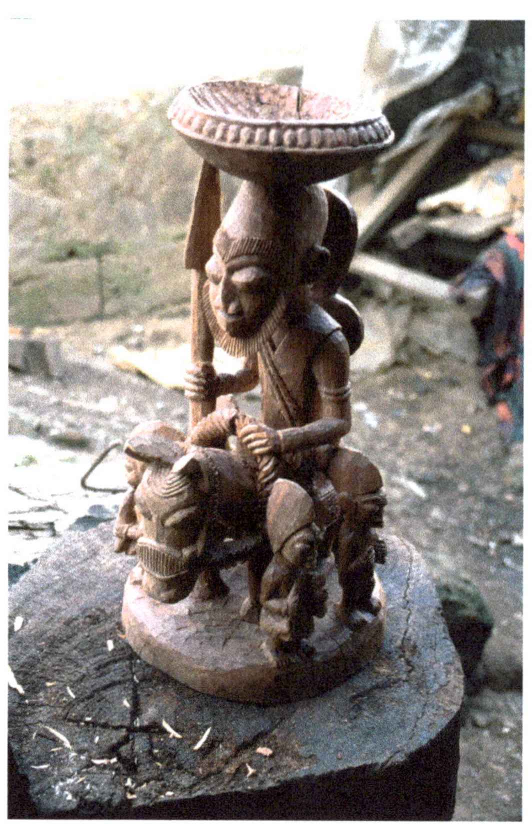

Work in progress.
A. Bankole shop, Ibadan

Contemporary images in Yorubaland

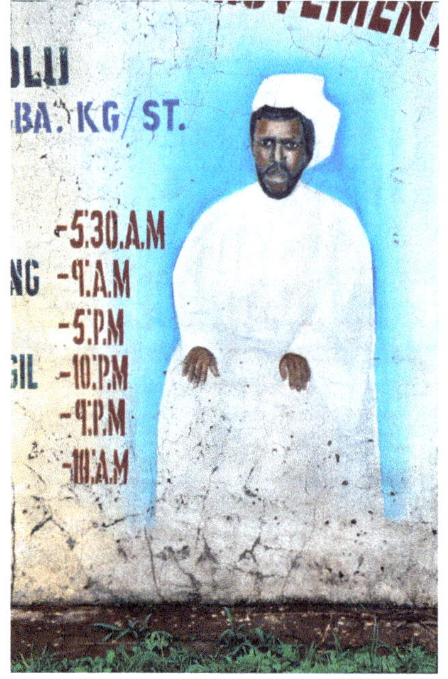

Cherubim and Seraphim Church,
Kabba

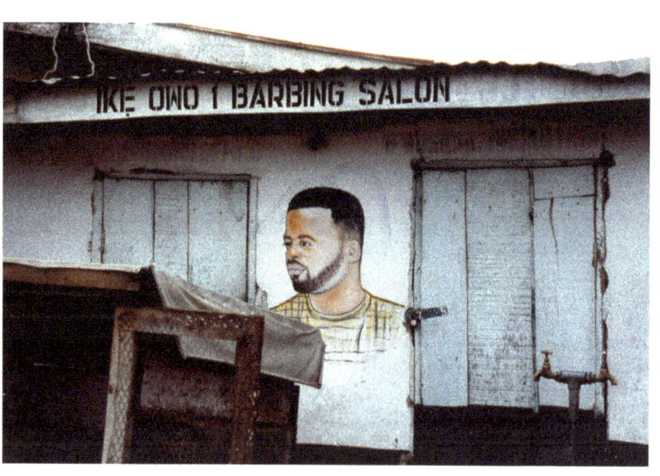

Osogbo

· 17 ·

Yoruba Art

We drove to the edge of the city so Prince could wire money home to Osogbo. On the way back I had a question for him. Writings about him divide. Some, built on early comments by Ulli Beier, stress his personality, his inherent talent and restless imagination. But Robert Plant Armstrong stressed culture, Prince's refiguring of the Yoruba tradition. Both opinions catch some of the truth, flashing off different facets of his integrated being, but who, I asked, was the more correct, Beier or Armstrong? Prince needed no time to think. Armstrong, he answered, without hesitation. Consistently, Prince's name for what he makes is "contemporary Yoruba traditional art."

Prince began the story of his life with culture, and in this chapter I begin to analyze his art, preparing you for the paintings assembled at this book's end, by considering the Yoruba strain in his creative action.

In *The Yoruba Artist*, John Picton welcomes diversity by putting it simply: Yoruba art is the art made by Yoruba people. Travel through Yorubaland and you will find art all around you. The clothing worn by women and men, spread in repose, splendid in motion, makes for one enveloping exhibition of art. Textiles attract the eye, so does pottery, but if one's vision of art reduces to the representational, variety remains. There are stylized carvings in wood, shaped faithfully on elder precedent. There are naturalistic statues in concrete and painted portraits in a photorealist style, some of them superb in craft and deserving close study. There are simplified faces painted quickly on commercial signboards, generally less numerous and fine than those of Ghana. There are innocent pictures of Jesus, competent documentary illustrations of traditional life, impressionistic landscapes, expressionistic spatterings of color on canvas, abstract paintings drawn from the designs of African textiles, and there are piles of paintings and batiks inspired by the works of Prince Twins Seven-Seven.

By virtue of its manifest excellence, Yoruba art has attracted many outstanding scholars who acknowledge diversity, yet speak easily of a single Yoruba style, a tradition that connects new work with old and distinguishes Yoruba art from the art of other people. Pieces floating free in the art market or museum collections can be confidently attached to Yoruba hands, identified by traits borne in silent forms. Those traits, carrying essential cultural values, are built into objects during creation to effect a communication between the maker and a viewer. They are, those traits, recognized immediately but hard to articulate in mere language.

In the nineteen-sixties, two American scholars, at work independently, set out to define the Yoruba essence, to put into words the feelings that enable attribution and judgment. By the early seventies, they had succeeded. The art historian Robert Farris Thompson conducted anthropological fieldwork to isolate the qualities—the "canons of excellence"—that govern the creation and evaluation of Yoruba sculpture. The anthropologist Robert Plant Armstrong employed phenomenological method, which he mastered as an editor of phenomenological texts, to clarify exactly what is Yoruba about Yoruba art. Their paths crossed on the fractured academic landscape. Thompson began in the humanities and followed his method toward the social sciences. Armstrong began in the social sciences and followed his method toward humanistic inquiry. Despite differences of training and procedure, they came to congruent conclusions. Their convergence provides a convincing intersubjective demonstration; they had articulated the Yoruba essence, achieving a thrilling victory for transdisciplinary thought. Meshing formal analysis with ethnographic understanding, their combined success inspired me to follow them as I searched for the essential qualities of Turkish art during the nineteen-eighties, and now their conclusions offer me firm footing for analysis. I am not an expert on Yoruba art, but standing on the foundation built by Thompson and Armstrong, I can reach out to gather insights from other writings, which amplify but do not contradict their conclusions, in order to consider the work of Prince Twins Seven-Seven in relation to the Yoruba tradition, expanding as I go to the matter of art in general.

The traits of Yoruba art that scatter through the scholarly texts can be bundled into three interrelated classes: a logic of representation, a logic of presentation, a logic of composition. Taken together, they define the Yoruba tradition. Since they are the means by which the inner invisibility of culture is given presence in the world, they connect Yoruba art with Yoruba ritual, dance, and sport, with Yoruba music, literature, and architecture. And since they combine into a tradition of art, they link Yoruba acts and intentions to the universal impulse to creation.

REPRESENTATION

I begin with the logic of representation because Robert Farris Thompson began, as many of his Yoruba critics did, with a key trait of representation. Thompson aptly called it "midpoint mimesis." The Yoruba critics recoiled from the extremes of abstraction and likeness, favoring a midpoint of integration where forms retained a recognizable relation with the things of the world, while remaining general and typological, capable of manifold reference. Midpoint mimesis centers the process of representation and locates the value of equilibrium, prevalent in Yoruba art and culture.

Yoruba art balances at the center of a wide span of possibility. In *The Blaue Reiter Almanac*, Wassily Kandinsky, who wrote about art nearly as magnificently as he made it, said that all art emerges between the poles of "total abstraction" and "total realism," blending these pure tendencies in palpable works that shift in one direction or the other, toward abstraction or toward realism. The "ideal" of an "absolute equilibrium" had been lost in the Europe of Kandinsky's day, when centuries of excessive realism had pushed modern artists toward an excess of abstraction, though it existed in the medieval, folk, and exotic works, including three from Africa, with which Kandinsky and Marc illustrated their almanac. That ideal abides in the Yoruba tradition, and—foreshadowing the conclusion—it exists in the art of Prince Twins Seven-Seven and generally in art inflected toward the spiritual, but Kandinsky's words fit, I feel, the little Western dilemma better than they fit the vast global reality.

By categorizing works as abstract or realistic we bring some order into the art of the late West, and those terms have been adopted by Yoruba artists with Western experience. Prince calls his works "abstract" if they "have no eyes," if they lack images of living creatures, and he calls paintings that are unlike his own "realistic," positioning his usual creations between the poles of abstraction and realism. In his autobiography, the Yoruba carver Lamidi Fakeye, who has, like Prince, spent much time in America, says that traditionally Yoruba carvers do not work "realistically" and he calls his own style "semi-abstract," a reasonable enough synonym for midpoint mimesis. The familiar words are handy, but others, I believe, would take us deeper.

Realistic works, as Sir Joshua Reynolds remarked long ago, are not real; they look real, matching visual experience. Consider perspective. A single vanishing point brings a scene into unity, but it falsifies reality. Roads do not really come to a point; they continue at an even width when you walk them. A friend of mine, a dyer in a Turkish village, was deeply disturbed by a photograph of a carpet that implied that one of its ends was narrower than the other, when he knew that it maintained a consistent width for its full length. What is seen conflicts with what is known, and that conflict, the conflict of appearance and reality, seeks resolution in art. In Indian miniature paintings, forms pile up; verticality suggests depth. Close things lie at the bottom, the main image fills the middle, and far things ride at the top, but all exist in proper proportion, one to the other; things are large or small because they are actually large or small, not because they are near or far. The cubists tried multiple perspectives in simultaneity, and Prince Twins Seven-Seven combines all these techniques—verticality, multiple perspectives, and vanishing points—creating depth and flatness at once to honor both subjective visual experience and objective understanding. When understanding is suppressed and artists commit enthusiastically to the visual, as old Uccello did in perspective, as Eakins did in form, as Monet did in color, the result is called realistic, but "visual"—or Duchamp's "retinal"—would be a more accurate name for one end of the spectrum of representation, and it would prompt a more logical term than abstraction for its opposite.

What is visible is the world out there. What is invisible is the world in here, the world locked in the black box of the brain. At the beginning of a career that would make him one of the leading scholars of Yoruba art, William Fagg generalized bravely in an essay, saying that African artists do not begin in nature. They begin conceptually. That is the word we need; it calls up consciousness, cognitive processes, memory and mental dynamics. Now set the conceptual against the visual and we have words that mark out the ends of the scale of representation at least as well as the conventional terms, abstraction and realism, and we have words that are existentially preferable. Artists work between abstraction and realism only in relation to the critical tradition of the late West, but every human being fuses the conceptual and visual in material creation. The Yoruba artist joins thought and sight, the shadowy inner windings of the mind with the outer lights that register on the retina. All artists do that, every one of them, but some lean this way, some that, while the Yoruba artist works to the middle. At the mimetic midpoint, the Yoruba creation embodies the virtue of equilibrium; it stands, as a mature person of high character stands, in balanced composure. It is ready to work in a place where, as Henry Drewal has argued, the visible and invisible, the physical and spiritual interact. The Yoruba work of art lives, as Yoruba people do, between the seen and unseen worlds, receiving and transmitting natural and supernatural energies.

Let me elaborate a bit on the conceptual. In one of its operations, the mind is abstractive (which validates the idea of abstraction). From the colors of nature, the mind abstracts the palette for an abstract-expressionist canvas. From the industrial landscape, the mind abstracts the forms of minimalist sculpture. If that were all the mind did, if consciousness were only a wind blowing toward a mountain, as Sartre put it, artists would be reduced to clever beasts responding to the stimuli in their environments. But the mind abstracts—and it projects. Here I am not following Freud or Jung—content is not at issue—but Noam Chomsky who held that the linguistic capacity is not derived from behavioral exchange. It is innate. Human beings are born with the ability to perform syntactic operations. With this inbuilt ability they project order into noise, converting racket into grammar. Chomsky was critical of the linguistic analogies, inspired by his genius, that once proliferated in academic discourse, but we do no violence to his thought to assert that people are born with the ability to bring order into visual chaos, to project into the world—as well as to abstract from the world—the geometric configurations and balanced, symmetrical relations that, abiding in the mind, enable the conjunction of concept and vision, and that, pleasing to the mind, abound in art.

Where Chomsky's work ends, the work of sociolinguists and poets begins. Linguistic analogy carries us on. Art issues from a performative act to run on its communicative errand through an endless series of social settings, accruing meanings that resist systematic formulation and require close ethnographic investigation. Art thrives in the poetic quality of ungrammatical surprise that rises from what Prince Twins Seven-Seven calls imagination.

Imagination is a mental operation that makes the invisible visible, that brings an image up from within, rather than in from without; it is visionary, not visual. Imagination is, along with abstraction and projection, a part of the conceptual apparatus. But where does it come from? From memory, from experiences distorted and traditions transformed in the unconscious, as John Livingston Lowes demonstrated in his delicate study of Coleridge's poetry. That answer satisfies the secular analyst, and it supplies a process for one of Prince's answers: meditation. Ideas come to him through meditation, through deep thought released to play strangely among memories, and they come to him in dreams. In the dreamlife, experience blends with the innate, abstraction and projection tumble together in a metaphoric jumble. But for Prince the dream opens one of the doors into the other world. He also hears voices, receives messages from the dead and gifts from God. If the skeptic replies that it is all in his head, that is true, it is all in his mind, but if the skeptic denies that it came into his mind from the other world, then a door slams on understanding, not only of Prince and other

Yoruba artists, but of most of the world's creators whose lives are turned at once by natural and supernatural forces. Through the conceptual, the spiritual enters artists and art.

It follows that Wassily Kandinsky would seek the spiritual through abstraction, and it follows that the conceptual—intellectual, imaginative, and pregnant with spiritual power—would prove to be a heavy counterweight to the visual, physical world in Yoruba art. Robert Farris Thompson theorized the conceptual and visual into a dialectic of equipoise, but in dialectic formulations one force or the other leads, and just as the visual, called the aesthetic, leads in the West, where art has surrendered its grand philosophical purpose, I think William Fagg is right: the conceptual leads in the Yoruba tradition where the philosophical abides in the ambit of the sacred (as once it did in the West) and retains its power in creative action.

If the visual is strong but the conceptual leads, then the traits that follow midpoint mimesis in the Yoruba logic of representation make perfect sense. Here is the first:

Though an image might refer to a specific individual, a dead twin or a great king, it does not narrow into visual likeness but widens through conceptualization into a generalized human form to which other forms are attached to indicate gender or status. The image becomes typological; its person stands in synecdoche for a whole class of human beings. The process is unlike the novelist's. In the novel given to psychological realism, details accumulate, the web of description thickens and tightens to reveal the personality of a unique individual. By contrast: in folktales, whether African, Asian, or European, the characters are types—the young hero, the wise king, the cannibalistic giant—who shake free of particular description to fill the roles demanded by the syntactic necessity of the narrative. Such generalized representation is generous. As Bengt Holbek said of Danish folktales and Michael Baxandall said of the religious paintings of Quattracento Italy, generalized images accept the particularities that different people project onto them to make them personally meaningful. Generalized figures can be moved around in metaphoric space toward personally useful conclusions. The image is open, capable of multiple, but not infinite, meanings. It is like that in Yoruba sculpture. People are rendered as generalized forms upon which signs must be hung to make them examples of types. They are, like the personages of oral literature, available for use as counters in philosophical discourse, being representations less of people than of cultural values.

That is clear in the trait of depiction to which Robert Farris Thompson attached the greatest importance. He called it "ephebism," and in *Wellspring* Robert Plant Armstrong approved of his word and his thought. People, even if they are broken and old, are portrayed as robust and young. Neither children nor elders, they rise between life's ends to exhibit the virtue of equilibrium. Round and full and smooth, not wrinkled and sagging, they are beautiful—realizations of aesthetic desire. Generally in African aesthetics, according to Susan Vogel, beauty aligns with moral virtue, with goodness, and connects to biological force, to health and fertility. She seems right to me. Poised in the prime of being, people in Yoruba art are swollen to tautness with *ase*, the power to make things happen. This power is the life force, the power, let us say, to father many children, to fight when attacked, to walk when wounded, to create works of art that others admire, to inspire other people into action, so they will follow you, dance for you, clear your fields, and honor you with chieftaincies. It is physical strength, mental strength, social strength, and it is the spiritual strength that signals the favor of the gods. The spiritual power that enters the process of creation through the conceptual takes form as enduring, timeless, otherworldly youthfulness.

Thompson names another representational trait "emotional proportion." It appears when physical appearances—as in ephebism—are intentionally distorted through conceptualization on behalf of meaning, when visual facts are traded for deeper significance, and the image becomes an essay in the hierarchy of value. The armed warrior is bigger than his horse, his head is big for his body, his eyes are big for his head. The stress rests on his power, his mastery of the beast beneath him, the head that he chose as the seat for his heroic destiny and noble character, the eyes that bulge with life force and provide him with the knowledge of the world that directs his bold moves. Less stressed, but hands and feet, too, are emotionally charged. With his hands he wields Ogun's weaponry to conquer his enemies, as babas employ the materials of magical action to defeat the witches hired by a client's enemies. The warrior's feet spread to give him a stable base, in truth, flat on the earth.

Stability bases the representational quality that Thompson's Yoruba critics termed "straightness." It begins in a practical consideration. What is called African art is largely the sculpture in wood from the continent's western and central regions, and generally the scholars of Yoruba art focus on carved wood. The carver must work, as the carver Lamidi Fakeye said, to assure that his wooden statue stands and stands straight, balanced into verticality on its base. The vertical axis provides a plumb midline around which a symmetrical composition is shaped. The figure stands in equilibrium, the eyes and shoulders, the hips, knees, and feet all aligned to the front. Ulli Beier looks and finds the word "static" for what he sees. Robert Farris Thompson sees the formal posture fit to public occasions, cool and rational, upstanding and vigorous. Robert Plant Armstrong looks too, and he sees the balanced management of worldly and supernatural forces, a contained intensity.

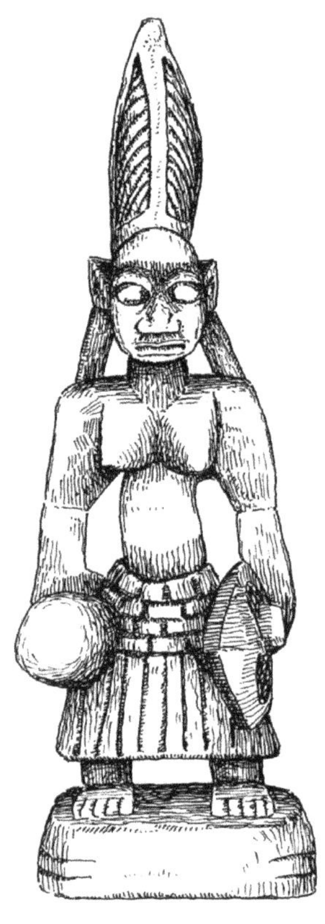

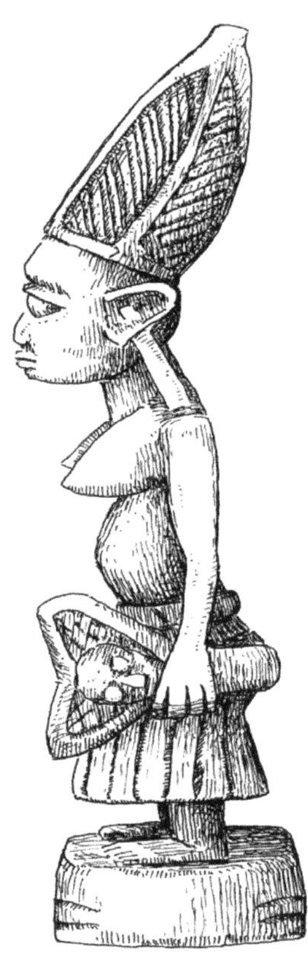

A priestess of Sango, carved by G. A. Dada in Osogbo (p. 301). In the Yoruba manner, the figure is unified vertically and divided horizontally, like many of Prince's paintings; see chapter 1, p. 10, and chapter 20, nos. 9, 20

The *ibeji* figures on the facing page, like G. A. Dada's Sango priestess, exhibit Yoruba forms and proportions; straight, frontal, and symmetrical, they have big heads and big eyes, long arms and short legs

Shift to the profile and you often find the posture of dance, of motion: the neck stretches, the lips press forward, the back is straight, the feet flat. Turn again to the front, and a deep shadow under the chin lifts the head—where the gift of the divine resides—into independence, while softer shadows cross horizontally, beneath the breasts, at the waist, beneath the knees, at the ankles, dividing the body into zones that are unified by the upthrust of verticality, by the inner dynamism that integrates the whole into a display of "intensive continuity." That is the term Robert Plant Armstrong developed to name the dominant visual quality of Yoruba art.

Stable and straight, vertical and symmetrical, segmented but intensively continuous, compressed, the figure is wound tight like the spring in a clock, stopped but ready to move and strike. An emblem of potentiality, it is poised in perpetual timelessness. The face is composed, alert or withdrawn, undisturbed by an expression, a smile or frown, that would connect it to the fleeting occasions of passing time. The body is still, taut but still. The man sits his mount holding a sword or flintlock musket in his right hand. The woman kneels and holds a bowl. In time, he will be victorious, she will be generous. But now they hold, hold

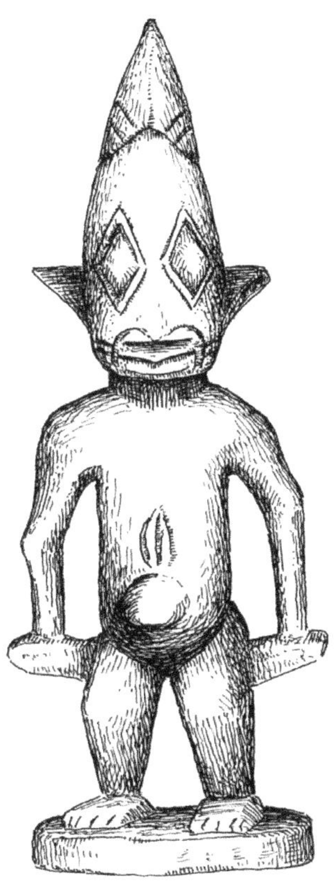 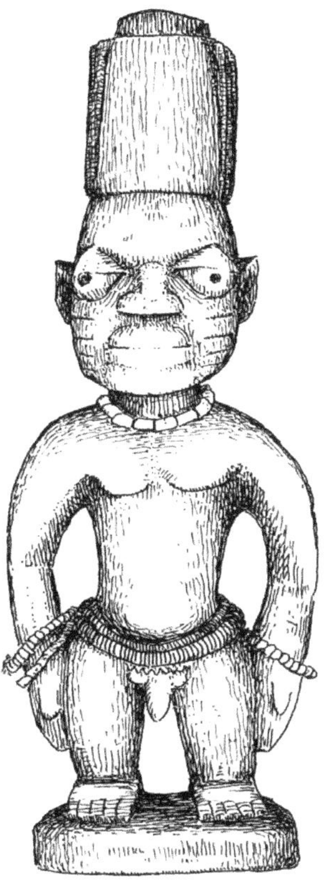 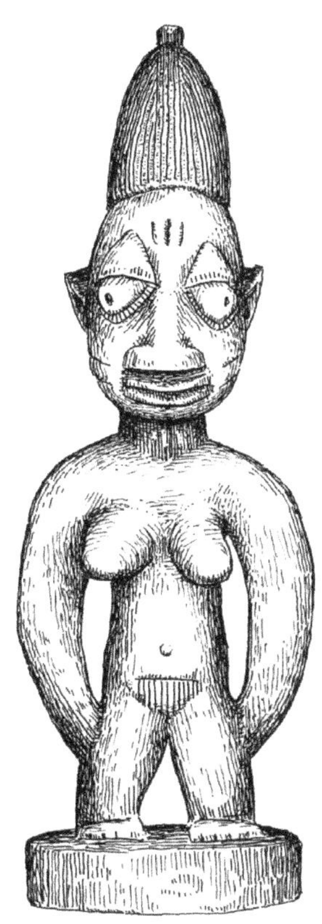

and do not act. They pose in a formal stasis of attentive readiness, only rarely disassembling into illustrative roles in time's events. They hold their disciplined positions, implying but not telling stories. Set beyond time, they are like the still, frontal icons of the Eastern church that rose between the extremes of narrative particularity and geometric symbolism when the doctors of Byzantium were shocked into conflict—the iconoclasts against the iconodules—by the appearance on their southern frontier of a spiritually purifying, aniconic Islam. Yoruba art comparably finds a central place of iconic balance, of power in tense suspension, and midpoint mimesis completes its mission in intensive continuity.

In tracing the logic of representation, we have come to the rationale that directs decisions of depiction. *Ibeji* figures provide scholars of Yoruba art with key texts for analysis and demonstration. *Ibeji* figurines are stable, straight, symmetrical, and frontal; their arms run down their sides like those of soldiers standing at attention. Their heads are big, their eyes are big, their forms are general—male and female faces look alike—and they separate into types by cicatrices of identification and conspicuous sexual characteristics. Out of time, they are at once the infants of the past and the adults of the future. Intensively continuous, occupying the mimetic middle ground, they do not represent deceased twins in the pitiful way that photographs record dead babies in Victorian albums. Propitiated to block the interference and win the support of the inhabitants of the other world, *ibeji* figures represent the living dead. It would distort their reality, it would be unrealistic, to shape them in conformity with the bouncy children who skip down the visual path into the mind. Through conceptualization, through the imaginative wit consolidated in tradition, they are shaped so they can refer to real babies while making the invisible visible. These are forms beyond the world, beyond time and sight. They are spirits.

The point is big. The Yoruba logic of representation is, in its outlines, the pictorial dynamic of the vast African wood-carving territory. Particular traditions slide along the scale to find their own midpoints. The Yoruba work closer to the Baule and Luba than they do to the Senufo or Fang; in the African expanse, their creations are relatively visual—"humanistic" is the word scholars find to distinguish them. But the pattern remains inclusively grand. Armstrong was searching for the African quality in all of African art when he lit upon the Yoruba. Thompson expanded gracefully from his knowledge of the Yoruba into a general treatment of African art. William Bascom and Frank Willett characterized African art compatibly with Armstrong, Thompson, and Fagg, and ranked the Yoruba high, granting them a place in African art like the French in nineteenth-century painting or the Kwakiutl—a comparison that would yield productive results—in Native American sculpture.

The representational pattern is clear. What of the cause: does African art look like it does, and unlike the art of the late West, because its creators are striving to depict spirits? Emboldened by his fieldwork among the Dogon, Marcel Griaule wrote a brief but brilliant book on the whole sweep of African art. His answer was yes. He noted the generalizing, typological tendency and declared African art to be more conceptual than visual, more spiritual than material. Griaule placed African art firmly in the formal and functional frame of religion. He joined the statue with the masquerade: both bring the invisible into visibility and the dead into life, connecting—as prayers and sacrifices do—people with supernatural power.

Not every figure depicts the living dead, as *ibeji* figures do, or beings from the other world, as Baule spirit partners do, but all are shaped similarly through the logic of representation. Deities, spirits, ancestors, priests and priestesses, kings and warriors, women and men—all are pulled away from the visual and toward the conceptual to make manifest the spiritual power that fills them. Yoruba artists represent the spirit in and through human bodies; Yoruba art is, according to Robert Farris Thompson, "primarily sacred." Yoruba art is African art. African art is spiritual art.

That conclusion needs at least this sketchy ramble through the world in its support. When Frank Willett noted the formal similarities of ancient Egyptian and recent African sculpture in his masterful survey *African Art*, his concern was historical connections. My concern is not with connection, contact, or influence, but with parallels of intentionality, with deep cause. My goal is to clarify the spiritual quality of Yoruba representation through comparison, preparing us for the art of Prince Twins Seven-Seven.

Consider, to begin, the parallels with Hindu art. Hinduism and the Yoruba religion both seem to be, as the religions of ancient Greece and Rome were, historical unifications of formerly disparate cults. Both acknowledge a high God—Bhagwan, Olodumare—who is, like the one God of Islam, an omnipotent force without form, who is remembered often but not imaged or worshiped in public ritual. In both there are a multitude of deities, including deified rivers, yet in each two great gods focus particular devotion—Vishnu and Shiva, Sango and Ogun—and there is a third who matches or surpasses them in power. In Hinduism, as it is practiced, this is Devi, the Goddess. In Yoruba practice it might be Ifa, the god of wisdom, who is also called Orunmila, or Ifa's friend Esu, the divine messenger, who is also called Elegba, and Prince Twins Seven-Seven is not alone in thinking it is Obatala, the creator.

Power in both religions expands and fragments through formal multiplicity. Devi appears as Parvati in wifely virtue, as Kali in rage, as Durga in supreme power, and Durga is the mother of four: Saraswati and Lakshmi, Ganesh and Kartikeya. Vishnu has taken form in ten avatars, including Rama, Krishna, and the Buddha. Shiva sits or dances alone, but he joins celestial society as the mate of Parvati or Kali, and some believe that Shiva, like Vishnu, has avatars, most significantly Hanuman who made possible Rama's defeat of Ravana. In the Yoruba tradition, the powers of Sango and Ogun scatter through their priests and priestesses who become, in effect and image, their avatars on earth. Obatala creates the fleshy form and provides the Ori, the head—the container of destiny, character, and spiritual force—that every human being carries through life. By Obatala's acts and their own choice all people combine the material and spiritual, becoming biological signs of the divine, wrong to represent as merely physical beings. Obatala's power spreads to all of humanity, and he brings feminine force into the world, as Devi does, for Obatala leads the white deities, including Osun.

In Abuja, Ayanwale Ayo Olayanju told me that Olodumare created four hundred and one deities, all male except Osun. Discord prevailed until Olodumare reminded the gods, busy with their warplay, that they should honor their mother, Osun. When they did, peace at last came to the universe. It was ready for human occupation. Obatala, the creator of human form, leads Osun, the goddess of fertility and healing, into human awareness.

Sango, like Vishnu, brings justice; both carry weapons. Ogun, like Shiva, balances creation and destruction; both associate with snakes. Then there is Osun. As Devi, in the form of Durga, brought order to the universe by suavely slaying the Buffalo Demon, much as Rama did by defeating the demon Ravana, Osun, the mother, calmed the childish gods into peace, preparing the world for human habitation. Combating negative force with positive, she brings hope to humankind through cures that are signs of the existence of a benign divinity. Vishnu, Shiva, and Devi, two gods and a goddess, make the Hindu trinity, and—in the practice of Prince Twins Seven-Seven—Sango, Ogun, and Osun, two red gods and a white goddess, make a Yoruba trinity.

Under the worst of conditions, the Yoruba religion spread to Brazil, Trinidad, Haiti, and Cuba. It is a world religion, like Hinduism; both are now practiced in the United States. The two are theologically comparable, and they are revealed similarly—though not identically—in visible form. The Hindu iconic repertory is more fixed upon images of the deities, called *murtis*. In them, the point of mimetic fusion shifts closer to the visual. The formal range of Hindu art spans wider. It opens to extension, to limbs flying free of the body; Robert Plant Armstrong used a cast statue of Shiva dancing in a ring of fire to establish contrast with the Yoruba inclination to intension. Yet, the Hindu tradition also closes into an intensive continuity tighter than that of the Yoruba, in, say, the images of Ganesh crafted by the potters of Rajasthan. But these are gods; this, too, is spiritual art. The similarities outweigh the differences.

Visions from nature do not lead in the creation of African art, nor do they in Hindu art. I asked the artists for the source of their ideas. In southern India, Pitchai Velar, a sculptor in Vilachery, Tamil Nadu, told me that he found his forms and proportions in *shastra*, in sacred writing. In northern India, Rajesh Kumar Gour, who manages the Jaipur Murti Bhandar in Banaras, told me that the men of his atelier—the workers who carve and polish the marble transported from Rajasthan and the masters who paint the statues—have two sources. When they carve and paint portraits of individuals, they use photographs to guide an exact likeness (as the portrait painters of modern Nigeria do). When they image the deities in *murtis*, they must rely on *kalpana*, on imagination, because, Rajesh said, no one has ever seen the gods. The visual channel is empty, so the conceptual capacity must fill from within. Memories of old *murtis*, melded in the mind, make the main source. To the east, in Bangladesh, prayer was the answer I got from Haripada Pal, a great master of the Bengali sculptural tradition. He begins work in his cramped, damp shop on Shankharibazar, Old Dhaka, by reciting mantras of praise that bring into his mind an image of the deity, a direct revelation of the divine. Then just as the artist of realism works to render an image that formed on the retina, Haripada works to shape in clay an image that formed in his mind's eye, that came to him through prayer.

Devoted work by Hindu artists yields figures that are—in Robert Farris Thompson's word—"ephebic." Less generalized than idealized, they are full and smooth, ripe with life, eternally youthful. Quite consciously, the artists accomplish idealization through geometric perfection, shaping bodies and their parts to match the pure forms of geometry. The resultant image is supernaturally beautiful, and beauty has a purpose. It attracts the devotee into worship. It pleases the deity who, flattered by the beautiful form, descends into the *murti*, called down by mantras of praise, just as mantras of praise called the deity into the artist's mind. Beauty brings the devotee to the deity, the deity to the devotee. The *murti*—Haripada Pal called it a mediator—brings them together. To some Hindu artists it is the god, to others it is a shell the god fills momentarily with power, but either way the *murti* is a device for communication between the worlds.

The *murti* is shaped to do its work, and in its shaping the parallels with African art continue. The *murti* is emotionally proportioned: the head is large for the body, the eyes are large for the head. From afar, the *murti*'s big eyes draw the eyes of the devotee into *darshan*, into connection through sight. Verticality integrates the Yoruba image. While Durga, the most powerful of all, stands in calm straightness to kill her demon, others sway or lean or reach, but all remain balanced on the midline, all turn frontally to the viewer to receive *darshan*. Iconic, they rarely illustrate narratives (Hanuman is the usual exception) but hold steady beyond time to stir inner mythic understandings. Their youthful, beautiful bodies bring male and female figures close. As in Yoruba art, the faces might be the same in symmetrical perfection, while the bodies differ by gender. Gods and goddesses divide, but their idealization requires the addition of signs for identification.

Lakshmi and Saraswati, the daughters of power, are both portrayed as beautiful young women, seated in composure, their eyes to the front. Color distinguishes them. Lakshmi is golden in hue, Saraswati is white as snow. They hold different objects. Lakshmi holds a pot, Saraswati holds the *vina*, the stringed instrument with which she shattered the sound of the beginning—*om*—into musical scales. They are accompanied by *vahanas*, Lakshmi by an

Hindu masters of art

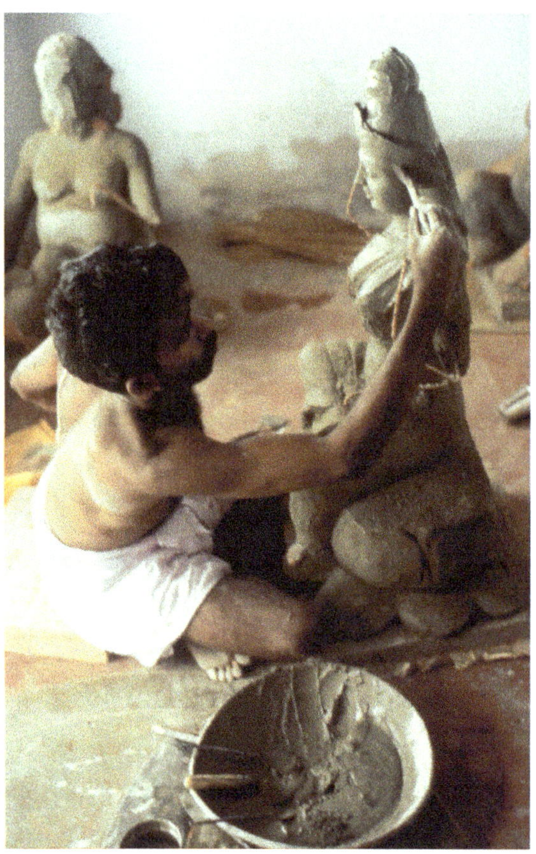

Pitchai Velar shaping Lakshmi in cement.
Vilachery, Tamil Nadu, India

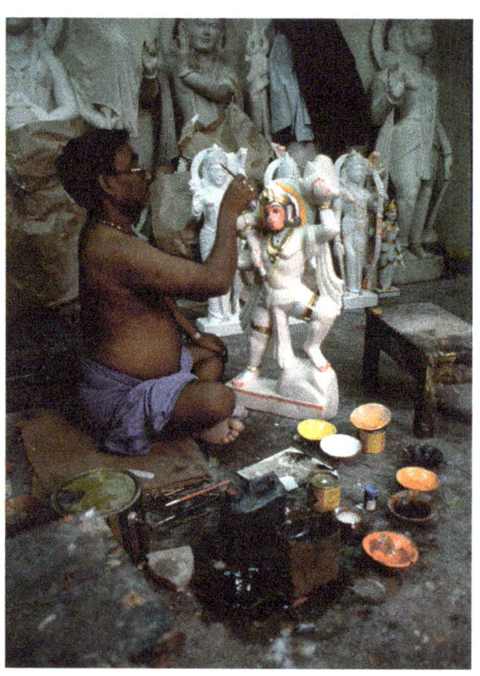

Sindranath Singh painting Hanuman.
Jaipur Murti Bhandar, Banaras, India

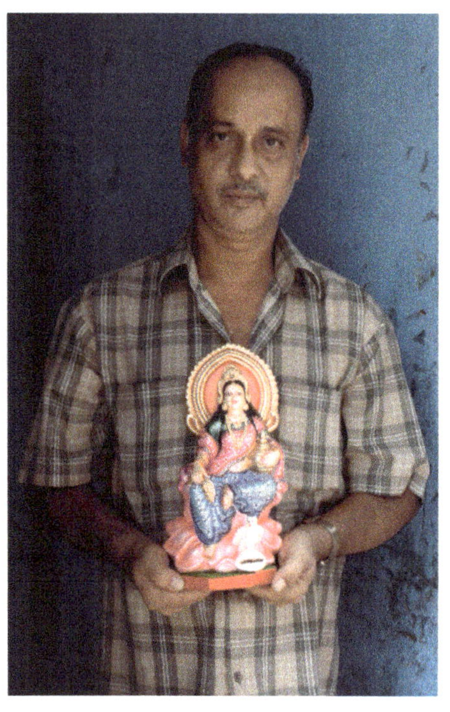

Haripada Pal with Lakshmi.
Shankharibazar, Dhaka, Bangladesh

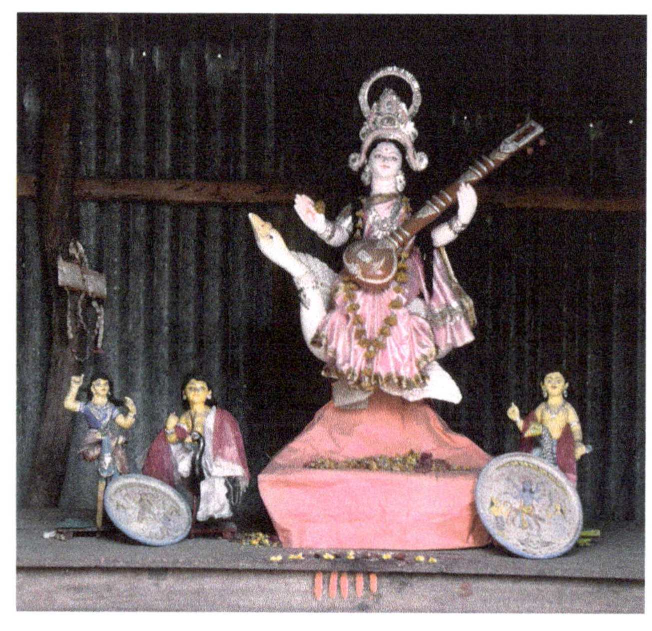

Saraswati by Haripada Pal.
Family temple, Norpara, Bangladesh

owl, Saraswati by the swan whose ability to separate the milk from the water in a liquid mix signals Saraswati's discriminatory capacity, her power as the goddess of wisdom. By these signs—color, object, and *vahana*—they are known. The devotee, sure of identity, knows which prayer to use in order to bring communication to its conclusion. Properly addressed, the goddess gets the praise she wants and delivers the boons the devotee wants. Incense fills the air, the drums beat, flowers go, sweets come, and the deal is done.

Like the Hindu image, the Yoruba image is generalized in formation, then particularized by signs. Osun's fish and Ogun's snake, like Durga's lion and Shiva's bull, Sango's axe like Krishna's flute—all signal the deity. The Hindu image, like the African image, represents the unseen powers of the other world, and it works for human benefit in this one.

(This hardly justifies the length of my comparison, but it is, in this context, interesting that the only piece of art in all of Prince's homes that is not the work of his own hands is a large painting on the wall of his country house outside of Ibadan. In the conventional manner, it shows Murugan, the Tamil form of the dapper Hindu god of war, Durga's son Kartikeya, instantly recognizable by his flamboyant *vahana*, the peacock. Prince was happy to learn when I told him about it, but he bought the picture in Sri Lanka and hung it on the wall because he liked its style. Once when we were together, we saw a strip of cloth embroidered with Hindu deities, and Prince said, "That is how I do my work too.")

Now look farther east, into the realm of Buddhism. In the Japanese cities of Hagi and Seto, potters work in the Zen frame, creating vessels for the tea ceremony and images of the deities. Their iconic repertory divides. When they portray the Seven Gods, the figures are—as African figures often are—short in the leg or seated to stress the trunk that holds the head aloft. The head is large, and in the case of the gods of Chinese origin, the elderly stars, Jurojin and Fukurokuju, that head is extravagantly elongated, emotionally proportioned to symbolize mental potency. They lean forward to show their age—the vitality of youth is here less important than the wisdom of age—but they are shaped symmetrically and aligned frontally like the deities of Indian origin: Benten (Saraswati) and the warrior Bishamon (Vishnu). Hotei, fat with compassion, smiles merrily, and the native gods, Ebisu and Daikoku, smile too, relaxing into familiarity, Ebisu with his fishing rod, the carpenter Daikoku with his mallet. Like the old Zen drawings that prefigure manga and anime, they provoke feelings of warmth and affection. Lovable, even cute (as Ganesh can be), the Seven Gods suit their locations on the altars in shops and homes. But when artists like Agawa Norio in Hagi or Kato Susumu in Seto depict the divinities of the temples and silent gardens—Jizo, Kannon, and the Buddha—the forms are erect in intensive symmetry, the faces composed in serene timelessness.

Turn now west to follow the Catholic expansion. The missionaries and colonial adventurers of Portugal and Spain carried the baroque style of the Counter-Reformation to places far flung from Iberia, providing the world with a projective test for spiritual art. The statues the provincial artists saw in the golden churches rendered the saints as startlingly real people, wrenched in the passion of faith. The statues the provincial artists carved stopped motion and relocated emotion in upright, frontal equilibrium. So it was in the Philippines, in Goa, in Puerto Rico, Brazil, Paraguay, Bolivia, Guatemala, Mexico, and the southwestern United States where the provincial style continues in the pale, stiff, symmetrical figures carved by the López family of Córdova, New Mexico. When we talked in Salvador da Bahia, Brazil, Edival Rosas, a great master of the baroque sculptural tradition, faulted the provincial work for its generalization, saying that the faces of male and female figures were the same, abstract and bland, differentiated only by the beards on the men. The monumental statues of saints that Edival carves out of cedar are proportioned precisely like the people of the world. The flesh is delicately tinted, the faces are alive with eyes of glass. They depict people who once walked the earth, and though they remain smooth and youthful—"saintly," Edival said—they contrast with the generalized figures to which attributes must be added, a staff for São Joaquim, birds for São Francisco de Assis, to enable identification.

Devotion to the saints aligns Catholic practice with the polymorphic traditions of Buddhism, Hinduism, and the Yoruba religion. One consequence was the syncretizing of the Yoruba gods with Catholic saints in the New World. Another was the displacement of the saints during the Reformation as Protestants sought to distance themselves from the Catholic past and, stiffened in stress, to distinguish themselves from their Catholic opponents in war. Iconoclasm returned in the Puritans' effort to eliminate ornament and match Judaism and Islam in their monotheistic concentration on the revealed word. Before the congregation, tablets bearing the words of the Ten Commandments replaced the Crucifix: stern instructions replaced the agony of sacrifice. The stark, seventeenth-century style of the Puritans endures in the old country churches of Ulster and the southern United States. But despite the Biblical injunction against graven images, the pictorial impulse could not be suppressed (even among the Puritans, whose carved slate gravestones were the first flowering of art on Yankee soil).

As though directed by Thomas Jefferson's editing of the Gospels to reveal the man Jesus in his Near Eastern setting, some Protestant artists—the Pre-Raphaelites, say—depicted

Variety in spiritual art

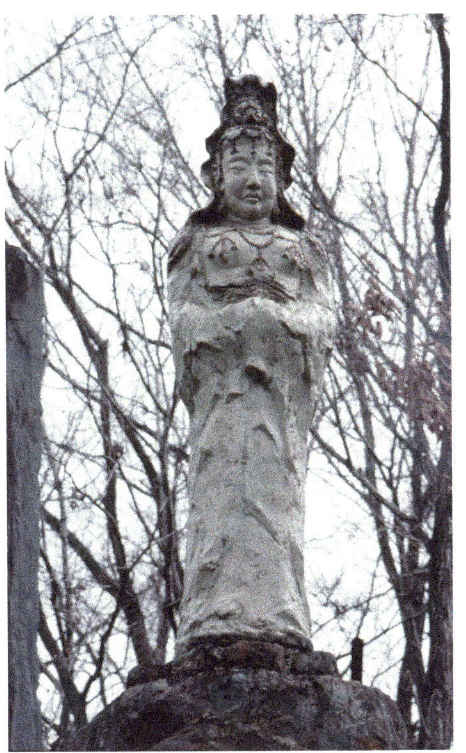

Kannon by Hoshiai Shinlei.
Glazed stoneware; Seto, Japan

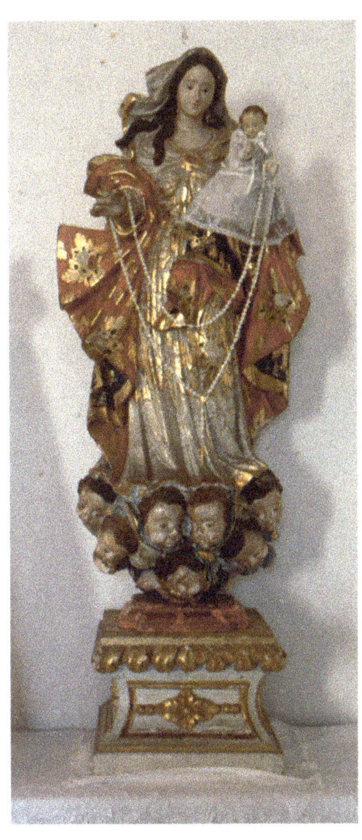

Nossa Senhora do Rosário.
Polychromed wood; São Domingos.
Salvador da Bahia, Brazil

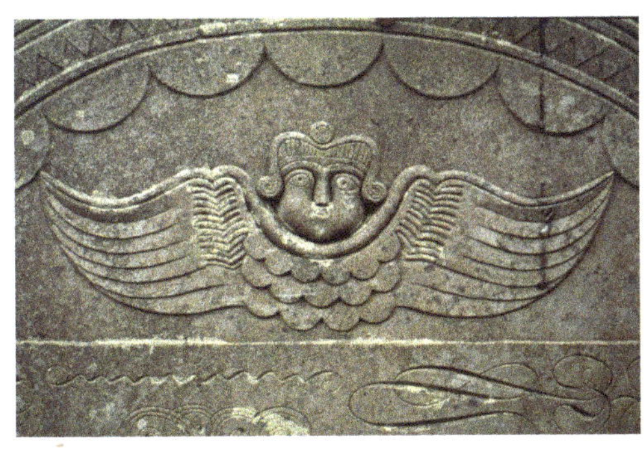

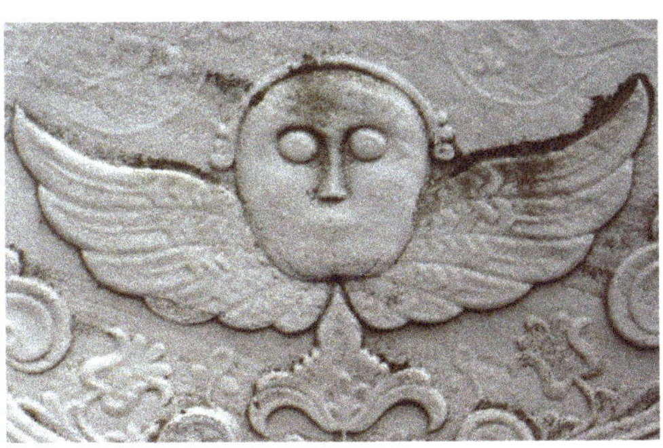

Protestant souls in stone.
Swimbridge, Devon, England.
Bennington, Vermont, U.S.A.

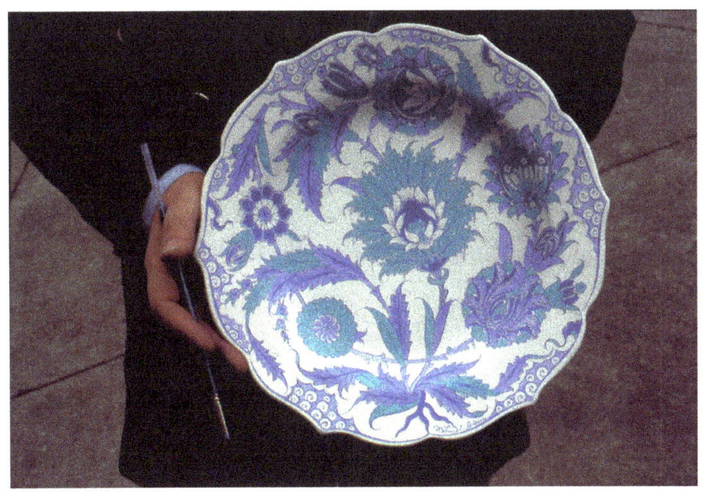

Muslim souls.
Çini plate by Mehmet Gürsoy.
Kütahya, Turkey

holy people naturalistically in mundane scenes awash with transitory light. But others—in the wall paintings of Sweden, the Staffordshire figures of industrial England, and the *fraktur* of the Pennsylvania Germans—worked in the manner of provincial Catholicism, creating what is called folk art. The sacred images of the old religion that survived in their churches might have provided the pattern, and John Brendel told me that the secret of the art of his people, the Pennsylvania Germans, was the retention among them, Protestants all, of a Catholic spirit. But whether or not they had seen the vertical, frontal, symmetrical figures of medieval European art, Protestant folk artists had surely seen printed pictures in which, through realism, art brinked on a collapse into materialism. In reaction, in resistance, and well in advance of the modern artists who turned from realism toward abstraction to recapture concept and spirit, Protestant folk artists—even when picturing people who were not saints, even when arranging figures in narrative scenes—created iconic, generalized forms.

Perhaps because they shared with their patrons a pictorial tradition that was rooted, like their oral literature, in an earlier age, and probably because their tradition was intellectual and philosophical, more than visual, and certainly because their thinking was at once religious and pragmatic, Protestant folk artists employed, by adoption or invention, the global norms of spiritual art in their creations.

Our comparison ends with Islam. Here the artistic orientation to the conceptual is most rigorous. Commitment to the primacy of the revealed word has made calligraphy the greatest of the Islamic arts. God is beautiful and loves beauty—that is the artists' guiding principle, and the word of God is drawn beautifully, when the breath is held and prayer fills the mind, just as the face of God is drawn beautifully in places where God has a face. Monotheistic, theologically similar, long in contentious contact, Islam and Christianity have purified themselves in opposition. Jesus Christ is represented by a bearded face in an icon; the Prophet Muhammad is represented by a written description in a *Hilye-i Şerif.*

The Holy Koran does not prohibit representation, but only the worship of statues, the profound error of confusing with God that which is not God. Representation is permissible, though in accord with *hadith* it is most favored when allied to utility. The splendors of Islamic textiles and ceramics logically follow, for both are at once beautiful and useful. The carpets on the floor and the tiles on the walls of the mosque carry geometric designs that expand syndetically toward infinity or contract synthetically into quadrilaterally symmetrical medallions. Both patterns evoke the encompassing wonder of the will of Allah. Calligraphy is highest, geometry most abundant, but things from the world are pictured too. The human form is not common, but it is not absent, and the human presence is pervasive in the objects most frequently pictured. Flowers, for example.

With Mehmet Gürsoy, a master of the Turkish ceramic tradition that runs back for more than half a millennium, let us consider the tulip, the carnation, the rose. The first thing that Mehmet will tell you is that the flowers he paints do not resemble the flowers of nature that wither and die. They are rendered full and flat, solid in color, outlined in black, and geometrically idealized at the peak of their bloom to reveal a timeless essence, making them supernaturally beautiful, making them symbolic. They stand for people. Mehmet says he is not interested in the transitory, distressed surface, the face worn with worry and age, but the inner power, the breath of God in the body, the shining immortal soul. The flowers are souls. They rise, all of them, from a single root, a symbol of God's will, and they stand in a floral assembly, swaying into a balanced composition that represents society as it ought to be, beautiful, integrated, and peaceful in the perfect circle of God's love.

Muslims have their ways, just as Christians, Buddhists, Hindus, and followers of the Yoruba faith have their ways to create spiritual art. Our comparative excursion concludes with the unsurprising observation that cultures develop through history into difference. In response to environmental conditions, as a result of social motion and encounter, every culture becomes an aggregate of retentions and borrowings, gathered around solved and unsolved problems. But culture is more than a peculiar stew of ideas. It is ordered by principles that people consolidate in traditions to bring their potential, their inbuilt abilities for creation and communication, into fruition through action. When acts are devoted, sincerely creative and sincerely communicative, their yield is art, and art functions to make sensate the principles that, at once, integrate and differentiate cultures. Art, then, provides the observer with an entry to cultural understanding, and it provides the creator with a way to express the self fully and to put into the world a view of the world, an understanding of reality that urges social cohesion.

In art, in poetry and oratory, in dance and sculpture, the Yoruba are the Yoruba and different from the Igbo, who are different from the Hausa, who are different from the English or Japanese. Our earth widens into an amazing array of ethnological difference, demanding a tolerant relativism and a history composed of thousands of histories. And yet, for all their particularity, cultures associate and divide by kind on the basis of their fundamental principles of construction.

The cultural principle that matters most in artistic representation is whether reality is imagined expansively to encompass the visible and invisible or restricted narrowly to the visible. When the Renaissance masters dedicated themselves to a scientific view—humanistic, empirical, and grounded on the knowable—they put art on the evolutionary track to realism. It did not take centuries to accomplish because realism is complicated or difficult; the artists of the Stone Age painted animals naturalistically and medieval artists in Africa and Japan achieved realism easily when getting a worldly likeness was the goal. It took centuries for European artists to clarify a materialistic understanding in opposition to a spiritual one, to banish the divine, forswear the miraculous, and peel away the desire to depict the unseen and unknowable. In their success, nearly reducing art to the pictorial and evaluation to resemblance, creators carried the "fine" art of the West into magnificent marginality, separating it from the "folk" art of the West in which a medieval spirituality endured, from the "primitive" art of the people who lived with the spirits of the forests, and from the refined art of the high civilizations of Africa, Asia, and the Americas that maintained a religious orientation and posed a threat to Western imperialistic expansion. From the art of these diverse traditions, the modernists drew their inspiration when, seeking to recover the spiritual and conceptual, they mounted their revolution at the beginning of the twentieth century and brought the art of the West back into touch with the art of the world.

In most societies, then and now, reality is understood to combine the seen and the unseen, the known and the unknowable. Extreme realism, an art meticulously restricted to the visual, would fail them. The key to categorical differentiation in art—folk and fine, primitive and progressive, provincial and cosmopolitan, spiritual and materialistic, traditional and contemporary, ours and theirs—is not excellence or expressivity, all art is excellent and expressive, but the culture, the worldview out of which artists create. The worldview of the traditional Yoruba artist—like that of the Hindu, Buddhist, Christian, or Muslim artist—opens to the unknown; it is expansive, doubled, spiritual in reach. And—this is the point—Prince takes the Yoruba view; his art witnesses to the presence of the spirits and deities.

We are ready for the art of Prince Twins Seven-Seven. As we go, I will refer to specific pictures in the collection assembled in chapter 20, where Prince's worldview unfolds. The conclusion will be that, in its representational logic, Prince's art is Yoruba art, African art, and spiritual art.

Prince is consistent in saying that his art is based on Yoruba mythology, that it is part of his effort to revitalize the Yoruba religion. Spiritual art, it is not drawn in from the world but up from his imagination. Prince will paint anything, but the works that matter most to him gather into three main classes: the other world, animals, and village life.

Scenes of village life, topically comparable to the genre paintings of the West, from Brueghel to Benton, seem poised for realistic rendition, but that is not what happens. "Modern life," Prince said, "is something you see every day, and I want to show that I am seeing something else." His paintings lack the artifacts of modernity. The houses are round and thatched, not squared off and roofed with sheet metal; the change from thatch to metal is a worldwide sign of modernization. Clothing and acts belong to the past. People labor with handtools in direct confrontation with nature, and they are committed to the old faith, worshipers, as he is, of Sango, Ogun, and Osun. When I asked Prince about this aspect of his art, I assumed that he chose village life as—in the vanguard of ethnology during the nineteenth century—Swedish artists chose rural subjects and American artists chose Native American subjects, recording the details of an imperiled culture. But Prince said he was born into a Nigeria that was already becoming modern. He has never seen what he depicts. Instead, he said:

"I follow my dreams. I follow my mythological thinking. I try to draw in some of my cultural beliefs that I have. At the same time, I don't want to paint what is existing in our world.

"Because: *that* I am leaving for other generations behind me."

In his village paintings, Prince scrapes away change to reveal a lost world, a world of coherence that preceded the disruption of colonialism—and that is the world of his imagination, his seeing. Rural scenes are often painted in the cities of Africa and South Asia where migrants from the countryside have settled. Such pictures frame through nostalgia an alternative, critical vision, and part of Prince's intent is critical. The colonial experience of his boyhood still angers him. Today's electronic distractions and ceaseless violence sadden and scare him. The life around him is not the life in his mind, nor the source of his ideas. He contrasts his paintings with the contemporary films that titillate their audiences with murder after murder; he paints with a purpose:

"Each artist have a reason, have a beginning; it is not just picking up a brush.

"When I began, I would pick stories; I would pick folklore stories to guide me in my paintings. I would pick animals' behavior in some of my paintings. And I would pick human behavior too. But if you look at my paintings, you don't see so much knife-stabbing people, killing people, and all that. Because in my heart, that's not what I belong to."

Prince belongs in another world, and his village scenes mount a critique of this one. They remember the collective labor and religious unity of the past; they oppose the violence of the present. In addition, Prince believes that viewers who miss his deep point will find his pictures engaging at the surface. "If I start painting," he said, "what everybody see every day, my paintings would not look new to everybody. But what I do here, when you look, you have to come back and look again." He does not depict what exists in our world. It is, Prince said, the task of other painters, painters who work "realistically," to make art out of the visible, mixed reality of contemporary Nigeria. His view of village life, at once oppositional and entertaining, is all from his head, entirely imaginary (see chapter 20, nos. 20–23).

The imaginary, the conceptual, directs Prince's depictions of the human figure. To see how his work relates to the Yoruba tradition we must allow for the shift from carving to painting, from a subtractive three-dimensional technique to an additive two-dimensional technique. If the traits of Yoruba art are, as the scholars insist, deep cultural values and not the surficial get of technical constraints, they will endure through a shift of medium in the way that African principles, according to Wole Soyinka and Chinua Achebe, endure through a shift of language. Painting is now, as English is now, as Christianity is now, a part of the general cultural resource; it belongs to the tradition of the Yoruba people.

The people in Prince's paintings are the plain people of Yorubaland. He draws them in the generalized way that Protestant folk artists draw the people of their places. The background fills with staring, symmetrical faces. They resemble the faces between the wings on the old gravestones of England and New England that represent the soul in ascent. Timeless, unaltered by expression, undifferentiated by gender or age, these faces represent, Prince said, "humanity"—humankind in the mass, in the abstract. The foreground figures are vertical and frontal, alike in the face, divided by dress into gender. Emotionally proportioned, they have large heads and large eyes. Iconic, like Prince's self-portrait in the last versions of *The Spirits of My Reincarnation Brothers and Sisters*, they stand straight and still, holding objects that identify them as musicians, as priests and priestesses, as kings, as farmers (see chapter 20, nos. 20–21, 29).

Statues offer a view from the front and a view from the side. Working on a flat surface, Prince uses both the frontal view and the profile in iconic representation, and in a simultaneity of perspectives, like that of pharaonic Egyptian art, he combines them: torsos are seen from the front, feet from the side. When Prince portrays people, shifts to the profile, as in *Barefoot President*, imply motion, but they are uncommon. He strongly favors the frontal view, the stable, timeless, formal pose of spiritual art that is adopted by the world's people when they stand to have their photos taken. Animals, though, are most easily recognized in profile. Once for a record jacket, Prince drew three elephants from the front. The rendering was unusual for his work; he called it commercial, simple, and realistic. Normally, having, he said, "no need to look at pictures of animals," Prince brings elephants out of his mind and draws them from the side. In profile, they are emblematic of elephantness as people posed frontally are emblematic of humanity (see chapter 20, nos. 12–13, 15).

Prince's birds are not sparrows or parrots or cranes. They are birds, essentialized categorically into birdness. By generalizing animal forms, Prince makes them symbolic, just as Mehmet Gürsoy makes floral forms symbolic by generalization. Prince's animals, like Mehmet's flowers, stand for people. Prince's inspiration for this move was, he told me, the stories he learned from his mother. As in the fables of old Aesop, the examples of the Irish countryside, and the rabbit tales of the African American South, animals in his mother's stories act like people, exposing human failings and virtues to urge children toward moral behavior. Prince said:

"You know, when we were very young, they used to make us sit under a tree, under the moon, and tell us stories, stories that can educate you from not doing bad things. This is the purpose of why they tell you stories in those days. Like a kind of communal education; educate the child from home.

"You see, all these stories—I never knew at that time I'd been given a goldmine."

Prince dug from that mine, traded sight for imagination, and painted birds that gestured toward birds but symbolized people. Birds represent witches, and, therefore, the mingling in life of positive and negative forces. Indicators of a fundamental precept, birds are the animals most abundant in Prince's work. Elephants come next. They are kings, signs of royal power, embodiments of good and bad governance. Elephants make a mirror for princes. Then come snakes. For Prince they evoke Ogun and symbolize "the end of the world": death. Like the bones and skulls of medieval European art, snakes provide a focus for contemplation when life's course is being charted. Discreetly, fish pop up everywhere, signifying the pervasive power of Osun, and among the infrequent creatures, leopards stand for chiefs, for people of deserved authority, tortoises stand for the lowly but cunning common folk, and the monkeys who come down to the ground then leap in the trees, nearly flying like birds, represent twins, people like Prince who know the low and know the high, who carry doubled spiritual gifts. Plucked out of nature and reconfigured typologically, like the characters in folktales, animals are good to think, as Claude Lévi-Strauss amply demonstrated; they are devices to deploy metaphorically in philosophical discourse. *Kissing Birds*, you will recall, is such an argument; it holds that in this world the powerful mistreat the weak and the political leaders do not care (see chapter 20, no. 13).

Painted, not carved, Prince's figures are flexible in posture, fluid in form, sprung loose in their symmetry, yet they are located between the seen and unseen realities in midpoint mimesis. To that rule there are two exceptions.

When Prince paints portraits, he uses photographs as the carvers of Banaras and the painters of modern Nigeria do. His mimetic midpoint slips toward the visual in his effort to get a good likeness. But he stops far short of realism. In comparison with the work of his contemporaries, the Indian sculptors and Nigerian painters, or with the marvels wrought by the old masters of Ife, Prince's pictures are highly stylized. His portrait of George fills with details of identification—George's beard and clothing, his house and pets—but the figure is vertical, frontal, and symmetrical, not much of an exception to the principles of Yoruba art, African art, or spiritual art (see chapter 20, no. 27).

Prince paints few portraits. He wants to depict what he thinks, not what he has seen, and his oeuvre floods with figures from the other world. In them, the point of mimetic fusion rests farther from the visual than it does in the old wooden statues of Yorubaland. Frontality remains. Individual spirits still balance on the midline and some take symmetrical shape. But among them power begins to shift from potentiality into actuality. The spirits awaken, stir, and sway like snakes, sometimes entwining into a writhing mass that represents spirituality as the massed faces represent humanity. Contrast is the point. Traditionally the Yoruba carver represents spirits by reconceptualizing the human form, but Prince knows the spirits do not look like the world's people. The spirits are real but invisible, known only through signs, so he seeks visions from nature, from clouds and the patterns in woodgrain, to envision the unseen. He dismembers nature and reorders its bits, combining animal and human forms, male and female characteristics into images of the spirits. All are distinguished by his large, veiled "trademark" eyes, and marked by distortion, dislocation, and multiplicity. Necks stretch and twist, birds have beards and breasts, human heads have horns, faces double and drop, eyes open everywhere (see chapter 20, nos. 1–7, 17, 28–29).

The carver who adheres to Robert Farris Thompson's canons of excellence will create a beautiful, powerful statue. Analysis of statues leads to recognition of an aesthetics of beauty and its subordination to an aesthetics of power. Masks stretch the visual paradigm. As Thompson has said, masks can be ugly, intentional contradictions of beauty designed to represent enemies through an aesthetics of the grotesque. As Prince Twins Seven-Seven has said, masks can be terrifying. They can incarnate an aesthetics of fear. Anesthetics deaden the senses; aesthetics do the reverse: they vibrate the senses into life. Beauty does that, ugliness does too. So does fear. Horror films and ghosts stories stimulate a thrill of uncertainty, an exciting shiver of apprehension, that deepens when we creep into the bush, encounter the babas, and remember that the living dead are all around us. Prince's paintings prod that memory, prick those feelings, and bring, as the masquerade does, the unseen into startling visibility.

Amos Tutuola used the conventions of oral literature to build a book of fear in *My Life in the Bush of Ghosts*. In her arresting first novel, *The Icarus Girl*, Helen Oyeyemi uses the conventions of realistic fiction to pull her reader along the narrative track. She draws delicate, closely observed scenes of childhood, and lifts her main character, Jess, into life through descriptions of girlish play, of juvenile tantrums, episodes of severe mental disturbance, and the surprising acts of an abiku, a ghost, the spirit of a dead twin. But not sure which is which, what is fact, what illusion, her reader—stopped in uncertainty by Oyeyemi's craft—has experienced the excitement of the Yoruba aesthetics of fear. Prince works toward the same end. A viewer in the right mood and taking time before a painting might be rewarded with a little rush of fear. But Prince works closer to the abstraction of Tutuola than to the realism of Oyeyemi, and he follows his own head in representation.

When Prince sets out to depict spirits and ghosts, Tutuola is one source of his inspiration. Others are his mother's tales and the frightening masks with multiple eyes that he saw in his boyhood. In his paintings, masks and spirits conflate; take a look at *The Last African Mask*, number 25 in the assembly of his works. Prince's spirits form out of the aesthetics of fear, but channeling his culture through his generous personality, he confines them in pictorial balance and softens them with whimsy. That softening has increased over time, along with formal regularity. Since they are real but invisible, spirits take form in the imagination, revealing the artist's personal vision, and Prince's vision of the spirits shapes close to the Japanese vision of the *yōkai*. No more terrifying, Prince's spirits blend horror and humor. Generating surprise, meshing in the grotesque, horror and humor run parallel in aesthetic operation. In the words Elliott Oring chose to define humor, Prince's spirits are appropriately incongruous. Incongruous in formation, they are consistent in type, appropriate in function. In artistic terms, they are conceptual, but not abstract, not unrealistic. Frankly portrayed like the characters in the spiritual realism of mythology, or the magical realism of Latin American fiction, calmly acknowledging the duality of reality, they are spirits.

Prince finds the spirits in his mind, just as Haripada Pal finds the gods in his mind. Haripada's *murtis* do not portray amazingly beautiful people; they are gods. And so it is with Prince. His shocking creatures are spirits, perfectly normal spirits, not bizarrely disfigured human beings.

Ambiguity diminishes, fear with it, but does not vanish. Since spirits do not resemble people, Prince uses them to symbolize human beings when he does not want to make a reference to particular individuals but does want to bring into visibility the negative spiritual force in all people that causes them to be, as the spirits can be, disorderly and malevolent (see chapter 20, no. 29).

Agbo and Egungun: the masquerade enacts a spirit; the mask provides precedent for Prince's scary spirits. But if his imagination carries him beyond the norms of Yoruba art, it does not carry him beyond the bounds of the Yoruba tradition. Prince did not find the spirits Alokolobo, Ogongo, Sigidi, Edun, and Ologbonkiyan in Yoruba art. He found them in Yoruba mythology (see chapter 20, nos. 1–5, 28–29). Literature—the stories his mother told, the stories that Tutuola recast in novels, that Soyinka and Ladipo recast in drama—was more insistently present in his life, more influential in his art, than the old carvings. He performed Agbo, listened to his mom, read Tutuola, acted in plays by Soyinka and Ladipo. Myth, as he says, guided his art. Prince's paintings align with the classics of Yoruba carving less because he saw them than because, as is the case with Tutuola, he and the old sculptors invented within the lineaments of Yoruba tradition.

When he pictures the deities who inhabit Orun along with the spirits, Prince works closer to the representational logic of Yoruba art. Traditionally, the carvers depicted few of the Yoruba divinities. Robert Farris Thompson used a fine statue of Sango to illustrate the Yoruba style and noted its rarity. Esu, the messenger, the bearer of sacrifices and transgressive opener of roads, is the god who most frequently gains visual presence in wood, but all feature in narratives and many appear in Prince's paintings. He draws from myth to picture Sango and Ogun as men, and, like the old carvers, he spreads the powers of the gods among their priests and priestesses, but, unlike the old carvers, Prince clarifies and emphasizes the fearful force of those priests and priestesses by imaging them more as spirits than people (see chapter 20, nos. 6–7, 11, 17). His rendition of Osun as a mermaid accords with Yoruba belief, but the elaborations are his own. Prince makes it clear that she comes into form through the swarming of fish. She holds a fish as a symbol of fertility. Her breasts bear faces, signs of vitality and vigilance which she shares with the spirits (see chapter 20, nos. 8–10).

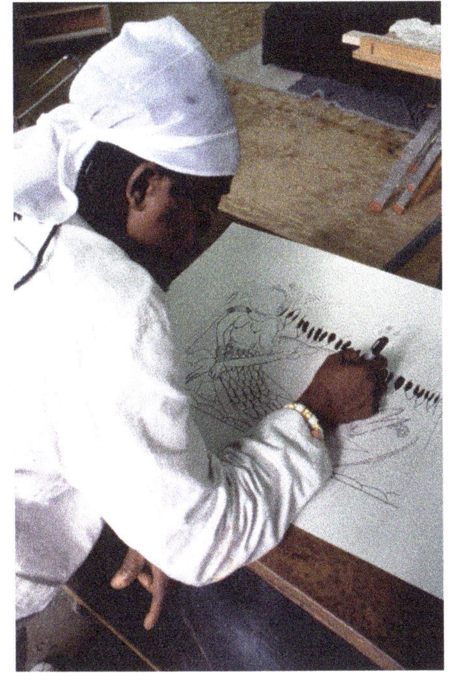

Prince paints Osun

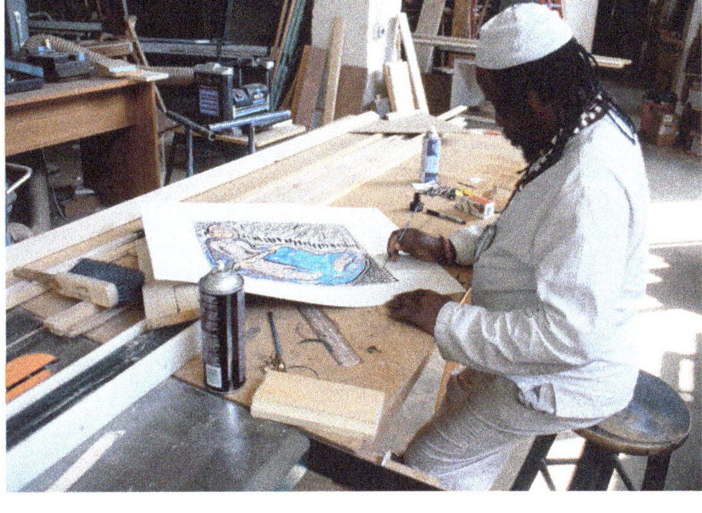

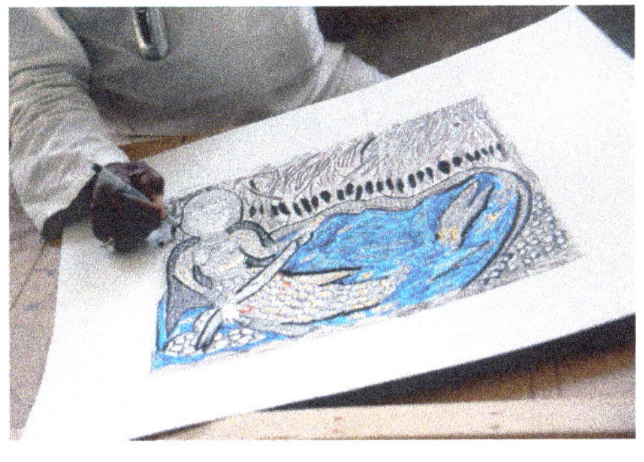

In Prince's usual rendition, Osun is a mermaid, her torso seen from the front, her tail from the side

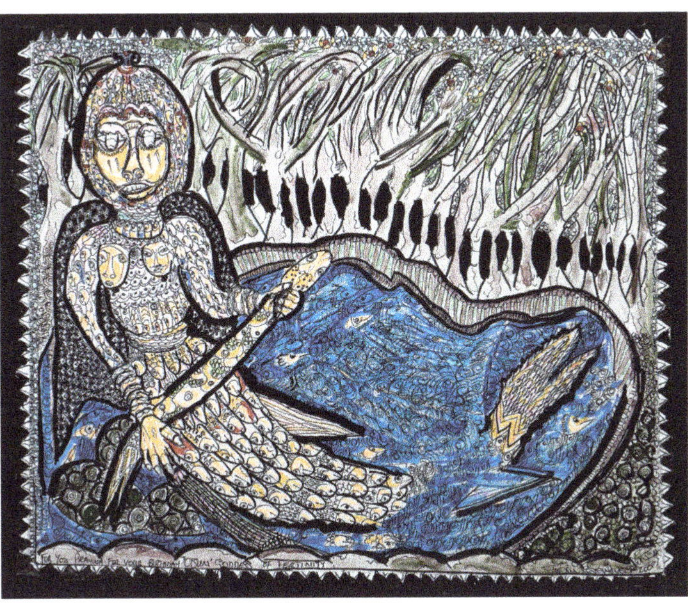

Osun, Goddess of Fertility. Ink and watercolor on paper. 18"x14". Philadelphia, October 2007

Of all Prince's subjects, Osun is pictured most often; "most of the time," he said, "I have river goddess in my paintings." Like all artists, Prince repeats ideas, sometimes with commerce in mind, sometimes because no new idea has come to him and he has to paint, as Beckett had to write. But his repetition of Osun is an act of devotion. Like Native American women who repetitively paint their pots with signs of dampness, like Muslim calligraphers who write once again the opening formula of the Holy Koran, Prince enters a meditative, prayerful state when he draws Osun. Spiritual art is repetitive in imagery precisely because it is repetitive in intent: images, like prayers, reiterate hope and praise. Prince's Osun is a visualized prayer.

Prayer joins beauty with power, affection with fear. It connects the worlds. Blood flows down the blades of iron, the host is lifted, lights whirl, voices surge in song, the forehead touches the carpet's soft surface: prayer in repetition brings it all together at the midpoint of existence.

The image brings it all together at the midpoint of representation. Erect in equilibrium, the figure perfectly balances the physical and spiritual realities. It might be a Buddhist bodhisattva, a Catholic saint, or a Yoruba priest, and the figure tightens mightily when it is both human and divine: Sango, Krishna, Christ. Purified toward the physical, the figure accumulates particularity until it becomes the portrait of an individual, warts and all as Cromwell put it. Purified toward the spiritual, imagery abandons appearances and yields to the perfect geometric patterning of Islam in which a simultaneity of extension and intension locates the unified principle that physicists have yet to capture in a mathematical equation.

With imagery as its task, the quest for purity rebounds from impossibility at both ends of the spectrum: at one end sunken in earthly darkness, at the other blinded by heavenly light. From one end, the physical, visual, and particular come. From the other comes the spiritual, the conceptual, and the general. All of this meets at some point, achieves integration, and consolidates into a tradition of representation.

When a tradition abandons the spiritual and embraces the sensate world, particularity takes over and a realism of measurement, appearance, and psychology results. When a tradition holds that the spiritual dimension of human nature is powerful and positive, a spark of the divine, the spiritualizing search replaces bodies with symbols of the soul: the angels of Christianity, the flowers of Islam that bloom eternally in Paradise. In the Yoruba tradition, as Prince describes it, the spiritual aspect of human nature is profound and double—twinned—at once positive and negative. Princes images this understanding as a bird, winged like an angel with its feet on the ground (see chapter 20, nos. 3, 5). The bird is a witch; witchcraft is both positive and negative. When Prince images the negative spiritual dimension of human nature, he paints a spirit, a ghost, an evil soul (see chapter 20, no. 29). Pure goodness lies beyond form, beyond sight, in God, in Olodumare, in Allah. But Prince joins and furthers the positive force in the world by lifting Osun out of the water into visibility. He is one of her devotees, like the fish who swarm to give her form. Sango and Ogun are red, mixed in nature as people are, but she is as white as light. When she bathes, a rainbow arcs in the sky (see chapter 20, no. 9). Osun is Prince's prayer for health, fertility, prosperity, and peace.

PRESENTATION

In its representational logic, the Yoruba tradition is distinct, and it is clearly African, clearly spiritual. Its distinctiveness sharpens in its logic of presentation, in the way that representational decisions are brought into being—into visibility Thompson would say, into presence Armstrong would say.

The Yoruba method for materializing thought follows the carver's process. The carver isolates a length of wood that will contain the figure he has in mind. He blocks it out, segmenting it into parts, then shaping them so that the pieces preserve integrity while cohering into formal wholeness. He smoothes and polishes the surface and ornaments it with passages of incising. Prince has carved, he has modeled wax for casting, and when he paints he creates through isolation, segmentation, smoothing, and ornamentation, striving, like the carver, for presentational clarity.

Figures in the foreground—people, beasts, and spirits—are singular and complete, from head to feet, isolated by solid black lines. In completeness, as in frontality, they are like Yoruba statues. Background figures might be partially obscured, but all are granted independence by thick outlines; nothing is lost into an atmospheric haze. The forms could be as readily carved out as painted on. Form's parts—eyes and heads, toes and feet—are also outlined in black, given separate presence within the figure's unity. In their book *African Sculpture*, designed to train Western eyes into appreciation, William Fagg and Margaret Plass note a plenitude of parallels between African and European art; this sharp segmentation of form they liken to cubism, and it is a signal trait shared by Prince's paintings and Yoruba carvings.

The carver's smooth surface is matched in Prince's paintings. He does not build paint into an impasto that records the strokes of his brush. Similarly, the Yoruba carver does not make a virtuosic display out of the rhythmic hacked tracks of his adze. Gestures trapped permanently in art are, as Paul Klee said, signs of time's passing, but smoothness erases the temporal dimension: a timeless, otherworldly perfection is the goal. The carver polishes, and Prince finishes his pictures, his drawings on paper as well as his oils on wood, with multiple coats of varnish. The surface shines. In its smoothness, in its sheen, the work is a sign of the craftsman's care. Unified and removed from its rough and dull surroundings, smooth and bright, it carries a fresh, luminous gloss. This brightness, a reach for the eternal, is general in spiritual art. Colors are strong and radiant, surfaces are buffed and reflective, settings sparkle and gleam. The effect, transcendently glorious to the devotee, seems kitsch to the materialistic observer who favors the suave, muted hues and shadowed matte surfaces of the workaday world. In this context, color points to one of the particular complexities in the art of Prince Twins Seven-Seven.

African sculpture can be painted, and Yoruba sculpture is particularly rich in color, in blue and brick-red, yellow, black and chalk-white. I recall an especially splendid *ibeji* figure in Robert Plant Armstrong's home that was stained a brilliant indigo. The scholars comment on color less than they do on form, possibly because works destined for the Western market are sometimes stripped to the bare wood, as American painted pine furniture once was. But Robert Farris Thompson remarked that, in the Yoruba tradition, blue is a cool hue of equilibrium, mediating between black and red. Prince employs three main palettes, each dominated by a trio of colors. In each of them, black and a light shade are balanced by a middle tone: black, blue, and pink; black, red, and yellow; black, brown, and green. Prince's bright, shiny surfaces cover two bright palettes, both comparable to those of Catholicism and Hinduism, one mediated by blue, the other by red. But the third, mediated by brown, is his most characteristic and common, and it is, I believe, a factor in his appeal to Westerners, who, accustomed to realism's dour tones and gritty subjects, prefer their African statues battered, their Indian statues bereft of the paint that once brightened them into life. The modern sculptor Elie Nadelman met this taste when, inspired by old pieces of American folk art, he painted his carvings to give them the worn look of antiques. And Prince, a modern painter, meets it with a naturalistic palette of black and brown, rust, clay, dust, and leaf-green.

Then in one of his invigorating contradictory moves, Prince gathers the earthy tones of the Nigerian landscape beneath a smooth, shiny spiritual surface. Here Prince and the old carvers converge. The bright paint on Catholic or Hindu carvings might lead you to expect paint on Yoruba carvings, but often the polished surface glows over the natural or darkened tones of the wood, and in Prince's brown paintings varnish coats a palette he calls dark. Dark and luminous, the work exhibits the ephebic flair of healthy flesh. Skin tones in Prince's paintings, as in the work of the African American artist Elijah Pierce, are lightened to signal vitality, to capture the bright, mirroring quality of deep, robust darkness.

Dark and bright, natural and supernatural, Prince's paintings belong to the Yoruba tradition, just as he says they do. As surely as Tutuola and Achebe developed an English capable of carrying African thought with grace, Prince has developed a style of painting that spreads an African aesthetic onto a flat surface.

Ornamentation ends the presentational task. The carver's incising abstracts the visual in representing hair and facial marks, becoming decorative through repetitive patterning. Then patches of rhythmic hatching extend the decorative effect, establishing contrast with the stretches of smoothness. Robert Farris Thompson and Henry Drewal both argue that cuts of Ogun's sharp iron blade bring civilization, converting the natural into the cultural. Cuts mark the land, claiming it and bringing it into cultivation, into productivity. Cuts mark the flesh, bringing the individual into social association and responsibility. The wooden carving, like the body, is civilized and beautified by decorative incisions.

Prince's painted parallel is found in the ornamental patterns he calls tattoo. As the name suggests, he took the idea from the cicatrices of identification and beautification, which Prince calls tattooing. By coating a figure's flesh with a webbing of black lines, Prince fills form's segments with subtle ornamentation. As he says, the more you look, the more you see. His tattooed patterns differ from those on carved wood or living flesh in that, while some are nonobjective, more are figurative. Parallels, though, continue. Some of his figurative tattoos are ornamental only, spontaneous rationalizations of smears, but others add an intimate layer of significance, as when the marks on the hands and feet of a drummer reveal on close inspection a patterning of fish, indicating that this musician, like Prince, has been blessed by Osun. Take your time: as you watch, Prince's work deepens and deepens (see chapter 20, nos. 23, 29).

Prince, you will recall, uses two ornamental patterns. His tattooing appears on the bodies of deities, spirits, and people, and sometimes on the heads of animals, signaling their metaphoric relation with humankind. His geometric patterning appears on clothing, spirits, and animals, and sometimes on objects in the background, extending energy and interest to the trees behind the figures, the ground beneath their feet. Though it is repetitive and generally nonobjective like the incising on statues, it is far more diverse, being derived not from Yoruba carving but from Yoruba textiles. It differs, too, when like a textile it spreads to fill a form. For this trait, so characteristic of Prince's paintings, there is some precedent in the

Prince with *The Lost Mask,* an old beaded picture he made that was cut from a wrecked theater set. The beaded technique, rare for Prince, was perfected by his Osogbo colleague Jimoh Buraimoh

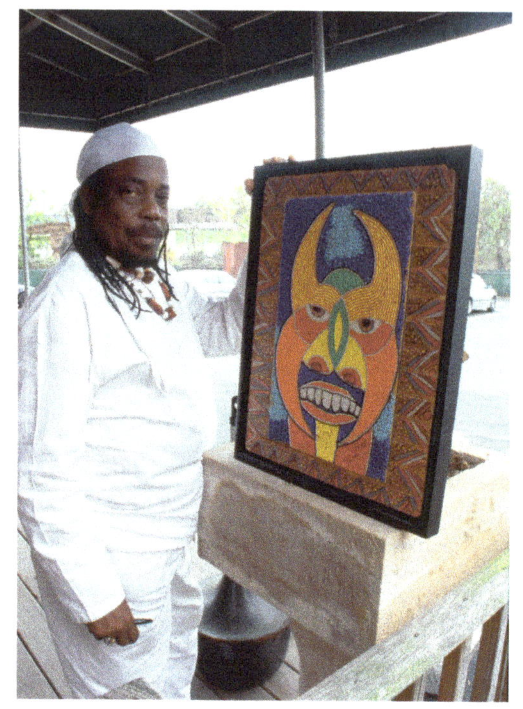

carver's art. The Yoruba carver Lamidi Fakeye says that his carvings have become finer and more elaborate over time (just as Prince's geometric patterns have), and he believes that if the old carvers had possessed his excellent tools, they would have also increased the ornament on their works. I have seen no Yoruba figure completely covered with incising, but Robert Plant Armstrong described an old carved figure that was painted with a geometric design of triangles, and some old pieces of Yoruba sculpture are coated with painted dots, unified, like Prince's figures, by an overall pattern at the surface. Farther afield, Doran Ross has gathered the carvings of a Ghanaian artist, his name unfortunately lost, who flourished early in the twentieth century and spread his forms with decorative incising. Stylized in profile, covered with geometric patterns, his carved animals resemble Prince's painted ones.

Carvings provide slight precedent, but, scanning wider, we find that Prince's geometric ornament brings to fulfillment a dimension of the Yoruba artistic tradition in which tiny forms repeat and accrete toward totality. Thompson sees it in the fine braiding of hair, and it is in depicting hair that Yoruba carvings are most consistently decorative. Armstrong sees it in beadwork, and—making indirect reference to Prince's paintings—he says that Yoruba traditional art contains a conatus to the pointillistic. Inspired by beaded crowns of the kind he wears, Prince has made beaded pictures by filling a shape on a board with glue, pouring colored beads on, then rolling them flat with a battery. The result, he says, is craft, not art, and he used the technique to create bright, shiny shapes on the backdrops for theatrical performances.

I would add the designs his father dyed on leather, since geometric patterns that head for infinity abound in Islamic art, but hatchings on statues, cicatrices and braided hair (for a man with cicatrices and braided hair), beadwork, and, above all, textile designs are enough to offer the idea that Prince drives to the limit in the endless sequences of lines and dots and scales that cover his forms with pattern.

Figures filled with pattern at once flatten and gain depth by intricacies of scale as smaller and smaller shapes recede from the surface. This concurrence of compression and depth, of concept and vision, extends to the whole when figures assemble in settings. As Prince recalls it, the first *Devil's Dog* had no background, and it was not unique among his earliest drawings in that respect. In exact isolation, the figure spread on the sheet like a flattened statue. Early on, Prince added backgrounds, and when he did, he did not shove the figure back into an environment of glancing light and cast shadow as Western realists do. Nor did he pull it forward with sculptural modeling as Indian painters often do.

Prince's figure occupies a shallow plane, unshadowed, unmodeled, that confects depth out of complexity. Behind it, he drops another plane, generally dark and forested, that provides a contrastive setting, effectively extending the figure's black outlines to the edge and isolating the subject in space as portraits by Ammi Phillips and Richard Avedon do. Many of Prince's prints and paintings stop there, stop at the layering of one plane on another, but in others he inserts a middle plane between the foreground and background, smoothing and complicating the transition from near to far (see chapter 20, nos. 20–21). At once visually continuous and conceptually layered, his work accumulates density and finds its perfection in the sculpture's painting, built literally layer upon layer. But through it all, Prince's free adoption of different perspectives creates interplay among the planes—backgrounds step forward, foregrounds step back—and the picture exquisitely exhibits the Yoruba style: segmented, but intensively continuous.

In Prince's pictures, his figures, their backgrounds, and their ornament combine into an extravaganza of contradiction: bright and dark, unified and divided, segmented and sequential, bold and delicate, free and disciplined, flat and deep, continuous and layered, critical and entertaining, frightening and funny, natural and supernatural, visionary and visual. These contraries abide in vibrant unresolution, held in precarious balance by the Yoruba virtue of equilibrium, released into presence through the Yoruba dynamic of additive composition, of ant work.

COMPOSITION

Segmentation and sequential arrangements—division and multiplication—are conspicuous signs of serial composition. Both appear in Prince's paintings and in the canonical classics of Yoruba carving, notably the divination boards rimmed with a series of images and the veranda posts composed of figures piled vertically. Its compositional dynamic seems to have become the definitive trait of Yoruba art as scholars have shifted focus, in line with the times, from form to process.

Formal properties trapped scholarly attention back when the aim was to locate African works of art in space through tribal attribution, much as Western paintings are located in time by style. Such connoisseurship is indispensable, basic, for once a work is pertinently located, objects in museum collections can be categorized and serious analysis can begin. Analysis then shaped in relation to the European concepts of realism and abstraction. Writers tended to reduce the European tradition to academic realism in order to sharpen the contrast with African (and African American) creativity, or to stress the abstraction of European modernism in order to ennoble African art during comparison. Both were useful rhetorical moves, heuristic ways to effect understanding in the West when it was still necessary to defend the African achievement against an ethnocentric evolutionism that functioned to support the virulent evil of colonialism. It is hard to believe, I know, but long ago in nations far away there were people who thought that African minds were different, that the African intellect was undeveloped, that African artists created as they did because they were incapable of advanced realism.

Time has passed. Scholars now look into Yoruba art to discover its own virtues, and they have fixed upon its compositional dynamic, as well as its individual creators and its cultural meanings, especially as they resonate in the space between art and oral literature, testimony, and ritual. In *The Yoruba Artist*, a volume of essays subtitled *New Theoretical Perspectives on African Arts*, Rowland Abiodun, Hans Witte, Ezio Bassani, and Henry Drewal all emphasize the seriate composition of Yoruba art.

Now, I follow old Confucius in thinking that it is a waste of time to concentrate on error, sophomoric to criticize the earnest efforts of others, since all scholarly work is flawed, all theories are deficient. But one of the essays in *The Yoruba Artist* struck me as strange. Its author objects to the black outlines of the Osogbo school, when, like Blake's outlining, they signal a reach for the spiritual, an escape from the mundane, and when, more to the point, those outlines—Prince's black upon black—are the consequence of the transfer to a flat surface of the compositional dynamic that distinguishes Yoruba art, that the rest of the excellent book celebrates.

It is exciting to watch Robert Plant Armstrong discover the Yoruba compositional dynamic—"an atomistic approach to continuity"—late in *The Affecting Presence*, published back in 1971. Then it was an understanding, a thought without a name, but in *Wellspring* and *The Powers of Presence*, the next volumes of his trilogy—blurbed by Robert Farris Thompson as "one of the most distinguished . . . in the history of aesthetics"—Armstrong gave it a name, syndesis, and traced its shape with patient precision. In *Wellspring*, he used the writings of Amos Tutuola and the paintings of Prince Twins Seven-Seven to exemplify syndetic composition.

Kissing Birds sufficiently exhibits Prince's process in painting, so I will turn to architecture. Syndesis is a general dynamic, not restricted to painting and sculpture (or to the Yoruba; it was, for example, the dynamic of the imperial Seljuk art of Anatolia in the thirteenth century, remains the dynamic of traditional art in eastern Anatolia today). Mature architectural works, such as the Olosun compound in Ibadan, show that Yoruba building is—like Yoruba verse and music—seriate, syndetic. Rooms string in sequence, assembling around courtyards from which other courtyards spring; the building grows as the family does.

In 1964, the year of *The Devil's Dog* and his first exhibitions, Prince bought a house on the outskirts of Osogbo. His "home of exile," it was a bungalow of one story. The plan, common in the region, was European in origin, symmetrical and synthetic in conception: a central corridor was flanked by two rooms on each side. Prince's house belonged to a big architectural family, along with his birthplace in Ijara, Aliratu's birthplace in Sekona, and Susanne Wenger's home in Osogbo. He called it the Art Man Gallery.

This small house was the given, the point of departure for Prince's expansive architectural design, just as the scrap sheet of plywood was the given at the beginning of *Kissing Birds*. Prince added a room to the left, then rooms to the rear and right, and then a second story to hold a library and gallery. The remodeling was complete by 1968, the year after his first trip to London. Then in 1979, with fame and fortune on the rise, he built a second house of three stories, behind the first and set off to the left. Unconnected internally, they were linked by a wall that defined a courtyard in front of the new house. The old house became a dormitory for his followers and a guesthouse for visitors. The new house provided apartments for his wives and on the top floor Prince arranged a gallery that became the place for parties. Closed

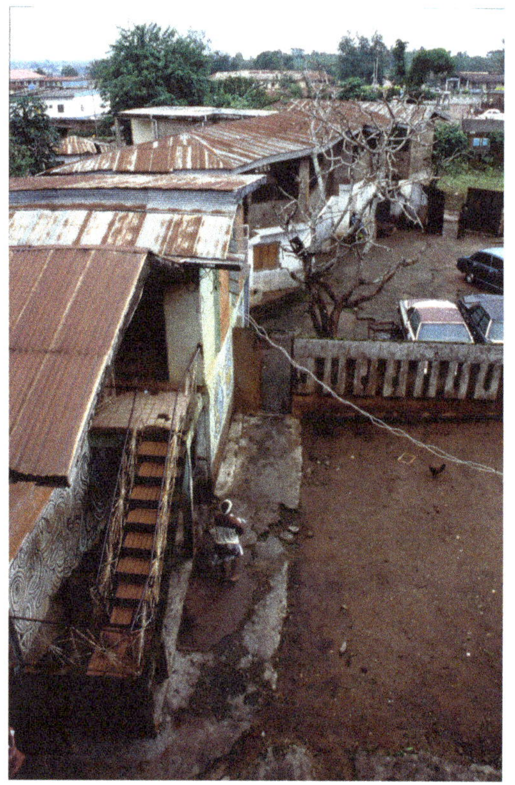

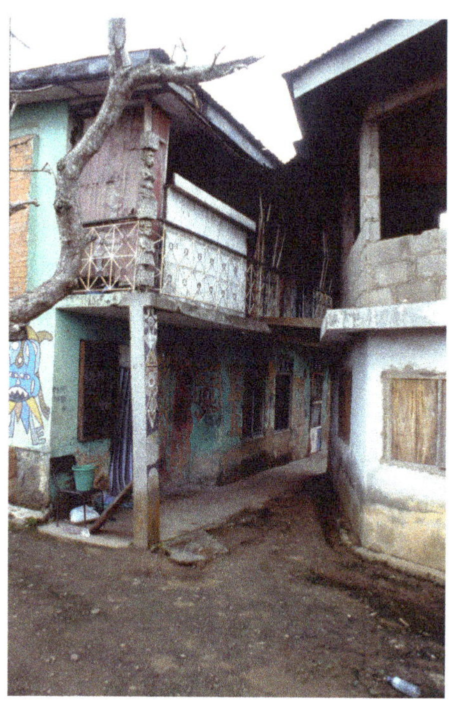

Prince's house in Osogbo.
The syndetic point where the parts do not join

The Beasts' Last Supper.
Detail of a 4'x8' sculpture's painting.
Osogbo, 1970

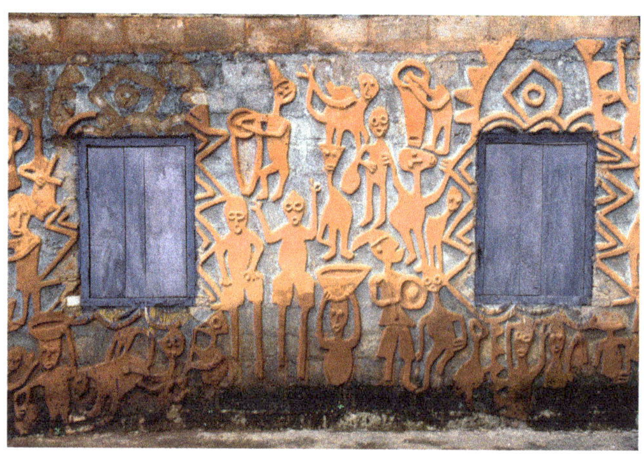

Relief by Prince, on the back of the first building.
Osogbo, 1968

rooms in the corners leave an open, irregular cruciform space in the middle, entered from a balcony on the side. The lower walls fill with framed awards and bleached photographs. A few early paintings hang high, and when I was there the main work on display was a large sculpture's painting, *The Beasts' Last Supper*, made in 1970. I took it for a witty comment on the good Christian people who sit on the soft sofas in this big room and eat up his food.

Walled on the right, the courtyard before the old house remained Prince's place for public performance. When his mother died in 1994, Prince buried her where she sat to hear his band play. He encased her arched tomb in a building that carries a recording studio on its second floor and makes the third wall of the courtyard. Earlier in the nineties, recovered from his wreck and fresh from successes in France, Japan, and Finland, Prince began work on the building that would become the fourth wall of the courtyard, planning it to be a computer school for local students. Raw concrete, not yet finished, it extends at a right angle from the building with his mother's tomb, approaching but not quite touching the building that incorporates the original house. Now Prince has four buildings, three in parallel alignment, two of them houses, each with a courtyard before it. On the other side of the unfinished school, there is a third courtyard, where cars are parked; it is entered through the main gate of the compound.

Forever in motion, Prince has plans for more; he would like to add a nightclub. But as it stands, a work perpetually in progress like the Resort de Paradise, his Osogbo house is an impeccable syndetic confection. It segments space for sequential experience. A gate separates the compound from the world. Passing through it, you enter the first courtyard, from which—by turning right through the unfinished school or walking straight ahead through the door in a wall—you enter a second courtyard in front of a house. At both you climb stairs up the side before finding yourself at last in a roofed, sociable enclosure.

Formally, the house divides. The three main buildings, neatly aligned in the composition, do not connect internally, and the narrow gap where the fourth building fails to touch the first and bring the courtyard into closure—where complete integration is denied—provides a sure sign of syndetic thinking. Assembled incrementally over time, slowly filled in like the farmsteads of the northeastern United States, sharply outlined and segmented by walls, Prince's house, like his paintings, comes into complex totality.

The house's parts gather toward a whole. Its ornament confirms its distinct character. Prince separated his Osogbo house from his earlier house in Ogidi and his later house in Abuja, as well as from the Resort, by not using his black-and-white technique. The decorative

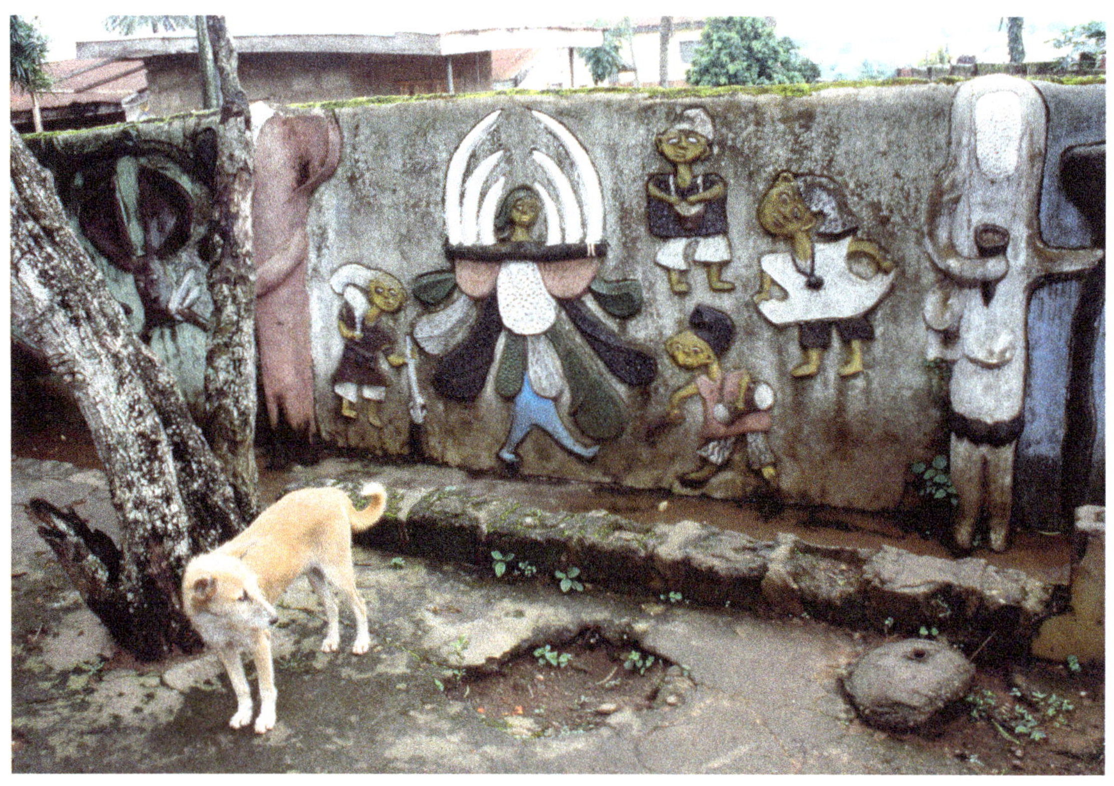

Ogboni masquerade by Prince. Osogbo, 1972

techniques he did use were not unified by a single program, a single style, or a single hand, being the work of both Prince and his friends.

The ornament, all confined to the exterior, concentrates around the first building. Over the concrete blocks of the back wall, in 1968, Prince created a flat, abstract relief of musicians and spirits. The door at the top of the stair was carved in panels of low relief by Prince's friend G. A. Dada, a pleasant, gentle man, a sculptor who works self-consciously in an older style. Two posts of piled figures on the front, carved by a sculptor named Alamu, also gesture directly to the Yoruba tradition. One door on the lower level, moved from his house in Ogidi, was painted by Prince in the sixties; it carries spirits in profile, coated with geometric patterns. Kalakuta Jasper, a painter who follows Prince's lead, has lived in this first building since 1977. He is the compound's watchman, and he drew a band of musicians high on the front wall. Jasper's picture would have floated above Prince's band when it played here. On the wall to the right, in 1972, Prince modeled and painted reliefs of Sango and a masquerade, not the leafy Agbo of his boyhood place, but one from the local Ogboni society with cloth flaps flying like Egungun. This masquerade comes accompanied by musicians, and in front of the wall stands a concrete statue of a woman drumming, created in the naturalistic style that Prince also used for the statue of Sango that stands guard over the front gate.

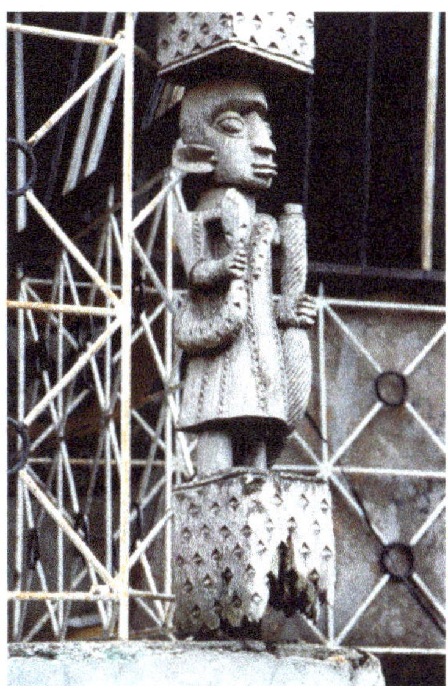

Post
by Alamu

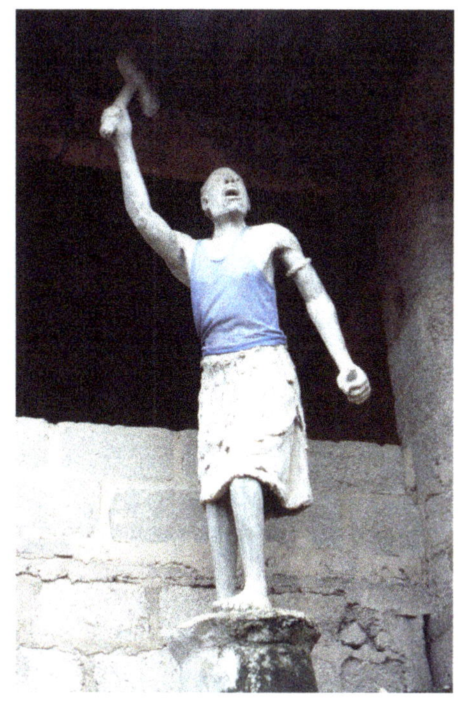

Sango
by Prince

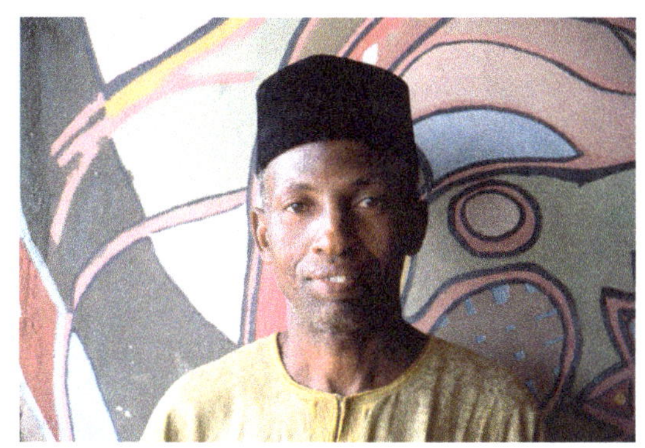

G. A. Dada

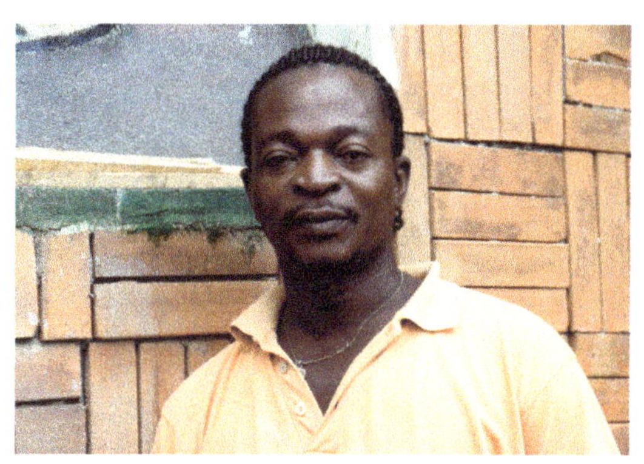

Kalakuta Jasper

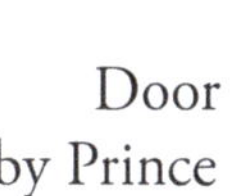

Door
by Prince

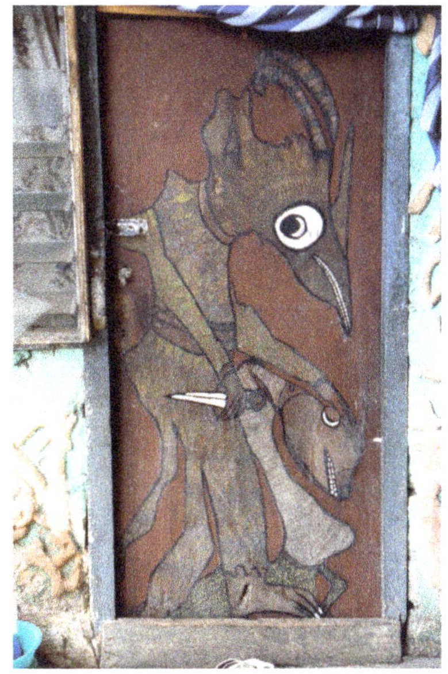

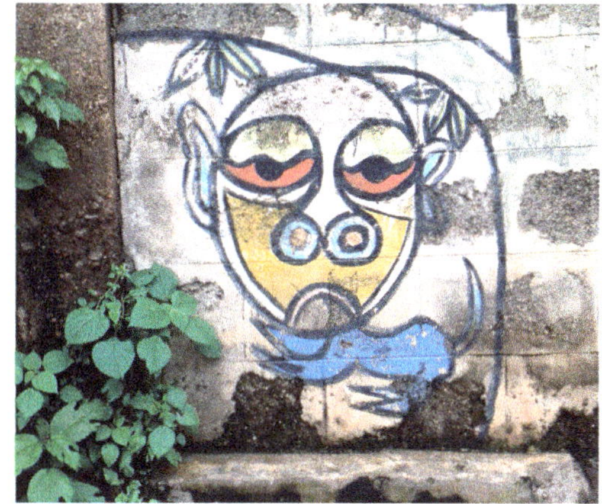

Creature by Wahabi Adisa

Musical imagery surrounds the place where music was made. Then ornamentation spills out of the compound, into the street. A large black mask on the exterior wall—based on a Senufo original and elaborated in Prince's style with a face in one of its eyes—signals Prince's home from afar. On the wall, back along the lane leading to the compound, creatures drawn by Prince and painted by one of his followers, Wahabi Adisa, mark the path for visitors. At the intersection of the lane with the main road, a man on a bicycle, welded to Prince's design out of scrap metal (like the muffler men of America), represents a palm-wine tapper. It is an homage to Tutuola, of course, but more than that it evokes a song Prince composed and recorded in which he hopes his enemies will be killed in an accident with a palm-wine tapper on a bicycle (see chapter 20, no. 24). Since tappers who ride bikes cannot afford insurance, the family of the deceased will receive no monetary compensation: the evil done by his enemies will bounce back to blast the next generation.

The sign above the tapper, on which another tapster is painted, proclaims that this is the entrance to The Living African Myth Palace, Gallery Home of Creative Art. And so it is. Myth and art, tradition and creativity: this is Prince's place. Syndetic formally, syndetic ornamentally, this is the house that Prince built—built, he says, like an ant, bit by bit, bit by bit, in the way he paints his pictures.

· 18 ·

Modern Art

By calling it contemporary Yoruba traditional art, Prince locates his work culturally and historically. Yoruba and new, it is traditional art.

Tradition is a historical process, the way that the future is created out of the past. Smoothing over the cracks in time, tradition brings continuity into the record, not by mere momentum, but through willed acts of recursion, through the retrieval of ideas from the past—from a minute ago or a millennium ago—and their repositioning in the moment from which the future unfolds. Such acts bring continuity, and, as William Morris argued in 1879, they always involve change, "the token of life."

Since Morris was right about change, and T. S. Eliot was right when he said that all art is traditional, historical evaluation must balance change with continuity, continuity with change. To make sense of it, traditional art needs to be subdivided to note the degree of connection between new work and old. Nothing comes out of nothing.

In replication, an old object is reproduced with exactitude. Reiteration is the goal; the old is made new, not by modifications of form and ornament, but by situation. An old proverb is repeated precisely in a new context, applied to a new predicament. Comparably, the Chinese potters of the Qing Dynasty replicated the porcelain masterpieces of the Ming Dynasty to satisfy new customers, and the cabinetmakers of the American Centennial reproduced colonial furniture to provide their patrons, whatever the genealogical reality, with a connection to the American beginning. In replication, continuity—the virtue of elder precedent—swallows change.

In restrictive creation, artists intentionally limit their resources to make new things in an old style. Self-consciously traditionalizing their effort, they effect revival by establishing certain creations as signs of a shared heritage. Such moves (which governments try to control through heritage policies) are common in American country music—and in craft disciplines throughout the world. For one example: this is how the carvers Lamidi Fakeye, G. A. Dada, and A. Bankole work in Yorubaland. For another: led by Liu Lizhong, potters today in Pengcheng, northern China, study old works and the shards found at the sites of their kilns, then combine the traits of the slipped and sgraffitoed Cizhou ware of the medieval era to make new pots that bespeak the continuity of their art and identity, despite the convulsive disruption of the Cultural Revolution. In restrictive creation, continuity overcomes change.

In categorical action, artists draw on the fullness of their experience to make new things that hold close to the generic qualities of old ones in order to communicate clearly. This is the normal process of folklore and folk art. The narrator, relating his harrowing encounter with a ghost, employs the conventional frame of the ghost story. The potter, thrilled again at the wheel, throws a brand new pot that is a jug, a crock, or a churn, useful to another. Connected firmly to the past, but vitalized by personal and local variation, the work exhibits the pattern of the *ibeji* figures of Yorubaland, and, when you think about it, this is the pattern of most art. Continuity and change coexist in interdependence.

In innovation, categories break down, styles combine, forms disassemble, and artists dig through things to principles. Dismantling objects to discover the fundamental principles of form, ornament, and technique, of content and style, category and function, artists reorder tradition to create new things—the things George Kubler called prime objects. Then these new things become the basis for new acts of replication, restrictive creation, and categorical action. The makings of the few, they are inspiration for the many. Tradition goes on, but change dominates continuity.

Prince Twins Seven-Seven is a rare kind of traditional artist: an innovator, an author of prime objects. He joined the content of Yoruba mythology with the ornament of Yoruba beadwork and textile design. He pulled in the palettes of his environments, dark in Nigeria, bright in America, and rolled the African carver's forms onto a flat European surface, bringing it all into anxious, contradictory order through additive, syndetic operations.

Prince's paintings are Yoruba in the way that John Millington Synge's plays are Irish, or Charles Rennie Mackintosh's buildings are Scottish, or Ralph Vaughan Williams's music is English, or Henri Matisse's paintings are French, or Rabindranath Tagore's poetry is Indian, or Kawai Kanjiro's pottery is Japanese. He is, in his place, as they were in theirs, a maker of the modern. Prince is a Yoruba artist, a traditional artist, and a modern artist. He calls his work "contemporary Yoruba traditional art," and he classes it solidly and correctly as "modern art," claiming—more bravely than accurately—that his was the first modern art in Africa.

"Modern" is a word nearly as vexed, as cumbered with multiple meanings, as "tradition" and "art." In one sense it means only "contemporary"—belonging to the present. Prince is a contemporary artist. Alive and at work, he belongs with the young artists, raised on television, whose videos roll in the latest biennial. And, lest we crush complexity and parochially constrict the present to our narrowness, he and they, as contemporary artists, belong with the potters of Seto, Hagi, Pengcheng, Jingdezhen, Kütahya, Kvidinge, Alto do Moura, Puebla, Acoma, Santa Clara, Seagrove, and Gillsville, with Haripada Pal who sculpts *murtis* in Dhaka, with Edival Rosas who carves baroque saints in Salvador, with Lamidi Fakeye in Yorubaland. There are millions of artists alive in our world, working in thousands of distinct styles, so I feel the common qualification of new African art as "contemporary" to be a bit of a dodge. Art is contemporary if it was made by a person who is, or was, alive in our times: the question is whether it is modern or not.

We call our historical epoch modern, knowing that it runs far deeper in time than the contemporary. No roll of the drum or clap of thunder announced the beginning, but slow and subtle changes, never to be complete, led to shifts in dominant values, making the world we inhabit. Events pulsed the flow: land reform and religious reformation, discoveries in the skies and on the seas, the rise of capitalism, the spread of colonialism and industrialization, political revolutions and cataclysmic wars, migration and urbanization. Changes from a religious to a scientific cosmology, from spiritual to materialistic motivations, from agricultural to industrial and commercial labor, from sustainable to profiteering economies, from local to national political orders, from custom to law, from direct to mediated communication—changes rearranged our priorities and set our conditions. We might call modern any artist who has worked in such a world—not Dante or Cimabue, but Shakespeare, Dickens, or Wole Soyinka, Caravaggio, Cézanne, or Prince Twins Seven-Seven. But late in the modern age, a modernist movement shaped in antagonistic opposition to the current modernity. The artists of that movement are the ones most aptly named modern. Prince belongs among them.

It is not hard, nor wrong, to argue that modernism began in Europe with a revolutionary generation that got to work before the First World War and continued after it, the generation of Kandinsky and Klee, Picasso and Duchamp, Stravinsky and Bartók, Yeats, Joyce, and Pound, Le Corbusier, Wright, and Gropius, Boas, Freud, and Einstein. We tinker, revise, and proclaim new paradigms, all the while fluttering in the cage they crafted. They were radical innovators, but they learned from others who learned from others, and threads of connection, strands of tradition drop from them back through time into the darkness. Their practice had precedent, and they were preceded by others in critical reaction to the drift of modern times, by the Levellers, Diggers, and Luddites, by the leaders of religious revivals, by the folk artists of Christendom. Modernism—a creative objection to contemporary norms—has no single point of origin, so I will step into the stream of time and search for modernism's causes and patterns of artistic response. We are bound for Nigeria, but I will start near home in America's shocking moment of newness, the half decade between 1850 and 1855 when Whitman published *Leaves of Grass*, Hawthorne published *The Scarlet Letter*, Longfellow published *Hiawatha*, Stowe published *Uncle Tom's Cabin*, Thoreau published *Walden*, and Melville published *Moby-Dick*.

In his early, enthusiastic biography of Herman Melville, Lewis Mumford linked Melville with Thoreau, saying that they were not rebels but men who reached beyond, then grew beyond their social settings. In reaching beyond, Melville went to sea as a boy, then as a man. He sailed the world, and in the novels of his twenties, *Typee* and *Omoo*, he sketched the virtues of exotic societies in counterpoint to his own, as professional anthropologists would do in later years. In his masterpiece *Moby-Dick*, written in one year when he was thirty-one, Melville tells the ethnographer's tale. An educator, bored with his routine, leaves home to learn about life by living as a participant-observer among others. He sails on a whaler, a wooden world freighted with human diversity; he records the work of the men and their customs, then returns alone to make his story theirs, their story his. Thoreau, by contrast, saw no need to travel; he preferred to sail the inner seas of the self. He went a mile into the woods to live simply, wisely, deliberately. There he planted beans in rows and built a cabin, framed of fresh timber, sided with recycled boards, near Walden pond. He recorded natural phenomena scientifically; he read and thought.

Melville's Ishmael likened his ship to a college. Thoreau said his cabin was better than a university. Both were handmade, wooden seats of learning. Melville's reach led to travel with others, to moments of love. Thoreau's reach led to solitude. Both reaches—one out, one in—were explorations compelled by dissatisfaction. Then as now, there was plenty to be dissatisfied about. America's imperialistic war with Mexico disturbed even the young officers in military service R. E. Lee and U. S. Grant. America's evil institution of slavery was hurtling the nation toward the Civil War. Thoreau, cantankerously certain and civilly disobedient, was perfectly clear about things: he would not pay taxes to a government that supported slavery and war, and he was jailed for it.

Henry Thoreau's dissatisfaction widened from the government to the people. An admirer of the simplicity of his Native American neighbors, he was pained by mad fashion and useless ornament, by progressive devices of communication used by people with nothing to communicate, by the reduction of farmlife to profit-making, by factories that enriched big corporations while immiserating the workers, by lives lost in drowsy desperation, squandered in hopeless labor.

At this moment of American glory, things were bad, but Thoreau and Melville believed they were worse in England where hereditary privilege split society, permitting the hidebound rich—Melville, who had been to England, called them snobbish and stupid—to live in opulence while the laboring poor endured in penury.

They can be excused their prejudices, being Americans born in the young republic—Thoreau in 1817, Melville in 1819—not long after the embattled farmers of Thoreau's place started the war that freed America from English colonial rule. But England, being advanced in modernization, clarified the complaint. Imperialism, new to America, was old in England. The English invaded Ireland in 1171. Colonization followed, establishing the pattern—orderly settlement for the planters, death and reservations for the natives—that would be applied in North America. Internal land reform began early in England, though it carried on for centuries, requiring parliamentary acts of enclosure to bring it near completion at the beginning of the nineteenth century. The enclosure movement destroyed the villages and fenced the fields, yielding economic advancement for the few, social disaster for the many. Displaced people were exiled to the colonies or pulled into the cities to become the whipped industrial laborers with whom Melville and Thoreau sympathized. England had abolished slavery and become a place of wage slaves. This is where industrialization, new to America, had begun.

Modernization was most advanced in England. So was righteous dissatisfaction. During the half decade that saw the publication of *Moby-Dick* and *Walden*, John Ruskin, who was born in the same year as Melville, published the three volumes of *The Stones of Venice*. When William Morris reprinted *The Nature of Gothic: A Chapter of The Stones of Venice by John Ruskin* at the Kelmscott Press in 1892, he called it in the first paragraph of his Preface, "one of the very few necessary and inevitable utterances of the century." In it, Ruskin celebrated the "imperfection," the "savageness," the "fantastic ignorance," and the "stern statues, anatomiless and rigid" of medieval art, reading them as signs of the worker's joy and freedom, and using Gothic art to attack the strict hierarchical orders of imperialism and industrialization that made men into tools, that ruined art and the laboring life. His essay was an assault on his England, where, Ruskin said, workers had been enslaved. (Slavery preoccupied the mind at the time.) The critique was like Thoreau's, but sharper, harsher, more informed.

John Ruskin wrote elegantly, incessantly. He had published books before, would publish many more later. In his Preface, William Morris praised Ruskin's writings on art, but said that his ethical and political writings, culminating in *Unto This Last*, were the more important, and it was that book, *Unto This Last*, published in 1860, which "gripped" Mahatma Gandhi, causing him to change his life, to put his principles into action, and ultimately to lead the nonviolent movement that would free India from English colonial rule.

When William Morris was a student at Oxford, where Ruskin had studied before, the argument of "The Nature of Gothic" hit him like a revelation. The medieval past had excited him in boyhood, but now it pointed "a new road on which the world should travel," a route to the future. Morris was a child of the next generation. In his maturity, things were only worse. The imperial expansion, begun in Ireland nearly eight centuries earlier, had produced an empire on which the sun never set, that sucked the world's wealth into London and left British boys dead on battlefields across the globe. Industrialization continued its crawl, blackening the skies with smoke, grinding the workers down, and depositing the commodities of Victorian times—stamped out, shoddily made, false to their materials, and foppishly ornate to fit the fashions contrived by capitalists to exploit the insecurities of the semi-prosperous populace. Morris hated it all. He wanted people to have work worth doing and satisfying rest, to have beautiful and useful things worth owning and a society of generous fellowship. Extreme conditions surrounded him. Extreme talent, vision, and energy filled him. Morris wanted, Yeats said, to remake the world, and he went into action.

Morris became a political activist, speaking in the streets and marching in protest, believing that socialism could alleviate the suffering of his fellow citizens. He was an environmentalist, a preservationist, a founder of the Society for the Protection of Ancient Buildings, seeking to stay the hand of fraudulent, intrusive restoration. Trained in architecture, he was a student of art, a theorist without peer, writing about the art of the past to discover the principles necessary to future creation. As a thinker, collector, and designer, Morris contributed to the development of the Victoria and Albert Museum where objects from Europe and Asia—ceramics from China, bronzes from India, carpets from Persia, and furniture from England—wait on display to inspire new work. An artisan at the dye vat and loom, an entrepreneur, he founded Morris and Company to offer crisply designed and carefully crafted goods to the public.

Reaching in, like Thoreau, Morris imagined an improved future, and he got it down, imperfections and all, in his visionary novel *News from Nowhere*. Reaching out, like Melville, he traveled to Iceland to find a living society that matched the ideals in his medieval dream. As a creator, a poet and designer, his expansive reach was double. He stretched backward, studying old books to guide the production of the most beautiful books of his age at the Kelmscott Press. He stretched outward, advising his colleagues to study the traditional carpets of western Turkey, for "they are designed on scientific principles which any good designer can apply to works of our day."

William Morris died in 1896, just as the modernist movement was beginning to form in Europe, but he had set the pattern for modern artistic action. It begins in dissatisfaction. Were that not so, the artist would be content to work within contemporary conventions; repetition would be the result, not revolutionary innovation. In the hunt for alternative sources, artists must reach beyond, back in time and out in space, to discover new things, things deserving study, things deserving preservation, things that hold the power to stir the imagination and guide art forward.

That pattern—a specifically situated version of the process of tradition in its innovative phase—held through the first generations of modernism. In Paris, then New York, artists were dissatisfied, oppositional, radical in politics. Picasso declared himself a Communist. They traveled in quest of fresh sources. Le Corbusier went east to find the ideas for a new architecture in Balkan folk pottery and Turkish vernacular building. They looked back to honor their forebears, bringing new appreciation to Cézanne, Manet, and Turner, to El Greco, Uccello, and Piero. They looked outward like folklorists and anthropologists, bringing appreciation to the neglected traditional arts—then divided into folk and primitive—of Europe, America, Asia, and Africa. In the first decade of the twentieth century, with Picasso's shock in Paris (or Kandinsky's in Berlin) as the epiphanic moment, the artists of modernism lifted African works of art out of the welter of ethnological specimens and set the taste that continues to guide the market in African traditional art.

Free in its vision and inclusive reach, the modernist operation was romantic. People who fear disruptions in the social, economic, and political order that provides them security are apt to use the adjective "romantic" pejoratively to label mushy, retrograde thought. But romanticism is an enduringly viable philosophy that values the undervalued in the search for ideas that, having proved workable elsewhere, might provide solutions for local problems and suggest ways to build a better future. Such hopeful thinking linked Morris back to the generation of Ruskin and Thoreau, forward to the generation of Yeats, Gropius, and Kandinsky.

In 1909, misreading in the twilight a painting of his own, Wassily Kandinsky discovered the absence of objects and became, he claimed, the author of the first nonobjective painting. He had been anticipated, of course, by the artists of Islam, by the calligrapher's *karalama*, the potter's interlocked geometry, the weaver's carpets that Morris admired. A thinker and theorist like Morris, Kandinsky looked back to Rembrandt and out to the Russian peasantry for inspiration. He became an ethnologist in order to "reach the soul of the people." He collected the folk paintings on glass that offered him bold, abstract forms. At work as an ethnographer, Kandinsky stepped into the splendid interior of a Russian peasant's dwelling, feeling that he had entered a painting, that art had engulfed him. Persuaded by his experience, he made paintings that invited the viewer to enter, forget, and "dissolve into the picture." Folk art and his art shared the "inner necessity"—the essence in all true art—that records the spirit's search for sensate presence and helps us escape from a "soulless materialistic life" to construct a "spiritual and intellectual life." That was how it looked by 1912, when *The Blaue Reiter Almanac* was published. Realism had become "unthinkable." Concept and spirit prevailed. New York's abstraction—Pollock, de Kooning, Kline, Still, Motherwell, Gottlieb, Rothko, Newman—followed directly.

In Paris, it had been the African art snatched from the colonies; in New York, in the nineteen-forties, when abstract expressionism was developing, it was the art of the Native American people of the Northwest Coast that excited the artists. The "imagination" of that art struck Franz Boas in a museum in Berlin. Born in Prussia and destined to become American anthropology's leading scholar and teacher, Boas had conducted ethnographic research in the Arctic, and when he returned to America in 1886, the complex cultures of Canada's Pacific coast claimed him. The collection of Northwest Coast artifacts that Boas assembled at the American Museum of Natural History in New York spread the art before the artists, whose interest had been aroused by an exhibition of American Indian art at the Museum of Modern Art in 1941.

With the art of Greece, Africa, and the Northwest Coast—Kwakiutl, Tsimshian, Haida, and Tlingit—in their minds, the painters Adolph Gottlieb, Mark Rothko, and Barnett Newman declared, in 1943, their "spiritual kinship" with the creators of "primitive" art—that was the word in those days. Gottlieb, a collector of African and Native American art, said that modern art took its impetus from primitive art. Rothko, an artist with a taste for art history, said that modern art announced a new Renaissance, and in the way that Renaissance art had been inspired by Greek sculpture, the art of the modern movement was inspired by the primitive sculpture that synthesized "sensibility and truth." Newman, an oppositional moralist, said that understanding modern art required an appreciation of the primitive art in which worldly appearances and "meaningless materialism" had been traded for "metaphysical understanding"—for, Gottlieb said, "spiritual meaning." Kandinsky's arguments of 1912 had been naturalized in North America in the forties and carried forward by the new artists.

Modernism is not a creation of the West alone. As Japan rose in industrial and imperial power, Yanagi Sōetsu, Kawai Kanjiro, and Hamada Shōji formed the Mingei movement in 1926. They opened themselves to European influence, to Blake and Morris in England, Hazelius in Sweden. They investigated the rural arts in Japan and Korea, collecting, preserving, and exhibiting examples of folk art that became canonical, just as the European modernists made certain works, like the whitened female masks of Gabon, canonical. They divided Morris's tasks. Yanagi became the theorist, his theories based on Buddhist precepts. Kawai and Hamada were the creators. Potters in a land where the ceramic arts hold a position as lofty as painting in Europe, they reordered the native tradition, innovatively fusing it with foreign ideas to create utterly new objects of clay. In 1920, Hamada had traveled west to England, to work with Bernard Leach who had gone east to learn in Japan, in 1909. Hamada collected the plain country furniture of England, the windsor chairs assembled of sticks, and he based new creations on the slipped masterpieces of the old English folk potters. Returning to Mashiko, Hamada developed a personal style that became as influential in international ceramic art as the styles of Kandinsky and Picasso became in painting.

Dissatisfaction with the status quo, courageous reaches back and out, innovative creation: the modernist pattern—Prince's pattern—is general. But it divides in intensity by conditions. Conditions are extreme in industrial, imperialistic nations. They are more extreme in colonial settings.

In William Morris's England, there was cause for anger and hope for change. The advanced position was self-critical. Among Morris's contemporaries in colonial Ireland, where self-criticism coupled with critical resistance to the invader, the causes were stronger, the need for change greater, the hope more fervent.

When, in Shakespeare's day, the chiefs of Ulster—Hugh Maguire of Fermanagh, Hugh O'Donnell of Donegal, and Hugh O'Neill of Tyrone—rose in rebellion, they were united by the passions of nationalism and Counter-Reformation. They beat the English at the Ford of

Biscuits and the Yellow Ford, and had they won at Kinsale, their Ireland—not the United States or France—would have set the model for the revolutionary origin of the modern nation-state. Instead, in death and surrender, they set the model for colonial resistance: rebellion and defeat. Rising after rising was put down, but in Morris's day hopes rose with the Home Rule movement, the Land League campaign, and the founding of the Gaelic League in 1893 by the folklorist Douglas Hyde who would become Ireland's first president. Home Rule promised a degree of political autonomy. The Land League promised rights of ownership to the farmers. The Gaelic League sought to counter English influence by restoring the Irish language, upon which, in the absence of political independence, the survival of Ireland as an entity seemed to depend.

In this context, laced with rage and braced with hope, revolutionary movements formed that would lead to the Easter Rising and an Irish republic, to partition and the persistence of armed resistance. In it, too, Irish modern literature took shape. In 1888, when he was twenty-three, William Butler Yeats published a collection of Irish folktales and composed two poems that gained him fame and prefigured the future. Yeats based the long narrative poem, "The Wanderings of Oisin," on a tale from the old Fenian cycle he found in a scholarly publication. (The story was localized and still told in the countryside when I was in Ireland.) To Saint Patrick, Oisin, the son of god-big Finn, tells how he followed his pearl-pale love to a glimmering land beyond time and change. Then, pining for home, he returned and, falling from his horse, aged suddenly, slumping under the centuries that had passed. The old gods and heroes were dead; Christianity had come and a feeble race labored on. A versified tale of marvels and loss, William Morris called it "my kind of poetry," and Yeats to the end called Morris "my chief of men." In the other poem, "The Lake Isle of Innisfree," Yeats bent inward, like Thoreau, locating a personal desire for simplicity, and *Walden* was his inspiration. Yeats was taking his measure, training his voice, and finding his sources—in Ireland first, in all the world next. Growing as a poet and dramatist, he was also an essayist who wrote knowingly about Irish folklore and English literature (Shakespeare, Blake, Shelley, Morris), about imaginative symbolist painting (for he was the son and brother of painters, schooled in art himself), about the Noh theater of Japan that helped him develop his theories for a modern drama.

Whether gently, sentimentally, or abrasively, innovative art carries political purpose in colonial environments. In his youth, W. B. Yeats supported Home Rule and composed a poem on the death of Charles Stewart Parnell—Ireland's uncrowned king, the leader of the Land League—exhorting his people to mourn and move forward in Ireland's cause. He worked to memorialize the heroes of the Rising of 1798 at the time of the centennial, and (the evidence is vague) he might have joined—and his art certainly inspired—the Irish Republican Brotherhood that brought on the Easter Rising of 1916. In 1922, Yeats became a member of the Senate in the first revolutionary government of the Irish republic.

Awarded the Nobel Prize for Literature in 1923, Yeats said in his acceptance speech that two forms should have been at his side when he received the medal: "an old woman sinking into the infirmity of age and a young man's ghost." The old woman, Lady Isabella Augusta Gregory, envious, she said, of Yeats's record of Sligo tradition in *The Celtic Twilight*, set out to gather the traditions of her Galway. Grounding her interest in the language of telling, open to the concerns of the people for history, mystery, and religion, Lady Gregory produced, as Douglas Hyde did, scrupulous, precociously modern and indispensable, collections of folklore. She was also a playwright, a leader in the Irish Dramatic Movement, along with Yeats and Synge. John Millington Synge was the young man whose shade should have appeared beside Yeats at Stockholm. As the story goes, Yeats told him to travel to the islands of the west, to live with the people, and "express a life that has never found expression." He did. Synge wrote *The Aran Islands*, the first great folkloristic ethnography, and found in his fieldwork the tales he recast in his plays, plays in the modernist manner that were first performed in the half decade—1904 to 1909—that also saw the breakthroughs in painting by Picasso, Matisse, and Kandinsky.

During a time of political struggle and painful victories, Irish writers turned to the Irish tradition and found the subjects and styles that enabled them to conquer the conqueror's tongue. Yeats became the greatest modern poet in English. If Synge was surpassed as a modern playwright, it was by Samuel Beckett who was born in Dublin, as Yeats and Synge and Joyce were. James Joyce left the rural twilight for urban turbulence and shaped his tale of Stephen and Bloom on a Greek rather than an Irish epic. Still, *Finnegans Wake*, named for an Irish folksong, drowns Irish allusions galore in its comic, mythic, cyclical effusion, and Joyce, Irish to the core, became the greatest modern novelist in English. Ireland was small, its population at once conservative and rebellious. Joyce escaped into exile and Beckett followed him to Paris, but for a moment the collision of genius and conditions made the Dublin of Yeats and Joyce one of history's great nodes of creativity, one with Leonardo's Florence, Sinan's Istanbul, Shakespeare's London, Manet's Paris, and Tagore's Calcutta.

The modernist pattern of colonial creation was pioneered in Ireland at one end of the British Empire and followed in India at the other. Morris's disciple Ananda Coomaraswamy studied the art of South Asia, becoming one of the world's most astute art historians, a theorist in the line of Morris and Yanagi. Yeats's friend Rabindranath Tagore meshed European romanticism with Bengali folk tradition to create the verse that won him the Nobel Prize for Literature in 1913. He had been preceded by Michael Madhusudan Dutt, who built old myths into new art in the nineteenth century, consolidating the culture in advance of political freedom, as Elias Lönnrot was doing in Finland by compiling the *Kalevala*. But in Tagore's day the freedom Ireland was winning seemed plausible in India. Tagore inspired the Swadeshi Movement that paralleled Ireland's Sinn Fein in time and intent, then pulled away, but he continued to give voice to the culture in works of art while Mohandas K. Gandhi—it was Tagore who named him Mahatma: Great Soul—was leading the political movement that would eventuate in the joy of independence and the nightmare of partition—in India as it was in Ireland. In time, the new countries of India and Bangladesh would both choose songs by Rabindranath Tagore for their national anthems.

Nigeria was late in the sequence, late, by comparison with Ireland and India, in exploration, conquest, and freedom from English colonial rule. The British took the land, piece by piece, between 1861 and 1903. Before the territory—the sprawling territory of contemporary Nigeria—was consolidated politically in 1914, anti-colonial protests had begun. Nationalistic aspirations matured in the thirties, consolidating at Lagos into the Nigerian Youth Movement, dedicated to the "development of a united nation out of the conglomeration of peoples who inhabit Nigeria." When the NYM split regionally and dissolved, the hope for freedom was carried forward, sometimes in cooperation, sometimes in rivalry, by three major parties, one for the West, one for the East, one for the North. In 1947, the year of Indian independence, a constitution was imposed on the Nigerian people. Subsequent constitutional reforms reinforced the sectional differences that would require, between 1967 and 1970, a civil war for resolution into national unity, but on October 1, 1960, Nigeria was free and independent from England. In the year of Independence, Chief Obafemi Awolowo, the political leader in Yorubaland, wrote that Nigeria had no Gandhi, but Nigeria had not suffered as India had, neither so long nor so violently, and British liberality and administrative ineptitude ensured a smooth transition to nationhood, but Chief Awolowo warned his people against sectionalism and a descent into "atheistic materialism."

In the generation born before Independence in 1960, we find what the examples of Ireland and India would lead us to expect. Native scholars were collecting, preserving, and analyzing instances of the native tradition. They were folklorists because folkloristic study, by virtue of its romantic heritage, was as implicated in the modernist project of creative resistance as anthropology, by virtue of its evolutionistic heritage, had been implicated in the imperialistic project of colonialism. In the way that Irish folklorists (Brooke and Croker, Hyde and Gregory) had been preceded by Irish historians (Geoffrey Keating and the Four Masters) who assembled the Irish story in the wake of defeat, Yoruba folklorists (Babalola and Abimbola) were preceded in the bad old colonial days of the nineteenth century by a Yoruba historian, the Reverend Samuel Johnson, who outlined the culture before narrating the events (including the rise to power of Prince's great-grandfather Osuntoki) in *The History of the Yorubas*. The writings of the old Irish historians provided materials for the artists of modern times—*Finnegans Wake* flocks with references to Keating and the Four Masters—and Johnson's *History* comparably served the creators of a later day. In that day, the time of the Mbari movement, the moment of Yoruba modernism, it was as it had been in Ireland and India. Scholarship and creativity ran in accord and gathered political force. Like Yeats and Tagore before him, Wole Soyinka acted politically; like them, he studied the tradition and blended it with foreign ideas in innovative creations that won him the Nobel Prize for Literature.

This was Prince's time too, the period of his beginning. He felt colonial rage, anger at the British who came to destroy his civilization, anger at his people who abandoned the old faith to embrace Christianity and Islam. In resistance, wishing to revitalize the native sacred tradition, he might have worked for artistic revival through replication and restrictive creation, becoming a carver like Lamidi Fakeye. But dissatisfaction coils in his nature. Prince escaped Muslim and Christian education to learn from the ants on the rock. He escaped Ogidi in youth, Osogbo in maturity, always seeking newness, needing, like Kandinsky, to create an art that met his inner necessity, that burst from his deepest, perpetually developing self.

Prince copied no one. But his art was not an innocent eruption. It was self-consciously oppositional. In his scenes of village life, he wipes out the colonial invasion. His animal pictures are often "political," critiques, like Soyinka's writings, of undemocratic governments. In the series of paintings entitled *The Beginning of the End* (chapter 20, no. 19), he stands against the intrusion of the new religions. In all of them, he stands for the elder faith. The son of a Muslim father and a Christian mother, he became an adherent of the Yoruba religion, and searching back into his tradition, as Yeats had, he sought the sources for a new art. Learning less from Yoruba art than from Yoruba folklore, Prince combined his ideas, as Soyinka did, with European techniques, learning from Europeans about painting and etching. Then, like the Irish masters, he conquered the conqueror's medium, winning his freedom by making paintings that were unshakably, distinctively Yoruba in subject and style, and he leapt to political prominence and artistic fame.

Modernism's signs are all there: dissatisfaction, reaches in and back and out, oppositional positioning, individualistic action, innovative creation, international recognition. The story, though, can be told in strictly Yoruba terms:

A baby sent by the spirits returned to the spirits until his mother remembered to honor Osun, as the gods had done at the dawn of time. Since the baby was the reincarnation of an old warrior who was a worshiper of Osun, his repeated returning was a request from the ancestors to continue devotion to Osun at a time when many, including the baby's mother, were leaving the old religion. Blessed by Osun, the baby lived and grew into a man capable of paying off his mother's debt to the spirits by dancing in the streets. As a dancer he was led by Osun to her place, where he worked to restore her shrine and learned to paint. He had chosen the head of an artist in Obatala's garden, and an abiku, a twin, a dada, creative from birth, he needed no instruction. Music welled up within him. His first picture fully realized his personal style in ink on paper. His art—his music, his painting—was part of his dedication to the old faith, and blessed by the gods, he ascended to fame. Fame as a singer and painter brought him high chieftaincies. Social power brought him down. He lost his inner balance as the Sango in him rose to dominate the Osun in him, the red overmastered the white. Jealous enemies worked sorcery against him, driving him into exile where Osun regained dominion and he turned back to art, choosing to picture Osun in paintings that were prayers, offerings to the goddess in ongoing devotion. Then she brought him home again.

His is Yoruba art. The surface carries the infinite depth and constant shocks of the enchanted reality. The images raise the unseen into visibility. It is, at last, not decorative, not entertaining: this is the twinned existence; these are the forces that make life and wreck it.

But Prince's acts are modernist, and his creations, true to his culture and personality, fit with the global modernist effort. Intentionally not realistic, dipped up from his bottomless imagination, Prince's paintings are conceptual and spiritual in the modernist manner of Kandinsky and Yeats. Issuing from ant work, from the syndetic Yoruba tradition, his works exhibit, through a simultaneity of contradictions, the processes of the artist's transforming mind and dancing hand as the great works of modernism do. Like the novels of Joyce and Faulkner, the paintings of Picasso and Rothko, Prince's works emit a whiff of the archaic, murmuring mythically to provoke the sensation that there is more than meets the eye, flowing under the surface, spreading beyond the edge.

Prince's paintings, without striving for it, appeal to foreign viewers—Ulli Beier being first and exemplary—whose eyes have been trained by European modernism, who are drawn, as the great modernists were, to alternative creations that seem familiar enough to appreciate, foreign enough to be exciting and inspirational. Prince's excellence met a peculiar moment in history and he was suddenly, without preparation, launched.

It was more than mere chance. Modernism was a critical reaction to modernization. Released by the division of religion, driven by the engine of commerce, modernization produced industrialization at home, and, through imperialism, subject colonies abroad. Progressively intricate and expensive technologies, developed to meet the needs of war, concentrated the power that spread over the world, propagating a scientific, materialistic culture with wealth and physical comfort as its main goals. In industrial nations and in their colonies, thoughtful artists responded. They rejected visual, physical realism, the artistic emblem of materialism, and they invented a conceptual and spiritual revolutionary art. In their opposition to contemporary norms, they valorized tradition, taking inspiration from the conceptual and spiritual creations of past times and distant places. Unable to escape from their times, for no one can, they melded the traditional and the visionary with the contemporary, and their works became advanced revelations of the common murmur.

Reacting to modernization, to internal decline and external intrusion, artists moved from dissatisfaction to innovation. They acted alike, though their means and motives differed. Precedents from the past and political purposes in the present were stronger in the colonies, stronger in Dublin and Ibadan than in Paris or New York, but materialistic realism seemed done for; concept and spirit took over. Prince acted as Soyinka did, as Yeats and Tagore had. Foreigners got it—at the surface at least—and my man was on the high road to success. Like all of his roads, though, it turned out to be rough. Modernism belonged to an expansive moment of caring and hope. It had nearly run its course in the West when Prince began in Nigeria, in 1964.

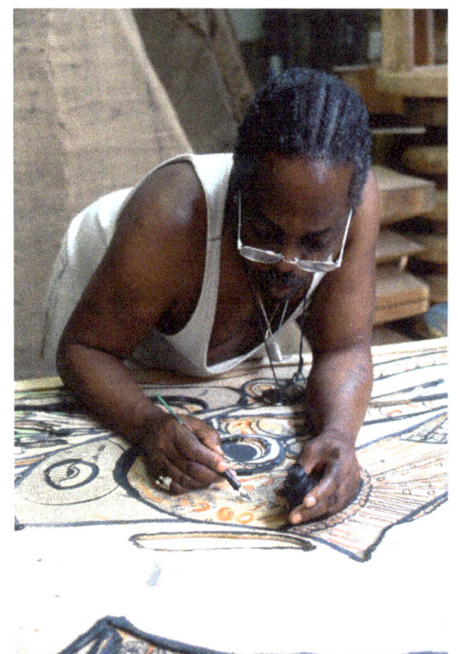

Prince at work in Philadelphia

Kissing Birds.
Chapter 1

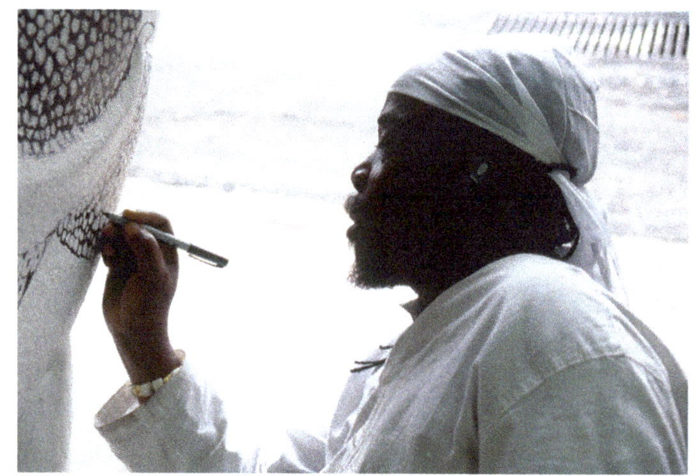

The dinosaur.
Chapter 16

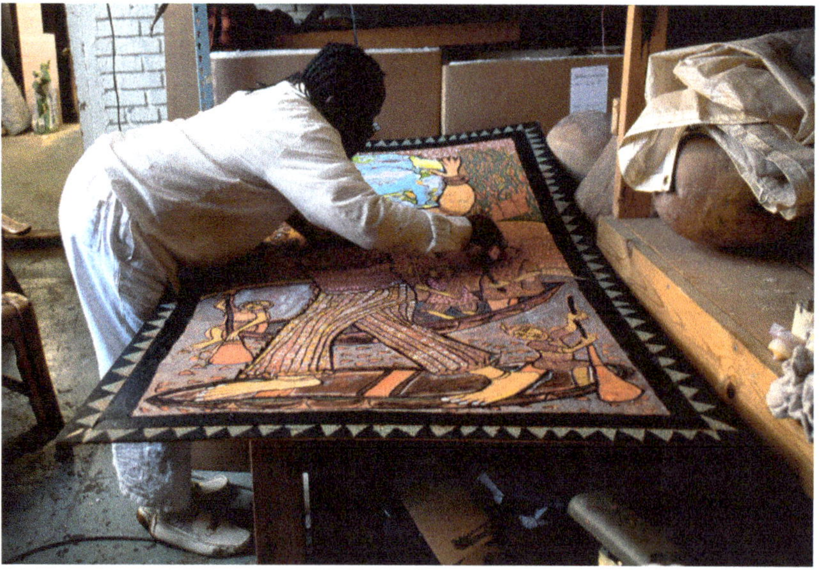

Barefoot President. Chapters 3, 16

· 19 ·

Postmodern Times

Over the forty-five years that lie between then and now, Prince's art has changed, but it has changed more by consolidation and refinement than by sudden shifts and departures. He has stopped, then started again, gone back and gone forward, all the while working to the core, exploring the shape of the unseen, and clarifying his style and intent. His art has advanced. His fortunes have declined.

Prince blames jealousy, witchcraft, and missteps of his own. He never should have worn that red beaded crown. But he is, as we all are, rolled by the tides of history, and events far beyond him have conditioned his life. His fortunes can be traced through a series of similarly named, broad accounts of African contemporary art that record Western critical opinion.

Ulli Beier witnessed the beginning in 1964. He placed Prince first among the artists of the Osogbo school in *Contemporary Art in Africa*, published in 1968, saying that Prince was the "best-known," the "most fantastic" of the painters, a musical young man with a limitless imagination and a grand sense of humor. "From the first minute," Beier wrote, "his talent was distinctive." He worked easily and fluently, creating "bizarre variations on Yoruba mythology and legend" in pictures filled with decorative patterns that developed spontaneously. Beier's characterization still fits, and he was followed closely in subsequent books.

In *African Art: The Years Since 1920*, published in 1974, Marshall Ward Mount calls Prince "the most interesting" of the Osogbo artists. He repeats Ulli Beier's story of Prince's beginning, repeats Beier's description of his art and personality. Mount features a painting by Prince from 1968, and noting the individuality of the artists, the absence of a "school style" at Osogbo, he credits the gentle direction of Ulli and Georgina Beier.

The Osogbo story gets retold briefly in the essays introducing *Contemporary African Artists*, the catalog of an exhibition held at The Studio Museum in Harlem in 1990. Quality declined after Ulli and Georgina Beier left Nigeria, Grace Stanislaus writes, but she lifts Prince out of the crowd as it descends to tourist art, saying he has "attracted national and international attention for his intricate and expressive drawings on paper and board." In the Foreword, arguing against narrow definitions of African art, Wole Soyinka uses "Twins Seven Seven's metaphysical explorations" as the very model of a modern authenticity; then Soyinka goes on to say, "Various creative expressions meet in Twins Seven Seven; it is not an afterthought to note that he is both a gifted musician and dancer, that his personality is at once febrile and dynamic."

The artist and art historian Jean Kennedy does more in *New Currents, Ancient Rivers: Contemporary African Artists in a Generation of Change*, published in 1992, shortly after her death. She tells again how Prince was the "best-known" of the artists discovered in the third Mbari Mbayo workshop, and how his first pictures were "distinctive" and "completely unrelated to the work of the others." Appreciating their "fantastic and amazingly alive" creatures, Kennedy brings Prince's paintings together with Tutuola's writings, since they "have the same haunting spirits and the same strange, fearful aura." Then she follows Ulli Beier and Robert Plant Armstrong in saying that their similarities were owed to a common source in Yoruba storytelling. Kennedy talked with Prince, quotes him briefly, adds biographical facts to the record, and comes to her own conclusions, praising "the ebullience of this man whose contagious, outrageous, and often whimsical enthusiasm for life has also motivated him to become a sometime politician. His enthusiasm and energy are embodied in every aspect of his being: his language, clothing, dancing, music, and painting." Her response was fresh, but the three works by Prince she chose to reproduce were all old ones, from the nineteen-sixties.

After the exhibition *Magiciens de la Terre*, held in Paris at the Centre Pompidou in 1989, André Magnin, the curator of the exhibit's African section, went to Africa to meet the artists. He reports the adventure he shared with Jacques Soulillou in *Contemporary Art of Africa*, published in 1996. Prince gets a page of text, a loose reiteration of the usual information (derived from Kennedy and Beier), but the color plates illustrate Prince's current, sharpening style through five sculpture's paintings, one from 1985, three from 1990, one from 1991.

At the end of the millennium, in 1999, Sidney Littlefield Kasfir published *Contemporary African Art*. The Osogbo story strings through the text. Ulli Beier, Georgina Beier, and Susanne Wenger get much ink and credit, but the artists remain a clump of uneducated Yoruba men, little differentiated by art or personality. Only one of the six successful painters discovered in the Mbari Mbayo workshops, Jimoh Buraimoh, gets individual attention. Prince is not mentioned. Three decades before, he was the first figure in the foreground; now he is lost into the background pattern, one of the abstract masks animated by the perceptive expatriates. My aim is not to criticize Kasfir's book, which I think is the best of the comparable volumes, but to read it as evidence of a change in taste. Kasfir writes that the "burning question" of the nineteen-sixties, the decade of independence, was whether one could be both an African and a modern artist. Prince is: that is exactly what Prince Twins Seven-Seven accomplished at exactly that time. But that time of colonial resistance, cultural revival, and nationalistic aspiration has passed in Kasfir's narrative, and a new era of postcolonial internationalism has come.

In an earlier day, Kasfir's book might have begun with a sketch of the elder tradition in which modernist efforts, like Prince's, were rooted. But *Contemporary African Art* begins with an engaging treatment of the African popular culture that flourishes in the cities and in regions without a wood-carving tradition. Most African people live in the countryside, but their arts, though contemporary, have ceased to matter. The artists who count, whether self-taught, trained in workshops, or educated in art schools, produce works that appeal to critics hip to the times. The interesting new artists respond to the Western art of the recent past or react wittily to globalization, to the materialistic surge that has swamped them. Their creations meet an excitable new taste.

That taste—modern in Africa, postmodern in the West—governed the selection of works in *African Art Now*, published in 2005. The catalog of an exhibition at the Museum of Fine Arts in Houston, it presents the collection of Jean Pigozzi, an Italian born in Paris. Prince is not represented, and that is telling because Pigozzi was first excited by the new African art in the *Magiciens de la Terre* exhibition in 1989, which included work by Prince. He sponsored André Magnin's jaunt to Africa, reported in *Contemporary Art of Africa*, and on his trip Magnin bought paintings by Prince for Pigozzi's collection, the CAAC in Geneva, curated by Magnin. When Pigozzi's collection was shown in the *Africa Hoy* exhibition in Las Palmas in 1991, Prince was included. But there was nothing by Prince in Houston in 2005. It was not because he was too old or too well known, for older and more famous artists appeared. He had lost his appeal, it seems; taste had changed.

Jean Pigozzi, a refreshingly frank, addictive collector, knows what he likes. "Most of the good African artists," he said, "get their inspiration on the street, in everyday life, on TV, radio." That does not describe Prince. It describes the artists, the "realistic" artists with whom Prince contrasts himself, the ones who make art out of the visible, mixed current scene. Prince's dedication to the Yoruba tradition, his boundless imagination, his conceptual and spiritual images belong to an earlier day, belong with the art of Kandinsky and Yeats in a finer time, now gone.

The books tell the story. In 1968, when Prince was twenty-four and unstoppably creative, he was the rising star of African contemporary art; a painting by him appeared on the cover of Ulli Beier's book. In 1989, at the time of the *Magiciens de la Terre* exhibition, Prince was forty-five and an established master of African contemporary art, recovered from his wreck and once again energetically productive. In 2005, the taste-makers of African contemporary art had abandoned him, though that was the year in which, at the age of sixty-one, Prince was named the UNESCO Artist for Peace and his artistic achievement was reaching new heights in Philadelphia.

African Arts is the leading journal in the field. Its publication history nearly matches the stretch of Prince's career. The computer's count of the magazine's articles that contain reference to Prince is not perfectly accurate, but it is close enough to suggest again the downward trend, not of his art, but of Western interest in him. From 1967 to 2007, the numbers descend, decade by decade, from 38 to 32 to 19 to 6.

The very first issue of *African Arts*, in 1967, carried an account of the exhibition Prince often remembers, the one in which his works were first shown in London. Then Prince's paintings reminded Dennis Duerden of Amos Tutuola's novels and Paul Klee's art. Five years later, Prince got an article all to himself. A. C. Mundy-Castle and Vicky Mundy-Castle visited Prince in Osogbo just before he left for his one-man show at the Merton Simpson Gallery in New York, where, you will recall, he made his first connection to Philadelphia.

Reports of interviews with Prince tend to be much alike because he has a routine for journalists, giving them quickly what they want, and because, forever in a hurry, they take weak notes in the field and fall back upon Ulli Beier's authority when crafting a scrap of prose. But the Mundy-Castles paid attention and captured valuable data in their brief piece, including eleven new works. They describe the "small low house in the middle of a large, well-tended garden," the little house at the beginning of his expansive compound where he lived at the time with Nike. They talked with his "sprightly" mother who told them the story Prince told me in our first interview: she gave birth to six sets of twins, but all of them died, and from the seventh set only Prince survived. They tell of his childhood and dancing, his beginning in art, his creation of "sculpture paintings," and they quote him as saying, "I am praying that I shall be able to live long to see if there is going to be any result in the field of art in this generation and the oncoming generation . . . . In the olden days nobody would like to be an artist. They told me that I must not be an artist; that it was a bad thing to be. Today I've got more than six or seven imitators."

That was 1972. A year before in *African Arts*, Robert Plant Armstrong had compared an old mask with a new painting by Prince to illustrate the quality of intensive continuity that unites Yoruba art. Prince had reached a high point in the early seventies. After that, writings in *African Arts* continue to help us get a grip on his situation. Prince kept working, and working well, but Westerners gradually lost interest. The question is: why?

In 1976, reviewing an exhibition at the Carnegie Institute, Irwin Hersey said that all of Prince's twenty-seven paintings were of "excellent quality" because they came from the artist's peak period between 1965 and 1971. What happened then, why Prince's later work was inferior, we do not learn; but a clear opinion had been stated. Prince's work had changed, and changed for the worse.

In 1981, Sidney Littlefield Kasfir reviewed an exhibition in London. Osogbo was overrepresented and Kasfir was disappointed by Prince's work. "It is ironic," she wrote, "that the artist best known to Western collectors, and easily the most lionized, has developed the least. Twins Seven-Seven, for all his early promise as a draftsman, and despite a horde of imitators he has inspired, has in the past few years turned out mainly repetitious versions of his earlier work." The complaint is not about quality. The problem is that Prince's work has not changed.

In 1989, Jeremy Lewison reviewed the *Magiciens de la Terre* exhibition—not in *African Arts* but in *The Burlington Magazine*—and he was excited by Prince's work, writing that "the imaginative and powerfully rich panel paintings of Twins Seven-Seven combine a Klee-like demonism with Nigerian primitive imagery." The language is steamy, but Lewison had looked at the work, abstract from the course of the career, and seen nothing wrong.

We have come to the last decade of the millennium. Prince, with shows in France, Spain, Finland, and Japan, is an old master of African contemporary art. Soon he will celebrate high chieftaincies in Nigeria, but his career has crested in the West; by the computer's count, seventy-two references in *African Arts* lie behind him, only twenty-three in the future. We have before us three opinions to ponder, and I am obliged to reconstruct the logic that undergirds them to discover what happened. One viewer looks straight at the painting and sees imagination and power, an African art that comports with European modernism. His logic is the one I sought to understand by writing the past two chapters, one apiece on Yoruba art and modern art. The complaints lodged in the other two opinions—that Prince's art changed and that it did not change—are the business of the balance of this chapter, after which his work will be arrayed so you can make up your own mind.

In considering change for the worse, I will accept for the nonce that Prince's early work was best, knowing that many critics still feel that way. Surrounded by paintings from 2005, the curatorial team of the Philadelphia Museum of Art selected a picture from the sixties. In the sixties, Prince attracted buyers from the West, but not from Nigeria. Not yet thirty, he was still near the beginning, new to his craft, and smoke stoked his imagination. It is no secret; he composed and recorded a popular song about smoking, and marijuana, he told me, gave him frightening and amusing hallucinations while he was painting. His best work, then, was weird in its vision, loose in drawing, and rough in its ornament—filled with the qualities he would lose when he mastered his craft and clarified his intent, dedicating himself, through serious opposition, to revitalizing the faith of his ancestors. The wild, fanciful imperfections of his early work struck Westerners as original, and needing a term to label what they saw, they chose "self-taught." Jean Pigozzi collects, he said, the work of self-taught artists, although his curator, André Magnin, said that few of the artists in Pigozzi's collection were actually self-taught. It is not a biographical fact, the actuality of autodidaction, but a certain look in the work that excites the Western observer. Prince had it, then lost it. He did not become less self-taught; he became more competent.

The term "self-taught" might serve collectors who buy what they like, as most certainly they should, but it needs careful handling in serious discourse. Agawa Norio, a true *sensei*, a master of the potter's art in Hagi, Japan, told me that all artists are self-taught. His argument—and Arthur Danto tells us that Kant once said something like it—was that what is most important in art cannot be taught. Craft protocols can be taught, technical tricks can be taught, but art cannot be. Not taught, it abides as potential until it is learned, learned by solitary study of admirable models, learned through practice, through long, lonely, tiring hours of trial and error during which artists teach themselves how to employ technical skills to shape objects that embody their deepest thoughts and feelings, that express satisfactorily their irrepressibly distinct selves. Reflect upon the writer's art, and you will find Agawa Norio to be right. All writers are taught, none are taught what makes them artists. Shakespeare went to school and his learning sprays through his poems and plays, but he taught himself through practice. He learned from his teachers, his readings, his fellow actors, from plays he had seen, but he learned the most from his own work.

So did Prince. The Osogbo school was once controversial. One critic faulted Ulli Beier for downplaying the degree to which the young artists were trained in the Western tradition, and Muraina Oyelami, who attended the third and final Mbari Mbayo workshop along with

Prince and Jimoh Buraimoh, wrote clearly about the process, saying that Georgina Beier was their "guardian and tutor." With her, they "began formal art analysis and learned technical discrimination and artistic concentration." Their first works were similar, but they achieved difference by practice, while "Twins Seven-Seven maintained his peculiar drawings and paintings." Prince, all agree, was the most distinct, the least influenced, but he told me that he was shown pictures of modern European art and trained in technique. The training was brief, the Beiers left Nigeria two years later, in 1966, but that training has led many critics to credit Ulli and Georgina for the art of the artists. Georgina deserves credit for teaching, Ulli for promotion, but to credit them for the art, to value patronage over creation, is to admit, unguardedly, a bias based on social class and probably on race too.

In a letter to me in 2007, Ulli Beier wrote, "I am NOT an artist, nor an art teacher and I could not have helped the dancer who advertised patent medicines to become an artist." He did help, and his help was crucial. Without the workshop Ulli set up, and the instruction Georgina provided, Prince would not have become a painter. He would not have become a creator of prime objects who blended native and foreign ideas in innovative works, just as Picasso did. And this is more important: he would not have known the European techniques he used to give new form to the Yoruba tradition and permanent form to his optimistic, introspective personality. The Beiers helped him begin, but his end was his own. To credit Ulli and Georgina for Prince's paintings would be like crediting Simon Hunt, the schoolmaster at the King's New School in Stratford-upon-Avon, for *Hamlet* and *King Lear*. Prince was taught, and just as most writings about him say, he was self-taught.

Every parent knows that children are born with distinct personalities. Every educator knows that when students arrive, life has already shaped them. Try as we might—I say with much experience as a parent and educator—we can bend others but not rebuild them. The young men in the Osogbo workshops were not empty vessels; Ulli Beier could not have filled them with foreign ideas, even if that were his goal, which it was not. They were, Oyelami wrote, musicians and actors in Duro Ladipo's troupe, adults full of the Yoruba experience that gained new presence in their work. The idea of self-taught art leads us toward education, and though the types of education provide a convenient means for classification, they will not provide the answer.

Artists are trained in family shops, working ateliers, and schools of art. In all they are urged, through loyalty, to further a particular tradition, maybe a folk tradition, maybe an academic tradition. The apprentice seems fated to follow the master, but that does not necessarily happen. Jackson Pollock's mature works do not look much like Thomas Hart Benton's. Artists not trained in such settings might be classed as self-taught, as outsiders. The supposition is that self-taught artists create outside, beyond the limits of tradition, bringing a deeper, freer, more private vision into their work. That is not necessarily so.

Artists who work beyond shops, ateliers, and schools, but live near them, can become, through imitation, rigorous practitioners of a tradition, though they are self-taught. In Córdova, New Mexico, José Mondragón carved cottonwood saints in the tradition of the López family, and his works are no more personally distinct than those of the artists within the family: José Dolores López who set the style, his son George who carried it on, Gloria and Sabinita in the next generation, Amy and Rafael in the next. In Kütahya, Turkey, thousands of potters are at work, some in vast, rumbly ateliers directed by masters, others alone and self-taught, beneath a bulb at the kitchen table, but all practice the city's venerable tradition. In Paris, Paul Gauguin was a stockbroker, self-taught as an artist, but he knew Pissarro and Degas, he lived for a couple of crazy months with Vincent van Gogh in Arles, and he painted in the avant-garde manner that got him into the big books of art history.

Artists who work beyond the gravitational tug of a vital tradition, who are wholly alone, socially outside like Henry Darger, still exist inescapably in environments flooded with objects that carry aesthetic directions. There are landscapes fashioned by farmers, buildings designed by architects, furniture inside, pictures on the walls, pots in the kitchen, toys on the floor, comic books, illustrated textbooks, photographs, advertisements, posters in the streets—all driving artistic values into the subconscious. Artists may not be taught, but they are born among things, and when they answer the impulse to creation, they pull up from within a personal vision that has been molded, confined and cajoled, during a lifetime of interaction with an aesthetically configured, culturally constructed world. That is true of Prince. He did not have to try to be a Yoruba artist any more than James Joyce had to try to be an Irish writer. He is a Yoruba artist as his father, the leatherworker, was.

The question is not whether artists are self-taught. All of them are, some more, some less. What remains at question is the source of their ideas, the tradition behind their practice. The artists customarily labeled self-taught learn—just as Jean Pigozzi said they do—from everyday life, from books in school, from advertisements they pass in the streets, from newspapers and television. The art they see is realistic (though "art" might be an overgenerous designation; they see pictorial objects that carry a diminished, accessible, popular kind of realism). The art they make is realistic, but, not being trained in realism, having taken no life classes, received no instruction in anatomy or perspective, they tend to mingle photographic accuracy, formal simplicity, and narrative fantasy in creations that have, at the best, a surreal quality. Surrealism might have been abandoned by the leading painters of the West, but as Susan Sontag argued brilliantly, it endures in arty photography—and it retains its appeal among collectors of outsider art.

Nothing in their work connects the artists who taught themselves, nothing at all, but the artists assembled in Western appreciation under the rubric "self-taught" create a surreal, abstracted realism. Prince's work veers in that direction when it slides toward the visual, in portraits and village scenes, but normally it differs radically, being conceptual in essence. He depicts, as spiritual artists do, the complexity of the invisible. Whether smoothly or roughly, the artists called self-taught simplify or exaggerate the visible, as cartoonists do. But back in the days when Prince's forms shook with uncertainty and drifted with the smoke, they gripped collectors who like the strange and search for the innocently original. Thinking of themselves as intrepid explorers in uncharted territory, collectors read pieces—self-taught or folk or primitive—as naive or nonconscious eruptions of the human spirit so they can credit their own sophistication, their own good eyes—and not the artists—for the objects in their collections.

Prince played along. He was young back then, funny and wild, a boy from the bush, low in the hierarchy of social relations. As you know, when Prince positions himself in that structure, he is paternal, aloof and generous to those below, and he is boyish to those above, humble and entertaining in the hope for boons, for support and monetary rewards. He told me that in the beginning he did not let Ulli Beier know who he was. He hid the facts of his education, hid his deep knowledge of the Yoruba tradition; Beier called him "alienated." By remaining simple and innocent, he guaranteed for himself the fatherly patronage of his protector. For collectors, he donned the mask of the merry, wise fool—a cute and canny, adaptive guise among subject people. He delighted the white folks, and their reactions track him right to the present. But as soon as he had imitators at home and exhibitions abroad, things looked different. He matured and so did his work.

In 1967, Prince went to London. In 1968, Ulli Beier published *Contemporary Art in Africa*. In 1969, Prince invented sculpture's paintings. In 1971, Robert Plant Armstrong wrote about him in *African Arts*. In 1972, Prince went to New York. That was the time of change. He was known, no longer innocent, no longer discoverable, and he was mastering his craft. Forms straightened out, spaces firmed and filled, the blobby dots of his early pictures transformed into neat lines of variable geometric motifs. He was not less self-taught, he was more self-taught, though his work looked less like that of the artists called self-taught. His art continued to change, gradually sharpening as it leapt over unproductive periods and passed through a new phase of experimentation in America. At the end, Prince's art is imaginative and syndetically spontaneous in execution, as it was in the beginning, but its craft—in his eyes and mine too—is better. Now Prince has collectors at home as well as abroad. But a line can be struck, about 1972, separating old work from new, better from worse if you like, but youthful from mature is right.

I turn from the complaint that Prince's work changed to the complaint that it did not change by observing that there is no paradox here. Change is constant in history, but things change more at the surface than they do in the depths. In Prince's work, the shallow look reveals change, the deeper look reveals continuity. Sidney Littlefield Kasfir was disappointed when, looking deeply, she found repetition, and she said that Prince worked like a "traditional artist." She was right, but why is that wrong? Tradition for Kasfir was not the process that produces all art, but a slow, conservative process that contrasts with a process of rapid change. I would call both processes traditions, but the word is not important; the idea is.

Slow traditions are based on spiritual values; they operate by perpetual transformations that shape a double helix of forward and backward motion around a timeless core of human concern. Once Prince had set his style and brought it to maturity, that is how he worked. Seeking the new, he ventured away, gathering fresh ideas, and then spiraling back to the steady center of his vision. By contrast, fast traditions are based on material values; they operate progressively, replacing one set of ideas with another in a linear sequence that parallels technological development and serves the needs of a technologically empowered capitalistic economy.

Claude Lévi-Strauss called the slow process "cool" (its goal is maintenance) and the fast process "hot" (its goal is the destruction of the old, the establishment of the new). Both processes yield art. Though the slow process is largely in the hands of the world's majority of poor and dark and female creators, surely the thought cannot be that, when it comes to art, the slow, cool process is inferior. It has produced most of the world's art, including the African and Native American sculpture that the great modernists judged to be superior to the contemporary art of hot—industrial and imperialistic—Europe.

The first function of an artistic tradition is to provide individuals with the means to create, to express themselves fully and satisfactorily. When the personal and cultural dimensions of their individualities fuse completely and they devote themselves totally to the task at hand, the result is art. By cultural convention, art might be casually identified by medium, by painting here or pottery there, but I think Turkish artisans are right when they argue that the medium is a biographical accident and art is the consequence of *aşk*, of a passionate dedication to the job, whatever the medium might be, gardening, perhaps, poetry, rug weaving, or the calligraphed inscription of the word of God. The medium is a matter of chance; art is a matter of choice. The work of art, a sensate sign of the devoted self, inevitably differs as cultures and personalities do. Some artists satisfy themselves through changes, as Picasso did, others through continuity, as Mondrian did, and most of them work like Prince: they find a style that meets their deep expressive needs and then continues to develop subtly during repetition and experimentation as they endure through life's ups and downs.

Communication is the second function of an artistic tradition. When makers and consumers of art share culture, as when speakers and listeners share a language, communication seems unproblematic, but artists regularly tell me that only another artist can fully appreciate what they do. Communication is always incomplete, imperfect, and always possible. Nobuhiko Kaneko, a master in Hagi, told me that he knows his work is excellent. He commands his métier, and, taking no shortcuts, he brings objects into the world with complete sincerity. What he does not know, he said, is whether other people will like what he makes. Their words, not being informed, are no help. He learns more from the look in their eyes, but direct interaction in polite Japan is of little use. Kaneko studies old works from his tradition and notes how his creations are used in order to imagine the desires of his buyers. Then building into his process an idea of the consumer, just as the storyteller gathers an idea of the listener into his narrative, Kaneko intends connection. Tradesmen strive to satisfy a market's demands, but Kaneko is an artist. Creation matters more to him than communication; commercial success is a happy consequence. As an artist, though, whose tradition enables him to express himself deeply and fully, personally and culturally, he makes things that do communicate. Others will react, connecting to him through the personality and culture his works must expose.

Culture—a collective patterning of thought—appears insistently in the art of slow, cool, spiritual traditions, like that of the Yoruba in the past. Creations are immediately identifiable, attributable to a people and a place. Early in the nineteen-fifties, William Fagg wrote that Yoruba art forms a "coherent whole because certain conventions are accepted throughout the territory." Then he went on to argue that traditional Yoruba art is rife with personality. He estimated that ninety percent of the anonymous works in Western collections could be attributed to individual creators if scholars would only go into the field and make inquiries. As Western works usually do, Yoruba works could have their artists' names, as well as dates and precise locations (in addition to a tribal affiliation), on their labels in museum exhibitions. What is true of Yoruba art is true of all art. It was made by people with names, with complicated biographies and idiosyncracies of practice, and close ethnographic research could prove it by discovering the names of unknown artists from the recent past. In the case of the Turkish carpets that have been scattered by commerce across the globe, the dealer can look at a carpet and name the region it came from, the local middleman can name the village, the women in the village can glance at the weave and name the particular weaver: Fatma or Rahime, Aysel, Sevgi, or Nezihe. William Fagg concludes that, among the Yoruba, as among European academics, "The artist's personal mode of expression communicates itself instantaneously."

Slow traditions and fast ones are alike in their capacity to enable creation and communication. They differ in historical conditions. Slow traditions employ the demonstrational techniques of shops and ateliers, and, based on spiritual values, their art is conceptual. Fast traditions employ the instructional techniques of schools, and, based on material values, their art is visual. That summation is too coarse, too general, though it is less coarse than the old notion of the Western academy which held that slow traditions produce folk or primitive (simple, repetitive, impersonal, marginal, inferior) art, which might not be art at all, but merely craft, while fast traditions produce fine (complex, inventive, personal, central, superior) art. No one, of course, thinks like that anymore. Such thinking, based on prejudices more than facts, was overturned by the modernists and patiently dismantled by the research of folklorists and anthropologists; yet, something like it seeps into the writings on African art when we are told that slow processes produce "traditional" art and fast processes produce "contemporary" art.

Since most contemporary art—contemporary in the sense of current, belonging to the present—is the product of slow traditions, it must be that the use of the qualifier "contemporary" is often a coded gambit of ethnocentrism, meaning art like ours. Apparently the art of the present is not all of the art of the present, but only that which resembles the modish art in the Western markets. Old colonial thinking dies hard. We and our art, it seems, belong to the present. They and their art might exist in the present, but they belong to the past. History is ours, oblivion theirs.

In *Africa Explores*, Susan Vogel objects, as I do, to the loose use of the word "contemporary," and in her book she and her colleagues, most usefully V. Y. Mudimbe, set out to crack African contemporary art into rational categories.

One kind of contemporary artist traditionalizes and revitalizes, working by restrictive creation to bring old styles into new presence. That is what Mehmet Gürsoy does in Turkey, Edival Rosas does in Brazil, and Lamidi Fakeye does in Yorubaland. All of them work as part of a massive worldwide movement to revive the local in opposition to the global. Prince shares their motives but not their practice, being an innovator who uses foreign techniques to give form to his native culture.

Another kind of contemporary artist produces the popular paintings of urban Africa, with their close parallels in Latin America and South Asia. Grounded in European realism, sleek and visually loquacious in the manner of the advertisement, this work, generally self-taught, records the everyday life that Jean Pigozzi likes and Prince, the spiritual artist, has left to those behind him. The painters of urban Africa, Vogel says, avoid the ethnic particularity that lies at the heart of Prince's art, which Robert Plant Armstrong called "profoundly Yoruba." This is not the class to which Prince belongs.

Susan Vogel locates Prince—"probably the most interesting of the Oshogbo painters," who "quickly created a highly original style"—among the "international" artists who tend to work in a flat, linear style. Her international artists divide. Some were trained in art schools and they follow their education and the trends in the West to create "modern" art. Their work fits into the slim slice of time called the present, but unlike them, Mudimbe says, Prince belongs to a select artistic set that is, at once, modern and traditional—belongs among artists, I would say, who are modernists, artists who look back to look forward, whose art answers their dreams and breaks beyond the limitations of current fashion. Prince is a certain sort of international contemporary artist, a man less of the present than of the past and the future: a modernist.

As an unreconstructed modernist, a gentle rebel, Prince has known victory and defeat. Changes of taste in the hot West brought into approval the art of urban Africa that, intentionally or not, looked "contemporary." By creating out of his inner necessity, by maintaining his integrity, Prince creates works that appeal to foreigners whose eyes have been trained by modernism but not to foreigners whose eyes have been trained by the art that succeeded modernism.

In New York, at exactly the time that Prince was making his beginning in Osogbo, Ad Reinhardt was locating the end of modernism in paintings of black and announcing that the next revolution would return art to "the folk-places and lower-depths where it all came from in the first place." Out of context, Reinhardt's words seem to reaffirm the modernist reach: Kandinsky and Yeats hunted in the old folks places. In context, they were prescient. Reinhardt's folk places were "the entertainment-field and junk-yard," and that is exactly where the next artists in the sequence of high fashions—Rauschenberg and Johns, Warhol, Lichtenstein, and Oldenburg—explored for their sources. They did not reach back into time or out into space, but snuggled into their urban, industrial, and emphatically American environment. Pulling back from pure abstraction, they depicted the common objects of their common place: American flags, maps of the United States, Ballantine Ale cans, Campbell's Soup cans, Brillo boxes, stop signs, clothespins and hamburgers, photographs of celebrities, comic book panels. The modernists had been there before—think of Duchamp's urinal and snow shovel, Bloom's dream house in *Ulysses*—but this art called "new" and "pop" was a decisive move in the creation of an era that was not comprehensively named until architects, recoiling from the functionalist excess of international modernist architecture, as the new artists recoiled from the abstracting excess of modernist painting, proclaimed a postmodern architecture.

For a while, everything from witty buildings to witless prose got called postmodern in the effort to give the era a distinct identity, though it was, like all of them, an inconsistent mix of unreconciled inclinations. I would place the beginning of postmodernism in the middle of the nineteen-fifties. I was in high school then; modernism seemed stale, sedately academic, and I remember how excited I was by the target and flags painted by Jasper Johns. It was a time of rising prosperity in the United States, a celebration of pop banality seemed in order, but most people paid no mind to the new art, and in the sixties, as postmodernism took shape, the abstract expressionists were still at work and young people took on the oppositional modernist task, listening to folk music, advancing the discipline of folklore, and marching in protest against the war and for civil rights. As it developed, many postmodern creators, who did not get it the first time around, reiterated the relativistic, critical theories of early modernism in their works. Some revived aspects of modernism, their abstraction following Newman, their expressionism following de Kooning. But others set the contemporary tone by wrestling with the ancestors to distinguish themselves, and as they tore away from the modernism that preceded them and fixed on the familiar, they drew appreciation away from artists like Prince Twins Seven-Seven.

The modernists sought to escape the decadent present by valuing the distant: the ancient and exotic. Postmodernists valued the near: the current and common, tin cans and graffiti, movies and television. In the modernist manner, Frank Lloyd Wright looked back through William Morris's eyes at medieval architecture and traveled to Japan in search of alternative sources. In the postmodern manner, Robert Venturi learned from Las Vegas.

The modernists sought the spiritual through abstraction. Postmodernists reveled in the material, moving from the incorporation of readymades in combines and the replication of industrial artifacts to the photographic new realism of Close, Estes, and Hanson, then on to the costly, campy kitsch of Koons. Confirmed materialists, they loved machines. For John Ruskin at the dawn of modernism, the ultimate evil was turning men into machines, but Andy Warhol said he wanted to be a machine, thought all people should be machines. From the Arts and Crafts Movement through abstract expressionism, from Morris to Pollock, the old romantics sentimentalized hand work. The new romantics sentimentalized technology, giving their abstract creations smooth, cool, machined surfaces from which all traces of process had been erased, and welcoming the camera, videocam, and computer into collaboration. The old romantics sentimentalized the placid green countryside. The new romantics sentimentalized urban grit.

In their search through cultural diversity for universal principles, the modernists favored the purity of precolonial artistic expressions. They liked the Dan mask or Fang statue that made the world seem larger; the modernists occupied an expanding universe. Postmodernists happily tracked the spread of their own culture, favoring the hybrid, impure creations of postcolonial times that recorded responses to the neocolonial ooze of globalization. They liked the Ghanaian barber boards that brought the world near; the postmodernists occupied a shrinking globe. Sincerity set the mood of modernism. Irony was the postmodern attitude.

Prince is puzzled. His art no longer gets the approval from foreigners that once it did. Excellent paintings remain unsold. Times change, change for the better, change for the worse. As postmodernism reached its peak, around 1990, Prince's fortunes began their steep decline, but, having changed, the times will change again, and he laughs and keeps at it, an ant on his own little hill. There is nothing ironic in him. Utterly sincere, he is devoted to his noble tradition, committed to the sacred, endlessly creative. A rare hero, Prince is the artist he must be.

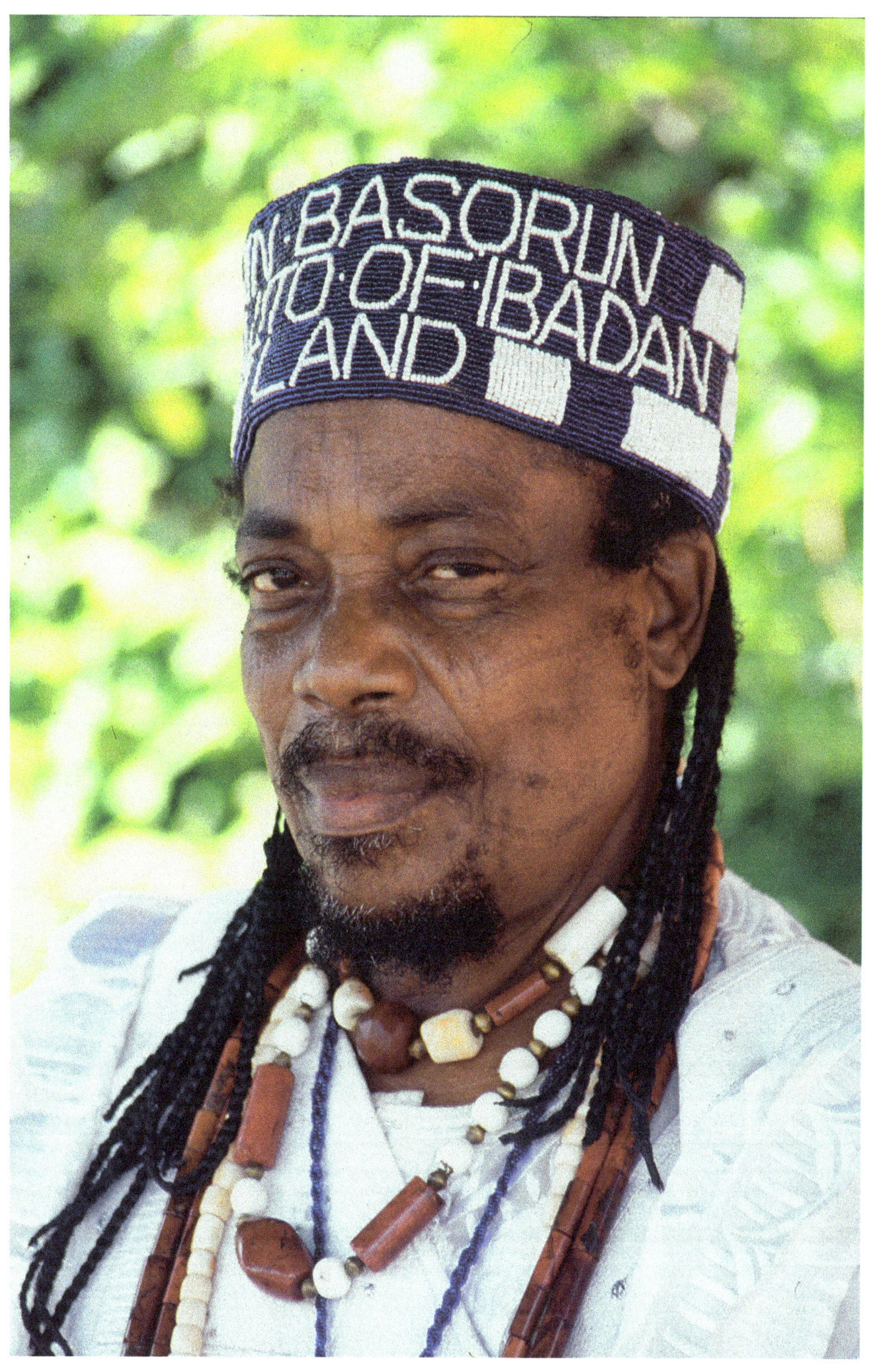

Prince Twins Seven-Seven. Philadelphia. June 5, 2008

· 20 ·

Dreams of the Abiku Child

A sampling from the oeuvre of Prince Twins Seven-Seven follows. Designed to display the range of his topics and techniques, the collection features, though not exclusively, the large finished paintings that he feels represent him best. Most of Prince's published paintings are early ones, so I have opted to balance the record: thirteen of the twenty-nine works, nearly half, are recent, created since 2000 during his American period.

All the information comes from Prince. The titles are those he prefers now (2009), but he has changed the titles of some pictures over time and uses alternative titles in conversation. Prince provided the media. Many of his works are not dated, and he drew the missing dates from his memory. Usually he was quite certain about their accuracy, and I was, of course, sure about those I watched him create. We talked at length about each picture, its title, media, date, and its interpretation. I build what I say on Prince's comments that I transcribed from tape-recordings of our talk, intending this to be an instance of correct folkloristic practice: a representative collection of texts accompanied by interpretations guided by the creator's understanding.

In telling the story of his life, Prince arranged his narrative by chronology and theme. Generally, as he spoke, chronology gave way to thematic organization. When I ordered the pictures in sequence, I followed him, attending to both chronology and theme, making sure that works from his whole career appear, that all of his common themes are represented, but I valued, as he did, themes over chronology and grouped his works thematically into the supernatural, the natural, and the cultural.

As the themes intersect, the works in this collection become facets of Prince's coherent worldview. Expressing a worldview, Mark Rothko wrote, is the artist's mission. Shortly before Prince's birth, when Rothko was developing the thoughts that would make him a great master of abstract expressionism, he said that artists join poets and philosophers by expressing "in concrete form their notions of reality," their ideas of "time and space, life and death," joy and despair, their preoccupation with "eternal problems." That is what Prince does.

When their notions of reality are framed by a scientific worldview—and, for Rothko, art and science generally run in accord—artists commit to the limits of the knowable, to the sensate reality. They realize the visual in "realistic" images that compare with the scientist's empirical reports, or they turn from particularity and generalize the visual into principles which they employ, as Rothko did, in the creation of "abstract" works that compare with the scientist's theoretical models. (Think of Lévi-Strauss's diagrams that look like Gabo's sculpture: the twentieth century was a time of abstraction in both art and science.)

The dichotomous economy of the realistic and abstract—as articulated by Kandinsky—usefully orders the works of artists who operate in terms of a scientific worldview, but it proves clumsy when applied to the works of artists whose worldview is spiritual. The scientific artist begins in nature, in the visible, and welcomes the conceptual into the task of refining and deepening understanding. The spiritual artist begins in the mind, in the conceptual, and welcomes the visual into the effort to give form to the unknown and unseen. Prince is a spiritual artist, like the old Yoruba sculptors who worked to the middle, like the artists of Islam and Hinduism who work toward the opposite ends of the mimetic scale, Muslims in an aniconic tradition, Hindus in a tradition that is iconic in the extreme. Like them, what Prince pictures, he has not seen; his errand is to bring invisibility into presence. A man of the present, he imagines the people of a lost past. A man on the earth, he imagines the gods and ghosts. His imaginings employ visual abstraction and conceptual reconfiguration to depict the fullness of a reality that brings all of time into the present and blends the supernatural into the natural. Like those of every spiritual artist, his "abstract" images are "realistic" renderings of a world that is incompletely known and only partially visible.

In Prince's worldview, as it is revealed in his work, human life is a struggle. Failed by technological progress, surrounded by signs of death's inevitability, people labor in forlorn contention with nature. They gain support from cooperation, delight from festivity, and hope from prayer, as they move through a world of forests and villages that exists only in relation to another. This world and the other, the twin dimensions of reality, interpenetrate: prayers go from this to that, power comes from that to this, so Prince's worldview would be incomplete, unreal, without the invisible spirits and deities. In Prince's view, human beings endure through a universe mixed of the seen and unseen, the good and the evil. The goddess Osun spreads goodness through Prince's world, but Sango and Ogun remain obliviously ambivalent, and the people and spirits, the living and dead, fuse benevolence and malevolence into a perpetually unstable uncertainty. Life is funny and frightening. It is this universe, natural and supernatural, good and bad, that Prince makes concrete—as spiritual artists, poets, and philosophers must.

Prince Twins Seven-Seven and Mark Rothko connect as artists, as modernists deeply interested in tradition—alike in achievement, different in worldview.

Primarily to present Prince's themes, the pattern and scope of his worldview, and secondarily to exhibit the sweep of his styles and techniques, his development as an artist, I have selected these works and arranged them like this:

Supernatural: Spirits (1–5), Deities (6–11).

Natural: Animals (12–17).

Cultural: Human Life (18–24), American Experience (25–29).

As for sources: nos. 1, 2, 3, 7, 8, 9, 13, 18, 21, 25, 27, and 29a come from various private collections; nos. 4, 5, 6, 10, 11, 12, 14, 15, 16, 17, 19, 20, 22, 23, 24, 26, and 29b are held by Material Culture in Philadelphia; and no. 28 is in the collection of the Philadelphia Museum of Art; it is, I believe, the only painting in this collection that has been published before.

1
The Dream of the Abiku Child

Ink, watercolor, and oil on brown wrapping paper, glued to plywood. 27" x 40". Osogbo, 1967

An early work, originally titled *Invisible Ghost and a Golden Fish in the Dark River*, this is a symbolic self-portrait, which in the typological manner of Yoruba art, and African art generally, signifies Prince without intending a physical likeness (chapter 17). At once Prince and all abikus, it records his preservation in life by the waters of the goddess Osun. Prince said: "This is an abiku child, felt he has been thrown into the water, and the fish—Osun—save him."

At birth, Prince was sinking toward death until his mother, advised by a babalawo, gave him the water of Omielja to drink (chapter 4). In maturity, far from home in Philadelphia, Prince was sinking toward spiritual death until, saved by his wife and friends, he took up painting again (chapter 14). Painting is a sign of his *ase*, his life force. The visions he paints are signs of the spiritual power of an abiku. In this painting, the abiku rises from the dark river, as though reborn from the water, as though he were one of the fish, the devotees of Osun. As a devotee, like the fish when they swarm, he gives form to Osun who gave life to him (nos. 8–10). His red hands, rendered in oil, reach up against the starry sky to shield his eyes. The hands claim the viewer's attention, but the artisan's hands matter less to Prince than the artist's eyes:

"You know, when an abiku child close his eyes, his eyes doesn't close properly. They still see his eyes: he's alive. He's alive."

Not dead, he has eyes that are "closed and open at the same time"—the eyes of a ghost, a spirit who sees simultaneously the visible and invisible realities. On this face, Prince painted an early version of the veiled eyes with slit lids that would indicate the spirits in his work for the length of his career (see no. 7).

It is the Yoruba belief, Wole Soyinka wrote, that the abiku is a "wanderer," a child "who dies and returns again and again to plague the mother." Three words from one line in Soyinka's poem "Abiku" position the abiku in time: "once . . . repeated . . . ageless." The abiku, like Prince, is a spirit child who has known death and known life, who lives in this world with knowledge of the other, who can envision the unseen. This image, then, of an abiku saved by Osun, describes Prince's artistic power.

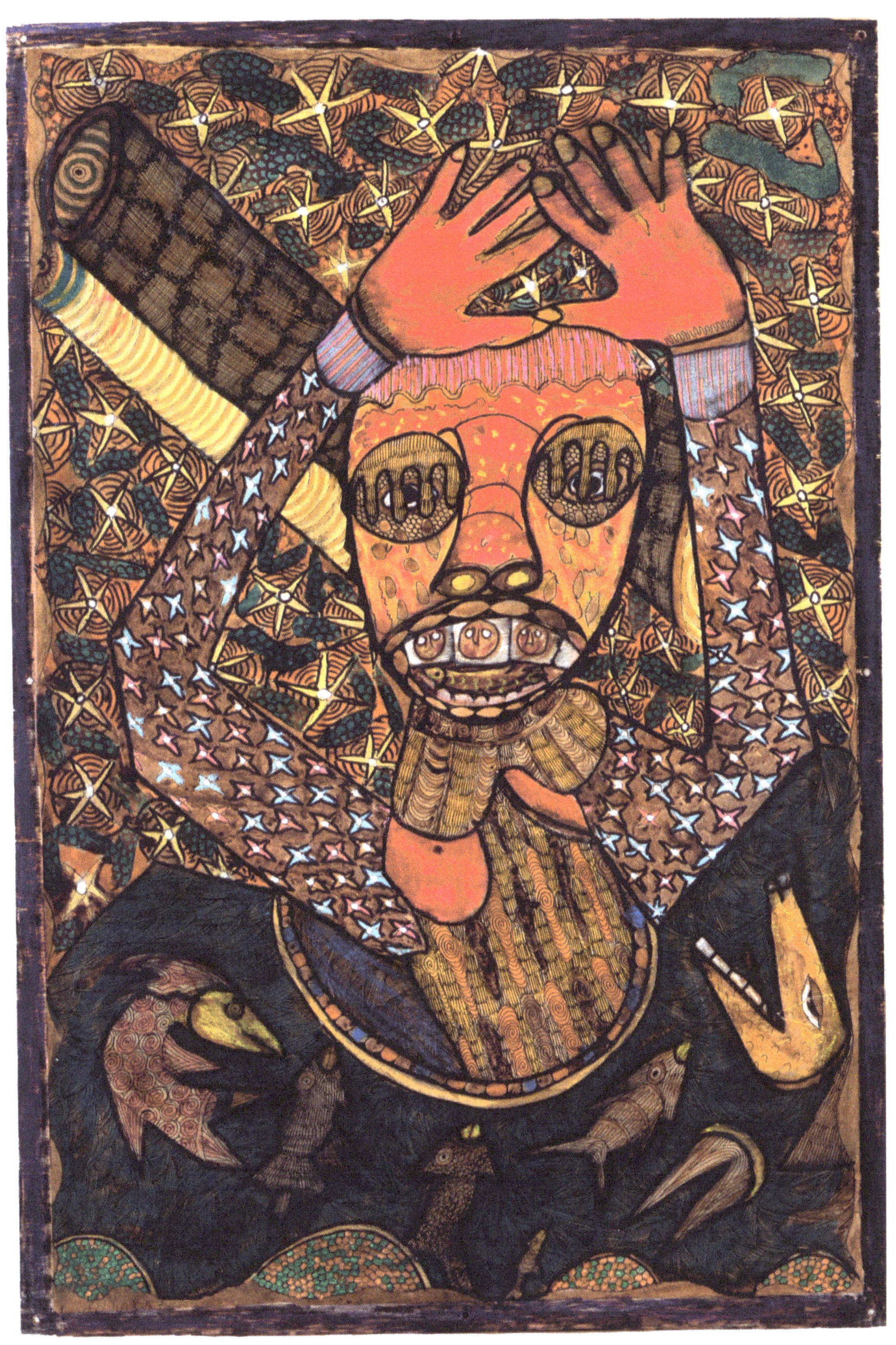

No. 1. *The Dream of the Abiku Child*. 1967

2
The Smelling Ghost

Ink, watercolor, and oil on brown paper. 31½" x 39½". Osogbo, 1966

In its drawing this painting is so close as to be a copy of the painting reproduced in Ulli Beier's *Contemporary Art in Africa* and titled *Elephant Man*, but the palette differs. The background of Beier's painting is a creamy buff; this one is vibrantly blue. This early work was framed and hung high in the gallery on the third floor of Prince's home in Osogbo, then brought to Philadelphia in 2006. Prince describes the spirit:

"It is called the smelly ghost. He lives among certain leaves that when he walk around in the evening, he have the smell of the leaves.

"The smelling ghost: like, when the baby is sick, and the babalawo need to go and look for certain leaves to make a potion for the sick baby, they look out for the smelling ghost because they believe if the smelling ghost is in some branches of trees around the house, the leaves will not work. So, they call it Ologbonkian. Wherever he is, everybody will hear the smell. He smells bad and he destroy the leaves so they would not touch. They look for a place where they don't hear his smells.

"I do have him at my house here—in this, my house in America. I smell him all the time. He lives among flowers.

"But you don't see it, but you hear it. He *smell* so bad. Rat, snake, anything will not go where he is. Because of his smell.

"Another rat that is in same relation to him is the small rat; you know, the rat with the long nose. We call it Arun, and this one, if it bites, it is more poisonous than a snake bite. So the rat with the long nose, it smells. They smell alike."

Ologbonkian, who smells like a venomous rat, destroys the herbs the babalawos use to cure sick babies. In the reality of mixed good and evil, he is countered by Osun who brings life to babies with her healing waters (nos. 7–10).

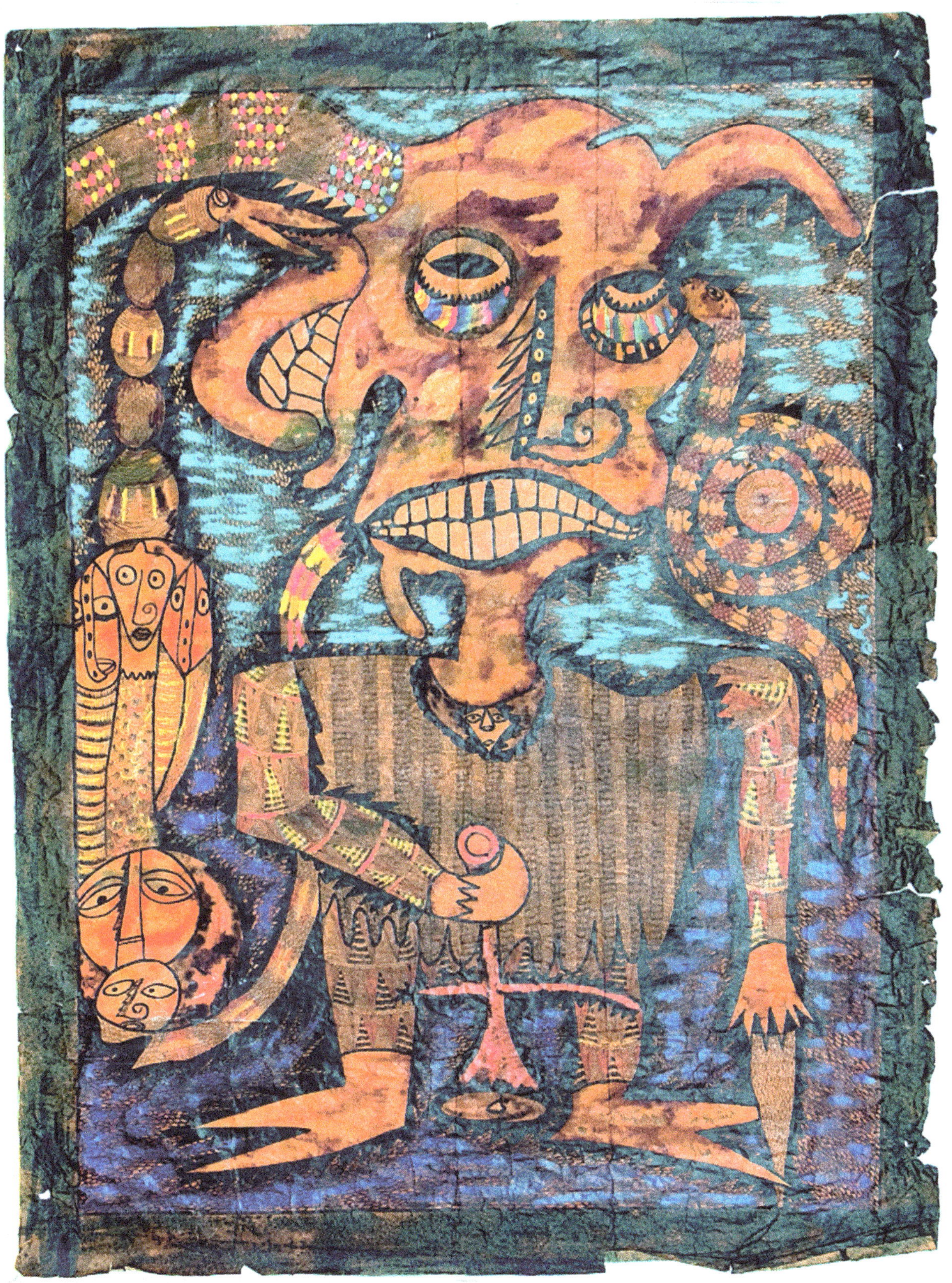

No. 2. *The Smelling Ghost*. 1966

3
Ogongo, The King of Birds

Ink, pastel, and oil on wood, a sculpture's painting of two layers. 2' x 4'. Osogbo, 1969

First titled *Kings of Birds* and also called *Longneck King of Birds*, this painting was crafted in the manner of *Kissing Birds* (chapter 1). In contrast to the preceding paintings, which come from his youthful beginning when his drawing was loose (chapter 19), this is an early instance of Prince's mature work, foreshadowing recent creations (chapter 14, p. 201, and no. 7). A sculpture's painting made in the year he invented the technique, it is ornamented with patterns inspired by "cloth work," by designs on textiles: the inked geometric motifs, filled with color, flow in orderly, repetitive succession. Prince said:

"It's like an ostrich that have a human face, but my concept of thinking here is like in the city of witches. Every Yoruba believe that the symbol of witches are birds.

"So, this is a strange bird that have a human head. And this we call King of Birds because many birds have beak; none of them have faces like this.

"So, this kind of imagination you can see from the plane when you look out in the sunset; you can see the red kind of cloud shapes in the sky. Or sometimes you can even see such things in the moon as well. It depends on how much you use the inner imaginative thinking.

"I call this Ogongo, The King of Birds."

Ogongo reminds me of Alokolobo (chapter 14, p. 201), and when I ask Prince about their resemblance, he laughs and says they look alike because he creates paintings in series, so the way he envisions an invisible spirit for one picture will influence the way he portrays a spirit in another. His work builds on itself:

"Yes. Because they are the same sort of area. You know when I do my painting, if I'm in one particular subject, before I jumped to another thing, a certain particular figure, it will be reflected back.

"That's the way I work. This is formally like Alokolobo. They are both powerful bird spirits. And because what I want to depict in my life—I want people to know that every living thing have their own shadow, have their own spirits."

The spirits, that is, have spirits, proliferating in infinite reformulation. Ogongo and Alokolobo shadow and reflect each other: invisibility reverberates into a mysterious shape that evokes witchcraft.

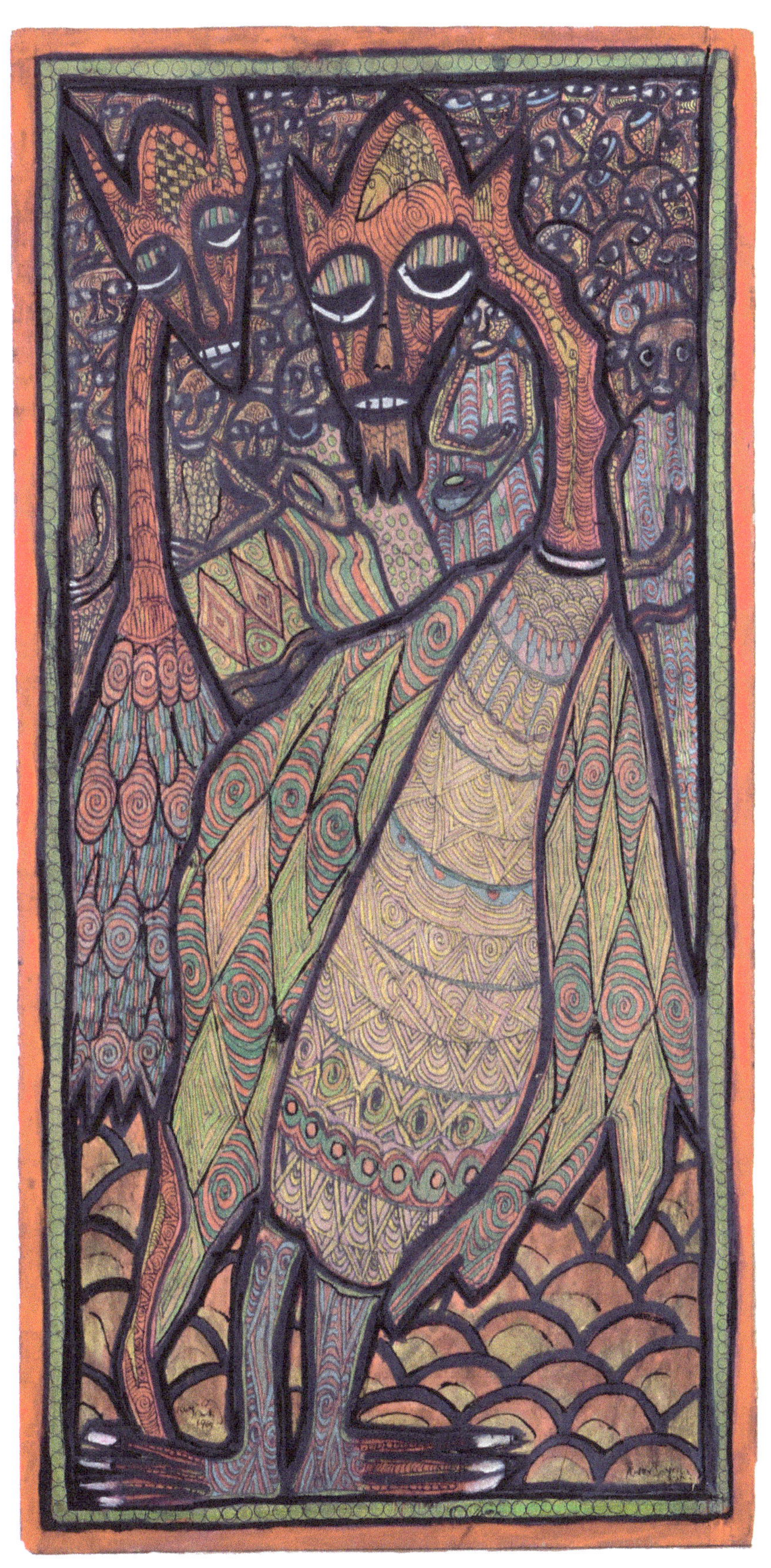

No. 3. *Ogongo, The King of Birds*. 1969

4
Dancing Spirits

Ink, batik dye, watercolor, and oil on cloth. 15½" x 24". Ibadan, 2007

This is one of fourteen pictures, vertical in format like most of his work, that Prince painted on cloth in his country house outside of Ibadan in the spring and summer of 2007. The image of Osun, *The Goddess of Fertility*, in chapter 3, p. 56, is another from this series. All were painted with the bright "rainbow" palette and "tattoo" ornament that he refined in the versions of *The Spirits of My Reincarnation Brothers and Sisters* he painted in Philadelphia in the winter of 2006–2007 (no. 29).

The Spirit of Twins, Prince said, could be an alternative title for this picture. In its doubleness, its multiplicity, the spirit incarnates the powers of the abiku twins behind it. Prince said:

"He lives in the other world, where twins come from; that's why he has so many heads. He have large eyes that can see so far."

On another day, Prince spoke of this spirit in more particular terms:

"You know, this one has to do with a certain destructive object in Yoruba life, called Sigidi.

"It's a kind of object that can—when it moves, it roll like a ball. But it has hands, has faces. They can send it to do anything, you know.

"Like, let me put it this way. Like, when my wife leave me—let's say she go and marry somebody, and I'm not happy with it, this kind of object can be used to terrify the new husband. While he sleep, one part of his head is shaved, and this"—his pubic hair—"is shaved.

"Imagine: you are asleep, and you wake up, and you find your head has been shaved, and you don't know who shaved it."

Prince laughs and continues:

"So. And then the people who fight on farms use that. When somebody want to take your father's land, and you are not happy with it, you can go to the priest that control this thing; you can use it. You can use it both for oppression and for positive purposes.

"When it moves, it can turn itself to anything. It can turn itself to a camel. It can turn itself into pangolin. The Sigidi. But when it moves, it moves like it's dancing, so that's why I call it Dancing Spirit.

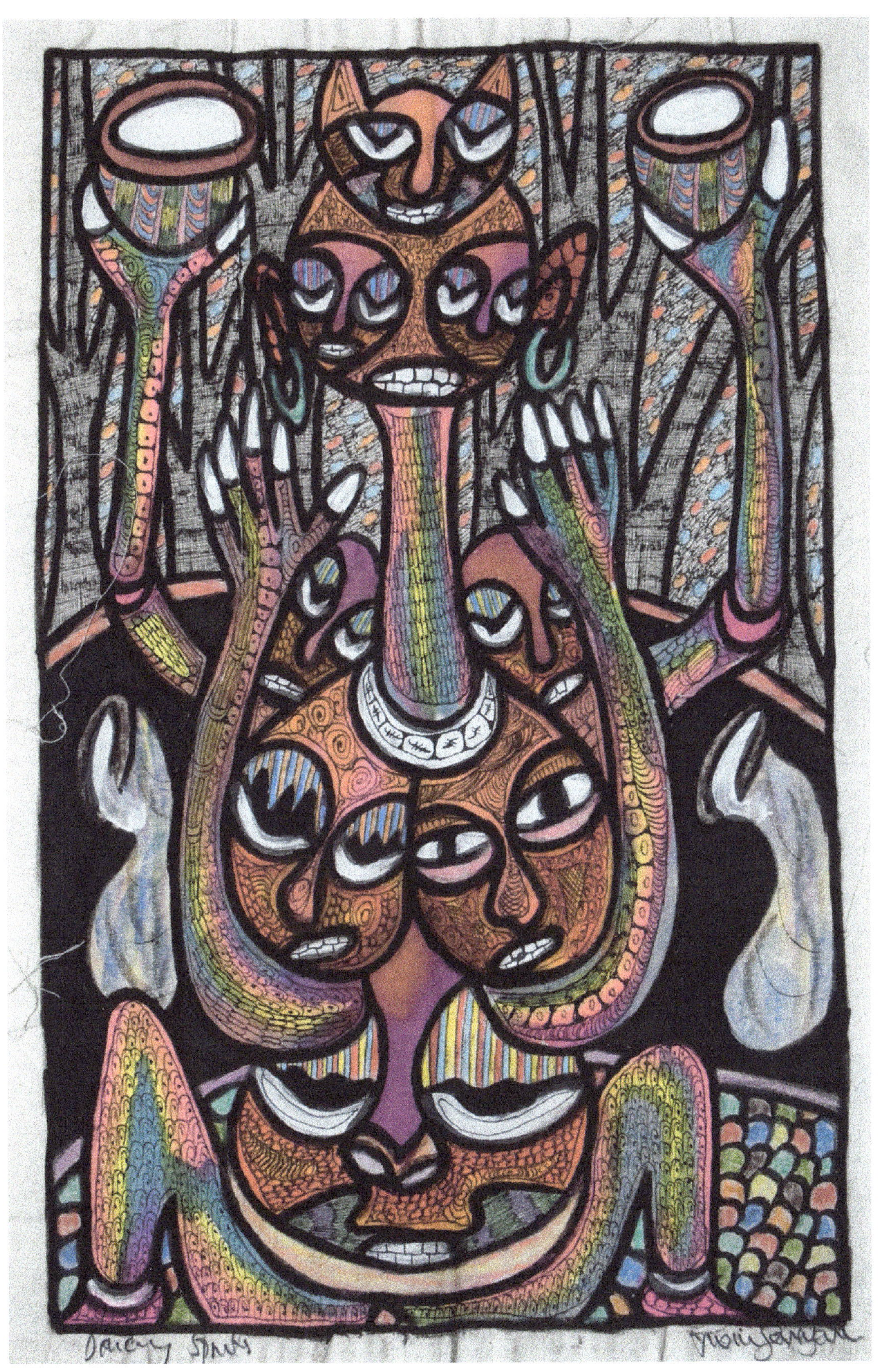

No. 4. *Dancing Spirits.* 2007

"But it came from the image of the large cloth. Spiritual thinking."

Spiritual thinking acknowledges the duality that spiritual images reveal. Osun is good (nos. 8–10), Ologbonkian is evil (no. 2), and Sigidi can be employed in acts both beneficial and malign. When Prince said that this spirit came from the large cloth, he meant that he plucked it from among the spirits who flank him in *The Spirits of My Reincarnation Brothers and Sisters* (no. 29). It is something he often does: he paints a masterpiece that might take months, then he creates small, quick pictures, like this one, out of its parts.

Prince points back at Sigidi, saying, "And then the eyes are my symbol, you know. The symbolic eye thing is there." Then he goes on to describe the technique he used in the series that began with *My Reincarnation Brothers and Sisters* and included this one:

"The technique on this is that you apply the color first. Then I put the drawing on top of the color. Unlike the other one"—*Kissing Birds* (chapter 1)—"that I do the drawing, and then do the color.

"Most of those spiritual paintings are in the same technique. This way is faster.

"So, this is the same tattoo technique, though it is harder on the fabric than the wood. Because when you work on wood, because the wood surface is smooth, and this one has a lot of stretching.

"And then, many years ago, when I am not here"—in Philadelphia—"when I cannot get all these material I am using now, I have to use, you know, the ink to edge out, but today I use the"—permanent, felt-tipped—"black pen.

"And then I use charcoal in Africa. Charcoal. The thing from fire. I put wood in the fire. When it burns, I put water on it. Two days, three days, I can use it, mix it with kerosene to give my black. Then I use it for black. And I varnish it, and when I varnish, it cannot remove. Because I don't have the color I have now. All the new material you have here, I don't have there.

"And that is why my coloring are getting brighter. Because I'm using American colors.

"Back in Africa, when I'm working, like, maybe I'm eating eba—you know, our food—sometimes I use eba when I'm eating, and I can use my eba and rub it on the wood, and when it dry, I smoothe it down. It's a color. Sometimes I use egg yolk mixed with color because I don't have all these bright colors.

"And why I love to use brighter color these days: more people are using colorful settee in their house. Then the chairs, the furnitures are getting more colorful.

"So, if you have a painting that, you know, come from my brownish period, you know, maybe they don't like it."

5
Conference of Noisy Birds

Ink, watercolor, and oil on wood, a sculpture's painting of two layers. 4' x 8'. Osogbo, 1978–1979

This painting comes from a "ghost series on wood" that was sent for sale to Germany. *Ghosts in Political Conference* in chapter 4, p. 74, also belongs to this group. The pictures in this series share a technique designed to display the natural tones of the wood beneath a transparent glaze of color. Prince said:

"There is no color. Only the wood itself.

"I put design on the wood with ink, drawing by ink, and after I finish, I just apply very lightly powder color with sponge, and rub it on with water.

"The wood itself shows. Except the black and white, you know."

As with *Kissing Birds* (chapter 1), the outlines are black, and the brown field is relieved with bright spots of thick, white oil paint. Amos Tutuola's novels were on his mind when Prince painted this series, and this painting was his example when he said he was not an illustrator, but he took from Tutuola a mood that inspired his work (chapter 8). Prince said:

"This had to do with the period I'm dealing with dream's ideas. This has to do with My Life in Bush of Ghosts, when I do some strange things—these are what many of my art collectors like to see."

Prince contrasts this painting with his paintings of village scenes (nos. 20–23), which, he says, are "social" in meaning. But:

"This is more spiritual, spiritual work.

"This is something you cannot see: a bird with a human head, a *big* python lady. See: the whole body is a python.

"This is a spiritual one.

"Sometimes I use the sky. Sometimes I look into the sky, and the shapes come in. If you sit in the place by the window, you look in the clouds."

A pandemonium, the mass of spirits represents spirituality in contrast to the massed faces that represent humanity in Prince's social scenes (nos. 20–21). Whether spirits or people, the beings in Prince's art suggest stories more often than they tell them (no. 13); they are posed or gathered—iconically (chapter 17)—in generalized frontality, offered as individual or collective portraits of the imaginary (nos. 2–4, 6–7, 9, 20–21, 25, 28–29).

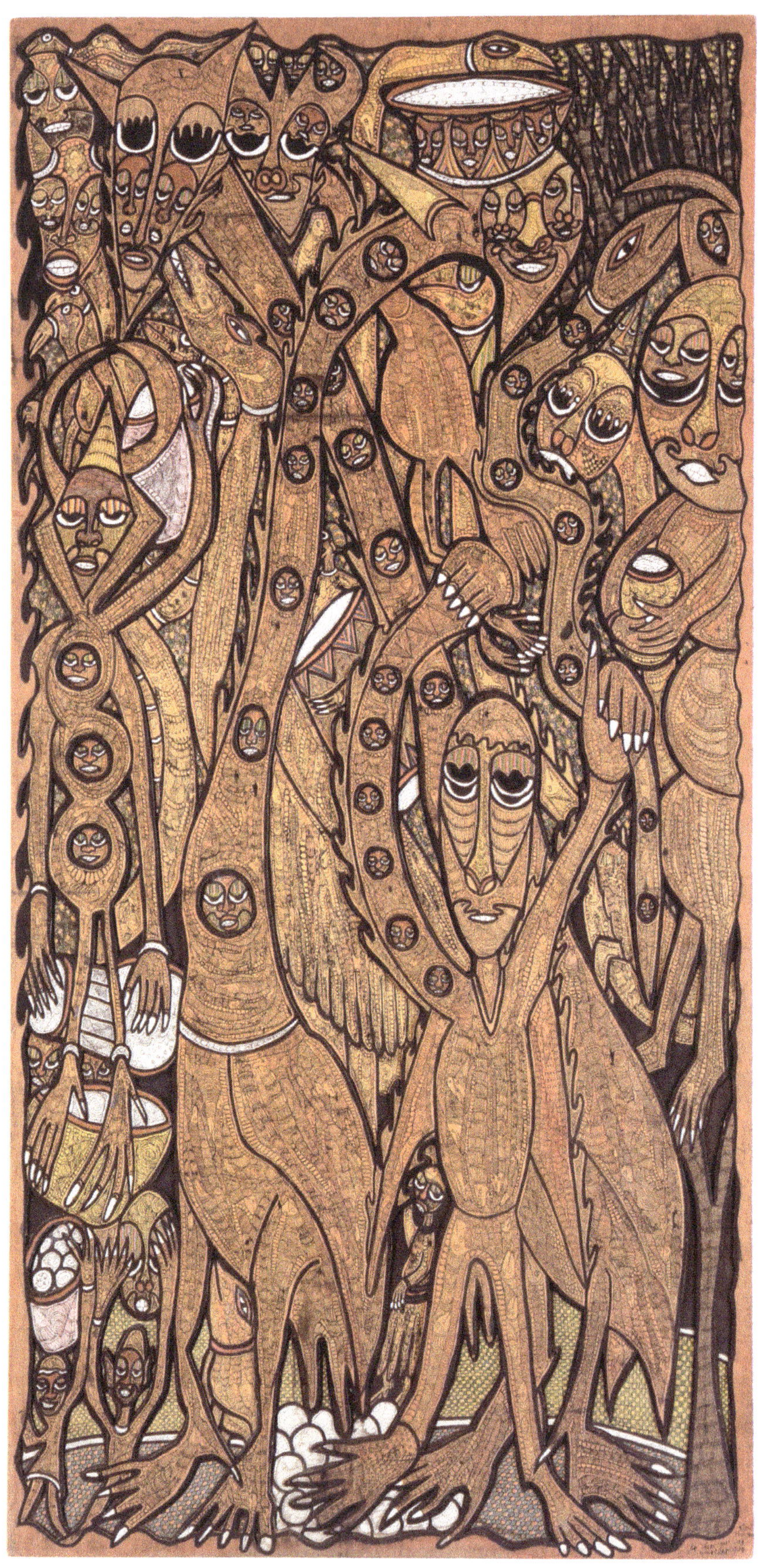

No. 5. *Conference of Noisy Birds.* 1978–1979

Prince calls this a conference of birds to connect spirituality with witchcraft (no. 3). Birds evoke witches; witchcraft embodies the philosophical proposition of the good and evil in all existence, in the people of this world, the spirits of the other. The forms of the unseen spirits come from stories, from dreams, from clouds, from the patterns in woodgrain, from birds and snakes and the human figure: the visual is dismembered and meshed in the mind, reconceptualized to unify what is divided in this world—man and beast, bird and snake—and bring the other world into this one, as African masks suddenly do.

Not everyone at the conference has avian features, and even those who do are not worldly birds. They are all spiritual beings, marked by the eyes that open everywhere—down the body of the python, along the snaky necks of the birds that cross to balance the composition—opening to reveal more spirit faces with more eyes. In their multiplicity, the vigilant eyes make visible the malevolent and benevolent, unseen presence of spiritual power in workaday life. The eyes are Prince's focus:

"Eyes. The eyes are a powerful thing. And this kind of painting—wherever you find them, you can't walk away without them follow you everywhere. Because of the eyes.

"The eyes follow you everywhere.

"That makes a Twins Seven-Seven painting: the eyes.

"Because, being an abiku child, most of these things you see are in your dreams. Most of these things come into your thinking. Most of these things is part of your practical thinking every day.

"The mythological thinking is part of the daily life.

"The eyes are part of spiritual life, also a trademark of my art."

6

Iyaogun

Ink, batik dye, and oil on cloth. 12" x 36". Osogbo, 1976

In the Yoruba wood-carving tradition, the deities, with the exception of Esu, are rarely depicted; they are represented, instead, by their agents and avatars on earth: a babalawo for Ifa, priests and priestesses for Sango and Ogun. This painting shows a priestess of Ogun, Iyaogun, who takes the form of a spirit, as priests and priestesses often do in Prince's work (no. 17). Prince made this painting on a scrap of fabric. "At that time," he said, "my wives are doing a lot of batik in the house. I use part of the leftover cloth." He made the painting for himself, and it hung for many years by the door of the gallery on the third floor of his Osogbo home, then he brought it to Philadelphia in 2006. *Snake Charmer*, Prince said, could be another title for this painting:

"Iyaogun is a snake charmer. Ogun priest can be a snake charmer. If you look at it, you will see people that have wings and can fly. Like angels. You see the wings? So, Iyaogun is the one in charge of all the snakes that were to be used for Ogun. She's a priestess in terms of taking care of snakes that were used for Ogun symbols."

She is pouring white snakes into a calabash, her hair is transforming into snakes. Prince continues:

"Like when she appear, according to the believer, the snakes, the hair moves. It depends on what sort of mood she is. When she calm down, the snakes relax on her body. And most especially, the people who were interested in sort of religion are mostly Ogun worshipers. God of Iron.

"She's a spirit.

"She has another head in the stomach. Which mean: it's like a tattoo, but it's not a tattoo; it's a moving tattoo. The stomach is like another *head*. And from her neck comes out a long arm that carry the special box that contain the white snakes."

In representing the god on earth, the priestess becomes a spirit, empowered by Ogun to control snakes as snake charmers can (see no. 17). Woman, priestess, and spirit, a link in the cosmic chain, her significance elaborates in Prince's recent rendition of Iyaogun (no. 7), next in this collection.

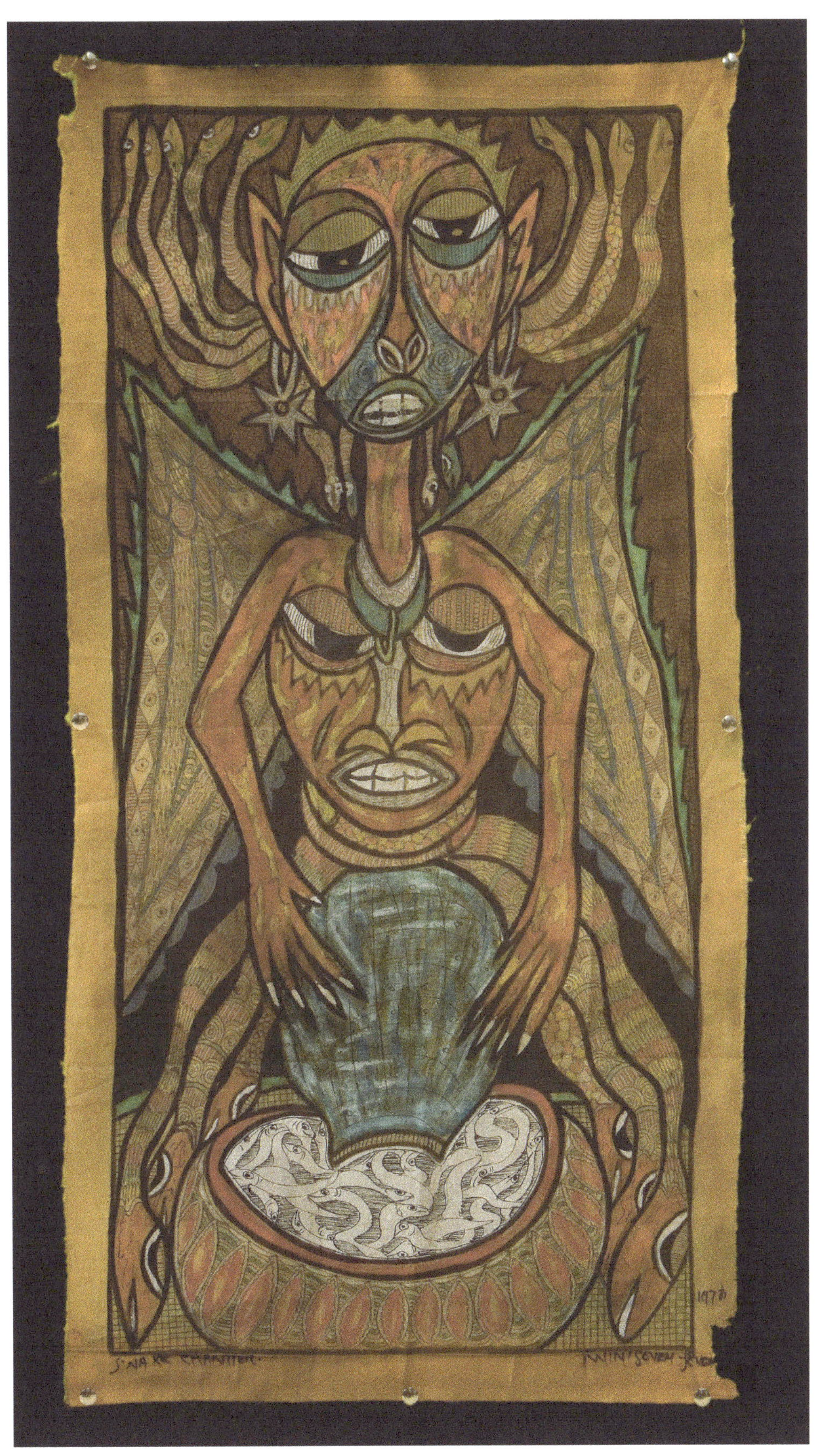

No. 6. *Iyaogun*. 1976

7
Ogun Goddess

Ink and oil on wood, a sculpture's painting of two layers. 12" x 24¼". Ibadan, 2008

The newest piece in this collection, this work exemplifies a presentational format that Prince used for many paintings at the end of the nineteen-nineties, then began to use again in 2007. Though their subjects are diverse, all the pictures are composed vertically—verticality being the axis of integration in Yoruba art (chapter 17). All are small, fastidiously finished sculpture's paintings, made for buyers who want something excellent but cannot afford Prince's large works. All have orange borders; the orange mediates in value between the black outlining and the white highlights, in hue between the red and yellow of the infill, and gathering the brown and contrasting with the green, orange tones the whole into a bright, but dark and earthy fusion. The image of Edun in this book's first chapter, p. 22, is an older piece from this set.

The painting shows Iyaogun, and, Prince said, *Iyaogun* could be its title. The subject, he said, is the same as the preceding painting (no. 6), but the image differs. Two decades lie between them. The calabash of white snakes below Iyaogun in the old picture rests on her head in the new one. Prince compares them:

"You see this one too is Iyaogun, having the snake around her body. And then the musicians behind her, and the calabash she is carrying here contains the same sort of white snakes that the woman is pouring into the calabash"—in the old painting.

"You see their faces: the ladies look similar, but it is different because this one is sculpture wood, because of the relief effect, and the other one is fabric."

That both are spirits is confirmed by the wings, spiky fingers, and second head of the old picture, the veiled eyes (nos. 1, 5, 9) of the new one. Of the new Iyaogun, Prince said, "She is a person and a spirit at the same time." Both blend with snakes. In the old picture, the braids of Iyaogun's hair lift into snakes. In the new one, snakes appear in the tattooed decoration on Iyaogun's arms, "because her spirit have to do with snakes, and everything on her have to do with snakes." A great snake coils around her (see no. 17); it is, Prince said, "a sign of her power; Ogun gives her power." As the title *Ogun Goddess* implies, she joins the god in power during ritual acts. The snake's tail, in Prince's clever design, replaces her left—spiritual—arm, rising to aid her in sacred performance:

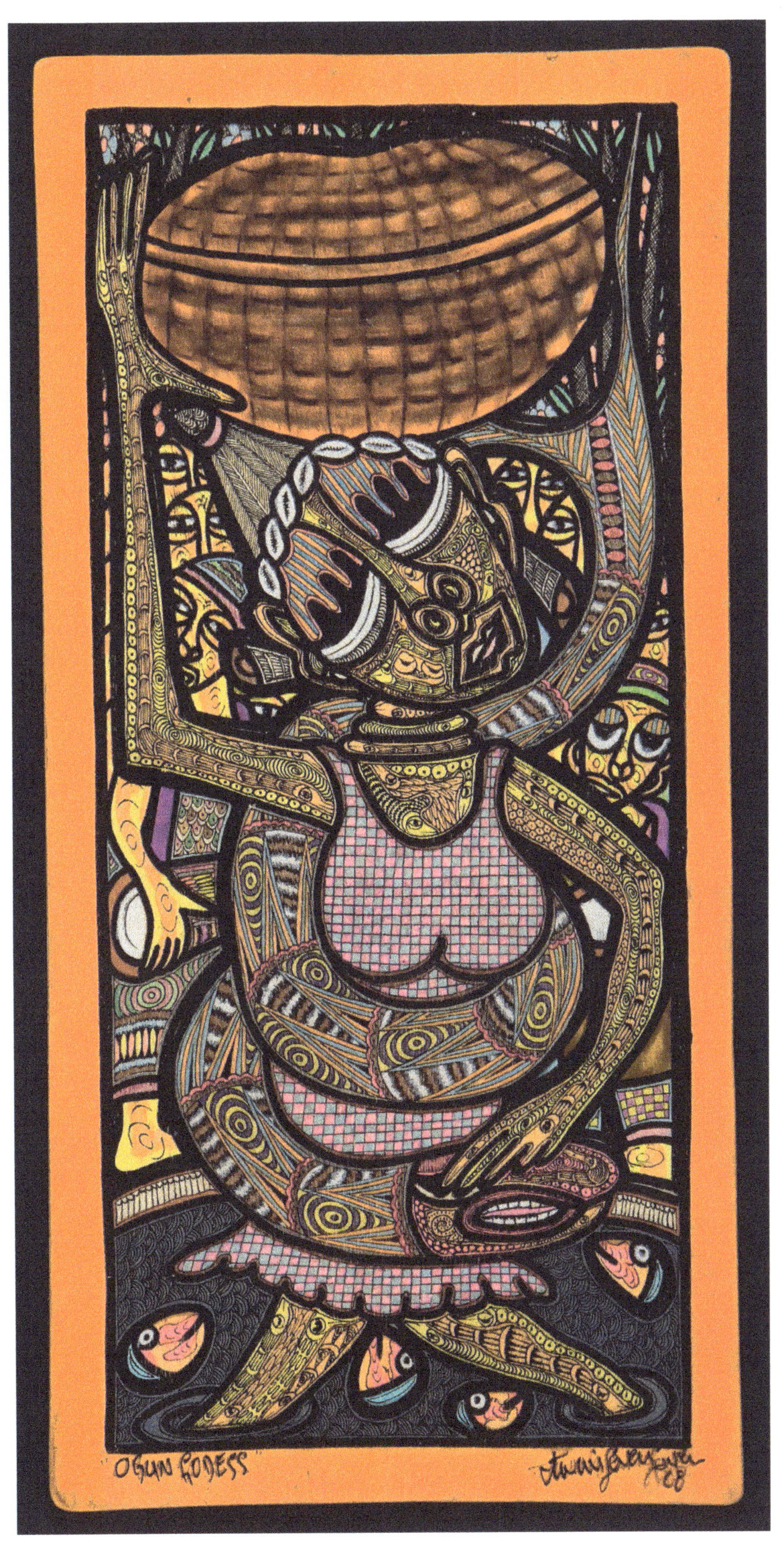

No. 7. *Ogun Goddess.* 2008

"You see it is not the arm. It is the *large* tail of the snake, holding the calabash for her. And you have the drummer here, the Ogun worshipers playing drum and all that."

The pictures differ in style and technique, but iconographically the chief difference lies at the bottom of the new painting. Fish appear in the water from which Iyaogun rises (see no. 1). Stylized fish ornament the furniture and walls of the Olosun compound in Ibadan, and fish swim subtly through Prince's paintings (nos. 23, 29). I assumed that these fish indicated the presence of the goddess Osun, and when I asked, Prince said:

"The fish are reference to Osun, because there is no way you talk about Osun without talking about Ogun. There is no way you talk about Ogun without talking about Sango. All the orisas are related to each other.

"And because to be Iyaogun she be somebody who have respect for Osun. Because whatever she do medicinally, it is Osun goddess that will make it possible for her.

"And because they have become my symbol. Hardly you see my painting without you find a fish there. Or snakes.

"The snakes have to do with death, but some snakes in our concept are positive. For Ogun, snake is a symbol of his power.

"Sometimes if you happen to be going to a farm, and you see a snake running across the street, it might mean somebody in the family is going to die. And sometimes if you are looking for a baby, and you sleep with your woman, and you have a dream of a snake, the baby is going to be a boy. We have all these concepts.

"Snake is like Ogun, both negative and positive, but the fish is always good. The fish is a symbol of fertility."

When the fish means fertility and the snake means death, they shape a symbolic antinomy, clarifying through human life and death the opposition of good and evil in all of existence. Osun, then, would seem to oppose Ogun. But pure difference is not Prince's point. Powers mix. The orisas—the deities—are related, he says, their forces mingle in reality. Osun, in his view, is the goddess of fertility, a healer, wholly positive (nos. 8–10). She exists—in Prince, in the universe—in relation to Sango and Ogun (chapters 3, 12–13). Like his symbol, the snake, Ogun is positive and negative. The god of iron, he empowers the smiths who hammer out the weapons of death and forge the farmer's tools that coax life from the soil. Ogun's priestess, wrapped in the god's power (see no. 17), calls upon Osun when healing is her task. Divine powers combine. In Prince's new painting of Iyaogun, the snake threatens death, but it means power, the power that will draw from Osun the blessing of life (no. 1).

Prince pictured this blend of powers more intensely in a painting from 1984—figure 18.4 in Henry Drewal's *Sacred Waters*—which meshed Osun and Iyaogun into a mermaid with snakes for hair, the bountiful hair possibly inspired by an image of Mami Wata (see no. 10). Powers combine, and Prince's new painting of Ogun's priestess rising from Osun's water—a fine instance of his craft and thought—provides a bridge to the pictures of Osun that are the most common sacred icons in his repertory (nos. 8–10).

8

Osun

Ink on paper. 4½" x 17". Osogbo, c. 1980

Prince's artistic career began with pen and ink, then, at Ulli Beier's suggestion, he turned to etching (chapters 8, 13). His sensibility remains linear, every painting builds on draftsmanship (chapter 1), and this piece is an instance of the "pen-and-ink, black-and-white work" he enjoys. We found it among the sodden papers in his Osogbo home. Cut at some point from a larger picture, it shows the river goddess as a mermaid, the form he normally gives her, the form she takes on the badges worn by pilgrims at the Osun Festival. The drawing, though, is unusual. It was inspired by the sculpture Susanne Wenger made for Osun's shrine at Osogbo, which, with some help from Prince, she worked to restore (chapter 15). Prince explains:

"This is an influence of Susanne Wenger.

"I went to the shrine that day with some guests. They come to visit my art gallery in Osogbo, and I took them to the shrine; that was a regular thing that I usually do.

"So, when we came back in the evening, I have food, and we were drinking. And I think one of the white guys was asking me: he would like to see how I work. Then I put the paper down, and when I sketched it, the influence of everything we saw in the afternoon were still in my mind. And I was thinking about: when Susanne Wenger is no more alive, will anyone preserve all the work that she did on the shrine. But by the time I was thinking about that happening, I made this drawing.

"So, if you look, the face here, and the tiny hands, are Susanne Wenger influence.

"She is wearing a wrapper, and she is having a basket containing some things she want to throw into the river. It's Osun, another kind of Osun.

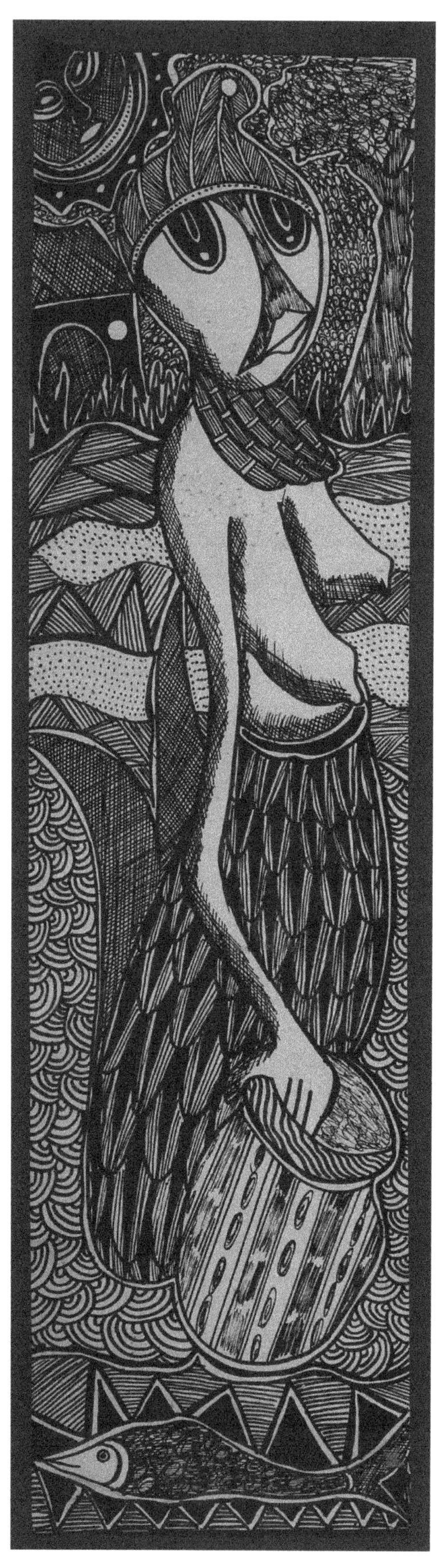

No. 8. *Osun.* c.1980

"But I don't usually make faces like this. This is Susanne Wenger influence. You see, part of the breast look like a big fish, and it doesn't have much neck because there's a lot of, like, cowrie things around its neck.

"This is Susanne Wenger influence. Which is not very common in my work. I don't always remember other people's work."

Prince has commented on the formal influences: the moderne face and sinuous, thin arms. The picture also departs from his norm, and meets Susanne Wenger's European style, in its shift to the visual: the shading, the tail's position, and the wistful turning of her head more than her body. Neither frontal nor profiled in Prince's usual way, she takes on a poignant, palpable reality, seeming to be both the goddess and her priestess—the priestess who wears a wrapper and carries offerings for Osun to the river (no. 20). In Prince's usual rendition of Osun, she holds the fish of fertility as a symbol of her power, paralleling Ogun's snake (nos. 6–7, 17) and Sango's axe (no. 11), but in this more earthly image, the natural contours of her breasts only suggest the fish that swims in the river beneath her, waiting for the offerings that will spill from her basket.

This Osun has appeared as a mermaid, an iconic form that probably entered Africa from the Mediterranean. The mermaid, the siren who lures mariners to destruction, is usually depicted in Europe, Africa, and the Americas as beautiful, voluptuous, and impossibly enticing. In Brazil, where she is generally imaged as a woman, not a mermaid, Osun is beautiful, flirtatious, and vain; her color is gold, a golden mirror is her symbol. William Bascom called Osun the Yoruba Venus, beguiling in appearance. Nothing in Prince's conception conflicts with all this, but as an initiate in her cult, his knowledge is deep, and he does not associate Osun with beauty, but with fertility, healing, prosperity, and peace. She is a river, and Prince chooses the form of a mermaid to bring her into visibility, just as she does. I asked why, and he said:

"Osun is a mermaid because she is a female goddess that come from the water.

"She is a human being first, but not a human being as such. She came from the water to become wife of Sango. But she's a woman with *large* ear."

Now Prince tells an abbreviated version of the story he told me two years earlier (transcribed in chapter 3), relating how she cut her ear into Sango's soup, how Sango preferred her food, how a jealous junior wife learned her secret and told Sango:

"So, he called her to his room, and as they were romantically playing, he untied her headtie.

"And the ears flipped down. One was halfly cut, and the other one was still long.

"And Osun get to know that somebody have divulged her secret.

"Then she fell down and became a river.

"But before that she was like a native doctor. She learned about herbs. She helped people to get pregnant. So, after she became a river, the people started singing, crying about the good things she has been doing.

"And then she tell them, If you continue worshiping me, I will continue to provide children, good luck to you. That's how they started worshiping Osun.

"And anytime she want to come, part of her body would be fish, would be in the water. And they would see the flesh side of her, but not just anybody can see *her*. You have to be a member of the cult, or to be a devotee.

"That's why I was able to bring her form out in different forms. Sometimes I give her two tails, sometimes I make her an invisible one that can swim away."

Osun is a river. She takes form as a mermaid, and Prince, her devotee, pictures her as a mermaid (with none of her charming, seductive encumbrances from European folklore). In the pen-and-ink drawing inspired by Susanne Wenger's sculpture, she has a woman's torso and the tail of a fish, but as Prince says at the end, he often gives her more complicated forms, like those that follow (nos. 9–10).

9

Rainbow Wealth Goddess

Ink, pastel, and oil on canvas. 33" x 55½". Osogbo, 1989

Generally Prince gives his paintings evocative titles for public consumption and reserves specific Yoruba names for conversational explanation and reference: the *Smelling Ghost* (no. 2) is Ologbonkian; the *Longneck King of Birds* (no.3) is Ogongo; the *Dancing Spirit* (no. 4) is Sigidi; the *Golden Bird* (chapter 14, p. 201) is Alokolobo; the *Masked Snake Charmer* (no. 17) is Abore; the *Foolish Elephant* (no. 13) is Erin; the *Mother Monkey* (chapter 1, p. 22) is Edun. The clear exception lies in pictures Prince made for himself, not the public: *Iyaogun* (no. 6), *Osun* (no. 8). Images of Osun are most often titled *The Goddess of Fertility*, but here she is the *Rainbow Wealth Goddess*, a title that stresses her gift of wealth rather than health.

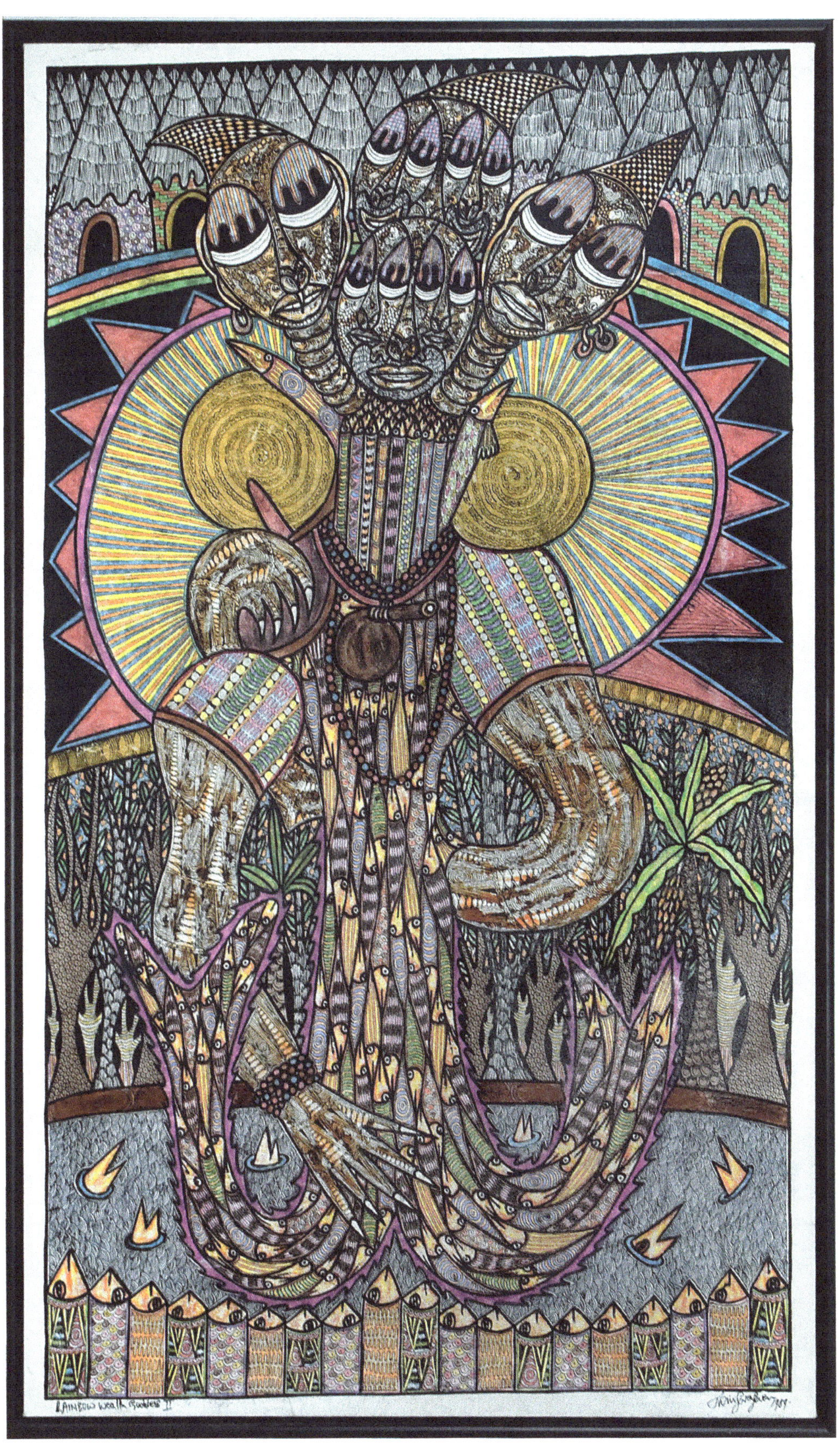

No. 9. *Rainbow Wealth Goddess.* 1989

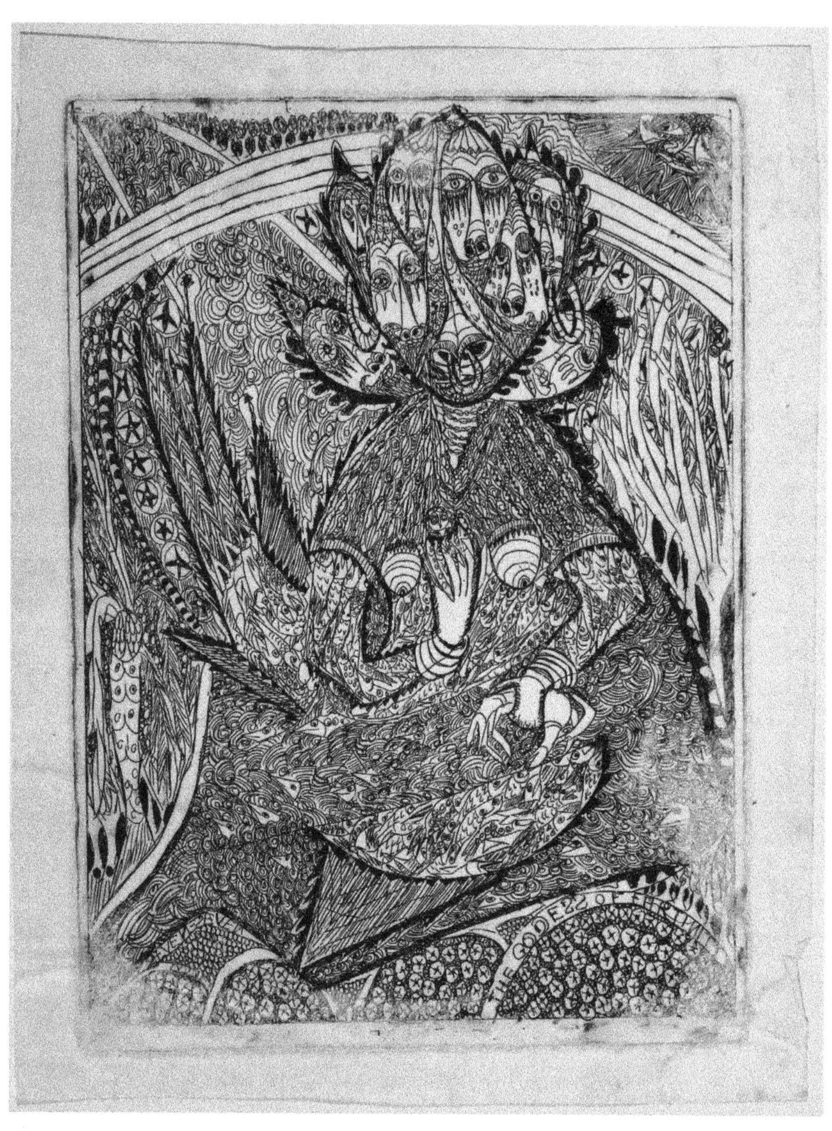

The Goddess of Fertility.
Etching. 8¾" x 12". Sydney, 1985.
Other impressions of this plate appear in Ulli Beier's *A Dreaming Life,* plate 13, and reversed in Henry Drewal's *Sacred Waters,* figure 18.3

The exhibition *Il ritorno dei maghi,* held in Orvieto, Italy, in 2000, included a sculpture's painting by Prince, dated 1969 and titled *Rainbow Goddess.* It shows an elongated Osun as a mermaid, holding two fish, her body composed of fish, a thick rainbow arcing behind her head. She has but one, and Prince first gave her many heads and a rainbow in a small etching from 1985. Prince followed this etching with a painting for the Fopma family of Amsterdam, then increased the color and brought the idea to perfection in the painting on the previous page. He thought it was from 1986, but it is dated 1989. Prince explains it:

"This is Osun with four major faces. You have a face during the rainy season. You have a face during dry season. You have a face for each weather: rainy season, dry season, muggy weather season, and when it is not raining but a lot of clouds, a time when you have a lot of whirlwinds, what you call hurricanes here.

"She always comes like multiples of small fishes—*thousands* of fishes glued together and form her. And at that time, the rainbow will appear in the sky. That was when we believed she come to bathe. But after she finish, and she want to go away, everything would just go. Dissolve. Like when you put soap, how it dissolve. Or like when you have stomach trouble, there is a special medicine you put in the water—like that."

It is basic to Prince's understanding that Osun is not a mermaid; she is a river, and the river's fish swarm to give her form. In his novel *Simbi and the Satyr of the Dark Jungle*, Amos Tutuola imagined a building constructed of birds who fly into architectural form, hold steady while the building is used, and then fly away, leaving nothing but air. Tutuola's image catches the mystery of the seen and unseen, and that is how Prince thinks of Osun. She is water, eternally flowing, taking visible shape only when the fish, her devotees, assemble. The shape she takes is that of a mermaid, so that is how Prince, her devotee, draws her. In the relatively naturalistic image inspired by Susanne Wenger's sculpture, her body is flesh, her tail is scaled, as in European mermaids (no. 8), but in Prince's usual depiction, her tail is clearly a fusion of fish, as it is in this painting, and though in most of his paintings she seems to be flesh above and fish below (see the images of *The Goddess of Fertility*, pp. 56, 289), her form is, in fact, always created entirely of fish: her hair, her eyes, her fingers—everything. Prince told me it is hard to represent this reality with the artist's tools, and usually he does not try, but he managed it in the next painting (no. 10). Fish swarm to give her momentary form, then disperse, while she, a river, flows on forever.

This painting makes plain that when the fish congregate and she appears, the world is altered: the seasons change, a rainbow arcs in the sky. Her power is great, expansive. "She has long arms," Prince says, "to stretch out, to connect to women and children." Prince continues the meteorological theme, pointing to the circles that surround her shoulders, "like a cape," and radiate, bristling with triangles that are flashes of light, "just like this kind of parking lights." He says:

"And then these represent the wind that blow after. These represent the wind, like the one you have here, you call tornado. But we don't have tornado there; we do have some beautiful whirlwinds. They can uproot the trees too. But don't act so dangerous like yours.

"Because when the wind was blowing, that the fishes would go in the water, and go away.

"So, my own imagination is all these heads. Originally it was supposed to come with only one head with different faces. I've done them a series of heads. There is some I did with cowrie shells covering the face. You see what I mean?"

I do: Prince, like the fish, gives form to Osun. They swarm; he meditates and dips from the deeps of his understanding as an initiate in her cult when he paints. Prince pauses, and I ask about Osun's double tail. It reminds me of a motif common in Yoruba traditional art, in which a figure's legs are replaced with rubbery, upcurled mudfish. William Fagg noted a formal resemblance to Meriterranean motifs—it could be, like the mermaid, a borrowing from Europe, designed to capture a native idea in a foreign form—and Fagg located the mudfish figure in the powerful Ogboni society of Yorubaland, saying it is called Onile and could represent Olokun, the sea deity, with whom Prince joins Osun in the next painting (no. 10). Prince laughs when I ask about the split tail and says, "Because she stand on those two tails. That is the imagination of an artist who think too much."

In the Yoruba manner (chapter 17), Prince's composition is unified vertically and divided horizontally. As in *Kissing Birds* (chapter 1), *Dancing Spirits* (no. 4), and *The Ritualist at the Osun Festival* (no. 20), a vertical unity is superimposed on a background broken horizontally into zones. Three of the zones correspond to those of Prince's painting of Osun's priestess (no. 20). At the bottom lies a fish-rich river. Prince says:

"That's my imaginative feeling: fish singing praises to her, coming out of the water. The fish at the bottom raising up to praise Osun.

"That's the River Osun. And there's trees around the water.

"At the top, the village is representing when everybody is asleep. And there's no light. You don't expect this kind of goddess to come out when there is so much noise. It's only when the place is quiet.

"That represent humanity. Because most of the time I don't want people to think I only see animals and beasts and ghosts."

Prince has given us one key to understanding his work. The spiritual figures stand vertically in front. Behind them, the background spreads horizontally with round thatched houses (no. 25) or with staring faces (chapter 14, p. 201, and nos. 3, 20). Both represent "humanity"—humankind massed into what Prince calls an "unnoticed crowd" (chapter 14, p. 201, and no. 21). I asked Prince what he meant by his term, and he said:

"I call it unnoticed crowd—unnoticed crowd because the goddess doesn't care about those people behind her. It is we who care about her.

"She only care about being there, listening to prayer."

Prince pictures division. The foreground figure does not care about humanity in the mass. The acrobats perform, bent on their tasks, without regard for the audience (no. 21): the artist creates without caring about the market. The god is a god, the spirit a spirit, in a world separated from the one filled with people (no. 11). But the goddess listens for the prayers that go from our world to hers, crossing the border between the seen and unseen, and this world's creatures divide. Her devotees at the bottom rise, sing her praises, and she appears to them, while the mass of humanity at the top remains unenlightened, unseeing. Framed by the zones at the bottom and top, this painting's division is not between deities and people, but between the devotees who join the goddess, who pray to her, who are awake to spiritual power, and the rest of the people who slumber in darkness.

Like every artistic, political, or religious performance, rituals for Osun (chapter 15) call some people into participation, leave others in the dark, dividing society into factions, cohorts, groups. In this painting, Osun's group is symbolized by fish, but in *The Ritualist at the Osun Festival* (no. 20), a zone opens between the river and the forest, shoving the forest up to the village and filling with devotees in human form. While the rest of humanity dozes in the village above (set deep in the distance by vertical perspective: nos. 11, 20), Osun's people gather, preparing for the festival, ready to offer their prayers to the goddess, as the fish have already begun to do.

Their prayers will bring them earthly boons: fertility, health, and prosperity. In this painting, Osun's promise (and Prince's prayer) is for wealth; its sign is the narrow rainbow that crosses behind her heads, beneath the dark village. When I asked him to explain the rainbow, Prince said:

"We have the belief that the python, when she form her eggs, and whenever she does that, there will be sort of shower rain, and the sun will appear, and when it shines on the eggs, the reflection of it is what show in the sky as a rainbow.

"That is what comes to the sky.

"It is only somebody that have powerful medicine that can go near it. If they can get it, they can turn into a very very rich person. *If* they can get it. I don't think it is so easy to get it," he laughs.

"Or, the rainbow happens when Osun is taking a bath.

"Or, sometimes it might be in a lake that a big tortoise—tortoise has over fifty years of age—can bring a rainbow too. By rolling out of the lake.

"You know, most of these reptiles that live in the water, sometimes they come out to take fresh air, when there is nobody around to disturb them. They will swim out; part of their body is in the lake, and maybe they need air. Snake does that. Big fish, too, does that."

When the sun shines on the python's eggs, when a creature surfaces in sweet water (as Osun does), when the fish assemble and Osun takes a bath, a rainbow appears in the sky. The rainbow connects Osun with the fish, the tortoise, and the python, and when it swings color over the heavens, the one who finds the python's eggs and the one who prays to Osun, as the fish do, will be rewarded with wealth. Through these connections, the Goddess of Fertility becomes the Rainbow Wealth Goddess. Here it is a rainbow; in the next painting (no. 10), Osun's signs are a calabash and a cowrie shell.

10
Mami Wata and the God

Black ink and tinted ink on canvas, glued to canvas. 5' x 3'. Philadelphia, 2005

In conversation, Prince titles every image of the goddess both *Osun* and *The Goddess of Fertility*, but not wanting to seem repetitious, he gives the same subject many titles. They lead, along with the complexity of his forms, to fanciful interpretations by scholars, which make internal sense but frequently stray far from his intent.

Here Prince calls Osun "Mami Wata." Henry Drewal has edited two new volumes, *Mami Wata* and *Sacred Waters* (both containing pictures by Prince), that provide an abundance of information about Mami Wata. Disparate phenomena are brought together by the name, Mami Wata (Mammy Water), and by two images. One is the usual international mermaid, the other is a female snake charmer with a glorious spray of hair; it began as a chromolithograph in Germany in the eighteen-eighties, which was reprinted in India and distributed through Africa. The new name and new images, often combined in a snaky mermaid, were applied to the old water spirits in Africa and the diaspora, and they were employed in a twentieth-century prosperity cult, driven by the anxieties of modernization. When Prince's Osun takes form as a mermaid and associates with a snake and a rainbow—as Oxumaré does in Brazil—she connects to the Mami Wata whose devotees wear white and pray for wealth. But Osun separates from the Mami Wata who is like a European mermaid: fair, vain, erotic, seductive, and destructive. When Mami Wata lures people to watery graves

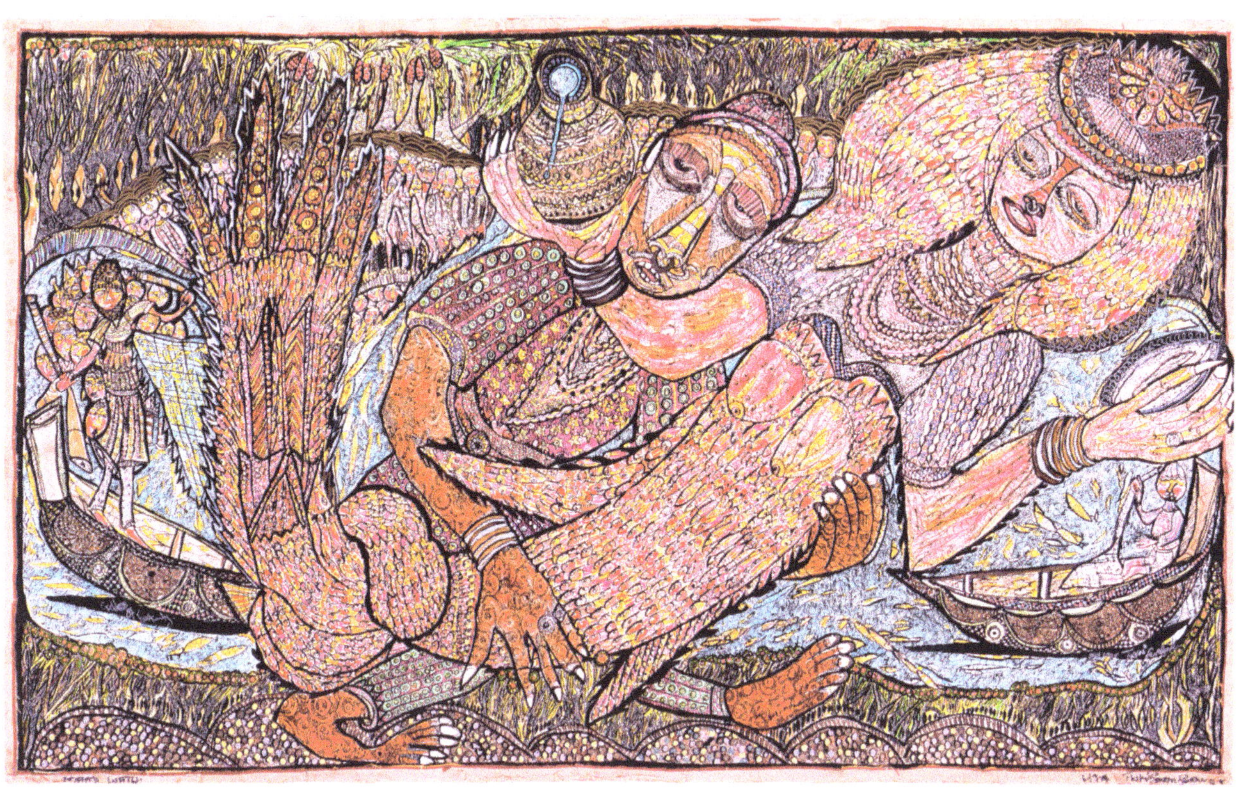

No. 10. *Mami Wata and the God.* 2005

or requires her followers to remain childless, when Mami Wata is male or the queen of the sea, she is no longer like Osun whose prime gift is fertility, children aplenty, and who is a goddess of the sweet, running water, distinct in Prince's mind from Olokun, the male deity of the deep sea.

For Prince, that is, Mami Wata is not more or less than another name for Osun. Others in Yorubaland use the name, and use it for Prince's pictures of Osun. He rarely does, but at the request of a friend, a pretty African American woman, Prince named this Osun "Mami Wata." He prefers the title *Olokun and Goddess of Wealth*, but feels stuck with the title he gave the picture while he was painting. It depicts Olokun, the god of the ocean, protecting Osun when her sweet water flows into the salt sea. Prince describes it:

"This shows the Goddess of Fertility. It is Mami Wata and the God.

"This is the creator. This is Olokun, Olokun the god of ocean, and the Mami Wata. And this was done with only ink, only ink; different color of ink is all I used to do this painting. No oil, nothing.

"The man on the boat"—to the left—"is the one who happen to see this happen. You know, fisherman when they are on the sea, there are so many things they can see. There are so many imaginative, unbelievable things *happening*. Sometimes they see *big snakes* in the ocean, or big whales, or something. Other people may not see it. Because they are always on the sea.

"It is like somebody who drove car all the time; he would be seeing car accidents and all that."

Again Prince divides humanity into people who see and do not see, into those who know, who believe, and those who abide in doubt and darkness (no. 9). He continues:

"The fisherman who see this thing: Olokun bringing the goddess—you can even see she was holding the calabash that contains the water of wealth.

"This is the type of Mami Wata that comes in tiny fishes. Millions of them form this shape. And when it want to disappear, the fishes will just go. Disappear.

"And she is holding here a big cowrie, eyowo-nla. This represent money.

"If I don't call it Mami Wata, it is supposed to be Goddess of Wealth: Olokun and Goddess of Wealth.

"The fish make her form. And when she want to go away, they will spread. Even when you look at the ocean, sometimes you can see this kind of thing. I've seen it myself: in some of the exploring channel on TV they show what is under the sea. Sometimes you can see

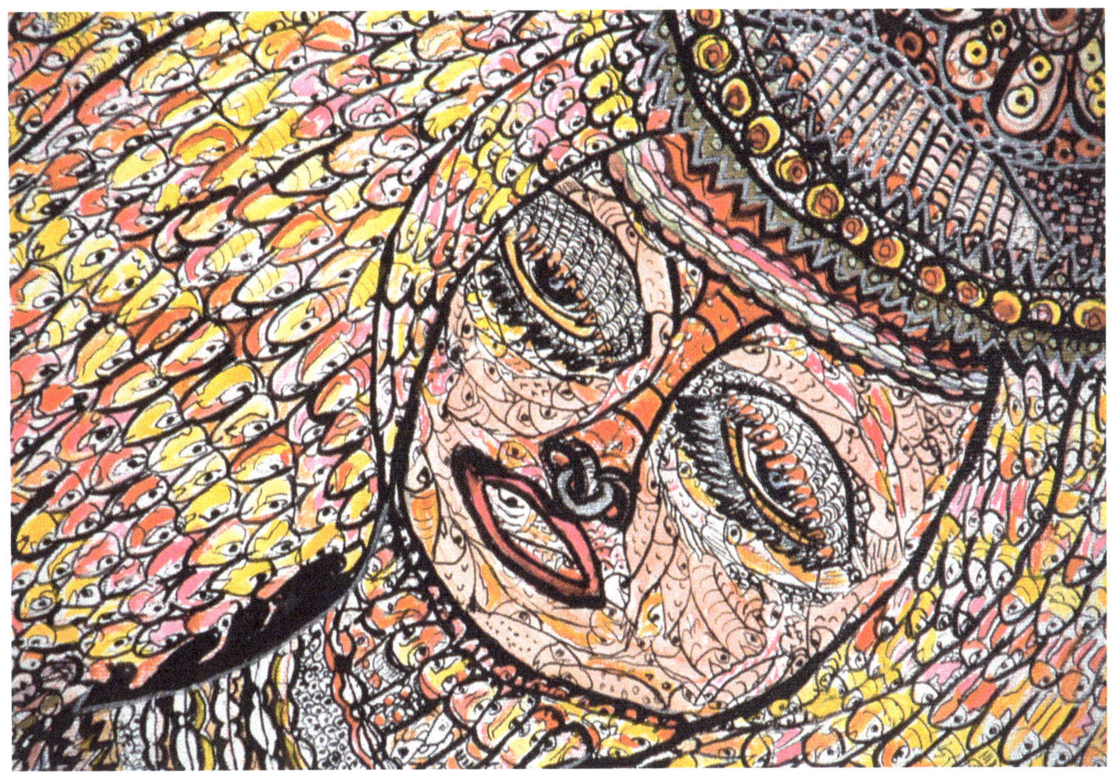

Osun. Detail from *Mami Wata and the God*

millions of tiny fishes swimming in one direction. Sometimes they can form like a ball, and sometimes they just: *wishoooo.*

"The fish come together and form her, and Olokun is carrying this object, this Mami Wata.

"Even her face, her fingers, even her hands—all fish. This is Osun. She has gone out in ocean from river and Olokun is protecting her. Olokun Jeniade, the god that wear crown of money.

"And you see this one doesn't have any rainbow. Instead of rainbow appear, that's why you have the Olokun Jeniade, the father of all the ocean people."

This time, taking his time, Prince has drawn Osun to make it clear that, a mermaid in form, she is entirely composed of fish. Instead of a rainbow (no. 9), Osun's calabash filled with the water of wealth, her gigantic cowrie—*eyowo-nla* in Yoruba—and the presence of Olokun Jeniade, crowned with cash, serve as signs of prosperity to those who pray. Prince's painting is a prayer (chapter 17), offered in 2005 when he was recovering from financial distress (chapter 14).

11
Sango and Traditional Musicians

Ink, batik dye, pastel, and oil on cloth. 33½" x 49½". Osogbo, 1994

"This about Sango, god of thunder; that's him with the bata drummers. This at the time when Nigerian journalists were writing about me, that I'm painting for the white people, that I didn't do realistic drawings.

"I'm trying to please them, to show I can do realistic drawings."

That is what Prince said to explain this unusual painting. It is "not so scary," he said, there are no weird eyes, because white people like frightening images but Nigerians do not. For Prince's work, the drawing is relatively "realistic." At the top of the pyramid, Sango raises his double-bitted axe of ambivalent, twinned power (see chapters 15, 17). Though he is pictured frontally, like the figure beneath him who faces out while his feet point in, Sango lifts a leg in danced motion. The musicians in traditional Yoruba attire move too, shifting from static frontality, some making the quarter turn that is, in Prince's work, a sure sign of a slide along the mimetic scale toward the visual (no. 8). There are hints of vanishing-point perspective in the group at the bottom, the houses at the top, but, as in Turkish, Persian, and Indian miniature paintings, depth in the forward plane is established primarily by verticality (see also nos. 4, 9, 20). It is instructive that Prince intended this move toward European realism to appeal, not to Europeans who were excited by modernism, but to Nigerians who were bent on becoming modern (chapters 6, 9, 18).

The technique is also unusual. By taping the big figures, Prince prevented color from bleeding into the white field beneath their feet. The lines are exceptionally crisp: the god and his entourage are laid over a ground filled with black-on-white drawings—"the way I do my etching," he said. Sango dances in Orun. On another plane, the quotidian world fractures into tiny vignettes of precolonial village life: round thatched houses, men, women, and children, a schoolboy, people pounding yams, musicians, dancers, masquerades, statues in the traditional Yoruba style, small animals, and big birds who are witches. In this painting, the two worlds, reality's simultaneous dimensions, do not connect, but in many of his paintings they do: people, gods, and spirits occupy a single setting (nos. 3, 10), or the tiny figures, here confined to the background, swim into the picture to cover the bodies with minuscule tattooing (nos. 22–23, 29).

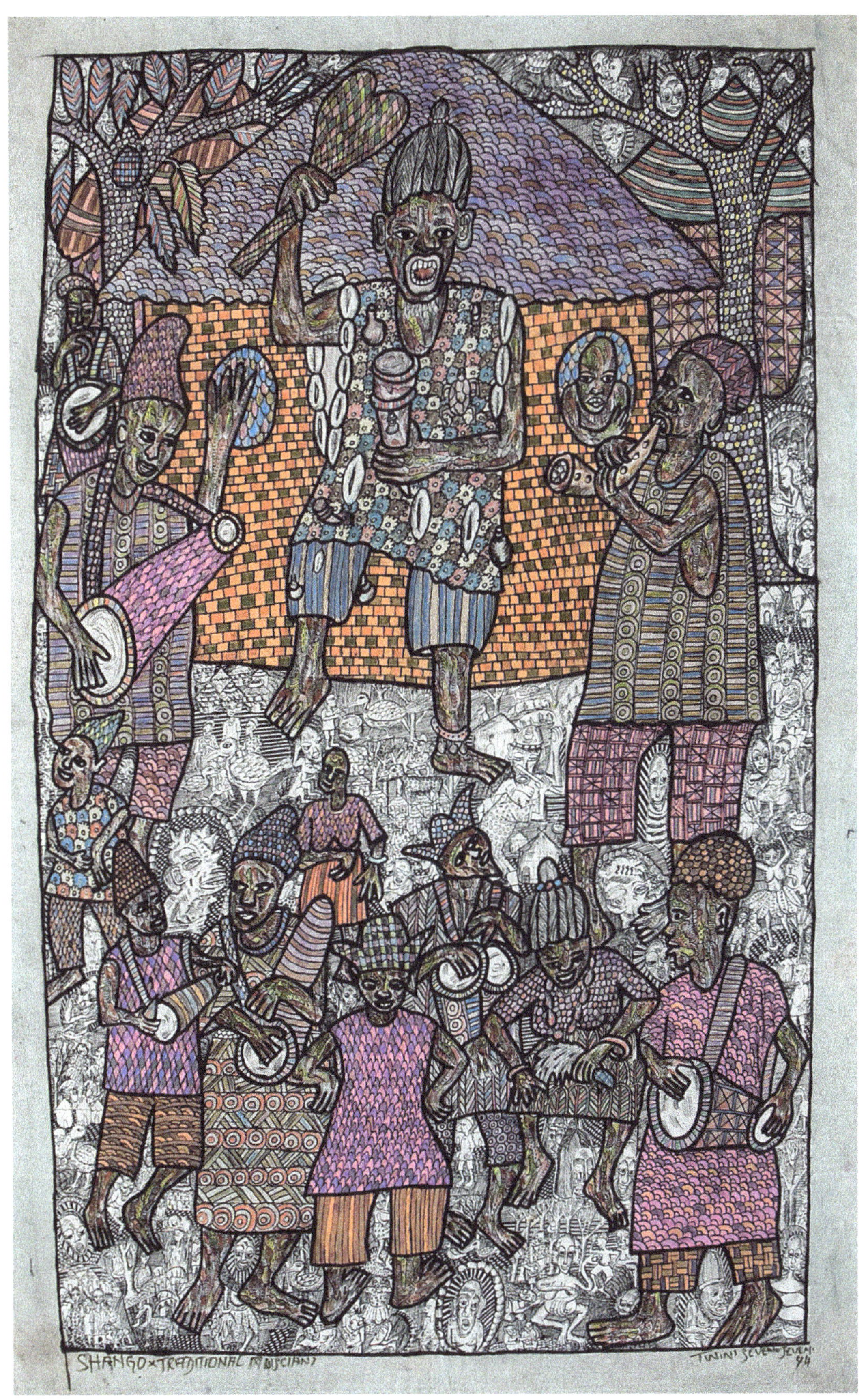

No. 11. *Sango and Traditional Musicians.* 1994

Performing in *Sango* for a Nigerian audience, Prince pulled the figures toward realism, eliminated the startlingly strange, and made his piece an exhibit of excellent craft (chapters 9, 16). In Western terms, though, it remains far from realism, and, conceptual in plan, it unfolds from Yoruba precepts and experiences.

12

The Father of Beasts and His Family Grazing

Ink and watercolor on paper, glued to a board painted black. 21¾" x 31¾". Osogbo, c. 1972

Grazing Elephants, Prince said, could be another title for this picture. It shows elephants "moving from one place that there is not enough food," grazing as they go, in search of sustenance. Prince had told me that his great-grandfather, his "father" Osuntoki, followed his grazing herd to Ibadan, where his cattle found food and he became king (chapter 3). Elephants, for Prince, symbolize kings. Of this painting, he said:

"I used to call elephant the Father of Beasts. It is a reference to power. Power. Because elephant represent *power*. That when somebody is a king, and he is ruling with iron fists, because he has the imaginative thinking of being untouchable. You know, the elephant is so powerful that you cannot push him."

Thinking of other paintings by Prince, I ask if this could be a mother with twins. No, he said, this is a leader with his followers, a great king protecting his people while they hunt for food:

"The big elephant is powerful over the other elephants, and he protect them.

"I call it The Father of Beasts and His Family Grazing."

Later Prince explained this unusually naturalistic painting:

"Let me tell you the truth. You know what I want to use this for? I want to use it for a record jacket. Erin Jo Gun Ola is a song that I wrote. Erin Jo Gun Ola means: The elephant inherited the position of honor among all the animals. That was the title of the music I was writing, and this particular drawing was meant to be used for the sleeve; you know, the old plates, the big ones, not the CD.

"This what you call drawing from the back. Drawing from the back. You have a mirror. You take a roller, like when you do woodcuts; the thing you apply black ink on the woodcut.

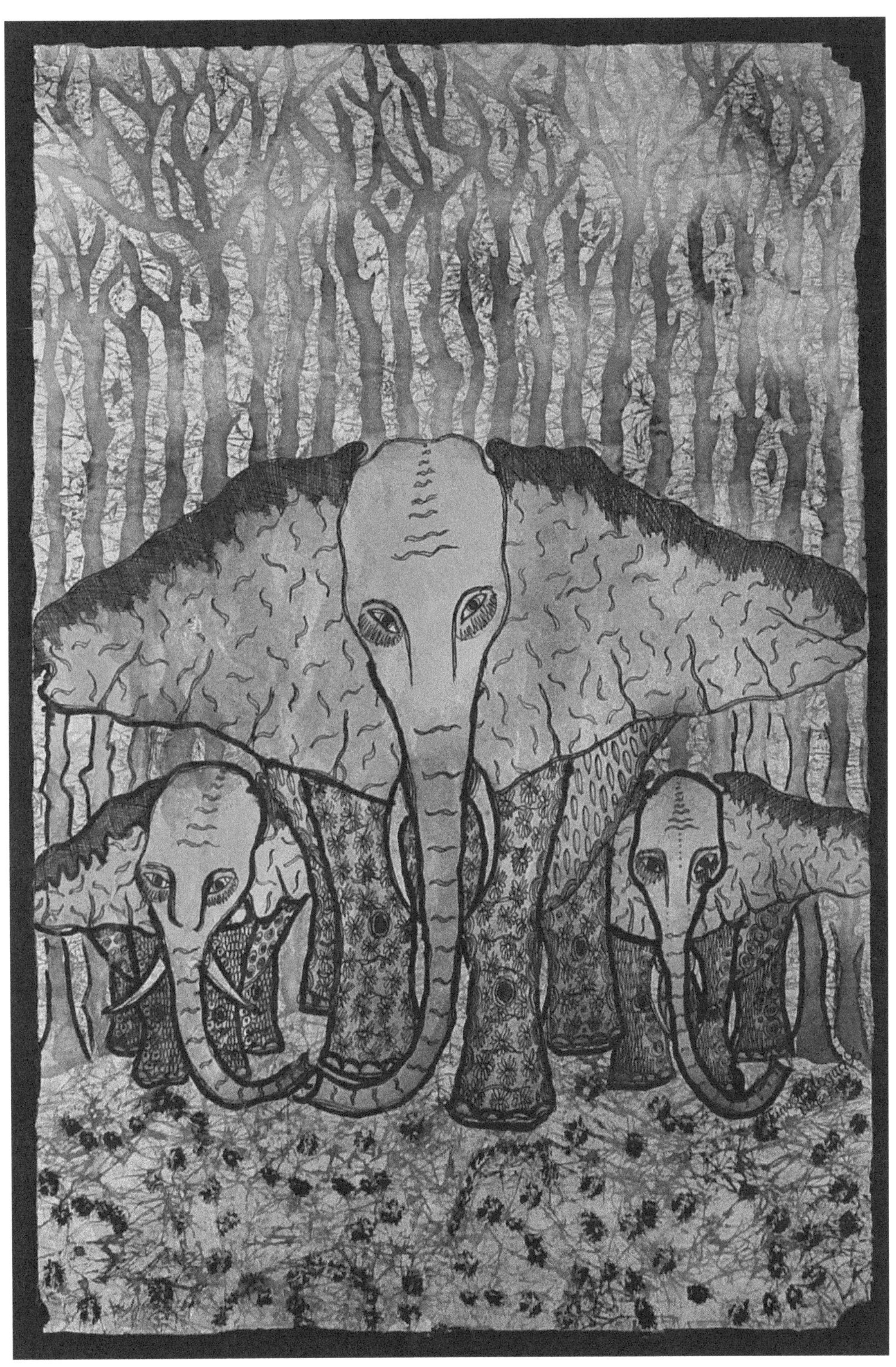

No. 12. *The Father of Beasts and His Family Grazing.* c. 1972

You push your roller on the glass. Fill it up. Then I pick a small broom straw or toothpick, and make a drawing here. And then take paper, put on it, rub it, and when you lift the paper, the drawing you put on the mirror will copy itself to the paper.

"Then when it dry, I come and use tiny drawing pens to rearrange the edges, so the paper can come out much better. It is drawing from the back.

"You see why I do this: it would make it more commercial. Some Africans may not want to have my paintings at the back of the jacket. That's why this one was done in a way whereby it do not look too scary.

"It is more realistic, and more simple."

As with the painting of Sango (no. 11), Prince pulled this picture toward realism to please the Nigerian consumer. An abstraction from the visual, a view from the front, it establishes one end of Prince's representational range. His midpoint, his representational norm, shifts toward the conceptual and fixes in the iconic profile (chapter 17), seen in the elephant he painted on the door of his house in Ogidi, in 1965, the elephants in *Kissing Birds* (chapter 1), and the elephant in *Dream of an Elephant Tusk Hunter* (no. 15). Farther from the visual—imaginative and conceptual—is the elephant in the next painting (no. 13), a two-legged creature, symbolized into elephantness (into royalty) with tusks and a trunk.

13

Mr. Tortoise, the Betrayer, and the Foolish Elephant

Ink, watercolor, and oil on wood, a sculpture's painting of two layers. 21¾" x 22½". Osogbo, 1989

Prepared for an exhibition of his work at the Taidemuseo, Hameenlinna, Finland, in 1991, this is one of a set of small, squarish sculpture's paintings that also includes *Elephant and Mr. Baboon*, reproduced in chapter 9, p. 128. Signed conspicuously—Twins Seven-Seven, Art Man Gallery, Box 68 Osogbo—and formerly titled *Elephant Playing Drum for Other Animals*, this painting illustrates one of the stories Prince learned from his mother in which animals exhibit human traits to guide children toward moral behavior (chapter 17). Prince explained:

"It is a painting with mythical thinking about the story of when the king was sick and they want the elephant heart.

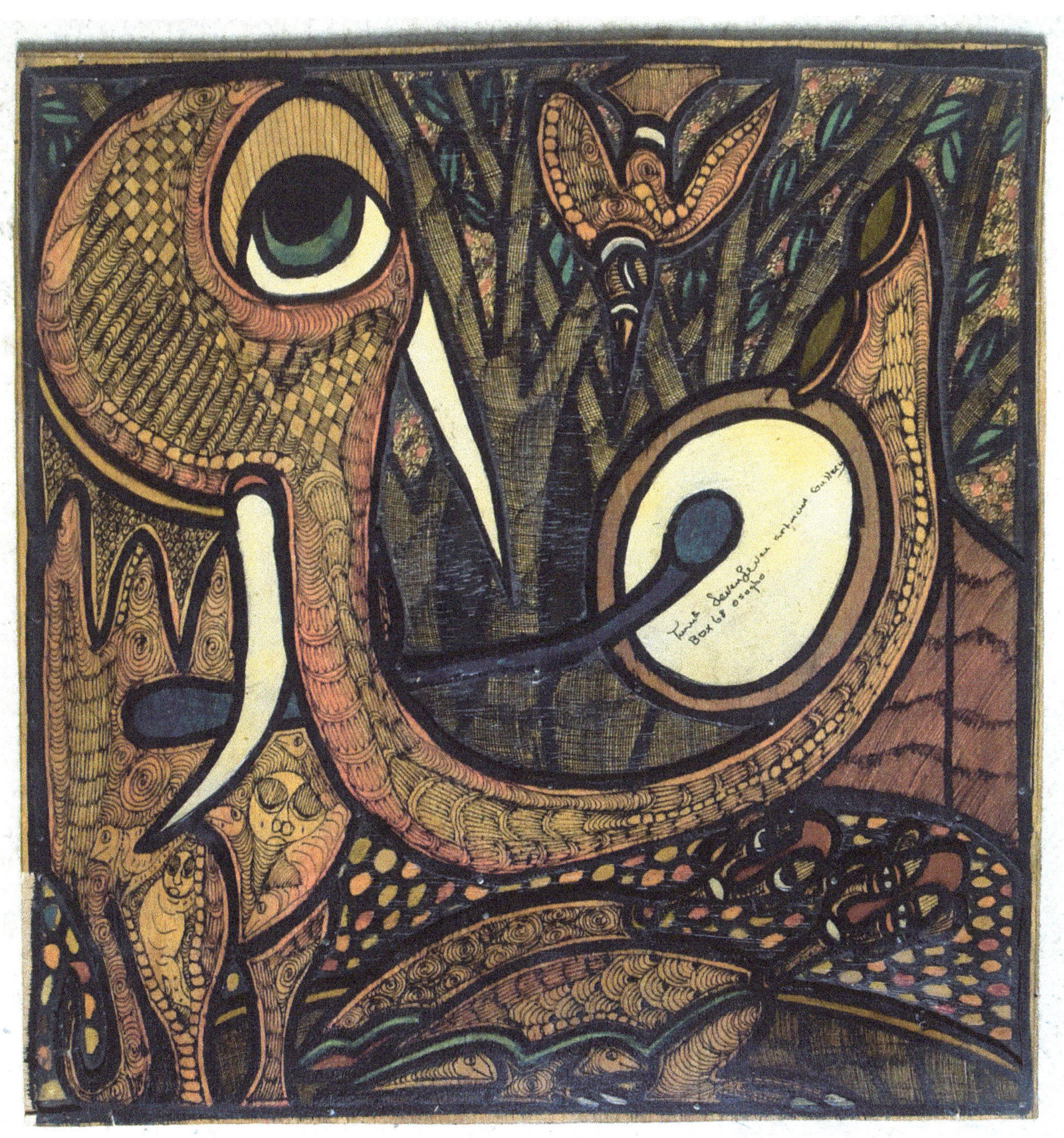

No. 13. *Mr. Tortoise, the Betrayer, and the Foolish Elephant.* 1989

"And the tortoise trick the elephant, and they going to make him king of all the human being. Already they have already made a big hole on the floor and cover it with carpet.

"And as soon as the elephant come to the carpet, he will fall down. Like a trap.

"But now the elephant was so surprised about the drumming of the people who came to visit him. So this is why the elephant hear the talking drum they use to bring him, and the bird were singing along with those people who came to visit him.

"So, it's called Ao Merin Joba: We Make the Elephant Be King: Ao Merin Joba. That's the name in Yoruba."

Prince points to the figures, to the singing bird above the drum, then to the pair below:

"And this the tortoise that want to fool him in coming. And this, the elephant, is dreaming how he will be ruling human being and other animals."

Narrators both report stories in referential synopsis and perform them fully with commitment. Prince has sketched his tale, but such stories in performance take cante-fable form, enlivened by passages of song, and eight months later, at my request, he told the whole tale:

"At the king's palace, the oba, and the crowd, and the palace jesters, chiefs, women, youth leaders, etcetera—in a big festival mood in the village. Then the oba consulted the Ifa priest. When the oba consulted the Ifa priest, he was told if he wanted to live long, for a long, long life, he must find a way to have a lively elephant, and have the heart, and eat it.

"Originally, you know, when somebody become an oba—you know, if I'm an oba today, if I die, they will remove my heart, keep it someplace secret in the palace. So, when another person come, want to take my position, he will *eat* my own heart. Then you ask him, What have you done? Then he will say, I have eat another oba. Then he become very powerful. Then they look at him as a special man.

"That's why they give such honor to the kings. It's a genuine situation; it's not gainsaying. It's not speculation. It will happen till tomorrow, till tomorrow.

"So, after consulting the Ifa priest, the oba was told he had to get a lively elephant, and get the heart, and eat it.

"Then, at the same time, all the animals in the forest in discussions of who will be king. Elephant, lion, every one of them, they want to be king of all the animals, but at the end of the day, it was the elephant that have the day.

"*Then*, at the oba's palace, the oba started getting sick. His life started getting deteriorated because he was trying to get the elephant heart, and he couldn't get. So, nobody can do anything about it.

"Then, they sent the hunters to the forest to go and bring—not kill him—bring an elephant. All the animals joined the elephant to throw away all the hunters. They came back without bringing an elephant home.

"Then, there is a young orphan boy in the village who volunteered to help them, because he has a small tortoise that he kept as a pet.

"And he talked to the tortoise.

"And the tortoise said, If you can promise that you will not ever, ever kill me in life, I will help the villagers.

"So, he went to the forest, and talked to the elephant, and told him he was sent by the people of the other village to bring all the animals. Because they would make elephant the king of all the human beings.

"Meanwhile, the animals were singing, praising the elephant, that one day he is going to become king of all the human being:

Erin karele kowajoba,
Erin karele kowajoba,

"Elephant, let's go home, so you will be installed as king.

"The tortoise was tricking the elephant to bring him back to the city, and all the animals were dancing and singing for him.

"And when he was coming, the elephant was coming, the people of the city see the elephant, and they sing:

Erin tide kowajoba,
Erin tide kowajoba.

"*But* they don't know how they are going to get the heart of the elephant. They don't know how they are going to kill the elephant because he is so huge.

"So, they asked the same young boy, who told them to make a special throne. Dig the *whole* grass and put very fragile branches of trees, and cover it with very expensive carpet.

"So, at the end, when Erin came to town—the elephant is called Erin—he was dancing with his hands up, and everyone was singing for him.

"And then he sat, and fell down.

"When the elephant dropped and fell into the trap, the sound of *poop*—everybody was running. Even the oba himself has run away. Because he scared them. And because the elephant drop into the big pit, he made a big *roar*, and everybody was running.

"Then the hunters who were brave enough started shooting.

"So, they kill him, and removed the heart, and give it to the king. And the king became very successful. And they used the other part of the meat for rituals.

"So, that's how they got him.

"That story was made to teach children not to be overambitious."

Since elephants symbolize royalty (nos. 12, 16), Prince identifies with the elephant whose fate in this story teaches children not to be overambitious. When Prince was at ambition's peak and he wore a red crown, he lost his balance, the Sango in him overcame the Osun in him, and things in his life began to fall apart (chapters 12–14).

14

He and She

Ink, pastel, acrylic, and oil on canvas. 30" x 48". Philadelphia, 2005

Having learned from his mother's stories how to employ animals metaphorically to reveal human values and predicaments (no. 13), Prince uses animals to depict indirectly incidents from his own life. Earlier he used this title for an image of a pair of affectionate birds. In this one, he portrays his wife Shola and himself as snakes. Prince said:

"This is a period I wanted to have affair with my wife. But she said, No. Because she felt we've already got too many children.

"And I came here"—to Material Culture—"and George told me, Can you make snakes?

"So then I do this drawing. It's called He and She. See that is me." Price points to the snake in front. "And that's my wife saying no." He points to the coiled snake in back.

"Look at the eggs down there.

"She is covering her thing, so I could not touch it, and she said, Look down there. We have so many eggs already.

"She makes it impossible.

"Because she felt we've got so many children already. I just call it He and She."

Prince has captured a tense, personal moment. She has withdrawn from him, coiled into herself. Half a year later, she, the love of his life, will leave him, take the boys and move to New York (chapter 16).

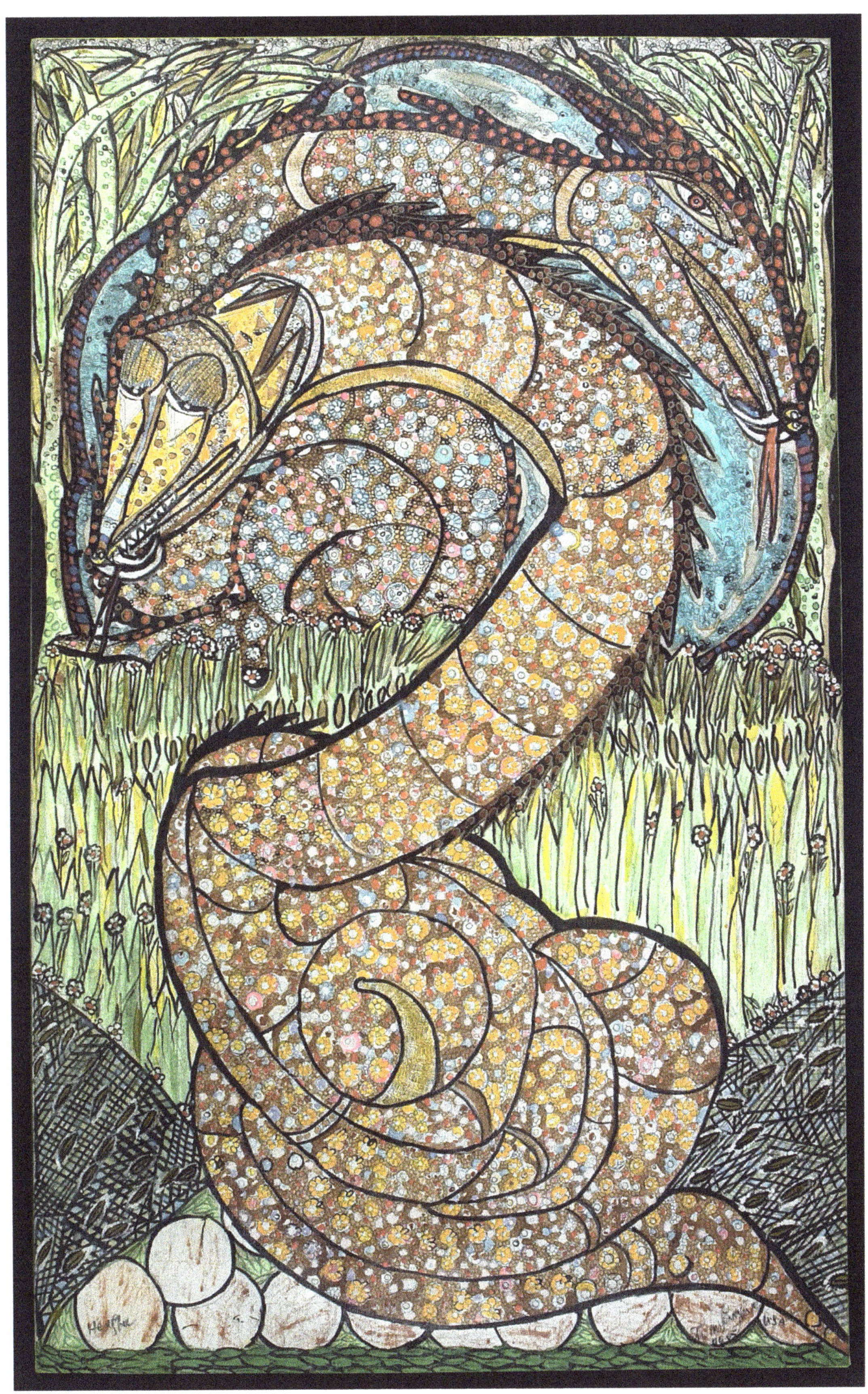

No. 14. *He and She.* 2005

15

Dream of an Elephant Tusk Hunter

Cut cloth, ink, pastel, and oil on canvas, glued on canvas. 5' x 3'. Philadelphia, 2005

In different techniques, Prince has created several images of elephants trampling hunters. The paintings display the weakness of human powers in relation to the powers of nature. At once the dream of an artist and the nightmare of a hunter who set out to lure elephants with fruit and kill them for the ivory of their tusks, this picture was described by Prince in these words:

"This is done with Ghana kente cloth. I was going around George's shop, and I saw these beautiful fabric. And George told me it is old, and he wanted to throw it away. So I said, Let me do something with it.

"So, I cut them in pieces. And I use it. And the painting is called Dream of Elephant Tusk Hunter."

Prince points to the man at the bottom:

"This is the collector here, being squashed by the elephant. Two elephants running after him. And in the basket you have fruits because elephant is eater of fruits. And the *wife* of the *hunter* is behind there, running with basket of fruit on her head.

"The collector is an African man. That's why you see tribal mark on his face. And that's why I give him hair braiding.

"And everything is done with the pieces of cloth, of fabric. Kente, kente cloth.

"This is fabric, very old Ghanaian kente fabric, or loom cloth, very old loom cloth, cut in pieces. There's oil paint; some places were finished with oil paint, pastel on canvas."

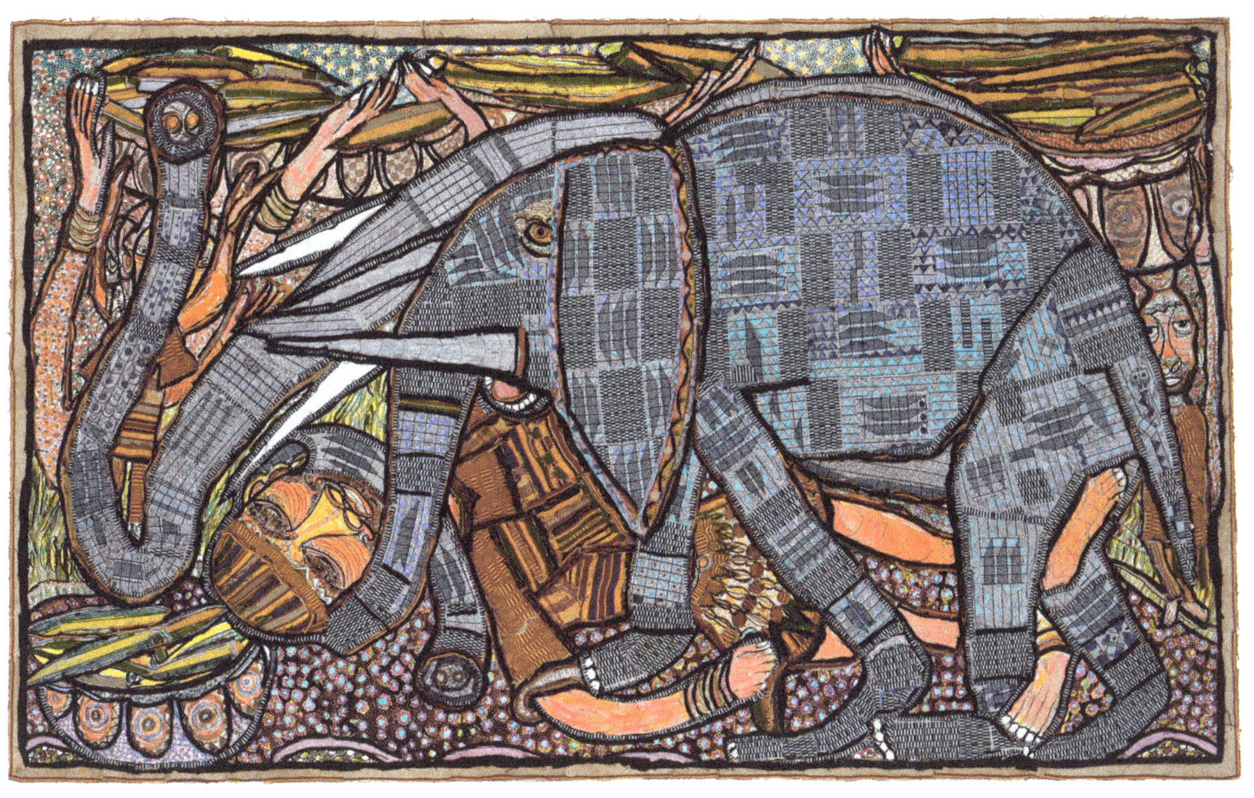

No. 15. *Dream of an Elephant Tusk Hunter.* 2005

16

Scientist in Animals' Kingdom

Ink and acrylic on canvas. 5' x 3'. Philadelphia, 2006

Called *Beast of No Nation* when it was in progress, this is, like number 15, an encounter of a man with nature. Prince said:

"This, I have no idea what I am doing when I started it. I put acrylic mixed with water. Then I drop it down; those are the stripes. I let it dry, and started the animals, one by one. And at the end, I find animals inside.

"It is a good period for me in this country."

The period was the spring of 2006, from February to April, when he also painted *The Coming to the World and the Golden Birds* (chapter 4, p. 73) and *Imaginative Dream of a Masked Snake Charmer* (no. 17). He was also experimenting by applying watery color, then tilting and turning the canvas to create drips, which, once they had dried, he worked into images, discovering forms with his pen in the way he creates his ornamental tattooing (chapter 14, p. 207, and no. 26). It was, Prince said, "a good period for me in this country, in my life anyway. It's the turning point of everything in my life." *Scientist in Animals' Kingdom*, the masterpiece of that period (chapter 14), began with drips in his "American style." Prince goes on:

"This was a style that I never did before. There's only one of its kind. And I never do anything like this in my life before, this technique:

"Mixing the acrylic with water.

"Spread it on the face of the canvas.

"Shake them around.

"And it brings some stripes.

"And I use the stripes: turn them into birds. If you turn it around, you see these are birds.

"And then while I'm cutting in the—designing all these things, by bringing from zero, zero, zero together, I have the form of seeing all these animals."

Prince finds forms in the accidents he has created, just as he finds forms in the natural patterns of woodgrain. He continues:

"And the title, if I remember, is The Scientist in Animals' Kingdom.

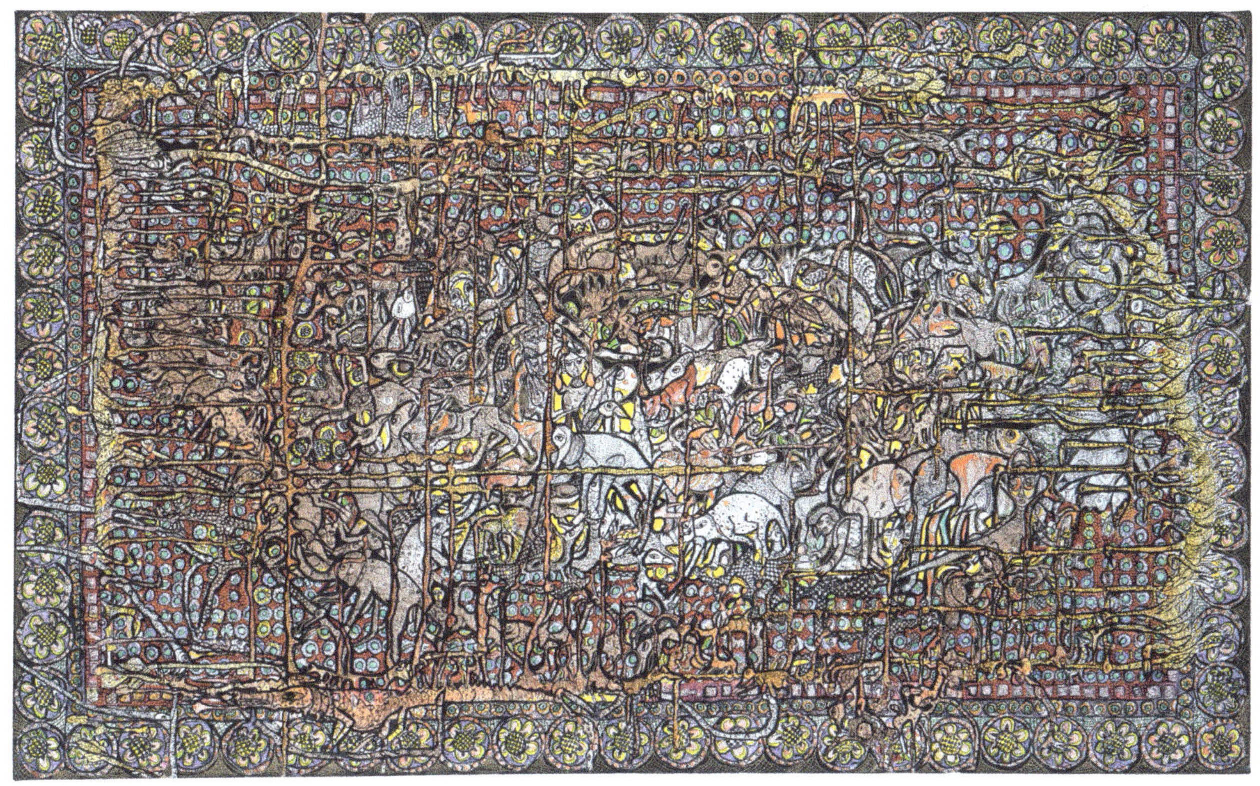

No. 16. *Scientist in Animals' Kingdom.* 2006

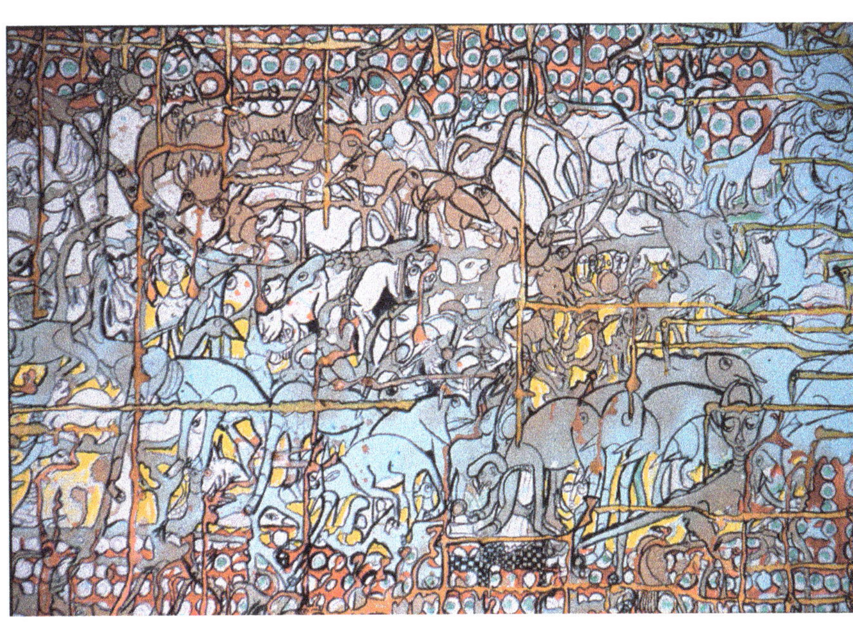

Scientist in Animals' Kingdom.
Detail of the painting in progress, March 2006.
The scientist is near the bottom, just right of center

"The scientist is down here with his glasses"—Prince points to the wee man in the painting's lower, right quadrant. "He has a magnifying glass. He thinks he can understand what the animals are trying to say.

"He has too many things to look in his magnifying glass."

That is: the scientist with his technology, like the hunter with his, is overmatched. Human plans are thwarted by nature's power, and Prince aligns himself with nature. In *Dream of an Elephant Tusk Hunter* (no. 15), the elephant (a royal personage like the artist Prince) crushes the "collector" who wants to take his precious ivory. For Prince, it seems, creation dominates consumption in art (no. 21). In *Scientist in Animals' Kingdom*, the artist's design engulfs and obscures the tiny scientist. For Prince, it seems, art surpasses science in producing knowledge of the world. Prince's hand brings more animals out of the pattern than the scientist can count, and, unlike the scientist bent over his magnifying glass, lost in the details, Prince understands that animals are more than objects of zoological study:

"Elephant is a symbol of power. And every time I think about my royal background, and every time my mind is there, I hardly do anything without touch elephants.

"And most of the time, I touch snakes too. Snakes have to do with death. So, I always believe that I end up one day I'm not going to be here.

"And then at the same time, snake is a symbol of Ogun, god of iron."

Human efforts and desires seem puny and pitiful in the context of natural and supernatural power.

In its border and its overall look, this painting was inspired by the oriental carpets Prince saw on the second floor at Material Culture where he was working at the time (chapter 14). He concluded:

"I never do anything ever like this. It is different. And if you are not here when I did it, somebody else will see it, will think I am not the one that did it."

17
Imaginative Dream of a Masked Snake Charmer

Ink and acrylic on canvas. 3' x 5'. Philadelphia, 2006

Taking on many forms, alive with interpretive potential, snake charmers appear often in Prince's work (no. 6). He describes this painting:

"This has to do with the book of Amos Tutuola, My Life in the Bush of Ghosts. This is called The Snake Charmer, Snake Charmer Ghost.

"He's playing the, like, horn-flute, but this snake charmer have so many heads himself, and his body is like and not like a snake, and he's playing his flute at this place where the branches of the tree have snake heads.

"My inspiration comes from My Life in the Bush of Ghosts, Palm-Wine Drinker—those are the Yoruba literature books that part of it was translated into English. The influence of it is in Chinua Achebe's book Things Fall Apart. Part of it Wole Soyinka used in most of his writings, the Nobel Laureate, Nigerian Nobel Laureate."

Prince's point is that the traditional oral literature of Nigeria—the "it" of his statement—was used by the great modern writers (Tutuola, Achebe, Soyinka) whose writings inspired him to use his own imagination and to turn back, as they did, to his native tradition. Prince continues:

"I got the idea from Tutuola because most of the time he talk about traditional magic, spiritual magic, things like snake charmer. And you know in those days, the people that have power, they communicate with anything. They communicate with the snake. They would communicate with animal, and all these animal are symbolic in their thinking.

"The snake: the snake is symbolic. You know, in coming into the world, the first person that started deceiving the first man in Christian thinking was happened to be turned into a snake. After that, God got angry with them. Since then, the snake has been part of the human being.

"It's only because you have cold weather here; that's why you don't see snakes so much. In Nigeria, there's so many snakes everywhere.

"So, it's part of our culture.

"The snake charmer can control it. Because when the snake is well-fed, it can be controlled, but not controlled when it is hungry.

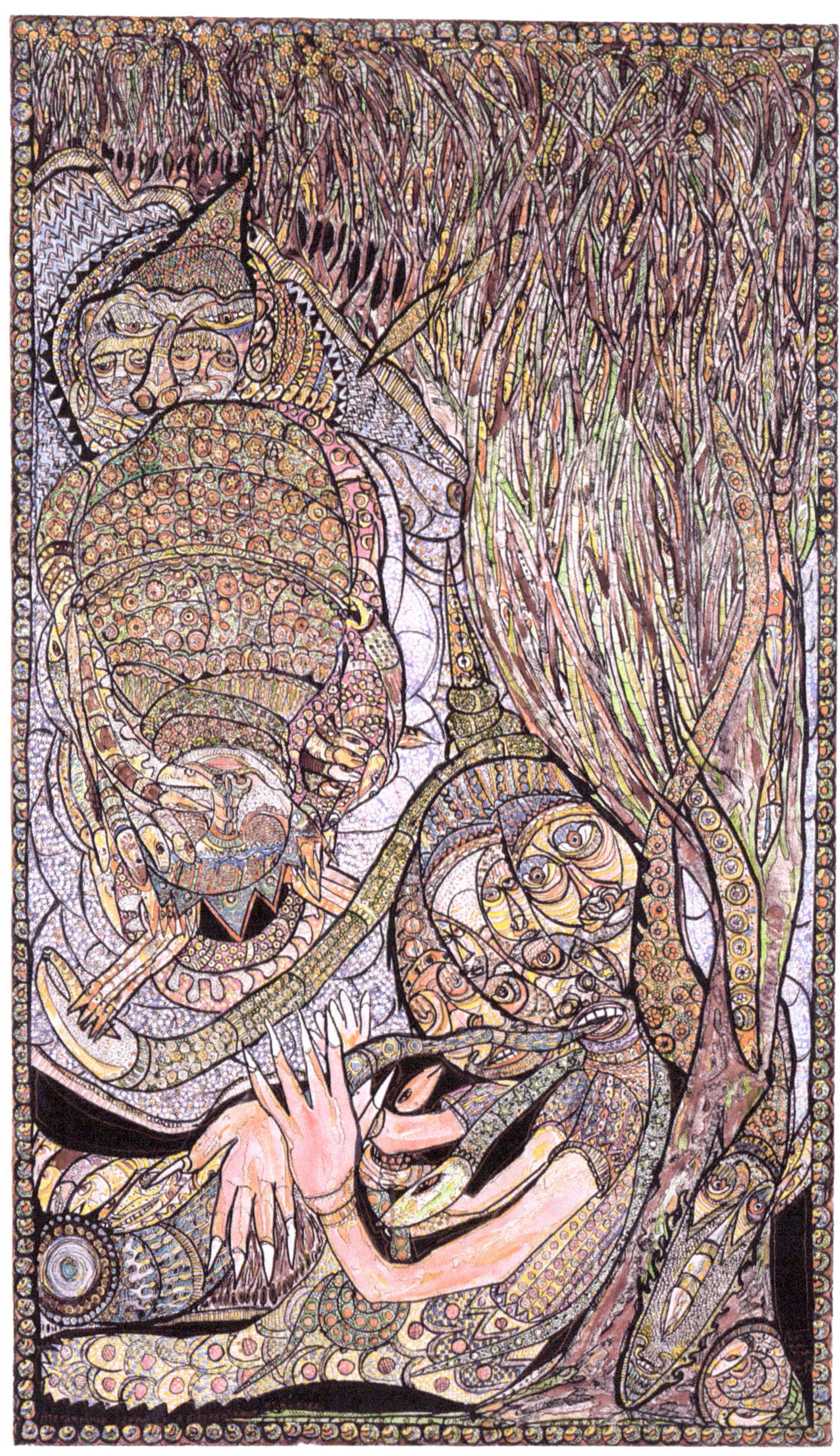

No. 17. *Imaginative Dream of a Masked Snake Charmer.* 2006

"You can call the snake charmer Abore if he is an Ogun priest; you call him Abore. And if it is just an ordinary snake charmer, you can call him snake charmer."

A rich instance of Prince's thinking, this picture is not a confusion of conflicting ideas that demands resolution into one meaning or another. Allegorically open, it is a layering, a syndetic accumulation of simultaneously valid meanings. It depicts a dream. Prince's early painting that served as the frontispiece for Robert Plant Armstrong's *Wellspring* was entitled *Oshogbo Man in an Intoxicated Dream*. The man (Prince) sits to one side, his dream of birds and monkeys (witches and twins) fills the other. In *Imaginative Dream of a Masked Snake Charmer*, the man sits to one side, the other fills with his dream, a dream in which he is wrapped in the coils of his snakes, controlled by the forces he strives to control. Both paintings doubly envision a dream (see no. 15). They make manifest the dream of the man in the picture, bringing his inner thoughts to the visible surface. And in both, the whole scene is the artist's invention; it spreads his "imaginative dream" onto the visible surface.

This painting, Prince said, could be titled simply *The Snake Charmer*. In that case it shows an "ordinary" snake charmer who keeps his snakes fed and trains them to rise and sway to the sound of his flute. His hellish dream is that the snakes he tries to control will rebel, wrap around his body, and bring on his death (see no. 15). Prince said the painting could also be titled *Snake Charmer in the Bush of Ghosts*, in which case this is an otherworldly snake charmer who occupies an enchanted realm of endless Ovidian transformation, where the branches of trees turn into snakes, snakes become people, and people become spirits. One title, the main one, implies a transformation by impersonation: a man in a mask, enacting a spirit. But Prince offers another title, *Snake Charmer Ghost*, and now this is surely a spirit, as his multiple heads suggest. Or, Prince said, the painting could be titled *Abore*, in which case this is a priest of Ogun, imaged as a spirit.

In Prince's paintings of Iyaogun (nos.6–7), the priestess of Ogun is at once a person and a spirit. She is also a snake charmer. In one image, Medusa-like, her hair turns into snakes. In the other, as in this one, a snake coils around her. The snake-charmer theme gathers Ogun, since Prince associates snakes with the god, and now the man, a priest, dreams that he is wrapped in the power of Ogun (no. 7). In this dream, snakes mean death to ordinary men, divine power to priests.

The animals in Prince's paintings are all symbolic. He was a happy dog as a boy (chapters 8, 13), an elephant in maturity who needed to be wary of his own ambitions (no. 13). In Prince's thought, the serpent's deceit lies at the origin of human existence, marbling life with evil (no. 18), and the snake symbolizes "the end of the world," the sunset, the individual's death. Prince's father, Aitoyeje, I remind you, died from the bite of a snake. In general, for Prince, the snake is a sign of Ogun's creative and destructive presence in the world, so the priest who has the power to communicate with snakes, as snake charmers do, can communicate with the god. When Ogun's priest merges with a snake charmer, his playing of the flute matches the acts priests use to call Ogun: the ringing of the hammer on the anvil, the spilling of a black cock's blood down the blades of iron (chapters 3, 5). This picture of a man who communicates with snakes, who seeks to control them, evokes the rituals in which priests, by prayers and sacrifice, beseech Ogun to use his power for human benefit. That is what happened after Alhaji Suleiman Otitoloju's divination for Prince at Kabba (chapter 5).

Building by contained ambiguity and manifold reference in the manner of Yoruba traditional art and oral literature, Prince's painting depicts a man having a dream, and it realizes the artist's dream in which the dreaming man is at once a snake charmer, a masquerade, a priest, and a spirit. This painting pivots centrally in Prince's worldview and oeuvre, combining many of his themes. It shows a man and his snakes—the connection between people and beasts that might collapse metaphorically into union (nos. 13–14) or shape antagonistically into a confrontation (no. 22), in which human will is overwhelmed by natural forces (nos. 15–16). It shows a man in a mask, a priest, a spirit—the connections between the inhabitants of the two worlds, revealing the formal multiplicity that signals the spirits (nos. 4, 25, 28–29), the power that unites spirits and priests (nos. 6–8), and then spills into whole realms of spirituality (no. 5). It shows a man who can and cannot control the powers beyond him, acknowledging life, death, and the inevitability in existence of good and evil (no. 18). Nothing is simple, nothing certain.

18

The End and the Beginning of the Fragile World

Ink, batik dye, watercolor, and oil on cloth. 31" x 60". Ibadan, 2007

One in the series begun in the winter of 2006–2007 with the two versions of *The Spirits of My Reincarnation Brothers and Sisters* (no. 29), this painting was made with Prince's "rainbow" palette and "tattoo" ornament (see no. 4).

The idea in this painting goes back at least to 1972, as can be seen in Prince's painting *Eve and Jupiter*, reproduced in the article by the Mundy-Castles in *African Arts*. In 2007, Prince also created a small sculpture's painting on this topic. He titled it *The Beginning of the Fragile World*, the title he usually uses for this one too. He also calls them both *The Beginning of the End*, connecting them with the series from which number 19 comes, in which Christianity, Judaism, and Islam arrive in Nigeria to end the dominance of the "traditional" Yoruba religion. Prince's point in *The Beginning of the Fragile World* is that human existence begins in an evil that will continue until the end of time. Here is what he said:

"With the title The Beginning of the Fragile World—you know, the world today is so fragile. And the beginning, from the concept of Christianity: they believe that Adam and Eve is the first human beings that were in the garden. And they were told not to eat certain apple, or certain fruit. But I know that fruit has to do with sexual something. In my mind, I know they were using the fruits"—metaphorically—"in order not to expose the minds of many people into sexual interaction among people. Because that is the beginning of destruction.

"If you have a lover and you haven't had sex together, you never get rid of each other. Your love is very strong. But the day you start having sex, then things start falling apart—even though your kids, your mom, but things start falling apart because you've seen the beginning of the end.

"So, this has to do with my own conception of those people who started the world, and the children they have. The first child they have is like a devil. Because it's the beginning of the fragile world.

"The beginning and the end. It's the beginning of everything, and the end of everything."

Prince laughs:

"The beginning of the end is sex.

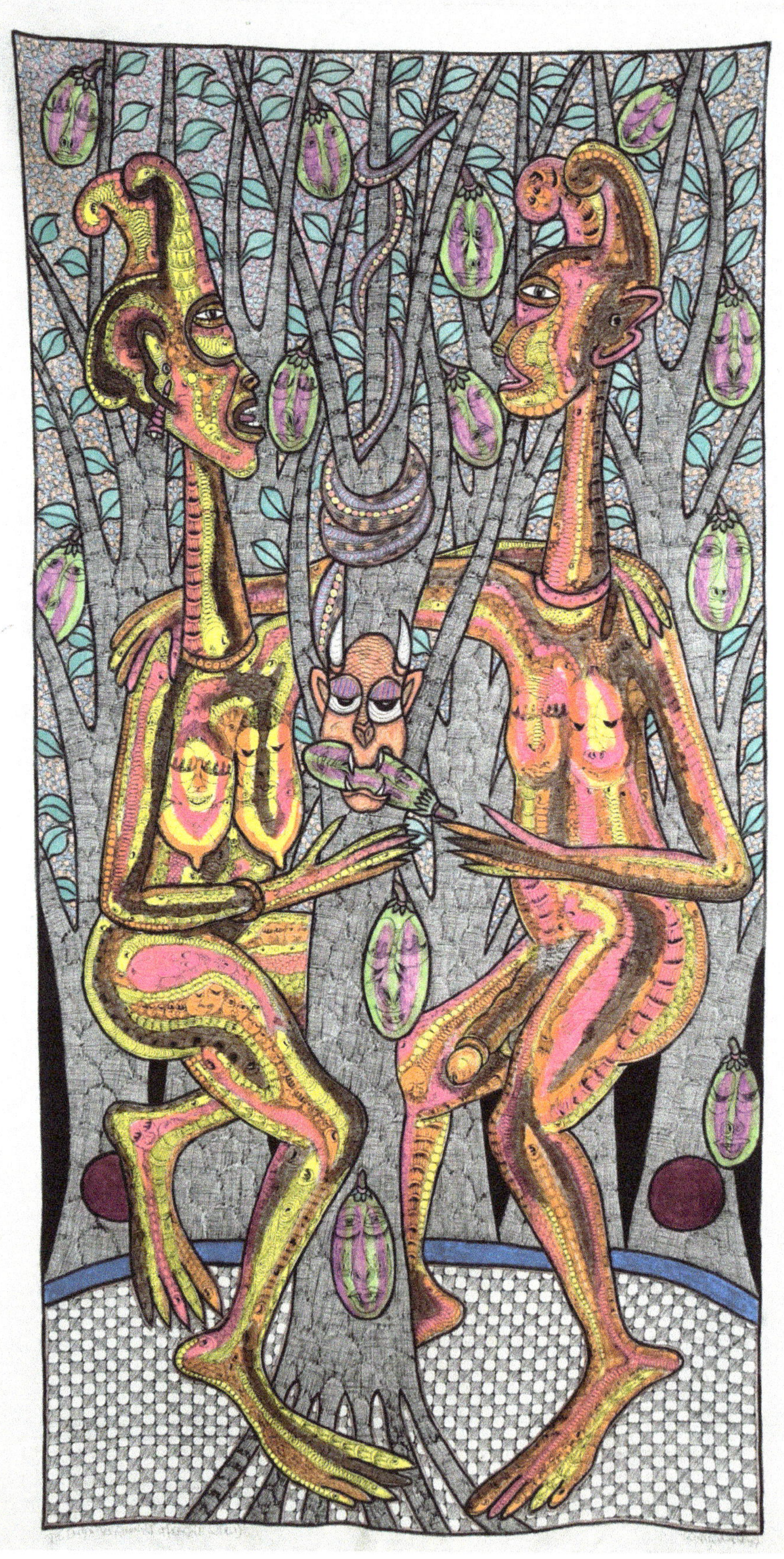

No. 18. *The End and the Beginning of the Fragile World.* 2007

"And then the forests with the faces represent different people that came into the world. Okay. All these heads of people.

"Because it's like you drop into the womb of Mama. Mama bring you into the world. The children grow up. They don't listen to Mama and Papa, because they are children from this beginning of the end.

"I started thinking about the world, how the first people came here. They started expanding, and the people who were expanding were bringing children that, when they grew up, some of them become killers, some become business people, some become a beautiful teacher, some become a beautiful artist. Some become criminals. Criminals.

"So, in the beginning, it is the end of everything."

Prince laughs again:

"And so, because of all these terrible children that have been born into the world, it become a fragile world."

Prince's argument is perfectly clear, but at the center of the painting, between the mother and father of this unholy family, there is an intentional ambiguity. Read first as the head of their baby, this is the head of the serpent who winds around the tree in the garden. In general, for Prince, snakes evoke death, the end. This snake is Satan, as the horned head attests. The fruit in Satan's mouth is their baby, the tricky gift of the Devil, the yield of their sexual transgression. Since Satan's head is also the devilish baby's head, the fruit is also the child of the baby, the grandchild of the first parents who will bear their evil, Satan's venom, forward in time. In generation after generation, their descendants, the "terrible children" symbolized by the heads that sprout from the trees, will create this fragile world of calamities, in which we, and all our children after us, are doomed to struggle.

The heads on the trees in the garden, symbolizing the descendants of the first couple, are visual reminders of the heads on the trees in Obatala's garden (chapter 16, p. 258) where the life of a Yoruba person begins. Yoruba and Christian precepts come into alignment. Note that, in the large painting on cloth (though not on the small sculpture's painting on the next page), Adam and Eve are horned like the Devil, complicit in deceit. The horned head between them is both the cause and result of the wickedness they perpetrated when, as all couples do, they traded love for lust. Then—Prince's argument continues—things fall apart. Children do not listen to their parents, social order disassembles. Some people are artists, others are criminals, but all, through endless copulation, carry the evil of the beginning on to the end. Prince explains:

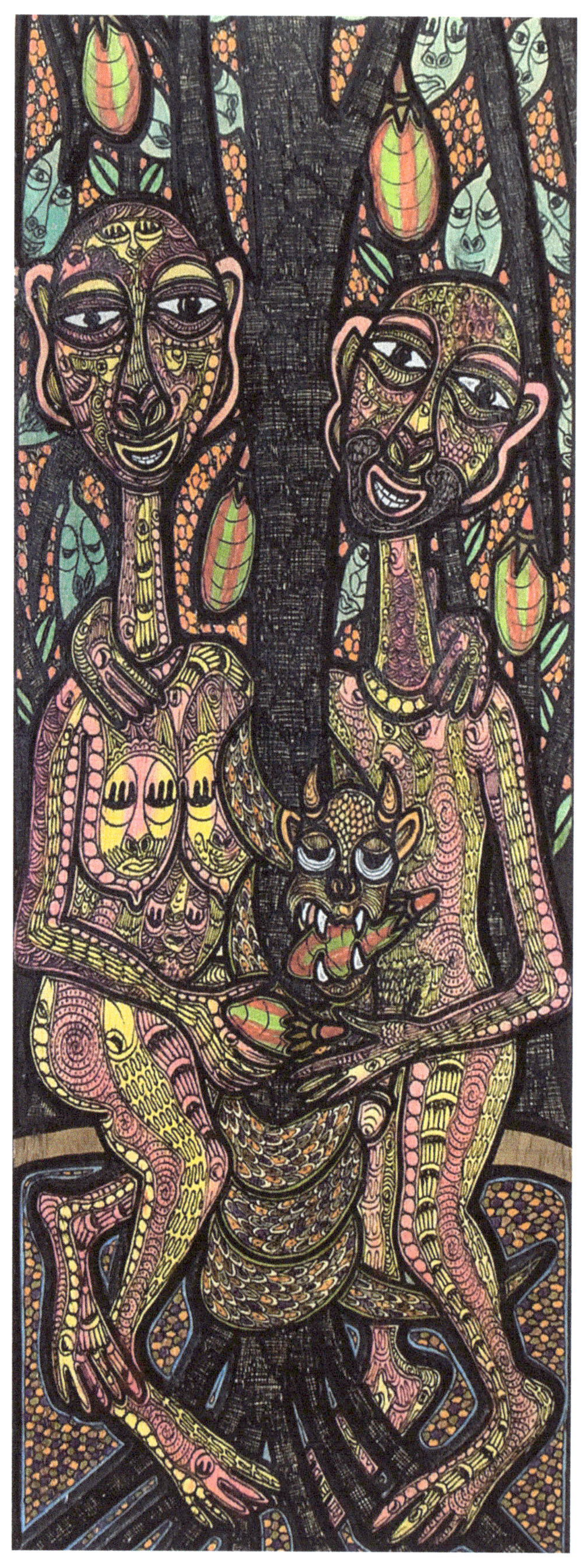

Detail of *The Beginning of the Fragile World.*
Ink and oil on wood; 2 layers. 12" x 36". Ibadan 2007

"You remember how Christians believe in Adam and Eve. The snake has tricked them, and the fact that I make the snake head look like the Devil's head. Because you see the way he tricked the lovers.

"It is how the whole world become, and how it became. That's why I call it The Beginning of the End. The baby is the end of the world. They have a devil baby. The baby is in the mouth of the snake, like a fruit. A negative baby in the mouth.

"The snake tricked them. And that is the baby that came out of the relationship. Okay. And the baby is holding this devilish thing in its mouth. That is the baby of the relationship. And that is *us*.

"*We*.

"We of the world. Because: see what is happening today. They brought the end of the world. The beginning of everything, and the beginning of the end. It started in this relationship."

It started with sex, and through sex, in this Yoruba redaction of original sin, it will continue.

19

The Beginning of the End

Paper, ink, and acrylic on canvas. 20" x 16". Philadelphia, 2005

This is one from a series of three distinctly different collaged paintings, each entitled *The Beginning of the End*. All record the presence of the new religions in Nigeria, the beginning of colonial intrusion, the end of social, cultural, and theological coherence in Yoruba life. In the modern—postcolonial—world, Prince said, people can turn back to their native traditions, so this picture is, like his ritual practice, a part of Prince's oppositional, revivalistic, modernist stance (chapter 18). He said:

"This is an interesting one. This one is called The Beginning of the End. It shows the religion thinking of the people of the world. They sold two; there were three pieces. They sold two.

"This is a Christian priest, telling everybody that God made the world."

Prince points to the text on the left with the first chapter of Genesis that continues on the slim pages beneath the cross on the right: "These are from Genesis. And these are the chapters and verses that I cut."

I ask about the passages in the Arabic script, and he answers:

"I don't know what it is, but I know it is about Christianity because there's a cross. It must be from the Koran.

"I must be crazy."

Prince laughs heartily, then says:

"Beginning of the End. These other religions are trying to kill out Yoruba religion.

"There's three of them; they bought two. There's one about Hebrew. There's one about a teacher teaching kids. And there's this one."

In this one a foreign Christian priest holds the book. On the book there is a bird. The text issuing from its beak reads, "I am the Alpha and Omega says the Lord, the beginning and the end." Prince points to the bird, laughs and says:

"The bird is telling. Like a parrot, repeating. The bird is a disciple, wants the other ones to learn the way of this religion."

At the beginning of the end, the bird, a form from nature, is a Nigerian, preaching to the crowd, parroting the Christian line, proselytizing for the new religion in the effort to end devotion to the Yoruba faith.

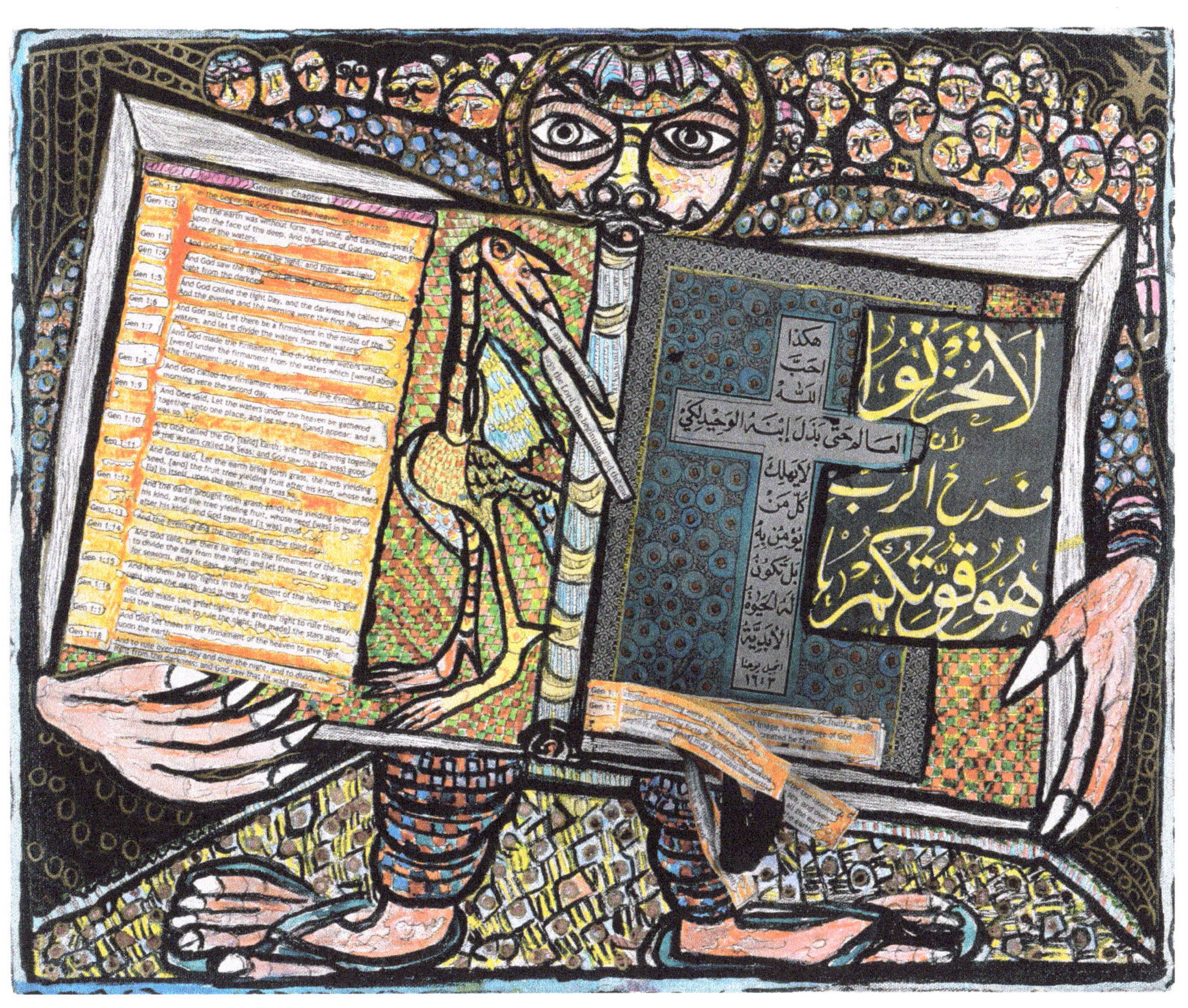

No. 19. *The Beginning of the End.* 2005

20

The Ritualist at the Osun Festival

Ink, batik dye, and oil on cloth. 34" x 52". Osogbo, 1991

Created with the bright palette and inked ornament Prince would later use in the series begun with the Philadelphia versions of *My Reincarnation Brothers and Sisters* (no. 29), this painting, also called *Preparing for the Osun Festival*, is composed in the traditional Yoruba manner. Like *Kissing Birds* (chapter 1) and *Rainbow Wealth Goddess* (no. 9), it is divided horizontally and integrated vertically, segmented but intensively continuous (chapter 17). The composition breaks into four zones, piled up to represent successively deepening circles in space: the river, the ceremony ground, the forest, the city. The horizontal zones are united by the bold upthrust of the symmetrical figure, a priestess bearing a covered and carved container of offerings to Osun that will be deposited in the river at the end (no. 8). Entailing at once the beginning of the Festival and its end, the virgin priestess rises out of the River Osun, aswarm with the natural devotees of the goddess (see nos. 1, 7). She lifts through the second zone of the ceremony, with musicians and dancers to the left, a king in a veiled crown to the right, the massed faces of humanity behind. Then the calabash on her head penetrates the third zone, the domain of nature, a forest with two monkeys, symbolic of twins, a lizard, and a snake, a sign of the end. The zone at the top, the farthest removed in space, fills with Osogbo, rendered as the village of round thatched houses from which the human devotees have come, and where those who are not devotees remain in oblivious sleep (no. 9).

Collapsing time and flattening space (at once a plan and elevation), this painting implies, but does not depict, the sequence of events at the Festival. As though it were a gathering of Yoruba statues on an altar, it collects generalized figures and poses them frontally. The narrative of the ceremony—the procession of dancers, the procession of the king, the sacrifice to Osun at the end—is not represented. Instead, this is a simultaneous assembly of the narrative's characters, waiting in stable, timeless, suspension for the viewer to project a sequential order upon them, as when the devotee, faced with a still, spiritually configured image of a deity, lifts from memory the myths of the god's origin and acts (chapter 17). This is not a stylized representation of an Osun Festival that Prince has seen (chapter 15), but the Festival as he imagines it was before the colonial intrusion, before the beginning of the end (no. 19). Prince describes it, pointing to the masked container that centers the composition:

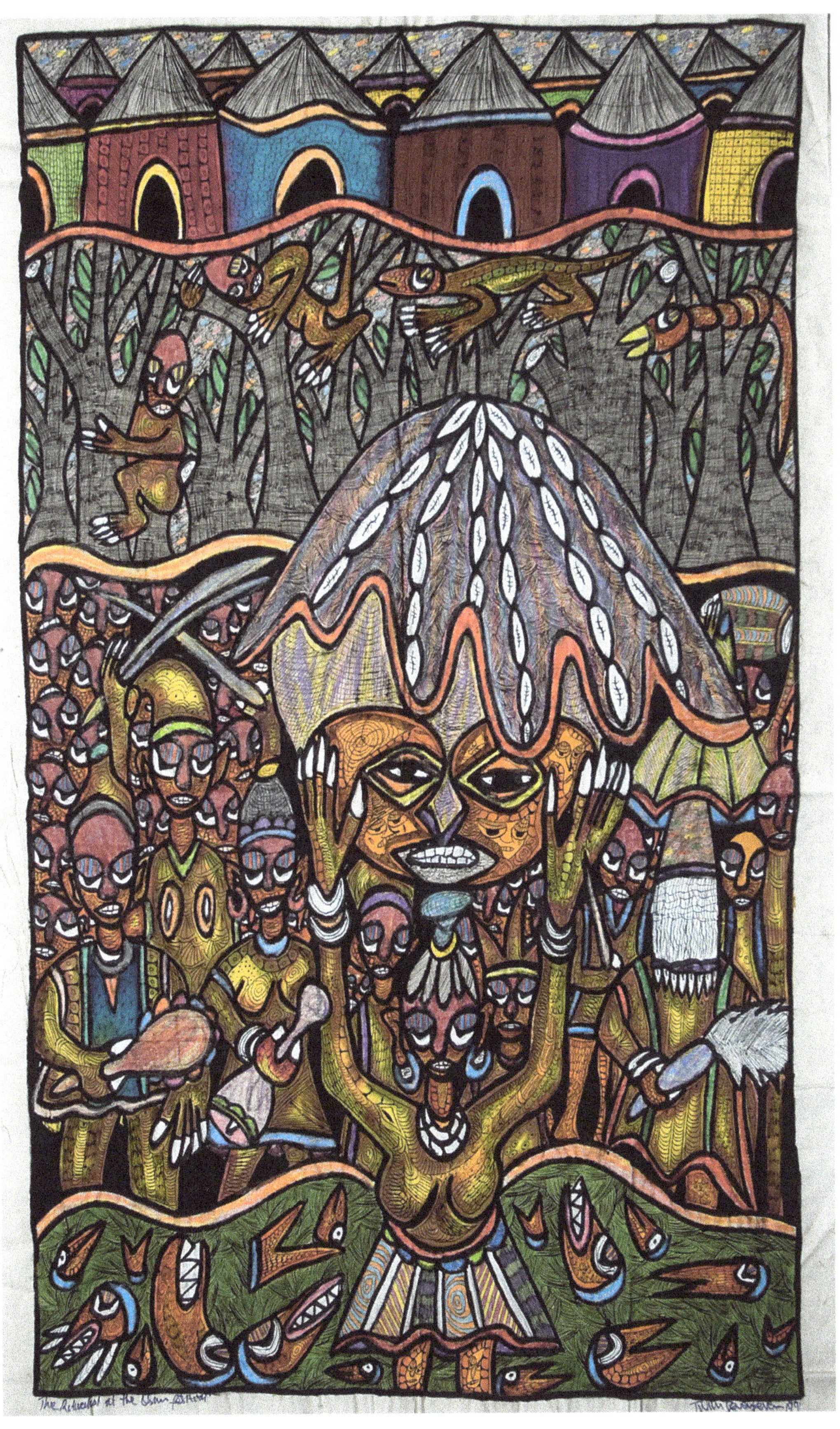

No. 20. *The Ritualist at the Osun Festival.* 1991

"This is about Osun. This is the calabash, the box that the Osun priestess carry. And it's covered with different colors, like basket or carpet or tapestry. It is the cloth they use to cover it. This head, this mask on the box was carved, but I think it is one of those wooden boxes, and it is being carried on the head of the young woman, a virgin woman.

"That begins the ceremony. It has the things they want to throw into the river whenever everybody leaves.

"And then there's crowds, masquerades, and there's a king, and the horsetail; he owns a horsetail"—the whisk of authority.

"And then, there's fish in the water. The only thing: I should paint the water blue, but at that time, sometimes Osun day, when it doesn't rain properly, the water is greenish.

"The background represent part of the city you walk past when you go to the Festival. Today you have a lot of modern buildings by the roadside, but at that time in Osogbo, this is what they have most: thatched."

21

The Acrobatic Dancers and the Unnoticed Crowd

Ink, watercolor, and oil on wood, a sculpture's painting of two layers. 24½" x 48¼". Osogbo, 1969

Originally titled *Priest and Village Dancers*, also called *Acrobatic Dancer Family* and *Acrobatic Dancers in the Village*, this, like number 3, is an early sculpture's painting. It pictures a common entertainment of the kind Prince arranged at the Olosun compound in Ibadan (chapter 15). He said:

"This one is very real. Like realistic. This is acrobatic dancers. Acrobatic dancers: the dancer, somebody is standing on him, and the drummers—like you see in Osun Festival.

"It's during the festival, carnival, from home in Nigeria."

When Prince put a cross in the left hand of the dominant figure, a priest, he was making, he said, a "political" comment, criticizing his people, as he regularly does, for professing Christianity by day and practicing the old religion at night (chapter 2). In his right hand the hypocritical priest holds a bowl of snakes, symbols of Ogun (nos. 6–7, 16–17). This critical mixing of religious emblems suggests that the beginning of the end has come (no. 19), but usually—and consistently in his mature work—Prince erases all signs of colonial presence

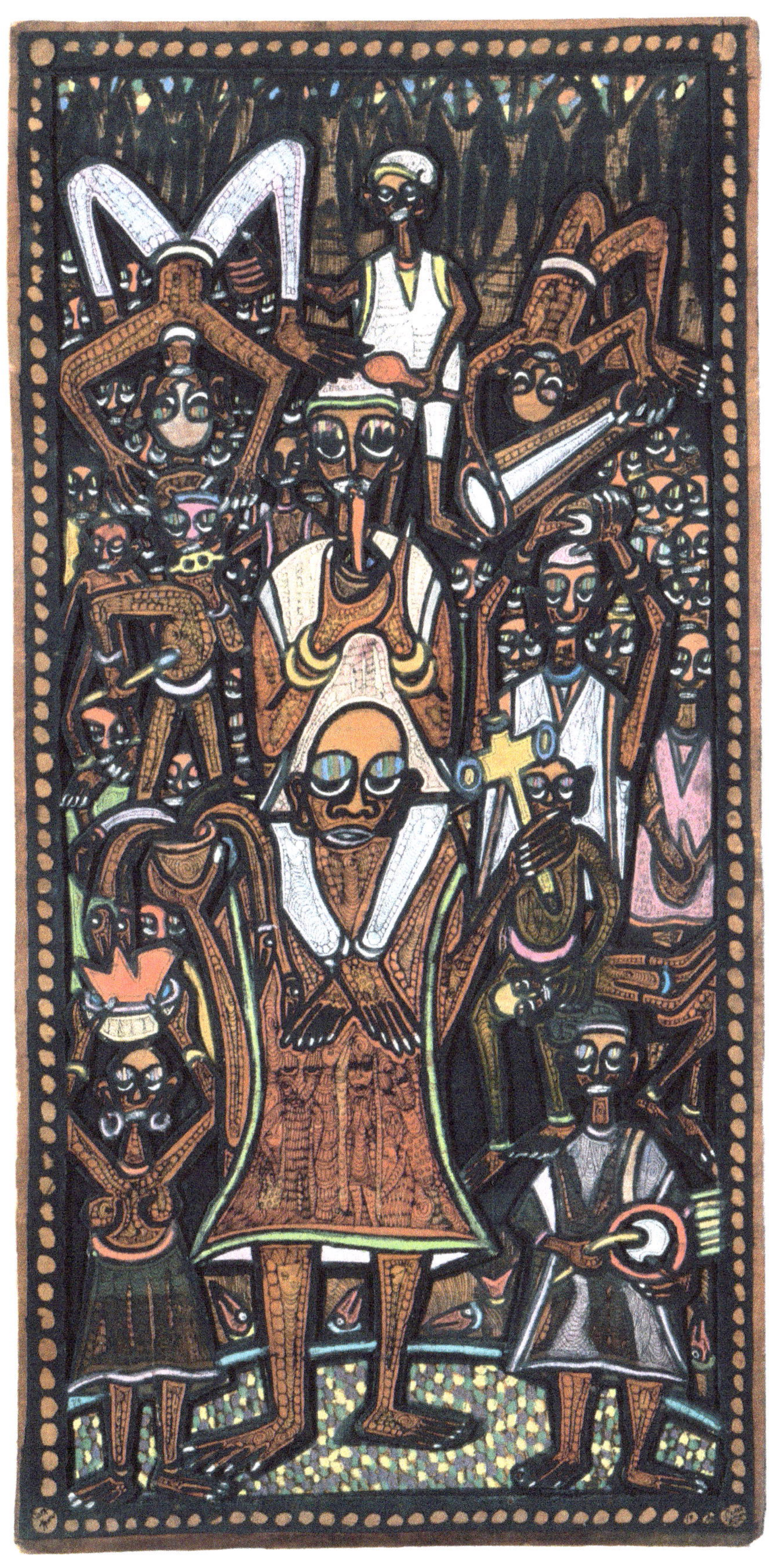

No. 21. *The Acrobatic Dancers and the Unnoticed Crowd*. 1969

from village scenes like this one. In 1991, Prince repeated this image in a large, bright painting on cloth. Titled *Acrobatic Dancer and the Culturalists*, it resembles number 20 in style and tone. In both, a man on the priest's shoulders establishes a firm, vertical axis, a boy tumbles high on both sides, and the background fills with the staring faces of the audience. There are, though, many small differences—a village rather than a forest at the top, no bare-breasted woman at the left, no glimpse of Osun's river behind the priest—but the main difference is that the priest, instead of a cross, holds the double-headed axe of Sango in his left hand, Ogun's bowl in his right. Signs of change have vanished.

22
Village Life under the Cocoa Tree

Ink, pastel, acrylic, and oil on wood, a sculpture's painting of two layers. 8' x 4'. Osogbo, 1978–1979

This painting and the next one (no. 23) belong to a set of six large sculpture's paintings that Prince made for an exhibition of his work in Italy. The show's organizer, an Italian collector, gave him a downpayment, and Prince gave him twenty-four small paintings. At the time, Prince feared that war would break out in Nigeria, so he sent the large paintings to his friend Dr. Klein Gunk, a gynecologist in Germany who collects Prince's work. Prince continues the story:

"So, Doctor Gunk told me, Don't take your paintings to Italy. Leave them with me here. Let him pay me; I keep your money.

"I waited ten years.

"Now, when I came here, and I have problem with my house, and I see that George love my work, and he's looking for some old ones, therefore I told him that I have these pieces in Germany. Because the gentleman from Italy didn't come, and he didn't pay me. He did not even pay me for the whole twenty-four paintings that he took away. He gave me three thousand dollars; he didn't pay the rest. He bought a huge painting of elephants for fifty thousand dollars. And we made paper and everything for it. I never see the money; I didn't ever see him again."

The Italian exhibition never happened. Eventually, George Jevremović paid for the shipping, Dr. Gunk sent the paintings, and they remain at Material Culture. Prince's story is but

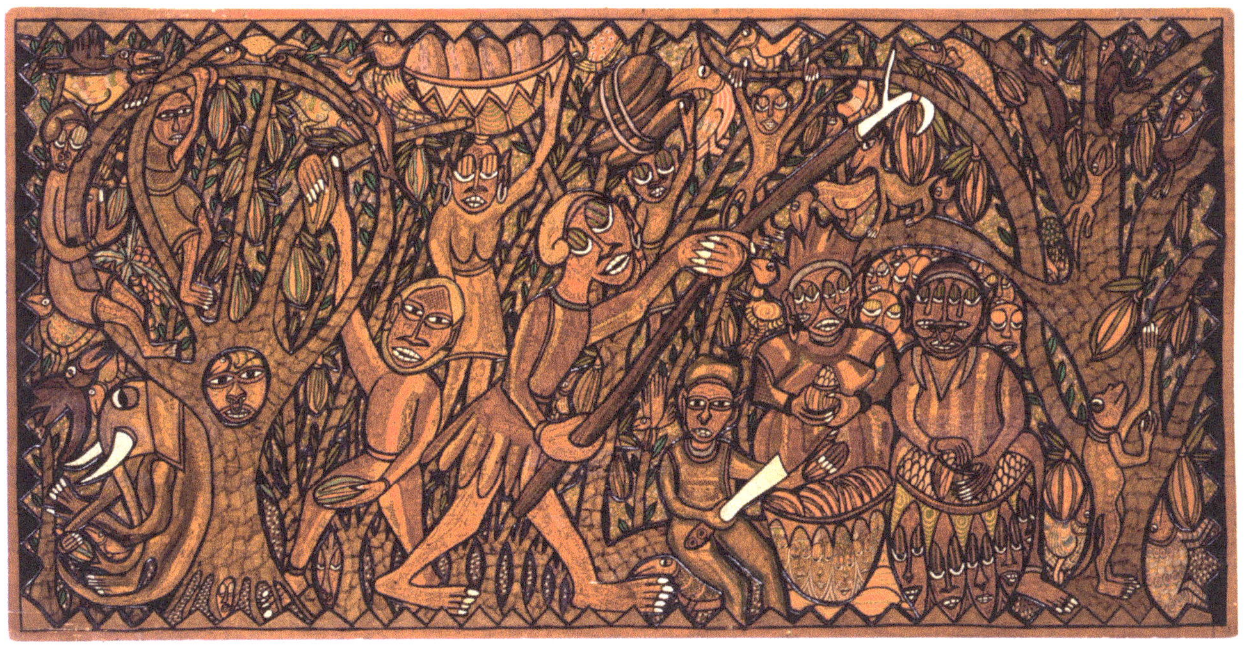

No. 22. *Village Life under the Cocoa Tree.* 1978–1979

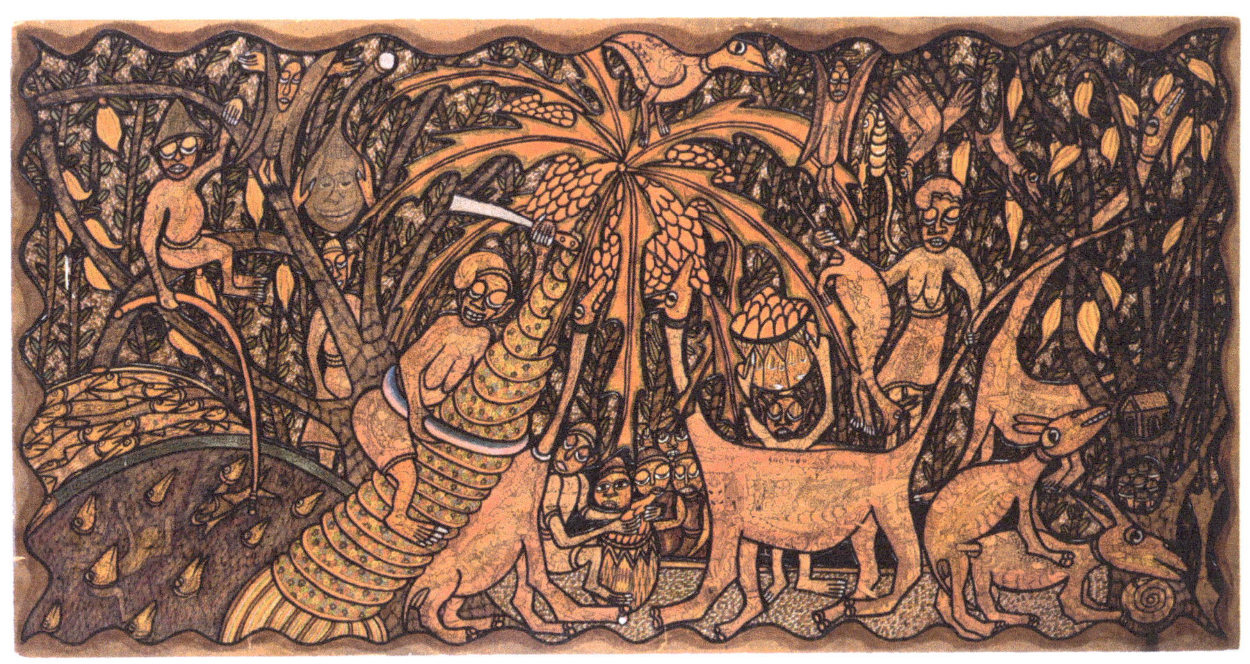

No. 23. *Village Life under the Palm Tree.* 1978–1979

one of many he tells to describe the disappointments and economic hardships that artists endure (chapters 14, 16). Sometimes Prince gets big money for his work; sometimes he is robbed by dealers and collectors. He laughs and keeps going, prevailing in the bemused, clever, resigned, and industrious manner of the peasant.

The paintings in this set all depict peasants at work in direct confrontation with nature, doing, Prince said, "what they can to survive." Another from the set, *Dream of a Reptile Collector*, shows men fishing, a man battling a crocodile, and a family gathering cocoa fruit. In this one, some people are picking and processing cocoa fruit while others pray and perform rituals to protect the harvest. Prince said:

"It's called Village Life under the Cocoa Tree. You see the person here; he's bringing down the fruit. And these ladies"—on the right—"are working, but they are not working as farmers; they were like priests, doing ritual something. See: they have masks on their faces. They were like two wives for a man, to a husband. And the old man was requesting blessings, hoping the animals would not take their products.

"The animals are trying to take part of their farm products, their food.

"And the tree has face like spirit—the natural form of a tree, like a face.

"Everybody is working to see what they can provide.

"It is my own imagination."

People and beasts contend for resources in a world blended of natural and supernatural forces. In such a world, as Malinowski understood, farming and prayer are both work, combined into a single technology in the effort to prosper.

23

Village Life under the Palm Tree

Ink, pastel, acrylic, and oil on wood, a sculpture's painting of two layers. 8' x 4'. Osogbo, 1978–1979

As in the other painting from this set (no. 22), country folks labor in a world of natural and supernatural causation. The tiny tattooed patterns that cover their bodies remove them from visible reality and suggest the presence of the other world in this one. Some of the patterns shape into the round thatched houses of a village, but more become fish, indicating that human health and prosperity flow from the goddess Osun (nos. 7–10). The lake filled with fish on the

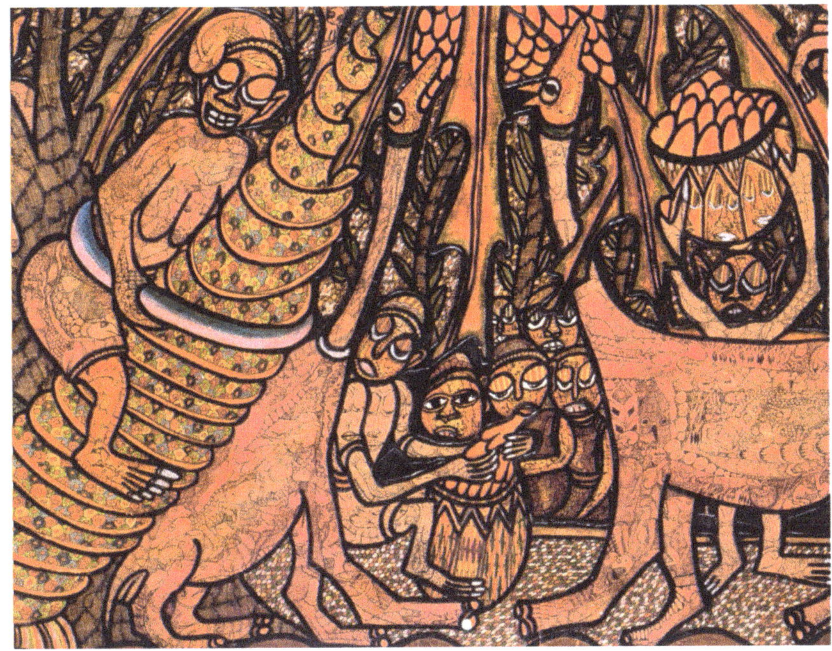

Detail of No. 23
Village Life under the Palm Tree

left alludes directly to the presence of Osun in the scene. "I hardly do any painting without me making a reference to Osun," Prince said when I asked him about the lake. All of these village paintings, Prince said, come from his imagination, and their imaginative quality, their joining of vision and concept, is clearest in the animals of this painting. He said:

"These animals in my own world. See the gentleman there on the cocoa tree, and you see this man climbing a palm tree, and you see the woman here, carrying a palm-wine keg. Okay. And these are strange animals from my own world, eating. It's not a giraffe; it's not an antelope. You know, this kind of animal comes from the shape of the wood"—the patterns in woodgrain—"like the way I do the Kissing Birds.

"See this shape"—in the grain of the wooden table before us. "I pull that shape up. I'm seeing something you don't see there. By the time I finish, this can become a mask. Because I'm so used to these that this thing just come by itself. It's like you're in a trance or something.

"So, you see these animals here, making love; these are strange animal making love. The goat-looking animal here." Prince points and laughs. "That's how it comes. Like, sometimes, like I told you, I can put water on wood, and you can see all these shapes."

Prince points again at the table top:

"If I pick my pen now, I could bring out a lot of shapes from all these patterns. Because it's inside my head."

24

Palm Wine Tapper

Ink, pastel, and oil on cloth. 30½" x 50½". Osogbo, c. 1978

At the entry to the lane that leads to Prince's compound in Osogbo, a palm-wine tapper sits on a bicycle, welded to Prince's design out of scrap metal (chapter 17). In Amos Tutuola's *Palm-Wine Drinkard,* the drinkard hunts for his dead tapster in the domain of the deads. This tapper could be dead then, a spirit as his spiky feet suggest, or it could be an ordinary rural worker with facial marks and a Yoruba cap, and it is certainly a reference to a popular song that Prince composed and recorded. He said:

"This is when I was working on the book of Amos Tutuola, like Palm-Wine Drinker, My Life in Bush of Ghosts, and something like that.

"I made a poem about whoever want me to die earlier will be killed by a palm-wine tapper bicycle, because palm-wine tapper bicycle have no insurance. It was a song from, like, nineteen seventy-four.

"It is one of my songs. You have palm-wine drinkers in real life, drinking palm-wine and singing songs."

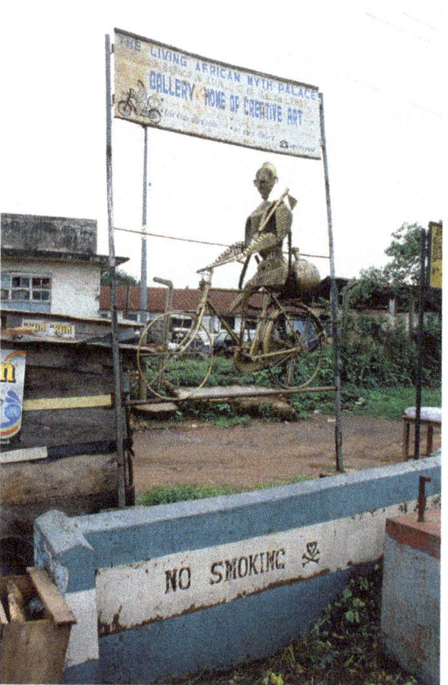

Palm-wine tapper on a bicycle.
The entry to Prince's home, Osogbo

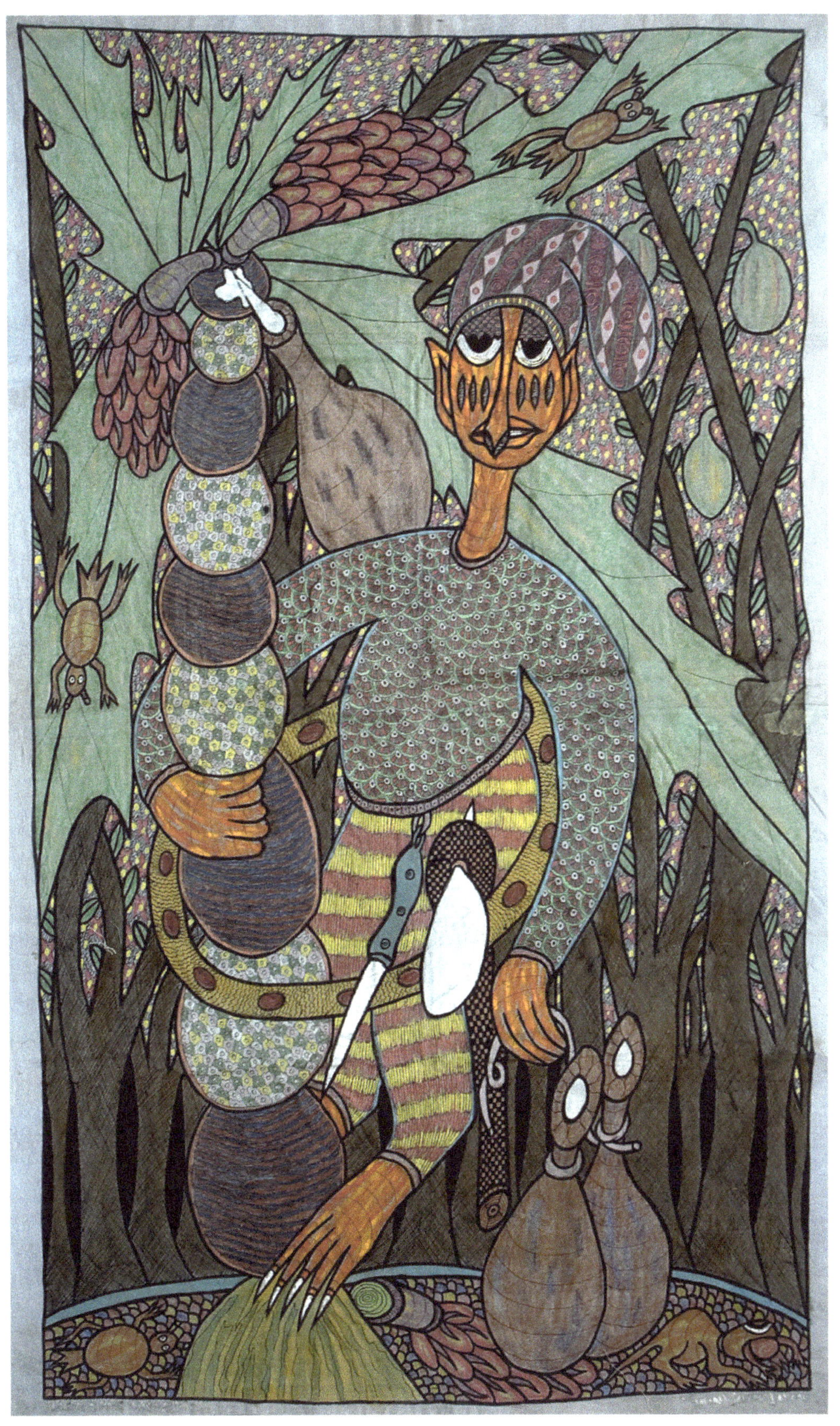

No. 24. *Palm Wine Tapper.* c.1978

25

The Last African Mask

Ink and oil on wood, a sculpture's painting of two layers. 38¼" x 27½". Philadelphia, 2004

Untitled on the list of Prince's works exhibited at Material Culture in 2005, also called *The Last Masks* and *My First Imaginative Dream about Masquerade in America*, this is the second sculpture's painting Prince made after coming to Philadelphia in 2000. He made the first, *The Golden Bird and the Unnoticed Crowd*, in his home (chapter 14, p. 201), and this was the first he made after George Jevremović provided him a place to work at Material Culture.

The painting presents a tight array of masquerades, lined up and posed frontally. Through the eyes of their masks, the performers' eyes stare forward, but the eyes of the masks on the left and lower right reveal spirit faces, the second from the right has multiple eyes and the veiled eyes of a spirit (nos. 1, 7), and little faces peek out of the bodies, showing that these are at once masks, masquerades, and spirits (see nos. 4–7, 17). As Prince has said (chapter 15), masks represent the dead, appearing in this world to portray spirits from the other. The mood is melancholy; Prince is longing for home, and for a lost, precolonial past. The tone is elegiac; these are the last African masks, witnesses to the beginning of the end (no. 19). Away in Orun, the spirits sadden as sacrifices cease, as people turn their attention to other immortals. In the dark village, the "unnoticed" people (no. 9) sleep, without caring, behind the masks. Prince was inspired by masks he had seen, the masks of the Dogon people of Mali, the Epa masks of his people, the Yoruba, but, as is the case with Amos Tutuola's novels (chapter 8), Prince is not illustrating, but drawing a mood from his sources into imaginative imagery. He said:

"This painting was during the Halloween time. You see the Halloween influence.

"These are masquerades with African village in the background. There's imagination, and there's some that look like Dogon, Dogon mask, or Epa mask—think of anything: Yoruba mask.

"And it was my *first* painting done in this place. In the workshop, the woodwork workshop."

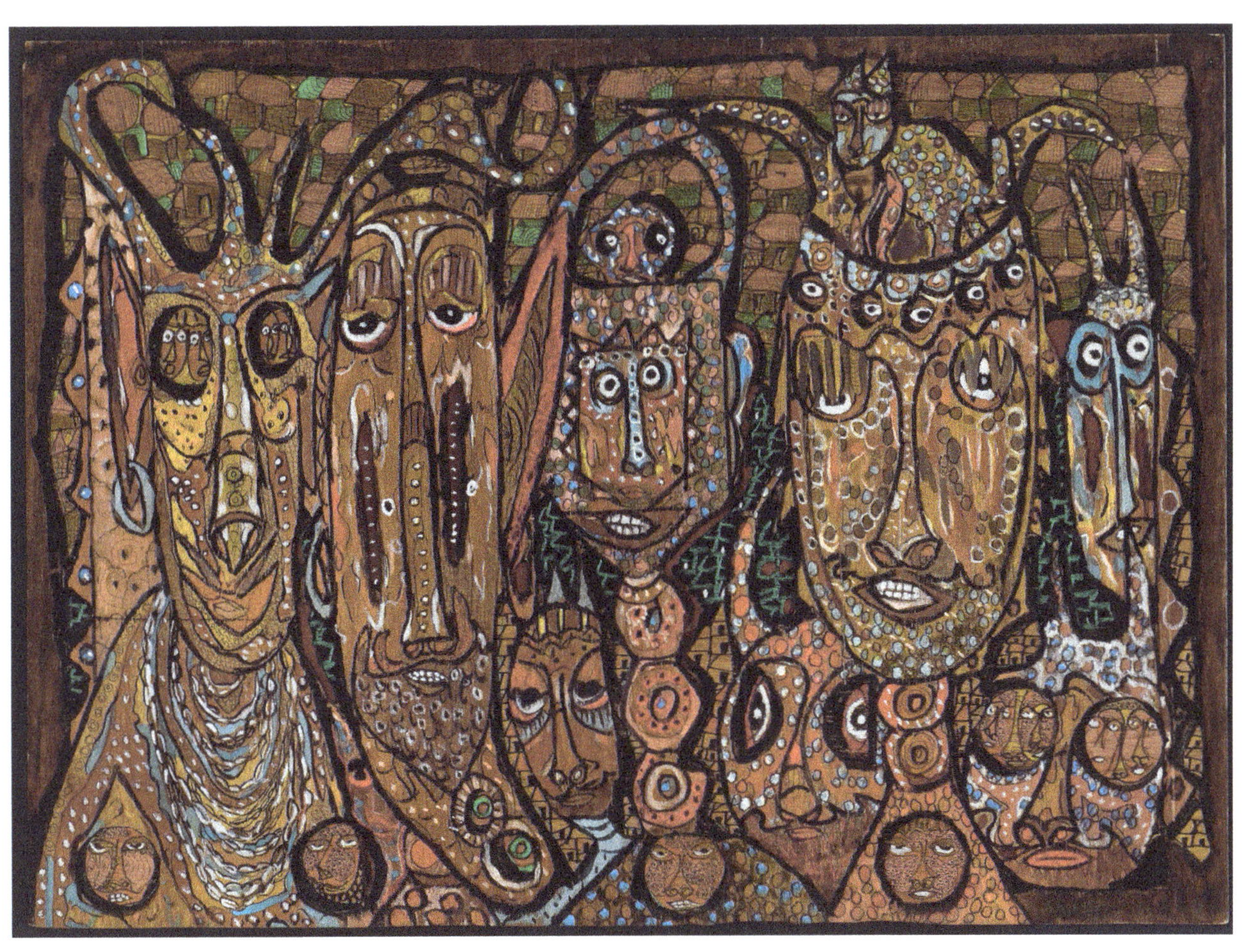

No. 25. *The Last African Mask.* 2004

26
Creative Shapes in God's Diary

Ink and acrylic on paper. 18" x 24". Philadelphia, 2005

The very first work in Prince's dripped "American style," this picture, also called *One of Its Kind*, was followed in 2005 and 2006 by many small paintings on canvas that began with spilled acrylics (chapter 14, p. 207, and see no. 16). Prince said:

"This is an experiment I started doing here. This lead to all the work I do on canvas.

"What I do here is a technique nobody teach me. I put acrylic color with water, and spill it down the paper, and start turning it around. And it turned out these shapes. By the time I finish applying some shapes I *see*, then you see all these animals, birds—everything come in.

"So, this is the first experiment that I started, which I say I never have seen anywhere before, that I started here in this place"—at Material Culture in Philadelphia.

"This is the first one. I think it is two thousand and four"—it is dated 2005. "Creative Shapes in God's Diary I call it. Or: One of Its Kind, because I've got other title like Creative Shapes in God's Diary, like on canvas.

"The God I'm referring to is my Yoruba God: Obatala, the god that create the head. I'm not referring to the Christian God; I'm referring to the Yoruba God: Olodumare.

"You see fish, owl, animals that come into my head when I'm doing it.

"They come into my head when I look at the shapes—the abstract form of it. Like, this is one like a snake here, a green snake with light eyes, getting a fish to swallow. And there is a bird here, too, waiting for an insect to pick. And there's a small bird's nest here."

Prince points to the painting and laughs with it all.

It is interesting that Paul Klee once experimented comparably, picturing the simultaneity of chaos and order by jolting himself with random patterns, then bringing them together with the draftsman's line. Klee provides the obvious comparison for Prince (chapter 19). His eloquent diaries, beginning in 1898, permit us to follow him as he strives for the modern, feeling that the age of the old masters has passed (medieval sculpture excites him, Raphael leaves him cold), that his training and study from nature retarded him, that he was unable to abandon the "crutch" of nature until 1911, when he met Kandinsky whose clarity of thought inspired him (chapter 18). Klee had to struggle to escape Western conventions and accom-

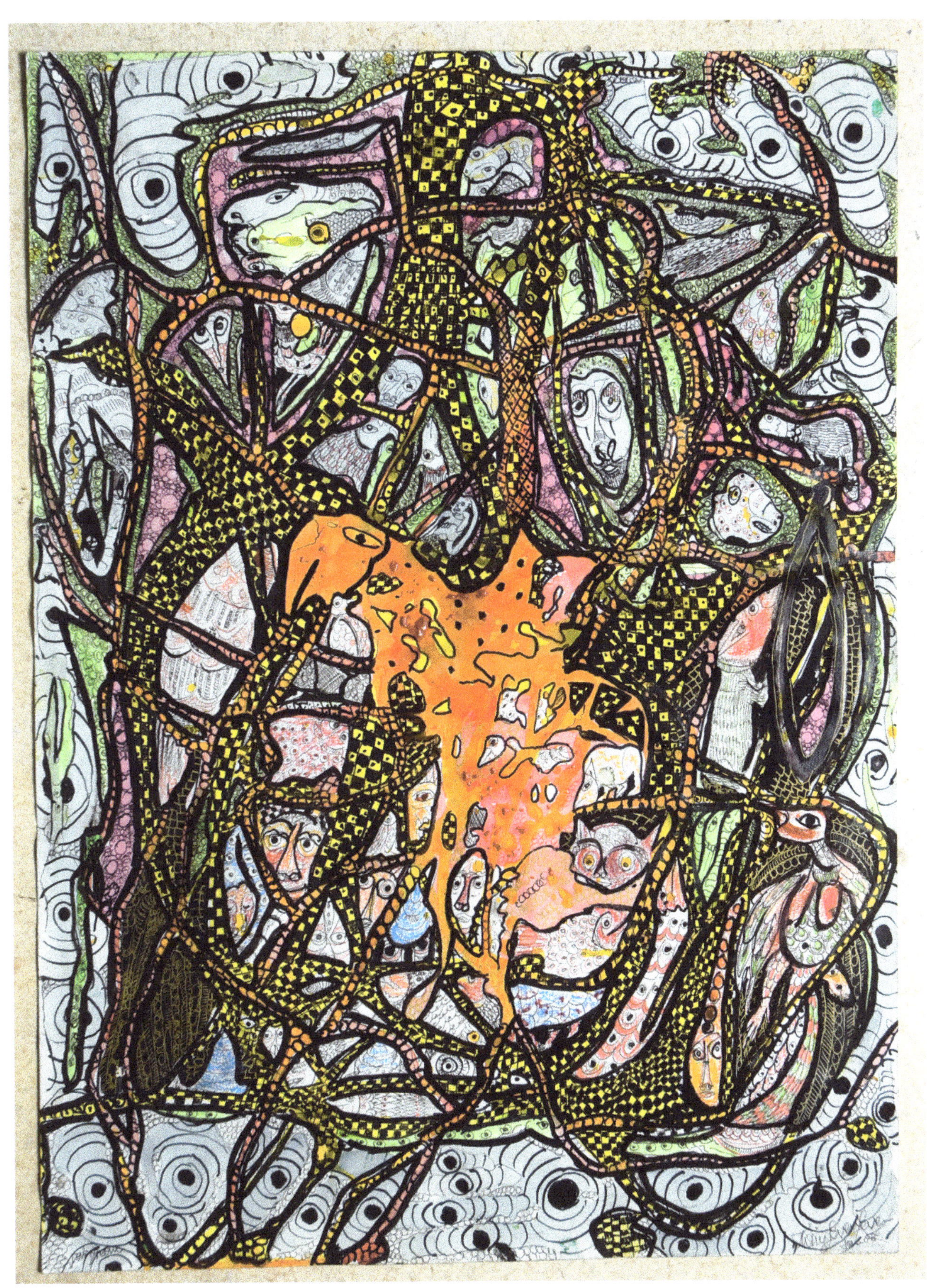

No. 26. *Creative Shapes in God's Diary.* 2005

plish the "absolute spirituality" of line that Prince found effortlessly in his first picture (chapter 8). Consistently Klee says in his diaries that he is an artist of the line; he found his first success with etching and engraving, remained uncomfortable with color until his trip to Tunisia in 1914.

Once Prince was moving on his career, he was shown pictures by Klee that must have reinforced his graphic tendencies, and Klee's example probably prompted Ulli Beier to recommend etching (chapters 8, 13) and drawing on glass (no. 12), but their similarities are not the result of influence, but of parallel inclinations to the linear. Prince, too, is an artist of line and form, to whom color came slowly. Klee, like Prince, was a gifted musician. They both use rhythm and melodic flights in their shared search for invisible shapes. Prince's work, like Klee's, builds on itself spontaneously. He had long been teasing smears into tattooed ornament (chapter 1, and nos. 4, 23, 29), so it was not much of a departure—and with no thought of Klee—when, a century later, he repeated Klee's experiments in Philadelphia. He began with spatters and spills, but not content to leave them alone—as Pollock and the potters of western Anatolia did—he worried them with the pen, as Klee had, into images of chaos and order (see also no. 16).

27

Portrait of George

Ink, batik dye, watercolor, and oil on canvas. 30" x 40". Philadelphia, 2007

In the winter of 2007, George Jevremović commissioned Prince to paint his portrait (chapter 16). Prince describes it:

"I used his photograph, but if I make him look exactly the way he is, it would not make him look like George. The idea here is that George, from the little I stay with him—he is a very kind man, but you better meet him when he is in good mood.

"I've never seen him screaming on anybody, and I've never seen him ignoring anybody, but when he has some personal problems, he doesn't want to talk. He acted like me sometimes. Like, I give, I give, I give to people, but occasionally when I have the feeling what I have is not enough for me, I don't want to give, and I don't want to say no. Then you get angry, but you don't show it. But it shows in your face. That's why I don't want to show his face.

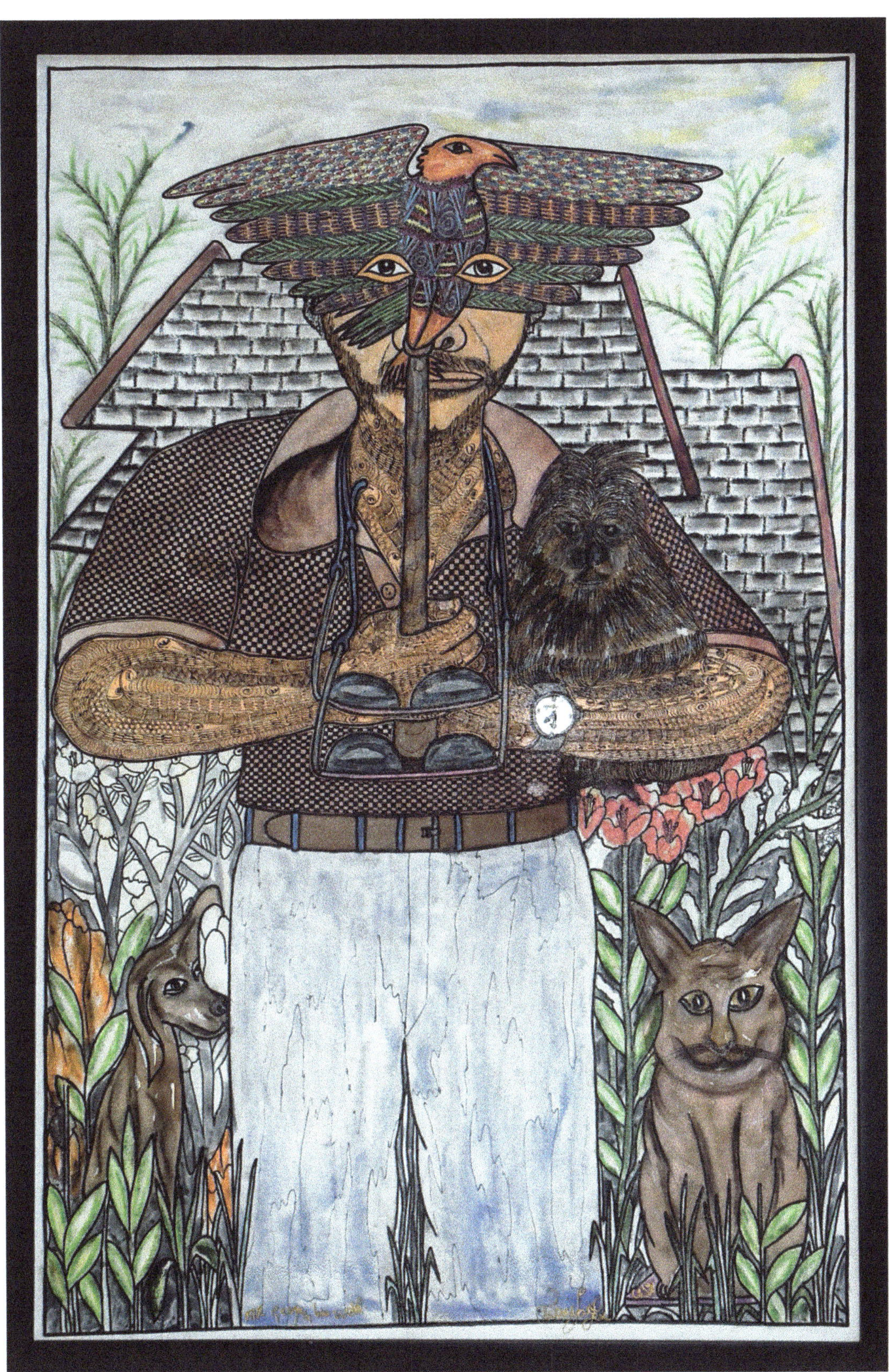

No. 27. *Portrait of George.* 2007

"I have to cover his face because he is different on different days; no one picture would get him perfectly."

Prince has explained why country people stand straight and do not smile when having their pictures taken, why artists of spiritual traditions draw people frontally, generalized and expressionless. The candid snapshot, rich with particularity, catches a specific, fleeting instant and but one of the subject's many moods; the whole person is lost. The generalized image is an attempt to capture a timeless identity, a stable essence, a soul. Prince posed George frontally and symmetrically, without motion. He attached signs for identification in the Yoruba manner (chapter 17), and he masked George to hide his shifting moods.

George liked it, saying Prince had "Africanized" him in the portrait. Prince continues, remembering a party he attended in Arizona, about 1986. It was thrown by wealthy people from Dallas who came masked to the party, and Prince gave George a mask like theirs—the mask of a dove—because he felt that George, though modest in appearance, belongs among such gracious, enviably affluent people:

"And then, I know as he is, even if he didn't tell me, he should belong to this kind of people. Because I was in Texas, couple of years ago, and I was invited to a real big, lot-of-people party. And everybody came in different kind of masks. Women have their own. And everybody rich, and everybody—white dress, black dress—everybody had some kind of mask. So, I made for him that kind. I said, Okay, George must have one. Let me cover that aspect of his face.

"And that time I look at him, he's always wearing two glasses. Even when he doesn't wear them, he have them hang on his neck. That's why you have those two.

"At that time, he always wear these short sleeves, checker, red-cloth shirt. And I notice that he loved this light-skinned jeans, you know. The jeans look like it is dirty, but it is new. So, I know he wear that."

Prince, a flamboyant dresser, is amazed that wealthy Americans dress so casually, masking differences of class:

"Back home, people when you are rich, or a big man, you wear *big* clothes. Here you don't wear no big clothes. You hardly know who's a rich man and who's not a rich man, because sometimes someone who is not even rich wear more expensive trousers than somebody who is rich. Or even what you call designer clothes worn by those who have no money—they buy it on credit. But those who have money will wear anything. Casual wear. You never know."

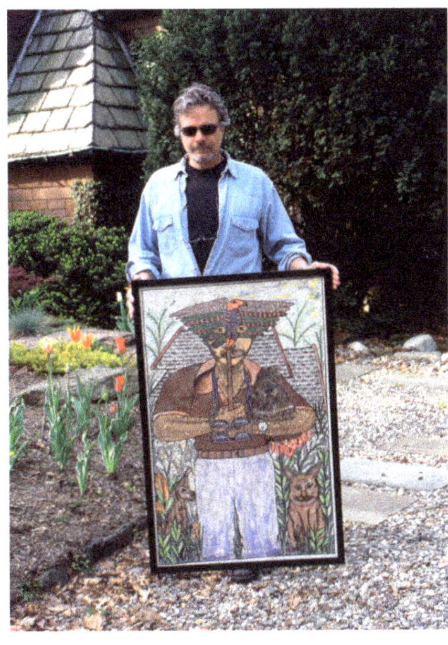

George Jevremović at home with his portrait by Prince. Philadelphia, 2008

George's modest dress disturbed Prince: "Even though he is very rich, he wear blue jeans, simple clothes." To clarify his status, Prince painted an expensive Rolex watch on George's left wrist, but George owns no such thing, and he made Prince repaint it. He did it roughly, then took his time and got it right. Prince caught George in casual attire, the glasses hanging around his neck, and further distinguished him by his pets: Simba, the "tiny dog with a lion's head," on his left arm, Henry the cat to the right, Smokey the dog on the left, but Smokey, Prince felt, was wrong:

"The only thing that I don't care about is the dog. I want to make the dog as small as possible. The dog should be bigger, but it would cover too much. Then I make the cat bigger than him."

Smokey was too small—too small because he was a big dog, far larger than the cat, and too small to balance the cat in the symmetrical composition of intersecting triangles—but Prince caught the slate roof of George's English vernacular house in Philadelphia. "I love it," Prince said of George's home, and then he concluded with an evaluation of his own work:

"You know, sometimes life can be funny. Sometimes you do something extraordinary, and sometimes you do something to *please* who wants it. It's like when I do his portrait here, I will not intentionally do a portrait like that, but something to make it unique and different from every other portrait.

"When you look at the way I paint Mister George portrait, some people will know I'm crazy. But they want to look and look and look. Because it's different from any other portrait.

"That's what I want—for them to look and look and look."

28
Spirits of My Reincarnation Brothers and Sisters

Ink, dye, and oil on linen. 6'x6'. Osogbo, 1968–1969. Collection of the Philadelphia Museum of Art. Purchased with funds contributed by John H. McFadden and with the gift of Material Culture, 2006

When the curatorial team of the Philadelphia Museum of Art came to the exhibition at Material Culture in the fall of 2005, this is the painting they chose (chapter 14). It shows, Prince said, "The spirits of *my* reincarnation brothers and sisters, the ones who came with me, and then they left." He represents the abiku twins who accompanied him into life, then died, as spirits in the other world. The long-necked one with breasts on the left is Alokolobo, pictured in *The Golden Bird and the Unnoticed Crowd* (chapter 14, p. 201). The devilish horned couple in embrace on the right resembles Adam and Eve from *The Beginning of the Fragile World* (no. 18). The monkey on the tree behind them is Edun, the protector of twins (chapter 4). The one on the far right is the destructive Sigidi (no. 4). Good and evil mix in the spirit world, as they do in this one. Prince remembers the creation of this painting:

"So, what is in my mind here is just dealing with the unseen world, the world of abikus. And this at the time that I always read Amos Tutuola's book when I do my paintings.

"It is an image of the other world.

"But in this period I smoked a lot. I smoked a lot. But now I don't smoke any; I slow down, get mellow. In those days I smoke a lot, and maybe—so, I think the smoking inspired a lot of my creativity. But now I don't smoke, and that is why my work is not as aggressive and scary. Because I remember I've done a painting, and I hang it, and I felt the painting is coming to get me," Prince laughs.

"I smoked but I never got too high to do what I am doing. It helped me a lot in my music too. When I'm driving, I hear sound in the air. I swear to Almighty God: most of the sounds in the music I play, I heard them when I'm driving. The beat of the air, by driving, become a background beat, and I started singing along, and some beautiful sounds would come from my mouth and—boom, it's a record.

"And I recorded a song on ganja:

It's true that I'm a smoker.
Rich people smoke, poor people smoke;
They smoke in America, they smoke in London.

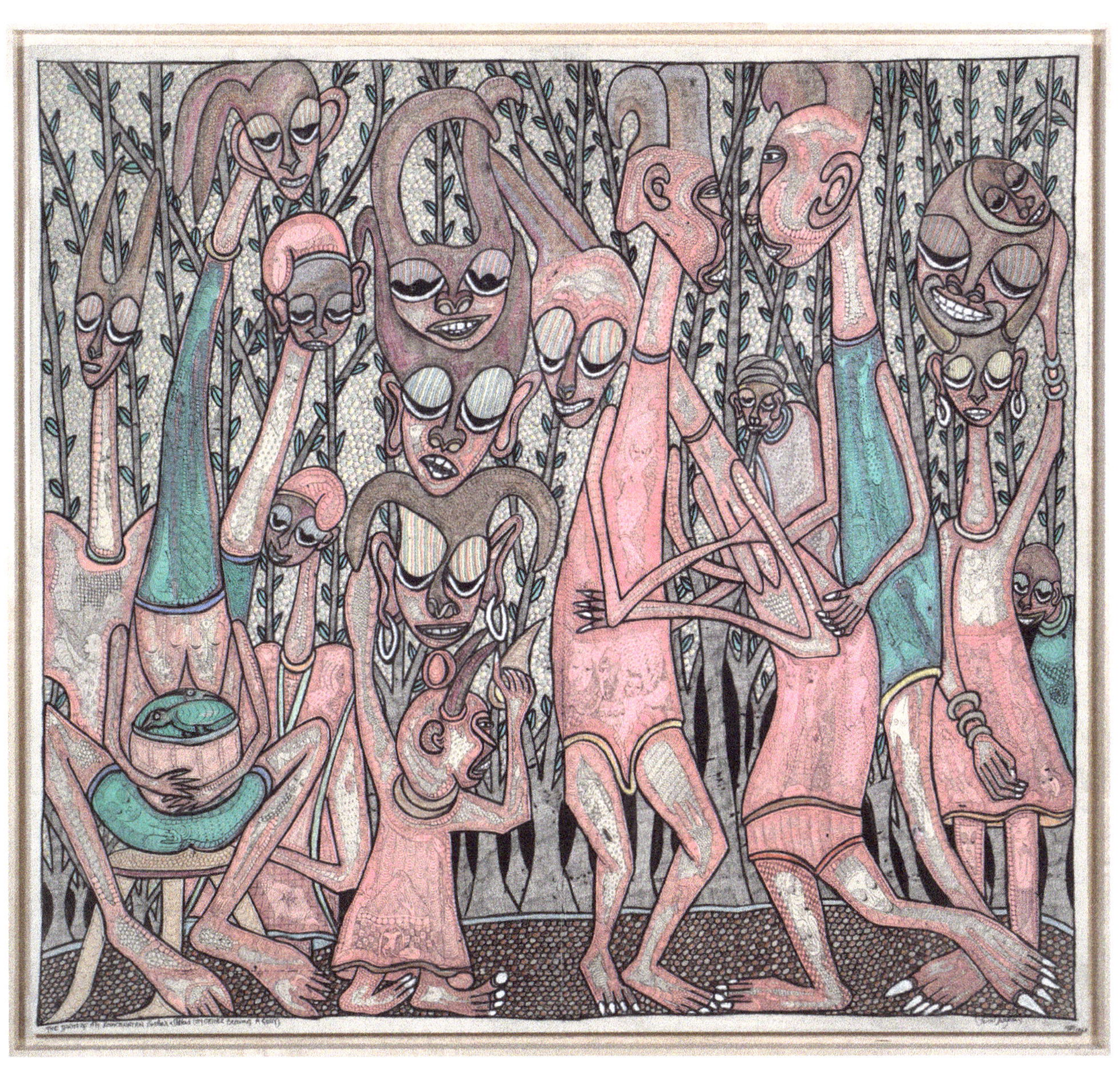

No. 28. *Spirits of My Reincarnation Brothers and Sisters.* 1968–1969

"I made that record," Prince laughs again.

From sounds in the wind, Prince creates songs. From patterns in woodgrain, he creates images. From this painting—excited by the most important sale of his American period—Prince created in quick succession two new paintings on cloth with the same title (no. 29).

29

The Spirits of My Reincarnation Brothers and Sisters

Ink, batik dye, watercolor, acrylic, and oil on cloth.
First version: 58" x 60". Philadelphia, 2006–2007. Second version: 65½" x 58". Philadelphia, 2007

Like the painting from the end of the sixties (no. 28), the new versions depict an assembly of spirits, with Alokolobo toward the left and Sigidi on the right. One difference is that the spirits make up a musical band. The major difference is the appearance of their leader on the midline. He stands straight while the spirits twist. This is Prince, not a likeness but—in the Yoruba style (chapter 17)—a generalized elder who signifies his presence and alters the interpretation. The spirits in the early painting represent his deceased brothers and sisters. Those in the new versions represent, through spirits blended of benevolence and malevolence, his "brothers and sisters" on earth who make Prince sad by making incessant demands on his resources of energy and money. The relation between the leader and his followers becomes clear in the "spiritual breast" Prince gave himself to feed them and in the figure he placed below him who licks from his *goje* and wears a clock around his neck to reckon the time difference between Nigeria and America, so he can call Prince on his cell phone and ask for cash (chapter 13).

Prince was amused by the glasses dangling from Alokolobo's neck in both of the new paintings. He borrowed them from the portrait of George Jevremović (no. 27) he was painting at the same time. George's glasses and Prince's self-portrait separate the Philadelphia paintings from the old one (no. 28), but for Prince the most important difference was the technique. The new works, he felt, were finer in craft. On them he used the combination of a "rainbow" palette with "tattoo" ornament (no. 4) that he developed early in the nineties (no. 20), brought to perfection in these paintings, and then continued in the series of fourteen paintings on cloth, including numbers 4 and 18 in this collection, when he returned to Nigeria in the spring of 2007 (chapter 16). In the old painting, Prince said:

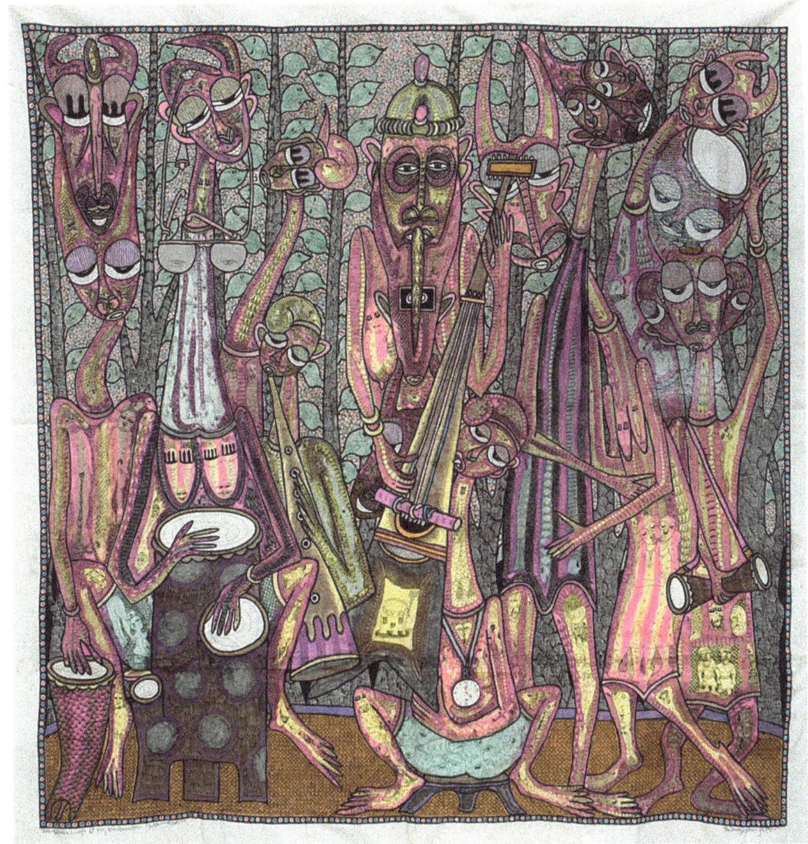

First version.
2006–2007.
See p. 174

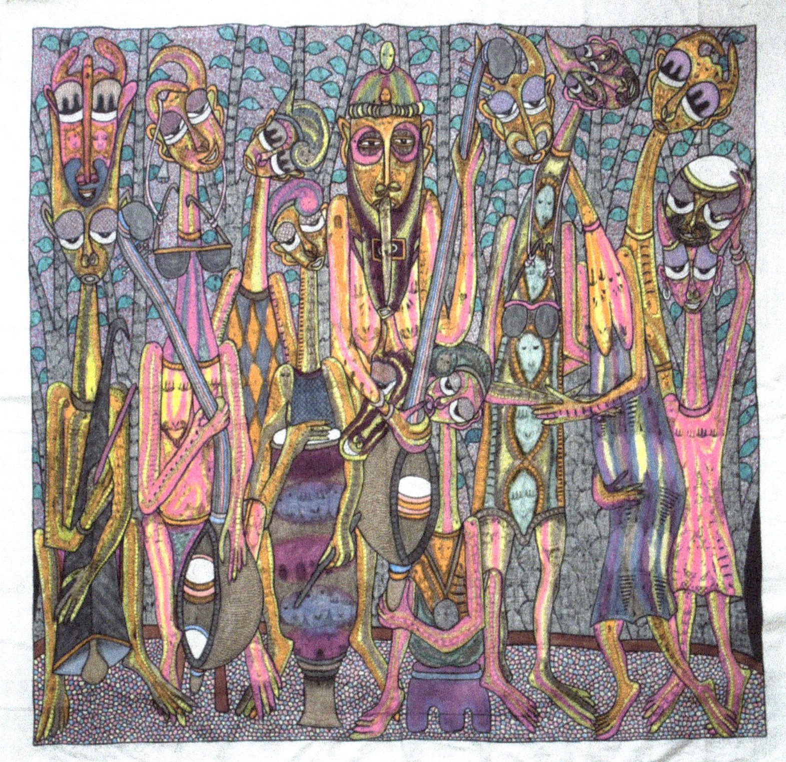

Second version.
2007.
See p. 417

The Spirits of My Reincarnation Brothers and Sisters

"I was thinking about the abikus. This is what I was thinking. The new one I do now have faces on the leaves. The leaves have faces. And there is more yellow; it is more yellowish. The new one has more color. Because I'm in America.

"The old one is different, but that one inspire me to go to this one, with this coloring.

"These colors are applied to the fabric already, and then you put the drawing on top of it.

"These are colors for making batik. You know, the dyeing, the fast color. The fast color that when you want to dye, you put it, you cover it with wax, and when you put it in dye and remove the wax, the color still remain there.

"That's the color I used there, and then I put pen and ink on it. Then I used oil and acrylic."

Color is bright in the American paintings and their tattooing deepens the meaning. In the first of the new paintings, there are musical instruments to echo the musical subject and a pair of Yoruba *ibeji* figures to reiterate on a different plane the theme of the twins. The ornamentation of the second incorporates a sketch from the painting *Barefoot President in a Fragile Boat with the World Tears Apart* (chapter 3, p. 53), which he had recently finished. In both paintings, drawings on the figures feature the most usual images in his repertory of tattooing: villages of round thatched houses that represent humanity (nos. 9, 25) and point backward in time, and the swarming fish who signal the pervasive goodness of the goddess Osun (nos. 7–10, 23). On both there are amorous couples, rare in his work, who stealthily establish causation: sexual desire led to all of this (see no. 18), to the twins who died and became spirits, to the man who lived to dance, make music, and paint, to the people around him who hound him for money (chapter 13).

Prince painted the first of the new versions to replace the old one that was sold to the Philadelphia Museum of Art (chapter 14, and no. 28). Then, finding it good and imagining its sale, he made a copy. Prince worked hastily on the copy, and he feels that he never quite finished it. The pen-and-ink work in the yellow stretches on the necks to the left is, in his mind, insufficiently complex. Prince concludes:

"I started the first one around November, two thousand and six. I work on it three weeks.

"It's a good one. A spiritual painting with ghosts.

"I hardly ever repeat myself, but one day I came and I think George, he feel like he wish he didn't sell the old painting to the museum. And that's why I did it. And then I did the other one. We have two, and you see the difference. They have more detail's work than the old one.

"Then I took the first one home, to look at it and try to copy. They are different, very different. When you put the two together and look, there's a lot of different things."

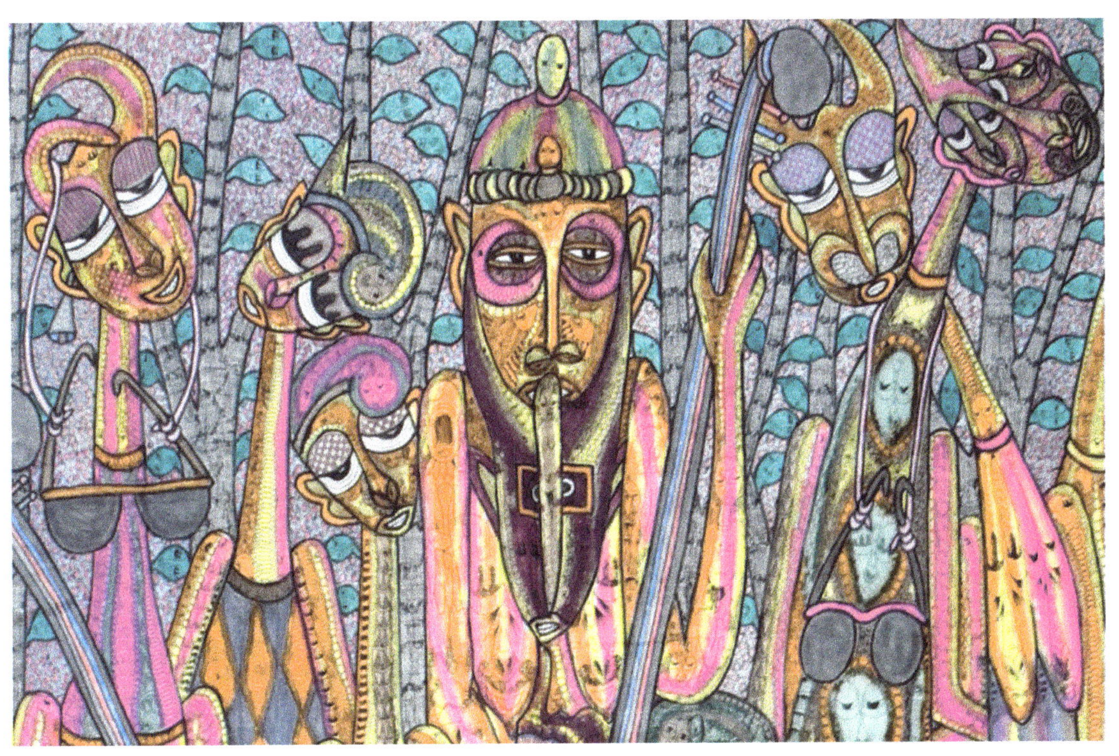

Prince among the spirits.
Detail from the second version of *My Reincarnation Brothers and Sisters.* 2007

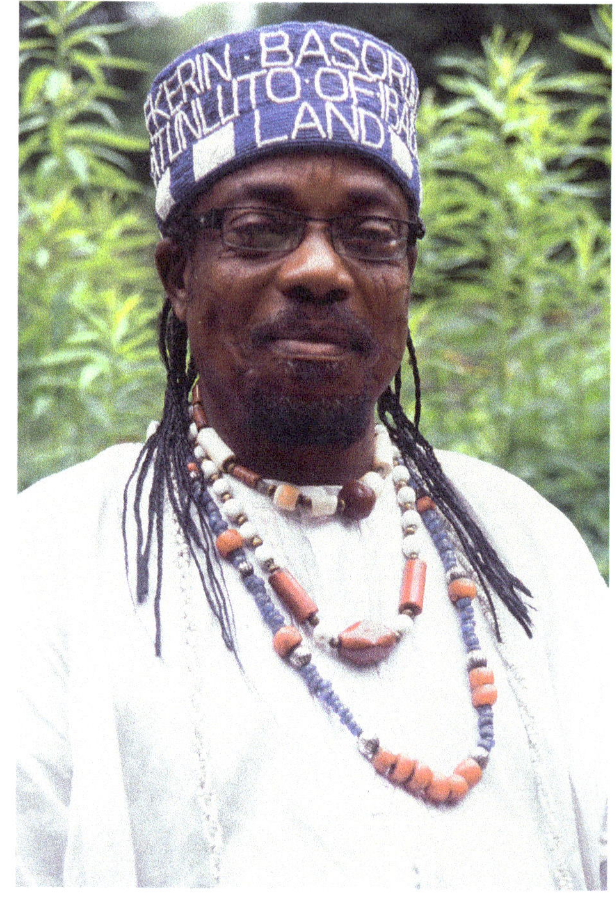

Prince Twins Seven-Seven.
Philadelphia. June 16, 2009

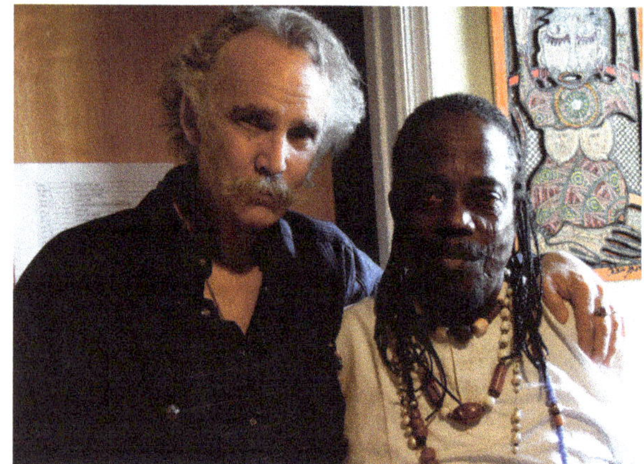

Henry and Prince. April 25, 2008

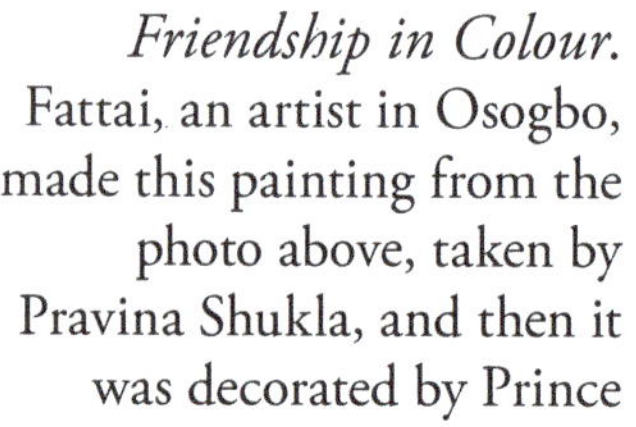

Friendship in Colour.
Fattai, an artist in Osogbo, made this painting from the photo above, taken by Pravina Shukla, and then it was decorated by Prince

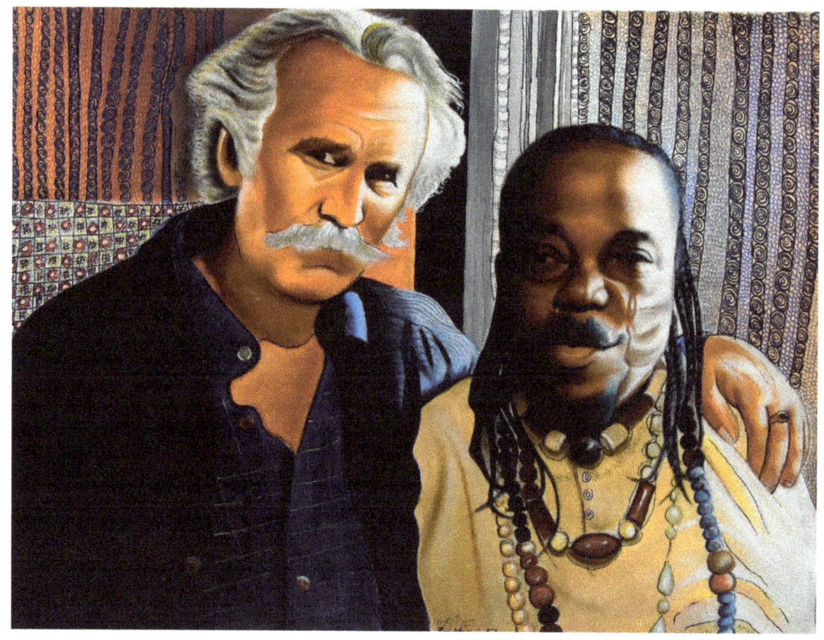

Afterword

Prince left America on June 9, 2008. When he called from home in July and August, Prince said he was "going around all the government people," hoping for a paying position, trying to get something done with the Resort. "What can I tell you, Doctor Henry? I'm just going around." When I asked in September how he was doing, Prince said, "The whole thing is just the same thing. I'm okay. I'm learning to live in Nigeria again." He laughed: "I'm here."

While one of the hopes he held in June moved from possibility to reality in the autumn, his calls became more frequent, and on the day after the election, Prince called me to praise Barack Hussein Obama's intelligence, to describe how Obama's acceptance speech had touched him. Prince was delighted that America would recover its "prestige in the world," and on the next day he called again to declare that Obama's victory was "a wonderful thing for America, and for Africa too. It is a symbol of revival of life for the *whole* world."

At the end of November Prince returned and we met for a couple of days of taped talk in Philadelphia, completing the collection in chapter twenty and enriching the commentary that accompanies his pictures. He called in December to say he arrived home safely after "a beautiful trip," called on New Year's Day to wish us the best, called on the day of the Inauguration to congratulate the United States for having, at last, a warm, brilliant, admirable president. Subsequent calls were regular but brief—reports of small events and continuing frustrations—until the first of April, when he called to tell me that, nine days earlier, Chief Busari Odunoye Osuntoki had died.

Chief Busari, the Mogaji, was gone, and, *inshallah*, Prince will become the Mogaji, a "stepping stone" to the throne of Ibadan, "the most important kingship in western Nigeria," Prince said. Eight lines descend from Osuntoki, who ruled from 1895 to 1897. Three are female lines, but the king must be chosen from a male line. Of the five male lines, three are extinct, leaving two candidates. The other man is younger than Prince and supports his selection, so Prince feels confident. What he needs are funds to sustain his campaign. Fortunately, a collector from Lagos bought some old works. Prince was able to buy goats to sacrifice and cloth so all the family's members could appear in identical dress at the funeral. On the phone, Sunday Ayantoye, Prince's driver and friend, told me, "Everyone is behind Twins because he is famous and popular. He gives lots of money away. They like it. You professors don't care about money, but we Africans love money. Twins gives money away, and everybody loves him. If you have money, people worship you."

Prince was gathering followers, consolidating his base. The men around him gave him new names of praise, names that will become part of the *oriki* sung to honor him—like the *oriki* still sung to honor the warrior Osuntoki—if Prince continues his ascent to the kingship. They call him Arikumasa (The man who sees death and refuses to run); his accident in 1982 brought him near death, but he recovered and fought back to fame. They call him Okunrinmeta (The man with three men's hearts), for he is a man of generosity and multiple talents, artistic, musical, and political.

"The most important part of my life is beginning," Prince told me, and during many calls in April and May he kept me abreast of developments. The mourning period lasts for five months. Chief Busari's widow will not leave the palace until August. In August, the selection will be made, and "public opinion polls," Prince said, indicate that he will be chosen, but the waiting is hard, the tension tremendous. To escape it all Prince flew to Philadelphia on June 8, 2009, a year after he left, and we met again in embrace.

Prince has lost weight. He is short of breath, feverish at night. The doctor's tests have revealed nothing serious, though he will have to go back to the hospital for further tests on June twenty-second, four days before he returns to Nigeria. The interviews are over; we sit, old friends, and talk. I ask how he will manage it. The Mogaji's task is to remain in the palace, listening to complaints, giving advice and rendering judgments, but he needs to travel, to get away, to meditate, to paint. Prince intends to set up a "kitchen cabinet" of wise men who can act in his absence, and he plans to renovate the palace, adding an upper story in the shape of a fish, since the fish is a symbol of Osun's power. Into the fish he will build a museum. The museum will teach the history of Yoruba war, celebrating his great-grandfather Osuntoki, and in it Prince will display his art and the art of other contemporary Yoruba creators. Once he has been selected, he will ask the Ifa priest to set an auspicious day for the coronation; Prince hopes it will fall in October. Becoming the Mogaji, the head of a lineage, is a requisite step in the lengthy process that leads a man, late in life, to the kingship of Ibadan. Prince says it could take ten years. But now this book is off to press, and Prince is waiting.

ACKNOWLEDGMENTS

My first debt is to Prince Twins Seven-Seven who was unfailingly generous with his time, who answered every question frankly and fully. George Jevremović was involved from the start—we dedicated this book to him—and he and Samantha gave me a place to stay when I was in Philadelphia, when Twins and I were talking. No expert on Africa, I was fortunate that my old friend Phil Peek, a genuine Africanist, was willing to read the manuscript and send me helpful reactions. Conventional it may be, but it must be said: what is wrong in this book is not Phil's fault. To bring this project to completion, I employed the currently fashionable digital technology; it slowed the process, increased the costs, and decreased the quality, but, living in this land famed for freedom, I had no other choice. I did have friends who struggled beside me. Karen Duffy got my hand-crafted manuscript into the computer with consummate care and diligence. The photographs of Prince's work were taken by members of the Material Culture staff and by my reliable, talented friends Michael Cavanagh and Kevin Montague. Matt Patterson, a man of skill and taste, worked to get their photographs and mine into the computer and bring them as close as possible to the high standard set by images on film. My colleague Dick Bauman let me borrow and draw two works from his splendid collection of African art. Harriet Schiffer, Prince's friend who works tirelessly to promote his art and music in the United States, compiled the list of his exhibitions that follows. John McGuigan, my pal of many years, took it all—text, pictures, and captions, notes, bibliography, and index—and working attentively to my design wrangled it into the form of a book on the computer. John is, as I am, a lover of books, and it was a pleasure to work with him on this one. Karen, Matt, and John made a fine team, and Dee Mortensen at the Indiana University Press was steady in the help she provided from the beginning to the end.

In the midst of it, the book a third done, I fell ill. Like Isaac Babel before his execution, what I wanted was to finish my work, to complete this scratch—the words are Faulkner's—on the wall of oblivion, and I am deeply grateful to the doctors who pulled me back from the brink of nothingness, to Jackie Trueblood, Eric Smith, and Rebecca Cohen. Administrators at Indiana University—Bennett Bertenthal, Bob Becker, Ruth Stone, and Sandy Dolby—proved kind at the time. My friends gathered around me: George and Samantha, Bill and Mary Beth, John and Pat, Nazif and Maha, Karen and Jim, Ray and Lorraine, Tom and Brooke, Michael and Joanna, Greg and Jennifer, David and Nick, Terry and Daphne, Mark and Carol, Vincent, Bob, Lee, Elliott, Ilhan, Takashi, Maggie, Dick, Fernando, Mehmet,

Ibrahim, Nurten, Ahmet, and three men named John. I can always depend on Judy, my sister, and my wonderful children came to my side, Harry, Polly, Lydia, and Ellen Adair. During that time Lydia brought the beautiful Maya into our lives, Ellen Adair's career in the theater took off, and during that time Pravina was heroic. She slept in the chair beside my bed when I was tangled up in tubes, little machines ticking, and she nursed me back. I am blessed that our lives are joined—Twins says we are as close as twins. Pravina, my wife, traveled with me to Nigeria, she read the manuscript closely, and she makes life worth living.

Here at this book's end, I look forward, excited by the rising generation of folklorists and ethnomusicologists, and I look back, remembering my masters who have passed, the men who made me: Fred Kniffen and Estyn Evans, Jim Deetz and James Marston Fitch, Kenny Goldstein, Erving Goffman, Bob Armstrong, Hugh Nolan, and Ahmet Şahin. I was lucky to have a father who was a scholar in his spare time, a grandfather who was a carpenter.

To all of them I am grateful. To Pravina I am more than grateful: to her I am bound forever in wondrous love.

Prince's Exhibitions

A List Compiled by Harriet Schiffer

1965

"Moderne Kunst aus Oshogbo." Neue Münchner Galerie, Munich, Germany.

"Third Anniversary Celebration of Mbari Mbayo." Osogbo, Nigeria.

1967

"Contemporary African Art." Institute of Contemporary Arts, London, England.

1968

"Contemporary Nigerian Art." Ori-Olokun Cultural Centre, Ile-Ife, Nigeria.

1969

"Contemporary African Art." Otis Art Institute, Los Angeles, California; Studio Museum in Harlem, New York; Cleveland Institute of Art, Cleveland, Ohio, U.S.A.

"Oshogbo Artists." Goethe Institut, Lagos, Nigeria.

"Contemporary African Art." Camden Arts Centre, London, England.

1970

Paintings by Twins Seven-Seven. Goethe Institut, Lagos, Nigeria.

"The Paintings of Twins Seven-Seven." USIS, Ibadan, Nigeria.

"African Painting at the BBC." Bush House, London, England.

"Oeuvres Africaines Nouvelles." Musée de l'Homme, Paris, France.

1971

"The Paintings of Twins Seven-Seven." Goethe Institut, Lagos, Nigeria.

"Moderne Malerei in Afrika." Museum für Volkerkunde, Vienna, Austria.

"Second Indian Triennial." Lalit Kala Akademi, New Delhi, India.

"Ten Artists from Nigeria." Arts Club of Washington, Washington, D.C., U.S.A.

"Mbari Mbayo Artists." Eighteenth Festival of the Arts, Virginia Union University, Richmond, Virginia, U.S.A.

"Contemporary Tapestries, Brass Castings, and Graphics from Nigeria." The Egg and the Eye, Los Angeles, California, U.S.A.

1972

Paintings by Twins Seven-Seven. Merton Simpson Gallery, New York, New York, U.S.A.

"New African Art in Czechoslovakia." Náprstek Museum, Prague, Czechoslovakia.

"Contemporary Nigerian Art." Montgomery College, Rockville, Maryland, U.S.A.

"Africa Creates '72." Union Carbide Gallery, New York, New York, U.S.A

"Oshogbo Artists." Goethe Institut, Lagos, Nigeria.

1973

Paintings by Twins Seven-Seven. Goethe Institut, Lagos, Nigeria.

"African Art." Colorado State University, Fort Collins, Colorado, U.S.A.

"Modern African Art." Everson Museum of Art, Syracuse, New York, U.S.A.

"Contemporary Nigerian Graphics and Textiles." National Center of Afro-American Artists, Boston, Massachusetts, U.S.A.

1974

Paintings by Twins Seven-Seven. National Museum, Lagos, Nigeria.

Paintings by Twins Seven-Seven. Goethe Institut, Lagos, Nigeria.

"Contemporary African Art." National Museum of African Art, Washington, D.C., U.S.A.

"Tradition and Change in Yoruba Art." E. B. Crocker Art Gallery, Sacramento, California, U.S.A.

"Graphics from Five Countries." Southern University, New Orleans, Louisiana, U.S.A.

"Art in Africa Today." Field Museum of Natural History, Chicago, Illinois, U.S.A.

"African Art Today: Four Major Artists." African-American Institute, New York, New York, U.S.A.

"African Prints: An Exhibition of Contemporary African Art." Kresge Art Museum, Michigan State University, East Lansing, Michigan, U.S.A.

"Contemporary Nigerian Art." Corcoran Gallery of Art, Washington, D.C., U.S.A.

1975

"Paintings by Twins Seven-Seven." Goethe Institut, Lagos, Nigeria.

"The Faces of Africa." Union Gallery, San Jose State University, San Jose, California, U.S.A.

"Modern Graphics by Ten Nigerian Artists." gallery rg, Curaçao, Lesser Antilles.

"Visions of Africa." Afro-American Cultural Center, Cleveland State University, Cleveland, Ohio, U.S.A.

"Art-Craft from Africa." Maryland Commission on Afro-American and Indian History and Culture, Annapolis, Maryland, U.S.A.

1976

"Two African Artists: I. M. Nour and Twins Seven-Seven." Carnegie Institute, Pittsburgh, Pennsylvania, U.S.A.

1977

"African Contemporary Art." Gallery of Art, Howard University, Washington, D.C., U.S.A.

1978

"National Art Exhibition." National Theatre, Lagos, Nigeria.

1979

"Moderne Kunst aus Afrika." Staatliche Kunsthalle, Berlin, Germany.

1980

"Twenty Years of Oshogbo Art." Goethe Institut, Lagos, Nigeria.

"Moderne Kunst in Afrika." Tropenmuseum, Amsterdam, The Netherlands.

"Contemporary Nigerian Artists: The Artists of the Oshogbo Workshops." New World Center Campus Art Gallery and Metropolitan Library System South Regional Library, Miami, Florida, U.S.A.

"Neue Kunst in Afrika." Mittelrheinischen Landesmuseum, Mainz, Germany; Universitat Bayreuth, Bayreuth, Germany.

"National Art Exhibition." National Theatre, Lagos, Nigeria.

1982

"De Goden Zijn Niet Dood." Provinciehuis, Zwolle, The Netherlands.

"Nigerianische Kunst-Ausstellung." Nigerian Cultural Centre, Bonn, Germany.

1983

"Oshobgo Arts." Elf House, Lagos, Nigeria.

1984

"Contemporary African Art." National Center of Afro-American Artists, Boston, Massachusetts, U.S.A.

"Evolution in Nigerian Art." Society of Nigerian Artists, National Theatre, Lagos, Nigeria.

1985

"Senegal bis Sambia: Neue Kunst aus Afrika." Bayreuth, Germany.

"Iwalewa: Afrikanische Kunst Heute." Städtische Galerie, Regensburg, Germany.

"Oshogbo Art." Commonwealth Art Institute, London, England; Commonwealth Institute, Edinburgh, Scotland.

"Silver Jubilee National Art Exhibition." National Theatre, Lagos, Nigeria.

"Myth and Image: An Exhibition of Works by 14 Nigerian Artists." Denton, Texas, U.S.A.

1988

"Art from the African Diaspora: Becoming Visible." Aljira Center for Contemporary Art, Newark, New Jersey, U.S.A.

"Uhuru: African and American Art against Apartheid." City Without Walls Gallery, Newark, New Jersey, U.S.A.

"Art by Metamorphosis: Selections of African Art from the Spelman College Collection." Department of Art, Spelman College, Atlanta, Georgia, U.S.A.

1989

"Tercera Bienal de la Habana." Centro Wilfredo Lam, Havana, Cuba.

"Les Magiciens de la Terre." Centre Georges Pompidou, Paris, France.

"Influences: Contemporary African and African American Art." Hodson Gallery, Tatum Arts Center, Hood College, Frederick, Maryland, U.S.A.

"Paintings and Drawings." Italian Cultural Institute, Lagos, Nigeria.

"Images of the Nigerian Nation." National Theatre, Lagos, Nigeria.

1990

"Songs of Power, Songs of Praise: Modern Visions from Haiti, Nigeria, and Papua New Guinea." San Jose State University Gallery, San Jose, California, U.S.A.

"West Africa: Powerful Patterns." Kauffman Museum, Bethel College, North Newton, Kansas, U.S.A.

1991

"Africa Hoy." Centro Atlántico de Arte Moderno, Las Palmas de Gran Canaria, Spain.

Paintings by Twins Seven-Seven. Taidemuseo, Hameenlinna, Finland.

1992

"Africa Now." Groninger Museum, Groningen, The Netherlands; Centro Cultural de Arte Contemporaneo, Mexico City, Mexico.

1994

Paintings by Twins Seven-Seven. Mucha Gallery, Philadelphia, Pennsylvania, U.S.A.

1996

"Er bestaat geen kunst in Afrika." Stadsgalerij Heerlen, Heerlen, The Netherlands.

1997

"Yoruba Diasporas I: Metamorphosis." October Gallery, London, England.

1998

Paintings by Twins Seven-Seven. Zak Gallery, Fürth, Germany.

1999

"New Colours from Old Worlds: Contemporary Art from West Africa." October Gallery, London, England.

2000

"A Concrete Vision: Oshogbo Artists in the 1960s." National Museum of African Art, Washington, D.C., U.S.A.

"Contemporary African Art: Five Artists, Diverse Trends." Indianapolis Museum of Art, Indianapolis, Indiana, U.S.A.

"Contemporary Art from Nigeria." October Gallery, London, England.

2001

"African Art: A New Perspective." African Art Museum of Maryland, Columbia, Maryland, U.S.A.

"The Short Century: Independence and Liberation Movements in Africa, 1945-1994." Museum Villa Stuck, Munich, Germany; Martin-Gropius-Bau, Berlin, Germany; Museum of Contemporary Art, Chicago, Illinois, U.S.A.

"Encounters with African Art." National Museum of African Art, Washington, D.C., U.S.A.

2002

"Prince Twins Seven-Seven: The Global/Living Myth Artist." Porter College Faculty Gallery, University of California, Santa Cruz, Santa Cruz, California, U.S.A.

2003

"The Global Living Myth of Africa: Past and Recent Works by Prince Twins Seven-Seven." The Allens Lane Art Center, Philadelphia, Pennsylvania, U.S.A.

"Twins Seven-Seven." James F. Lewis Museum of Art, Morgan State University, Baltimore, Maryland, U.S.A.

2004

"African Art, African Voices: Long Steps Never Broke a Back." Philadelphia Museum of Art, Philadelphia, Pennsylvania, U.S.A.

2006

New Acquisitions Display: *Sprits of My Reincarnation Brothers and Sisters*. Philadelphia Museum of Art, Philadelphia, Pennsylvania, U.S.A.

2007

"Twins Seven-Seven." Galerie in der Promenade, Fürth, Germany.

"Contemporary African Art from the Collection of William Jones." Aljira Center for Contemporary Art, Newark, New Jersey, U.S.A.

2008

"George Lilanga, Kivuthi Mbuno, Cheri Samba, Twins Seven-Seven." ARTCO Gallery, Herzogenrath, Germany.

"Mami Wata: Arts for Water Spirits in Africa and Its Diasporas." Fowler Museum at UCLA, Los Angeles, California; Chazen Museum of Art, University of Wisconsin, Madison, Wisconsin.

Notes

Introduction

P. 1. Spelling: Osogbo, Osun, Osuntoki, Sango, *ase*, and *orisa* are the contemporary spellings that Prince prefers. Like many in Yorubaland, he generally does not use the diacritics that would make it clear that these words would be pronounced by a speaker of English as Oshogbo, Oshun, Oshuntoki, Shango, *ashe*, and *orisha*. Depending on the one I am quoting, both spellings will appear in this book. Some Nigerian names are spelled in more than one way—Prince's birthplace is both Iyara and Ijara—but I steadily adhere to Prince's choice in spelling. Nigerian opinion: Ogundele, *Omoluabi*, p. 145; Adenaike, "The Oshogbo Experiment," p. 205.

P. 3. Armstrong's trilogy: *The Affecting Presence*, *Wellspring*, and *The Powers of Presence*. My essay on *Wellspring:* Glassie "Source for a New Anthropology." Bob Armstrong was remembered at his death in "Robert Plant Armstrong: A Memorial," *African Arts* 20:1 (1986): 30–31.

P. 4. Mister Imagination: Patterson, *Reclamation and Transformation*, pp. 34–63; Wardlaw, *Black Art*, pp. 186, 225–27, 271; Cerny and Seriff, *Recycled, Re-Seen*, pp. 50–54.

P. 5. Beier's book: *A Dreaming Life*, Prince told me, was based on his diaries, which he read aloud to Ulli Beier. Prince left his diaries with Ulli in Australia, but recently, Prince said, they have returned with Ulli Beier's papers to Osogbo where they will be housed in a cultural center dedicated to Beier's admirable work. A conspicuous difference between my book and Ulli Beier's lies in the representation of Prince's voice. I transcribed directly from tape and left myself in the text to make questions clear and preserve the integrity of unlinked statements, while Beier smoothed Prince's speech toward conventional prose and ran statements together creating larger units, though, I believe, he did not distort Prince's main message. More important is the fact that—see Briggs, *Learning How to Ask*—interviews are communicative occasions, constructed by both parties. When speaking to Beier, who knew much of the story already, Prince emphasizes the details of interpersonal relations, his connections to his colleagues in the Osogbo school, his collectors, his women, and he is careful to give credit politely to Ulli's wife, Georgina. In speaking to me, since I was less knowledgeable about his life and society, he placed more stress on my interests in art and culture, and he was more apt to construct explanatory narratives. But time is the main difference between Ulli Beier's book and mine. *A Dreaming Life* was published in 1999, but it is based on interviews from 1984–85, with some interviews from earlier dates. Coincidently, in Jegede's *Contemporary African Art*, published in 2000, the information about Prince also comes from an interview in 1985. These recent books do not cover recent events, do not tell of his chieftaincies in 1996 or his coming to America. The last quarter of a century is missing. Bringing the story up to date is one reason for this book, but a full analysis of Prince's art, attempted in no earlier writing, is a more important reason. Of significance, too, are the changes in the man between 1985 and the present, and the most important is the maturing of his thought, the shift of emphasis from magic to religion, from personal to cultural purpose, as he has refined his philosophy. *A Dreaming Life* and this book catch Prince at different stages of his development, so I felt it was important to keep his statements from 1984–85 separate from those of 2006–08. I have imported nothing from *A Dreaming Life* into my text, but in these notes I will comment on the relation between what Prince told me and what he told Ulli Beier. Southern pottery: Rinzler and Sayers, *The Meaders Family*; Burrison, *Brothers in Clay* and *Cousins in Clay*; Zug, *Turners and Burners*; Sweezy, *Raised in Clay*; Hewitt and Sweezy, *The Potter's Eye*.

P. 6. Method: My practice is sketched in Glassie, *Material Culture*, chap. 2, and in chaps. 3–4 of Glassie and Mahmud, *Living Traditions*, but it is best exemplified in these full studies: Glassie, *Turkish Traditional Art Today*; Glassie, *Art and Life in Bangladesh*; Glassie, *The Stars of Ballymenone*. The great poet's words: Heaney, *Finders Keepers*, p. 14. On Agee: I do not refer to Agee's knowledge of George Gudger (Floyd Burroughs)—see Bergreen, *James Agee*, pp. 164–77; Maharidge and Williamson, *And Their Children After Them*, pp. 88–96, 252—but to Agee's rhetoric of the ultimate unknowability of the living other in *Let Us Now Praise Famous Men*, pp. 12, 100, 105–11, 239–40, 245–46, 366. Categories of art: I have considered art's conventional subdivisions in *The Spirit of Folk Art*, concluding that art is art and such categories as fine, folk, pop, and primitive might be handy in conversation, but they are faulty in logic.

P. 7. Subjective revelation: I tell you what Prince said, and, Prince's friend, undistracted by rumors, I tell you about the man as I know him. Biography: *Sun Chief* by Simmons excited me when I was an undergraduate student in anthropology. Nabokov's *Two Leggings* is another of the Native American autobiographies I admire. Oscar Lewis's writings on Mexican people also inspired me in my student days. Biographies of writers, like Ellmann's on Joyce or Foster's on Yeats, in which the work and the life are read into each other, and the standard monographs of art history that include a biography and an assembly of works, like Panofsky's on Dürer or Grohmann's on Kandinsky, have guided me, but I would locate my effort along with that of my fellow folklorists who attend to both the life and the works in their studies of individual creators: narrators, poets, singers, and musicians: Hyde on Thomas Casey; Ó Duilearga on Seán Ó Conaill; Dégh on Zsuzsanna Palkó; Pentikäinen on Marina Takalo; Ferris on Ray Lum; Narayan on Urmila Devi Sood in *Mondays on the Dark Night of the Moon*; Ives on Larry Gorman, Lawrence Doyle, and Joe Scott; Abrahams on Almeda Riddle; Morton on John Maguire; Bird on Seydou Camara; Pearson on Archie Edwards and John Cephas in *Virginia Piedmont Blues*; Hansen on Richard Seaman; and the painters, sculptors, and artisans: Bascom on Duga of Meko, Goldstein on William Robbie; Jones on Chester Cornett in *Craftsman of the Cumberlands*; Peek on Ovia Idah and Eture Egbedi; Burrison on Lanier Meaders in *Brothers in Clay*; Zug on Burlon Craig in *Turners and Burners*; Vlach on Philip Simmons; Ferris on James Thomas; Davis on Elijah Pierce; Hunt on Roger Morigi and Vincent Palumbo in *The Stone Carvers*; Duffy on Virgil Boruff; George on A. D. Pirous in "Ethical Pleasure, Visual Dzikir, and Artistic Subjectivity in Contemporary Indonesia"; Kirshenblatt-Gimblett on Mayer Kirshenblatt; and Cochran on Dorris Curtis. I began working in this folkloristic tradition of the study of creative individuals with a paper on a basketmaker from upstate New York, William Houck, published back in 1967, and carried it on in my books on Ireland, Turkey, and Bangladesh. In this book it is not Matthew Hewell in Georgia, Hugh Nolan in Ireland, Ahmet Şahin in Turkey, Haripada Pal in Bangladesh, or Agawa Norio in Japan, but Prince Twins Seven-Seven who is my hero.

Chapter 1

P. 11. Sprung symmetry: Wilson, *Patriotic Gore*, pp. 484–85; Agee and Evans, *Let Us Now Praise Famous Men*, pp. 38–39, 140–46, 171, 202–4, 230.

P. 12. Carpet: Glassie, *Turkish Traditional Art Today*, chaps. 18–21. Chair: I base what I say on time spent in the Daud and Yusuf shops, Kwazakhela, Swat, Pakistan, in 1997; the chairs were like those in Kalter, *The*

Arts and Crafts of the Swat Valley, pp. 130–35. Gothic virtue: Ruskin, "The Nature of Gothic" from the second volume of *The Stones of Venice*, published in 1853. Teabowl: Glassie, *The Potter's Art*, pp. 100–107.

P. 13. Heroic ritual: Soyinka, *Myth, Literature and the African World*, chap. 1. Material subjectivities: Armstrong, *Wellspring*, pp. 42–44, 73; Armstrong, *The Powers of Presence*, pp. 3–6.

P. 15. The wedding of sky and earth: Soyinka, *A Shuttle in the Crypt*, p. 4.

P. 20. Birds and witches: W. Abimbola, *Ifá*, p. 152; Awolalu, *Yoruba Beliefs*, pp. 86–88; Bascom, *The Yoruba of Southwestern Nigeria*, p. 95; Armstrong, *The Powers of Presence*, pp. 57–58; R. F. Thompson, *African Art in Motion*, pp. 199–203; R. F. Thompson, *Black Gods and Kings*, chap. 11; M. T. Drewal, *Yoruba Ritual*, pp. 172, 178; Drewal and Drewal, *Gẹlẹdẹ*, pp. 71–75, 203.

P. 21. Elephants: In "Image and Indeterminancy," Henry Drewal provides a fine overview of the symbolic significance of the elephant among the Yoruba. Drewal's paper appears in an excellent volume, *Elephant*, edited by Doran Ross, in which a painting by Prince (p.135) and a batik by his former wife Nike (p. 274) show people riding elephants as signs of their power.

P. 32. The need for descriptions of the artist at work: F. Klee, *The Diaries of Paul Klee*, p. 239. Assemblage: In the conclusion to *African Art*, p. 380, Michel Leiris generalizes that the tendency to incorporation and collage is a major feature of African art.

P. 33. Seriate, syndetic composition: Armstrong, *The Affecting Presence*, pp. 121, 143, 154, 164–70; Armstrong, *Wellspring*, pp. 59, 101–50; Armstrong, *The Powers of Presence*, pp. 13–33, 49–51, 67–72, 78, 83–86, 90–93, 106–7; H. J. Drewal, in Abiodun, Drewal, and Pemberton, *The Yoruba Artist*, pp. 194–95; H. J. Drewal, "Beauty and Being," pp. 91–95; H. J. Drewal, in Ross, *Visions of Africa*, pp. 70–74; and Drewal, Pemberton, and Abiodun, *Yoruba*, pp. 16–18.

P. 34. Architecture: When I was writing about old houses in Virginia, in 1972, searching for the material signs of the change from the medieval to the modern, I used Robert Plant Armstrong's intensive-extensive opposition from *The Affecting Presence*, but the chief definitive oppositions were open-closed and asymmetrical-symmetrical, which accord with the syndetic-synthetic opposition that Armstrong would develop in *Wellspring* and *The Powers of Presence*. Continuing to learn, I found that W. G. Hoskins had anticipated my conclusions in *Provincial England*, chap. 7, and I would go on to discover comparable contrasts in Ireland and beyond, coming to believe that the change from open and asymmetrical to closed and symmetrical designs—from syndetic to synthetic designs—is a clear index to the shift to the modern that has happened in different places at different times. See: Glassie, *Folk Housing in Middle Virginia*, chaps. 6–7; Glassie, *Passing the Time in Ballymenone*, chap. 13; Glassie, *Turkish Traditional Art Today*, chap. 9; Glassie, *Vernacular Architecture*, pp. 51–61, 116–38, 146–59. I worked closely on this matter with my dear friend Jim Deetz—we dedicated books to each other—and his account of this massive historical change, built into the material world, can be found in his excellent book *In Small Things Forgotten*. Beckett: Harvey, in Knowlson, *Beckett Remembering, Remembering Beckett*, pp. 133–37. What Beckett wanted to do in drama—trading form for motion—is what Pollock did in his famous dripped paintings.

Chapter 2

P. 37. Abiku: Johnson, *The History of the Yorubas*, pp. 83–84, 137; W. Abimbola, *Ifa Will Mend Our Broken World*, pp. 41, 127; Soyinka, *Idanre*, pp. 28–30; Soyinka, *Aké*, pp. 16–19; Bascom, *The Yoruba of Southwestern Nigeria*, p. 74; Armstrong, *Wellspring*, p. 131; Drewal,

Pemberton, and Abiodun, *Yoruba*, pp. 15, 26; Quayson, *Strategic Transformations in Nigerian Writing*, pp. 122–24. Prince refers to his birth as an abiku in Beier's *A Dreaming Life*, pp. 73, 80, 83–84, but he elaborated more on the matter when speaking with me, and, p. 79, he lists, as he did in our first interview, the twins who preceded him and died; the details differ, but the pattern is the same. "In those days": Prince uses this phrase to refer generally to the distant past and specifically to the era before the British colonial intrusion.

P. 40. On the eastern origin of the Yoruba: Johnson, *The History of the Yorubas*, pp. 3–7; Adegbola, *Traditional Religion in West Africa*, pp. 410, 429–30; Turnbull, *Man in Africa*, p. 212. The rise of Ibadan as the successor to Oyo during the nineteenth century: Johnson, *The History of the Yorubas*, pp. 13–14, 94, 238–46, 282, 285–89, 293, 324–26, 403, 636–38; Lloyd, Mabogunje, and Awe, *The City of Ibadan*, chaps. 1–2; Falola and Heaton, *A History of Nigeria*, p. 76.

P. 42. Islam and Christianity: Johnson, *The History of the Yorubas*, pp. 26, 38–39, 296; Lloyd, Mabogunje, and Awe, *The City of Ibadan*, p. 249; Falola and Heaton, *A History of Nigeria*, pp. 87–89. Incomplete conversion: W. Abimbola, *Ifa Will Mend Our Broken World*, pp. 84, 149; Awolalu, *Yoruba Beliefs*, pp. 193–95. Prince speaks similarly of his people who profess Christianity and still follow the old faith in Beier's *A Dreaming Life*, pp. 14, 33. Inclusive polytheism: Gibbon, *Decline and Fall of the Roman Empire*, I, pp. 46–48.

P. 43. Nation: Johnson in *The History of the Yorubas*, chap. 2, says the Yoruba are not a tribe with subtribes, but a nation with tribes. W. Abimbola calls the Yoruba a nation in *Ifa Will Mend Our Broken World*, pp. 96–99, and nation is the word Achebe uses for his people, the Igbo, in *Home and Exile*, p. 3. Nation seems right to me.

P. 44. Cicatrices: Henry Drewal provides an excellent introduction to Yoruba marks in two papers, "Art or Accident" and "Beauty and Being." See too: Johnson, *The History of the Yorubas*, pp. 104–9; Soyinka, *Aké*, pp. 144–49; Bascom, *The Yoruba of Southwestern Nigeria*, pp. 43, 56; R. F. Thompson, *Black Gods and Kings*, chap. 12.

Chapter 3

P. 47. Agbeni market: Johnson, *The History of the Yorubas*, pp. 247–48. Yoruba palaces, expandable compounds with impluvium courtyards: Dmochowski, *An Introduction to Nigerian Traditional Architecture*, II, chap. 2, pp. 10–63; Johnson, *The History of the Yorubas*, p. 98; Willett, *African Art*, pp. 121–27; Vlach, "Architecture," in Peek and Yankah, *African Folklore*, p. 9. For comparable compounds beyond Yorubaland, see: Moughtin, *Hausa Architecture*, chap. 4; Prussin, *Architecture in Northern Ghana*; Oliver, *Shelter in Africa*, chaps. 3–4; and, above all, the books by Bourdier and Minh-ha, with their magnificent photographs and drawings: *African Spaces*; *Drawn from African Dwellings*, especially pp. 89–115; and *Habiter un Monde*. Sacred space: R. F. Thompson, *Face of the Gods*, pp. 146–47; Awolalu, *Yoruba Beliefs*, pp. 114–17.

P. 49. Osuntoki: The career of Prince's great-grandfather can be traced, though not easily or quite to the end, in Johnson's *The History of the Yorubas*, which was composed in 1897 when Osuntoki was in the second year of his reign in Ibadan. Johnson tells of Osuntoki's positions as Maye (Generalissimo) and Otun Bale, his victory in the Jalumi War of 1878, and his rise to power in Ibadan; see pp. 370, 426–36, 548, 550, 582, 636–37, 655, 670.

P. 50. Yoruba reincarnation: W. Abimbola, *Ifa Will Mend Our Broken World*, p. 35; Awolalu, *Yoruba Beliefs*, pp. 54, 60; Soyinka, *Myth, Literature and the African World*, pp. 10–11, 132; Bascom, *The Yoruba of Southwestern Nigeria*, chap. 7; Bascom, *Ifa Divination*, pp. 114–15; Bascom, *Sixteen Cowries*, pp. 35–36.

Prince speaks generally of reincarnation in Beier's *A Dreaming Life*, pp. 99, 104–5, much as he did to me, but the specific case of most importance was markedly different. Prince said, pp. 74–75, that his great-great-grandfather was a healer who worshiped Osun, that his father's people followed Osun, but he called himself, p. 110, a reincarnation of "Ogundaisi." In 1985, that is, it seems that he had not developed his understanding of his relation to Osuntoki, nor had he fully consolidated his dedication to Osun—aspects of his life that were foundational to his thought when our interviews took place in 2006–08. English proverb: Shakespeare, *Julius Caesar*, act 3, scene 2.

P. 52. Dilemma tales: Bascom, "African Dilemma Tales," and Lee Haring, "Dilemma Tales," in Peek and Yankah, *African Folklore*, pp. 90–91. Yoruba deities: The Indiana University Press has published two edited volumes, with excellent introductions, that treat particular Yoruba deities in their African presence and transatlantic expanse: Barnes on Ogun, Murphy and Sanford on Osun, and the Press promises for the future a comparable volume on Sango, edited by Tishken, Falola, and Akinyemi. (Those three, Sango, Ogun, and Osun, make a trinity for Prince.) Wande Abimbola's excellent *Ifá* can also be counted as a book on a god. Ifa is both the name of a procedure of divination and the name of a god, so the Muslim, who professes that there is no god but God, can mean, when he says he learned from Ifa, that he learned from the system, while a follower of the old faith means he learned from the god. In *Yoruba Beliefs*, pp. 23–24, Awolalu says Ifa is not a god, but a procedure, and Orunmila is the god, but Abimbola offers the view which I find to be general—it is certainly Prince's view—that Ifa and Orunmila are different names for one god, the god of wisdom. For more on the Yoruba deities: Soyinka, *Myth, Literature and the African World*; W. Abimbola, *Ifa Will Mend Our Broken World*, pp. 2, 20, 70–80, 95–96; K. Abimbola, *Yoruba Culture*, pp. 51–52, 72; Bascom, *The Yoruba of Southwestern Nigeria*, chap. 8; Fagg and Pemberton, *Yoruba*, pp. 195–200; Drewal, Pemberton, and Abiodun, *Yoruba*, chaps. 1, 6.

P. 55. Red, a dangerous color: W. Abimbola, *Ifá*, pp. 190, 239; M.T. Drewal, *Yoruba Ritual*, p. 147.

P. 60. The Oyo Empire and Sango: Johnson, *The History of the Yorubas*, pp. 11–14, 34–37, 149–52, 186–88, 190, 193–242, 268; Falola and Heaton, *A History of Nigeria*, pp. 48–52, 54, 56, 65, 74–77; Adegbola, *Traditional Religion in West Africa*, pp. 412–18; W. Abimbola, *Ifa Will Mend Our Broken World*, pp. 78, 101–2; Pemberton, in Drewal, Pemberton, and Abiodun, *Yoruba*, chap. 6; R. F. Thompson, *Face of the Gods*, pp. 152–54, 163, 232. The tale of Osun's origin: Bascom, "Oba's Ear"; W. Abimbola, *Ifa Will Mend Our Broken World*, p. 125. Verger's version in *Lendas Africanas*, pp. 47–49, is the usual story. Oba and Osun, two of Sango's three wives, are rivals. When Oba asks why Sango prefers her food, Osun, whose ears are hidden by her headtie, says she cuts her ears into his soup, that the mushrooms in the soup are her ears. Then Oba, in culinary competition for Sango's affection, cuts one of her ears into his soup, and Sango, furious, finds the soup and Oba repulsive. Osun reveals that her ears were not cut; the co-wives fight and turn into rivers. In Ulli Beier's brief version in *Yoruba Myths*, pp. xii–xiii, the central episode of the usual tale, lacking any account of origins, reduces the myth to what Beier calls "a typical Yoruba trickster tale, of the type we associate with the character of tortoise, rather than a Yoruba *orisha*." Beier's judgment of generic distinctions is apt, and when I asked Prince about the difference between his story and the usual version, Beier's in particular, Prince said that Beier's small, comic story of trickery is the one generally known, while his full, serious version is known only by people, like himself, who have been initiated into Osun's cult. Prince told me his story three times, all of them different in length but alike in their plots and characters (see chapter 20, no. 8). Adepegba offers a different story of how Sango's three wives became rivers in Murphy and Sanford, *Osun* *across the Waters*, pp. 103–4 (a book that also includes a brief report of the usual story, pp. 72–73, apparently from Brazil).

P. 61. *The Beginning of the End*: chapter 20, no. 19. Sacrifice for Osun: Prince offers her vegetarian fare, and, in general, though she is also given blood sacrifices, vegetarian food predominates: W. Abimbola, *Ifá*, p. 140; Awolalu, *Yoruba Beliefs*, pp. 47, 163 for Osun, pp. 37, 163 for Ogun.

Chapter 4

P. 63. Abiku: See the notes to p. 37. Two worlds: Drewal, Pemberton, and Abiodun, *Yoruba*, pp. 14–16; Bascom, *The Yoruba of Southwestern Nigeria*, chap. 7; K. Abimbola, *Yoruba Culture*, pp. 36, 51–52; W. Abimbola, *Ifa Will Mend Our Broken World*, p. 3; M. T. Drewal, *Yoruba Ritual*, pp. 26, 33, 47.

P. 65. Omielja: Prince also speaks of the lake in Beier's *A Dreaming Life*, pp. 73–74, saying it was drained in a ritual every seven years. Beier spells it Omi Eleja; I spell it as Prince told me to spell it.

P. 71. Wild hair: Bewaji, *Beauty and Culture*, pp. 129, 132. Prince calls himself a dada child in Beier, *A Dreaming Life*, pp. 80, 109–10, 147.

P. 75. Twins and names: Pemberton, in Drewal, Pemberton, and Abiodun, *Yoruba*, pp. 170–76; Fagg, pp. 15–17, and Pemberton, pp. 80, 162, in Fagg and Pemberton, *Yoruba*; R. F. Thompson, *Black Gods and Kings*, chap. 13; R. F. Thompson, *African Art in Motion*, pp. 51–52, 111; Johnson, *The History of the Yorubas*, pp. 79–83; Bascom, *The Yoruba of Southwestern Nigeria*, p. 74; Bascom, *Sixteen Cowries*, pp. 35–36; Fakeye and Haight, *Lamidi Olonade Fakeye*, pp. 52, 71, 75–76, 80–81; Drewal and Drewal, *Gẹlẹdẹ*, pp. 58, 134–36, 229–31, 250–52; W. Abimbola, *Ifa Will Mend Our Broken World*, p. 81; K. Abimbola, *Yoruba Culture*, pp. 118–19; Adams, *Designs for Living*, pp. 51–52.

Chapter 5

P. 79. Spatial history: Momaday, *The Man Made of Words*, pp. 36, 74–76, 207; Momaday, *The Names*, pp. 97, 142. In *Conversations with N. Scott Momaday*, Schubnell usefully gathers the transcripts of many interviews in which Momaday graciously, patiently answers repetitive questions, at points raising the connection of history with place, oral tradition with the landscape, implying parallels between his writing and Faulkner's: pp. 38, 112, 158–60. Nabokov describes the general orientation to space in Native American histories in *A Forest of Time*, chap. 5. Among many Native American people, prophecy works, as divination does among the Yoruba, to bring the past and the future into the present; see Mould, *Choctaw Prophecy*. For Hugh Nolan and Irish spatial history: Glassie, *The Stars of Ballymenone*, chap. 8 and pp. 377–80. The past has not passed: Faulkner, *Requiem for a Nun*, p. 92.

P. 82. American ghosts: Jones, *Things That Go Bump in the Night*, chap. 1. Ghosts and wraiths: Glassie, *The Stars of Ballymenone*, chap. 19. Divination brings all of time into the present: W. Abimbola, *Ifá*, p. 10; W. Abimbola, *Ifa Will Mend Our Broken World*, p. 87; and see Soyinka, *Myth, Literature and the African World*, pp. 144–46.

P. 85. Koranic concoction: Mungo Park's reports of his tortured trips to Africa, one at the end of the eighteenth century, the other concluding with his death early in the nineteenth, make great reading and provide historical depth for many practices later observed by anthropologists. Park got to the Niger but did not get into Yorubaland, so his book is of slight use to me, but he does describe making a potion like the one Sule makes for Prince: *Travels in Africa*, pp. 137, 213.

P. 86. Divination among the Yoruba: W. Abimbola, *Ifá*; Bascom, *Ifa Divination*; Bascom, *Sixteen Cowries*. Those are the primary texts, but see too: Johnson, *The*

History of the Yorubas, pp. 32–34, 160; Onaiyeken, in Adegbola, *Traditional Religion in West Africa*, pp. 48–51; Awolalu, *Yoruba Beliefs*, pp. 122–32; W. Abimbola, *Ifa Will Mend Our Broken World*, pp. 85–95; K. Abimbola, *Yoruba Culture*, pp. 80–82, 95; Bascom, *The Yoruba of Southwestern Nigeria*, pp. 70–71; R. F. Thompson, *Black Gods and Kings*, chap. 5. African divination in general: Peek, *African Divination Systems*, pp. 11–14, 79–80, 89, 117–18, 183, 193, 195, 214; Peek, "Divination: Overview," in Peek and Yankah, *African Folklore*, pp. 91–92. Prince's talk of divination in Beier's *A Dreaming Life*, pp. 87–96, is excellent, and it complements my treatment in this chapter, for traveling with Prince, I concentrated on the performance of the procedures, but *A Dreaming Life* concentrates on the accuracy of prediction. The two come together, since Prince's main hope in 1985 was the same as his main hope in 2006: that he would become the king of Ibadan.

P. 87. Northeastern *agbigba* divination: Bascom, *Ifa Divination*, pp. 6–7, 9, 11; Bascom, *Sixteen Cowries*, p. 22; W. Abimbola, in Murphy and Sanford, *Osun across the Waters*, p. 141.

Chapter 6

P. 93. Scottish authenticity: Currie, Prefatory Remarks in the biographical first volume, pp. 1–31, of *The Works of Robert Burns*. Stay a while with Burns. A century after his death, Henderson ended his historical survey *Scottish Vernacular Literature*, chap. 14, with a tempered assessment of Robert Burns, arguing that his authenticity, his dedication to a particularly Scottish tradition, prevented him from becoming one of the greatest masters of English verse. And so it is with Prince: though he is as innovative and talented as many of the acknowledged luminaries of modern art, his work is too thoroughly Yoruba to permit smooth assimilation into the big books of art history. Both Burns and Prince worked, oppositionally, for local cultural revival. Henderson quotes Burns as saying that he composed easily, then polished fastidiously. His work was bold and caring. So is Prince's; fluid and swift in the beginning, it is refined delicately at the end. Something in their personalities joins them. Henderson opines that, a great poet, Burns was an even greater personality, robust and attractive; he might have made a better politician than a poet. Prince's personality is comparably striking; see Jegede, *Contemporary African Art*, p. 42. Ulli Beier begins *A Dreaming Life*, p. 11, by saying that Prince's great creation is himself. And, for better or worse, Prince is drawn to politics. Their shared authenticity, rooted and extravagant, fills their creations, and even more, perhaps, it grounds their charisma. Bold and charming, Burns and Prince gathered people around them; both had many problems with many women.

P. 101. Serial, syndetic composition: See the notes to p. 33.

Chapter 7

P. 111. Ulli Beier meets Prince: Beier, *Contemporary Art in Africa*, p. 113. Ulli Beier tells this story again in *A Dreaming Life*, p. 7, and Prince tells it in that book, pp. 16–17, 29.

Chapter 8

P. 113. Ulli Beier and the Mbari Mbayo Club: Ogundele, *Omoluabi*, pp. 31, 36, 59–61, 97, 104–25, 140–50, 154–70, 194, 244; Beier, *Contemporary Art in Africa*, part 2; Kennedy, "I Saw and I Was Happy"; Fanilola, "Theater: Duro Ladipo and Yoruba Folk Theater," in Peek and Yankah, *African Folklore*, pp. 464–65.

P. 115. On Wole Soyinka: Soyinka's memoirs *Aké*; *Ìsarà*; *Ibadan*, pp. 60–61, 66 (quoted), 70–71, 208, 230–32 (quoted), 265, 290, 372; and *You Must Set Forth at Dawn*, pp. 46–47, 112, 154–55, 242–49. Ogunbiyi and Awe provide useful biographical information in their contributions to Adelugba, *Before Our Very Eyes*, pp. 48–85. In advance of his skilled chronological reading of the plays—the treatment of *Death and the King's Horseman*, pp. 117–27, is excellent—James Gibbs provides a biography (up to 1984) and surveys the playwright's field of influence in *Wole Soyinka*, chaps. 1–2. A drama of tradition, disruption, and death: In his useful critical edition, *Wole Soyinka, Death and the King's Horseman*, Gikandi includes Soyinka's play, pp. 1–63, Ladipo's play, translated by Ulli Beier, pp. 74–89, and a chronology of Soyinka's life, pp. 223–25. The traditional practice at the foundation of the plays was described by Johnson in *The History of the Yorubas*, pp. 56–57. Soyinka on revival and shifts of medium: Soyinka, *Ibadan*, pp. 9, 66, 187; Soyinka, *Myth, Literature and the African World*, chap. 4; and Soyinka, "Theatre in African Traditional Cultures." Brian Crow accurately locates Soyinka's action within the romantic tradition of modernism in Adelugba, *Before Our Very Eyes*, pp. 147–69. In *Isuma*, Michael Evans provides a rich instance of how, as Soyinka argued, shifts of medium bring myth into new life.

P. 117. Ulli's account: Beier, *Contemporary Art in Africa*, pp. 113–14. Beier tells again of Prince's beginning in art in *A Dreaming Life*, p. 8, and in that book Prince tells the story on p. 18. Jegede offers another version in *Contemporary African Art*, p. 43. The details differ, but all accounts end with Prince using a pen to draw.

P. 118. Tutuola: Parrinder's Foreword to *My Life in the Bush of Ghosts*, especially p. 11. Quayson's reading of Tutuola in *Stragic Transformations in Nigerian Writing* concludes with, pp. 58–59, an independent corroboration of syndetic ordering. He had not read Armstrong on Tutuola and syndesis, nor Drewal on seriate composition, but he writes that Tutuola's stringing of stories denies closure. On Tutuola's importance: Achebe, *Morning Yet on Creation Day*, pp. 76, 110; Achebe, *Home and Exile*, pp. 44–45, 54–55, 60, 68–69. Tutuola and Prince: Beier, *Contemporary Art in Africa*, p. 116; Armstrong, *Wellspring*, pp. 62–82, 143–44. The designer of the City Lights edition of Tutuola's *Feather Woman of the Jungle* glimpsed the connection and put a painting by Prince—*The Anti-Bird Ghost*, an early version of a common subject—on the book's cover. The novel itself is instructive. Presenting a series of stories, set like *The Arabian Nights* in a narrative situation, it exhibits the materials—synthetically structured tales—out of which Tutuola constructed the syndetic strings in his earlier, more acclaimed, novels.

P. 119. Illustration: Panofsky, *The Life and Art of Albrecht Dürer*, pp. 188–90.

P. 121. Barbara Ann Teer: Prince brought her into the story in 2006, but when he spoke with Ulli Beier two decades earlier, his relation with Barbara Ann Teer, who died in 2008, was a major topic; *A Dreaming Life*, pp. 81, 156–58, 179–87.

P. 123. Prince and Ladipo: Beier, *A Dreaming Life*, p. 7. Also in *A Dreaming Life*, p. 18, Prince tells that Ladipo did not take him to Germany, but he does not speak of the despair that caused him to consider suicide.

Chapter 9

P. 125. The art story: Soyinka, *You Must Set Forth at Dawn*, pp. 188–221. Historical time: Braudel, *On History*, especially part 2.

P. 126. Western reactions to Prince's art: See chapter 19, and pp. 423–26.

P. 132. Hagop Barın's story: Glassie, *Material Culture*, chap. 3. The car accident: When Prince visited Ulli Beier in Australia to narrate his autobiography, it was only two years after the wreck, so the account in *A Dreaming Life*, pp. 47–50, is fresh, detailed, and emotional.

P. 133. Decline in productivity: Adenaike, "The Oshogbo Experiment," p. 205. Picasso opposes simple developmental schemes: Ashton, *Picasso on Art*, p. 5. Ulli favors the imaginative: Beier, *Contemporary Art in Africa*, pp. 116–18.

P. 134. Nigerian market: In Beier's *A Dreaming Life*, pp. 60–64, Prince was angry that foreigners believed his work was appreciated only by Europeans. After usefully describing his expat buyers, pp. 57–60, and saying he depended on European customers until 1970, Prince said that now—1985—he had more Nigerian than European patrons, and he spoke at length about Babs Akerele, his brother-in-law, who owned the largest collection of his art.

P. 136. Commercial beginning: The story of his sale to an Israeli is important to Prince, and in "the Ulli book," Beier's *A Dreaming Life*, pp. 20, 23, 57, he identifies the buyer as Joel Spitzer and calls him "the first real collector of my work."

Chapter 10

P. 143. Political history. For the national events in this chapter, I relied on Falola and Heaton, *A History of Nigeria*, chaps. 7–9; Williams, *Nigeria*, pp. 23–30; and Wole Soyinka's writings: Soyinka, *The Open Sore of a Continent*, pp. 12, 15, 37–40, 95, 98–106, 152–53; Soyinka, *You Must Set Forth at Dawn*, pp. 15–18, 55–58, 132, 184–87, 347–48, 373–96, 413, 427, 461.

P. 144. Election fraud: Prince also tells how he was elected to the House of Representatives but his name was not forwarded in Beier's *A Dreaming Life*, p. 51.

P. 145. "Osogbo is part of Ibadan": At the time Osogbo lay in Oyo State, of which Ibadan was the capital; the new state of Osun, with Osogbo as its capital, was not erected until 1996: Falola and Heaton, *A History of Nigeria*, pp. 192–93.

P. 147. Abiola and Abacha: Soyinka, *The Open Sore of a Continent*, pp. 15, 48, 152–53.

P. 150. Speech is not prose; oral narratives shape poetically: Hymes, *"In Vain I Tried to Tell You,"* chap. 9.

Chapter 11

P. 153. Prince's wives: The account of his wives is longer and more detailed in Beier's *A Dreaming Life*, pp. 22, 96–98, 100, 147–69, 172–77. It was apparently a topic of high interest for Prince and Ulli in 1985. His story in this chapter is shorter, shortened not out of deceit but out of a desire for drama and clarity. Prince holds nothing back, and he would have told more if I had asked, but *A Dreaming Life*, which he gave me as a gift, had gotten the information into print. Had Prince gone back to add Iyabo to his list of wives, then he would have had two, not one, when his mother urged him into polygamy, and he would have had eight wives, not seven. His wives did not leave suddenly after his wreck; their departure began earlier, continued for a while after. Still, the outline holds and it is clear: his polygamy began in earnest after Bintu's attack (the lead story of this chapter, which he told to Beier, pp. 149–50, much as he told it to me); he had, at any one time, no more than seven wives before his wreck; all of them left, and he had five—only two of whom had arrived when he talked to Beier—afterward.

P. 156. Fela and the musical scene when Prince was young: Waterman, "Yoruba Popular Music," pp. 480–85; Ewens, *Africa O-Ye!*, pp. 94–105; Williams, *Nigeria*, pp. 53–54, 336; Soyinka, *You Must Set Forth at Dawn*, pp. 27–30; Falola and Heaton, *A History of Nigeria*, pp. 196–97.

P. 159. Nike: Williams, *Nigeria*, p.163; Scott, "Nike Olaniyi." Prince often speaks of Nike in Beier's *A Dreaming Life*, pp. 152–55, 159, 168, 172–73, saying she was the one who helped him with his art and she was the wife with artistic talent. Though she says bad things about him from a distance, Prince said, "she wants to have her own life, and I don't bother her about it." Nike provides her version of events in Vaz, *The Woman with the Artistic Brush*. Things fall apart: W. B. Yeats, "The Second Coming," Allt and Alspach, *The Variorum Edition of the Poems of W. B. Yeats*, pp. 401–2. Achebe continued the historical line of *Things Fall Apart* in *No Longer at Ease*, and Adichie carried it on in *Purple Hibiscus*, which recalled Achebe (and Yeats) in its opening sentence, "Things began to fall apart at home. . . ." Achebe turned back to explore once more the horrific moment of change in *Arrow of God*, a novel as great as *Things Fall Apart*, and Adichie returned to that moment in a recent story, "The Headstrong Historian." These fine Igbo writers of different genders and generations caught the instant when things began to fall apart, historically, socially, and traced the disastrous consequences.

Chapter 12

P. 162. Prince also tells the story of his Ilobu chieftaincy in Beier's *A Dreaming Life*, p. 70. Beier spells the title Omolodun; Prince spells it Amuludun. Prince's later and more important chieftaincies in 1996 are not described in Beier's book because, though it was published in 1999, its chronology ends in 1985.

Chapter 13

P. 171. Smiling beast: The Spider's Bush in Tutuola's *My Life in the Bush of Ghosts*, pp. 89–95, provides the setting but not the beast who is the subject of Prince's etching.

P. 177. Deracinated self-interest: Turnbull, *The Lonely African*, pp. 35–36, 53, 59, 68, 125, 129, 204, 250; see too: Turnbull, *Man in Africa*, pp. 280–82; Bohannan, *Africa and Africans*, p. 25. Turnbull pictured an individual of amoral self-interest, suspended between religions in a colonial setting. The novelist Richard Wright located a comparable social type, particularized as the fictional Bigger Thomas in *Native Son*, a man stuck low in the hierarchy of class in the United States. As Wright explains in his essay "How 'Bigger' Was Born," which has been appended to later printings of his novel, including the 2008 edition that commemorates the centennial of Wright's birth, the man, whether black or white, who rejects the old-time religion and folk culture of his raising and orients himself to the pop culture of capitalism, but who, uneducated and untrained, cannot succeed financially, comes to embrace in bravado a life of spontaneous action. Wright's Bigger Thomas, like Turnbull's Lonely African, personifies deracination and frustration, isolation and selfishness; they are the casualties of modernization. Failure, though, is not inevitable, as Wright made plain in his jolting, heroic memoir *Black Boy*. Despite a hard, fatherless, impoverished childhood, Wright's self-interest led him to success in art, just as Prince's did. Prince was loose in the world, but he anchored himself in tradition, charismatically gathered followers, and, blessed with exceptional talent, succeeded in the brave new world, as Bigger did not, as Richard Wright did.

P. 187. Spiraling stories: Glassie, *The Stars of Ballymenone*, pp. 261–64.

Chapter 14

P. 205. Environmental palette: Ashton, *Picasso on Art*, pp. 6, 59. *Scientist in Animals' Kingdom*: chapter 20, no. 16.

P. 206. Idea into art: Shahn, *The Shape of Content*, pp. 51–53, 61–65, 70, 124.

P. 208. The early version of *My Reincarnation Brothers and Sisters*: Dykstra, *Philadelphia Museum of Art Annual Report, 2006*, pp. 35, 59. See chapter 20, no. 28.

Chapter 15

P. 219. Ethical connections: Nuttall, *Shakespeare the Thinker*, pp. 314–15; see too Ribner, *Patterns in Shakespearian Tragedy*, pp. 139–42.

P. 222. Masquerade: Griaule, *Folk Art of Black Africa*, pp. 60–61, 68–70, 79–82, 89, 90–92, 126. See too: Leiris and Delange, *African Art*, pp. 128–43, 272–73; Cole, *I Am Not Myself*, pp. 16–25.

P. 229. Egungun: Bascom, *The Yoruba of Southwestern Nigeria*, pp. 92–97; R. F. Thompson, *African Art in Motion*, pp. 213–25; Adedeji, in Adegbola, *Traditional Religion in West Africa*, pp. 117–27; Euba, in Abiodun, Drewal, and Pemberton, *The Yoruba Artist*, pp. 161–69; Pemberton, in Drewal, Pemberton, and Abiodun, *Yoruba*, pp. 175–87; Drewal and Mason, *Beads, Body, and Soul*, pp. 266–75; M. T. Drewal, *Yoruba Ritual*, pp. 90–98; Cole, *I Am Not Myself*, pp. 61–63.

P. 230. The Osun Festival in Osogbo: Olupona, in Murphy and Sanford, *Osun across the Waters*, pp. 54–61; Falade, *The Comprehensive History of Osogbo*, pp. 42, 44, 66, 174–90 (a book that says Osogbo is distinguished in art, the home of Prince Twins Seven-Seven, pp. 220, 222).

P. 234. Susanne Wenger: Ogundele, *Omoluabi*, pp. 36, 59–61; Soyinka, *Ibadan*, pp. 231–32; Soyinka, *You Must Set Forth at Dawn*, pp. 68–69; Beier, *Contemporary Art in Africa*, chap. 9; Kennedy, *New Currents, Ancient Rivers*, chap. 5.

P. 236. Susanne Wenger's sculpture: Don Cosentino's clever, engaging essay "Afrokitsch" stumbles a bit when it passes through Osogbo. He seems to think that Susanne Wenger's controversial statues at the Osun shrine were made by the painters, Prince and his colleagues from the third Mbari Mbayo workshop, Oyelami and Buraimoh, but they were not, and he thinks there is no market for the artists in Nigeria, which was once true, but was not the case when Cosentino wrote in Susan Vogel's *Africa Explores*, published in 1991.

P. 242. Twenty-eight children: When Prince offers a grand total of his children, it includes both children and grandchildren. The total impresses the people around him. An old friend of his told me that each of his seven wives gave him seven children—an exaggeration and mysteriously neat, which suggests how others view his power.

Chapter 16

P. 259. Interviews: Truesdell, "A Life in the Field," which includes, p. 61, a photo of Prince and me.

Chapter 17

P. 263. A reasonable definition: "Yoruba art is the art Yoruba people do," John Picton writes in Abiodun, Drewal, and Pemberton, *The Yoruba Artist*, p. 23.

P. 264. Following Thompson and Armstrong in Turkey: Glassie, *Turkish Traditional Art Today*, pp. 91–119, 178–86, 332–68, 783–869. Yoruba style: R. F. Thompson, "Aesthetics in Traditional Africa"; R. F. Thompson, "Yoruba Artistic Criticism" (the fullest account of his project); R. F. Thompson, *African Art in Motion*, chap. 1; R. F. Thompson, *Black Gods and Kings*, chap. 3; Armstrong, *The Affecting Presence*; Armstrong, *Wellspring*; Armstrong, *The Powers of Presence*. Also: Fagg, "On the Art of the Yoruba," in Fagg and Pemberton, *Yoruba*; Fagg, "The African Artist"; Fagg, *Nigerian Images*; Abiodun, Drewal, and Pemberton, *The Yoruba Artist*; Drewal, Pemberton, and Abiodun, *Yoruba*; Bascom, *The Yoruba of Southwestern Nigeria*, chap. 9 (he refers to Thompson's work on p. 112); Gillon, *A Short History of African Art*, chap. 11. And in general: Griaule, *Folk Art of Black Africa*; Leiris and Delange, *African Art*, chap. 7; Willett, *African Art*, pp. 106, 150–52, 190–205, and he usefully summarizes Thompson's project, pp. 195–98; Bascom, *African Art in Cultural Perspective*, pp. 4–19; Bascom, "Creativity and Style in African Art"; Vogel, *African Aesthetics*, pp. xi–xvii; Adams, *Designs for Living*.

P. 265. Midpoint mimesis: R. F. Thompson, "Aesthetics in Traditional Africa," pp. 376–77; R. F. Thompson, "Yoruba Artistic Criticism," pp. 32–34; R. F. Thompson, *African Art in Motion*, pp. 26–27; R. F. Thompson, *Black Gods and Kings*, chap. 3, p. 1. Abstraction and realism: Kandinsky, in Kandinsky and Marc, *The Blaue Reiter Almanac*, pp. 158–60. Also Kandinsky, *Concerning the Spiritual in Art*, pp. 50–52. Lamidi Fakeye: Fakeye and Haight, *Lamidi Olonade Fakeye*, p. 142. The book includes an excellent autobiography of Fakeye; for more on him see: Ogunwale, "Lamidi Fakeye"; Willett, "An African Sculptor at Work"; Willett, *African Art*, pp. 209–19, 228–31; Mount, *African Art*, pp. 33–38, 194–95.

P. 266. Conceptual beginning: Fagg, *The Webster Plass Collection of African Art*, p. 10. Also: Fagg, *Nigerian Images*, pp. 118–19; Cole, *I Am Not Myself*, p. 18. Physical and spiritual interaction: Drewal, Pemberton, and Abiodun, *Yoruba*, pp. 16–17, 63, 71; Armstrong, *The Powers of Presence*, p. 12; Sieber and Rubin, *Sculpture of Black Africa*, p. 16; Peek, "Ovia Idah and Eture Egbede," p. 54.

P. 267. Noam Chomsky: I refer you to these of his writings: Chomsky, *Syntactic Structures* (the theoretical breakthrough); Chomsky, *Cartesian Linguistics* (the philosophical setting); Chomsky, *Problems of Knowledge and Freedom* (chap. 1 is especially clear on the innate); and Chomsky, *Language and Problems of Knowledge* (not only clear on the innate, but also entertains parallels in the visual and geometric realms, permitting my use of his work: pp. 4, 134–35, 152, 171–72, 184). Poetic imagination: Lowes, *The Road to Xanadu*.

P. 268. Philosophy in art: Danto, *The Philosophical Disenfranchisement of Art*. Typological representation: R. F. Thompson, *Black Gods and Kings*, chap. 3, pp. 1–2; Armstrong, *The Affecting Presence*, pp. 104, 118; Fagg and Plass, *African Sculpture*, p. 143; Pemberton, in Drewal, Pemberton, and Abiodun, *Yoruba*, p. 202; Ogundele, *Omoluabi*, p. 92. Also: Griaule, *Folk Art of Black Africa*, pp. 94–98, 106–7, 115; Adams, *Designs for Living*, p. 13; Bravmann, *Islam and Tribal Art in Africa*, p. 166; Fernandez, "Principles of Opposition and Vitality in Fang Aesthetics," p. 363; Boyer, *Baule*, pp. 20, 27–28, 34, 68–70. Generous generalization: Holbek, *Interpretation of Fairy Tales*, pp. 442, 445; Baxandall, *Painting and Experience in Fifteenth-Century Italy*, pp. 46–48.

P. 269. Ephebism: R. F. Thompson, "Aesthetics in Traditional Africa," p. 378; R. F. Thompson, "Yoruba Artistic Criticism," p. 56; R. F. Thompson, *African Art in Motion*, pp. 5, 7; R. F. Thompson, *Black Gods and Kings*, chap. 3, p. 3; Armstrong, *Wellspring*, p. 34. Aesthetics: Vogel, *African Aesthetics*, pp. xiii–xvii. Also Leiris and Delange, *African Art*, pp. 40–46. Proportion: R. F. Thompson, "Yoruba Artistic Criticism," pp. 42–48; R. F. Thompson, *African Art in Motion*, pp. 51–52; Armstrong, *The Affecting Presence*, pp. 96, 106; Armstrong, *The Powers of Presence*, pp. 60, 64; Fagg, *Nigerian Images*, p. 24; Leiris and Delange, *African Art*, pp. 229, 231; Bascom, "Creativity and Style in African Art," p. 118; Willett, *African Art*, pp. 150–52. Straightness and symmetry, verticality and frontality, segmentation and unity: R. F. Thompson, "Yoruba Artistic Criticism," pp. 53–55; R. F. Thompson, *African Art in Motion*, pp. 9, 20, 24, 26, 51, 143; R. F. Thompson, *Black Gods and Kings*, chap. 3, p. 2; Armstrong, *The Affecting Presence*, p. 114; Armstrong, *Wellspring*, p. 36; Armstrong, *The Powers of Presence*, pp. 55, 87–88; Fakeye and Haight, *Lamidi Olonade Fakeye*, p. 174; Drewal and Drewal, *Gẹlẹdẹ*, p. 263; Fagg, *Nigerian Images*, p. 42; Pemberton, in Fagg and Pemberton, *Yoruba*, p. 126; Willett, *African Art*, p. 106; Boone, *Radiance from the Waters*, pp. 158–60. Straightness concludes in intensive continuity: Beier, *African Mud Sculpture*, p. 41; R. F. Thompson, "Yoruba Artistic Criticism," pp. 58–59; R. F. Thompson, *African Art in Motion*, pp. 43–49, 80, 112, 143; Armstrong, *The Affecting Presence* (intensive continuity is the conclusion); Armstrong, *Wellspring*, chap. 1; Armstrong, *The Powers of Presence*, p. 12.

P. 271. Twins: See the notes to p. 75.

P. 272. Yoruba importance in art: Armstrong, *The Affecting Presence*, pp. xiii, 65–66; Bascom, *African Art in Cultural Perspective*, pp. 85–92; Willett, *African Art*, p. 18; Fagg, *Nigerian Images*, p. 9; W. Abimbola, in Abiodun, Drewal, and Pemberton, *The Yoruba Artist*, p. 137. Spiritual conclusion: Griaule, *Folk Art of Black Africa*, pp. 60–61, 68–70, 79–82, 89, 94–98, 108–9. Spirit partners: Ravenhill, *Dreams and Reverie*; Ravenhill, *The Self and the Other*, pp. 26–31; Boyer, *Baule*, pp. 8–9, 20–29. Sacred art: R. F. Thompson, *African Art in Motion*, p. 191.

P. 273. Comparison: Willett, *African Art*, p. 106. Hinduism and Hindu art: Chaudhuri, *Hinduism*; Coomaraswamy, *The Indian Craftsman*; Coomaraswamy, *The Arts of India and Ceylon*; Coomaraswamy, *The Dance of Śiva*; Dutt, *Folk Arts and Crafts of Bengal*; Michell, *Hindu Art and Architecture*; Blurton, *Hindu Art*; Shearer, *The Hindu Vision*; Pal, *Hindu Religion and Iconology*; Eck, *Darśan*. I have selected a few admirable works to recommend out of a massive bibliography, but I base what I say on my fieldwork in India and Bangladesh; for the *murti*, see especially Glassie, *Art and Life in Bangladesh*, pp. 128–67, 211–23, 313–66, 441–53. Three gods: For Wande Abimbola, they are Sango, Ogun, and Ifa; *Ifa Will Mend Our Broken World*, p. 48. For Wole Soyinka, they are Sango, Ogun, and Obatala; *Myth, Literature and the African World*, chap. 1. Scattered power: In *Flash of the Spirit*, pp. 5–6, Thompson says that *ase*—spiritual power, creative force—scatters through creation. The deities have *ase*, and *ase* comes from the gods and abides differently in every human being, profoundly in the Ori, the head provided by Obatala and chosen by the individual, so every human being partakes of the divine, and divine power rises with particular strength in the priests and priestesses who are imaged as avatars of the gods in the Yoruba tradition. This power guides Prince to depict priests and priestesses as spirits (chapter 20, nos. 6–8, 17), positioned during ritual between deities and people. But all people have *ase*—the Ori is a divinity—and their energy causes their images to be pulled from the particular toward the general, from the physical toward the spiritual, to reveal the simultaneity within them of the biological and spiritual dimensions of their being, to expose their possession of *ase*. See: R. F. Thompson, *Black Gods and Kings*, chap. 9; Armstrong, *Wellspring*, pp. 26–31; Fagg, *Nigerian Images*, pp. 24, 122–23; Drewal, Pemberton, and Abiodun, *Yoruba*, pp. 16–17, 26; Drewal and Drewal, *Gẹlẹdẹ*, pp. 5–6; W. Abimbola, *Ifá*, p. 113; W. Abimbola, *Ifa Will Mend Our Broken World*, pp. 5, 83.

P. 274. Olayanju's myth of Osun (401 deities): K. Abimbola, *Yoruba Culture*, pp. 126–27; Fagg and Pemberton, *Yoruba*, p. 198. In Murphy and Sanford, *Osun across the Waters*, Abiodun (pp. 16–18, 28–29), Adepegba (pp. 106–7), W. Abimbola (pp. 144–46), Ogunbile (pp. 191–94), and R. F. Thompson (p. 252) offer a different but parallel myth. In the beginning, Olodumare created seventeen deities. Osun was the last and only female. (The deities were 16 + 1, as in the other tale they were 400 + 1.) When Oldumare was asked why things were going wrong, the gods were informed that it was because Osun had been left out of their plans. When she was brought into consultation, when her beneficent power was included, the world was brought into order. Shiva in extension: Armstrong, *Wellspring*, p. 53; Armstrong, *The Powers of Presence*, p. 21. Hindu artists: I talked with Pitchai Velar in 1999, Rajesh Kumar Gour in 2003, and during my years in Bangladesh, beginning in 1987, Haripada Pal became the main source of my understanding of *murtis*: Glassie, *Art and Life in Bangladesh*, pp. 307–66; Glassie, *The Potter's Art*, pp. 19–34.

P. 275. Illustration: Scholars of religion who are familiar with Christianity and Judaism tend to base understanding on written texts. That works for Islam. But polytheistic religions, having many deities, have many conflicting texts and no single text that is as fundamental as those of the monotheistic religions that arose in the Middle East, in which the word, not the image, is basic. During interpretation, scholars of the Yoruba religion use the verses of Ifa divination as the scholars of Islamic art use the Holy Koran, and they report myths, though rarely in full, verbatim texts. Myths, that is, seem to be valued more as information than as art, and Robert Plant Armstrong told me that, in his view, the great works of the Yoruba religion, its affecting presences, are not verbal, but visual: they are statues, masks, masquerades, spectacles in which power enters the mind through all the senses at once, but most immediately through the eye. Drewal and Drewal begin their outstanding book *Gẹlẹdẹ*, pp. 1–14, with the idea of the spectacle. They characterize the masquerade of western Yorubaland as an instrumentality, a worldly manifestation of otherworldly power, as a "multimedia production," a spectacle, defined, p. 78, as a combination of "actual sights and mental images of ethereal entities." In spectacle, the seen and unseen become visible in the manner of spiritual art. The masquerade is central to the artistic expression of the Yoruba religion, and its spirit, its startling revelation of the unseen into visibility, is central to the art of Prince Twins Seven-Seven. Its parallel in Hindu art is the *murti* in *puja*, a visible device for communication between the worlds. Hinduism has great texts that can be employed in interpretation like the Bible or Koran, but the prime works of the sacred—the key texts—are, as Bob Armstrong believed to be the case with the Yoruba, visual, not verbal. They are the statues of the gods that focus the spectacle. The Christian image illustrates a myth, but the Hindu myth illustrates an image; see Glassie, "Mud and Mythic Vision."

P. 277. African religions (as they function in a manner parallel to Hinduism): Bascom, *The Yoruba of Southwestern Nigeria*, chap. 8; Bascom, *African Art in Cultural Perspective*, pp. 11–12; M. T. Drewal, *Yoruba Ritual*, pp. 182–85; Griaule, *Folk Art of Black Africa*, pp. 24, 44, 50–51, 58, 68–70, 89–92; Leiris and Delange, *African Art*, pp. 220–23; Cordwell, "African Art," pp. 41–43; Fagg, *Nigerian Images*, pp. 122–24. My point is parallels in culture, in logic and action, but if, as Claude Lévi-Strauss argues in *Tristes Tropiques*, pp. 396–410, an aniconic monotheism interrupted the expanse of an older iconic polytheism, if there was once in history a religious unity of Europe and Asia (that, likely, included northern and western Africa), then it is interesting that in ancient Greece and Rome, as in India and Yorubaland, there were two worlds and deals were struck in ritual between them, between the gods of that world who wanted praise and sacrifices and the people of this world who wanted the aid of the deities as they struggled on. For ancient Greece and Rome, see Hansen's excellent *Handbook of Classical Mythology*, pp. 43–46. Japan: Suzuki, *Zen and Japanese Culture*; Chiba, *The Seven Lucky Gods of Japan*; Wilson, *Inside Japanese Ceramics*; Kawano, *Hagi*; Cort, *Seto and Mino Ceramics*. Those are among the many books that provide some background, but I base what I say on fieldwork, begun in 1992, and partially reported in Glassie, *The Potter's Art*, pp. 91–116.

P. 278. New Mexico (historical images): Espinosa, *Saints in the Valleys*; Wroth, *Christian Images in Hispanic New Mexico*. The López family: Briggs, *The Wood Carvers of Córdova*; Salvador, *Cuando Hablan Los Santos*, pp. 62–71, 95; Rosenak, *The Saint Makers*, pp. 32–33, 103–6. I have visited with the López family occasionally since 1967. Brazil: Pravina and I talked with Edival Rosas in Salvador, in 2007, then again in 2009 when he told us that, unlike the provincial carvings, his figures of saints are properly proportioned, but their faces must not resemble faces you have seen in the world. They must be "saintly," a quality he cannot teach his apprentices. It can be learned only during long years of practice. Forty percent of artistic techniques, Edival estimated, can be taught; the rest must be learned during self-directed experience. Edival's contrast of the baroque and provincial is perfectly illustrated by the images of São Miguel Arcanjo in Marino, *Iconografia de Nossa Senhora e dos Santos*, pp. 133–34. Baroque masterpieces dominate in the books; see Whistler's lovely *Opulence and Devotion*. But Herstal provides a rich collection of provincial work in *Imagens Religiosas do Brasil*, and introducing the collection, pp. 22–29, he says the provincial images are imperfect but sincere, authentic expressions of Brazilian culture in which splendid simplification yields essential forms that appeal to modern artists. Yankee gravestones: Ludwig, *Graven Images*; Benes, *The Masks of Orthodoxy*.

P. 280. Sweden: Svärdström, *Dalmålningar*; Bringéus and Tellenbach, *Dalmålningar*. England: Oliver, *The Victorian Staffordshire Figure*; Pugh, *Staffordshire Portrait Figures*. Pennsylvania: Shelley, *The Fraktur-Writings or Illuminated Manuscripts of the Pennsylvania Germans*; Weiser and Heaney, *Pennsylvania German Fraktur*. Islamic art: Burckhardt, *Art of Islam*; Nasr, *Islamic Art and Spirituality*; Brend, *Islamic Art*; Al-Qaradawi, *The Lawful and the Prohibited in Islam*, pp. 100–120. Calligraphy: Serin, *Hat Sanatı ve Meşhur Hattatlar* is the masterpiece, but Safadi, *Islamic Calligraphy*; Schimmel, *Calligraphy and Islamic Culture*; and Derman, *Letters in Gold*, provide fine introductions in English. Again, these are among the works I have found useful and wish to recommend, but my knowledge has been built during fieldwork, many years in Turkey and Bangladesh, with trips to Kuwait and Pakistan as well. On the process of oppositional purification: Lévi-Strauss, *The Way of the Masks*, pp. 14, 30–32, 64–67, 93, 123–25, 236.

P. 281. Turkish ceramics: Lane, *Later Islamic Pottery*, chap. 5; Atasoy and Raby, *Iznik*; Carswell, *Iznik Pottery*; Denny, *Iznik*. Those books provide the history; for Mehmet Gürsoy and the current *çini* tradition, see: Glassie, *Turkish Traditional Art Today*, chaps. 14–17; Glassie, *The Potter's Art*, pp. 56–90.

P. 282. The modernist revolution: That is the subject of chapter 18.

P. 283. Thatch to metal: Glassie, *Vernacular Architecture*, pp. 25–36. Bascom comments on the change among the Yoruba in *The Yoruba of Southwestern Nigeria*, p. 38. Rural scenes: Kasfir, *Contemporary African Art*, pp. 29–30; Glassie, *Art and Life in Bangladesh*, pp. 28–38, 420–38.

P. 284. Language and change: Soyinka, *Myth, Literature and the African World*, chap. 4; Achebe, *Morning Yet on Creation Day*, pp. 10, 27, 83, 94–96.

P. 285. Fables: Ireland: Glassie, *The Stars of Ballymenone*, pp. 229–30. African American South: Joel Chandler Harris's collections, beginning in 1880 with *Uncle Remus: His Songs and His Sayings*, brought popular attention to the animal tales of the South, many of them clearly African in origin, proofs of the courageous preservation of an African heritage in the United States. One of the stories Prince learned from his mother tells of the tortoise trickster who won a race with a rabbit by positioning members of his family along the route; they sprang up, one by one, the last one crossing the finishing line ahead of the weary rabbit. It is number 1074 in Aarne and Thompson, *Types of the Folktale*, and number 2.3.1074 in Haring's *Malagasy Tale Index*, known in India as well as Africa, and Richard Dorson collected it twice in the United States from African American tellers from the South: Dorson, *Negro Folktales in Michigan*, pp. 37–38, 205; Dorson, *American Negro Folktales*, pp. 86–87. Metaphoric beasts: From *Totemism* through the volumes of the *Mythologiques*, Lévi-Strauss demonstrated how animals are good to think. An excellent, more recent example, a model instance of his thinking, is Lévi-Strauss, *The Story of Lynx*.

P. 286. Ife: Willett, *Ife*; Eyo and Willett, *Treasures of Ancient Nigeria*, pp. 10–14, 32–39; Fagg, *Nigerian Images*, pp. 36–37. Yoruba aesthetic hierarchy (power over beauty): Armstrong, *The Powers of Presence*, p. 6.

P. 287. Grotesque masks: R. F. Thompson, *African Art in Motion*, pp. 120, 125, 159. The African mask, it seems—Willett, *African Art*, p. 144; Segy, *Masks of Black Africa*, p. 40—is often double-coded, amusing for adults, terrifying for children. That is, like Prince's art, the masquerade is both funny and frightening, and, like his art, it is at once serious and playful. For these mingled traits of the masquerade, see the excellent accounts of masquerades by Anderson, Peek, H. J. Drewal, Kpone-Tonwe, and Salmons in Anderson and Peek, *Ways of the Rivers*, pp. 148–61, 184–85, 194–213, 278–90. In that book, Henry Drewal describes a Yoruba masquerade called Agbo, but neither it, nor the Agbo described in Drewal and Drewal, *Gẹlẹdẹ*, pp. 237–38, seem to be much like the Agbo who came into this book in chapter 15. Fear: Oyeyemi, *The Icarus Girl*; see especially pp. 174–76, 181, 199–201, and 204 for the abiku, twins, and ghosts. *Yōkai*: In his new book *Pandemonium and Parade*, Michael Foster presents excellently the culture of the funny and frightening monsters of Japan. Humor and horror: These tendencies mesh constantly in Prince's paintings and Tutuola's novels. A couple of especially clear instances appear in Tutuola's *Feather Woman of the Jungle*, when, pp. 27–28, the narrator and his sister find a human disaster hilarious—amusement is the father of sorrow, the narrator says, as Orwell or Beckett might—and when, p. 67, the narrator is dismayed to think of all the coffins that will have to be made for the people listening to him, then realizes, with sudden delight, that many will die in miserable ways that will require no coffins. Making disaster and death into a joke was basic to the philosophy of endurance held by the Irish storytellers I celebrate in *The Stars of Ballymenone*. Humor: The first chapters in Oring, *Jokes and Their Relations*, and in Oring, *Engaging Humor*.

P. 288. Yoruba deities are rarely represented: R. F. Thompson, "Aesthetics in Traditional Africa," pp. 380–81; Bascom, *The Yoruba of Southwestern Nigeria*, p. 111; Pemberton, in Fagg and Pemberton, *Yoruba*, p. 92; H. J. Drewal, in Drewal, Pemberton, and Abiodun, *Yoruba*, p. 230.

P. 291. Visibility and presence: R. F. Thompson, "Aesthetics in Traditional Africa," p. 377; R. F. Thompson, "Yoruba Artistic Criticism," pp. 33–37; R. F. Thompson, *Black Gods and Kings*, chap. 3, p. 2; Armstrong, *The Affecting Presence*, chap. 2. The carver's process: Fakeye and Haight, *Lamidi Olonade Fakeye*, pp. 60–61; Willett, "An African Sculptor at Work"; Bascom, "A Yoruba Master Carver," pp. 65, 67, 69, 70–77; Drewal and Drewal, *Gẹlẹdẹ*, pp. 260–70. Cubism: Fagg and Plass, *African Sculpture*, pp. 33–41.

P. 292. Trapped gestures: F. Klee, *The Diaries of Paul Klee*, pp. 177, 374. Smooth and luminous: R. F. Thompson, "Yoruba Artistic Criticism," pp. 37–40; Armstrong, *The Affecting Presence*, p. 116. The aesthetic of smooth, shiny darkness is analyzed elegantly by Boone in her study of feminine beauty and Songe masks among the Mende in *Radiance from the Waters*, pp. 119–20, 155–60, 236–38. Paint: Wingert, *The Sculpture of Negro Africa*, p. 31; Willett, *African Art*, p. 143; Vogel, *Africa Explores*, p. 24; Pemberton, in Fagg and Pemberton, *Yoruba*, p. 132; Bascom, "A Yoruba Master Carver," pp. 70, 72. Blue: R. F. Thompson, "Aesthetics in Traditional Africa," p. 379; R. F. Thompson, *Black Gods and Kings*, chap. 3, p. 6; Armstrong, *The Powers of Presence*, p. 78. Nadelman: Kirstein, *The Sculpture of Elie Nadelman*.

P. 293. Pierce: Livingston and Beardsley, *Black Folk Art in America*, pp. 116–21; Connell, *Elijah Pierce*; Davis, "Elijah Pierce, Woodcarver." Cicatrices and civilization: R. F. Thompson, "Yoruba Artistic Criticism," pp. 35–36; R. F. Thompson, *African Art in Motion*, p. 18; R. F. Thompson, *Black Gods and Kings*, chap. 12; R. F. Thompson, in Abiodun, Drewal and Pemberton, *The Yoruba Artist*, pp. 229–30; H. J. Drewal, "Art or Accident"; H. J. Drewal, "Beauty and Being"; Bascom, *The Yoruba of Southwestern Nigeria*, pp. 43, 56; Bascom, *Sixteen Cowries*, pp. 46–47.

P. 294. Carved detail: Fakeye and Haight, *Lamidi Olonade Fakeye*, pp. 145–46, 190. Geometric painted surface: Armstrong, "Aesthetic Continuity in Two Yoruba Works," and, in general, Armstrong, *Wellspring*, pp. 54–55, 76. Dotted surface: Fagg, *Nigerian Images*, fig. 81; Leiris and Delange, *African Art*, p. 310; R. F. Thompson, *Black Gods and Kings*, chap. 14; Cole, *I Am Not Myself*, pp. 11; Drewal and Mason, *Beads, Body, and Soul*, p. 79; Drewal and Drewal, *Gẹlẹdẹ*, pp. 254, 256. Ghanaian incised surface: Ross, *Visions of Africa*, pp. 60–61. Hair: R. F. Thompson, "Yoruba Artistic Criticism," pp. 46–48. Beadwork: Armstrong, *The Powers of Presence*, p. 67, fig. 60; R. F. Thompson, *Black Gods and Kings*, chap. 8; Bascom, The *Yoruba of Southwestern Nigeria*, pp. 11–12, 30; Drewal, Pemberton, and Abiodun, *Yoruba*, p. 38; Clarke, *Power Dressing*, pp. 19–20. Henry Drewal and John Mason (with Pravina Shukla) provide a beautiful overview of Yoruba beadwork in Africa and the diaspora in *Beads, Body, and Soul*. In it, the third section of Drewal's "Yoruba Beadwork in Africa" is rich with information on crowns, and it includes beadwork pictures by Prince's Osogbo colleague Jimoh Buraimoh, pp. 81–83, and by Olabayo Olaniyi, pp. 84–85, who is Prince's son.

P. 295. Islamic design: The repetitive, expansive patterns of Islam have influenced the design of Yoruba textiles; see Drewal and Drewal, *Gẹlẹdẹ*, pp. 94–95, 191. Whether the source is his father's leather, the textiles of his people, or something else that caught his eye, I believe Prince's flat patterns spread an Islamic sensibility over the forms of his imagination, just as, constantly in Yoruba life, a Muslim or Christian veneer lies over a framework built on Yoruba cultural suppositions.

P. 296. Seriate composition: Abiodun, Drewal, and Pemberton, *The Yoruba Artist*, pp. 46, 59, 92, 152–53, 194, 221.

P. 297. Syndesis: Armstrong, *The Affecting Presence*, pp. 169–70, also 121, 143, 154, 164–69. After *The Affecting Presence* and before *Wellspring*, in 1974, Armstrong wrote an article, "My Collection," in which he said, pp. 42–43, that what he called "atomism" in *The Affecting Presence* he now saw as "perhaps *the* cardinal dynamic of Yoruba art." Then in the books that followed, he expanded rigorously on that understanding: Armstrong, *Wellspring*, pp. 101–50; Armstrong, *The Powers of Presence*, pp. 13–33, 49–51, 67–72, 78, 83–93, 106–7.

P. 299. Northeastern farmsteads: Glassie, "The Wedderspoon Farm"; Hubka, *Big House, Little House, Back House, Barn*.

P. 300. Architectural ornament: Prince's house and the Resort recall Idah's house in Benin City, excellently described by Phil Peek in "Ovia Idah and Eture Egbede," pp. 56–58.

Chapter 18

P. 303. Tradition: D. Ben-Amos, "The Seven Strands of Tradition"; Hymes, "Folklore's Nature and the Sun's Myth"; Glassie, "Tradition." Change: Morris, "Making the Best of It," *Hopes and Fears for Art*, p. 158. Continuity: Eliot, *Notes towards the Definition of Culture*, pp. 106–7, 114. Qing replication: Li, *Chinese Ceramics*, pp. 10–11, 266–67; Kerr, *Chinese Ceramics*, pp. 14–28, 51, 66.

P. 304. Early Cizhou ware: Yataka, *Freedom of Brush and Clay*; Satō, *Chinese Ceramics*, chap. 15; Medley, *The Chinese Potter*, pp. 123–35. I learned about the current state of affairs when I visited Pengcheng with my colleague Wang Juan in 2000. Prime objects: Kubler, *The Shape of Time*.

P. 306. Reaching beyond: Mumford, *Herman Melville*, p. 107, also pp. 41, 123, 147, 183–84, 365–66, and *Moby-Dick*. American complaint: Thoreau, *Walden*, pp. 4, 7, 20, 23, 29, 41, 56, 72–74, 79, 136, 156, 169, 253–54. Soldiers disturbed by the imperialistic Mexican War: Pryor, *Reading the Man*, p. 158; Bunting, *Ulysses S. Grant*, p. 19.

P. 307. Enclosures: Tate concludes *The Enclosure Movement*, p. 175, saying that, an economic success, enclosure was a social "disaster." Gothic critique: Ruskin, *The Nature of Gothic*, especially pp. 13–23, and Morris's Preface. In 1853, when the volume of *The Stones of Venice* that included "The Nature of Gothic" was published, Ruskin gave four lectures in Scotland, published as *Lectures on Architecture and Painting*. The last two lectures offered his perceptive, persuasive appraisals of the English painters of his day, Turner and the Pre-Raphaelites. In the first two, Ruskin criticized contemporary architectural practice and found in the architecture of the far past a prescription for the future: modern architecture in Britain, he argued, should be based on Gothic, not Greek, precedents. Ruskin began his second lecture, as he had to in his time, as he would have to in ours, by contending that romanticism is not nostalgic or utopian, but a way to locate unexpected virtue and use it as a guide to future creation (pp. 56–59), and he repeated in the addenda to the lectures (pp. 108–11), his assessment of the virtues of the Gothic, holding that the Gothic artist was not reduced to a slave or machine; he was freed to be a man in full humanity. My point is not that modernism began in England in the eighteen-fifties. There was an earlier English revolutionary moment, Wordsworth's moment in the last decade of the eighteenth century, as E. P. Thompson showed in his final book, *The Romantics*, and before that, of course: Rousseau. But conditions were such that critique, retrieval, and hopes for improvement were all part of the general intellectual discourse in the eighteen-fifties, and Ruskin brought them together. Connect his essay and his lectures, and Ruskin, in 1853, had outlined modernist action, the romantic dynamic that begins in a complaint (current architecture is degenerate, aesthetically and socially), leads to appreciation of an alternative (the Gothic), and concludes in a futuristic solution (an architecture better in artistic and human terms). It was left to Morris (and Gropius, Le Corbusier, and Wright) to put these ideas into action. As part of his action, Morris gave a lecture in 1889, which he printed auspiciously as a small book, *Gothic Architecture*, during the Arts and Crafts Exhibition in London in 1893. In it, he honorably follows Ruskin (see especially pp. 30–34, 51–53, 57–58, 61–68), and in our day, Bill Ivey, active in Washington circles, argues that Ruskin, Morris, and the Arts and Crafts Movement continue to hold rich implications for the future of art: Ivey, *Arts, Inc.*, pp. 287–89. For chronology, I relied on Collingwood's *The Life and Work of John Ruskin*, but in this chapter I am proceeding in the progressive-regressive manner, outlined by Sartre in *Search for a Method*, chap. 3, believing that linear histories omit too much, and hunts for ultimate origins are vain.

P. 308. *Unto This Last*: Gandhi, *Autobiography*, p. 265. On Morris: Mackail, *The Life of William Morris*; E. P. Thompson, *William Morris*; MacCarthy, *William Morris*; Harvey and Press, *William Morris: Design and Enterprise in Victorian Britain*; Peterson, *The Kelmscott Press*; Watkinson, *William Morris as Designer*; Crossley, Hassell, and Salway, *William Morris's Kelmscott*; Yeats, "The Happiest of the Poets," in his *Ideas of Good and Evil*; Faulkner, *William Morris and W. B. Yeats*; Pevsner, *Pioneers of the Modern Movement: From William Morris to Walter Gropius*. By Morris: From his writings—twenty-four thick volumes in *The Collected Works*, edited by his daughter May Morris—I select these as especially pertinent to his views on art in life: Morris, *Hopes and Fears for Art*; Morris, *Signs of Change*; Morris, *Architecture, Industry, and Wealth* (p. 59 quoted); Morris, *A Dream of John Ball*; Morris, *News from Nowhere*.

P. 309. Opposition and extension: Hess, "A Tale of Two Cities"; Penrose, *Portrait of Picasso*, pp. 67, 92; Le Corbusier, *Journey to the East*, pp. 14–19, 60, 103, 167, 195, 240. Picasso's shock: Leiris and Delange, *African Art*, pp. 8–14; Goldwater, "Judgments of Primitive Art," pp. 32–34; Willett, *African Art*, p. 34; Vogt, *The Blue Rider*, p. 92. Modernist art was inspired by artistic alternatives, but it is too simple to locate the origin of European modernism in one artist's discovery, in, say, 1907, of African sculpture. Native American art had been appreciated before, so had Japanese art, and European folk art before that, and before that the medieval art of Europe and the archaic art of the Mediterranean. Certainly European medieval and folk art readied the artists to receive the African message. And all of these alternatives carried the seeds of modernism and inspired a host of artists, working independently and in association, who were romantic in their action and futuristic in their vision. Bowe's *Art and the National Dream* demonstrates the breadth of the movement at the end of the nineteenth century.

P. 310. Kandinsky: Kandinsky, "Reminiscences," pp. 22–24, 28–29, 38; Kandinsky, *Concerning the Spiritual in Art*, pp. 9, 24, 30, 50–54, 66, 71; Kandinsky and Marc, *The Blaue Reiter Almanac*, pp. 37–40, 72, 147, 160, 186–87, 192, 252, 258–60; Grohmann, *Wassily Kandisky*, pp. 54–55. In *Sounds*, a book of poems and woodcuts from 1912, Kandinsky speaks of the ordinary things you always imagine and never see (p. 17), of the wide modernist reach (p. 21), of difference and sameness, of abstraction (pp. 71–73), and shows two images (pp. 27, 53) that were based on folk paintings on glass. Islamic precedent: *Karalama* is a spontaneous, abstract art that was practiced by Muslim calligraphers for centuries before the rise of abstraction in the West: Edgü, *Turkish Calligraphic Art (Karalama/Meşk)*. A more familiar traditional art that was allied to calligraphy is *ebru*, marbled paper, once called Turkish paper in Europe. Blending control and chance like abstract expressionism, and thoroughly nonobjective (before the figurative innovations of Necmeddin Okyay in the twentieth century), marbled paper is a clear, early precursor to Western abstract art: Derman, *Türk Sanatında Ebru*; Türkmenoğlu, *Sudaki Nakış: Ebru*. In *Marbled Paper*, Wolfe deals largely with marbling after it got to Europe, but see chaps. 1–2, and especially plates IV–V. On Boas: Jonaitis, *From the Land of the Totem Poles*, chaps. 4–5; Jonaitis, Introduction to *A Wealth of Thought*; Goldschmidt, *The Anthropology of Franz Boas*, pp. 25, 54, 64, 126. By Boas: Boas, *The Central Eskimo*, pp. 146, 150–53, 240; Boas, *Primitive Art*; Boas, *Kwakiutl Ethnography*, chaps. 7–8, 10.

P. 311. New York: Rothko, *The Artist's Reality*, pp. 54–55, 59–62, 106–8, 113–16, 122; López-Remiro, *Mark Rothko*, pp. 30–40, 95, 130–38; Alloway and MacNaughton, *Adolph Gottlieb*, pp. 20, 33–34, 37–38, 40–42, 45, 169–71; O'Neill, *Barnett Newman*, pp. 58–65, 75–77, 98–108, 144–47, 165, 287; O'Connor, *Jackson Pollock*, pp. 32, 40, 75, 79; Ashton, *The New York School*, pp. 20–22, 38–42, 54–74, 113, 126–38; Ashton, *American Art Since 1945*, p. 26. Claude Lévi-Strauss begins *The Way of the Masks* by recalling that, in 1943, he thought Boas's galleries of Northwest Coast material culture at the American Museum of Natural History were magical and the art was "not unequal to the greatest." He was, as usual, right on both counts. In 1945, Barnett Newman, who had read Boas and curated an exhibition of Northwest Coast painting, called it "an abstract symbolic art of the highest sophistication"; O'Neill, *Barnett Newman*, p. 75, and see too pp. 105–8. Mingei: Sōetsu Yanagi, *The Unknown Craftsman*; Uchida, *We Do Not Work Alone*; National Museum of Modern Art, *Kanjiro Kawai*; Leach, *Hamada: Potter*; Leach, *A Potter in Japan*; Leach, *A Potter's Book*, chap. 1; Peterson, *Shoji Hamada*; Wilcox, *Shoji Hamada*; Sōri Yanagi, *Mingei*: Moes, *Mingei*, chaps. 1–3; Moes in Weeder, *Japanese Folk Art*, pp. 20–27; Brandt, *Kingdom of Beauty*. Gabon masks: An example appeared in Kandinsky and Marc, *The Blaue Reiter Almanac* (1912), p. 190, and others appeared regularly after: Wingert, *The Sculpture of Negro Africa*, p. 50, plates 71–72; Griaule, *Folk Art of Black Africa*, p. 17; Leiris and Delange, *African Art*, pp. 158, 328–30; Willett, *African Art*, pp. 172–73; Bascom, *African Art in Cultural Per-*

spective, p. 131; Vogel, *Art/Artifact*, pp. 38, 60–61; Segy, *Masks of Black Africa*, no. 194.

P. 312. Irish history: Ellis, *Ireland in the Age of the Tudors*, especially pp. 334–57; Kee, *The Green Flag*; Jackson, *Home Rule*; Clark, *Social Origins of the Irish Land War*; Ó Tuama, *The Gaelic League Idea*, especially pp. 45–46, 94–97. Yeats: Foster, *W. B. Yeats*, I, chaps. 2–3, 5–7, 11, 17; Foster, *W. B. Yeats*, II, chap. 6; Hone, *W. B. Yeats*, chaps. 3–7; Allt and Alspach, *The Variorum Edition of the Poems of W. B. Yeats*, pp. 1–63, 117, 737–38. Yeats's tale of Oisin in tradition: Glassie, *The Stars of Ballymenone*, pp. 308–11, 513–16.

P. 313. Writings on folklore by Lady Gregory: Gregory, *Poets and Dreamers*; Gregory, *A Book of Saints and Wonders*; Gregory, *The Kiltartan History Book*; Gregory, *Visions and Beliefs in the West of Ireland*. For her life, see her autobiography, *Seventy Years*. By Synge: His great ethnography is *The Aran Islands*; his plays are collected in *The Works*. Particularly useful is Bourgeois, *John M. Synge and the Irish Theatre*. The example of Synge prompts me to stress this point. Modernism, at once innovative and appreciative of alternative traditions, was both an artistic and scientific movement. Its art was architecture and literature, painting and sculpture. Its science was anthropological and folkloristic. J. M. Synge was a naturalist and an ethnographic photographer; see Stephens, *My Wallet of Photographs*. Synge was a folklorist and a playwright, just as Kandinsky was an ethnologist and a painter. Their match in Brazil was the fictional Pedro Archanjo of Amado's *Tent of Miracles* (see especially pp. 153–54, 200, 221–23, 365). A follower of the old faith, like Prince, a man of Xangô, he was a poetic modern writer, an admirer of Boas, and the father of folkloristic study in Bahia. Archanjo published his first book on Bahian folklife in 1907, the year in which Synge published *The Aran Islands* and *The Playboy of the Western World*.

P. 314. Coomaraswamy: His early book *The Indian Craftsman* (1909) follows William Morris's direction and parallels Yanagi's *The Unknown Craftsman*. Coomaraswamy's masterpiece, *The Transformation of Nature in Art* (1935), offers fine guidance to anyone studying artistic representation, as I have in this book. Tagore: Dutta and Robinson, *Radindranath Tagore*, chaps. 15, 17–18, 30; Bose, *Tagore*, pp. 5, 23–26, 68–70; and Tagore, *Reminiscences*, pp. 188–89, 192, 269. Dutt: Gupta, *The Writings of Michael M. S. Dutt*; Sen, *History of Bengali Literature*, pp. 197–224. Finland: Wilson, *Folklore and Nationalism in Modern Finland*. Indian nationalism: Wolpert, *A New History of India*, chaps. 17–23. Nigerian nationalism: Falola and Heaton, *A History of Nigeria*, chaps. 4–6; Awolowo, *Awo*, chaps. 10–14, 16, especially pp. 116, 121–23, 131–32, 160, 223, 294, 298–300, 312. The old Irish historians: O'Donovan, *Annals of the Kingdom of Ireland, By the Four Masters*; Comyn and Dinneen, *The History of Ireland by Geoffrey Keating*. These seventeenth-century historians gather at the *Wake*; see Glassie, *Passing the Time in Ballymenone*, pp. 753–54. Johnson: Ulli Beier describes Duro Ladipo's debt to Johnson's *The History of the Yorubas* in *Three Nigerian Plays*, pp. viii–xii. I expand on Yoruba modernism in chapter 8.

P. 316. Modernist style: Picasso said that his paintings changed while he worked on them—Ashton, *Picasso on Art*, pp. 8, 27–31, 158—and proceeding syndetically, Yoruba-style, that is what Prince does. The work records the process of its creation. Jackson Pollock's dripped paintings provide an extreme instance of this key modernist trait in which form is traded for action. Prince has dripped paint on canvas (see chapter 20, nos. 16, 26), and though this is not his normal process, and though his work is referential in a way that Pollock's dripped pictures are not, there is much in the look of the work that brings them together: the flat surface on which depth is confected out of density and scale, the large spaces filled with tiny detail, the black lines of connection and containment, the simultaneity of frenzy and calm, the musical rhythms, the spontaneous modifications of accidents, the complexity in balance. Pollock's works and Prince's record the action, reveal the unconscious, embrace the contradictions, and exhibit the modernist look.

P. 317. Tradition: James Marston Fitch, an architect and theorist who participated in the modernist movement, argued that there is, of necessity, something archaic in the modern, and that the postmodern abandonment of the archaic was part of a regression to Victorian snobbery and irresponsibility: Sawin, *James Marston Fitch*, pp. 44–45, 62–65, 80, 147, 155, 161, 194, 239–41.

Chapter 19

P. 319. Beier in 1968: *Contemporary Art in Africa*, pp. 113–19, 169. Mount in 1974: *African Art*, pp. 147–58.

P. 320. Stanislaus and Soyinka in 1990: *Contemporary African Artists*, pp. 8, 20, 23–24. Kennedy in 1992: *New Currents, Ancient Rivers*, pp. 69–77. Magnin in 1996: *Contemporary Art of Africa*, pp. 7, 61–64.

P. 321. Kasfir in 1999: *Contemporary African Art*, pp. 16, 50–57, 77–78, 133–38, 152, 166, 178–81, 205–7. In her fine new book *African Art and the Colonial Encounter*, pp. x–xi, 21, Kasfir explains how the academic fashion shifted among the Africanists of her generation from rural to urban subjects. Pigozzi in Houston: Magnin, Greene, Wardlaw, and McEvilley, *African Art Now*, pp. 10–19 (interviews with Pigozzi from which, p. 13, I quote), 20, 35–37.

P. 322. Not forgotten: Though the taste-makers had abandoned him, Prince was, along with Lamidi Fakeye and Jimoh Buraimoh, one of the few living artists Frank Willett used to represent contemporary work in the 2003 edition of *African Art*, pp. 239–45. In another of the similarly named books, *Contemporary African Art*, the catalog of an exhibition at the Indianapolis Museum of Art in 2000, Dele Jegede treats five artists. One of them, pp. 41–51, is Prince. Jegede supplies information from an interview and briefly interprets six works, ranging in date from 1964 to 1996. London in 1967: Duerden, "Letter from London," p. 67.

P. 323. Prince in 1972: Mundy-Castle and Mundy-Castle, "Twins Seven Seven." Prince in 1971: Armstrong, "Aesthetic Continuity in Two Yoruba Works." Prince in 1976: Hersey, "Two African Artists." Prince in 1981: Kasfir, "Art from Africa," p. 77. Prince in 1989: Lewison, "Paris and Cologne," p. 585.

P. 324. Pigozzi: Magnin, Greene, Wardlaw, and McEvilley, *African Art Now*, pp. 11, 30, 36–37. Agawa Norio: Glassie, *The Potter's Art*, pp. 98–116. Kant: Danto, "Artifact and Art," p. 27.

P. 325. Critic: Naifeh, "The Myth of Oshogbo." Georgina's instruction: Oyelami, "Mbari Mbayo and the Oshogbo Artists." Prince describes learning from Georgina Beier in Beier's *A Dreaming Life*, pp. 30–32. Simon Hunt: Greenblatt, *Will in the World*, pp. 18–19, 26, 96–97.

P. 326. Pollock and Benton: O'Connor, *Jackson Pollock*, pp. 16–20, 24–25, 32, 43, 51. López family; see the notes to p. 278. Gauguin: Cachin, *Gauguin*, pp. 16–17, 49–57.

P. 327. Surrealism survives in photography: Sontag, *On Photography*, pp. 46–51, 162–64.

P. 328. A deeper look: Kasfir, "Art from Africa," pp. 77–78. Cool and hot: Charbonnier, *Conversations with Claude Lévi-Strauss*, chap. 3; Lévi-Strauss, *The Savage Mind*, pp. 232–36.

P. 329. Passionate devotion: The artists' definition of art as the consequence of intense commitment governed my treatment of art in *Turkish Traditional Art Today*; see especially pp. 118–19, 806–13, 847–69. Other thinkers from other societies define art comparably as the yield of care and sincerity, soul and devotion: Kandinsky, *Concerning the Spiritual in Art*, p. 75; Leach, *A Potter's Book*, p. 17; Coomaraswamy, *The Transformation of Nature in Art*, p. 90; Suzuki, *Zen and Japanese Culture*, p. 226. For them, for me, and for the Turkish artisan, art does not lie in the medium or in the eye of the beholder (the patron, collector, or critic), but in the mind and heart and hand of the artist. Kaneko: Glassie, *The Potter's Art*, pp. 98–116.

P. 330. Cultural consistency and identifiable artists: Fagg, in Fagg and Pemberton, *Yoruba*, pp. 13–14, 32–33. William Fagg repeated his assertion about identifiability in Fagg, *Nigerian Images*, pp. 117–20, and in Fagg and Plass, *African Sculpture*, pp. 90–93. Dan Crowley wondered if Fagg was right in "An African Aesthetic," p. 327. Boyer agreed with Fagg in *Baule*, pp. 78–79, but did not put his idea into practice; most of his pictured works remain, unfortunately, without the artists' names. With rich experience among the Baule behind her, Susan Vogel meditated productively on the problem in "Known Artists but Anonymous Works." Her notion that the attachment of names to works is of little importance in African society (though see Roslyn Walker's fine piece in *The Yoruba Artist*) seems convincing; still, my studies in many different societies lead me into sympathy with Fagg. What is needed is inquiry during long association with the artists. My time with the weavers of carpets in Turkey, reported in *Turkish Traditional Art Today*, part 4, taught me that, though the merchants and consumers (and the scholars) were not interested in the names of the creators, the weavers certainly were. For more on this matter in Africa: Leiris and Delange, *African Art*, pp. 49–51, 113, 336, 380; Kasfir, *African Art and the Colonial Encounter*, pp. 170–80, 253. Patiently dismantled: I expanded this clause into a book: Glassie, *The Spirit of Folk Art*.

P. 331. Contemporary art and Prince: Vogel in *Africa Explores*, p. 182, also pp. 25–26, 95, 105, 114, 176, 178, 185, 188–90, and Mudimbe, pp. 281–84, 287. Armstrong argues that Prince's work is "profoundly Yoruba" in *Wellspring*, pp. 74–80, 143–44.

P. 332. Manifesto for the new art: Reinhardt, "Writings," p. 204. Next in the sequence: Ashton, *American Art Since 1945*, chap. 2, and pp. 119, 128, 143–44; Alloway, *Topics in American Art*, the three sections on the sixties, especially pp. 76–97, 119–22, 155–59, 171–81; Battcock, *The New Art*, pp. 68, 213, 230–34, 245; Lippard, *Pop Art*, pp. 9–10, 22–25, 69–70, 75–77, 82–86, 96–100, 106–7. In the Foreword to *Jasper Johns*, Leo Castelli describes the thrill of his initial encounter with the artist. Castelli first exhibited Johns's work in his gallery in 1958, and it was in that year or the next when—a high school kid who often took the train north to New York to get a grip on what was hip—I was excited by the targets and flags.

Chapter 20

P. 335. Worldview: Rothko, *The Artist's Reality*, pp. 21, 79; see also López-Remiro, *Mark Rothko*, pp. 14–15.

P. 336. Science and art: I wrote about structuralism as scientific modernism in Glassie, "Structure and Function, Folklore and the Artifact." Lévi-Strauss actually built his scientific models into three-dimensional objects that he likened to Calder's mobiles: Eribon, *Conversations with Claude Lévi-Strauss*, p. 170.

P. 337. Material Culture: There is no conflict in my interest here. All studies of art, whether frankly, clandestinely, or accidentally, connect to the art market; they are inextricably tangled up in money matters. My main purpose in writing about living artists is to enrich my understanding, and, it is to be hoped, the general understanding of art, but another purpose is to bring attention and financial gain to the artists. Ethnographers intrude in the quiet lives of other people; their intrusion will have consequences, and those consequences should benefit the people about whom they write as well as the writers who, gaining little by way of royalties, gain much by way of promotion and pay. As I stated clearly in this book's introduction, my hope is to benefit Prince, bringing him new appreciation, new buyers. He, like the contemporary artists redundantly celebrated by the critics, needs to live. Most of Prince's work for sale is held by Material Culture, and it involves a generous arrangement for sharing the profit with Prince. If buyers turn from this book to find works by Prince—just as buyers have gone from my book on Turkish art to find works by Mehmet Gürsoy, Ibrahim Erdeyer, and Nurten Şahin—then one expressed, if secondary, goal of my writing will have been met. My intention is to help my friend Prince, but if there are people who think that the exhausting labor required by a book of this kind was done to sell a few pictures, I would say that their view of the difficult, untidy world we occupy is confused and immature. In pure money terms, it would have been far less expensive for me to have bought all of Prince's paintings at full prices and then to have burned them. I did buy four paintings by Prince. I would have been most insincere if I had not wanted to own his work. He gave me two more. This book might increase their value, but I would be most insincere if I wanted to sell them. Living with Prince's works, which mellow and meld in time, is one of life's little delights.

P. 338. Abiku: Soyinka, *Idanre*, pp. 28–30; see the notes to p. 37.

P. 340. *Elephant Man:* Beier, *Contemporary Art in Africa*, p. 94.

P. 342. Birds and witches: See the notes to p. 20.

P. 357. Osun as the Yoruba Venus: Bascom, *The Yoruba of Southwestern Nigeria*, p. 90; Bascom, *Sixteen Cowries*, p. 43.

P. 360. The Goddess of Fertility: In Murphy and Sanford, *Osun across the Waters*, pp. 150–51, Wande Abimbola writes that Osun has many attributes, but she is certainly a goddess of fertility. For Prince, fertility is her prime power. *Rainbow Goddess*: Mascelloni and Sarenco, *Il ritorno dei maghi*, p. 143; see too pp. 142–45, 168.

P. 361. A house made of birds: Tutuola, *Simbi and the Satyr of the Dark Jungle*, pp. 109–15.

P. 362. Mudfish figure: Fagg, in Fagg and Pemberton, *Yoruba*, pp. 19–20, 49; Eyo and Willett, *Treasures of Ancient Nigeria*, pp. 47–48, 154–55, where Willett argues against Fagg, probably correctly, saying that Onile is not Olokun; H. J. Drewal, *Mami Wata*, pp. 41–49; Drewal, Pemberton, and Abiodun, *Yoruba*, p. 136.

P. 364. Mami Wata: I generalize from H. J. Drewal, *Mami Wata*, pp. 37, 52–56, 64, 84–87, 167, 180–81, 193; and H. J. Drewal, *Sacred Waters*, pp. 1–3, 33–39, 92–93, 96, 108, 119–21, 127–33, 145–46, 178–79, 183–84, 217–22, 229–41, 271–72, 280–87, 294, 310–11, 351–52, 361, 385–86, 405–6, 427, 483–85, 499, 566, 587–88. Also: Vogel, *Africa Explores*, pp. 18, 39–40, 132, 164, 170, 286; Anderson, in Anderson and Peek, *Ways of the Rivers*, pp. 160–65; Himmelheber, "The Present State of Sculptural Art," p. 194 and fig. 2; Boyer, *Baule*, pp. 71–73. In *Sacred Waters*, p. 3, Henry Drewal says that Mami Wata is "absent among the Yoruba." He is right, I presume, because he is referring to the German snake-charmer image and the twentieth-century prosperity cult, but "Mami Wata" is used in Yorubaland, as in other places, as a name for old water deities; for a couple of instances: Soyinka, *Ìsarà*, p. 46; Falade, *The Comprehensive History of Osogbo*, pp. 42, 66.

P. 374. Narrators both report and perform: Hymes, *"In Vain I Tried to Tell You,"* chap. 3; Bauman, *A World of Others' Words*, chap. 6; Glassie, *The Stars of Ballymenone*, pp. 79–84.

P. 378. Doran Ross produced a monumental study of kente cloth in *Wrapped in Pride*.

P. 400. Labor and prayer are parts of one technology: Malinowski, *Argonauts of the Western Pacific*, pp. 59–60, 142, 387, 413–14.

P. 408. Experiments and linear work: F. Klee, *The Diaries of Paul Klee*: experiments, pp. 8, 176, 238; formal inclination, pp. 49, 66–67, 69, 112, 136, 141, 147, 150–51, 184, 231–32, 243–44, 265, 278, 297, 402. Klee's spontaneity: Barr, Sweeney, and Feininger, *Paul Klee*, p. 8. The gestural ceramic ornamentation in the old Ottoman lands, in Turkey and the Balkans, that anticipated dripped paintings by centuries: Bakurdjiev, *Bulgarian Ceramics*; Glassie, *Turkish Traditional Art Today*, chap. 13.

P.414. Pictorial narrative: Prince is a storyteller, as the first part of this book demonstrates. His paintings provide occasions for narrative when he opens their Yoruba content for a viewer. Some of his works illustrate stories (nos. 13–15), but usually, in the manner of spiritual art, they are iconic; they present characters upon whom a knowledgeable viewer can project a narrative (nos. 2–4, 6–9, 12, 20, 25). Configured typologically, the spirits and deities, beasts and people will accept a range of interpretations, but one must know what Prince knows to locate true meanings. The semantic dynamic of his work parallels the folklorist's genre of the legend: a phenomenal anomaly, a past event, or a personal experience is brought into communicative order, shaped artfully into sensate presence; see Glassie, *The Stars of Ballymenone*, part two. The versions of *My Reincarnation Brothers and Sisters* (nos. 28–29) provide instructive examples. The figures stand iconically—twisted when they are spirits, straight when they are human—bringing into vision the phenomenal anomaly of abiku birth and the personal experience of the demanding requirements of fame.

Prince's Exhibitions

P.423. The list of Prince's exhibitions, generously prepared by Harriet Schiffer, differs from the list I found in the program published to celebrate Prince's chieftaincies in Ibadan, in 1996, from which, with Prince's help, I developed the generalizations in chapter 9 of this book. Notably, Harriet's list has more shows from Nigeria, fewer from Europe, but the final counts are close: about eighty-four shows up to the year 2000. Prince has kept no running list of his exhibitions, or of his works and their publication, so the biographer of the future will find it hard, maybe impossible, to compile a perfect list. No extant list is complete, but Harriet's list will be a place to begin, and as it stands her list suggests the range of venues in which the art of Prince Twins Seven-Seven has been exhibited.

Bibliography

Aarne, Antti, and Stith Thompson. *The Types of the Folktale: A Classification and Bibliography.* FFC 184. Helsinki: Suomalainen Tiedeakatemia, 1973.

Abimbola, Kola. *Yoruba Culture: A Philosophical Account.* Birmingham: Ikoro Academic Publishers, 2005.

Abimbola, Wande. *Ifá: An Exposition of Ifá Literary Corpus.* Ibadan: Oxford University Press Nigeria, 1976.

———. *Ifa Will Mend Our Broken World: Thoughts on Yoruba Religion and Culture in Africa and the Diaspora.* Ivor Miller, ed. Roxbury: Aim Books, 2003.

Abiodun, Rowland, Henry J. Drewal, and John Pemberton III, eds. *The Yoruba Artist.* Washington: Smithsonian Institution Press, 1994.

Abrahams, Roger D. *A Singer and Her Songs: Almeda Riddle's Book of Ballads.* Baton Rouge: Louisiana State University Press, 1970.

Achebe, Chinua. *Things Fall Apart.* New York: Anchor Books, 1994 [1959].

———. *No Longer at Ease.* London: Heinemann, 1960.

———. *Arrow of God.* New York: Anchor Books, 1989 [1964].

———. *Morning Yet on Creation Day: Essays.* Garden City: Anchor Press, 1975.

———. *Home and Exile.* New York: Anchor Books, 2001.

Adams, Monni. *Designs for Living: Symbolic Communication in African Art.* Cambridge: Carpenter Center for the Visual Arts, Harvard University, 1982.

Adegbola, E. A. Ade, ed. *Traditional Religion in West Africa.* Ibadan: Sefer, 1998 [1983].

Adelugba, Dapo, ed. *Before Our Very Eyes: Tribute to Wole Soyinka.* Ibadan: Spectrum Books, 2005 [1987].

Adenaike, Tayo. "The Oshogbo Experiment," in Havell, ed. *Seven Stories about Modern Art in Africa,* 1995, pp. 202–7.

Adichie, Chimamanda Ngozi. *Purple Hibiscus.* Lagos: Farafina, 2004.

———. "The Headstrong Historian," *The New Yorker* (June 23, 2008): 68–75.

Agee, James, and Walker Evans. *Let Us Now Praise Famous Men.* Boston: Houghton Mifflin, 1960 [1941].

Ajuwon, Bade. *Funeral Dirges of Yoruba Hunters.* New York: Nok Publishers, 1982.

Alloway, Lawrence. *Topics in American Art Since 1945.* New York: W. W. Norton, 1975.

Alloway, Lawrence, and Mary Davis MacNaughton. *Adolph Gottlieb: A Retrospective.* New York: The Arts Publisher, 1981.

Allt, Peter, and Russell K. Alspach, eds. *The Variorum Edition of the Poems of W. B. Yeats.* New York: Macmillan, 1971.

Al-Qaradawi, Yusuf. *The Lawful and the Prohibited in Islam.* Indianapolis: American Trust, 1960.

Alver, Bente Gullveig. *Creating the Source through Folkloristic Fieldwork.* FFC 246. Helsinki: Suomalainen. Tiedeakatemia, 1990.

Amado, Jorge. *Tent of Miracles.* Barbara Shelby, trans. Madison: University of Wisconsin Press, 2003 [1971].

Anderson, Martha C., and Philip M. Peek, eds. *Ways of the Rivers: Arts and Environment of the Niger Delta.* Los Angeles: UCLA Fowler Museum of Cultural History, 2002.

Armstrong, Robert Plant. *The Affecting Presence: An Essay in Humanistic Anthropology.* Urbana: University of Illinois Press, 1971.

———. "Aesthetic Continuity in Two Yoruba Works," *African Arts* 4:3 (1971): 40–43, 68–70.

———. "My Collection," *African Arts* 7:3 (1974): 38–45.

———. *Wellspring: On the Myth and Source of Culture.* Berkeley: University of California Press, 1975.

———. *The Powers of Presence: Consciousness, Myth, and Affecting Presence.* Philadelphia: University of Pennsylvania Press, 1981.

Arnoldi, Mary Jo, Christraud M. Geary, and Kris L. Hardin, eds. *African Material Culture.* Bloomington: Indiana University Press, 1996.

Ashton, Dore. *Picasso on Art: A Selection of Views.* Harmondsworth: Penguin, 1980 [1972].

———. *The New York School: A Cultural Reckoning.* Berkeley: University of California Press, 1973.

———. *American Art Since 1945.* New York: Oxford University Press, 1982.

Atasoy, Nurhan, and Julian Raby. *Iznik: The Pottery of Ottoman Turkey.* London: Alexandria Press, Thames and Hudson, 1989.

Awolalu, J. Omosade. *Yoruba Beliefs and Sacrificial Rites.* Brooklyn: Athelia Henrietta Press, 2001 [1979].

Awolowo, Obafemi. *Awo: The Autobiography of Chief Obafemi Awolowo.* Cambridge University Press, 1960.

Bakurdjiev, Georgi. *Bulgarian Ceramics.* Sofia: Bulgarski Hudozhnik, 1953.

Barnes, Sandra T., ed. *Africa's Ogun: Old World and New.* Bloomington: Indiana University Press, 1989.

Barr, Alfred H., Jr., James Johnson Sweeney, and Julia and Lyonel Feininger. *Paul Klee.* New York: Museum of Modern Art, 1941.

Bascom, William. *The Yoruba of Southwestern Nigeria.* New York: Holt, Rinehart and Winston, 1969.

———. *Ifa Divination: Communication Between Gods and Men in West Africa.* Bloomington: Indiana University Press, 1969.

———. "Creativity and Style in African Art," in Biebuyck, ed. *Tradition and Creativity in Tribal Art,* 1969, pp. 98–119.

———. "African Dilemma Tales: An Introduction," in Dorson, ed. *African Folklore,* 1972, pp. 143–55.

———. *African Art in Cultural Perspective: An Introduction.* New York: W. W. Norton, 1973.

———. "A Yoruba Master Carver: Duga of Meko," in d'Azevedo, ed. *The Traditional Artist in African Societies,* 1974, pp. 62–78.

———. "Oba's Ear: A Yoruba Myth in Cuba and Brazil," in Crowley, ed. *African Folklore in the New World,* 1977, pp. 3–19.

———. "Changing African Art," in Graburn, ed. *Ethnic and Tourist Arts,* 1979, pp. 303–19.

———. *Sixteen Cowries: Yoruba Divination from Africa to the New World.* Bloomington: Indiana University Press, 1993 [1980].

Bascom, William R., and Melville J. Herskovits, eds. *Continuity and Change in African Cultures.* Chicago: University of Chicago Press, 1959.

Battcock, Gregory, ed. *The New Art: A Critical Anthology.* New York: Dutton, 1966.

Bauman, Richard. *A World of Others' Words: Cross-Cultural Perspectives on Intertextuality.* Malden: Blackwell, 2004.

Bauman, Richard, and Charles L. Briggs. *Voices of Modernity: Language Ideologies and the Politics of Inequality.* Cambridge: Cambridge University Press, 2003.

Baxandall, Michael. *Painting and Experience in Fifteenth-Century Italy: A Primer in the Social History of Pictorial Style.* Oxford: Oxford University Press, 1988 [1972].

———. *Patterns of Intention: On the Historical Explanation of Pictures.* New Haven: Yale University Press, 1985.

Beck, Horace P., ed. *Folklore in Action: Essays for Discussion in Honor of MacEdward Leach.* Philadelphia: American Folklore Society, 1962.

Becker, Howard S. *Art Worlds.* Berkeley: University of California Press, 1982.

Becker, Howard S., Robert R. Faulkner, and Barbara Kirshenblatt-Gimblett, eds. *Art from Start to Finish: Jazz, Painting, Writing, and Other Improvisations.* Chicago: University of Chicago Press, 2006.

Beier, Ulli. *African Mud Sculpture.* Cambridge: Cambridge University Press, 1963.

———, ed. *Three Nigerian Plays.* London: Longmans, 1967.

———. *Contemporary Art in Africa.* London: Pall Mall Press, 1968.

———. *Yoruba Myths.* Cambridge: Cambridge University Press, 1980.

———, ed. *A Dreaming Life: An Autobiography of Twins Seven-Seven.* Bayreuth African Studies 52. Bayreuth: Bayreuth University, 1999.

Ben-Amos, Dan. "The Seven Strands of Tradition: Varieties in Its Meaning in American Folklore Studies," *Journal of Folklore Research* 21 (1984): 97–131.

Ben-Amos, Paula Gershick. *The Art of Benin.* Washington: Smithsonian Institution Press, 1995.

Benes, Peter. *The Masks of Orthodoxy: Folk Gravestone Carving in Plymouth County, Massachusetts, 1689–1805.* Amherst: University of Massachusetts Press, 1977.

Bergreen, Laurence. *James Agee: A Life.* New York: E. P. Dutton, 1984.

Bewaji, John Ayotunde Isola. *Beauty and Culture: Perspectives in Black Aesthetics.* Ibadan: Spectrum Books, 2003.

Biebuyck, Daniel P., ed. *Tradition and Creativity in Tribal Art.* Berkeley: University of California Press, 1969.

Bird, Charles. *The Songs of Seydou Camara.* Bloomington: African Studies Center, Indiana University, 1974.

Blurton, T. Richard. *Hindu Art.* Cambridge: Harvard University Press, 1993.

Boas, Franz. *The Central Eskimo.* Lincoln: University of Nebraska Press, 1964 [1888].

———. *Primitive Art.* New York: Dover, 1955 [1927].

———. *Kwakiutl Ethnography.* Helen Codere, ed. Chicago: University of Chicago Press, 1966.

Bohannan, Paul. *Africa and Africans.* Garden City: Natural History Press, 1964.

Boone, Sylvia Ardyn. *Radiance from the Waters: Ideals of Feminine Beauty in Mende Art.* New Haven: Yale University Press, 1986.

Bose, Buddhadeva. *Tagore: Portrait of a Poet.* Bombay: University of Bombay, 1962.

Bourdier, Jean-Paul, and Trinh T. Minh-ha. *African Spaces: Designs for Living in Upper Volta.* New York: Africana, 1985.

———. *Drawn from African Dwellings.* Bloomington: Indiana University Press, 1996.

———. *Habiter un Monde: Architectures de l'Afrique de l'Ouest.* Paris: Editions Alternatives, 2005.

Bourgeois, Maurice. *John M. Synge and the Irish Theatre.* London: Constable, 1913.

Bowe, Nicola Gordon. *Art and the National Dream: The Search for Vernacular Expression in Turn-of-the-Century Design.* Dublin: Irish Academic Press, 1993.

Boyer, Alain-Michel. *Baule.* Visions of Africa. Milan: 5 Continents Editions, 2008.

Brandt, Kim. *Kingdom of Beauty: Mingei and the Politics of Folk Art in Imperial Japan.* Durham: Duke University Press, 2007.

Braudel, Fernand. *On History.* Sarah Matthews, trans. Chicago: University of Chicago Press, 1980 [1969].

Bravmann, René A. *Islam and Tribal Art in West Africa.* African Studies Series. Cambridge: Cambridge University Press, 1974.

Brend, Barbara. *Islamic Art.* Cambridge: Harvard University Press, 1991.

Briggs, Charles L. *The Wood Carvers of Córdova, New Mexico: Social Dimensions of an Artistic "Revival."* Knoxville: University of Tennessee Press, 1980.

———. *Learning How to Ask: A Sociolinguistic Appraisal of the Role of the Interview in Social Science Research.* Cambridge: Cambridge University Press, 1986.

Bringéus, Nils-Arvid, and Margareta Tellenbach, eds. *Dalmålningar i jämforande perspectiv.* Leksand: Dalarnas Museum, 1995.

Brooke, Charlotte. *Reliques of Irish Poetry.* Gainesville: Scholar's Facsimiles and Reprints, 1970 [1789].

Bunting, Josiah, III. *Ulysses S. Grant.* New York: Henry Holt, 2004.

Burckhardt, Titus. *Art of Islam: Language and Meaning.* Westerham: World of Islam, 1976.

Burrison, John A. *Brothers in Clay: The Story of Georgia Folk Pottery.* Athens: University of Georgia Press, 1983.

———. *Cousins in Clay: The Continuing Story of North Georgia Folk Pottery.* Athens: University of Georgia Press, 2010.

Cachin, Françoise. *Gauguin: The Quest for Paradise.* I. Mark Paris, trans. New York: Harry N. Abrams, 1992.

Carswell, John. *Iznik Pottery.* London: British Museum Press, 1998.

Cashman, Ray. *Storytelling on the Northern Irish Border: Characters and Community.* Bloomington: Indiana University Press, 2008.

Castelli, Leo. *Jasper Johns.* New York: Universe Publishing, 1997.

Cerny, Charlene, and Suzanne Seriff, eds. *Recycled, Re-Seen: Folk Art from the Global Scrap Heap.* New York: Harry N. Abrams for Museum of International Folk Art, 1996.

Charbonnier, G. *Conversations with Claude Lévi-Strauss.* John and Doreen Weightman, trans. London: Jonathan Cape, 1970.

Chaudhuri, Nirad C. *Hinduism: A Religion to Live By.* New York: Oxford University Press, 1979.

Chiba, Reiko. *The Seven Lucky Gods of Japan.* Rutland: Charles E. Tuttle, 1996 [1966].

Chomsky, Noam. *Syntactic Structures.* The Hague: Mouton, 1969 [1957].

———. *Cartesian Linguistics: A Chapter in the History of Rationalist Thought.* New York: Harper and Row, 1966.

———. *Problems of Knowledge and Freedom: The Russell Lectures.* New York: Vintage Books, 1971.

———. *Language and Problems of Knowledge: The Managua Lectures.* Cambridge: The MIT Press, 1994 [1988].

Clark, Samuel. *Social Origins of the Irish Land War.* Princeton: Princeton University Press, 1979.

Clarke, Christa. *Power Dressing: Men's Fashion and Prestige in Africa.* Newark: The Newark Museum, 2005.

Clunas, Craig. *Art in China.* Oxford: Oxford University Press, 1997.

Cochran, Robert. *Vance Randolph: An Ozark Life.* Urbana: University of Illinois Press, 1985.

———. *Singing in Zion: Music and Song in the Life of an Arkansas Family.* Fayetteville: University of Arkansas Press, 1999.

———. *Come Walk With Me: The Art of Dorris Curtis.* Fayetteville: University of Arkansas Press, 2004.

———. *Louise Pound: Scholar, Athlete, Feminist Pioneer.* Lincoln: University of Nebraska Press, 2009.

Cole, Bruce. *The Renaissance Artist at Work: From Pisano to Titian.* New York: Harper and Row, 1983.

Cole, Herbert M., ed. *I Am Not Myself: The Art of African Masquerade.* Los Angeles: Museum of Cultural History, UCLA, 1985.

Cole, Herbert M., and Doran H. Ross. *The Arts of Ghana.* Los Angeles: Museum of Cultural History, 1977.

Collingwood, W. G. *The Life and Works of John Ruskin.* 2 vols. Boston: Houghton, Mifflin, 1893.

Comyn, David, and Patrick S. Dinneen, eds. *The History of Ireland by Geoffrey Keating, D.D.* Irish Texts Society. 4 vols. London: David Nutt, 1902–1914.

Connell, E. Jane, ed. *Elijah Pierce: Woodcarver*. Seattle: University of Washington Press for Columbus Museum of Art, 1992.

Coomaraswamy, Ananda K. *The Indian Craftsman*. New Delhi: Munshiram Manoharlal, 1989 [1909].

———. *The Arts and Crafts of India and Ceylon*. New Delhi: Today and Tomorrow's Printers and Publishers, 1971 [1911].

———. *Rajput Painting*. 2 vols. Varanasi: Motilal Banarsidass, 1976 [1916].

———. *The Dance of Śiva: Essays on Indian Art and Culture*. New York: Dover, 1985 [1924].

———. *The Transformation of Nature in Art*. Cambridge: Harvard University Press, 1935.

Cordwell, Justine M. "African Art," in Bascom and Herskovits, eds. *Continuity and Change in African Cultures*, 1959, pp. 28–48.

Cort, Louise Allison. *Seto and Mino Ceramics*. Washington: Freer Gallery of Art, 1992.

Cosentino, Donald John. "Afrokitsch," in Vogel, ed. *Africa Explores*, 1991, pp. 240–55.

Croker, T. Crofton. *Researches in the South of Ireland*. Blackrock: Irish Academic Press, 1981 [1824].

Crossley, Alan, Tom Hassall, and Peter Salway, eds. *William Morris's Kelmscott: Landscape and History*. Macclesfield: Windgather Press, 2007.

Crowley, Daniel J. "An African Aesthetic," in Jopling, ed. *Art and Aesthetics in Primitive Societies*, 1971, pp. 315–27.

———, ed. *African Folklore in the New World*. Austin: University of Texas Press, 1977.

Currie, J., ed. *The Works of Robert Burns*. 4 vols. London: Cadell, Davies, and Creech, 1801.

Danto, Arthur C. *The Philosophical Disenfranchisement of Art*. New York: Columbia University Press, 1986.

———. "Artifact and Art," in Vogel, ed. *Art/Artifact*, 1989, pp. 18–32.

Davis, Gerald L. "Elijah Pierce, Woodcarver: Doves and Pain in Life Fulfilled," in Hall and Metcalf, *The Artist Outsider*, 1994, pp. 290–311.

d'Azevedo, Warren L., ed. *The Traditional Artist in African Societies*. Bloomington: Indiana University Press, 1974.

Deetz, James. *In Small Things Forgotten: An Archaeology of Early American Life*. New York: Anchor Books, 1996 [1977].

Dégh, Linda. *Hungarian Folktales: The Art of Zsuzsanna Palkó*. Vera Kalm, trans. New York: Garland, 1995.

———. *Narratives in Society: A Performer-Centered Study of Narration*. FFC 255. Helsinki: Suomalainen Tiedeakatemia, 1995.

Denny, Walter B. *Iznik: The Artistry of Ottoman Ceramics*. London: Thames and Hudson, 2004.

Derman, M. Uğur. *Türk Sanatında Ebru*. Istanbul: Ak Yayınları, 1977.

———. *Letters in Gold: Ottoman Calligraphy from the Sakıp Sabancı Collection, Istanbul*. New York: Metropolitan Museum of Art, 1998.

Dmochowski, Z. R. *An Introduction to Nigerian Traditional Architecture, Volume Two: South-West and Central Nigeria*. Lagos: The National Commission for Museums and Monuments, 1990.

Dorson, Richard M. *Negro Folktales in Michigan*. Cambridge: Harvard University Press, 1956.

———. *American Negro Folktales*. Greenwich: Fawcett, 1967.

———, ed. *African Folklore*. Garden City: Doubleday, 1972.

Drewal, Henry John. "Art or Accident: Yoruba Body Artists and Their Deity Ogun," in Barnes, ed. *Africa's Ogun*, 1989, pp. 235–60.

———. "Image and Indeterminancy: Elephants and Ivory Among the Yoruba," in Ross, ed. *Elephant*, 1992, pp. 187–207.

———. "Beauty and Being: Aesthetics and Ontology in Yoruba Body Art," in Rubin, ed. *Marks of Civilization*, 1995, pp. 83–96.

———, ed. *Mami Wata: Arts for Water Spirits in Africa and Its Diasporas*. Los Angeles: Fowler Museum at UCLA, 2008.

———, ed. *Sacred Waters: Arts for Mami Wata and Other Divinities in Africa and the Diaspora*. Bloomington: Indiana University Press, 2008.

Drewal, Henry John, and Margaret Thompson Drewal, *Gẹlẹdẹ: Art and Female Power among the Yoruba*. Bloomington: Indiana University Press, 1990 [1983].

Drewal, Henry John, and John Mason. *Beads, Body, and Soul: Art and Light in the Yoruba Universe*. Los Angeles: UCLA Fowler Museum of Cultural History, 1998.

Drewal, Henry John, and John Pemberton III, with Rowland Abiodun. *Yoruba: Nine Centuries of African Art and Thought*. Allen Wardwell, ed. New York: Harry N. Abrams for the Center for African Art, 1995.

Drewal, Margaret Thompson. *Yoruba Ritual: Performers, Play, Agency*. Bloomington: Indiana University Press, 1992.

Duerden, Dennis. "Letter from London: The London Exhibition of Contemporary African Art / 1967," *African Arts* 1:1 (1967): 27–29, 67.

Duffy, Karen M. "The Work of Virgil Boruff, Indiana Limestone Craftsman," *Midwestern Folklore* 22:2 (1996): 4–71.

Dutt, Gurusaday. *Folk Arts and Crafts of Bengal: The Collected Papers*. Calcutta: Seagull, 1990.

Dutta, Krishna, and Andrew Robinson. *Rabindranath Tagore: The Myriad-Minded Man*. New York: St. Martin's Press, 1995.

Dykstra, Gretchen, ed. *Philadelphia Museum of Art Annual Report 2006*. Philadelphia: Philadelphia Museum of Art, 2006.

Eck, Diana L. *Darśan: Seeing the Divine Image in India*. Chambersburg: Anima Books, 1985.

Eco, Umberto. *Art and Beauty in the Middle Ages*. New Haven: Yale University Press, 1986 [1959].

Edgü, Ferit. *Turkish Calligraphic Art (Karalama / Meşk)*. Istanbul: Ada Press, n.d. [c. 1988].

Eliot, T. S. *Notes towards the Definition of Culture*. London: Faber and Faber, 1948.

Ellis, Steven G. *Ireland in the Age of the Tudors, 1447–1603: English Expansion and the End of Gaelic Rule*. London: Longmans, 1998.

Ellmann, Richard. *James Joyce*. New York: Oxford University Press, 1959.

Eribon, Didier. *Conversations with Claude Lévi-Strauss*. Paula Wissing, trans. Chicago: University of Chicago Press, 1991.

Espinosa, José E. *Saints in the Valleys: Christian Sacred Images in the History, Life and Folk Art of Spanish New Mexico*. Albuquerque: University of New Mexico Press, 1967.

Evans, E. Estyn. *The Personality of Ireland: Habitat, Heritage and History*. Cambridge: Cambridge University Press, 1973.

Evans, Michael Robert. *Isuma: Inuit Video Art*. Montreal: McGill-Queen's University Press, 2008.

Ewens, Graeme. *Africa O-Ye!: A Celebration of African Music*. New York: Da Capo Press, 1991.

Eyo, Ekpo, and Frank Willett. *Treasures of Ancient Nigeria*. New York: Alfred A. Knopf, 1982.

Fagg, William. *The Webster Plass Collection of African Art*. London: British Museum, 1953.

———. *Nigerian Images*. Lagos: National Commission for Museums and Monuments, 1990 [1963].

———. "The African Artist," in Biebuyck, ed., *Tradition and Creativity in Tribal Art*, 1969, pp. 42–57.

Fagg, William, and John Pemberton III. *Yoruba: Sculpture of West Africa*. Bryce Holcomb, ed. New York: Alfred A. Knopf, 1982.

Fagg, William, and Margaret Plass. *African Sculpture: An Anthology*. London: Studio Vista, 1964.

Fakeye, Lamidi Olonade, Bruce M. Haight, and David H. Curl. *Lamidi Olonade Fakeye: A Retrospective Exhibition and Autobiography*. Holland: De Pree Art Center and Gallery, Hope College, 1996.

Falade, S. Ade. *The Comprehensive History of Osogbo*. Ibadan: Tunji Owolabi, 2000.

Falola, Toyin, and Matthew M. Heaton. *A History of Nigeria*. Cambridge: Cambridge University Press, 2008.

Faulkner, Peter. *William Morris and W. B. Yeats*. Dublin: Dolmen Press, 1962.

Faulkner, William. *Requiem for a Nun*. New York: Random House, 1951.

Feintuch, Burt, ed. *Eight Words for the Study of Expressive Culture*. Urbana: University of Illinois Press, 2003.

Fernandez, James W. "Principles of Opposition and Vitality in Fang Aesthetics," in Jopling, ed. *Art and Aesthetics in Primitive Societies*, 1971, pp. 356–73.

Ferris, William. *"You Live and Learn. Then You Die and Forget It All": Ray Lum's Tales of Horses, Mules, and Men*. New York: Doubleday, 1992.

Ferris, William, and Maude Southwell Wahlman. *James "Son" Thomas*. Las Cruces: New Mexico State University, 1985.

Foster, Kathleen A. *Thomas Chambers: American Marine and Landscape Painter, 1808–1869*. Philadelphia: Philadelphia Museum of Art, 2008.

Foster, Michael Dylan. *Pandemonium and Parade: Japanese Monsters and the Culture of Yōkai*. Berkeley: University of California Press, 2009.

Foster, R. F. *W. B. Yeats: A Life, I: The Apprentice Mage, 1865–1914*. Oxford: Oxford University Press, 1998.

———. *W. B. Yeats: A Life, II: The Arch Poet, 1915–1939*. Oxford: Oxford University Press, 2003.

Gandhi, Mohandas K. *Autobiography: The Story of My Experiments with Truth*. Mahadev Desai, trans. New York: Dover, 1983 [1948].

Gauguin, Paul. *Noa Noa*. O. F. Theis, trans. New York: Greenberg, n.d. [1926].

Geertz, Clifford. *Works and Lives: The Anthropologist as Author*. Stanford: Stanford University Press, 1988.

George, Kenneth M. "Ethical Pleasure, Visual Dzikir, and Artistic Subjectivity in Contemporary Indonesia," *Material Religion* 4:2 (2008): 172–93.

Georges, Robert A., and Michael O. Jones. *People Studying People: The Human Element in Fieldwork*. Berkeley: University of California Press, 1980.

Gibbon, Edward. *The History of the Decline and Fall of the Roman Empire*. 12 vols. London: Cadell, Davies, and others, 1807 [1776–1788].

Gibbs, James. *Wole Soyinka*. New York: Grove Press, 1986.

Gikandi, Simon, ed. *Wole Soyinka, Death and the King's Horseman*. New York: W. W. Norton, 2003.

Gillon, Werner. *A Short History of African Art*. London: Penguin, 1991 [1984].

Girardot, Norman J. *Bad and Nasty Art: Quantity and Quality in the Career of Howard Finster*. Bethlehem: Lehigh University Art Galleries, 2004.

Glassie, Henry. "The Wedderspoon Farm," *New York Folklore Quarterly* 22:3 (1966): 165–87.

———. "William Houck, Maker of Pounded Ash Adirondack Pack-Baskets," *Keystone Folklore Quarterly* 23:3 (1967): 163–85.

———. "Structure and Function, Folklore and the Artifact," *Semiotica* 7:4 (1973): 313–51.

———. *Folk Housing in Middle Virginia: A Structural Analysis of Historic Artifacts*. Knoxville: University of Tennessee Press, 1975.

———. "Source for a New Anthropology," *Book Forum* 2:1 (1976): 70–77.

———. *Passing the Time in Ballymenone: Culture and History of an Ulster Community*. Philadelphia: University of Pennsylvania Press, 1982.

———. *The Spirit of Folk Art*. New York: Harry N. Abrams, Museum of International Folk Art, 1989.

———. *Turkish Traditional Art Today*. Bloomington: Indiana University Press; Ankara: Ministry of Culture of the Turkish Republic, 1993.

———. *Günümüzde Geleneksel Türk Sanatı*. Istanbul: Pan Yayıncılık, 1993.

———. *Art and Life in Bangladesh*. Bloomington: Indiana University Press, 1997.

———. *Material Culture.* Bloomington: Indiana University Press, 1999.

———. *The Potter's Art.* Bloomington: Indiana University Press; Philadelphia: Material Culture, 1999.

———. *Vernacular Architecture.* Bloomington: Indiana University Press; Philadelphia: Material Culture, 2000.

———. "Mud and Mythic Vision: Hindu Sculpture in Modern Bangladesh," in Schrempp and Hansen, eds. *Myth*, 2002, pp. 203–22.

———. *Mark Hewitt: Outside.* Wilmington: Louise Wells Cameron Art Museum, 2002.

———. "Tradition," in Feintuch, ed. *Eight Words for the Study of Expressive Culture*, 2003, pp. 176–97.

———. *The Stars of Ballymenone.* Bloomington: Indiana University Press, 2006.

———. "Virtuous Conventions: Thoughts on a Survey of Japanese Ceramics," *Museum Anthropology* 31:1 (2008): 47–50.

Glassie, Henry, and Firoz Mahmud. *Living Traditions.* Cultural Survey of Bangladesh 11. Dhaka: Asiatic Society of Bangladesh, 2007.

Goldschmidt, Walter, ed. *The Anthropology of Franz Boas: Essays on the Centennial of His Birth.* Memoir 89. Menasha: American Anthropological Association, 1959.

Goldstein, Kenneth S. "William Robbie: Folk Artist of the Buchan District, Aberdeenshire," in Beck, ed. *Folklore in Action*, 1962, pp. 101–11.

———. *A Guide for Field Workers in Folklore.* Hatboro: Folklore Associates, 1964.

Goldwater, Robert. "Judgments of Primitive Art, 1905–1965," in Biebuyuck, ed. *Tradition and Creativity in Tribal Art*, 1969, pp. 24–41.

Graburn, Nelson H. H., ed. *Ethnic and Tourist Arts: Cultural Expressions from the Fourth World.* Berkeley: University of California Press, 1979.

Greenblatt, Stephen. *Will in the World: How Shakespeare Became Shakespeare.* New York: W. W. Norton, 2004.

Gregory, Lady. *Poets and Dreamers: Studies and Translations from the Irish.* Dublin: Hodges, Figgis, 1903.

———. *A Book of Saints and Wonders.* London: John Murray, 1908.

———. *The Kiltartan History Book.* London: T. Fisher Unwin, 1926 [1909].

———. *Visions and Beliefs in the West of Ireland.* 2 vols. New York: G. P. Putnam, 1920.

———. *Seventy Years.* Colin Smythe, ed. New York: Macmillan, 1976.

Griaule, Marcel. *Folk Art of Black Africa.* Michael Heron, trans. Paris: Les Éditions du Chêne, 1950.

Grohmann, Will. *Wassily Kandinsky: Life and Work.* Norbert Guterman, trans. New York: Harry N. Abrams, n.d. [c. 1958].

Gupta, K., ed. *The Writings of Michael M. S. Dutt.* Calcutta: Sahitya Samsad, 1974.

Hall, Michael D., and Eugene W. Metcalf, Jr., eds. *The Artist Outsider: Creativity and the Boundaries of Culture.* Washington: Smithsonian Institution Press, 1994.

Hammond, Dorothy, and Alta Jablow. *The Africa That Never Was: Four Centuries of British Writing About Africa.* New York: Twayne, 1970.

Hansen, Gregory. *A Florida Fiddler: The Life and Times of Richard Seaman.* Tuscaloosa: University of Alabama Press, 2007.

Hansen, William. *Handbook of Classical Mythology.* Santa Barbara: ABC-CLIO, 2004.

Haring, Lee. *Malagasy Tale Index.* FFC 231. Helsinki: Suomalainen Tiedeakatemia, 1982.

Harris, Joel Chandler. *Uncle Remus: His Songs and His Sayings.* New York: Appleton, 1895 [1880].

Harvey, Charles, and Jon Press. *William Morris: Design and Enterprise in Victorian Britain.* Manchester: Manchester University Press, 1991.

Havell, Jane, ed. *Seven Stories about Modern Art in Africa.* London: Whitechapel, 1995.

Heaney, Seamus. *Finders Keepers: Selected Prose, 1971–2001.* London: Faber and Faber, 2002.

Helm, June, ed. *Essays on the Verbal and Visual Arts: Proceedings of the 1966 Annual Spring Meeting of the American Ethnological Society.* Seattle: American Ethnological Society, 1967.

Henderson, T. F. *Scottish Vernacular Literature: A Succinct History.* London: David Nutt, 1898.

Herbert, Robert L., ed. *Modern Artists on Art.* Mineola: Dover, 2000.

Hersey, Irwin. "Two African Artists: Amir I. M. Nour and Twins Seven-Seven," *African Arts* 10:1 (1976): 82.

Herstal, Stanislaw. *Imagens Religiosas do Brasil.* São Paulo: Sociedade Brasileira Expansão Comercial, 1956.

Hess, Thomas B. "A Tale of Two Cities," in Battcock, ed. *The New Art,* 1966, pp. 161–78.

Hewitt, Mark, and Nancy Sweezy. *The Potter's Eye: Art and Tradition in North Carolina Pottery.* Chapel Hill: University of North Carolina Press, 2005.

Himmelheber, Hans. "The Present State of Sculptural Art Among the Tribes of the Ivory Coast," in Helm, ed. *Essays in the Verbal and Visual Arts,* 1967, pp. 192–99.

Hofer, Tamás, and Edit Fél. *Hungarian Folk Art.* Oxford: Oxford University Press, 1979.

Holbek, Bengt. *Interpretation of Fairy Tales: Danish Folktales in a European Perspective.* FFC 239. Helsinki: Suomalainen Tiedeakatemia, 1987.

Holm, Bill. *Smoky-Top: The Art and Times of Willie Seaweed.* Seattle: University of Washington Press, 1983.

Holtzberg, Maggie. *Keepers of Tradition: Art and Folk Heritage in Massachusetts.* Lexington: Massachusetts Cultural Council and National Heritage Museum, 2008.

Hone, Joseph. *W. B. Yeats: 1865–1939.* New York: Macmillan, 1943.

Hoskins, W. G. *The Making of the English Landscape.* London: Hodder and Stoughton, 1955.

———. *Provincial England: Essays in Social and Economic History.* London: Macmillan, 1965.

Hubka, Thomas C. *Big House, Little House, Back House, Barn: The Connected Farm Buildings of New England.* Hanover: University Press of New England, 1984.

Hunt, Marjorie. *The Stone Carvers: Master Craftsmen of Washington National Cathedral.* Washington: Smithsonian Institution Books, 1999.

Hyde, Douglas. *Beside the Fire: A Collection of Irish Gaelic Folk Stories.* London: David Nutt, 1910.

———. *Mayo Stories Told by Thomas Casey.* Irish Texts Society 16. Dublin: Educational Company of Ireland, 1939.

Hymes, Dell. *Foundations in Sociolinguistics: An Ethnographic Approach.* Philadelphia: University of Pennsylvania Press, 1974.

———. "Folklore's Nature and the Sun's Myth," *Journal of American Folklore* 88 (1975): 345–69.

———. *"In Vain I Tried to Tell You": Essays in Native American Ethnopoetics.* Philadelphia: University of Pennsylvania Press, 1981.

Ives, Edward D. *Larry Gorman: The Man Who Made the Songs.* Bloomington: Indiana University Press, 1964.

———. *Lawrence Doyle: The Farmer-Poet of Prince Edward Island: A Study in Local Songmaking.* University of Maine Studies 92. Orono: University of Maine Press, 1971.

———. *Joe Scott: The Woodsman-Songmaker.* Urbana: University of Illinois Press, 1978.

Ivey, Bill. *Arts, Inc.: How Greed and Neglect Have Destroyed Our Cultural Rights.* Berkeley: University of California Press, 2008.

Jackson, Alvin. *Home Rule: An Irish History.* London: Weidenfeld and Nicolson, 2003.

James, John. *Chartres: The Masons Who Built a Legend.* London: Routledge and Kegan Paul, 1985.

Jegede, Dele. *Contemporary African Art: Five Artists, Diverse Trends*. Indianapolis: Indianapolis Museum of Art, 2000.

Jencks, Charles. *What is Post-Modernism?* London: Academy Editions, 1986.

Johnson, Samuel. *The History of the Yorubas*. O. Johnson, ed. Lagos: C. S. S. Bookshops, 1969 [1921, 1897].

Jonaitis, Aldona. *From the Land of the Totem Poles: The Northwest Coast Indian Art Collection of the American Museum of Natural History*. New York: American Museum of Natural History, 1988.

———, ed. *A Wealth of Thought: Franz Boas on Native American Art*. Seattle: University of Washington Press, 1995.

Jones, Louis C. *Things That Go Bump in the Night*. New York: Hill and Wang, 1959.

Jones, Michael Owen. *Craftsman of the Cumberlands: Tradition and Creativity*. Lexington: University Press of Kentucky, 1989 [1975].

Jopling, Carol F., ed. *Art and Aesthetics in Primitive Societies: A Critical Anthology*. New York: E. P. Dutton, 1971.

Joyce, James. *Ulysses*. Paris: Shakespeare and Company, 1922.

———. *Finnegans Wake*. New York: The Viking Press, 1939.

Kalter, Johannes. *The Arts and Crafts of the Swat Valley: Living Traditions of the Hindu Kush*. London: Thames and Hudson, 1991.

Kandinsky, Wassily. *Concerning the Spiritual in Art and Painting in Particular*. New York: George Wittenborn, 1964 [1912].

———. *Sounds*. Elizabeth R. Napier, trans. New Haven: Yale University Press, 1981 [1912].

———. "Reminiscences," in Herbert, ed. *Modern Artists on Art*, 2000 [from 1913], pp. 19–39.

Kandinsky, Wassily, and Franz Marc, eds. *The Blaue Reiter Almanac*. Klaus Lankheit, ed. New York: Da Capo Press, 1989 [1912].

Kasfir, Sidney Littlefield. "Art from Africa," *African Arts* 14:4 (1981): 76–78.

———. *Contemporary African Art*. London: Thames and Hudson, 1999.

———. *African Art and the Colonial Encounter: Inventing a Global Commodity*. Bloomington: Indiana University Press, 2007.

Kawano, Ryōsuke. *Hagi: 400 ans de céramique*. Paris: Maison de la culture du Japon à Paris, 2000.

Kee, Robert. *The Green Flag: A History of Irish Nationalism*. London: Weidenfeld and Nicolson, 1972.

Kenaan-Kedar, Nurith. *Marginal Sculpture in Medieval France: Towards the Deciphering of an Enigmatic Pictorial Language*. Aldershot: Scolar Press, 1995.

Kennedy, Jean. "I Saw and I Was Happy: Festival at Oshogbo," *African Arts* 1:2 (1968): 8–16, 85.

———. *New Currents, Ancient Rivers: Contemporary African Artists in a Generation of Change*. Washington: Smithsonian Institution Press, 1992.

Kerr, Rose. *Chinese Ceramics: Porcelain of the Qing Dynasty, 1644–1911*. London: Victoria and Albert Museum, 1986.

Kirshenblatt-Gimblett, Barbara. *They Called Me Mayer July: Painted Memories of a Jewish Childhood in Poland before the Holocaust*. Berkeley: University of California Press, 2007.

Kirstein, Lincoln. *The Sculpture of Elie Nadelman*. New York: Museum of Modern Art, 1948.

Klee, Felix, ed. *The Diaries of Paul Klee, 1898–1918*. Berkeley: University of California Press, 1968.

Klee, Paul. "On Modern Art," in Herbert, ed. *Modern Artists on Art*, 2000 [from 1924], pp. 102–15.

Klein, Barbro, and Mats Widbom, eds. *Swedish Folk Art: All Tradition Is Change*. New York: Harry N. Abrams, 1994.

Knowlson, James and Elizabeth, eds. *Beckett Remembering, Remembering Beckett: A Centenary Celebration*. New York: Arcade Publishing, 2006.

Kubler, George. *The Shape of Time: Remarks on the History of Things*. New Haven: Yale University Press, 1962.

Lane, Arthur. *Later Islamic Pottery: Persia, Syria, Egypt, Turkey*. London: Faber and Faber, 1957.

Leach, Bernard. *A Potter's Book*. Levittown: Transatlantic Arts, 1973 [1944].

———. *A Potter in Japan: 1952–1954*. London: Faber and Faber, 1960.

———. *Hamada: Potter*. Tokyo: Kodansha, 1990 [1975].

Le Corbusier. *Journey to the East*. Ivan Zaknić, ed. and trans. Cambridge: The MIT Press, 1989 [1966].

Leiris, Michel, and Jacqueline Delange. *African Art*. Michael Ross, trans. New York: Golden Press, 1968.

Lévi-Strauss, Claude. *Tristes Tropiques*. John and Doreen Weightman, trans. New York: Penguin, 1992 [1955].

———. *Totemism*. Boston: Beacon Press, 1963.

———. *The Savage Mind*. Chicago: University of Chicago Press, 1968 [1962].

———. *The Way of the Masks*. Sylvia Modelski, trans. Seattle: University of Washington Press, 1982.

———. *The Story of Lynx*. Catherine Tihanyi, trans. Chicago: University of Chicago Press, 1995.

Lewis, Oscar. *Five Families: Mexican Case Studies in the Culture of Poverty*. New York: Basic Books, 1959.

———. *The Children of Sánchez: Autobiography of a Mexican Family*. New York: Random House, 1961.

———. *Pedro Martínez: A Mexican Peasant and His Family*. London: Secker and Warburg, 1964.

———. *A Death in the Sánchez Family*. New York: Random House, 1969.

Lewison, Jeremy. "Paris and Cologne: 'Bilderstreit' and 'Magiciens de la Terre,'" *The Burlington Magazine* 131:1037 (1989): 585–87.

Li, He. *Chinese Ceramics: A New Comprehensive Survey*. New York: Rizzoli, 1996.

Lippard, Lucy R. *Pop Art*. New York: Frederick A. Praeger, 1966.

Livingston, Jane, and John Beardsley. *Black Folk Art in America: 1930–1980*. Jackson: University Press of Mississippi for Corcoran Gallery of Art, 1982.

Lloyd, P. C., A. L. Mabogunje, and B. Awe, eds. *The City of Ibadan*. Cambridge: Cambridge University Press, 1967.

Lomax, John A., and Alan Lomax. *Negro Folk Songs As Sung by Lead Belly*. New York: Macmillan, 1936.

López-Remiro, Miguel, ed. *Mark Rothko: Writings on Art*. New Haven: Yale University Press, 2006.

Lowes, John Livingston. *The Road to Xanadu: A Study in the Ways of the Imagination*. Boston: Houghton Mifflin, 1927.

Ludwig, Allan I. *Graven Images: New England Stonecarving and its Symbols, 1650–1815*. Middletown: Wesleyan University Press, 1966.

MacCarthy, Fiona. *William Morris: A Life for Our Time*. New York: Alfred A. Knopf, 1995.

Mackail, J. W. *The Life of William Morris*. 2 vols. London: Longmans, Green, 1899.

Magnin, André, with Jacques Soulillou. *Contemporary Art of Africa*. New York: Harry N. Abrams, 1996.

Magnin, André, Alison de Lima Greene, Alvia J. Wardlaw, and Thomas McEvilley. *African Art Now: Masterpieces from the Jean Pigozzi Collection*. London: Merrell, 2005.

Maharidge, Dale, and Michael Williamson. *And Their Children After Them: The Legacy of Let Us Now Praise Famous Men: James Agee, Walker Evans, and the Rise and Fall of Cotton in the South*. New York: Pantheon, 1989.

Malinowski, Bronislaw. *Argonauts of the Western Pacific: An Account of Native Enterprise and Adventure in the Archipelagoes of Melanesian New Guinea*. London: George Routledge, 1922.

Marino, João. *Iconografia de Nossa Senhora e dos Santos*. São Paulo: Banco Safra, Museu de Arte Sacra, 1996.

Mascelloni, Enrico, and Sarenco. *Il ritorno dei maghi: Il Sacro nell'arte Africana contemporanea*. Milano: Skira, 2000.

McNaughton, Patrick R. *A Bird Dance Near Saturday Night: Sidi Ballo and the Art of the West African Masquerade*. Bloomington: Indiana University Press, 2008.

Medley, Margaret. *The Chinese Potter: A Practical History of Chinese Ceramics*. Ithaca: Cornell University Press, 1976.

Melville, Herman. *Moby-Dick; or, The Whale*. Berkeley: University of California Press, 1981 [1851].

Michell, George. *Hindu Art and Architecture*. New York: Thames and Hudson, 2000.

Mino, Yutaka. *Freedom of Clay and Brush through Seven Centuries in Northern China: Tz'u-chou Type Wares, 960–1600 A.D.* Bloomington: Indiana University Press, 1980.

Moes, Robert. *Mingei: Japanese Folk Art from the Montgomery Collection*. Alexandria: Art Services International, 1995.

Momaday, N. Scott. *The Names: A Memoir*. New York: Harper and Row, 1976.

———. *The Man Made of Words: Essays, Stories, Passages*. New York: St. Martin's Press, 1997.

Monroe, Arthur. "Tradition and Change in Yoruba Art," *African Arts* 7:4 (1974): 75.

Morris, May, ed. *The Collected Works of William Morris*. 24 vols. London: Longmans, Green, 1910–1915.

Morris, William. *Hopes and Fears for Art: Five Lectures. Delivered in Birmingham, London, and Nottingham, 1878–1881*. London: Longmans, Green, 1898 [1882].

———. *Signs of Change: Seven Lectures*. London: Longmans, Green, 1903 [1888].

———. *A Dream of John Ball and a King's Lesson*. Hammersmith: Kelmscott Press, 1892 [1888].

———. *Gothic Architecture: A Lecture for the Arts and Crafts Exhibition Society*. Hammersmith: Kelmscott Press, 1893 [1889].

———. *News from Nowhere: Or, An Epoch of Rest, Being Some Chapters from a Utopian Romance*. Hammersmith: Kelmscott Press, 1892 [1891].

———. *Architecture, Industry, and Wealth: Collected Papers*. London: Longmans, Green, 1902.

Morton, Robin. *Come Day, Go Day, God Send Sunday: The Songs and Life Story, Told in His Own Words, of John Maguire, Traditional Singer and Farmer from Co. Fermanagh*. London: Routledge and Kegan Paul, 1973.

Moughtin, J. C. *Hausa Architecture*. London: Ethnographica, 1985.

Mould, Tom. *Choctaw Prophecy: A Legacy of the Future*. Tuscaloosa: University of Alabama Press, 2003.

Mount, Marshall Ward. *African Art: The Years Since 1920*. Bloomington: Indiana University Press, 1974.

Mumford, Lewis. *Herman Melville*. New York: Literary Guild of America, 1929.

Mundy-Castle, A. C., and Vicky Mundy-Castle. "Twins Seven Seven," *African Arts* 6:1 (1972): 8–13.

Murphy, Joseph M., and Mei-Mei Sanford. *Osun across the Waters: A Yoruba Goddess in Africa and the Americas*. Bloomington: Indiana University Press, 2001.

Nabokov, Peter. *Two Leggings: The Making of a Crow Warrior*. Lincoln: University of Nebraska Press, 1982 [1967].

———. *A Forest of Time: American Indian Ways of History*. Cambridge: Cambridge University Press, 2002.

Naifeh, Steven W. "The Myth of Oshogbo," *African Arts* 14:2 (1981): 25–27, 85–86, 88.

Naipaul, V. S. *Reading and Writing: A Personal Account*. New York: New York Review Books, 2000.

Narayan, Kirin. *Storytellers, Saints, and Scoundrels: Folk Narrative in Hindu Religious Teaching*. Philadelphia: University of Pennsylvania Press, 1989.

———. *Mondays on the Dark Night of the Moon: Himalayan Foothill Folktales*. New York: Oxford University Press, 1997.

Nasr, Seyyed Hossein. *Islamic Art and Spirituality.* Albany: State University of New York Press, 1987.

National Museum of Modern Art. *Kanjiro Kawai: Catalogue of Kawakatsu Collection.* Kyoto: National Museum of Modern Art, 1983.

Norberg-Schulz, Christian. *Nightlands: Nordic Building.* Cambridge: The MIT Press, 1996.

Nuttall, A. D. *Shakespeare the Thinker.* New Haven: Yale University Press, 2007.

O'Connor, Francis V. *Jackson Pollock.* New York: Museum of Modern Art, 1967.

O'Donovan, John, ed. *Annals of the Kingdom of Ireland, By the Four Masters, From the Earliest Period to the Year 1616.* 7 vols. Dublin: Hodges, Smith, 1856.

Ó Duillearga, Séamus. *Seán Ó Conaill's Book: Stories and Traditions from Inveragh.* Dublin: Comhairle Bhéaloideas Éireann, 1981 [1948].

Ogundele, Wole. *Omoluabi: Ulli Beier, Yoruba Society and Culture.* Bayreuth African Studies 66. Bayreuth: Bayreuth University, 2003.

Ogunwale, Titus A. "Lamidi Fakeye: Nigerian Traditional Sculptor," *African Arts* 4:2 (1971): 66–67.

Oliver, Anthony. *The Victorian Staffordshire Figure: A Guide for Collectors.* London: Heinemann, 1971.

Oliver, Paul, ed. *Shelter in Africa.* New York: Praeger, 1971.

Ollman, John, and Brendan Greaves. *"Cigarmaker, Creator, Healer, and Man": The Artwork of Felipe Jesus Consalvos.* Philadelphia: Fleisher/Ollman Gallery, 2005.

O'Neill, John P., ed. *Barnett Newman: Selected Writings and Interviews.* Berkeley: University of California Press, 1992.

Oring, Elliott. *Jokes and Their Relations.* Lexington: University Press of Kentucky, 1992.

———. *Engaging Humor.* Urbana: University of Illinois Press, 2003.

Ottenberg, Simon, ed. *The Nsukka Artists and Nigerian Contemporary Art.* Seattle: University of Washington Press, 2002.

Ó Tuama, Seán, ed. *The Gaelic League Idea.* Cork: Mercier Press, 1972.

Oyelami, Muraina. "Mbari Mbayo and the Oshogbo Artists," *African Arts* 15:2 (1982): 85–87.

Oyeyemi, Helen. *The Icarus Girl.* New York: Anchor Books, 2006.

Pal, Pratapaditya. *Hindu Religion and Iconography According to the Tantrasara.* Los Angeles: Vichitra Press, 1981.

Palmer, Gabrielle G. *Sculpture in the Kingdom of Quito.* Albuquerque: University of New Mexico Press, 1987.

Panofsky, Erwin. *The Life and Art of Albrecht Dürer.* Princeton: Princeton University Press, 1971 [1943].

Park, Mungo. *Travels in the Interior of Africa.* Edinburgh: Adam and Charles Black, 1860.

Patterson, Tom. *Reclamation and Transformation: Three Self-Taught Chicago Artists.* Chicago: Terra Museum of Art, 1994.

Pearson, Barry Lee. *Virginia Piedmont Blues: The Lives and Art of Two Virginia Bluesmen.* Philadelphia: University of Pennsylvania Press, 1990.

Peek, Philip M. "Ovia Idah and Eture Egbede: Traditional Nigerian Artists," *African Arts* 18:2 (1985): 54–59, 102.

———, ed. *African Divination Systems: Ways of Knowing.* Bloomington: Indiana University Press, 1991.

Peek, Philip M., and Kwesi Yankah, eds. *African Folklore: An Encyclopedia.* New York: Routledge, 2004.

Penrose, Roland. *Portrait of Picasso.* New York: Museum of Modern Art, 1957.

Pentikäinen, Juha. *Oral Repertoire and World View: An Anthropological Study of Marina Takalo's Life History.* FFC 219. Helsinki: Suomalainen Tiedeakatemia, 1978.

Peterson, Susan. *Shoji Hamada: A Potter's Way and Work.* Tokyo: Kodansha, 1974.

Peterson, William S. *The Kelmscott Press: A History of William Morris's Typographical Adventure.* Berkeley: University of California Press, 1991.

Pevsner, Nikolaus. *Pioneers of the Modern Movement: From William Morris to Walter Gropius*. London: Faber and Faber, 1936.

Pound, Ezra. *Confucian Analects*. London: Peter Owen, 1980 [1951].

Price, Sally. *Primitive Art in Civilized Places*. Chicago: University of Chicago Press, 1991.

Price, Sally, and Richard Price. *Maroon Arts: Cultural Vitality in the African Diaspora*. Boston: Beacon Press, 1999.

Prown, Jules David. *Art as Evidence: Writings on Art and Material Culture*. New Haven: Yale University Press, 2001.

Prussin, Labelle. *Architecture in Northern Ghana*. Los Angeles: University of California Press, 1969.

Pryor, Elizabeth Brown. *Reading the Man: A Portrait of Robert E. Lee Through His Private Letters*. New York, Penguin, 2007.

Pugh, P. D. Gordon. *Staffordshire Portrait Figures and Allied Subjects of the Victorian Era*. Woodbridge: Antique Collectors' Club, 1987.

Quayson, Ato. *Strategic Transformations in Nigerian Writing: Orality and History in the Work of Samuel Johnson, Amos Tutuola, Wole Soyinka and Ben Okri*. Bloomington: Indiana University Press, 1997.

Ravenhill, Philip L. *The Self and the Other: Personhood and Images among the Baule, Côte d'Ivoire*. Los Angeles: Fowler Museum of Cultural History, 1994.

———. *Dreams and Reverie: Images of Otherworld Mates among the Baule, West Africa*. Washington: Smithsonian Institution Press, 1996.

Reed, Daniel B. *Dan Ge Performance: Masks and Music in Contemporary Côte d'Ivoire*. Bloomington: Indiana University Press, 2003.

Reinhardt, Ad. "Writings," in Battcock, ed. *The New Art*, 1966, pp. 190–209.

Ribner, Irving. *Patterns in Shakespearian Tragedy*. New York: Barnes and Noble, 1960.

Rinzler, Ralph, and Robert Sayers. *The Meaders Family: North Georgia Potters*. Smithsonian Folklife Studies 1. Washington: Smithsonian Institution Press, 1980.

Robertson, Pamela, ed. *Charles Rennie Mackintosh: The Architectural Papers*. Wendlebury: White Cockade, 1990.

Rosenak, Chuck and Nan. *The Saint Makers: Contemporary Santeras y Santeros*. Flagstaff: Northland, 1998.

Ross, Doran H., ed. *Elephant: The Animal and Its Ivory in African Culture*. Los Angeles: Fowler Museum of Cultural History, 1992.

———, ed. *Visions of Africa: The Jerome L. Joss Collection of Art at UCLA*. Los Angeles: Fowler Museum of Cultural History, 1994.

———. *Wrapped in Pride: Ghanaian Kente and African American Identity*. Los Angeles: UCLA Fowler Museum of Cultural History, 1998.

Rothko, Mark. *The Artist's Reality: Philosophies of Art*. Christopher Rothko, ed. New Haven: Yale University Press, 2004.

Rubin, Arnold, ed. *Marks of Civilization: Artistic Transformations of the Human Body*. Los Angeles: Museum of Cultural History, 1995.

Ruskin, John. *The Stones of Venice*. 3 vols. London: Smith, Elder, 1851–1853.

———. *Lectures on Architecture and Painting, Delivered at Edinburgh, in November, 1853*. New York: John Wiley, 1864 [1854].

———. *Unto This Last*. London: George Allen, 1902 [1860].

———. *The Nature of Gothic: A Chapter of the Stones of Venice*. Hammersmith: Kelmscott Press, 1892.

Safadi, Yasin Hamid. *Islamic Calligraphy*. London: Thames and Hudson, 1978.

Salvador, Mari Lyn C. *Cuando Hablan Los Santos: Contemporary Santero Traditions from Northern New Mexico*. Albuquerque: Maxwell Museum of Anthropology, 1995.

Sartre, Jean-Paul. *Search for a Method*. Hazel E. Barnes, trans. New York: Alfred A. Knopf, 1963 [1960].

———. *Between Existentialism and Marxism*. John Matthews, trans. New York: William Morrow, 1976 [1972].

Satō, Masahiko. *Chinese Ceramics: A Short History*. New York: Weatherhill / Heibonsha, 1981.

Sawin, Martica, ed. *James Marston Fitch: Selected Writings on Architecture, Preservation, and the Built Environment*. New York: W. W. Norton, 2006.

Schildkrout, Enid, and Curtis A. Keim. *African Reflections: Art from Northeastern Zaire*. Seattle: University of Washington Press, 1990.

Schimmel, Annemarie. *Calligraphy and Islamic Culture*. New York: New York University Press, 1990 [1984].

Schjeldahl, Peter. "A Coming of Age in Africa," *The New York Times* (June 13, 1971): D23.

Schrempp, Gregory, and William Hansen, eds. *Myth: A New Symposium*. Bloomington: Indiana University Press, 2002.

Schubnell, Matthias, ed. *Conversations with N. Scott Momaday*. Jackson: University Press of Mississippi, 1997.

Scott, Victoria. "Nike Olaniyi," *African Arts* 16:2 (1983): 46–47.

Segy, Ladislas. *Masks of Black Africa*. New York: Dover, 1976.

Sen, Sukumar. *History of Bengali Literature*. New Delhi: Sahitya Akademi, 1960.

Serin, Muhittin. *Hat Sanatı ve Meşhur Hattatlar*. Istanbul: Kubbealtı, 2003.

Shahn, Ben. *The Shape of Content*. Cambridge: Harvard University Press, 1957.

Shearer, Alistair. *The Hindu Vision: Forms of the Formless*. London: Thames and Hudson, 1993.

Shelley, Donald A. *The Fraktur-Writings or Illuminated Manuscripts of the Pennsylvania Germans*. Pennsylvania German Folklore Society 23. Allentown: Schlecter's, 1961.

Shukla, Pravina. *The Grace of Four Moons: Dress, Adornment, and the Art of the Body in Modern India*. Bloomington: Indiana University Press, 2008.

Sieber, Roy. *African Textiles and Decorative Arts*. New York: Museum of Modern Art, 1972.

———. *African Furniture and Household Objects*. Bloomington: Indiana University Press, 1980.

Sieber, Roy, and Arnold Rubin. *Sculpture of Black Africa: The Paul Tishman Collection*. Los Angeles: Los Angeles County Museum of Art, 1968.

Simmons, Leo W. *Sun Chief: The Autobiography of a Hopi Indian*. New Haven: Yale University Press, 1942.

Sontag, Susan. *On Photography*. New York: Farrar, Straus and Giroux, 1990 [1977].

Soyinka, Wole. *The Jero Plays*. Ibadan: Spectrum Books, 1995 [1964].

———. *The Lion and the Jewel*. Ibadan: Mosuro Publishers, 2004 [1964].

———. *The Interpreters*. New York: Africana, 1972 [1965].

———. *Idanre and Other Poems*. New York: Hill and Wang, 1987 [1967].

———. *A Shuttle in the Crypt*. New York: Hill and Wang, 1972.

———. *Death and the King's Horseman*. New York: Hill and Wang, 1987 [1975].

———. *Myth, Literature and the African World*. Cambridge: Cambridge University Press, 2005 [1976].

———. *Aké: The Years of Childhood*. Ibadan: Spectrum Books, 2004 [1981].

———. "This Past Must Address Its Present," Nobel Lecture of 1986, in *Nobel Lectures from the Literature Laureates, 1986 to 2006*. New York: The New Press, 2007, pp. 268–90.

———. "Theatre in African Traditional Cultures: Survival Patterns," in Gikandi, ed. *Wole Soyinka, Death and the King's Horseman*, 2003 [from 1988], pp. 89–103.

———. *Ìsarà: A Voyage Around "Essay."* New York: Random House, 1989.

———. "Twice Bitten: The Fate of Africa's Culture Producers," *PMLA* 105:1 (1990): 110–20.

———. *Ibadan: The Penkelemes Years: A Memoir: 1946–1965*. London: Methuen, 2001 [1994].

———. *The Open Sore of a Continent: A Personal Narrative of the Nigerian Crisis*. New York: Oxford University Press, 1997.

———. *You Must Set Forth at Dawn: A Memoir*. New York: Random House, 2006.

Stanislaus, Grace. *Contemporary African Artists: Changing Traditions*. New York: The Studio Museum in Harlem, 1990.

Steiner, Christopher B. *African Art in Transit*. Cambridge: Cambridge University Press, 2001 [1994].

Stephens, Lilo. *J. M. Synge, My Wallet of Photographs: The Collected Photographs of J. M. Synge*. Dublin: Dolmen Editions, 1971.

Stoller, Paul, and Cheryl Olkes. *In Sorcery's Shadow: A Memoir of Apprenticeship Among the Songhay of Niger*. Chicago: University of Chicago Press, 1987.

Stone, Ruth M., ed. *Africa. The Garland Encyclopedia of World Music, I*. New York: Garland Publishing, 1998.

Suzuki, Daisetz T. *Zen and Japanese Culture*. Princeton: Princeton University Press, 1993 [1959].

Svärdström, Svante. *Dalmålningar i urval*. Stockholm: Albert Bonniers, 1975.

Sweezy, Nancy. *Raised in Clay: The Southern Pottery Tradition*. Washington: Smithsonian Institution Press, 1984.

Synge, John M. *The Aran Islands*. Boston: John W. Luce, 1911 [1907].

———. *The Works*. Boston: John W. Luce, 1912.

Tagore, Rabindranath. *Gitanjali (Song Offerings)*. London: Macmillan, 1913.

———. *Reminiscences*. Delhi: Macmillan India, 1980 [1917].

Tate, W. E. *The Enclosure Movement*. New York: Walker and Company, 1967.

Thompson, E. P. *William Morris: Romantic to Revolutionary*. New York: Pantheon, 1977.

———. *Customs in Common*. New York: The New Press, 1991.

———. *The Romantics: England in a Revolutionary Age*. New York: The New Press, 1997.

Thompson, Robert Farris. "Aesthetics in Traditional Africa," in Jopling, ed. *Art and Aesthetics in Primitive Societies*, 1971, pp. 374–81.

———. "Yoruba Artistic Criticism," in d'Azevedo, ed. *The Traditional Artist in African Societies*, 1974, pp. 18–61.

———. *African Art in Motion: Icon and Act*. Berkeley: University of California Press, 1974.

———. *Black Gods and Kings: Yoruba Art at UCLA*. Bloomington: Indiana University Press, 1976.

———. *Flash of the Spirit: African and Afro-American Art and Philosophy*. New York: Vintage Books, 1983.

———. *Face of the Gods: Art and Altars of Africa and the African Americas*. New York: Museum of African Art, 1993.

Thoreau, Henry David. *Walden*. London: J. M. Dent, 1995 [1854].

Truesdell, Barbara. "A Life in the Field: Henry Glassie and the Study of Material Culture." Pioneers of Public History. *The Public Historian* 30:4 (2008): 59–87.

Tulku, Tarthang. *Sacred Art of Tibet*. Berkeley: Dharma, 1988 [1972].

Türkmenoğlu, Turan. *Sudaki Nakış: Ebru*. Istanbul: Milenyum Yayınları, 1999.

Turnbull, Colin. M. *The Forest People*. New York: Simon and Schuster, 1961.

———. *The Lonely African*. New York: Simon and Schuster, 1962.

———. *Man in Africa*. Garden City: Anchor Press, 1976.

Tutuola, Amos. *The Palm-Wine Drinkard and his dead Palm-Wine Tapster in the Dead's Town*. New York: Grove Press, 1953.

———. *My Life in the Bush of Ghosts*. London: Faber and Faber, 1978 [1954].

———. *Simbi and the Satyr of the Dark Jungle*. London: Faber and Faber, 1955.

———. *Feather Woman of the Jungle*. San Francisco: City Lights, 1988 [1962].

Uchida, Yoshiko. *We Do Not Work Alone: The Thoughts of Kanjiro Kawai*. Kyoto: Kawai Kanjiro's House, 1972.

Vaz, Kim Marie. *The Woman with the Artistic Brush: A Life History of Yoruba Batik Artist Nike Davies*. Armonk: M. E. Sharpe, 1995.

Venturi, Robert. *Complexity and Contradiction in Architecture*. New York: Museum of Modern Art, 1966.

Verger, Pierre Fatumbi. *Lendas Africanas dos Orixás*. Salvador: Corrupio, 2006.

Vlach, John Michael. *Charlestown Blacksmith: The Work of Philip Simmons*. Columbia: University of South Carolina Press, 1992 [1981].

Vlach, John Michael, and Simon J. Bronner, eds. *Folk Art and Art Worlds*. Ann Arbor: UMI Research Press, 1986.

Vogel, Susan Mullin. *African Aesthetics: The Carlo Monzino Collection*. New York: The Center for African Art, 1986.

———, ed. *Art / Artifact: African Art in Anthropology Collections*. New York: Center for African Art, 1989.

———, ed. *African Explores: 20th Century African Art*. New York: Center for African Art, 1991.

———. "Known Artists but Anonymous Works: Fieldwork and Art History," *African Arts* 32:1 (1999): 40–55, 93–94.

Vogt, Paul. *The Blue Rider*. Joachim Neugroschel, trans. Woodbury: Barron's, 1980.

Wardlaw, Alvia J., ed. *Black Art: Ancestral Legacy: The African Impulse in African-American Art*. New York: Harry N. Abrams for Dallas Museum of Art, 1989.

Waterman, Christopher A. "Yoruba Popular Music," in Stone, ed. *Africa*, 1998, pp. 471–87.

Watkinson, Ray. *William Morris as Designer*. New York: Reinhold, 1967.

Weeder, Erica Hamilton, ed. *Japanese Folk Art: A Triumph of Simplicity*. New York: Japan Society, 1992.

Weiser, Frederick S., and Howell J. Heaney. *The Pennsylvania German Fraktur of the Free Library of Philadelphia*. 2 vols. Breinigsville: Pennsylvania German Society, 1976.

Whistler, Catherine. *Opulence and Devotion: Brazilian Baroque Art*. Oxford: Ashmolean Museum, 2001.

Wilcox, Timothy, ed. *Shoji Hamada: Master Potter*. London: Lund Humphries, 1998.

Willett, Frank. *Ife in the History of West African Sculpture*. New York: McGraw-Hill, 1967.

———. "An African Sculptor at Work," *African Arts* 11:2 (1978): 28–33, 96.

———. *African Art: New Edition*. London: Thames and Hudson, 2006.

Williams, Lizzie. *Nigeria: The Bradt Travel Guide*. Guilford: Globe Pequot Press, 2005.

Wilson, Edmund. *Patriotic Gore: Studies in the Literature of the American Civil War*. New York: Oxford University Press, 1962.

Wilson, Richard L. *Inside Japanese Ceramics: A Primer of Materials, Techniques, and Traditions*. New York: Weatherhill, 1995.

Wilson, William A. *Folklore and Nationalism in Modern Finland*. Bloomington: Indiana University Press, 1976.

Wingert, Paul S. *The Sculpture of Negro Africa*. New York: Columbia University Press, 1950.

Wolfe, Richard J. *Marbled Paper: Its History, Techniques, and Patterns*. Philadelphia: University of Pennsylvania Press, 1990.

Wolpert, Stanley. *A New History of India*. New York: Oxford University Press, 1982 [1977].

Wright, Richard. *Native Son*. New York: Harperperennial, 2008 [1940].

———. *Black Boy: A Record of Childhood and Youth*. New York: Harper and Brothers, 1945.

Wroth, William. *Christian Images in Hispanic New Mexico: The Taylor Museum Collection of Santos*. Colorado Springs: Taylor Museum, 1982.

Yai, Olabiyi Babalola. "Tradition and the Yoruba Artist," *African Arts* 32:1 (1999): 32–35, 93.

Yanagi, Sōetsu. *The Unknown Craftsman: A Japanese Insight into Beauty*. Bernard Leach, trans. Tokyo: Kodansha, 1989.

Yanagi, Sōri, ed. *Mingei: Masterpieces of Japanese Folkcraft*. Tokyo: Kodansha, 1991.

Yeats, W. B. *Fairy and Folk Tales of the Irish Peasantry*. London: Walter Scott, 1888.

———. *Irish Fairy Tales*. London: T. Fisher Unwin, 1892.

———. *The Celtic Twilight*. London: A. H. Bullen, 1902 [1893].

———. *Ideas of Good and Evil*. Dublin: Maunsel, 1905.

———. *The Cutting of an Agate*. London: Macmillan, 1919.

———. *A Vision*. London: Macmillan, 1937.

Zug, Charles G., III. *Turners and Burners: The Folk Potters of North Carolina*. Chapel Hill: University of North Carolina Press, 1986.

Index

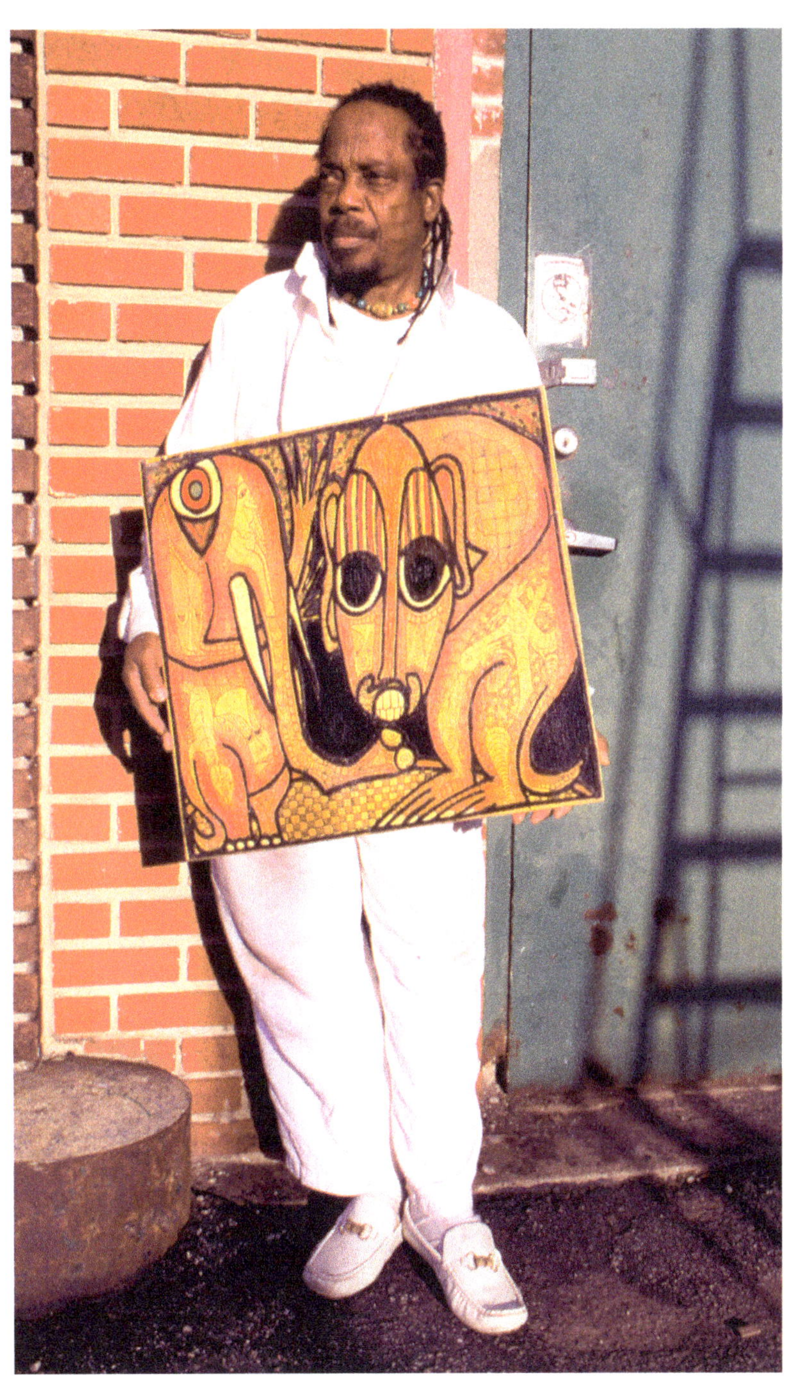

Prince Twins Seven-Seven: His Art,
His Life in Nigeria, His Exile in America
was designed by Henry Glassie,
composed by John McGuigan,
and published by Indiana University Press

www.ingramcontent.com/pod-product-compliance
Lightning Source LLC
LaVergne TN
LVHW070403060826
844660LV00009B/288
* 9 7 8 0 2 5 3 3 5 4 3 9 6 *